Maria Woodworth-Etter

The Complete Collection of Her Life Teachings

Compiled by
Roberts Liardon

Albury Publishing
Tulsa, Oklahoma

All Scripture quotations are taken from the *King James Version* of the Bible.

Maria Woodworth-Etter:
The Complete Collection of Her Life Teachings
ISBN 1-57778-122-8

P. O. Box 30710
Laguna Hills, California 92654

Published by Albury Publishing
P. O. Box 470406
Tulsa, Oklahoma 74147-0406

Contents

Table of Photographs

FOREWORD

In recent years, the name Maria B. Woodworth-Etter has resurfaced in the Pentecostal churches. In her own lifetime, her meetings were legendary because of how God showed His approval of His faithful servant with thousands being saved and healed of all kinds of afflictions.

It wasn't long after she turned her life over to the Lord that He baptized her with the Holy Ghost and fire, much like He did the twelve disciples on the day of Pentecost. The anointing she received that day stayed with her throughout her life and ministry. Few have prayed the prayer of faith with such power and confidence.

She was described by her contemporaries in the following manner:

She seems to consider her life as belonging wholly to God and not her own. Out of her eyes a spirit radiates which spells purity, consecration, earnestness, separation, and zeal for Jesus' cause.

The anointing she received of Him abode, probably because she waited on Him in secret prayer, fellowship, and communion, consecrated unto death if necessary and with an entirely humble, obedient spirit.

It is with great pride and affection that I speak of my great-great-great grandmother. I can only speak *of* her from the research I have done over the years, since she passed away long before I was born. But I believe everyone will enjoy reading the words that were spoken in her great meetings by a little woman who fought the good fight and kept the faith for so many years.

— Thomas A. Slevin

ACKNOWLEDGMENTS

I would like to thank Wayne Warner, a foremost expert on Maria Woodworth-Etter, and the staff at the Flower Pentecostal Heritage Center for their assistance. Mr. Warner kindly provided many news articles to add to my collection to make this book complete.

Note from the Editor:

The materials published by Maria Woodworth-Etter and the periodicals of her time have been treated in the following manner:

- The words have been quoted exactly as they were published except for minor updating of spelling.
- Punctuation has occasionally been added or eliminated to bring these materials into conformity with modern practices.
- Some long paragraphs have been broken into smaller paragraphs for ease of reading.
- Old style Bible references have been rewritten in the currently accepted style (For example, Ps. 6.2 has been changed to Psalm 6:2).
- Words added for clarification are in brackets.
- Words interpolated from an unclear newsprint copy are in brackets with a "?" following to indicate uncertainty.
- Illegible text is signified by empty brackets.
- Some errors necessary to the text, such as a newspaper misspelling Mrs. Etter's name throughout an article have been denoted by "(*sic*)". When the newspaper spells it correctly in the article with one misspelling, the misspelling is corrected without notation.

When the same sermon has been printed in several publications under different titles, and with minor changes, only one has been included here, usually the longest one.

Maria Woodworth-Etter

Section One

Maria Woodworth-Etter: Trailblazer for God

TRAILBLAZER FOR GOD

y some supernatural power she just knocks 'em silly when they are not looking for it, and while they are down she applies the hydraulic pressure and pumps the grace of God into them by the bucketful."[1]

No woman has had to blaze as many trails for God as Maria Woodworth-Etter. Not only did she have to preach the Gospel at a time when the public frowned upon women preachers, but God also used her to spread the fire of the Holy Spirit at a time when the Church had forgotten just what that meant. In the face of opposition from churches and unbelievers alike, she had to sacrifice her reputation and her own ideas of what she as a woman could do for God. Instead she chose to gain a reputation in heaven.

Born in 1844 in Lisbon, Ohio, Maria Woodworth-Etter answered the call to salvation at the age of thirteen. At the same time, she also heard God's call to be an evangelist. She later wrote, "I heard the voice of Jesus calling me to go out in the highways and hedges and gather in the lost sheep."[2]

It was some time before she could bring herself to answer that call. She tried at first to answer it by going to school, hoping to marry a missionary who would help her in her work. This plan didn't work when her father died and she had to leave school to help support her family. During the Civil War, she set God's call aside for a while and married P. H. Woodworth, a Civil War veteran.

After having six children, Maria continued to hear God's call, but she never knew how she could answer with all her responsibilities. Woodworth himself had no desire for the ministry, and Maria was sickly which made it even harder for her to answer this call. When disease carried away five of her children and she began to search God's Word for comfort, Maria found that women in the Bible

---

For a more complete biography of Maria Woodworth-Etter and other important ministers who lived during and after her lifetime, refer to *God's Generals* by Roberts Liardon (Tulsa: Albury Publishing, 1996).

[1] Liardon, Roberts, *God's Generals* (Tulsa: Albury Publishing, 1996), 55.

[2] Ibid., 47.

were used by God. God's call continued, and His Word answered all her objections one by one. Finally she had a vision in which angels came into her room and showed her a long, wide field of grain which fell like sheaves as she preached. Then she heard Jesus tell her, "Just as the grain fell, so people [will] fall." He said this would happen as she yielded to His call to preach.[3] She agreed, but it was some while later before she had the courage to step out in front of people and obey the call to preach the Gospel.

Maria's first act of obedience occurred in her community among a crowd that included mostly relatives: "She opened her mouth, and the crowd began to weep and fall to the floor. Some got up and ran out in tears."[4] She was thirty-five. This first meeting set the tone for a ministry that would increase from house and church gatherings to huge tent revivals, for in each of these increased gatherings, God's Spirit moved through the people in life-changing ways. These moves of the Holy Spirit also caused the churches around her to divide between those who opposed the new things God was doing and those who accepted them. In spite of this, God would use her to convert towns that were known for sin and hostility towards the Christian faith when no one else could gain their ear. But many religious people were hostile toward Maria, not just because she was a female preacher, but also because they were so unfamiliar with the work of the Holy Spirit.

This Christian evangelist became a trailblazer for God's Spirit as she preached the Gospel. At one meeting in western Ohio, people began to have what they called, "trances."[5] Maria wrote: "Fifteen came to the altar screaming for mercy. Men and women fell and lay like the dead. I had never seen anything like this. I felt it was the work of God, but did not know how to explain it, or what to say."[6] This move of God continued in her meetings from that time on. The vision Maria had of the falling sheaves of wheat was fulfilled.

---

[3] Ibid., 49.

[4] Ibid., 50.

[5] Ibid., 51.

[6] Ibid.

The people who experienced these trances would arouse themselves and go on to live changed lives as a result of their encounter with the Holy Spirit. Many of them had visions of heaven and hell and were saved. They also experienced other manifestations of the Holy Spirit such as tongues. Etter accepted all of these manifestations as normal for the Holy Spirit. As "the only leading evangelist of the Holiness Movement who embraced the Pentecostal experience of speaking in tongues," she explained simply that the Church had lost these experiences before this time.[7]

Later in her ministry she began to pray for the sick, and God healed them miraculously. All these things earned her the hostility of the press. The religious community continued their hostility too, but the faithful Maria never stopped obeying the call of God. She preached at revivals in the Midwest and then turned her eyes to California, where she held a large revival in Oakland in 1890. At this time, she experienced a great deal of persecution by the newspapers and threats from hoodlums, who vandalized her tents several times. In addition, she suffered the blow of learning her husband was unfaithful. The two divorced in 1891. He died in 1892.

Maria continued to faithfully preach the Gospel wherever God called her to do so. She met her second husband in 1902. Samuel Etter was from Hot Springs, Arkansas, and he became a real asset to her ministry, especially with publishing and distributing her books.[8] Now known as Mother Etter, she published several books:

Life, Work, and Experience of Maria Beula Woodworth, Evangelist.

Marvels and Miracles God Wrought in the Ministry of Mrs. M. B. Woodworth-Etter for Forty Years.

Signs and Wonders God Wrought in the Ministry of Mrs. M. B. Woodworth-Etter for Forty Years.

Songbooks.

Questions and Answers on Divine Healing.

Spirit-Filled Sermons.

Holy Ghost Sermons.

[7] Ibid., 61.

[8] Ibid, 60-61.

Acts of the Holy Ghost (later published as *A Diary of Signs and Wonders*).[9]

Samuel Etter worked with his wife for twelve years until his death. He was with her during the famous Dallas revival in 1912 which F. F. Bosworth planned and about which he later wrote. These meetings lasted six months and "as a result, Dallas became a hub of the Pentecostal revival."[10]

In 1913, Mother Etter took part in the Worldwide Camp Meeting in Los Angeles. Though she was forced to minister in the afternoon because of doctrinal controversies that took up the evening meetings, many were healed at her meetings. Forced to end before she was able to minister to the huge crowd that had come one day, she often would "raise her hands toward heaven as she was leaving the tent, and at that moment, many were healed."[11]

After her husband's death, Mother Etter continued to minister as a traveling evangelist until 1918. She was seventy-three. At that time, she returned to the Midwest to build The Tabernacle in Indianapolis, Indiana. Here, she continued to minister to those who came to hear her or to be healed, giving more and more of her responsibilities to her associates. During this time Aimee Semple McPherson came to see her preach. Many feel that her trailblazing ministry provided a model for McPherson who admired her.[12]

In 1924, an aging Mother Etter, suffering from failing health, lost her only surviving daughter to a streetcar accident. She mustered the strength to conduct the funeral and exhorted the people to look to heaven and not the grave.[13] Later that year, after telling her closest associates that the end was near, she died peacefully in her sleep at the age of eighty.[14]

---

[9] Ibid.

[10] Ibid., 65.

[11] Ibid., 66.

[12] Ibid., 70.

[13] Ibid., 71.

[14] Ibid., 72.

Section Two

Maria Woodworth-Etter Tells Her Story

Synopsis of My Early Life and Experience in the Work, Condensed

PART 1: MY BIRTH AND MARRIAGE

Life's Dawn—
Early Sorrows—
Discouragements and Losses

was born in New Lisbon, Columbiana County, Ohio, July 22, 1844, and was the fourth daughter of Samuel and Matilda Underwood. My parents were not Christians; therefore I was left without the religious teachings and influence with which so many homes are blessed. My father and mother joined the Disciple church one year before my father's death, which occurred in July, 1855. The death of my father was the first great sorrow of my life. He had gone away to harvest in usual health, and I will never forget the night he was brought home, cold in death. Some neighbor children and I were out watching a terrible storm raging when we saw two strangers approaching the house. They came to bring the sad intelligence of what had happened; and as we looked out, we saw the conveyance approaching, bringing the remains of our dear father. It was a terrible blow to our young hearts to see our father carried into the house cold and stiff in death and my mother fainting as fast as they could bring her to. We children were screaming and the storm was raging in all its fury. Father died of sunstroke. He was only sick a few hours and died praying for his family.

MY FATHER

My father was a fine-looking man, very intelligent and full of energy, but addicted to the accursed cup. He could control his appetite very well until he went to a town or city; then when his friends would persuade him to take a drink, he was large-hearted and easily persuaded. When he took one drink, he was like a crazy man for more and thought he was rich and would give his last penny away. Then when he had no money to buy drink with, he would pawn his clothes and come home to his large family and brokenhearted wife without a penny to buy food, and all in rags. And we little children would run and hide. Our young lives were full of terror and hardships. This is the reason we were left in poverty with a sickly, brokenhearted mother and eight helpless children, not one in the wide world to come to our rescue.

My mother was left with eight children to provide for and almost destitute. Then began the battle of life with us all. My mother was obliged to seek work in various ways. My oldest sisters and myself had to leave home and work by the week. We had not only ourselves to provide for, but also our brothers and sisters at home. It was very hard for my sensitive nature to go among strangers. I was discontented and homesick. I wanted to go to school where I could learn, for I longed for an education; and I often cried myself to sleep over this matter. I would have my books in the kitchen, where I could read a verse and commit it to memory; then read another, and so on, thus improving every opportunity while at my work. I had no opportunity of going to church from my earliest recollection. My heart went out in strong desire to know of God when eight years old. Two of my sisters were converted in a Methodist meeting. I went once or twice. My heart was melted with the Savior's love, but they seemed to think children had no need of salvation, and I was kept back.

My Conversion

At the age of thirteen, I attended a meeting of the Disciples church. My family were all Disciples at this time. When I heard the story of the Cross, my heart was filled with the love of Jesus. My eyes seemed to be fountains of tears.

I was seated in the back of a large audience and was the first to make the start to seek the Lord. It seemed so far to the front seat that it looked like I could never make it, but I said,

> I can but perish if I go.
> I am resolved to try,

For if I stay away I know
I shall forever die.[1]

The minister took great interest in me and said many good things to encourage me and prayed that my life might be a shining light. If he could have looked forward and have seen my life's work for the Master, he surely would have rejoiced to know how kindly he had talked to the poor little orphan girl.

But I did not get converted then. They did not believe in a change of heart and nature; but praise the Lord, He did not leave me in the dark. The next day, as they took me down to the creek to baptize me, there was a great crowd around. I heard someone say, "Maybe she will be drowned." It scared me a little. I thought, *Maybe I might*. But I said, "Lord, I will go through if I do." So I asked the Lord to save me fully, trusting myself in His hands; and while going into the water, a light came over me, and I was converted. The people saw the change and said I had fainted.

God Calling Me to the Work

Then began my new life of peace and joy in a Savior's love. Then I was contented and happy, singing and praising God all the day long. I never went to any place of amusement. I attended four meetings on Sabbath and three or four during the week. I did not stay away from meeting once a year unless I was sick. I was more anxious now than ever for an education, for I wanted to work for Jesus and be useful in the vineyard of Christ. Soon after I was converted, I heard the voice of Jesus calling me to go out in the highways and hedges and gather in the lost sheep.[2] Like Mary, I pondered these things in my heart for I had no one to hold counsel with.[3] The Disciples did not believe that women had any right to work for Jesus. Had I told them my impression, they would have made sport of me. I had never heard of women working in public except as missionaries, so I could see no opening—except, as I thought, if I ever married, my choice would be an earnest Christian and then we would enter upon the mission work. A few years after this I married Mr. Woodworth.

[1] Title and source of verse unknown.

[2] See Luke 14:23.

[3] See Luke 2:19.

We settled in the country and thought by industry and honest toil to gain a little of this world's goods to sustain these physical bodies, but my health failed and everything we undertook seemed to be a failure. I was away from all Christian influence and could not often attend the house of God. Often, when hearing the church bells ringing, which had been the signal for me to repair to the house of worship, and knowing that I could not go, I would cry myself to sleep. I had one trial after another, and temptations and discouragements beset me on every side. The angel of death came to our home and after hovering around for a few days, he bore away our only little boy, a bright, blue-eyed darling. As he was passing away, he looked up and smiled. He looked like an angel and seemed to say: "Mamma, do not weep for me; I am going to a better world." It almost broke my heart to lay him away in the cold grave; but I could see the loving hand of God and hear Him calling me to build up higher, to set my affections on heavenly things and not on the things of the earth.

Georgie's Conversion and Sickness

One year had hardly passed by when the angel of death came again to our home and took away our baby Freddy, and at the same time, I lay for weeks between life and death. In all this I could see the hand of the loving Father calling me to leave all and follow Him. About this time our little daughter Georgie was converted. She was about seven years old. She was a great comfort to me. She loved to talk of the goodness of God and our Redeemer. Many happy times we enjoyed talking together of the beautiful home over the river where her brothers had gone. I did not think she would leave me so soon to join their ranks and raise her voice with theirs in singing salvation to our God, who sitteth upon the throne, and to the Lamb forever.[4] She was taken sick with that dreadful disease, scrofula,[5] and lingered about eight months. Her sufferings were great, yet she never murmured or complained but only said it was for her good.

[4] See Revelation 7:10.

[5] "scrofula"—Tuberculosis of the lymphatic glands, esp. of the neck. *(Webster's New World College Dictionary,* Third Edition, [USA: Macmillan, 1997]).

She loved to read about Jesus and the beautiful mansions He was preparing and the robe and crown that were waiting for her. She would talk to all who came to see her of Jesus and His love and tell them to meet her in heaven.

She sent messages to her Sabbath school teacher and scholars, and to her friends far and near, to meet her in heaven. For weeks before she died, her face was all lighted up with the glory of God. The angels seemed to be hovering about her bed. She could hear them singing. Her body was with us, but her spirit seemed to be above the earth communing with God. She was willing to go and be with Jesus, but it seemed hard for her to leave me. She would say: "O Mamma, if you could go with me I would be so happy. I hate to leave you; but oh, say you will meet me in heaven."

I said, "Georgie, I will try."

But that would not do. She said: "O Mamma, say you will: I cannot die unless you promise to meet me in heaven."

I said: "Georgie, by the grace of God I will meet you in heaven."

She said: "Now I am ready; I know you will come, Mamma; I shall always be looking for you, and when you die, I am coming for you."

Georgie's Death

The Sabbath before she died, she called me to her bedside and said: "Mamma, I am going to leave you this week," and she began to set her house in order. She talked of dying as we would talk of going to visit a dear friend. She gave away all of her earthly possessions. To me she gave her testament—said she would like to see all her friends once more. She selected her burial robe and place to be buried and requested us to leave room for me to be buried by her side. She stayed with us until the last of the week and was frequently heard to say:

> I am coming, Lord,
> Coming now to Thee;
> Wash me, cleanse me in the blood
> Which flowed on Calvary.

She kept inviting everyone to come to Jesus and be saved. Her sufferings were intense toward the last. When she could not speak, and we would ask her if she was happy and if Jesus was with her, she would smile and nod her head. She thought she was going. She put up her mouth to kiss each one and gasped good-bye between her struggles, saying, "Meet me in heaven;" but she rallied and lived two [more] hours. In this way she talked on till the last, and her face shone with the glory of heaven. Looking up she said: "O Mamma, I see Jesus and the angels; I see my little brothers; they have come for me." And they bore her away in triumph to the heavenly land. It seemed to me that I could see them as they went sweeping through the gates in the New Jerusalem.

It was like death to part with my darling. But Jesus was very precious to my soul. Heaven was nearer, Christ was dearer than ever before. I had one more treasure in glory.

My health had been very poor all through her sickness. Three weeks before her [Georgie's] death, little Gertie was born. She was the picture of Georgie and seemed to have her sweet disposition, and I thought as she grew older she would take her place; but the precious bud was not permitted to bloom in this world of sin. At the age of four months, the angels bore her away where the flowers never fade nor die, there to join her sister and brothers who were waiting to welcome her at the golden gates. I could say with David, they cannot come back to me, but I will go to them.[6] Praise the Lord for the Christian's hope.

[6] See 2 Samuel 12:23.

PART 2: PREPARATION FOR SERVICE

Visions of Heaven – Needed Help – God Calling Me to Preach

rom the time of the sad occurrences which have just been narrated in the previous chapter, my health was very poor, and many times I was brought near the brink of the grave. Everyone who saw me thought I would die. But the work the Lord was calling me to do came up before me so plainly that I thought He would raise me up and open the way; and at these times, when I seemed to be hovering between life and death, I would have such glorious visions.

At one time I was praying for the salvation of sinners, and the Savior appeared on the cross by me and talked with me; I laid my hand on His mangled body and looked up in His smiling face. Another time I was meditating upon the love of God in giving His only Son to die for sinners and of the beautiful home He was preparing for those who love Him, and I seemed to float away and was set down in the Beautiful City. Oh, the glorious sight that met my view can never be expressed by mortal tongue! Heaven is located. It is a real city. Its inhabitants are real and not imaginary. If mothers could see their children as I saw them, in all their shining glory, they would never weep for them, but would leave all and follow Jesus. They would let nothing keep them from meeting their children in heaven, where they are shining in dazzling beauty around God's throne and are watching to give welcome to the Beautiful City. I never think of my children as being in the grave. Oh, no. The loved form that we laid away in the cold grave is nothing but the casket that contained the jewel which is now shining in the Savior's crown.

Often now when I am pleading with sinners to come to Jesus and telling them of the love of God, [of] the beautiful home in heaven, of the mansions bright, of the robe and crown, and of the great multitude who have been washed in the blood of the Lamb, the veil seems to be taken away and I feel lost in the love and glory of

Christ. I feel as though the congregation was left behind, and I was floating upward in a cloud of glory. Oh, the wonderful love of God! The half has never been told. It never can be told. It will take all eternity to tell of the redeeming love in the wonderful plan of redemption to a dying world. Dear readers, will you not give up all and follow Jesus and meet me in the beautiful land where sorrow will never come?

I do praise God for His lovingkindness to me in always raising up the best of Christian friends in my behalf. In all my sickness and trouble, the ministers and people came from the different churches in the town and had prayer meetings in my room. They prayed in the churches for my recovery. I was willing to die and leave my little girl and boy, feeling that God would care for them, but the work God was calling me to do loomed up before me. All these years God had been preparing me—for I was not willing. I felt like a worm in His sight. It seemed impossible for me to undertake the work for the salvation of souls; but the time had come to promise or die. I promised God that if He would restore my health and prepare me and show me the work, I would try to do it. I began to get better immediately.

The Perishing Multitudes

We then moved to a Friends' settlement, and they came and took me to church. They had glorious meetings. God seemed to say to me, "I brought you here; go to work." Now the struggle commenced. I was very timid and bound as with chains in a man-fearing spirit. When I arose to testify, I trembled like a leaf and began to make excuses—"Oh God, send someone else!" Then the Lord, in a vision, caused me to see the bottomless pit, open in all its horror and woe. There was weeping and wailing and gnashing of teeth. It was surrounded by a great multitude of people who seemed unconscious of their danger; and without a moment's warning, they would tumble into this awful place. I was above the people on a narrow plank-walk, which wound up toward heaven; and I was exhorting and pleading with the people to come up onto the plank and escape that awful place. Several started. There was a beautiful, bright light above me, and I was encouraging them to follow that light and they would go straight to heaven.

This vision left quite an impression on my mind. When the Spirit of God was striving with me to talk or pray in a meeting, I would resist as long as I could. Then this awful vision would rise before me, and I would see souls sinking into eternal woe. The voice of Jesus would whisper, "I am with you; be not afraid." Then I would be on my feet or knees in a moment. I would forget everything but the love of God and dying souls. God seemed to speak through me to the people, but I had so much opposition to contend with. My people were opposed; my husband and daughter fought against it; and my whole nature shrunk from going to stand as a gazingstock for the people. But the Lord was showing in many ways that I must go and perform the work He had for me to do.

Death of Willie

Several ministers whom I had never seen before told me, at different times, that God was calling me to the ministry and that I would have to go. I said, "If I were a man, I would love to work for Jesus." They told me I had a work to do which no man could do; the Lord was calling me to the West to labor for lost souls. I said, "O Lord! I cannot take Willie with me, nor can I leave him behind." Then the Lord saw fit to take him out of the way, so He laid His hand on my darling little boy and in a few days took him home to heaven.

He was the joy of my life, nearly seven years old. He was very bright for one of his age—in fact, far beyond his years. He was the pet of the whole neighborhood. He seemed to know when taken sick that he would not get well. He talked of dying and going to see Georgie, who had been dead three years that month. He said he would have to die sometime, and that he would rather go now if we could go with him—that he would never be sick any more, nor have to take any more medicine. He bid us all good-bye and said he was going to be with Jesus. He died very happy.

He had talked and fretted much about his little sister and said he could not live without her. By faith, I could see her meeting him at the beautiful gates and welcoming him into the golden city of God. This sad bereavement nearly took my life. The dear Savior was never so near and real to me before. He was by my side and seemed to bear me up in His loving arms. I could say, "The Lord gave and the Lord has taken away; blessed be the name of the Lord."[1]

When alone, I missed my darling so much that I wept as though my heart would break. Then I would always pray; and as I prayed, I would forget everything earthly and soar away by faith to the Golden City and there see my darlings all together shining in glory, looking at me and saying, "Mamma do not weep for us, but come this way." I would always end in praising and giving glory to God for taking them to such a happy place. Lizzie, our oldest child, aged sixteen, was all we had left of six sweet children.

Satan Hinders Me

In all these trials, God was preparing me and opening the way for the great battle against the enemy of souls; and now the great desire of my heart was to work for Jesus. I longed to win a star for the Savior's crown. But when I thought of my weakness, I shrank from the work. Sometimes when the Spirit of God was striving and calling so plainly, I would yield and say, "Yes, Lord; I will go." The glory of God came upon me like a cloud; and I seemed to be carried away hundreds of miles and set down in a field of wheat, where the sheaves were falling all around me. I was filled with zeal and power and felt as if I would stand before the whole world and plead with dying sinners. It seemed to me that I must leave all and go at once.

Then Satan would come in like a flood and say, "You would look nice preaching, being a gazingstock for the people to make sport of. You know you could not do it." Then I would think of my weakness and say, "No, of course I cannot do it." Then I would be in darkness and despair. I wanted to run away from God, or I wished I could die; but when I began to look at the matter in this way, that God knew all about me and was able and willing to qualify me for the work, I asked Him to qualify me.

God Baptizes Me With the Holy Ghost

I want the reader to understand that at this time, I had a good experience, a pure heart, [and] was full of the love of God but was not

[1] See Job 1:21.

qualified for God's work. I knew that I was but a worm. God would have to take a worm to thresh a mountain. Then I asked God to give me the power He gave the Galilean fishermen—to anoint me for service. I came like a child asking for bread. I looked for it. God did not disappoint me.

The power of the Holy Ghost came down as a cloud. It was brighter than the sun. I was covered and wrapped up in it. My body was light as the air. It seemed that heaven came down. I was baptized with the Holy Ghost and fire and power, which have never left me. Oh, praise the Lord! There was liquid fire, and the angels were all around in the fire and the glory. It is through the Lord Jesus Christ, and by this power, that I have stood before hundreds of thousands of men and women, proclaiming the unsearchable riches of Christ.

The Friends wanted me to travel a year with a minister and his wife and work in revivals, and they would pay all expenses. But my husband was not willing for me to go or to engage in the work anyplace.

PART 3: PROGRESS IN PREPARATION

Excuses—
The Burden for Souls—
The Neglected Talent

I thought I would go through a course of study and prepare for the work, thinking the Lord would make my husband and people willing in some way to let me go out and work. But I could not get my mind fixed on my study. Everything seemed empty and vacant, and I was restless and uneasy.

The dear Savior stood by me one night in a vision and talked face to face with me and asked what I was doing on earth. I felt condemned and said, "Lord, I am going to work in Thy vineyard."

The Lord said, "When?"

And I answered, "When I get prepared for the work."

Then the Lord said to me, "Don't you know that while you are getting ready souls are perishing? Go now, and I will be with you." I told Him that I could not talk to the people; I did not know what to say, and they would not listen to me. Jesus said, "You can tell the people what the Lord has done for your soul; tell of the glory of God and the love of Jesus; tell sinners to repent and prepare for death and the judgment, and I will be with you." Still, I made one excuse after another, and Jesus would answer, "Go and I will be with you."

I TALK WITH THE SAVIOR IN A VISION

I told Him I wanted to study the Bible, that I did not understand it well enough. Then, there appeared upon the wall a large, open Bible, and the verses stood out in raised letters. The glory of God shone around and upon the Book. I looked, and I could understand it all.

Then Jesus said again, "Go, and I will be with you."

I cried, "Lord, I will go. Where shall I go?"

And Jesus said, "Go here, go there, wherever souls are perishing." Praise the Lord for His wonderful goodness in revealing His Word and will in such a wonderful way, to such a poor weak worm of the dust. I saw more in that vision than I could have learned in years of hard study. Praise His holy name. I saw that I must not depend on anything that I could have learned in years of hard study. Praise His holy name. I saw that I must not depend on anything that I could do, but to look to Him for strength and wisdom. "Not by might, nor by power, but by my spirit," saith the Lord.[1] I was to be the vessel of clay God was going to use to His own glory. I was to be God's mouthpiece. I must trust God to speak through me to the people, the words of eternal life.

There was all this time a secret monitor within, telling me that I should be calling sinners to repentance. I could not get clear of that reflection by day or by night. Awake or dreaming, I seemed to have a large congregation before me, all in tears as I told them the story of the Cross. Thus for months and years did I debate; and yet did I falter and hesitate, and like Jonah, trim my sail for Tarshish. I thought if I were a man it would be a pleasure for me; but for me, a woman, to preach, if I could, would subject me to ridicule and contempt among my friends and kindred and bring reproach upon His glorious cause.

I Keep My Talent Hidden Away

Always when I had trouble, I would flee to the stronghold of faith and grace and prayer. But when I went in secret to pray, the words seemed to come to me, "You deny Me before men, and I will deny you before my Father and the holy angels."[2] Then I would go to my Bible and search for teachings and examples.

When the Lord put His erring people in remembrance of His great blessings to Israel He said, "Did I not send thee Moses and Aaron *and Miriam* to be your leaders?"[3] And again, the prophets were ordained of God. And when there was trouble on hand, Barak dare

[1] Zechariah 4:6.

[2] Matthew 10:33, paraphrased.

[3] See Micah 6:4.

not meet the enemy unless Deborah led the van.[4] And the noble woman, always ready to work for God and His cause, said, "I will surely go. God's people must not be a prey to the enemy. Oh no; call out the men of Israel, Sisera's mighty hosts are gathering."[5]

God Used Women

As I continued to read my Bible, I saw that in all ages of the world the Lord raised up of His own choosing, men, women, and children—Miriam, Deborah, Hannah, Hulda, Anna, Phoebe, Narcissus, Tryphena, Persis, Julia, the Marys, and the sisters who were co-workers with Paul in the Gospel, whose names were in the Book of Life, and many other women whose labors are mentioned with praise.[6] Even the children were made the instruments of His praise and glory. (See 1 Samuel 3:4; Jeremiah 1:6; and Numbers 22:28[7]). The more I investigated, the more I found to condemn me. There was the Master giving one, two, and five talents and the moral obligation of each person receiving them and their several rewards.[8] I had one talent, which was hidden away.

By the prophet Joel, we learn that one special feature of the Gospel dispensation shall be "your sons and your daughters shall prophesy, your old men shall dream dreams, your young men shall see visions: and also upon the servants and the handmaids in those days will I pour out my Spirit."[9] It seems by the prophet Joel, that the last days were to be particularly conspicuous for this kind of prophesying. We cannot reverse God's decree, for it is said: "Heaven and earth shall pass away, but the Word of God shall endure forever."[10]

---

[4] See Judges 4:9-10.

[5] See Judges 4:14.

[6] See Micah 6:4; Judges 4:4; 1 Samuel 1 & 2; 2 Kings 22:14; Luke 2:36; Romans 16:7,11-13,15; Luke 1:30; Luke 10:42; John 11:2; and Mark 16:9.

[7] Numbers 22:28 mentions a donkey that was used to speak to the prophet.

[8] See Matthew 25:14-30.

[9] Joel 2:28-29, paraphrased.

[10] Matthew 24:35, Mark 13:31, or Luke 21:33, paraphrased.

The first meeting that I undertook to hold was in a little town where we had lived some years before, right among my husband's people. It was a cross for me to talk to those people; but I said, in the name of God and by His sustaining grace, I will try and leave the result with Him. As I rose to speak, this text came to my mind: "Set thine house in order; for thou shalt die, and not live."[11]

When I began to talk upon the subject, the man fearing spirit left me and the words came to me faster than I could give them utterance. My sister-in-law broke down and left the house. We continued the meeting a few days and twenty claimed to be converted. People were converted all through the neighborhood. One who came to this meeting afterward became my son-in-law.

I continued to keep house and spent as much time in holding meetings as I could, to give my husband a chance to attend his work. I was anxious to raise money for us to go West. I would ride seven miles and hold a meeting on Saturday evening and three meetings on the Sabbath—sometimes in different churches—and then ride home over a hilly and rough road. By this time I would be nearly exhausted and hardly able to walk around to do my work. But the last of the week I would go again. Often through the week, I held meetings in the towns around where I was born and raised, where we had lived since we were married.

Good Results

It was a cross for me to speak before my own folks and the people whom I had always known. But God wonderfully blessed my labors in every place. Wherever I went, the house was crowded. I did not write my sermons or have sketches of sermons. I would take a text and trust God to lead me in His own way.

I was holding meetings for a few days where I was raised, and the house was crowded every night. One night I could not get a text. The people came pouring in until the house was packed. I began to get frightened. A brother said to me, "The Disciples[12] are turning out tonight." There I was, with several hundred people before me and no text—nothing to talk about. Everything was empty. I began

[11] 2 Kings 20:1 or Isaiah 38:1.

[12] Possibly members of the Disciples of Christ church.

to plead with Jesus. I told Him He had called me to preach, that here was this starving multitude, and I had no bread to give them. To verify His promise and to glorify Himself in manifesting His power to this people, the words came to me, "What are you going to do with Jesus, that is called the Christ?" and also the place to find the text.[13]

Jesus seemed to whisper in my ear, "I am with you; be not afraid." I opened the meeting and repeated the text. As I did so, the power[14] came and it seemed that all I had to do was to open my mouth. The people all through the house began to weep. I talked one hour and a quarter. The power came as it did when I received the baptism of the Holy Ghost. It seemed as if the house was full of the glory of God. I felt as if I was drawn up over the people. Glory to God for helping a worm of the dust.

Taken from *Spirit Filled Sermons Preached by Mrs. M. B. Woodworth-Etter, Evangelist,* by Maria Woodworth-Etter (Indianapolis: Mrs. M. B. Woodworth-Etter, 1921).

---

[13] Matthew 27:22, paraphrased.

[14] "The power"—This term refers to the empowerment of the Holy Spirit for ministry. In some Holiness groups this experience constituted the third stage of spiritual growth, coming after justification (conversion) and sanctification (power over sin).

Church built in 1918 by Etter in Indianapolis, Indiana, known as the Etter Tabernacle.

Brief Summary of the Woodworth-Etter Tabernacle Work

Established over Three Years—Many Souls Are Finding God—The Easter, Mid-Summer, Christmas, and New Year Special Revivals Are Annual Affairs

little over three years ago, God showed me one night that I was to build a tabernacle here at West Indianapolis, Indiana, so that people from all parts of the country could come in and spend some time in a good spiritual mission and get established in God. He showed me that the meetings should be of old-time fashion and power, where people can get spiritual food to supply their needs for soul and body; also that there was a tendency in these last days to depart from the old paths and seek new paths that the Son of Man never trod. We see these side paths on the right and on the left today.

Tabernacle Meetings Prove a Blessing

Ever since the Tabernacle has been built, the meetings have been going on, unabated in interest and power. Many special campaigns have been held during these years. The Word has gone forth, and multitudes have heard and published it and are still doing so. During these special efforts, people generally have to be turned away for lack of room, and the Tabernacle is crowded to its capacity.

People have come and are coming from all parts of this country and Canada to get help for soul and body, and nearly all go back saying they received what they came for. Our desire is to help such and to get them rooted and grounded in the faith of Jesus Christ our master so that they can be lighthouses for Jesus in their community.

God Heals People

Many wonderful healings have taken place. God, at times, shows people definitely that He wants them to come. One time a woman living in the East had a large tumor, which gradually got worse. Most of her relatives and the doctors wanted her to be operated on at once. She felt she should come to the Tabernacle and be prayed for but did not wish to come against the desire of her loved ones. She finally decided to get God's mind by putting her finger on a text in the Bible without knowing where. She asked, "Lord, what will You do if I go to the hospital?" When she looked on the text, where she had placed her finger, it said, "The Lord will do nothing."[1] She closed the Book and put her finger on another place without knowing on what text it was and asked, "Lord, what will You do if I go to Sister Etter's meeting?" This time she had her finger on a text that read, "Before you call I will hear and answer."[2] This settled the matter in her mind. She came with her nurse, suffering intensely, was prayed for, and God healed her.

A few weeks ago a woman came into the Tabernacle who had such a large tumor that she could not dress herself. After she was prayed for, she felt relieved and that she was healed. The next day she came back with a smile on her face and said, "The tumor is going down and today I dressed myself." A week later she testified that the tumor was all gone.

People Get Saved and Baptized

There is somebody getting through to God in practically every meeting. Scores of people get saved and baptized in water, also with the Holy Ghost and fire. God greatly blesses at the baptismal services. On one occasion recently, the power of God fell on all those around the baptistery and a number fell as though dead. An ordained evangelist who witnessed the scene, but was in a rather backslidden condition, was suddenly shown by the Spirit to reconsecrate her life to God and be baptized. When she went in under the water, she was carried away by the Spirit into the other world.

[1] Amos 3:7, paraphrased.

[2] Isaiah 65:24, paraphrased.

She had to be carried out and lay for eighteen hours under the power with scarcely a move. When she came out, she told what Jesus had shown her while she was in heaven in the Spirit.

The power comes in waves of glory over the meetings as we worship God in Spirit and in truth, so that some touch God almost daily and get what their hearts long for.

A few days ago, a backslider made his way to the altar and there the power struck him. He got saved and baptized, and for about ten minutes he had the floor, telling what Jesus had done for him.

Last Sunday, a woman who never had been in the Tabernacle before came to be healed of rheumatism. As she knelt down at the altar, the power of God struck her and she got up on the platform and demonstrated by leaping and dancing that God had healed her at the altar.

Messages in other tongues with interpretations come forth at almost every meeting. Recently, a stranger came to the Tabernacle who testified that he spoke and understood seven languages and that he understood, in the natural, some of the messages in tongues.

Come During Special Campaign

We purpose to have special campaigns every year. At Easter, midsummer, Christmas, and New Years, they are annual affairs. We desire all those who can to write us beforehand and arrange at some time to attend these campaigns. During these periods, we generally have three meetings daily and continue from two weeks to a month or longer. We also have extra ministers with us during these periods, who will prove to be a great blessing. I do not expect to go out in evangelistic campaigns in various parts of the country as much as I used to, but intend to give most of my time to the work at home here.

Anointed Handkerchiefs

There are many who have read my books and are suffering from sickness but cannot arrange to attend the meetings here. Many have written asking me to pray over and anoint handkerchiefs and return them to them. Like in the days of Paul, God is healing people through these anointed cloths. "God wrought special miracles by the hands of Paul: So that from his body were brought unto the sick handkerchiefs and aprons, and the diseases departed from them, and the evil spirits departed out of them" (See Acts 19:11-12).

We have prayed over thousands of these cloths and handkerchiefs and send them out in the name of Jesus. It is wonderful, the reports that come in daily, how God heals people. And others get saved and baptized through these prayers.

Many people wonder how we live and get along at all. Others are careless about giving as they think that we have a financial backing that we can depend upon, but we have not. We are living a life of faith and are not looking to any special ones; but trust God, that through the people, He will supply all our needs.

In my ministry of forty-five years, I have never asked anyone individually for even one dollar, amidst all the mighty healings; but have left it with them and the Lord. Many people think because it is a life of faith we do not need anything and so do not give anything. If the people were more faithful on lines of giving, there are many things we could do for the Lord's work from which we are now hindered for lack of means.

Our work here is very heavy. We get calls at all hours from various parts of the city to pray for the sick and afflicted, and if at all possible, some of the workers visit these people.

Also telegrams and long distance messages and special delivery letters come from the Atlantic to the Pacific, at all hours of the day and night, to pray for someone that is dying. May the Lord's blessing be upon us all. Amen.

This City Is a Good Place to Live

Indianapolis, Indiana, is a good place to live, being approximately the center of the U.S.A. It means much for you and I (*sic*) to live at a place where we can get the spiritual food we need in these last days. We give you all a hearty welcome to become one of our band here, to take part in the Gospel work. Surely if we do this, Jesus will have a reward for us when He comes.

And, behold, I come quickly; and my reward is with me, to give to every man according as his work shall be.

—Revelation 22:12

The Spirit and the bride say, Come. And let him that heareth say, Come. And let him that is athirst come. And whosoever will, let him take the water of life freely.

—Revelation 22:17

Taken from *Spirit Filled Sermons Preached by Mrs. M. B. Woodworth-Etter, Evangelist* (Indianapolis: Mrs. M. B. Woodworth-Etter, 1921).

SECTION THREE

What the World Saw

NOTE FROM THE EDITOR:

The news articles that follow have been arranged chronologically to allow the reader to trace the course of Maria Woodworth-Etter's ministry from 1885-1924. Hostile reporters wrote some of the news clippings, demonstrating many of the obstacles this ground-breaking evangelist had to overcome each time she came to a city. They also demonstrate the truth that when God does a work, no one can remain neutral. Some clippings, therefore, do not accurately represent her, some perpetuating lies about her and her ministry. On the other hand, some clippings report accurately the mistakes that Mrs. Etter made as she attempted to follow the will of God. The prophecies which she mistakenly affirmed in Oakland, California are an example.

Some news articles will not flatter this servant of God, but the overall impression will be that of a faithful, hard-working minister whom God used to perform some remarkable and miraculous conversions and healings. By preaching seven days a week, twice a day (most days), she often earned the grudging admiration of her harshest critics. Like Wesley, she brought thousands to Christ whom the Church ignored. In addition, the excitement and turmoil that stirred in a town as she went about the task of soulwinning can be communicated best by those who experienced it.

February 25, 1884

Unknown Source[1]

An Evangelist Appears

ne week later, Wednesday, Feb. 25, Mrs. Maria B. Woodworth, a famous evangelist of the era, was scheduled to appear but failed to show up, "sorely disappointing" a large crowd that had gathered to hear her. Mrs. Woodworth finally opened on Thursday evening, March 12. The *Post* described her as "a terror to sin and the devil," but allowed that her act would be "severely tested" in Columbia City with its 13 saloons. She drew large crowds, the largest being that of Sunday evening, March 22. During all this evangelistic period, the roller skaters became more and more restive for Mrs. Woodworth to vacate the rink; however, she remained on stage until Sunday, March 29, after which the revival moved to Larwill.

[1] Note to reader: The article which was published mid- to late-twentieth century is included for its reference to the *Post* (Columbia, Indiana) and its treatment of Etter. It is taken from a book chapter of an unknown source, which discusses the construction of the skating rink in which Etter preached.

May 13, 1884

Ft. Wayne Gazette (IN)

[Noble Work]

aria Woodworth is doing noble work in the cause of the Lord at New Haven. She has been there for the past week, and her success has been nothing short of phenomenal. Monday she was greeted by many of her friends, who spoke many words of encouragement and praise, wishing her unbounded success in her noble calling, and assuring her of their hearty cooperation. Many have repented and become true Christian men and women through the efforts of this laborer in Christ's vineyard. The best proof of her success is that the number converted through her intercession now reaches well up in the hundreds. Fifty advanced Sunday night and buckled on the armor in the cause of Jehovah.

January, 1885

Cincinnati Enquirer (OH)

[A Very Remarkable Revival]

I have endeavored to give a true and impartial account of the very remarkable revival of religion at the Methodist Episcopal Church in this city, and I am impressed with the magnitude of the undertaking, at present more than ever before, and am convinced that it is beyond the "ken of tongue or pen," to give an accurate description of the scenes enacted at each meeting. Scores have been stricken down at these meetings, and whatever form the limbs or body chanced to assume, in that position, immovable as a statue, they remained—sometimes the hand uplifted far above the head, the eyes open wide, and not a muscle of the entire body moved; they were as immovable as in death. Many have gone to these meetings in a spirit of jest and were the first to be under the influence pervading the assembly. The people are wonderfully excited, and neighbor asks neighbor, "What is it?" Is it what is known as catalepsy,[1] or is it a form of ecstasy, where the mind absorbs an idea until every faculty of the soul is under its control and the body becomes stilled as though dead—naught but circulation and the act of respiration remaining to signify life? The features are as pale as marble, the pulse week and feeble.

This morning a young lady was found in a trance or ecstasy in bed, and could not be aroused for hours. The eyes were lifted to the ceiling, and the hand pointed to heaven. When she was restored to consciousness, she shouted, clapped her hands, and sang hallelujahs for an hour, and said she was perfectly oblivious and totally unconscious to all about her. Is it contagious, or infectious; epidemic, or endemic; good, or evil? Many think it is mesmerism[2]; others attribute

Quoted from *Trials and Triumphs of Maria B. Woodworth* by Maria Woodworth-Etter (Published by Maria Woodworth-Etter, 1886), 187-190. (Editor's Note: A combination of the following two articles also appeared in the *New York Times* on January 24, 1885.)

[1] "catalepsy"—A condition in which consciousness and feeling seem to be temporarily lost, and the muscles become rigid (Webster's N. W., 1997).

[2] "mesmerism"—The nineteenth-century term for hypnotism arising from the disputed claims of a European physician, Anton Mesmer, to affect his subjects by magnetism.

attribute it to the works of Satan, while the believers tell us it is the work of the Divine Spirit. We are loth[3] to give other than facts in regard to the wonderfully marvelous influence being brought to bear for bringing sinners to repentance, but we have observed that all, without a single exception of those affected, are very impressible in their natures, quite excitable in their dispositions, and ready believers in the wonderful, mysterious, and supernatural.

The lady evangelist, Mrs. Woodworth, is a lady of fine physique, comely and commanding appearance; and while not highly cultured and refined, yet she is an impressive speaker, and when speaking keeps her hands in constant motion. She was first to become a subject of this form of catalepsy or ecstasy, and soon others were subjected to the same influences. Each and all of them tell of wonderful transition from grief and woe to joy and peace, and many of them assert that while thus unconscious they are feasting upon heavenly manna and drinking from the fountain of life, conversing with father, mother, or loved ones in the spirit land.

The older and sedate Christians are amazed and startled at the scenes enacted and transpiring before them, and already mutterings of discontent are being heard. To them it is a new departure—"something new under the sun." At each and every meeting the entire populace is in attendance and other towns and the country around are helping to swell the great numbers that flock to see and hear the wonderful and mysterious scenes.

For the last few evenings a colored barber named Ananias Frazier has been a constant and devoted worker and sings with a fervor and inspiration that enlivens and awakens enthusiasm to its highest tension. His songs are plantation melodies, and they help to give variation to the meetings.

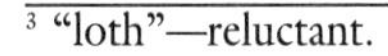

[3] "loth"—reluctant.

January, 1885

Cincinnati Enquirer (OH)

[The Half Has Not Been Told]

The half has not been told concerning the wonderful revival at this place. No pen could have exaggerated the scenes that have occurred, nor tongue given expression to words that would have painted, in the least, incidents that have transpired. The evangelist lady said she received scores of letters from all parts of the country, many requesting her presence to carry on a revival. Among the list on Saturday was a letter from a distinguished physician, an infidel, stating that he had read the accounts descriptive of the scenes enacted at the meetings, of the tranced condition of so many persons. He wanted the evangelist's opinion of the cause and wished her to tell him how to obtain such "a pearl of great price"[1]—that these things were to him truly a mystery.

Yesterday John M. Ruckman, ex-editor of the *Hartford City News* and postmaster at this place, expressed conversion, and his glowing and impressive account of the wonderful transition from darkness to light, and his earnest appeal for others to taste of the riches of salvation, awakened an enthusiasm seldom witnessed. Last evening the evangelist delivered her farewell exhortation. Her voice, rendered hoarse and feeble by long continued labor and overexertion, was freed from any embarrassment by these conditions and rang out clear and distinct, and her plea was the most impressive of all and had a wonderful and telling effect upon the audience. We are not exaggerating when we say that at least two hundred of that vast audience were engaged in prayer in an audible voice at once.

As many as twenty reporters have been here from different states to see, hear, and give an account of these meetings. This morning a Boston paper sends a representative, but he comes at the eleventh hour. Yesterday's quarterly meeting services were held at the church, Elder Robinson officiating. In the afternoon they gave way for Mrs.

Quoted from *Trials and Triumps of Maria B. Woodworth* by Maria Woodworth-Etter (Published by Maria Woodworth-Etter, 1886), 191-194.

[1] See Matthew 13:46.

Woodworth, and a class meeting or experience meeting was instituted in which all of the young converts participated, giving evidence of the change in their condition from death to life, from sin and condemnation to favor with God.

Seven were tranced, or in an ecstatic condition last night. The shouts of "newborn souls," prayers by the saints, and singing by that immense concourse of people, together with the senseless gibberish of a thoughtless and giddy throng of dudes and dudesses, was "Babel confused." Yesterday about forty united with the Methodist Episcopal Church, and one hundred and twenty-seven expressed conversion as the result of the revival. The evangelist asks not, and apparently cares not, for assistance, only to supply her wants, and her husband's, who is dependent upon her for a living. The lady recognizes the great good done her by the publication of her meetings in the *Enquirer* and makes public acknowledgement of the same in the presence of the vast throngs that assemble to hear her.

By a wise and prudent course, an upright and chaste walk, and godly conversation, she has silenced the tongue of calamity and secured to herself praise and adulation from the very lips that fired their venom and anathemas at her, while she was trying to bring them to repentance.

Last night was the last of this series of meetings, and the evangelist made the finest plea of all her ministrations at this place. She could have been heard blocks away. She cried out at one time in a voice that startled everyone of that large assembly: "Open your hearts to God, and He will open heaven to you." Almost every town and neighborhood around this city for miles has been represented. Last night a gentleman from Indianapolis was present and participated. The evangelist does not indicate her destination when she takes her departure today, but Union City is earnestly laboring to secure her services, and she probably will engage in revival services there.

The closing scene was wonderful. In the presence of the elder and pastor of that charge, several clergymen, and nearly three thousand persons—many were struck down and lay as if dead around the pulpit, and scores were wounded—and amidst the fire from the battlements of heaven, the earnest appeals of the evangelist, and the hallelujahs of the blood-washed, stood that mass of people, wondering.

January 23, 1885

Ft. Wayne Gazette (IN)

Sister Woodworth

SHE KNOCKS 'EM COLD AT HARTFORD CITY—THE UNREGENERATE FALL IN SPASMS OF RELIGIOUS EMOTION

ister Woodworth, the Methodist lady evangelist who labored so long in this county, is now at Hartford City, about forty miles from this city, and has repeated her wonderful success in snatching souls from the burning.

On Sunday evening, at the M. E. [Methodist Episcopal] church a scene was enacted seldom witnessed. Mrs. Woodworth, after delivering a sermon on the "Ten Virgins," called for seekers and a score went to the anxious seat; and soon many of them gave expression of conversion, four of the number going into a trance, and lay for hours. One of them, a young lady, was carried home on a stretcher. The meeting continued until 4 o'clock on Monday morning. A young man, who sat in derision and was scoffing at the scene before him, at once was struck down and lay for hours apparently dead, and when he came to, proclaimed the tidings of a separation from all sin. Sister Woodworth has captured the people and magnetizes her audience, and the number increases at each meeting. The lady will return to Allen County in a few days and proclaim the Word of Life in a hall in this city. The Methodist clergymen of Fort Wayne are not inclined to give her an opening in any of the sanctuaries as her methods are of the extreme order and not sanctioned by the bishops of the church.

January 25, 1885

Indianapolis Journal (IN)

A Remarkable Revival

EXTRAORDINARY CHARACTER OF THE MEETINGS NOW IN PROGRESS AT HARTFORD CITY

Special to the *Indianapolis Journal*

HARTFORD CITY, IND., JAN. 24.—

he great revival at the M. E. [Methodist Episcopal] Church is still in progress under the supervision of the evangelist Mrs. Woodworth. The meeting continues with unabated zeal, and the scenes enacted on one night are but repetitions of the scenes of the preceding night. Never before have the people of our town witnessed such a spectacle. Large numbers from neighboring towns come for the purpose of investigating, traveling salesmen arrange to return to this place each night, and overwhelming masses from the country rush in to witness the proceedings. Last night, two young women and one young man passed into a trance and at the close of the services were carried into the classroom and anxiously watched by near friends till consciousness should return. Your correspondent examined the young man as he lay perfectly oblivious and unconscious, limbs outstretched and rigid, hands lifted toward heaven, eyes open, fixed and staring, and his pulse, which was examined by a physician, ranging from thirty to forty. His mother, on being interviewed, spoke freely and stated that this was the seventh time he had passed into a trance; that he remained in that condition sometimes half a day, and that when he revived he spoke each time of the glory of the celestial world and of a happy communion and reunion with loved ones who had already "joined the innumerable caravan." There is no limit to this supernatural visitation, and sinners in the rear of the room laughing, scoffing, and jesting are stricken down in the aisles. It is pronounced by physicians to be a form of catalepsy, as the pulse is kept up and respiration continues; yet the entranced are insensible to all surroundings.

Day meetings are held with as much fervor. The evangelist herself has passed into that state three different times, and while in that condition, pleads with sinners to flee from the wrath to come. A lady from Bluffton, who is personally acquainted with her, was interviewed last night and stated that the evangelist bore an excellent reputation and was a woman of integrity, of honor, of merit. She possesses great magnetism, is pleasant and affable in conversation, and is an impressive speaker, though not a polished rhetorician. Upon the streets and in the stores great excitement prevails, and nothing else engages attention. The oldest citizens are much amazed, and the aged followers of the Lamb wonder at her marvelous success.

January 27, 1885

Indianapolis News (IN)

[Unabated Interest]

he remarkable revival at Hartford City continues with unabated interest. Mrs. Woodworth, who takes the entire conduct of the meetings, is a woman of slight education, thirty-five years old, medium size, and dark complexion. She is a tireless worker, rarely sits down, and when singing or speaking, keeps her hands uplifted and in constant motion. She remains at her post of duty from early afternoon till late at night. She is accompanied by her husband. They are in indigent circumstances and have no home, having spent all in preparation for Mrs. W.'s mission. Twenty-five sinners have fallen entranced up to present advices,[1] remaining insensible for some time. The church is crowded afternoon and evening.

[1] "up to present advices"—according to the latest reports.

January 27, 1885

Indianapolis Journal (IN)

The Hartford City Revival

SOME FEATURES OF THE REVIVAL SERVICES NOW BEING CONDUCTED BY MRS. WOODWORTH

Special to the *Indianapolis Journal*

HARTFORD CITY, IND., JAN. 26.—

he remarkable revival now in progress at the M. E. [Methodist Episcopal] Church in interest and results is unprecedented in the annals of the city. Mrs. Woodworth, the evangelist upon whom rests the burden of the triumphs of success, hails from Syracuse, Ind., and is reported as belonging to the Church of God for the Indiana Eldership. The meeting has been in progress two weeks. The achievements and reputation of the evangelist preceded her arrival. Her first appearance electrified the people, and they at once reposed confidence in her integrity. She assumes entire control of the meeting, alternately singing, praying, and entreating and pleading with lost souls.

Every night scores rush to the altar. Aged pilgrims gather about to comfort them and invoke blessings from on high. She sends workers here and there among the congregation and in the gallery, and simultaneous supplications are offered up for penitent souls. All at once there comes a pause; the audience arises to its feet, someone is stricken down in his sin; and the audience, irretrievably lost to order, blockades the aisles to grasp a view at the entranced. Several of these have been interviewed, and there appears to be two divisions of this wonderful state, viz.: First, those who are stricken down in their sins represent all as dark as a mighty chaos, not a single ray of light. Second, those who claim to be converted see a halo of light, a dazzling effulgence; see multitudes of angels, hear seraphic songs, sonatas of praise, and meet and greet those who have died. Their faces bask in the sunshine of happiness, their hands uplifted and motioning to sinners to come to Christ. Up to this time there have been twenty-five entranced. One young man of excellent character has passed into the ecstatic state five times. A majority of these are young. The church, which is large and capacious, is too small to accommodate the crowds that endeavor to secure admission. The mutterings and discontent which were heard at first have subsided, and the tongue of vituperation and calamity has been quelled and hushed since laughers, scoffers, and jesters have been stricken down in the aisles.

Mrs. Woodworth, the evangelist, is thirty-five years of age, of medium height, dark complexion, prepossessing appearance, and wears continually a pleasant smile that wins approbation wherever she goes. Her constant study and devotion to her work has rendered her accomplished and refined, though bereft of the early advantages of education. She has written a book entitled *My Experience,* which meets with rapid sale. She is a tireless worker, rarely sits down, and when singing or speaking, keeps her hands uplifted and in constant motion. She remains at her post of duty from early afternoon till late at night. She is accompanied by her husband. They are in indigent circumstances, and have no home, having spent all in preparation for Mrs. W.'s mission. She has just received an invitation to go to Cincinnati, but she declined on the ground that the half is not yet done here. The excited populace anxiously await the final result.

January 30, 1885

Indianapolis Journal (IN)

Mrs. Woodworth's Converts

Hartford City Special

mong the conversions is a man familiarly known about town, whose name is withheld from publication, a man of convivial habits, and who, on this occasion, was loaded to the guards.[1] Determined on breaking up the meeting, he marched within ten feet of the pulpit and began a torrent of profane abuse until, as he says, his tongue failed him. He sat silent, annoyed at being overcome by a woman who had caused

[1] "loaded to the guards"—drunk.

this result without making any special effort in his direction. He seems, as he says when asked what his sensations are like, not to understand what it is, but replies in the injured tone of a man who has been personally affronted: "Go up yourself and find out."

All sorts of theories are out as to the secret of the evangelical power. The belief generally seems to be that of mesmerism, although she bitterly denies her power of mesmerism and says that it is truly the power of God. If mesmerism it is, she must have some way of securing private interviews with her subjects and bending them to her ways afterwards, for she certainly does not have an opportunity for it in church. In no instance can the writer find out that this has been done and for this reason we have to give it,[2] in that we know not of what power it is. A strange phase of this revival and one not attendant on the ordinary meetings is the prostration of people away from the church. One young woman went to an evening service and, at its conclusion, went home where she talked on the usual topics before retiring. A whole night intervened, and at breakfast the young lady did not appear. She was found sitting up in bed, cold and apparently stiff, with wide staring eyes, her pulse barely perceptible, and not able to speak.

When two or three hours later she came out of the so-called trance, she seemed greatly worried, and when rested told that with one exception the scenes that she had witnessed were glorious. The exception was that of a body of angels marching down to hell with the lost souls. Viola McDermot is a lady above the average height, with a very pale face that is saved from being plain by a pair of handsome dark eyes which have anything but a restful look when she is interviewed. She says:

"I know as well as anything when the trance is coming on, for I have been in one now five times. My hands get cold as ice, and I feel my arms stiffening. My eyes get hard, and the inside of the church or room gets smaller. The darkness begins at the outer edges of the room and comes toward me from all sides and gets closer. I get more icy and stiff, and then the sight is gone. I can't talk and don't want to talk. I am in both worlds—in this because I can hear

[2] "give it"—Possibly, to accept her explanation or give it credence.

everything that is said around me, and in the other because I can see the Great White Throne."

"How does it look?" was asked.

"I hardly know how to tell you: it is something like a chair, only a great deal larger than any I ever saw."

"Did you see anything else?"

"Yes, golden streets, with angels passing around through them. There are habitations or paradises, as you would call them. They rise up on each side, glorious and magnificent. The light is not white, but radiant and bright—oh, so bright and glorious! I got here by two ways—one with nothing on my mind and all is happiness; the other is to have a sinner to save, and then I am praying and pleading for him. That is hard work and I suffer. My coming back is just the same as my going. There is no time of total unconsciousness between. I am always very much worried afterward."

This young lady has been a member of church about two years.

January 30, 1885

New York Times (NY)

Religious Craze in Indiana

One of the Female Converts Explains the Sensations of a Trance

INDIANAPOLIS, IND. JAN. 29.—

he reports from the Hartford City religious craze, carried on under Mrs. Woodworth, are beyond belief. Mrs. Woodworth is well known in the state and enjoys a good reputation. A letter from there gives some instances of the so-called conversions, which rival and outdo the celebrated "Yerks"[1] in Kentucky a half-century ago. Among the conversions is a man familiarly known about town, whose name is withheld from publication, a man of convivial habits, and who on one occasion was "loaded to the guards." Determined on breaking up the meeting, he marched within ten feet of the pulpit and began a torrent of profane abuse until, as he says, his tongue failed him. He sat silent, annoyed at being overcome by a woman who had caused this result without making any special effort in his direction. He seems, as he says when asked what his sensations are like, not to understand what it is, but replies in an injured tone of a man who has been personally affronted, "Go up yourself and find out."

All sorts of theories are out as to the secret of the evangelical power. The belief generally seems to be that of mesmerism, although Mrs. Woodworth denies that she possesses any power of mesmerism. She says that it is truly the power of God. If mesmerism it is, she must have some way of securing private interviews with her subjects and bending them to her will afterward, for she certainly does not have an opportunity for it in church. In no instance can the writer find out that this has been done. A strange phase of this revival, and one not attendant on the ordinary meetings, is the effect that the revival fever has on persons away from church. One young woman went to an evening service, and at its conclusion went home, where she talked on the usual topics before retiring. A whole night intervened, and at breakfast the young lady did not appear. She was found

[1] "Yerks"—The word means jerk or move abruptly and could possibly refer to the phenomenon called the "jerks" in which people jerked and trembled under the influence of the Holy Spirit.

sitting up in bed, cold and apparently stiff, with wide staring eyes, her pulse barely perceptible, and not able to speak. When two or three hours later she came out of the supposed trance, she seemed greatly worried, and when rested told that with one exception the scenes that she witnessed were glorious. The exception was that of a body of angels marching down to hell with lost souls.

Viola McDermot is a woman above the average height, with a very pale face that is saved from being plain by a pair of handsome black eyes, which have anything but a restful look when she is interviewed. She says: "I know as well as anything when the trance is coming on, for I have been in a trance five different times. My hands get cold as ice and I feel my arms stiffening. My eyes get hard and the inside of the church or room grows smaller. The darkness begins at the outer edges of the room and comes toward me from all sides and gets closer. I become more icy and stiff, and then the sight is gone. I can't talk and don't want to talk. I am in both worlds—in this because I can hear everything that is said around me, and in the other because I can see the Great White Throne."

"How does it look?" was asked.

"I hardly know how to tell you. It is something like a chair, only a great deal larger than I ever saw."

"Did you see anything else?"

"Yes; golden streets with angels passing around through them. There are habitations or paradises as you would call them. They rise up on each side, glorious and magnificent. The light is not white, but radiant and bright—oh, so bright and glorious. I go there by two ways—one with nothing on my mind, and all is happiness; the other is to have a sinner to save, and then I am praying and pleading for him. That is hard work and I suffer. My coming back is just the same as my going. There is no time of total unconsciousness between. I am always very much worried afterward."

This young woman has been a member of the church about two years.

January 31, 1885

Indianapolis Journal (IN)

Mrs. Woodworth's Revival

THE MEETING DRAWING TO A CLOSE—EXTRAORDINARY EXPERIENCE OF A MERCHANT

Special to the *Indianapolis Journal*

HARTFORD CITY, IND., JAN. 30.—

he wonderful revival is still in progress, and daily and nightly new names are added to the list of converts. The evangelist, after almost a three week's siege, still plies her mission with the same calmness and judgment that distinguished her earlier efforts. The interest never wanes; instead it seems to wax warmer, stronger, and deeper as the meeting nears its end. As another day fades and evening comes it brings with it a renewed effort, increased courage, and better results. Although invitations are rapidly coming in and better inducements are offered Mrs. Woodworth, she has not finally determined when to leave nor where to go. The last few meetings have been unique and incomparable.

On Wednesday night six persons, five of whom were adults, passed into a state of ecstasy and were carried from the room rigid. Happy conversions were experienced; and the tumultuous audience, after dismissal, had to be almost forced to leave the room. On Wednesday a merchant, not a member of any denomination, passed into a trance, and upon being questioned said: "I was reading a Bible in my place of business and almost instantly I felt a numbness, as if exhausted, and immediately lost consciousness. When I recovered, my wife informed me that when found, I was lying supinely upon my back with one hand uplifted and the other clasping the Bible. All seemed dark to me. When I recovered I soon passed into that state of ecstasy, and I saw two visions as plain as day. One was the infernal regions, which seemed to consist of eight squares. I could hear wailing and gnashing of teeth. It seemed then like an abyss into which victims were constantly falling and some standing on the edge. They appeared of all ages. Then I could look to the right and see the celestial world, shining with a glorious light, could hear the angels singing, but could recognize no one." Last night, upon further inquiry, he stated: "This afternoon I attempted to tell and describe my heavenly vision, but found I could not do so, for fear I should pass into another trance. I could describe the infernal regions, but could not the other."

The evangelist was interviewed about this singular inability to describe the heavenly vision, and she stated that such had been her observation and even her own experience. They can portray the vision in its common phase but cannot enter into the details. Yesterday afternoon the evangelist again passed into the ecstatic state and remained so for two hours. She stated, upon inquiry, that she saw heavenly visions but did not attempt to describe them.

Within the last week, a score of editors from neighboring counties have witnessed the proceedings. The meeting is nearing its end. The evangelist thinks some of removing to Fort Wayne.

February 5, 1885

Kokomo Dispatch (IN)

[Like a Footpad Tackles His Prey]

On writing of superstition, my mind instinctively reverts to the great Hartford City religious revival. I do not pretend to say why, but it does. Of one thing I am morally certain: unless Hartford City has much changed since my last visit, it stands much in need of a religious revival and a strong disinfectant. A town of more iniquity and bad odors to the square inch it has never been my misfortune to encounter. A more importunate set of gamblers and whiskey-sellers and a dirtier set of loafers have never escaped the penitentiary, and it is pardonable exaggeration to say that the carrion crows fly a mile from the courthouse to get fresh air.

Mrs. Woodworth has undoubtedly shown great wisdom in her manner of converting Hartford City. She goes at it like a footpad tackles his prey. By some supernatural power, she just knocks 'em silly when they are not looking for it; and while they are down, she supplies the hydraulic pressure and pumps the grace of God into them by the bucketful. While in this semi-comatose condition, her subjects go "gallivanting" over the gold-paved streets of the New Jerusalem, conversing with departed friends, and having a good time in general. Business—what little business there is—in Hartford City entirely suspends when meeting "takes up," and even the skating rinks don't stand a ghost of a show. The excitement extends to neighboring places, and one railroad has taken advantage of the occasion and carries passengers to the very door of Saint Peter's lodge at excursion rates.

I hope I do not blaspheme, but indeed I cannot think seriously of this strange way of getting religion. The man or woman who is carried away in a religious trance is not the person whom I should like to trust in position requiring will, nerve, and good judgment. Put me on the fast express and let me discover that the locomotive driver is given to trances, and I will thank him to stop and let me off at his earliest conv[en]ience. And I know no reason why I should trust his judgment more in a spiritual journey than a temporal one.

Mrs. Woodworth may be a most excellent and most earnest woman, and I hope her mission in Hartford City may be productive of much good. As I have remarked before, Hartford City needs it, and I have always thought that nothing less than a theological pile driver could churn the fear of God into its sinful denizens. But, on general principles, I quarrel with her methods. I object to attributing to a spiritual agency that which is obviously a physical phenomena—the ecstasy of nervous bodies and mercurial minds. I dislike this making the holy face of the Almighty so vulgarly familiar—that one in sin may look on it and turn from it to sin again. The manner of conduct in these revivals smacks too strongly of sensationalism to assure much sincerity. There is too much of the "biggest show on earth" about one which seeks converts under strain of mental excitement and rushes them all unprepared to the baptismal font. In this matter the Hartford City evangelist out-Herrods Herrod (*sic*);[1] and while the morals of that place may justify her, I object to a general spread of such evangelism.

[1] Harrods, a British department store founded in 1834. During the time of this article, the store had expanded into selling a wide range of goods. Harrods sales were renowned in the twentieth century and possibly in the late nineteenth century.

February 6, 1885

Marion Chronicle (IN)

[Mrs. Woodworth Leaves Hartford City]

rs. Woodworth, the revivalist, has left Hartford City. On Tuesday she came to Marion on her way north and remained at the depot until the C., W., & M. train arrived. On Sunday evening she preached her farewell exhortation. Seven were "tranced." Mrs. Woodworth made the finest plea of all her ministrations. She could have been heard blocks away. She cried out at one time in a voice that startled everyone of that large assembly. "Open your hearts to God, and He will open heaven to you!" Almost every town and neighborhood around that town for miles have been represented. At the afternoon service, forty united with the M. E. [Methodist Episcopal] Church, and one hundred and twenty-seven expressed conversion as the result of the revival.

February 16, 1885

Cincinnati Enquirer (OH)

[A Contagion That Pervades the County]

HARTFORD CITY, IND. FEB. 16.—

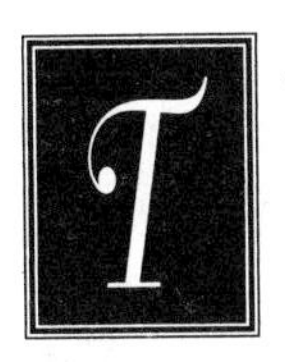

he wonderful revival at this place assumed its maximum proportions on Saturday night at the opera hall. Over one thousand persons were present, and hundreds turned away that could not gain admission. Several were in a trance, and a general petition to the heavenly throne by hundreds rendered the scene most remarkable. On Sunday, John Cantwell and Elisha Pearce, both men of influence and leading attorneys at the bar, were at the anxious seat. Mr. Cantwell expressed conversion. Mr. Cantwell's daughter, a Mrs. Moller, was tranced for several hours. It seems the influence of this great evangelist began its work first upon the lowest stratum of society. Some of the worst citizens, a few of whom had been incarcerated in jail for misdemeanors, were first to go to the anxious seat and become recipients of pardon; now all phases of society are gradually but surely becoming impressed in a manner never before experienced. It is simply a contagion that pervades all this county. No such religious demonstration has ever been witnessed here. The Methodist Episcopal Church still conducts its meeting at the sanctuary; and the church was crowded last evening, and a grand, good time was had. The very atmosphere seems impregnated with a religious fervor, and Satan's bulwarks are threatened with a final and complete overthrow in our midst.

Mrs. Woodworth expects to visit Cincinnati when her work here ceases, which will probably be next Sunday.

Quoted from *Trials and Triumphs of Maria B. Woodworth* by Maria Woodworth-Etter (Published by Maria Woodworth-Etter, 1886), 190-191. (Editor's Note: A combination of the following two articles also appeared in the *New York Times* on January 24, 1885.)

February 20, 1885

Marion Chronicle (IN)

The Evangelist

H. Woodworth, husband of the evangelist, was in Marion on Monday evening and left for Syracuse, Indiana, the following morning, where he was called by the illness of their granddaughter. The meetings at Hartford City closed on Sunday night, and Mrs. Woodworth left for New Corners, about fifteen miles from Hartford City, to continue her religious work. She will remain there a week when she will probably go to Columbia City. Although the revival season has been the most successful ever held in that town, having been reported in every newspaper in the United States and stirred up the people of the entire surrounding country, the converts have not been munificent in their contributions to the support of Mr. and Mrs. Woodworth. Mr. Woodworth informed a reporter of the *Chronicle* that the total receipts, except from the sale of books and pictures of the evangelist, amounted to about forty-two dollars. He shows no disposition to complain; on the contrary, he seems perfectly satisfied with the result and says the Lord is the best paymaster and gives the biggest rewards.

Mr. Woodworth says his wife has remarkable endurance. In thirteen series of meetings such as those in Hartford City, she has never failed to be at her post: morning, noon, and night. She usually retires at 11 or 12 o'clock at night and gets up at 7 or 8 o'clock in the morning. She is often restless and cannot sleep. Often he awakens to find her at his side in a trance, rigid and cold, and nothing can be done for her until she recovers. She is always industrious and cannot find contentment except in her evangelistic work.

Mr. and Mrs. Woodworth have received hundreds of letters from cities and towns all over the country imploring their aid in religious work.

February 27, 1885

Indianapolis Journal (IN)

Mrs. Woodworth at New Corner—in a Trance

The following, from an occasional correspondent, will give an idea of the methods used by Mrs. Woodworth, the evangelist, who recently created such excitement at Hartford City

NEW CORNER, DELAWARE COUNTY, FEB. 18.—

On yesterday Mrs. Woodworth opened services by singing, "Let Me in the Kingdom." Her gestures, voice, and countenance seem not of earth, and she sees her crown almost within her grasp. Her text was Acts 2:17: "Young men shall see visions and old men dream dreams." She said the last prophecy is being fulfilled.

> Signs and wonders follow God's Word in His way. Don't expect blessings in your way, but cry, "What shall I do?" And be ye also as clay in the potter's hands. Remember you are doing business for eternity. Oh, do it well. May God make sinners sin-sick and place great thorns in their pillows. Sinners, don't resist the Spirit. You can resist until the key is turned on your heart. Don't stray away from God. Don't cross the deadline. Change your course; there are breakers ahead. Leave the poor old stranded wreck and get into our boat. It's a lifeboat. Christ is our pilot; He never leaves the helm. He will guide us safely into port. Passage is free for all. We will soon sail for the kingdom. Your country is in the sky. Oh, come, come now.

Many lay entranced for hours. Those who resisted most were first stricken. Many related visions they had seen. Rev. Robinson of the Methodist Episcopal Church said he stood face to face with God. But the reception was not at first pleasant. God showed him he was weak and erring. Then with a sharp knife He pruned from his body a branch called impatience; also another branch, that of passion. Then He passed His loving hands over the wounds and healed them. "Then," said Mr. Robinson, "He bade me arise, and led me to the edge of an awful pit and showed me its terrors." He saw persons there whom he had known, and others God told him must go there if they did not repent at this meeting. Then He took him up into heaven and showed him green fields and bright flowers, singing birds, and many other beauties of that glory land. He also permitted Mr. Robinson to see many friends who had gone before and many white-robed angels.

Another said he ascended a ladder with golden rounds, and at the top, in great golden letters, was the word "God," and above that His crown.

No pen save that of the recording angel could describe the scenes enacted here tonight. Almost the whole house was transformed into an altar, and cries of mercy from many scores were mingled with shouts of victory. No one can prophesy where this work will end. Many superstitious persons stay away for fear of Mrs. W.'s power to overcome them. Others refused to shake her hand.

She came to us, as she does at all her appointments, with the earnest and hearty recommendations of her former neighbors and friends. Letters are now in our midst, and can be seen at any time, from prominent citizens of her former home at Syracuse, Indiana, which sustain her as an energetic, whole-souled Christian lady. Whatever may be said of the trances, there is no denying the fact that her meetings are productive of great good and that, when the sheaves are finally bound for eternity, many will bless the name of the great evangelist.

March 13, 1885

Marion Chronicle (IN)

Mrs. Woodworth at the Helm of "The Life Boat"

To the Editor of the *Chronicle:*

FAIRMOUNT, IND., MARCH 11, 1885.—

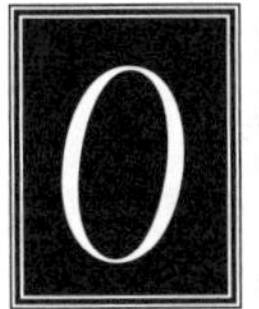n Wednesday evening of last week Mrs. Woodworth, the great evangelist, arrived in this beautiful and enterprising village and received a hearty welcome. After resting for a short time at the Maddy House, she was escorted to the Wesleyan church, from which the seats had been removed and a double altar erected the entire length of the house. Mrs. W. opened the service with that thrilling song, "Let Me in the Life Boat," followed by an earnest season of prayer and an impressive sermon. She then conducted an altar service, and many rushed to the altar, pleading for mercy. The interest increased with each meeting. Services continued from 9 A.M. until 3 P.M., and from 4 P.M. until 9 P.M. Many superstitious persons were afraid to go near Mrs. W., thinking her a mesmerist. But their fears were soon dispelled, and others who came through mere curiosity were convicted and brightly converted. Many others were stricken down and lay entranced from ten minutes to fifteen hours. Little Ida Pressnall, six years old, said that Jesus had blessed her and she was going to bless Him; that she had seen Him and His angels and an awful deep ditch with many people burning, and "one girl in there I knew."

A young man named Howell was permitted to view all the horrors of hell and the dazzling beauties of heaven, while others saw only "The distant ties of the golden strand/That the Savior gives on the border land."[1]

Quite a number of avowed infidels have been converted saying that Mrs. W.'s arguments have broken down their walls and that they could see no more floating straws to catch at.

Herman Newberger, of New Cumberland, who has been reared in the Jewish faith, says he is now fully convinced that the Christian

[1] Source unknown.

religion is a reality and that he expects to seek until he finds that reality.

Mrs. W.'s sermons on such subjects as "The Wedding Garment," "Will a Man Rob God," and "The Resurrection," were full of power and carried conviction in almost every sentence. Her sermon on "The Unpardonable Sin" has been published in pamphlet form and can be had by addressing her at Columbia City, Indiana, or later at Tipton, Indiana.

The number of conversions here she estimates at 350, but there have been many at their homes, of which there are no definite account. The conversion at Summitville exceeded two hundred, and those at New Corner five hundred, making a total of more than one thousand for the three meetings.

Still the work goes on. At the closing service tonight, almost the entire house was transformed into an altar, the deep wails of anguish being mingled with the joyful shouts of victory.

News, 5th.—

March 13, 1885

Marion Chronicle (IN)

Mrs. Woodworth at Fairmount

he Woodworth revival was removed to this place yesterday. The Wesleyan church was cleared of its seats and arranged as we last week described the church at New Corner. Mrs. Woodworth preached last night from the text: "Am I my brother's keeper?"[1] Whatever may be said of her manner of working, there seems nothing unscriptural in her sermons. She is listened to attentively, except by the "sightseers," who last night acted very disgracefully. Several attempts were made while she was preaching to restore quiet, and after the sermon, during the singing of songs and hearing testimonies, such confusion was surely never known before inside the walls of a church. Scores of people up to within a few feet of the mourner's bench were talking and laughing, apparently oblivious of the fact that a religious meeting was in progress in the same room. The meetings begin at 9 every morning and at 4 in the evening and are announced to at least continue over Sunday. It is reported that there were a thousand conversions at New Corner and Summitville.

Mrs. Woodworth delivered a good sermon on the theme, "Shall we rob God?"[2] this forenoon. One person fell in a trance, and the meeting was still in session at 1:30 P.M.

[1] Genesis 4:9.

[2] See Malachi 3:8.

April 24, 1885

The Weekly Review Democrat (Anderson, IN)

Elwood Column

rs. Woodworth, the great paralyzer, arrived in Elwood one week ago last Wednesday and has been creating more excitement than "a bull in a china shop." She holds three services each day, and they are attended by people from all parts of the country. No system regulates the proceedings; no text is taken, no particular subject is discussed, but a general exhortation to sinners, interspersed with lively songs, is indulged in by the evangelist and her converts. The meetings are held in the M. E. [Methodist Episcopal] church from which the greater number of seats have been removed, leaving only a few for a "mourner's bench" around which the sinners are invited to gather and plead for God's mercy.

The proceedings are strange and startling but are taken part in by some of the oldest and most respected citizens of our town. While a great number of church members attend the meetings and take part in the exercises, there are those from all churches who discountenance the meetings and condemn their fellow members for their actions. A number of converts have been made and several have visited the other world, via a trance. The converts seem to be changed and immediately fall into a line and begin a warfare against the sinful. The meetings are pictures for the young man who is blessed with a girl.[1] A bartender remarked the other day that he wanted the meeting to stop as they kept waiting on the sightseers who stepped out between scenes.

[1] "The meetings are pictures"—In other words, the meetings are entertainment and provide a place to go on a date in the same way that a photography or art exhibition would.

April 24, 1885

The Weekly Review Democrat (Anderson, IN)

County News

Elwood indeed has been quite a business place in the last week, especially in a spiritual point of view. People are coming daily from a distance to attend the series of meetings conducted by Mrs. Woodworth. [H]er meetings are rapidly growing in interest, and the prospect is that there will be the greatest work accomplished in Elwood—by way of a general reformation, morally speaking—that was ever experienced before, notwithstanding the opposition she has met with by a few cranks that are always on the side of the devil and would scorn at Christ if He was to make a visit here. You can see a few gathered here and there in the streets and corners hissing and making sport and show[ing] by their words, deeds, and actions that they are doing all they can to raise the standard of immorality, and some of these parties are citizens of our town who ought to be glad that such a good work is being done.

The cloven foot has been revealed at last; it now tells who is in favor of a reformation and who is opposed to it. It is no wonder our town has a bad reputation far and near; anyone with half an eye can see that in the last few days (laying aside prejudice) that the morals of Elwood is (*sic*) five hundred per cent better than before; and if the reformation fire goes on, Elwood will soon be a desirable place to live. It is said from good authority since Mrs. Woodworth's stay with us here that there have been over one hundred sound conversions. Some are children, some are fathers, some are mothers, and in some instances whole families—people of firm wit and intelligence. If any one doubts this, let them visit this place in a few months and see for themselves; facts are stubborn things—truth will prevail.

The correspondent to the *Herald* from this place is one who is a stumbling block to some extent to the progress of the moral condition of this place, when he says in last week's issue that "Mrs. Woodworth, the paralizer (*sic*), has arrived and the agitation has begun." Whether the seats will be removed from the church and the saloon plan of covering the floor with sawdust is a question yet to be decided. We wonder whether this correspondent did compose the number who made public sport of Mrs. Woodworth on the streets on her arrival here in words, motions, signs, and gestures, observed by citizens and strangers; and it is still practiced, but the number of scoffers are diminishing and are passing away. And what few may be left, it is to be hoped they will hunt their holes or get out of town and hunt up a class elsewhere, where it will be more congenial for them. Mrs. Woodworth goes from here to Tipton.

—Bruno

May 7, 1885

Kokomo Dispatch (IN)

Conversion by Trance

Something of Mrs. Woodworth, the Wonderful Evangelist

WHAT SHE IS DOING AT TIPTON—WILL VISIT KOKOMO SOON

hile on a business trip to Tipton on Monday, I attended the services conducted by Mrs. Woodworth, the lady evangelist, who has been creating such a religious awakening in Elwood, Columbia City, and other places. I reached the Methodist church, where the meetings are being held at 10 o'clock A.M. The meeting was not large, the house not being more than half full. The meeting was being conducted as day services usually are, in serial meetings, the time being devoted to songs, prayers, and short talks from new converts and others. The peculiarity of the lady's work lies in the great number of powerful conversions and in quite a number of the congregation going into a trance state.

Mrs. Woodworth is about forty years of age, of medium size, of active temperament. Her intellectual development is good. She is a strong, well-developed woman physically. Phrenologically speaking,[1] she has a well-balanced organization, of which, by her permission, I may speak at another time.

I attended her meetings throughout the day, and until the 8 o'clock train at night. During that time there were several well-defined cases of trance and a large number of bright conversion[s]. I had all possible opportunity given me to investigate the trance cases, both while the subjects were in that condition and also to talk to them after they came out of it, and can say without hesitation that there was no deception in any case. They all varied from each other, no two having the same experience and no one having the same experience twice.

The one that gave me the most information concerning her trance experiences was a Mrs. Dr. Grey, of Tipton, a practicing physician

[1] "Phrenology" was a nineteenth century pseudo-scientific fad in which the practitioners claimed to be able to perceive character qualities and talents by locating the various bumps on a person's head. They used a map of the head in which certain locations were labeled. Bumps in these locations indicated a strong predisposition toward that quality.

of good repute, a large fleshy woman of about forty years of age, a very intelligent lady, of strong willpower and a mind of her own. She has been in the trance state three times during these meetings, one of which I saw. Her experience as she related it to me was very wonderful indeed. She said she was a skeptic, if not an entire infidel to the Christian religion, and especially was she an unbeliever as regards the trance state. As she stated to me, she had been attending the meetings regularly; and she and some others were having some fun seeing the performance when she felt this wonderful power, which she regards with the greatest confidence as the Spirit of God.

She was standing near the back part of the house not taking any part in the exercises of the meetings when some invisible power seemed to take possession of her and impelled her forward, not so strong at first but what she could have easily resisted it. But she gave up to do as the force inclined her; and it pushed her forward along the aisle with rapidly increasing pace until she reached the space between the altar and the front seats; this power then threw her onto the floor in an unconscious state, and she remained in this condition for several hours.

During this time she had no consciousness of earth or physical existence. All this time she was being carried as though floating in the air to the abode of those who have passed from this life into the spirit land. She said she was here permitted to see the abode of both the good and the bad. She gave me an interesting description of this, but it would be too long to give in this article. Let this suffice: She said that she was permitted to see what she recognized as representing the regions of the damned and also the home of the saved, of which there were three degrees, reaching to the highest conception of joy, beauty, and grandeur. This story of her experience was connected by an interesting chain of thought covering the idea of salvation through righteousness and damnation a result of sin. I heard her speak beautifully in the meeting of God's merciful dealings with her, her face beaming with emotion and thankfulness for the great truth of the religion of Christ.

There was another interesting case, because of the contrast both in organization and circumstances surrounding it, with the one just mentioned. She was a young married lady, rather small, of a delicate fine organization, fair complexion, and flaxen hair. She was an intelligent woman with marked nervous temperament. She was a member of the Presbyterian Church and a professing Christian. She had been attending the meetings and took some part in the exercises by joining in the singing. On last Friday she felt some strange sensations which she thought must be the "trance coming on." She left the meeting, went home, and the feeling all disappeared. She did not return to the meeting until Monday morning. She took a seat in the center of the house and took no part in the services whatever. During the exercises I noticed quite a stir in that part of the church and saw that this lady was manifesting symptoms of the trance, which is an indescribable half-sleep, half-dead appearance. She seemingly became entirely unconscious of everything around her and remained in this state for several hours. She also gave me an interesting account of her experience. What I have related of these cases I obtained from their own words with the exception of what I saw.

Do I believe that there is such a thing as a trance? Yes, I have known of trances through history and from the writings of mental philosophers, but this is my first opportunity of seeing anything of the kind. I regard it as a great truth in mental and psychological science; and it is also fully corroborated by the science of phrenology, which teaches that the brain is divided into organs, each of which controls its own particular character of thought. While in the trance, that portion of the brain through which God's Spirit comes to us and teaches us of Him is in supreme control and all the rest of the brain is dormant, or is held more or less inactive for the time. Yes, the grand principles of truth underlie the trance state; and all truth is philosophical truth, a scientific truth. God is the author of all truth, and there can be no complications.

These things I write because there is an inquiry in regard to this thing but let this suffice: Mrs. Woodworth will soon be in Kokomo and you will hear for yourselves. I will say to those who will likely attend her meetings to scoff at religion, you had better be a little careful. Her religion is of such a character that scoffers are very likely to be humbled and brought to the dust. They are often caught in the midst of their scoffing. At Tipton that class has been brought the lowest.

And to you, Christians of the Methodist and Quaker order, who have been praying so long and loud for the fullness of that religion of which you have been permitted to have a little taste, let me say that this woman, only, has that fullness for which your souls have long panted; so be careful how you treat her when she comes among you, that you may not be made ashamed before she goes away. Be careful that you do not so act that sinners who will be converted by the hundreds will not be ashamed of you.

And you, Christians, who have received Christ the best you know, with honest minds and yet think God is not now revealing Himself to the children of men only through His written Word, come and see and hear for yourselves what God is doing through little children.

—Dr. T. V. Gifford

Dr. A. B. Pitzer of Tipton, is reported to have succumbed to the evangelical influence of Mrs. Woodworth, the trance evangelist, who has been holding meetings for some time in Tipton.

May 11, 1885

The Indianapolis Times (IN)

A Farcical Religion

THAT OF MRS. MARIA WOODWORTH

More About the Cataleptic Epidemic Which is Likely to Spread to Kokomo—The Singular Visions That Are Seen—Citizens' Opinions

TIPTON, IND., MAY 10.—

grand windup of Mrs. Woodworth's revival took place today, and there were the usual number of cataleptic victims. The excitement was unprecedented, and a stranger visiting the meeting would doubtless have been impressed with the belief that one-half of the people of Tipton were temporarily out of their heads. They indulged in the most extravagant demonstrations; a greater burlesque of true Christianity could not be imagined.

The visions, that are alleged to appear to those who go into the so-called trances, are ludicrous in the extreme. One woman reports that when she knocked at the gate of heaven, God admitted her and conducted her through three departments—the first set apart for the good, the second for the better, and the third for the best. The descriptions of halos are more appalling than those contained in "Dante's Inferno,"[1] and the singular feature of the visions is that Tipton folks predominate in these regions of torture—though yet alive—and the converts, when they "come to," resort to every device to scare the unbelievers into repentance. The evangelist herself does likewise; and she, by the way, can go into a trance on the shortest notice, whenever the situation seems to demand such action. She frequently appeals to a sinner by name, telling him to turn then and there and be saved; and should he announce himself not ready or prove obstinate, she gravely informs him that the gates have closed against him, that he will be forever damned. God appears to the victims in diverse forms. Some describe Him as a patriarch with the proverbial long, white hair and beard, while others say He is young and smooth-faced. It is the repentant young women usually who see visions of a youthful Almighty.

[1] "Dante's Inferno"—Dante Aliguieri (1265-1321). The first part of an epic poem called *The Divine Comedy.*

Mrs. Woodworth will take away from Tipton much more of a worldly nature than she brought. The proceeds of the sale of her life and photograph (at forty cents each) have been large, and over one hundred dollars have been donated to compensate her for her two weeks' sojourn here. The result of her work is yet to be realized, but none save those who have given away to the craze believe that any lasting good will be felt by the community. The conservative people have been disposed to countenance the farce because one prominent citizen suddenly experienced reformation, which he was sadly in need of. But the large percent of the population—who, whether they be Christians or sinners, respect religion in proper form—will feel joyful that the noted travesty has been brought to a timely end.

Mrs. Woodworth is in a somewhat unhappy frame of mind in consequence of the numerous press criticisms of her peculiar style of work and has come to the conclusion that some very wicked papers are published. She failed to convert any of the Tipton editors, although she made a desperate effort to entrap one of them into a trance. After a short rest, she will go to Kokomo and endeavor to introduce catalepsy there—under a different name.

May 12, 1885

The Indianapolis Times (IN)

Visions in Trances

As Seen by Mrs. Maria Woodworth

THE EVANGELIST VISITS INDIANAPOLIS AND TELLS WHAT HAS BEEN REVEALED TO HER BY THE ALMIGHTY—SOME VERY ASTONISHING STATEMENTS

rs. Maria B. Woodworth, the evangelist who has recently stirred up such a religious excitement in the town of Tipton, came to the city yesterday with her husband and engaged a room on Indiana Avenue. A *Times* reporter called on Mrs. Woodworth during the afternoon. She is of medium size, forty years of age—though she does not appear thirty-five—has brown hair worn in a high knot above her head, gray eyes, fairly good-looking, dressed in no unusual fashion, and has in the corners of her mouth a firmness suggestive of the picture of Andrew Jackson. She is not particularly intellectual, does not look like a fanatic, and as a talker is coherent and evidently sincere. Once started on the subject of religion, she can get in as many words to the hour, and as many hours to the day, as the most accomplished lightening red agent[1] that ever plied his calling. Her husband is full of hostility toward newspaper reporters. He sat on the trunk and exercised a lawyer-like surveillance over the interview with Mrs. Woodworth. He denounced unsparingly the articles that have been published in the *Times* concerning the Tipton meetings and remarked that, "but for the name of the thing," he would "crack that paper for libel in a hurry." He thought no good could come of the proposed interview. On being told that the present reporter did the religious features, and was not the one who visited Tipton, he subsided and sat in silence on the trunk.

Being asked about her church affiliations and the call she had received to do evangelistic work, Mrs. Woodworth said: "I was converted when thirteen years old and joined The Disciples or Campbellite church, in Columbiana County, Ohio. I began to receive calls to the work soon after and all my life have fought against them. I felt an inward [?] to do this work, but the flesh and the devil resisted and [?]

[1] "lightening red agent"—unknown term, possibly a salesperson of some kind.

me [against] making a laughingstock of myself until almost two years ago when I had been broken down in health almost by the [urgency] of the call. [unreadable sentence].

"Starting out two years ago I saw a [vision?] of a cloud of glory, which came and bore me up and carried me far into the West and set me down in a field of grain where the stalks were falling thickly around me. The first trance happed in this [manner]: A man fell down, and I did not understand until a [sudden] vision sweeping over me showed me that this falling grain in the first vision represented the man and that this manifestation of God's power was for converting this man and others."

When asked what a cloud of glory looked like, she answered: "Not like anything we see here. It reminds me most of a red sunset, but the light is heavenly light. Hundreds of people have been in trances at my meetings. Sometimes they go to heaven and sometimes they are shown the bottomless pit. A real rank infidel is shown the pit as a warning, and others are put directly into heaven and play on harps and their faces shine like the sun."

The reporter suggested that he would like to go into a trance awhile, if he could get back in time to get in the copy for today's paper.

"Do you know that sounds like blasphemy to me," she said. "I don't put people into trances and have no knowledge that they are coming. They come from God, though they don't come unless I pray for them as helps. It is in fulfillment of the prophecy that the sons and daughters of men shall prophesy and the old men and young men dream dreams and see visions. A young lady at Tipton, who had never played on a harp and didn't know a string, went into a trance and sat playing on a harp and fingering perfectly. She was in heaven playing on a golden harp. People who go through trances once want to do so again. I have talked with Jesus and laid my hand on His mangled body."

"How is it that Moody and other evangelists don't put people in trances?"

"They haven't the right kind of faith."

Mrs. Woodworth continuing said that at times her voice, though naturally weak, had been heard preaching and singing a mile

In her early years as an evangelist Maria Woodworth-Etter often wore a decorative scarf called a fichu, something reporters often noted in their descriptions. In many of her portraits she points to heaven with one hand while displaying a Bible with the other.

distant. This, she held, was a miracle. She did not think of what she should say before she rose to speak but depended on the Lord to furnish the logic and the rhetoric. (Both, by the way, are very faulty.) Her husband was also under authority to preach. She had been very badly treated, she said—by the Campbellite church particularly. She was receiving calls at all times with offers of large pay, but she depended on the contributions taken up at the meetings and went where the Lord seemed to call.

In the wickedest towns she had been highly successful, and the infidels have fallen before her like the wheat before a brand new reaper. In spite of the wickedness of the Indiana Legislature and its effects upon Indianapolis, she has received no definite call to come hither. She will remain here to rest for a few days, then go to Kokomo, and thence to Fort Wayne and Onion City, holding meetings in each of those places. She reminded the reporter as he took his leave that she would confront him at the judgment seat in the event of an improper report of the interview.

May 12, 1885

Kokomo Gazette Tribune (IN)

The Tipton Trance Meetings

WHAT I SAW AND HEARD—
MRS. WOODSWORTH (*SIC*),
THE EVANGELIST

EDITOR'S *GAZETTE TRIBUNE*—

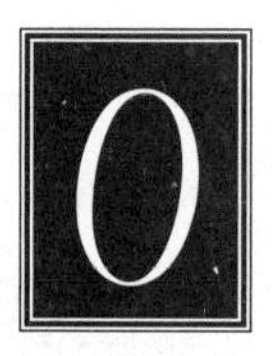

On Thursday, Wm. Trueblood and myself took the train for Tipton. Arriving there at 2:30, we soon found our way to the Methodist church. The church building is about the size of the Friends church in Kokomo and was three-fourths full of people. Soon a large, fine-looking lady came in the side door and stepped at once to the platform and asked the audience to sing a hymn. This was Mrs. Woodsworth (*sic*). She was attired in a black dress and white fichu[1] around her neck. She has an expressive face, high check bones, dark hair, and dark eyes. She seemed to be in a tired condition, pale in features, but soon became animated in her speaking. After the singing she took for her text, "The Great Supper," as described in the 14th chapter of Luke, and delivered a very good sermon, ending in many strong appeals for all to come to the Marriage Feast. She also spoke of the eternal damnation spoken against those who should sin against the Holy Ghost. She then asked all to kneel and pray, and at least twenty-five persons knelt on and around the platform and altar, and all prayed at the same time. I could not hear more than two or three voices nearest me, but the enthusiasm shown was very great. In singing hymns, Mrs. Woodworth was very enthusiastic in leading in each chorus. At five o'clock the meeting adjourned, no person appearing in a trance.

At 6:30 my friend and I again went to the church and secured seats within four feet of the altar. Before 7 o'clock, every seat and chair and foot of standing room was occupied. A more dense audience I never saw. At 6:30 Mrs. Woodsworth (*sic*) came upon the platform and asked, as usual, for all to sing a hymn. She took her text from Acts 2nd chapter and 17th verse: "And it shall come to pass in the last days, that I will pour out of my Spirit upon all flesh, and your

[1] "fichu"—a three-cornered lace or muslin cape for women, worn with the ends fastened or crossed in front *(Webster's N. W.,* 1997).

sons and your daughters shall prophesy, and your young men shall see visions, and your old men shall dream dreams." She quoted from Job and Daniel and many other books in the Bible as to the truthfulness of the prophecy and delivered a good, plain, forcible sermon on the subject.

Sometimes her language is not grammatical. She is not eloquent, but her earnestness and forcible manner of expression, with many upward waves of her hands, keeps her audience in rapt attention. After her sermon she again called on all to kneel and pray. I am speaking within bounds when I say that at least fifty, two-thirds young men and young women and some boys and girls about fourteen years of age, all joined in vocal prayer at the same time. Such a sight is seldom seen. After this she asked all to rise and sing. The hymn sung, and especially the chorus, seemed to fill the house more than full, and many were shouting and clapping their hands, beating time and swaying right and left and eyes full of tears. Many were called to the altar and that was crowded more than full.

Whilst the vast audience was singing, Mrs. Woodsworth (*sic*) stopped and looking upward with both hands upraised, attracted the attention of all. Her face became pale, her eyes fixed, and her right hand was making a graceful circular movement. Two ladies stepped to her side and placed their arms around her. She remained standing there, apparently insensible to all around her. Her face wore a most beautiful, and I might say, angelic expression. She spoke not a word nor moved her eyes. Fifteen minutes having passed, all singing and many shouting, when suddenly a large, handsome lady, directly in front of the lady who sat by my side, began to waver in position and sank back into the arms of my nearest neighbor. Her eyes looked upward, her hands clasped, and a happy smile was on her features. I took hold of her hand and felt her pulse; it seemed as quiet but not as strong as usual.

A few minutes later, and a young man about eighteen years old sank back upon the seat in front of us; and my friend Mr. Trueblood holding out his hands caught his head and held it for the time that he seemed unconscious, his eyes were directed upward, his hands pointing upward, his mouth open, and slowly waving his right hand in a circle. He did not speak or move his body. Two of his friends came and upheld him in his seat until he recovered. While these two ladies and the young man were in this condition, attention was drawn to another young man a few feet in front of us who was passing into a trance. The lady nearest me recovered in ten minutes, and her first remark was "Oh, how happy I have been."

Next Mrs. Woodsworth (*sic*) recovered, having been some forty-five minutes in that unconscious condition. The boy in front of us remained about twenty minutes in his trance whilst the young man in the "amen corner," laid out on two or three chairs, seemed perfectly rigid. I called a physician and asked him to examine his pulse and asked him if that was a condition of catalepsy. He replied that it was not. It was now 11 o'clock, and the benediction being pronounced, all retired save the young man and a few of his friends who remained to watch him.

During the time that the three other persons were unconscious, Mrs. Woodsworth (*sic*) did not come near them or place her hands upon their person in any way. The query is at once, "What is it?" Can it be explained upon a medical or scientific or psychological basis? Several physicians, who examined these parties on the evening named, say it was not catalepsy, as the limbs in that condition are perfectly rigid. They say it is not hysteria, nor is it epilepsy. One physician said it looked more like extasia,[2] but he was not satisfied on that point. Fully one-half of the physicians I talked with, as to the scenes occurring that evening, said it was "the power of God," and the other half said it was wonderful and they could not explain it. The people generally in attendance say that it comes from God, and that it is not human power.

It will not do to say, no man can say who has seen these cases of trance, that there is any deception or sham on the part of the subjects entranced. It does not seem to affect weakly, nervous persons so easily as strong, able-bodied men and women. Wm. Trueblood and I, both of a nervous temperament, were not affected in the least by the feeling manifested; and yet we stood for an hour or more closely watching and attending those entranced. Mrs. Woodsworth (*sic*) says and believes that it comes from God. She is without

[2] "extasia"—the experience of ecstasy.

doubt an earnest, loving, whole-souled Christian, working for the salvation of souls. So far as observation extends, no harm has ever come from these trances or from any meetings which she has held, and good has resulted therefrom, as many know that sinners have been converted.

Mrs. Woodsworth (*sic*) seems fatigued by her constant labors, and after resting for a week or ten days, she stated that she desired to come to Kokomo and hold a series of meetings. We earnestly hope she may do so, and then all can see for themselves.

—N. A. Trueblood

May 22, 1885

The Indianapolis Times (IN)

The Trance Evangelist

Pendleton Excited Over the Conversion of a Blasphemous and Vindictive Citizen

PENDLETON, IND., MAY 21.—

The announcement yesterday afternoon that Mrs. Woodworth, the evangelist, was in a trance caused hundreds of people to make a break for the place of meeting. She lay on the platform from 2:30 in the afternoon until 8:30 at night before recovering her senses. The daughter of John Malone soon after was similarly affected and so death-like was her appearance that some of the members thought that she was dying, and her father was summoned. As he was known to be a man of violent temper, trouble was looked for. He was aroused from sleep and at once commenced vowing all kinds of vengeance on Mrs. Woodworth and her assistants, keeping it up until he was inside the church. He soon weakened, however, and in ten minutes he was the noisiest convert in town, praising the Lord and shouting that he was glad he had found Christ. The converts are few in number, and people generally are slow to be convinced that the so-called trances are else then cataleptic fits. At the meeting held this afternoon, the house was crowded and several converts and mourners were thrown into the "trance" state.

May 25, 1885

The Indianapolis Times (IN)

Mrs. Woodworth at Kokomo

KOKOMO, IND. MAY 24.—

rs. Woodworth, the great trance evangelist, arrived in this city Saturday and held her first meeting the evening of the same day at the Friends church. The text of her first sermon in this city was the memorable words of Elijah, the prophet: "How long halt ye between two opinions?"[1] She was greeted by an immense concourse of people (the first meeting) of all churches and classes, some coming fifteen miles on foot. Every available inch of standing room was taken and hundreds went away unable to gain admittance.

Today (Sunday) "The Bulwarks of Satan and the Walls of Jericho" were stormed in the large auditorium of the courthouse. Many of her converts from Elwood and Tipton are here assisting her in song, prayer, and exhortation. Fully four thousand people have visited her meetings here today. The last one has not yet closed. She speaks of being well-pleased with the grand opening here and predicts, with a faith that characterizes the prophets of old, a great religious awakening in Kokomo; and so far as outward demonstrations are concerned, her faith far exceeds in size the biblical mustard seed. It is really amusing to see with what eagerness every motion she makes is watched by the multitude, who seem anxious for some evidence of a superhuman power. Yet many are actually afraid to come in contact with her.

To say the least, she is a remarkable woman, full of zeal and desperately in earnest. As yet no one has gone into a trance or visited the paradisien abode. But she promises the denizens of this fair city a wonderful outpouring of what she calls the Holy Spirit. In this city, her following is from the ranks of the better class of people; and as Kokomo never does anything by halves, it is not unreasonable to presume, with the southern countermand, that it must be now that the kingdom is coming, etc. She is to religion what Dennis Kearney[2] was to the body politic—an agitator, but on a much grander scale.

---

[1] 1 Kings 18:21.

[2] "Dennis Kearney"—A political agitator in San Francisco who started The Workingmen's Party.

May 26, 1885

Kokomo Saturday Tribune (IN)

The Woodworth Revival

AN IMMENSE OUTPOURING OF THE PEOPLE TO HEAR THIS STRANGE WOMAN

rs. Woodworth, the far-famed trance evangelist, accompanied by her husband, arrived in this city Saturday afternoon and held her first meeting Saturday evening at the Friends church. At an early hour, the church was packed to overflowing and large numbers went away unable to get in.

The text of her first sermon in this city was the memorable words of Elijah the Prophet: "How long halt ye between two opinions?"[1]

Three services were held at the courthouse Sunday, all of which were attended by hundreds of people, many from idle curiosity and others from pure and honest motives. It is estimated that her audience on Sunday night numbered fully twelve hundred people. Many of our best Christian people are assisting her in her labors in this city. She was also assisted by several of her young converts from Elwood and Tipton in testimony, prayer, and song. In regard to this new religious departure, our reporter does not feel like assuming the role of a critic. So far as Mrs. Woodworth is concerned, she is a very zealous woman and appears to be desperately in earnest. So far as the public is concerned, they seem to be divided as to her motives and by what power she operates; this, however, is always the case during unusual religious awakenings. So far as the doctrine she preaches, it is strongly backed up by the "thus saith the Lord."

As yet no superhuman power or trance demonstrations have been exhibited. The singing is devoid of time and consists of many repetitions of choruses. In passing out of the courthouse Sunday, an aged Methodist said to us, "It's nothing but good, old-fashioned religion." Another not so spiritual in his inclinations says, "It's hypocrisy and is nothing more than a mockery." The better plan is for all to go with an honest purpose to see and hear and not be too hasty in passing judgment. A leading pastor of one of our churches

[1] 1 Kings 18:21.

said to us a few days ago that the preachers had been expending their energies upon the strongholds of sin for three or four years with no effect and that if this lady could come amongst us in the name of God and wake up the people, he would shout lustily, "Amen!"

May 26, 1885

Muncie Daily News (IN)

Packed to Suffocation

KOKOMO ALREADY STIRRED TO THE DEPTHS BY THE FEMALE EVANGELIST

KOKOMO, IND., MAY 25.—

The Woodworth revival is becoming contagious and spreading out among all classes of our people. The large courthouse was packed tonight to suffocation. It is estimated by those who ought to know that fully fifteen hundred people were crowded into the large auditorium, jury rooms, and corridors, and that as many more went away unable to get in.

People came in from the country on horseback and in carriages by scores. Her severest opposition comes from the churches and those whom she has a right to expect to assist her. Men and women who have fixed up a pet system of theology hold her aloof because it conflicts with their formal church etiquette and many preconceived notions. Still, in the face of all this opposition, she is backed up by a strong following of earnest workers who are rallying to her support.

She made a very touching and tearful appeal tonight to the wandering prodigals to come home. While there are many who perhaps do not believe in her methods, yet there is seldom one found who is foolhardy enough to ridicule this work or to doubt her honesty of purpose. The signs of the times point to the greatest religious awakening ever seen in Kokomo. These signs are strengthened by her prophetic declarations. Thus far the multitude of curiosity-seekers have been disappointed in trance performances, as yet nothing but the simple, unvarnished old story of the Cross has been indulged in. Every noise or unusual sound brings the audience to their feet. They are evidently "seeking for a sign," and it remains to be seen whether it will be given them.

May 27, 1885

The Indianapolis Times (IN)

Kokomo in a Trance

Under the Spell of Woodworth

TABOOED BY THE CHURCH PEOPLE, YET HER MEETINGS ARE WITHOUT PARALLEL IN THE HISTORY OF THE WICKEDEST CITY IN THE STATE—GLORY GALORE

KOKOMO, IND., MAY 26.—

Today has marked a memorable epoch in the history of Kokomo. Thousands of people are flocking to what seems the religious mecca of the Hoosier Commonwealth. The Woodworth meetings today and tonight are without a parallel in the history of this city. Hundreds of anxious people are unable to get within hearing distance of the speakers and go away disappointed. Tonight, large delegations came from Jerome, Greentown, Alto, New London, Tipton, and many other suburban towns. The meeting tonight was addressed by Dr. J. B. Puckett and many other leading citizens.

The afternoon meeting was one of great power, and a genuine old hallelujah time, similar to the primitive days of Methodism, was enjoyed and which culminated in several powerful conversions. Slowly but gradually, the scales of prejudice are dropping from the people's eyes, and they are rallying to the support of this noted woman who seems to bring the message of glad tidings to the hearts of the people. The Macedonian cry of "Come over into the vineyard and help us"[1] has been heeded, and many recruits from Tipton and other points arrived this evening to give new life and zeal to the work. There seems to be no chance by those inclined to stay the tide that threatens to lash over and swallow up the strongholds of sin in this city. Many seekers surrounded the altar tonight pleading for pardon and a better experience.

Mrs. Woodworth displays remarkable tact in the management of her meetings. She seems very desirous of working in harmony with the churches and is receiving some royal support from the Society of Friends, while others seem fearful of having their beautiful temples

[1] See Acts 16:9.

defiled and would rather have this evangelist depart in order that their peace and quiet may not be disturbed and anxiously await further developments.

May 28, 1885

Kokomo Dispatch (IN)

Trance Religion

Mrs. Woodworth Opens Her Batteries on this City

THE CURIOUS ARE ATTRACTED IN GREAT NUMBERS

Personal Sketch of the Trance Evangelist

Mrs. Woodworth Interviewed—Opinions of Representative Citizens

Mrs. Maria B. Woodworth, the famous trance evangelist, began a series of revival meetings in this city on last Saturday night. She is accompanied by her husband and two young men—R. H. Dempey of Toledo, and J. W. Sweeney of New Corner, Indiana. The only business apparently of her two young helpers is to sing and pray. Mrs. Woodworth does all the preaching herself. The first meeting was held in the Friends church, and to say the church was packed like sardines in a box is no exaggeration. The people flocked to see the noted evangelist with the same curiosity that will draw the crowd to Kokomo today to see the Forepaugh show.[1] We are safe in saying that fully three-fourths of Mrs. Woodworth's audiences are drawn together out of sheer curiosity to see this noted woman and the results of her work.

The text of her first discourse was "How long halt ye between two opinions?" There was nothing peculiarly striking about her preaching except her earnestness and sincerity. Nearly everybody gives her credit of being sincere, however opinion may differ on other points. She is doubtless an honest Christian woman, whatever else may be said of her. She can't preach, as we understand the common acceptance of the meaning of that word, and she is only a tolerable talker. She is preeminently an exhorter, and the burthen[2] of her discourses is "Come to Jesus."

Her meetings are characterized by much singing and prayer. Sometimes three or four long prayers will be made in succession and after the meeting is fully under headway, the workers and seekers for salvation all pray aloud at the same time. At this stage of the meeting the

[1] "Forepaugh show"—the name of a circus that came to town.

[2] "burthen"—burden.

excitement runs very high, and that strange things should happen under these conditions is not to be wondered at. Frightened souls coming within the current of this mighty whirlpool are snatched up and saved, as it were by a miracle, from the wrath to come.

The place of meeting was transferred to the courthouse on Sunday where three services have been held every day since at 10 o'clock A.M., 2 P.M., and at 7 in the evening. The courthouse has been packed almost to suffocation at the night meetings, and the day meetings are very largely attended. Every evening from fifty to a hundred country teams[3] may be seen hitched around the public square belonging to people living all the way from one to fifteen miles from town.

Personal Appearance

Mrs. Woodworth, in appearance, is a plain, unassuming woman of a common type. She is of medium size, light complexion, and dark blue eyes. She is of the sanguine nervous temperament and has the appearance of one who has drained the cup of bitterness to the dregs. She does not possess the magnetic power[4] some have attributed to her. On the contrary she appears to us to be deficient in this attribute. But when preaching, and when in animated conversation, her face lights up with an angelic smile that well becomes her. She cannot be called a handsome woman. She is forty years old and is the mother of six children, only one of whom is living.

That she has not had the advantages of even a common school education is evident from her preaching. She scarcely utters a sentence that does not contain errors of grammar, but she has the faculty of making herself understood. She dresses plainly and displays no jewelry. She wears her hair in a roll on the crown of the head and eschews bangs and frizzes[5] as the devil's own implements of war.

Mrs. Woodworth Talks

A *Dispatch* reporter had the temerity to call on the distinguished evangelist at her hotel, the Central House, where she is stopping,

---

[3] "teams"—refers to teams of horses which pull carriages.

[4] "magnetic power"—hypnotic power.

[5] "frizzes"—hair that is curled into small, tight curls.

and had an interesting interview with her. Mrs. W. received him in the parlor very cautiously; and learning the purpose of the call, readily granted the request and in the same breath cautioned him to be very careful to report her fairly and correctly. She instanced the purported interview recently published by the *Indianapolis Times* as the result of criminal incompetence and unfairness in reportorial work. She said she had lots of trouble with the press, and she had come to be very chary of her favors to reporters—it was so difficult to get her interviews fairly and properly reported.

Of course the representative of *The Dispatch* was too gallant not to accept this reasonable condition and commenced the pumping process by asking her to state something of her birth, parents, family, etc.

"I was born," she said, "in New Lisbon, Ohio, July 22, 1845, and am consequently now nearly forty years of age. I was the fourth daughter of a family of eight children. In 1856, I was left an orphan by the death of my father. My parents belonged to the Church of the Disciples. We were poor and the battle of life was a hard-fought one for us."

[K. D.] "When and how were you converted to Christianity?"

[M. B. W.] "Although I had no opportunity to go to church in my early youth, at the age of eight I was profoundly impressed with a desire to know God. The first time I remember of attending religious services, my heart was melted with the Savior's love. I was soundly converted at the age of thirteen and joined the Disciples' church. Soon after I was converted, I heard the voice of Jesus calling me to go out in the highways and hedges and gather in the lost sheep. I resisted the call to work in God's vineyard until God had taken five of my six children, and then I consecrated myself to Him and His work. I had many visions urging me . . . [bottom portion of column missing] . . . sickness or death come between me and the work. God accepted the offering and the blessing and power came to me. I began systematically the evangelical work five years ago."

[K. D.] "What success has attended your labors?"

[M. B. W.] "My success has been really marvelous. The number of converts to Christianity under my preaching would run far up into the thousands. You can have a better idea of my success by taking the result of my work in a few towns. At Hartford City the number of converts was not less than five hundred; at New Corner five hundred; at Summitville about four hundred; at Columbia City, six hundred."

[K. D.] "Do the churches generally affiliate with your work?"

[M. B. W.] "No, not as a general thing. The preachers seem to be envious of my great success. The Christian, or Campbellite, church, especially, antagonizes me. But I defy them to prove that I do not preach the pure Gospel of Christ, a thing some of the preachers don't do by a long ways."

[K. D.] "Do you attribute the religious trance directly to the power of God?"

[M. B. W.] "Certainly. To what other influence could it be attributed? I know it is God's work."

[K. D.] "How do you know it?"

[M. B. W.] "Because I have experienced it. Personal knowledge and experience is the best possible proof."

[K. D.] "How often are you entranced?"

[M. B. W.] "Sometimes twice in one day, and at other times I may go for weeks without enjoying this experience."

[K. D.] "How does the trance affect you?"

[M. B. W.] "In different ways, but generally I return to a normal condition in an hour or so, feeling much afreshed instead of prostrated as some think. I remember what I saw while in the trance state, and this revelation aids me greatly in my work. I often see the very persons in my meetings that I had seen in the trance, and I warn them of their imminent danger and thus often save them. It affects different persons differently."

[K. D.] "Does the trance leave any delirious effect?"

[M. B. W.] "No. It is strengthening rather than debilitating."

[K. D.] "There is much conjecture, Mrs. Woodworth, as to the pay you receive for your work. Will you satisfy the curiosity of the public on this point?"

[M. B. W.] "I demand no stipulated sum. I go where the Lord calls me without regard to the pay there is in it. I have been offered three hundred dollars a week to go to this place and that, but I am not working for money. I am working for the Lord and He will abundantly repay me back in His own good time and way."

[K. D.] "How long will you remain here, Mrs. Woodworth?"

[M. B. W.] "That is impossible to say except that it will be until the Lord calls me elsewhere."

Opinions

Opinion is much divided touching the salient points of the Woodworth mode of conversion. Some approve her work and at the same time deny that she possesses the power she claims. Others accord her honest motives and a good heart but do not approve her methods. She antagonized many of our best people right at the start by declaring that the churches had done more to make skeptics than everything else combined. She antagonizes the preachers, and it is but natural that the preachers and their friends should reciprocate the compliment, wherefore the clergy and the leading members of our churches are conspicuous for their absence at her meetings. So far only a few prominent church people and none of our ministers, except Doctor Puckett, have taken an active part in her meetings; in fact their silent influence is against this new mode of saving sinners. In order to get the drift of public opinion, we have interviewed a number of our representative citizens on this subject. Doctor R. Q. Wilson visited Tipton while Mrs. W. was holding meetings there and had a good opportunity to study the question in all its phases.

Doctor R. Q. Wilson

[K. D.] "Doctor," queried a Dispatcher, "have you attended any of Mrs. Woodworth's meetings?"

[Dr. W.] "I have."

[K. D.] "Well, what is your opinion of her methods and plans of conversion?"

[Dr. W.] "She appears to be a very earnest and devoted woman. She preaches the Gospel, as I understand it, but in a manner peculiar to herself and differing greatly from most ministers in her method of presenting it. Her plans of conversion are the same that I saw forty years ago at camp meetings among the mountains in Pennsylvania."

[K. D.] "Do you think the Woodworth trance is the result of supernatural agency, or can it be accounted for on rational principles?"

[Dr. W.] "I am of the opinion that the trance manifestations can be accounted for on physiological and psychological principles."

[K. D.] "By what name then would you designate the condition known as 'trance'?"

[Dr. W.] "I would call it ecstasy."

[K. D.] "What is 'ecstasy,' Doctor? Please explain it."

[Dr. W.] "In ecstasy the mind is wholly absorbed in one idea and utterly oblivious to all else. The nervous system is excited to its utmost tension; and if continued, it must end either in trance spasms or complete exhaustion and relaxation. During this condition hallucination often occurs, for the mind is active all the time and the 'visions' are distinctly and even vividly remembered afterward."

[K. D.] "Is that not the same thing as catalepsy?"

[Dr. W.] "No. In catalepsy the mind ceases to act—is suspended for the time being; consequently the person can have no hallucination and no after-recollection, for the simple reason that there is nothing to recollect."

[K. D.] "How, then, in your opinion, is this condition called ecstasy brought about?"

[Dr. W.] "By intense excitement, the mind being concentrated on a single subject and insensible to everything else for an indefinite period."

[K. D.] "In your opinion, are the results likely to be beneficial or injurious?"

[Dr. W.] "It is hard to tell. From my standpoint, one would not draw a favorable conclusion. Being myself an old Blue Stocking Presbyterian, I could not naturally have much sympathy in that direction. But after all, who knows to an absolute certainty who is right and who is wrong?"

Rev. C. G. Hudson

"With reference to Mrs. Woodworth and her work, I can scarcely call myself qualified to judge, having thus far only attended one evening.

"I have advised with several of the pastors, in whose churches she has labored, and with others who have been with her, as to the general results of her work on the prosperity of the church; and, from all I can understand, I think she is a devout, sincere, earnest, and enthusiastic worker, and that she is orthodox in her teachings concerning the necessity of repentance of sin, conversion, or a change of heart, and leading a new life.

"I understand that she has been successful in reaching many hardened cases who have resisted every other good influence brought to bear upon them.

"If by her labors here such persons can be reached and saved, I wish her a hearty Godspeed and abundant success; for there are many in every community who can only be reached by some unusual agency. Certainly, in this land of religious freedom, where everyone can worship God according to the dictates of his own conscience, no one should set up any cast iron rule by which all others must believe and act, or indulge in denunciation of those who may harbor a different opinion, or offer any opposition to those who are sincerely working for the glory of God.

"As to the peculiar manifestations connected with the work of this lady, which are called trances, I have not seen any of them so as to judge. From such reports as have come to me, it seems that they are the same manifestations which have been seen in all ages. Manifestations of a similar character occurred in the medieval Roman church. They were not uncommon in Scotland some two hundred years ago. Jonathan Edwards[6] records them abundantly in his account of the Great Awakening in New England. Whitefield[7]

[6] "Jonathan Edwards"—(1703-1758) a preacher and Theologian in eighteenth century America during the time of the Great Awakening.

[7] "Whitefield"—George Whitefield (1714-1770) was an English evangelist who brought revival to eighteenth-century America and spurred the Great Awakening, a revival which transformed America.

found them in New Jersey. Very remarkable instances occurred in the early camp meetings of the Presbyterians and others many years ago, such as trances and jerks.

"In the beginning of Mr. Wesley's preaching, near London and New Castle, the wicked were stricken to the earth and converted, although without any visions or revelations. While Mr. Wesley looked upon these manifestations with favor at first, he afterward repressed them as far as possible.[8] Some of these manifestations he believed to be wholly from God and others to be imitations. He never confounded them with noise, clamor, or screaming in public worship, and these latter he always severely repressed.

"In the history of these peculiar manifestations connected with religious excitement, we find that they were seldom or never followed by any morbid physical effects. Although they are peculiar to religious excitements, yet, as far as one can judge, they are in themselves physical affections. The most devout have not been the most subject to them. They have not always been followed by moral results. They have attended the worst as well as the best forms of religions.

"The Rev. Silas Comfort, in an exhaustive article concerning them, in the *Quarterly Review* for April, 1859, calls them 'religious catalepsy'—'a suspension more or less of the functions of the cerebrum, attended by an abnormal activity of the cerebellum: the rational powers—the will, judgment, or reason—are temporarily put in abeyance, and the involuntary susceptibilities left subject to the prevailing impression or influence.' He says, 'To be thrown into the cataleptic state in conversion is no criterion of the genuineness of the change. The proof must be sought and will be found elsewhere. Religious catalepsy is not a safe standard by which to estimate a religious state, growth in grace, or personal piety in any stage of experience.'

"Richard Watson,[9] the great commentator, gave as his advice, which was approved by the Methodists of his time and which has been the

[8] That Wesley repressed manifestations of the Holy Spirit is disproved by a careful reading of his journal, in which he indicated the same kind of trances occurred throughout his preaching ministry and labeled them as signs of the Holy Spirit's presence during conversion.

[9] "Richard Watson"—Richard Watson (1781-1833) was the first Methodist to publish a systematic theology. He also wrote sermons and a dictionary of Jewish culture.

general sentiment of the Methodist church, that 'in no such case should the occasional occurrence of noise and disorder be taken as a proof that a work of grace is not being wrought in the hearts of men by the Spirit of God, that, as far as possible, they are to be repressed by a firm discipline, for the power of the work does not lie in them; yet that discipline should be discriminating for the sake of the real blessing which at such seasons may be attending the administration of the truth.'

"Time and the results in men's lives, will best show the nature of these manifestations in connection with the work of Mrs. Woodworth. If good be done, let all rejoice and endeavor to make it permanent."

Rev. Robert McCune

Rev. Robert McCune declined to be interviewed at this time, preferring to withhold comment until the meetings have run their course for fear that he might be charged with attempting to impede or obstruct the work.

Rev. Smith

Our reporter could not find Rev. Smith, but he is quoted by his friends as being very much opposed to the Woodworth methods.

Dr. Lewis Kern

"I believe it is genuine, old fashioned Methodist religion, just such as we had in the times of Finley,[10] Mrs. Fletcher,[11] and Peter Cartwright,[12] all wool and a yard wide.[13] No one who believes in the Methodist doctrine can say naught against Mrs. Woodworth's plan and teachings."

I. H. Ellis

"I like it the best of anything I ever saw in the way of a religious meeting. Hope it will go on till every sinner in Kokomo is stretched out stiff on the mourner's bench."

[10] "Finley"—Possibly, Charles Finney (1792-1875), a well-known evangelist.

[11] "Mrs Fletcher"—Julia A. Fletcher, a ninteenth century moralist and poet who wrote "Little Things" (1845).

[12] "Peter Cartwright"—(1785-1872) a Methodist Episcopal evangelist whose travelling ministry covered Kentucky, Tennessee, and Illinois.

[13] "all wool and a yard wide"—The context suggests that this expression means that these people and Mrs. Woodworth are genuine, high-quality examples of Methodist spirituality.

Elder E. L Frazier

"I do not at all endorse it nor accept her claims. The whole work and results may be accounted for without God. Her claims that she holds conversations with God and the Christ are very presumptuous and to me seem impious. Her style and talk are without reverence. No one who has respect for holy things or reverence can give bold utterance to such as "a cyclone of the Holy Ghost." She does a good deal of rubbing and patting to get her seekers through. Everyone who knows anything of mesmerism, magnetism, and electricity will understand this. Does the Holy Ghost have no power over men without first getting up a storm of excitement? I have not witnessed the like since I attended the meetings of the poor black slaves in Kentucky, thirty years ago. The behavior is that of the prophets of Baal—they need only the stones to cut themselves with. Heaven's first law is order."

Father Lordermann

[K. D.] "Well, Father, it is hardly necessary to ask your opinion of the Woodworth revival. Your position on all phases of emotional conversion is so well-known."

[F. L.] "Yes, you can put me down every time as opposed to excitement of every description as a means of turning people to God. I believe Mrs. Woodworth's meetings are a reproach and a disgrace to the religion of God."

J. B. Carter

[K. D.] "As representing the conservative class of quiet, calm thinkers, *The Dispatch* would be pleased to lay before its readers your views of Mrs. Woodworth and her work."

[J. B. C.] "I speak for myself and nobody else. I believe Mrs. Woodworth is a sincere, honest Christian, whose sole object is to save souls. I have no objection to her manner or means. However, I believe the trances produced under her preaching are caused by natural causes which in turn, I admit, may very properly be attributed to God, in the same way that He is said to be the fountainhead or source of everything—the Great Creator of the physical universe and every living thing. I think Mrs. Woodworth is reaching a class of people that the churches cannot—or do not—reach, and I say 'amen' to her work."

Elder Joseph Reese

"I don't believe the Woodworth theory of conversion. Don't believe God has anything to do with the so-called Woodworth trance. The plan is not rational, neither is it desirable."

W. S. Armstrong

"I will give Mrs. Woodworth $50, needy as I am, if she will down one side of me,[14] and I will give her every opportunity and all the time she wants."

W. B. Elson

"It's nawthun but flap-doodle and wind."

N. A. Trueblood

"I believe Mrs. Woodworth is a good woman and doing a good work. I can't say what the power is that causes people to go into trances under her preaching."

Side Notes

The book and picture business has opened.

For a little woman, Mrs. Woodworth has a wonderful voice.

"When the Bridegroom Comes" and "Palms of Glory" are the prevailing songs.

Mrs. Woodworth says that more than one year ago, Little Joe Sayiors told her to come to Kokomo.

Thus far no trance manifestation has developed whereat the curious and the sightseers are disappointed.

Mrs. W. pitched into the churches, hammer and tongs,[15] on Sunday evening—she will not forgive them for not embracing her system of religion.

---

[14] "down one side of me"—overthrow or knock down; in this case he will give $50 if he will put him in a trance which will throw him to the ground.

[15] "hammer and tongs"—with all her might (refers to blacksmithing).

No church in Kokomo, save the Quaker, would open their doors to Mrs. Woodworth. They take no stock in the religious hysteria that she teaches.

To Taylor McNiel (*sic*),[16] more than all else besides, is due Mrs. Woodworth's presence in our midst. He worked up the matter and is the directing force of the meetings.

This talk of entranced persons seeing Jesus and walking the streets of the New Jerusalem is all poppycock. As well argue the existence of ghosts to scare little children.

The pilgrim singers that attend the evangelist, are "like sweet bells jangled and out of tune." As singers they are most dismal failures. They ought to be accompanied by a pair of cymbals.

Old man McChristian is a sort of aid-de-camp. He prays loud and long, and his voice is like the old-time Hepsidam wong-doodle preacher.[17] When he lets loose, the audience think a vocal cyclone has struck them. He is so full of "oh, Lord—ahs" that one wishes the machinery would fly a cog so as to give his powerful lungs a rest for a while.

Mrs. Woodworth's husband is a trifle above medium size, has short, coarse, sandy hair, short mutton-chop whiskers, and a countenance that does not betoken any vast degree of intelligence or religious veneration. We learn that he calls himself "Elder," but as yet he has not opened his mouth in the way of exhortation to flee the wrath to come. Mrs. W. and her husband are stopping at the Central Hotel.

The reports of the meetings sent daily to the metropolitan press, notably the *Indianapolis Times,* are colored beyond warrant and exaggerated beyond the truth. It looks like an arranged scheme to

[16] Another news reporter (May 30, 1885, "Mrs. Woodworth in Trance") spelled the name "McNeil." Both spellings are maintained as they appear in these and other articles.

[17] "Hepsidam wong-doodle preacher"—Alf Burnett, a comedian during the Civil War created a soliloquy of a hypocritical, uneducated Baptist preacher who quotes a verse he claims is from the Bible, "For they shall gnaw a file, and flee unto the mountains of Hepsidam, what the lion roareth and the wangdoodle mourneth for his first born." ("Frontier Humor," webpage. accessed 14 April 2000. Http://www.towson.edu/~duncan/wangdood.html). The expression insults Old Man McChristian whose name also may be a pseudonym for one of the local people helping Maria Woodworth.

write Mrs. Woodworth into fame that she does not deserve. There is too much gush and flapdoodle about the newspaper reports.

Mrs. Woodworth is not an educated woman. Her grammar is bad but she talks glibly and at times eloquently for all that. Her catch words are "cyclone" and "fire." She trips upon the verbs as witness—"Something must be did," "I have came," etc. She is not so magnetic as Mrs. Russell, the temperance evangelist, nor so intelligent, but she has a great deal more endurance.

The meeting Tuesday night was a perfect jam, so anxious everybody seemed to see someone go off in a trance. But this morbid curiosity was not gratified. The report that several had been entranced during the day was the loadstone that attracted the sightseers. Some fifteen persons from Tipton, and many from other distant points, were in attendance, most of whom addressed the meeting. Among this number was Dr. A. Pitzer of Tipton, a recent convert to Mrs. Woodworth's preaching.

May 30, 1885

Kokomo Journal (IN)

Mrs. Woodworth in Trance

THE EVANGELIST PASSES INTO THE ECSTATIC STATE IN HER MEETING AT KOKOMO

A Specimen of Her Exhortation, and the Methods She Pursued in Rousing Excitement—An Epileptic Convert

FROM A STAFF CORRESPONDENT OF THE JOURNAL, KOKOMO, MAY 30.—

rs. Maria B. Woodworth, the evangelist, has now been here a week. Her first service was held on last Saturday in the Friends church. On Monday she was given the large room in the courthouse, a room capable, when filled, of holding fifteen hundred people. It is filled at night—packed. Mrs. Woodworth is everywhere the topic of conversation. Kokomo is divided as to the acceptability of her methods—some approving, others condemning them. It stands in the way of her success that the disapproval does not take the form of vigorous condemnation, but is rather apathetic. There are few who have seen her who do not acknowledge, even while disapproving of her methods, that she is an earnest, honest woman trying to win souls to Christ.

Thus far she has had few converts, the pastors of the strong churches of the city, Methodist, Congregational, and Christian, taking no part in the services. The singing, for this reason, is poor, the choir singers of the several churches not lending their voices. The last desertion is more serious than the first, as her services need the assistance of song to develop the enthusiasm. "Mrs. Woodworth," said a gentleman yesterday, to your reporter, "is displeased with the way that they (the church people) are doing here. She told me if they did not take hold of the work better that she would stay all summer—it is a dreadful threat." Said a pastor of one of the strongest churches, "We have been overworked with excitements and many of our best people think no good can come of them. They remember the temperance revival here of last winter a year ago conducted by Jimmy Dunn. It continued thirteen weeks until everyone was sick and tired of it. It was reported that twenty-five hundred persons donned the red ribbon. There was certainly a great number, but they were already temperance people—men, women, and children. There were few chronic drinkers, and of the drinkers, the last one flopped back again at the last election."[1] In consequence of these things, Mrs. Woodworth's co-workers are few in number and mostly [come] from outside of Kokomo. She brings with her a husband and two young men, R. H. Dempey of Toledo, Ohio, and J. W. Sweeney of New Corner, Indiana, whose business appears to be only to sing and pray, Mrs. Woodworth doing the preaching herself. Her husband takes no part in the meetings.

Yesterday was the red-letter day in the revival. Previous to that time there had been no trances, and those who had been attracted wholly by curiosity began to express themselves as disappointed. Yesterday morning, as Mrs. Woodworth stepped upon the raised platform in the courthouse where the jury sits, it was plain to be seen that she was extremely tired and worn. Little wonder when it is taken into account that she has for several weeks been holding two or three meetings a day.

She is about forty years old and dresses in black, with extreme plainness. She wears a white lace kerchief about her neck, coming down over her bosom. Her dress sleeves are trimmed with black lace at the bottom, and loose, enabling her arm to escape free and white showing nearly to the elbow. Her face is not full and her features are strong rather than handsome, her nose being prominent, her mouth wide and thin. She is short in stature but well-rounded and well-knit. Her wrists are large and round, her fingers long. She is evidently capable of great fatigue. Her hair is dark brown, coiled at the top of the head. It is difficult to determine the color of her eyes—at times they seem blue, at other times gray, and at still others light hazel. She has a strong contralto voice, the most sympathetic of all voices and one capable of arousing much emotion in a nervous person. It may easily be seen that that kind of a voice, when used at its best, might bring many persons where they would not know what they were about. When she exerts it to its full power, it

[1] "at the last election"—It was not uncommon for people competing for office to have stands near the polls where they served alcoholic beverages to those who voted for them.

comes out strong and clear, and can easily be heard many squares away through the opened windows of the courthouse.

At the meeting yesterday afternoon, the second held that day—for she works hard, not sparing herself, and her labor being such as few preachers could stand—the audience was not large, not filling more than one-fourth of the room. After singing and prayer, Mrs. Woodworth spoke. She does not preach as the following, taken from her talk, will show. What she says is delivered with great earnestness, striking her hands together repeatedly and stamping her foot upon the platform:

> Let us ask God to search our hearts. Search my heart and try me. If anything is in my heart that should not be there, oh take it out. I come to tell you of religion that will keep you all the year round, that will be good for the harvest field or any place. Jesus says let your light be burning. Then there will be some attraction about you—something the sinner can understand. If our lamps are burning, the world is coming to see the light. Take a candle out on a dark night and people will see it far and near. Oh, let your light shine. You can tell a true child of God as soon as you see one. I can go round and lay my hand on them every one and not make a mistake once. I see it in the face every time. Call it what you will. Call it electricity, if you please; I say it's the Holy Ghost shining through the face.
>
> If ever you are saved, you must lie down at the feet of Jesus. Jesus says unto you, "Come unto Me if you are weary and heavy laden, and I will give you rest.[2] Go to Him and drop your burdens at His feet. Bless the Lord. And more than that, He blots out our sin, covers it up with His blood. Your sins, once blotted out, will never come up again—never! Glory to God! Some men's sins come before judgment and some follow after. If you die a Christian, not a single sin will be charged against you. David was a happy Christian: "I will praise the Lord with

[2] Matthew 11:29, paraphrased.

my mouth. I will magnify His name continually. Bless the Lord. O my soul! He calls upon the nations; let the redeemed of the Lord say so."[3]

If we are climbing Jacob's ladder as we should, we will be happy Christians and will be praising God, telling the good things He is doing for us continually. Shout and make a joyful noise to God. Yes, my friends, if we are redeemed we shall say so. We will not be afraid to say so. We will rejoice always in the Lord. Let us speak out and tell what the Lord has did (*sic*) for us. Glory to God! God has promised to fill all our hearts with the fullness of God. The reason so many of our hearts are not filled is because we have not allowed Him to fill them. Christ is a satisfying portion. If we go in a right way, He will come and fill us with all the fullness of God. Let us test the Word. Let us bring all our trials to Him. "Prove me, says the Lord of hosts."[4] He will shower down the blessings from heaven.

We want today to get our hearts filled to overflowing. God will send the power down, my friends, so that we shall all be filled if we ask it. And then we shall shout. That is what makes people shout; when you are a Christian, you cannot keep it to yourself. You will want to make other people Christians. Glory to God! Let us place our vessel at the fountain, and let it remain there until it is filled and God will fill it—fill it to overflowing. The woman of Samaria came out to draw water, but the Lord filled her pitcher from heaven and she went into the city and told of it—became a street preacher. Yes she did, glory to God! She was a child of God and they were compelled to listen to what she said. . . .[5]

Let us humble ourselves, let us get down. What are we but worms of the dust? Why should we not humble ourselves? Thus saith the Lord; you cannot go back on it. I want to show you that the noise that goes up from a full heart to

[3] Possibly, Psalms 145:21; 103:1; 107:2-3 paraphrased.

[4] See Malachi 3:10.

[5] See John 4:28-30, 39.

> God is pleasing to Him. The Lord wants us to rejoice. They rejoiced in the olden time, making a loud noise and weeping for joy. That is the old-fashioned religion. People seem afraid to open their mouths in these times. They were not afraid then, as we are, of having it called "excitement." They were people of God and the old-time religion. Christ is our burden bearer if we take our burdens to Him. Don't think to please the people here. Let us shout to please our God; let us be happy Christians. Let us give our whole hearts to Jesus, remembering that Jesus is our captain, that He fights our battles and has never lost a battle. Never mind the mocks and laughs, the more need that we should stand firm for Jesus.
>
> Let us be filled with the joys of His salvation. What scores and hundreds are yours for eternal rewards—others are damned. If any go down to hell through your neglect or mine, how dreadful that will be. We must be burdened for souls. (Then she stamped her foot repeatedly.) Yes, burdened for souls. God never sent us to this place for nothing. Some say money is our object. A great many reports are going around. I go where the Lord sends me if I don't get a penny. Dear friends, God has sent us here to warn you of the life to come. We will warn you faithfully in spite of the designs of Satan. God help you to come to Jesus and be saved. God help us to get into line. If we are not ready, let us get ready. Like Nineveh, in less than forty days many of us are to be sealed for heaven or for hell. Oh, give your hearts to God! Let us get "Nearer my God to Thee, nearer to Thee."

After the sermon there was singing and praying, Mrs. Woodworth's method being to have everybody pray at the same time and pray aloud. This sort of conglomerate prayer is very confusing to the disinterested listener; but apparently has a strong effect upon those who are engaged, and the voices of the contestants rise higher and higher, and they become more and more excited. Suddenly a man about twenty-eight years old fell in what was called "a trance." His legs and arms were rigid while the muscles of his face worked with every indication of epilepsy. At this incident, the shouts grew wilder and wilder but were continued to fewer than twenty persons, the workers most of whom were women and several of them well advanced in years. There were cries of "Glory to God, another son is saved," and similar expressions.

Mrs. Woodworth's face is working strangely and its color has changed to a grayish white. Suddenly she drops into a chair. Her face is turned upwards, her eyes open, staring, the pupils dilated. One arm is raised above her head, the fingers all but one, the index finger, and that pointing upward. Her other arm is rigid, the hand bent in an unnatural and uncomfortable position, the index finger pointing to the floor. She moves the uplifted arm, the right arm, slowly above her head, the pointing finger quivering. Her teeth are clenched and the right side of her mouth perceptibly drawn. This distortion gave the appearance of a smile, but there was in it more of discomfort than of happiness.

One of the workers explained that the rigid evangelist was pointing heavenward with one finger and toward hell with the other, and "Oh, dear friends, which way will you go?" After this "trance" had continued nearly three-quarters of an hour, Mrs. Woodworth, with her eyes still fixed and unwinking, the pupils dilated, rose from her chair and began slowly to walk the platform. As she did so she sighed, repeated and faintly whispered, "Oh, Jesus. Oh, my God," and afterwards extending her arms and then drawing them towards her as if to embrace, murmured, "Oh Jesus, oh my God, save the people." Many of the women who were standing about betrayed great emotion at this, some weeping and wringing their hands, while others shouted and still others prayed. One elderly woman gave a shout and scream, and throwing her hands above her head, seemed as if she had gone entirely deranged. It was some minutes before she came out of it, which she did with a flood of tears, after which her face fairly shone with happiness. Mrs. Woodworth, instead of recovering went into another "trance," and afterwards into still another, making an hour and three-quarters in which she had been in that condition, from 5 o'clock until a quarter of 7. The news went out over the city that the evangelist was in a trance; and though it was the supper hour, hundreds flocked in to see her—men and women, young girls and boys, some mothers bringing babies in arms, a little one or two tagging at the apron strings.

To add to the excitement just before Mrs. Woodworth "came out of hers," a young man was "taken" and fell bloodless and rigid. He was vigorously fanned while the singing and praying and shouting continued.

This young man's name was John Moon. He looked extremely silly as he was coming out of his "trance" which lasted nearly an hour. "What did you see?" was inquired of him. "I did not see much of anything," was the answer. "I was so busy wrestling with the Lord." The other man who had the "trance," the writer was told by a physician who has frequently attended him, is an epileptic and frequently has fits. It was asked if Mrs. Woodworth did not take great risks in working herself up to the point of having "trances," an ecstatic state frequently noted by medical writers and not uncommon even when unaccompanied by religion. "Oh, no," was the reply of a worker, "she had one down to Pendleton the other day, that lasted five hours. Besides if she died in one of 'em she would go straight through the gates to glory."

"Well," said another, an able-bodied man of twenty-five, "I dassen't look her in the eye when she has one of them spells. I feel it in my bones that if I did it would knock me. I'd have one sure."

It was nearly half past 7 in the evening before Mrs. Woodworth had fully recovered from her trance. She did not go to the hotel where she and her husband are putting up, though it is only three-quarters of a square from the courtroom, but ate sparingly of a lunch that was sent her, bathed her face, and soon afterward opened the evening service.

The courtroom was crowded, many going away unable to gain entrance. The services were opened by the singing of a new hymn, composed by Newton A. Trueblood of Kokomo. It was sung to the air, "Let the Lower Lights Be Burning," and was as follows:

> Jesus said to souls in sorrow
> Come to Me when tempest toss'd

Help today perchance tomorrow
Some poor sinner may be lost.

Chorus—

Come my father, come my mother
Sin abounds in Christian lands
Come my sister, come my brother,
Do not sit with folded hands.

Help the sinner to salvation
By the Cross that Jesus bore
Lead him far from sin's temptation
Point him to the other shore.

Many souls in sin are weeping
You can do what heaven demands
Harvest now is ripe for reaping
Do not sit with folded hands.

Taylor McNeil, a hardware merchant of the place, and heretofore not considered even a Christian but who was chiefly instrumental in getting Mrs. Woodworth to come to Kokomo, spoke. He said that this evangelist's methods had brought many to Christ, and he believed in them, that they were good and that he himself would take his chances for her doing good, that he had been done good. Mrs. Woodworth seemed disinclined to talk much, evidently being worn out by her exertions of the afternoon. She did no preaching and there was much singing and praying. The meeting, while uncomfortably large, was orderly and without fainting or trances. As in the afternoon, everybody was asked to pray aloud and at the same time as before; the supplications took the form of a vocal race.

As the praying went on Mrs. Woodworth, pacing the platform with clasped hands, would cry, "Oh, my God, must this people perish? Oh, God, the destiny of so many souls is at stake. Jesus, awaken this people! Oh, my God, save them! Now pray, oh, my God, everybody pray. Oh, Jesus, have mercy; Thou Son of David, have mercy!" etc. In the meantime, in the midst of this distress, Mrs. Woodworth kept an eye on all sides and gave frequent whispered directions to her lieutenants. Those who crowded round the altar were for the most part girls, several of them little girls. The helpers went through the audience, but the supplicants who came forward were few. Later on she referred with considerable bitterness to the fact that the pastors had not come to her aid in the meetings she held. Nearly all the pastors of this town stayed away. Some have even said this is hellish work. "Why should we stand and be criticized and persecuted as we have been? Why should I have come to this town? It is for precious never dyings (she weeps). Oh, don't try to drive away the Spirit. I pray sleep may be taken away from your eyes and that you may be restless until you repent and give yourselves to Him."

Your correspondent failed to find among the pastors or the body of religious people any persecution of Mrs. Woodworth: they simply leave her alone. Many think the giving of the courthouse room to her has set a precedent that may in the future be a very annoying one, and the judge who did so is already meeting with some criticism. Next week as there will be court, the meetings will probably be held in a large tent. The general opinion is that Mrs. Woodworth will meet with little success here. Her success heretofore has been in small towns and villages where there were few excitements. Kokomo is a brisk, thriving little city, with many and diverse interests and no lack of either occupation or amusement. Besides this—and the writer heard considerable comment on the matter last evening—Mrs. Woodworth's trances are not pleasant to look upon.

Still, as I remarked in the beginning of this communication, there is no doubt that she is an earnest Christian woman, with her whole soul in the work, and entitled to respect whether her methods are considered objectionable or not. She has, perhaps, been given undue prominence and her powers have been greatly magnified by the newspapers, as she is in no wise a great evangelist. She is no sermonizer, her talks being merely shreds and patches—exhortations and not arguments.

—C.D.

June 2, 1885

The Kokomo Gazette Tribune (IN)

The Woodworth Meeting

The great Woodworth meeting still goes on with swelling numbers and increasing interest. The courthouse was again packed on Wednesday night. After the grand preliminary of song and chorus, the meeting was baptized with a spirit of prayer led by Rev. J. L. Puckett and Elder Ervin, followed by a sermon of great earnestness and power by Mrs. Woodworth, taking as a foundation for her remarks, the building of the ark and the subsequent destruction of the antediluvian world. After the sermon an appeal was made to wandering prodigals to come to the ark of safety whose captain is King Jesus. A large number surrounded the altar, penitently seeking the better way, and several were converted. The meetings during the day were well attended and marked with great spiritual power. As prejudice gets out of the people and the churches go to work, the interest deepens and widens.

June 2, 1885

The Kokomo Gazette Tribune (IN)

Mrs. Maria B. Woodworth

AN INTERVIEW WITH THE GREAT TRANCE EVANGELIST—HER LIFE, HISTORY, AND METHOD OF WORK

Wednesday a representative of the *Gazette Tribune* sought and obtained a very pleasant interview with Mrs. Woodworth, the noted trance evangelist who at the present time is so wonderfully shaking up the city of Kokomo by her rehearsal of the story of the Cross—a grand theme that has interested mankind in all ages of the world, from the days of the patriarchs of old to the present time.

Mrs. Woodworth was born July 22, 1845,[1] at New Lisbon, Columbiana County, Ohio, and was the fourth daughter of a very large family. Her parents were members of the Disciples church. At the age of 13 she was converted and joined the church under the preaching of Dr. Belding; but owing to the fact that this church did not and does not believe in special dispensations of Providence, and that a woman had no business in advocating the cause of Christ from the pulpit, she soon left them. She entered the field as an evangelist at the age 30.

During the War[2] she was married to her present husband. Five children have blessed their union, all of whom are dead. Mr. Woodworth was a gallant soldier in the army of the Potomac and was wounded in the head from which he has long been a sufferer in both mind and body.

Mrs. Woodworth is an intelligent lady, well informed on general topics, and a very interesting conversationalist. In speaking of going into a trance, she referred to it as "the power of God," and said that it was nothing more than the Holy Spirit taking complete control of both soul and body, and the willpower becoming as clay in the hands of the potter. While in these trance conditions, she says that

[1] 1845 is incorrect. Maria Woodworth was born in 1844.

[2] "War"—the American Civil War.

she frequently beholds the future state with all its grand and glorious possibilities. She also says that many people falsely accuse her with claiming this power, that she can control all these things at will. This she emphatically denies, stating that it comes alone from God and that those who set her and this power at defiance are only blaspheming the power of God.

Mrs. Woodworth is well-pleased with the outlook in Kokomo and of her treatment by the newspapers of this city. The meeting Tuesday afternoon was one of unusual power. Many were at the altar under conviction. There were also one or two conversions and an old-fashioned shout went up from the camps of Israel. The meeting at night was attended by an immense concourse of people, many going away unable to get in. By some power, much of it curiosity, no doubt, the people are being wonderfully stirred up. So far as it goes towards bettering the condition of our people, the *Gazette Tribune* will bid Mrs. Woodworth Godspeed. Dr. Puckett addressed the meeting Tuesday night with great earnestness. Many people are coming in from the country and the remote townships and taking part in these meetings. A number of our best citizens are assisting her in the work. On the other hand, there are many good citizens who are skeptical and are inclined to look with doubt, if not with contempt and ridicule, upon her methods and theories. There is, of course, opposition also from that element found in all communities that is desirous of tearing down the work of God, no matter by whom it is built.

Storming the Fort

The evangelistic labors of Mrs. Maria Woodworth are increasing in numbers and deepening in interest. Since our last report, Mrs. Woodworth and several others have passed into the trance state and given an account of glorious visions. Dozens of penitents crowd the altar at every meeting seeking a better experience. A good many of the Christian people are becoming more inclined to lay aside their prejudices and assist in the work. Since Saturday afternoon, the meetings have been held in the mammoth rink of R. T. Groves, which is much more convenient and better adapted to the work. On Sunday was held perhaps the largest, longest, and most remarkable meeting ever held in this city. The services began promptly at ten o'clock in the morning and closed at eleven at night. The audience at night was estimated at from 2,500 to 3,000.

The meeting was addressed by Dr. Pitzer of Tipton, Dr. Manning of New Corner, Freeman Cooper, R. T. Groves, Taylor McNiel, and others, and had a wonderful shaking up effect upon the people. Several persons professed conversion during the day.

Contrary to all expectations from a worldly point of view, the meetings of Mrs. Woodworth were largely attended Thursday, in spite of the show. It had been predicted by many for several days that she could not stem the Forepaugh tide that was coming. In order to test the matter, a reporter went to the courthouse just at the close of the street parade, which was pronounced by many to have been the best and most attractive ever in the city, and to his surprise he found fully one thousand people packed in the courthouse and the evangelist walking the rostrum leading in the soul-stirring song, "Are you washed in the blood, in the soul-cleansing blood of the Lamb?" The afternoon services were attended with great spiritual power and some happy conversions. Mrs. Woodworth and two others were entranced. And since the demonstrations of Thursday, it is believed that had the great showman remained a week, Mrs. Woodworth would have worn him out and monopolized the crowd.

J. D. Higgiman, a shorthand reporter for the New York, New Orleans, and Atlanta papers, is in the city attending the Woodworth meetings and reporting the sermons which will be published in book form. He is an intelligent gentleman and was converted at the Pendleton meetings.

Dr. Ambrose Manning of New Corner, this state, one of Mrs. Woodworth's new converts, spent the day and Sunday in the city and contradicts the statement that people have gone crazy at New Corner as a result of the Woodworth's meetings in that place. It is as hard to get the exact location of these [(possible missing word)?] people as it is of the smallpox.

June 4, 1885

Kokomo Dispatch (IN)

The Woodworth Meetings

Transferred from the Courthouse to the Skating Rink

A LARGE ATTENDANCE—NUMBER OF SEEKERS AND CONVERTS

The Trance Business Introduced With Mrs. W. as the Chief

Fighting the Churches—Random Notes, Queries, etc.

Today marks the twelfth in the series of Woodworth meetings. Owing to the opening of court on Monday, the meetings were transferred to Groves' Skating Rink on Saturday evening, where services are conducted three times a day—at 10 A.M., 3 P.M., and 7 P.M. Rude seats have been constructed and daily the attendance is large. It cannot be said that the interest is increasing, but certainly it is not flagging. Up to date there have been 125 seekers and 75 conversions, ranging in years from 60 to 10. It is a common sight to see little girls not more than 10 years old at the "mourners' bench."

In a Trance

The climax of interest and excitement culminated on Friday in two so-called trances. The first was a young man of about 30 years, Fred Adamson, an invalid subject to epileptic fits, who lives near Vermont. He lay for an hour in a rigor, stretched out on the platform and the curious flocked about him—some scoffing, some awestricken and filled with superstition, and yet others calmly indifferent. While Adamson lay in a trance, Mrs. Woodworth was seized by one also. She sat in a chair on the elevated platform with head thrown back and the right arm pointing upward and the left downward. She kept swaying her arms gently backward and forward and was evidently conscious some of the time, at least, for she beat time to some of the songs with her hands.

The word spread like wildfire and citizens of all degrees abandoned their offices, stores, and shops and hurried to the courtroom to "see the show." After the trance had continued nearly three-quarters of an hour, [Mrs. Woodworth] with her eyes still fixed and unwinking, the pupils dilated, rose from her chair and began slowly walking the platform. As she did so she sighed repeatedly and faintly whispered: "Oh, Jesus! Oh, my God!" and afterwards extending her arms, then drawing them toward her as if to embrace, murmured: "Oh, Jesus! Oh, my God! Save the people!" Many of the women who were standing near betrayed great emotion at this, some weeping and wringing their hands, while others shouted and still others prayed. One elderly woman gave a shout and a scream, and throwing her hands over her head, seemed as if she had gone entirely deranged. It was some moments before she came out of it, which she did with a flood of tears, after which her face fairly shone with happiness.

Mrs. Woodworth, instead of recovering, went into another trance, and still another, making an hour and three-quarters in which she had been in that condition. To add to the excitement, just as Mrs. Woodworth was recovering, a young man was "taken" and fell to the floor lifeless and bloodless. He was vigorously fanned while the singing, shouting, and praying continued. The young man was John Moon, of near Greentown. He looked extremely silly as he was coming out of his trance, which lasted about an hour. "What did you see?" was enquired of him.

"I did not see much of anything," was the answer, "I was too busy wrestling with the Lord." It was nearly 7:30 in the evening before Mrs. Woodworth fully recovered from her trance. She did not go to her hotel but ate sparingly of a lunch that was sent her, bathed her face, and soon afterward opened the evening services.

Up to date there have been but four trances, as follows:

Fred Adamson, aged about 30, lives near Vermont.

John Moon, aged about 25, lives near Greentown.

Mrs. Woodworth.

Jonas Harris, aged 60, lives at New London.

Others have been momentarily overcome, notably one Rev. Spon, pastor of a congregation at Rosebud, Grant county, but not with the pronounced symptoms of the trance state.

Opinion is very much divided as to the genuineness of the trance, some holding that it is largely "acting," but the great majority of the people regard it as genuine and explainable on purely physical and scientific principles, scouting the idea of anything supernatural. It is observable, and it is a noteworthy fact that the trance subjects are generally weak-minded people, highly excitable and emotional, or subject to fits, epilepsy, etc. As yet, no resident of the city of Kokomo has been affected—and this we say to the intelligence and mental equipoise of our people. The meetings will be conducted all of this week and probably next, although this has not been decided upon. The rental of the rink is $35 a week, several gentlemen having guaranteed the rent for the first week. As soon as she closes here, Mrs. W. will return home to rest up and will next work Indianapolis.

Fighting the Churches

As is well-known, none of the churches of this city would open their doors to Mrs. Woodworth, save only the Quaker—and the members of this church were much divided as to the propriety of such proceedings. Mrs. W. was stung to the quick by this initiatory procedure and has ever since evinced a very hostile spirit towards them. She has poised[1] as a martyr, as a victim of persecution—yet she is more sweeping in her denunciation of the churches than they have been of her. They have simply declined to take any part in her meetings, while she openly attacks them. She said in her talk on Monday night that not five out of three hundred—one out of sixty—church members had ever been converted, and that two-thirds of the churches did not believe in the Holy Ghost religion, and those that did, did not preach it.

As we understand it, every Christian denomination on the face of the globe believes in the Holy Ghost religion. As to the charge that not one in sixty of the church members have been converted, we shall not presume to pass judgment. We will leave that for Mrs. W. to do. With the words—"Judge not lest ye be judged"[2]—in her mouth, she judges by wholesale the entire church membership of the globe. By her speech and action she is teaching her followers to

[1] "poised"—posed.

[2] Matthew 7:1, paraphrased.

hate the churches. By and by she will retire from her labors here, leaving her converts full of prejudice and hatred against the churches. What is to become of them when she is gone? Will they unite with God's people, spite[3] their prejudice? Or will they stay away and lapse back into the world? These are thoughts that may well engage the attention of Mrs. W. and us all.

Queries

A churchman hands in the following queries with the request that they be printed:

Is it the Holy Ghost or the people who make the noise at the rink?

How many people who saw Mrs. W. Friday believe she was in a trance?

In all her talk about Pentecost, why does not Mrs. W. tell her seekers to do what Peter, speaking by the Holy Ghost, told his seekers to do?

When the people go to hear a preacher who acknowledges that no time has been spent in reading or preparation, what kind of preaching do they expect to hear?

Why does Mrs. W. declare that the Holy Ghost made a great noise on Pentecost, when the Bible does not say so? It was the "sound from heaven" that filled the house.

When God measured arms with the Egyptians, He broke them down and triumphed. If He has sent Mrs. W. here sustained by miraculous power, why don't (*sic*) He break down the opposition to her work?

If the Lord, or the Holy Ghost, tells Mrs. Woodworth so many things, why did they not tell her on Monday that that man at the altar was drunk, so that her prayers and energies might not have been wasted on him?

Was it just right for the Lord to kill five innocent children who had the natural and divine right to life and its possibilities, as all have, to induce a mother to go out preaching? And will not the husband and other child be very anxious to have her keep on preaching lest the Lord shall take them?

[3] "spite"—despite.

Notes

So far no Kokomoan has "gone into a trance."

The most wonderful thing about Mrs. Woodworth is her physical endurance.

Mrs. Woodworth went into another trance of an hour's duration yesterday afternoon.

Three-fourths of the audience are non-residents of Kokomo, mostly people from the country.

W. H. Hackley had his pockets picked of eleven dollars at the Woodworth meeting Tuesday evening.

Is the *Gazette Tribune* for or against the trance humbuggery? Its editors talk against it in private while "Old Pantaloons" endeavors to commit the paper to it. Come, no dodging. Yes or no?

On Monday afternoon, a street man—Charles Snowden, of Richmond, a graduate of Earlham College—sauntered into the rink to attend the Woodworth meeting. He was quite drunk and went up to the altar as a seeker. After working with him a while, his condition was discerned and a policeman sent for. Constable Immel arrived and arrested Snowden at the altar and lugged him off to jail. In the morning, both the constable and Snowden returned and both went to the mourners' bench and were converted. Snowden has frequently spoken in the meetings.

The *Gazette Tribune,* true to its instincts, is trying to carry water on both shoulders anent[4] the Woodworth meetings. A few weeks ago it was very pronounced against the trance nonsense—now it pipes halfheartily in its praises. The truth is, the *G. T.* is afraid of losing a penny by the expression of an honest opinion—hence its shuffling on this matter. A fine moral guide is the *G. T.* to be sure! It has no opinions that are not measured by dollars and cents. It is afraid of its shadow and is a moral coward. Mr. Hoss is a professing Christian—a member of the Disciples church—yet he is as silent as an oyster; Mr. Johnson is an infidel, and he is as silent as death; Mr. Turpen is a reformed Shaker, and he has committed the columns of

[4] "anent"—concerning (Webster's N.W. 1997).

the *G. T.* to the trance poppycock. Privately each of this triplet pretends to be opposed to the Woodworth religion, yet they seek to make their paper face both ways. Come out of your concealment, boys, and say your say. Be a man or a mouse. Don't trifle with the public any longer. If you endorse the trance religion, say so openly like men; if you are opposed to it, have the courage of your convictions and "speak out in meetin'." Don't play the hypocrite any longer. Say "yea" or "nay".

EDITOR'S *GAZETTE TRIBUNE*—

June 9, 1885

Kokomo Gazette Tribune (IN)

Some Plain Questions

hy should any orthodox Christian refuse to work with Mrs. Woodworth? What is orthodox Christianity? Is it not mainly a belief in Christ, His divinity, His immaculate conception, His miracles, His crucifixion, His resurrection, and His ascension? That through His sacrifice and our faith herein humanity is to be redeemed, if redeemed at all? Mrs. Woodworth advocates this doctrine.

Does not orthodoxy preach that God will and does answer prayer for physical and material blessings or effects? Mrs. Woodworth preaches this doctrine.

Does not orthodoxy proclaim the demonstration of God's power to move the hearts of men through the Holy Spirit? Mrs. Woodworth proclaims this doctrine.

Does not orthodoxy pray to be guided in all earthly affairs by the power of God? Mrs. Woodworth claims to have realized answers to just such petitions.

When orthodoxy so prays, it does not dictate to the Almighty how, or in what manner the answer shall come. Does orthodoxy then dare to challenge the conscientious declarations of those who claim to have experienced the power of God in response to an orthodox prayer for a manifestation of His power amongst men? Is orthodoxy surprised at the practical and logical results of its own theories? Does it limit the power of God?

It can easily be understood how an "outsider" can doubt the spirituality of the trance, because he does not believe that physical or material results follow prayer. He may believe in prayer to God as a necessary agency for soul elevation and spiritual improvements, of raising the moral nature "out of the mire and the clay and placing it upon the Rock of Ages." But he may not believe that prayers for health, to prevent shortage in crops, to prevent Asiatic cholera from coming this way, and the other hundreds of prayed-for effects will change one iota the course of nature or of law. Therefore he is skeptical of the trance manifestation.

Yet this class is slower to condemn these manifestations than many orthodox Christians. They have more charity and are not so free to deny the power as of God; neither do they say it is the power of the devil. They see every evidence of honesty and faith in the workers at these meetings, and believing that God, the universal Father of humanity, has created man in infinite variety, both in mind and body, are free to acknowledge the truth of the spiritual, as well as the literal, application of the adage, "what is one man's meat is another man's poison." I cannot think that the God of love, justice, and mercy looks down with approval upon intolerance. "Faith, hope, and charity, these three; but the greatest of these is Charity,"[1] from every standpoint.

So long as a man or woman is trying in any way consistent with common decency to raise humanity up, to replace despondency with hope, to smooth the rough path of human life, to make people better in their everyday walk, constraining them from evil unto good, so long they should have the support of all good people. Whenever it is proven that the logical results of any line of work are weakening and undermining the moral foundations of society—leaving a community in a worse condition than before its operations began, these evil results to be manifest to the general intelligence and judgment of a community, not to the imagination of a jaundiced few—then it should be condemned, and not until then. Let there be liberty of thought and freedom of conscience to that extent.

— FAIR PLAY

[1] 1 Corinthians 13:13, paraphrased.

EDITOR'S *GAZETTE TRIBUNE*—

June 9, 1885

Kokomo Gazette Tribune (Indiana)

The Reason Why

n Tuesday's *Gazette Tribune* "Fair Play" asks, "Why should any orthodox Christian refuse to work with Mrs. Woodworth? I am one of those who refuse and am willing to tell the reason why. My answer will perhaps voice the sentiment of all Kokomo Christians (and they are many) who refuse to work with Mrs. W.

There are two reasons, each involved in the other, and either sufficient to keep me from participation in that work.

First, because I do not believe it is God's work.

Second, because I think it will result in evil, not good. "Fair Play" says, "So long as a man or a woman is trying in any way consistent with common decency to raise humanity up, and etc. they should have the support of all good people." Amen. But the "common decency"—well just go to the rink and look at it.

Then "common decency" is not enough. When one comes in the name of the Lord, that one must work on the Lord's plan or forfeit his claims on "orthodox, right-thinking Christians" for their support. There is a choice bit of the "droppings from that sanctuary." A fruit of the spirit (of the rink meeting) in "Fair Play's" little piece, when in a very spiritual frame of mind, perhaps just from a fresh "baptism of the Holy Ghost," he speaks of certain of the dear Christian brothers and sisters as a "jaundiced few." Perhaps if he would look around and count noses—take the number of Kokomo Christians who do work with Mrs. Woodworth and the number of those who do not—he would have a "revelation" as to where are the few and where are the many, and if he could see with the eyes of the great majority of the Christians of Kokomo, and everywhere, he would be surprised to find where the symptoms of jaundice are located. Some who suffer with jaundice are so jaundiced that it gets into their eyes and then everybody looks yellow to them.

Kokomo refuses to be swept back into the darkness of the past, when the people of the past had few schools and not everyone had a Bible or could read it, and consequently general intelligence and Scripture knowledge being low, the good people received the illiterate preacher who came from his anvil or plow to do the best preaching he could under the inspiration of the hour, honestly thinking as he told them that God put the words in his mouth. But [Kokomo] demands a higher order of intelligence and more Scriptural teaching; [Kokomo] demands sense, not sound, while districts more rural and less informed have been moved by this "cyclone" of empty sound and wild confusion; it is that much in Kokomo's favor. If "Fair Play," or any other wishes to know why the meeting at Kokomo has been a failure, the answer is in this. The intelligence of Kokomo is too great and too far above such methods and scenes. Kokomo intelligence and reverence are outraged with the monstrous story that God murdered five innocent children to induce one woman to go preach such a Gospel as the peaceful, pure, just Gospel of Jesus Christ. If "Fair Play" will keep his eyes and ears open at the rink, he will not need to ask why intelligent, reverential Christian people do not work there.

— Orthodox Christian

June 14, 1885

The Indianapolis Times (IN)

Baptized in Wild Cat

Eighty-two of Mrs. Woodworth's Converts Immersed in the Presence of 6,000 Persons

KOKOMO, IND. JUNE 14.—

ll day the city has been filled with a dense throng of people, variously estimated at from eight to twelve thousand. Between 12 and 1 o'clock today, Rev. Wm. Hile of Greensborough, assisted by Mrs. Woodworth, baptized eighty-two persons in Wild Cat, the religious Ganges[1] of Howard county. The ceremony was a beautiful one and very impressive and was witnessed by six thousand people. The very best of order prevailed. Between forty and fifty converts will be baptized tomorrow morning. Mrs. Woodworth closed her sixty-sixth meeting in this city tonight. Notwithstanding the weather was suffocating, the rink was jammed, and a large overflow meeting was addressed from a goods box in the street by Revs. Hile, Riley, and Spurgeon.

There have been over four hundred conversions during these meetings. Twenty-eight trances have been reported and a people's church, without a creed, has been organized with a large membership. Mrs. Woodworth will go to North Manchester and rest a week, and then she will return. During her absence, the meetings will be continued night and day by Revs. Hile, Riley, and Spurgeon. The oldest inhabitant has been interviewed. He never saw the like before, it even eclipsing the scenes of our grandfathers' days. The evangelist says she has no engagement in Indianapolis and don't (*sic*) know that she will hold a meeting there.

The Sunday closing law was enforced today by our new Republican city administration.

[1] "religious Ganges"—The Gangee River in India is a sacred river to the Hindus.

June 16, 1885

Kokomo Gazette Tribune (IN)

The Revival

There were two thousand perspiring people packed into the Religio-Skating Rink Thursday night. After an offhand address by Rev. Spurgeon, an Indianapolis evangelist who spoke on "The Faith of the Israelitish Maid and the Cleansing of Naman, the Leper,"[1] the large audience was worked for a collection to, in part, compensate Mrs. Woodworth for her faithful and untiring labors in this city. eighty-eight dollars and seventy-five cents was raised and presented to her in a few minutes. S. A. Stephens of Rochester, NY, through W. H. Higgins, kindly donated two thirds of the gas bill. After the collection, Mrs. Woodworth stated that she proposed to organize a "Daniel's Band" composed of new converts and members of the various churches, not for the purpose of antagonizing the churches, but for the purpose of keeping alive the work that has already been accomplished. She spoke at length upon the Hebrew children—of the prophet Daniel and two fellow Babylonish students as the first Daniel's Band who dared to do right in the midst of a proud, idolatrous people. After the exhortation, over two hundred names were handed in who desired to become members of the band. It is believed that the number will reach four hundred. The meeting closed near midnight with the usual altar services. On Sunday the meeting, if the weather permits, will be conducted as a basket meeting[2] in Haskett's grove in the western suburbs of the city, after which the ordinance of baptism will be administered to all who desire it, in Wild Cat. A large outpouring of the people is expected.

On Thursday, the stand at the Woodworth meeting was adorned by five Methodist clergymen. We will stake our reputation as a prophet by stating that there is more good, old-fashioned, orthodox religion in Kokomo at the present time and fewer yellow-legged chickens than ever known before.

[1] See 1 Kings 5:1-19.

[2] "basket meeting"—a picnic meeting.

June 16, 1885

Kokomo Gazette Tribune (IN)

Kokomo's Big Sunday

rom a religious standpoint, Sunday eclipsed anything ever seen in this city or section of Indiana. Saturday night closed the third week of Mrs. Woodworth's evangelistic labors in this city. It had been previously announced that all her converts so desiring would be baptized in Wildcat (*sic*) on Sunday. Early Sunday morning, the people began pouring into the city by hundreds from all points of the compass, and by noon the multitude that overflowed the rink and thronged the streets was variously estimated at from seven thousand to twelve thousand people. The morning meeting was a grand one and consisted in song and testimony, conducted on the gospel volunteer plan, with Mrs. Woodworth as leader. Over one hundred and fifty bore testimony to the saving power of the Gospel and of having been greatly benefited by this series of meetings.

After the morning services were over, all repaired[1] to the placid waters of Wildcat, the religious Ganges and Howard county's Jordan. The banks on either side of the river and the mouth of Washington Street, together with the railroad and wagon bridges, was one vast sea of humanity that had assembled to witness the return of the Pentecostial (*sic*) day. At 11:30 A.M., Rev. Wm. Hile, a brilliant young Wesleyan Methodist preacher of Greensborough, entered the water, and one by one the applicants, assisted by Mrs. Woodworth, entered the water, knelt down, and were buried with Christ in baptism at a rapid rate until 82 persons, ranging all the way from youth to old age, of both sexes, were baptized. This beautiful ceremony was conducted without even a jar and lasted about an hour. The weather was clear and sultry, and the order was as good as ever witnessed in a church. Fully six thousand people lined the banks of the river to witness the scene, which on all sides was pronounced the grandest event ever witnessed in this part of the country.

The meeting again convened at the rink at three o'clock, and Mrs. Woodworth made a powerful appeal to sinners to come home and

[1] "repaired"—went.

be saved. This was followed with an altar lined with penitents pleading for a better experience. The meeting telescoped itself into the night meeting which was addressed by Mrs. Woodworth and others in the rink, and a large overflow meeting was addressed at the corner of Main & Mulberry Streets by Revs. Riley and Spurgeon. This closed the sixty-sixth meeting held in the city with the following result: About four hundred persons claim conversion during this series of meetings. There have been reported twenty-eight cases of trance or paradisal visions. On Thursday night a "Daniel's Band" was organized with over two hundred members. The object of this organization is to keep up prayer and gospel meetings and to work auxiliary to the various churches and is designed to be missionary in its labors. A new church organization to be known as "St. Paul," or the "People's Church," is on foot and starts off with a large list of names composed of many of our best citizens.

Mrs. Woodworth left Monday for Elwood where she will remain until Wednesday, when she goes to Rochester to rest and visit her daughter until Saturday, the 27th, just when she will return to Kokomo and resume her work. At the meeting Sunday night, D. T. McNiel requested all who desired Mrs. Woodworth to return after a few days rest and resume her evangelistic labors, to say "aye." A simultaneous response from probably twenty-five hundred voices went up in her favor. It was decided to continue the meetings night and day during her absence. The services will be conducted by Rev.'s Hile, Riley, and Spurgeon.

A collection was taken up and presented to Mrs. Woodworth, and many substantial evidences of aid were promised her for future work. She states, seemingly with an abiding faith that takes no denial, that the work is only fairly begun in this city. There is no denying the fact that this meeting has reached a large class of our people thus far that the churches have failed to get, and many good citizens both in Kokomo and all over the county testify to its benefits and heartily endorse the work. Thus far the writer has heard nothing but good, sound gospel doctrine preached in these meetings, strongly backed up by the "thus saith the Lord." As we have stated heretofore, the *Gazette Tribune* heartily endorses anything that has a tendency to better humanity. We are not yet ready to ridicule all these people who have been zealously laboring in these meetings. Thus far we have heard of no evil results and until such is reported and proven, the *Gazette Tribune* will find no fault with them.

Notes

The 66 meetings above referred to do not include an 8 o'clock morning service each day.

Two cases of trance were reported Sunday, Mrs. Woodworth and Miss Hostetler.

Does our religious contemporary still think this is all "flapdoodle," and will it dare to reiterate that it is all "poppycock?"

Mrs. Woodworth appointed J. L. Puckett and D. T. McNeil elders, and J. F. Morrison and Samuel Brown deacons, in the "Daniel's Band."

On Thursday night, E. N. Taylor went into a trance in his buggy a mile west of the city and was laid by the roadside by a friend. He remained in that condition four hours.

At the meeting this morning, thirty-five stood up and requested to be baptized. The ordinance will be performed on Sunday, June 28. One person was baptized this afternoon.

Dr. Scott and family, D. T. McNiel and family, Taylor Jackman and family, Dr. Puckett and family, L. W. Hercules and family, Seth Slyter and family, Dr. L. Kern and family, Dr. Cooper, father and mother, C. E. Hendry and wife, and many others are leading off in the new church organization.

June 23, 1885

Kokomo Gazette Tribune (IN)

The "Daniel's Band"

A COMPLETE ORGANIZATION WITH 320 MEMBERS

ccording to previous arrangements, the Daniel's Band met Friday evening at the rink, and in connection with the religious services of the evening, completed their organization, which starts out with a determination full of golden promise, offered as follows:

Elders—Rev. J. L. Puckett and D. T. McNiel.

Deacons—N. B. Brown and J. F. Morrison.

Sec.—W. H. Turpin.

Treas.—W. C. Amos.

Finance and executive committee—D. P. Boyd, W. C. Amos, and David Smith.

One week ago, 269 names were procured for this organization and fifty-one new names were added to the roll Friday night, making in all 320. The object of this Band is not for the purpose of tearing down or antagonizing the churches but is to sustain an auxiliary relation to them. This band is made up of members of all churches, as well as those who have no church relationship. The main object is to broaden and strengthen the bonds of union and Christian brotherhood and is missionary in its designs. Many of our best citizens hold a membership in this new organization. Meetings will be held night and day during the coming week under the spiritual direction of Rev. Wm. Hile.

The Revival

Dr. J. L. Puckett preached a splendid sermon Thursday night to a very large and appreciative audience. He spoke at length upon the wickedness of Jacob during the early period of his life and closed with a most eloquent appeal to those who were strangers to God to begin to make a preparation for the life beyond the grave. Previous to the sermon, a social meeting was held and over 10 persons spoke of the power of the Gospel to save from sin. The meeting closed with an altar lined with seekers.

July 2, 1885

Kokomo Dispatch (IN)

A Storm Cloud

Tearing Asunder the Disciples of Trance Religion

TWO RIVAL FACTIONS WITH TWO RIVAL SCHISMS AT WAR

The Shepherds Lock Horns Over the Matter of Creed

Another Baptism on Sunday—Mrs. Woodworth's Farewell

hen the pious Aeneas propounded the conundrum—"can such resentment dwell in heavenly minds?"[1]—he voiced a query that stands unanswered to this day. That the disciples of Mrs. Woodworth, the trance revivalist, who have been a unit in fighting the churches for four long weeks, should at the very close of the great revival fall to wrangling over a matter of creed is at once a subject of amazement and regret. But that the brethren are torn asunder and at religious war with each other, under the banners of opposing shepherds and all about the questions of creed, is now an open secret—an undeniable fact.

One week ago, a Mission church organization was effected after a careful survey of the field and much prayerful consideration. The object of the organization was announced to be a purpose to do general evangelical or mission work. There was to be no creed but the Bible, and the organization was to serve as an auxiliary to all the churches. This much was seemingly settled, and it was further understood that Rev. W. A. Hile was to be the shepherd, or pastor, to lead and direct the flock. This he could do without recanting his faith—that of a Wesleyan Methodist, inasmuch as it was to be a church without a creed. It was further talked that an edifice for worship would be erected and the battle against sin waged unceasingly in Kokomo.

But there is a reverse side to every picture, and this praiseworthy project was doomed to speedy assaults by an opposing faction. The

[1] A reference to Juno's resentment of Aeneas. Dryden's translation reads,

> For what offense the Queen of Heav'n began
> To persecute so brave, so just a man;
> Involv'd his anxious life in endless cares,
> Expos'd to wants, and hurried into wars!
> *Can heav'nly minds such high resentment show,*
> Or exercise their spite in human woe?

opponents to the mission idea wanted a church with a creed, and it was whispered that Dr. Puckett was to be the pastor of the new faction. This movement, or rebellion, was headed by Dr. Puckett, D. T. McNiel, L. W. Hercules, W. C. Amos, and others. The leaders of the mission, or no-creed movement, were C. E. Hendry, J. F. Morrison, Dr. L. Kern, H. Y. Wooton, Dr. Wm. Scott, David Smith, N. B. Brown, W. H. Turpen, James Hockett, Wm. Imbler, and others.

This brings us up to the return of Mrs. Woodworth on Sunday to take her final leave-taking of this people. While Mrs. W. was conducting morning services in the rink, the McNiel faction was in a room upstairs effecting a regular church organization, which they christened the St. Paul's Christian as contradistinguished from the Union Mission, or no-creed organization. After the regular services, Rev. Hile, assisted by Mrs. Woodworth, baptized 86 converts in the presence of several thousand people, lining either bank of the Wildcat from the Wabash bridge to the Washington Street bridge. This makes in all 148 baptisms arising out of the revival meetings.

During the afternoon gospel meeting, the opposing factions were in separate rooms upstairs, talking, organizing, etc. The Union Mission faction elected officers as follows:

Elders—N. B. Brown, H. Y. Wooten, C. E. Hendry, and Dr. L. Kern.

Stewards—James G. Hockett, Dr. Wm. Scott, Jaennie Hendry, and Maggie Sharp.

Secretary—W. W. Turpin; Assistant Secretary, Eva Pleas.

A committee of six was appointed to formulate rules and by-laws for church government as follows: C. E. Hendry, Dr. Kern, Dr. Scott, Rev. Hile, J. F. Morrison, and W. H. Imbler. This committee met in the W.C.T.U.[2] hall last night to prepare rules for the mission, after which regular services were held in Sharp & Armstrong's hall. The only test of membership in the Union Mission will be a Christian character. Rev. W. A. Hile has been employed as a regular pastor. He will preach only every other Sunday until after the Wesleyan Conference meets, in September, when he will locate here

[2] "W.C.T.U."—Woman's Christian Temporance Union.

permanently. Arrangements have been made to hold the meetings in Sharp & Armstrong's hall.

The St. Paul church folks organized on Monday and elected the following officers:

Elders—J. L. Puckett, W. H. Tunis, Dr. Wm. Cooper, Mrs. Hepsy Hercules, Mrs. Dorcas Tucker, Miss Lizzie Carter.

Deacons—W. C. Amos, Taylor Jackman, E. Payne, Samuel Bolinger, C. W. Lee.

The membership on Tuesday footed up 156. Meetings for future church organization will be held every night this week at the rink or some other place to be announced. It is their purpose to secure a pastor and rent a hall for six months at least.

Thus closes the Woodworth revival in Kokomo—ending in a religious row and torn asunder by factions that give little promise or hope of reconciliation. "'Tis true, 'tis pity; and pity 'tis, 'tis true."[3]

Notes

There were six trances on Sunday night.

Herman Statz, of Clay township, is said to have developed a new kind of trance.

"Behold, how pleasant and good it is for brethren to dwell together in unity."[4]

Six months will probably develop which was right—the churches or the Woodworth methods.

The clergy of the city can now lay their index fingers alongside their noses and ejaculate—"I told you so."

Some worldly one has fastened the appellations of "Mugwump" on the St. Paul faction and "Rinkwump" on the Mission.

Now that the rival factions of the Woodworth converts have fallen to fighting among themselves, we presume the churches will get a rest.

The Woodworth revival is at an end; one hundred forty-eight persons were baptized; three hundred converted; five hundred

[3] Polonius's line concerning Hamlet's madness from Shakespeare's *Hamlet* (Act 2, Scene 2).

[4] Psalm 133:1, paraphrase.

seekers; and a split of the followers into two hostile and irreconcilable factions.

> The *Kokomo Dispatch* gives me credit for capturing six of them. Well, I want to capture six more—yes six hundred and would not be willing to stop unless the editor of *The Dispatch* was among my captors.
>
> — Saml. Brannen, Greentown, Ind.

"Captor" is one who captures; "captive," one who is captured. Does Samuel really confess that *The Dispatch* has captured *him?* See, Sam?

The second and third editions of the *Trance-Evangelist,* organ of the Woodworth meeting, were printed at *The Dispatch* office. Well, whether they endorse *The Dispatch* or not, they have to come to it to get their printing done at fair rates and in first-class style.

> Ministers and editors were arrayed against her, and a reply to things written about the meeting and those who worked in it was not allowed in the city papers.
>
> —*Trance-Evangelist.*

Nothing could be further from the truth. *The Dispatch* has not at any time denied its columns to a hearing of the Woodworth following, but *per contrary* has repeatedly invited such contributions.

The organ of the trance revival says that Decoration Day in Kokomo was almost a failure on account of the interest in the Woodworth meeting and that Forepaugh's circus lost three hundred dollars on account of it. This is not true. Our Memorial Day services were largely attended, but the attendance was much diminished on account of the heavy rain that fell. As to the circus, we do not know, yet we are confident that the attendance was fully up to the average. It is well to stick to the facts, even in praising the drawing powers of the trance evangelist.

The little *Trance-Evangelist* apologizes for its second appearance on the ground that "a hearing was denied in the city press." This is false so far as *The Dispatch* is concerned. For three weeks we have urged Mrs. Woodworth's followers to write something in behalf of her methods, and last week "Vindex" responded in a three-column article. *The Dispatch* is not a one-idea paper. While it is free at all times to express its opinions, it always gives the opposition a courteous and respectful hearing. So it has been in the trance religion controversy.

To the Editors of the Dispatch:

> I have been requested to ask you for enlightenment on your two, or double, opinions as to Mrs. Woodworth and her methods. You say you think her works are the worst of travesty on religion, and so do we; and then again you say you think she is a sincere, Christian woman, working in the vineyard of the Lord. Now the conundrum with us is, how you are going to make the assertions reconcile with each other.
>
> — A Subscriber

The query is answered easily enough. One may be sincere and yet error (*sic*). Mrs. W. may be as sincere as the apostles and yet may be in error. She may do good in bringing about conversions though she may teach a heresy. Saul was as sincere in his persecution of the Christians as he was when he became a great Christian leader. Sincerity has no bearing on right or wrong motives. The Southern States were honest and sincere in their notions of rebellion, but they were wrong all the same. So when Mrs. W. teaches divinity of trances, in our judgment she teaches an untruth or an error, yet she may be as conscientious in it as is possible for humanity to be sincere.

Still Another View

TO THE EDITORS OF THE DISPATCH:[5]

Seeing that you are so kind and liberal with your columns, giving all an opportunity to express their views touching the merits or demerits of the so-called religious cyclone that has struck a corner of our city, and being inflated with a desire for truth for truth's sake, I am constrained to ask your further indulgence while I "give a reason for the hope"[6] I have outside of the "rink" and its environments. And in order that I may be specific, I must first deal in general. But first of all I

[5] What follows is a long letter to the editor authored by another writer.

[6] 1 Peter 3:15, paraphrased.

would, like the apostle Paul, give them credit for every known excellency, hence would say that they are full of fervor and appear to be full of faith and hope, and *ad interim*[7] some profess a superfluity of the Holy Spirit. They preach the Gospel in part and in part they don't. A few of our best Christian people, both from city and country, gladly participate and a few don't. That some good may come from the meetings, many believe; that some harm will result is apparent to all.

Saint and sinner, this is, (latter day saint) have been alike profuse in instructing the churches and ministers here in their duty in the premises, and severally and jointly they imprecate the "dry bones"[8] because they will not materialize and come to the "rink's" rescue. Do you ask why the ministers and so many Christian people pay no attention to the rink meetings? And why should they? Or what is there in these meetings to cause ministers to violate the established custom? When an accredited minister comes here, or goes elsewhere, all are *invited* to come and hear him preach, but none are forced. Those who so desire and those who prefer to stay away, stay away. "Is thy servant a dog that he should do these things?"[9] This is a free country and in matters of conscience, on religious questions, all have the right to do as they please. It will be a sorry day for America when from any species of pressure men are compelled to attend church or to sanction every new-fangled dogma or women's fables. I am now past 43 years of age, have attended church all my life, and I never heard a true minister of the Gospel of Christ publicly censure another minister for not assisting in a meeting and feel sure I never will. A preacher, to say the least, undignifies himself and disgraces his profession when he goes whining around and asserting that other preachers are not doing their duty. "Where the Holy Ghost is, there is liberty,"[10] and where the Holy Ghost is *not,* there is sometimes noise, confusion, backbiting, etc.

Now when this strange woman was ushered in upon us as minister plenipotentiary and convoy extraordinary from the courts above,

[7] *"ad interim"*—in the meantime.

[8] See Ezekiel 37:1-14.

[9] 2 Kings 8:13, paraphrased.

[10] 2 Corinthians 3:17, paraphrased.

demanding that the church doors stand wide for her reception and that our ministers make her paths straight, a plea in abatement was overruled, and a motion to quash was answered in two paragraphs—first, that she is a woman and that that will draw the curious; and, second, that her *trance* trick will draw the credulous. No one daring to gainsay either of these propositions, business begins. And in her first sermon at the Friends church (not sizing her audience exactly, having just emerged from the mountains of an adjoining parish where the thing seemed to take), she boldly averred that through faith and her prayers, a woman who had been confined to her bed for many months in great suffering was at once healed of her disease, sprang from her bed, "And, thank God, has been able to do her own work ever since." And for further proof that she comes with healing in her wings, she related that once on a time, when a little girl was in a trance, her drunken father rushed into the church with oaths in his mouth and murder in his fist to take her (his daughter) therefrom. But the fiat went forth (from what authority I know not) that he should not do this, but that he, the profane drunkard, "should either be killed or converted right then and there," and the Lord chose the former, and threw him down and converted him.

Moreover, she says that she speaks by direct authority from the Lord; that she studies but little—"hasn't time to study"—but that the Lord "puts it on her" to say things and she says them; that "the Lord put it on her" to say that all the ministers and professors of religion who do not affiliate with her in these meetings are "dry-bones," "unconverted," and "hypocrites"; that when she goes into a trance, she is trance-planted into heaven and talks with the Lord; that He often tells her who is hanging over hell by a brittle thread; who are nearing the "deadline," and who have "crossed the deadline." Just why this *trance* action, in these particular cases, is necessary at all, since she is in continued communication, is not apparent, per adventure it has a better effect on the one sought after, whom she sees hanging by the hair or nearing the "deadline." Now when the people heard these sayings, they were amazed and many were taken in, saying: "Surely, this woman is from God. Let's build her a tabernacle. Let's rent the rink." And so it was. And herein is the prophecy made above in two paragraphs fulfilled, to-wit: That the curious and the credulous can be "drawed."

In those days in the city of Kokomo, there were diverse ministers of the Gospel of Christ, men approved of God and revered by all who knew them best, "whose feet are shod with the preparation of the gospel of peace";[11] "who *study* to show themselves workmen that need not be *ashamed*, rightly dividing the word of truth";[12] who have, in season and out of season, through evil as well as through good report, upheld the crimson ensign of the crucified yet risen Lord;[13] who, "in every condition, in sickness, in health, in poverty's vale or abounding in wealth,"[14] most willing and cheerfully minister to the wounded soul and bleeding heart; who have ever clung to the Bible, and it alone, as the Magna Carta of the Church of Christ and have defended it against all comers and will continue to do so when the chaff engendered at the rink will be scattered to the four winds of heaven.[15]

Yes, it is these ministers—God bless them, every one!—and the little bands of God-fearing men and women who, "by a faithful continuance in well doing,"[16] have advanced the Redeemer's kingdom in our midst. They have visited the widow and the orphan,[17] the sick and afflicted, buried the dead, and solaced the bleeding hearts of suffering friends. Their church, prayer meetings, and Sunday schools they will not abandon, nor will they swerve from the ways of righteousness. What our city is today, religiously, is the rich fruit of their handiwork. Their untiring labors made the meetings at the rink possible and the field at all desirable. Yet, strange as it may seem, these "veterans of the Cross," these fathers and mothers in Israel, together with others who have borne the heat and burden of the day in the Master's service, are the ones and the only ones, who come under the especial condemnation of this woman. By them our ministers and Christian people have been denounced openly, defiantly,

[11] Ephesians 6:15, paraphrased.

[12] 2 Timothy 2:15, paraphrased.

[13] 2 Timothy 4:2.

[14] Philippians 4:12, paraphrased.

[15] Psalm 1:4.

[16] See Romans 2:7.

[17] See James 1:27.

and brazenly time and again as hypocrites and "dry-bones." In this Kokomo is outraged, and it owes it to itself, its honor, and its fair name to spit on the infamous slander. I know not the antecedents of these itinerants, but whether good or bad, he, she, or they are doing the work of Satan here by a large majority and are as carbuncles and excrescencies upon the body politic of the church militant.

But as this "balm of Gilead"[18] physician, Mrs. Woodworth, and her assistant, Rev. Hile, and many of their abettors in this unjust crusade against the churches, are so minutely described in Romans, 10th chapter, I quote it:

> For I bear them record that they have a zeal of God, but not according to knowledge.
>
> For they being ignorant of God's righteousness, and going about to establish *their own* righteousness, have not submitted *themselves* unto the righteousness of God. . . .
>
> But the righteousness which is of *faith* speaketh on this wise, Say not in thine heart, Who shall ascend into heaven (that is, to bring Christ down from above:)
>
> Or Who shall descend into the deep? (that is, to bring up Christ again from the dead.) But what saith it? The word is nigh thee, even in thy mouth, and in thy heart.[19]

Yes, brother Hile goes about to establish his own righteousness by pleading sanctification, and Mrs. W. not satisfied with violating the command, "say not in thine heart, who shall ascend into heaven," professes to absolutely make the trip, and that her *trans*-ition[20] is guided by the same Holy Ghost that guided Paul when he condemned *even the thought* of such a *trans*-ition. And again, in Paul's last letter to his son Timothy, he exhorts him in the fear of God to

> Preach the *word*. . . .
>
> For the *time will come* when they will not endure sound doctrine; but after their own lusts shall they heap to themselves teachers, having itching ears; . . .

[18] See Jeremiah 8:22.

[19] Romans 10:2-3, 6-8.

[20] *Trance*-ition. A play on the similarity of "trans-" and "trance."

> And they shall turn away *their* ears from the *truth,* and shall be turned unto *fables.*[21]

A fable (I speak now to the little folk) is something that is not true; it's something that we sometimes call a fib. For instance: the report that God, who "notes the sparrow's fall"[22] killed five little children in order to bring one bad woman to time—that's a fable, children, a fib. That God downed a bad, old drunk man while he was drunk and swearing and made a Christian out of him in the presence of a woman who didn't care a red whether he was "converted or killed"—that's a fable, too. When a woman says she prayed for another woman who had been "sick abed" for years and that God-cured the woman through faith—that's a fable. God don't (*sic*) do that way now. If He did, He certainly would have cured poor Garfield, for a Christian nation prayed for him.

When people tell you that all our home preachers and church members are bad folks and that these new male and female preachers have wings—that's a fable. When a young man that you never saw before tells you forty or fifty times that he is so much better than you, in fact, that he is just so good that he can't do, or even think, a wrong (he calls it "sanctified")—"keep your eye pealed," for that's a fable. When a woman tells you that she can trance or dance herself into [line missing], that's a fable. When a man tells you that he felt awful good last night and that he had a "change of heart," and you don't notice any particular change of "cheek"—why, I expect that man's mistaken. When a woman tells you that she is full of charity and is running over with the "Holy Ghost" and then keeps saying naughty things all the time about good people and scolds all the time she is preaching, why, I expect—I expect, she's a fraud. Say, Mister, if this "old-time religion" has sidetracked everybody in forty years' time, won't it do the same thing again if we get on at the same depot and take the same train? That would seem reasonable and logical, my son, but then you mustn't reason on religious matters—it's wicked.

Mister, has the Daniel's Band got brass horns? Oh yes, but they call them elders and deacons, however. Say, if the Bridegroom was to

[21] 2 Timothy 4:2-4; italics as printed in news article.

[22] Matthew 10:29, paraphrased.

come to the rink and find two brides and one little kid, that they called Daniel, wouldn't He think that more than five of 'em were foolish? I expect He would. What are Mugwumps? "Mugwump" has been defined to mean "goody-goody." In olden times they were called Pharisees who "thanked God that they were not like other people."[23] They would just make loud, long, noisy prayers and although God told them that the quiet, humble, publican who would not look up nor allow the preachers to turn his face up, but in humility simply said, "Lord be merciful to me, a sinner," was justified rather than they, still they wouldn't pay any attention to what God told them and just kept hammering away. And then God told them again, "But when you pray, use not vain repetitions, as the heathens do: for they think that they shall be heard for their much speaking."[24] But they thought that that meant "head religion," and feeling that (the muscle called) the heart was all right, they set God's authority aside and go in on their muscle, just like they do in Africa.

In modern times, Mugwumps, for the most part, are men who can't get an office or position in their own party and then they leave it and sometimes start a new party. They say they haven't left their old party, but then they have all the same. They say that the old parties are dead and that they want to build up a live party out of dead material. They say that they are agreed in almost everything but then they ain't—except in making a noise. They say they have great faith, but I don't think they have, for faith is "the *evidence* of things *not seen,*"[25] and they are all the time wanting to see something, even if they have to send someone up to get a peep. It is based on the testimony of the apostles and prophets, and yet they put absolute confidence in the testimony of their own feelings. "I feel, I feel," is their shibboleth,[26] "that my heart is all right." "It is well, if it is well," so says the Hindoo (*sic*) mother, as she tears her babe form her breast

[23]See Luke 18:10-14.

[24]Matthew 6:7, paraphrased.

[25]See Hebrews 11:1.

[26]"shibboleth"—In the Bible, the test word used by the Gileadites to distinguish the escaping Ephraimites, who could not pronounce the initial sh: Judges 12:6; hence, any test word or password, any phrase, formula, custom, etc. considered distinctive, as of a party, class, faction, etc. (*Webster's New World Dictionary of the American Language,* College Edition, [Cleveland and NY: The World Publishing Company, 1960]).

and casts it into the river. "I feel, oh, I feel, that my poor wounded and bleeding heart is all right in the sight of my god (idol)."

Oh, ye, of little faith. "These things are written that ye might *believe,* and believing, have life through His name."[27]

Say, Mister, what did you say fables were for? They are for men with "itching ears."[28] They heap to themselves teachers (preachers), bring them in on the trains, heaps of them, and then they tell them ghost stories and such things, and they like to hear them. Say, what do these folks want to climb "higher and higher" for? Isn't there danger of their falling? Sonny, hush; go home!

— Untranced

[27]John 20:31, paraphrased.

[28]See 2 Timothy 4:3-4.

July 9, 1885

Kokomo Dispatch (IN)

To the Editors of the *Dispatch*

Knowing the native fairness of The *Dispatch*, and believing that it would not willingly engage in misrepresentations, I venture to make some remarks upon my relations to religious meetings in this city and also to correct some mistakes in your editorial of last week concerning the organization of the "St. Paul Church," which occurred a week ago last Sabbath evening.

Since I have been a resident of this city, I have had the pleasure of attending divine services at nearly all the churches in the place and have been treated with true Christian courtesy. I have been favored with invitations to preach in four of the churches, two of which I accepted. My motto is to assist all Christians in whose company I may chance to fall in the work of leading men to a better life.

When Mrs. Woodworth came to this city, I attended her meetings, and being requested to state publicly my attitude toward her work, I did so. I said that so far as the work was to lead men to a higher life it should have my support, but should things be said or done that my judgment could not approve, I should reserve the right to withhold my sanction from the objectionable features. I would "prove all things and hold fast that which is good."[1]

This series of meetings have now passed into the history of religious work of this city. I believe that much and lasting good has been done. I do not regret the part that I took in it but am sorry that I was not able to do more. There is one thing, however, that I do regret deeply (this I have often spoken of privately and once publicly: I refer to the spirit of crimination and recrimination that was developed during the meeting. My view of the matter is that all who desired to go and assist in the meetings at the rink should have been permitted to do so without bitter aspersions being poured out upon them, while those who for conscience's sake remained away should have been unimpeached in their motives.

[1] 1 Thessalonians 5:21, paraphrased.

But permit me to correct the errors referred to above concerning the organization of the "St. Paul Church." Perhaps the best way to make the corrections is to state plainly the facts in the case. When the series of meetings were nearing their close, there was a feeling entertained by many that there should be a church formed for the benefit of those who were without a religious home. There was, accordingly, a mass meeting held by those interested in the work to consider this question. This meeting appointed a committee of thirteen to formulate resolutions, and this committee brought in a report recommending the organization of an independent church to be called the "Union Mission Church of Kokomo" (the Bible to be its only creed and Christian character its only test of fellowship.) This report was adopted by the mass meeting, which at once appointed a committee on the reception of members. When this committee met to engage in its work, it was discovered that there was a material difference of opinion entertained, not only by members of the committee, but also by others outside, as to what the proposed organization was really intended to be. Some thought it was to be simply a missionary society and not a church in fact, while others thought it to be a church in every sense of the word, having the same powers as other churches.

Some of the members of the committee had doubts as to its power to settle so important a question, so a mass meeting was again called of all those favoring the new organization that they might settle the question for themselves. This mass meeting voted by an overwhelming majority that the organization should be a church in fact and not simply a missionary society, and as it seemed the name "Union Mission" was liable to mislead the public as to the nature of the organization, the mass meeting voted that that name be dropped and the name "St. Paul Church" be substituted. This meeting also appointed a committee on the reception of members and organization, and the "St. Paul Church" was organized in accordance with the instructions of the mass meeting (with no creed but the Bible and making Christian character the only test of fellowship.)

I do not write this article to argue the point with anyone but because justice and truth demand that the public should have the facts as they have occurred. Our Christian friends who favored the forming of a mission society have established their organization, as they had a right to do, and they will no doubt accomplish great good. I am quite sure *The Dispatch* is mistaken when it says the forming of these two societies was the result of a "row," but I must confess as a "rinker," that I am just a little proud that two such societies as the St. Paul Church and Union Mission have sprung out of the "Woodworth meetings." It must be a rich soil that produces two such vigorous plants. I must still be allowed to believe, however, that other churches and other ministers in this city are doing, and will continue to do, good work. If they chose to remain away from the rink, they had a right to do so, so long as they are faithfully engaged in their respective fields of labor. Let us have liberty—just a little.

— J. L. Puckett

August 18, 1885

Indianapolis Journal (IN)

Mrs. Woodworth in Miami County

Special to the *Indianapolis Journal.*

WABASH, AUG. 17.—

rs. Woodworth, the evangelist, pitched her tent near Xenia, Miami County, last week, and throngs have attended her meeting. Yesterday, however, she was greeted with a tremendous outpouring—people coming in carriages from every direction. Fully ten thousand persons were in and about the tent, and the road was blocked with carriages for about half a mile in each direction. The woods nearby were also crowded with vehicles. Xenia has taken in Mrs. Woodworth with open arms, and nearly every man, woman, and child in the little town is an ardent believer in the teachings of the trance medium. Any dissent from this view is treated as sure evidence of hardness of heart by the enthusiastic Xeniaites; among the visitors were many of this ungodly class.

Mrs. Woodworth was dressed yesterday in her customary black dress, matching her dark hair, with a fichu of white mull extending to the waist, while her hair was done up in a French twist on the top of her head. Her arms were bared to the elbow, revealing a plumpness and beauty which some of her sacrilegious listeners declared to be "the only pretty thing about her." The lady walked back and forth across her improvised platform, and waved her arms up and down as she spoke, after her customary fashion. It is thought that this constant movement exercises a sort of magnetic[1] influence over her converts.

A well-known divine[2] in Xenia occupied a seat on the platform and materially assisted in conducting the exercises. Unlike other places where the evangelist has appeared, the clergy of Xenia are in hearty accord with her and will operate as a powerful auxiliary to her success. Mrs. Woodworth employed her usual methods for making

[1] A reference to nineteenth century belief in "animal magnetism" which many related to the power that some hypnotists had over their subjects.

[2] "divine"—clergyman.

conversions yesterday, exhorting and singing. Her powerful contralto voice could be heard for a great distance. The favorite song was "Five of Them Were Foolish," the air[3] of which was utilized by the boys in the campaign last fall. The lady occasionally went off into a trance, after which she would exhort her hearers with powerful utterances to "get on the gospel boat," which was about to leave, adding, "no seasickness on this boat." During a trance period an ugly-looking fellow on the stage who ranked as one of the converts, constantly "guyed"[4] the evangelist, making the whole performance seem ridiculous. Only a handful of converts were made yesterday who were dragged off to the smaller tents when they felt the effect of the trance power. While the meeting progressed attachés[5] of the evangelist circulated about, about [remainder of article missing].

[3] "air"—tune.

[4] "guyed"—ridiculed.

[5] "attachés"—staff attached to the ministry of Woodworth.

August 18, 1885

Indianapolis Times (IN)

The Trance Evangelist

Mrs. Woodworth Laboring With Multitudes of Sinners at Xenia

WABASH, AUG. 17.—

esterday was a big day in the history of Xenia, south of this city. Fully twelve thousand visitors were attracted to the place by the presence of Mrs. Woodworth, the now famous trance medium, who has been holding forth in a grove near Xenia for several days past. She was greeted yesterday with the largest audience that has listened to her. The country was depopulated for several miles around. Lines of carriages blocked the roadway for long distances from the tent.

Mrs. Woodworth exhorted after her usual manner and with much power. Her full, rich voice could be heard in every direction for a long distance. Listeners were implored to "get on the gospel boat" right away. A few responded and were taken off to the smaller tents to recover. A Xenia clergyman occupied the platform with the lady. The clergy of Xenia are in hearty sympathy with the movement, and general public sentiment sustains the lady in her work. A collection amounting to about seventy-five dollars was taken up for her benefit. During the meeting Mrs. Woodworth's husband turned an honest penny selling peanuts and circus lemonade to the crowd. The lady announced that she would remain for a week longer in Xenia, and it appears that she has struck a rich field for her labors. Saturday night a gang of Kokomo roughs attempted to break up her meeting, alleging that she had driven several Kokomo persons into the asylum. It is reported that Somerset, this county, has made a bid for Mrs. Woodworth, and that she will next pitch her tent there.

August 21, 1885

Marion Chronicle (IN)

Mrs. Maria Woodworth

Her Evangelistic Work at Xenia—Her Methods and Success

or the past two weeks, Mrs. Woodworth has been engaged in revival work at Xenia. The place of the meetings is a large grove one-half a mile east and a quarter south of the town. Here are a dozen or more tents of various sizes used for restaurants over which Mr. Woodworth presides in a truly enterprising and businesslike fashion. Here Mrs. Woodworth has her tent with the necessary fixtures to make her home as comfortable as the circumstances will permit.

Although the meetings have been in progress for several days, yet they are losing none of their former interest. They are a constant novelty to the people who flock there by the thousands each day. Mrs. Woodworth, as a worker, seems indefatigable and untiring as she holds meetings both day and night and preaches upon all occasions. She is surrounded by a host of workers, among whom are Revs. Elkin, Leasenby, Ervin, Jeffery, Evans, and Cork, of New Corners and others. Many good people of Xenia and the surrounding community are her earnest supporters. There are some however, who "take no stock" in her methods and even denounce them. Notwithstanding this, Mrs. Woodworth is meeting with surprising success and is attracting immense crowds. On Sunday it is said that there was never such a gathering in Miami County, with perhaps for exception of the Democratic barbecue held at Peru last autumn.

A *Chronicle* reporter visited the meeting on Monday. He made his way to the far-famed Mrs. Woodworth whom he found in her tent ready to preach another sermon that afternoon. Mrs. Woodworth is of medium size. It is a common expression of those who have seen her that she is "neither beautiful nor homely." She is far from homely. She has a high forehead, gray eyes which wear a wearied expression when in repose. Her countenance is pleasing and intelligent in appearance. She wore black, fashionably but not ostensibly made. Mrs. Woodworth spoke of the attitude of the churches of Xenia toward her, the constancy of her labors, and the merits of her work.

She said that she was meeting with the earnest support of most of the churches. She referred to Rev. Elkins in particular. "Rev. Elkins" she said, "is an earnest Christian and is throwing his whole soul into the work." She said that long before she held her revival at Hartford City she had been working day and night. "I have been constantly preaching all this time," she said, "and I have to speak extemporaneously, that as I have no time to prepare beforehand. I can outwork six men. That has been acknowledged." Speaking of the merits of her beliefs and work, she referred to two ladies who were then walking about the grounds in a semi-trance state. She said: "Did you notice the happy expression on their faces? No one can be skeptical enough to say that this is not the power of God—the Holy Ghost—shining through and illuminating their faces. The world cannot deny it." She estimated her audience Sunday at ten thousand persons.

When the *Chronicle* representative made his appearance upon the ground, the first and most prominent sight that met his eyes was a crowd of about thirty men and women, mostly women, standing in a huddle and singing a popular camp-meeting song. Upon closer inspection he found that they were crowded around a middle-aged woman who had just recovered and was yet in a semi-trance condition. At times she would move her lips as if in prayer; at other times she would pray audibly. She had seen the "visions" common to this condition. "O, God," she would murmur, "why does one want to live so long? Why have I lived so long?" Several old women in a state of ecstasy, who had crowded around her, would exclaim, "Why sister, it is because He was not ready to receive you. You were not prepared for it." The entranced woman would then roll her eyes back; the tears would flow profusely, she breathed heavily and appeared as if her condition gave her almost unbearable fatigue. She finally recovered.

In a short time two ladies—those to whom Mrs. Woodworth referred—appeared upon the ground. Their countenances bore a truly happy and bright expression. They walked arm in arm aimlessly about the ground. They appeared to be in a dreaming condition and paid no attention to anyone, but most constantly kept their eyes rolled upward as if something pleasing attracted their attention. They would wave their hands outward from above their heads as if signaling to a vision seen or as if trying to expel a cloud between themselves and [God]. One would occasionally turn and whirl about and shade her eyes as if the vision would flit about to different places. They came up to the place of speaking and one of them sat down. She waved her hands continually until she finally appeared exhausted and fell back in the arms of friends into a partial trance state. She rolled her eyes far back at times and sought God to "remove the cloud" which intervened between herself and glory as the tears rolled down her cheeks.

"O, God," she would murmur, "remove the cloud, remove the cloud. I am Thy child; remove the cloud." She appeared an object of distress and exhaustion, while a lot of old men and women were encircled about her howling and singing dolefully. "Pray on, sister; have faith, sister," they would shout. It appeared that the girl's object was to dispel a cloud which yet rested between herself and God. For half an hour she prayed pitifully that this cloud might be dispelled. She had been in a trance state before, yet she did not consider that she was as happy as her companion with whom she was walking a few minutes before. One little cloud yet remained before her vision. That must be dispelled before she was truly happy. At last a bright smile lit up her countenance. "But one little cloud remains and it is passing away." At last it was entirely gone, and she appeared happy the rest of the day. No such demonstrations as appeared from her at noon escaped her. She appeared in a pleased and thoughtful mood. Her friend, however, waved her hands almost continually throughout the afternoon, with the exception of speaking time. The latter's name is Miss Powell, the former's, Lillie Niles. Both are residents of Xenia. Both have been in the trance state before. Miss Powell has been in the condition almost continuously for two or three days. One man, a resident of Xenia, sat back and looked on the proceedings coldly. Said he to the *Chronicle* reporter, referring to the Powell girl: "It is a shame, she will be as crazy as a loon in a few days if her condition continues as it is and has been."

While Miss Niles was in her trance condition, a young man, short of stature, of stout and heavy build, with a well-formed head, a square face, stout-looking jaws, a short neck, a sandy and light moustache, a freckled complexion, light gray eyes and light hair, sat by her and held the lady's head. He seemed one of Mrs. Woodworth's lieutenants and was earnestly working in the cause. He was dressed in a brown sacque coat, a dark vest, and a pair of pants of the same color. The *Chronicle* representative afterwards learned from him that he had led a dissipating life, and his appearance did not belie the assertion, although he wore a subdued and reflective expression.

This young man was holding Miss Niles' head while she was in the trance. She had asked him to pray for her. As quick as a flash, he threw up his hands and with a painful "Oh," which would do justice in the death yell of a Mohawk brave, he fell back heavily upon the board seats, apparently lifeless. His eyes were closed. His countenance was fixed and somewhat paler than usual. His pulse was weak. He did not breathe as it seemed for several seconds. His hands were cold. In a few minutes he moved his hands and held them partially up as if in supplication. His lips quivered and finally his eyes opened with a vacant stare. He turned his head about him and looked around. "I am a child of God, you bet." He exclaimed. "God was away up yonder before, but He is right here now," striking his breast. "Oh, my poor father who has talked to me so much of my waywardness," he would say.

He recovered and went to an eating stand and took dinner after which he enjoyed a fragrant cigar and stood about in a dazed and reflective state of mind. He said that his name was Kelly Frasee and that his home was in LaGro. He was reared at LaFontaine. He belongs to the Daniel's Band at Kokomo. This was not his first experience, as he had been in the trance state on Thursday before. He said that he was praying that the cloud would be removed from the lady's vision, and at this moment, a bright light appeared to him. He experienced no pain but on the contrary a glorious feeling. Nothing appeared to him but a bright light, and he regretted that he could see nothing else that others on the ground had seen. He had experienced a great change of life. Said he, "I was a wonderful player at poker and could beat all those around me. Why, a man at Tipton—I have his name—desired me to form a partnership with him in a poker establishment. I told him, "No, sir." He then pulled from his vest pocket a piece of yellow envelope on which was written the man's name to whom he referred.

Speaking began at 2 o'clock in the afternoon. Besides Mrs. Woodworth, half a dozen others were on the platform. An audience of five hundred, perhaps larger, had gathered on the seats. Mrs. Woodworth's methods of conducting a revival, with few exceptions, do not differ from those pursued at the ordinary camp meeting. Two gentlemen and a colored lady exhorted for a few moments. The order was excellent. Mrs. Woodworth arose to speak and was the picture of self-possession. She had a very bad cold and experienced hoarseness which vanished as she continued to talk. Her followers were flocked around her, and all seemed happy and perfectly at home. She talked in conversational tones but could be heard distinctly. When she made a striking point, she met with an ever-ready "amen." No one was afraid to speak, and from all sides came a thought or a suggestion.

Mrs. Woodworth used terms and illustrations in her talk which are strikingly forcible and energetic. This strikes the popular heart. The meeting was not by any means characterized by dolefulness, and everybody was ready to smile or laugh outright at any forcible remark the speaker might make. The colored lady, a woman of perhaps two hundred pounds, was especially demonstrative. She would sit and clap her hands, laugh and pass judgment upon the speaker's remarks. Her husband was sitting by her, and she would engage in earnest conversation with him at times. Her remarks were complimentary to the sermon.

Mrs. Woodworth preached for about a half-hour. She talks fluently. Her voice is good and strong. Her gestures are frequent, forcible, and graceful. In the course of her remarks, she would often end a sentence with an excellently inflected "Praise the Lord, glory hallelujah!" which would ring throughout the surrounding woods. She spoke principally in answering the question, "What is a Christian?" She took her text: "He that commits sin is of the devil,"[1] etc. and commented on each thought or word.

[1] 1 John 3:8, paraphrased.

Christianity, she said, means something. The path of the Christian is straight and narrow. He cannot take false steps, he must not waver in his course. Too many presumed Christians possess the attributes of sinners. They make professions of Christianity, yet entertain malice, hate, [and] jealousy. These are not the attributes of a Christian. He that possesses them is of the devil. This true Christian is filled with the love of God. This must be the position of the true Christian wherever he may be, whether in the field, in the kitchen, or at the washtub.

She then exhorted them to Christianity. "Let us pray God," she said, "to send converting power in our midst as well as in the surrounding community. Let us have faith today in His converting power. At Hartford City people fourteen miles away, whom I had never seen, experienced the power of God. May it be so today in the surrounding community as well as in our midst. How many want [that] experience today? Let all such come around this altar." At this a half dozen women went to the altar to seek repentance while others crowded around them. One was a young lady. A number of old men and women collected around her and prayed and shouted and howled until they got her to crying and praying for forgiveness.

Mrs. Woodworth was on the platform walking about and exhorting. The faces of two old women in the audience became as expressionless as putty. They attempted to clap their hands which disobeyed the will and often missed each other while they feebly shouted to give expression to their happiness. They almost fell several times but did not go into the trance state. In a few minutes Mrs. Woodworth shouted to the audience to kneel about the altar and the repentants and pray. A hundred or more promptly obeyed. They all prayed as loudly as they could, and such a babel of tongues can better be imagined than described.

The old crone of a colored woman was the most prominent figure. She was, perhaps, the most happy person there, or at least she gave the most expression to it. She stood up and clapped her hands. When a sinner had become converted, her happiness was boundless. While singing was in progress, she would stand with her head thrown back, smile, and keep time with the music with both her hands and feet. While they were singing a camp meeting song and while the penitents were yet at the altar, two young men were standing near the speaker's stand. While they sat they rolled their eyes toward heaven in an apparent effort to go off into a trance.

"Look at those fools," said a bystander to the *Chronicle* reporter, "they want to become entranced. If someone would hit them a good lick on the head with a stone, it would waken (*sic*) them up." They became interested in the singing, however, and forgot their desire. One of them again rolled his eyes up, and after standing in this way for about five minutes, he fell at full length on the ground. His condition was the same as that of the former young man who has been mentioned. In a few minutes he arose and walked about evidently pleased at the effort. In the meantime the young suppliant at the altar, who has been mentioned, was growing weaker. She was yet crying and praying but less audibly. She was now on her knees and had thrown herself back into the arms of friends. It is growing late, the *Chronicle* reporter must go. Whether the "cloud" departed from her vision, he is not able to say, but as he leaves he hears the echoes of a howling mob of toothless old women and long-faced old men crying, shouting, and singing over her.

Notes

The young man who was last entranced was from near Amboy. His name is Tom Sullivan. He is about eighteen years of age. Some who were present said that he was half witted, but they evidently drew their conclusion from his being entranced. "Why," they said, "he has not good sense or he wouldn't be there." Others said he had reasonably good sense.

Marion was almost depopulated Sunday, her people being in attendance at the Woodworth meeting.

Misses Niles and Powell, who were so demonstrative last Monday, have been in the trance state several times.

The preaching was interspersed with camp meeting songs, the most popular being "I belong to the Union Band."

"I believe in Mrs. Woodworth; I believe her an earnest Christian," said a good old resident of Xenia to the *Chronicle* man.

The Seventh Day Adventists have their tents pitched in the west part of the town. In view of the Woodworth meeting, they draw small crowds.

There is a peculiar difference between the manner of the men and women who fall into the trance condition, as shown by Monday's meeting. The men would drop over suddenly as if struck by a thunderbolt. They would remain in this condition for several minutes apparently lifeless. They would then recover and appear with their usual demeanor. The women would go off first into a semi-trance condition, making demonstrations all the time. They would then roll their eyes back and become unconscious while they would breathe heavily and appear greatly fatigued. They would then become conscious and then again pass into the trance state. Their countenances all the time showed great distress or pleasure while the men's countenances were fixed and expressionless.

September 9, 1885

Indianapolis Journal (IN)

A Case That Passes for a Faith Cure Reported from Madison County

THE SO-CALLED
FAITH CURE OF A
MADISON COUNTY LADY

Special to the *Indianapolis Journal*

MUNCIE, SEPT. 8.—

n conversation with Dr. T. J. Bowles, one of the leading physicians of this city, your correspondent was given the following facts concerning a most remarkable faith cure. Somewhat over a year ago, Dr. Bowles was called to treat a lady, the wife of Mr. C. P. Diltz, living just over the line in Madison County, a distance of perhaps fifteen miles from this city. She had then been a long time sick. The doctor used every remedy which he thought would reach the case, but in spite of his scientific treatment and the most careful nursing, she gradually grew weaker until she became absolutely helpless, being unable to feed herself or turn her body in bed.

She had the greatest confidence in her physician but appeared void of the proper willpower and was entirely effortless. Her friends despaired of her recovery and daily expected her death. Dr. Bowles remained hopeful and believed that she would recover, for she was afflicted with no particular constitutional disease, but a general wasting away of strength due to what the doctor calls paralysis of the will.

Late in the spring, when she was reduced to that point where death seemed imminent, Mrs. Maria Woodworth came into the neighborhood and conducted one of her wonderful revival meetings, which aroused all the people to a state of religious fervor to them before unknown. Learning of the illness of Mrs. Diltz, she visited her home, and by permission of the physician, prayed for her recovery. Mrs. Diltz is a devout Christian woman and was at that time a fervent believer in the efficacy of prayer and at once placed implacable confidence in Mrs. Woodworth.

At the close of the prayer, she appeared of better cheer and the next morning surprised her friends by getting out of bed, dressing herself, and taking her place at the table—a thing she had not done for several months before—ate a hearty breakfast. For one so thin, she seemed to possess unusual strength, and from that time on she rapidly improved until now, in the language of the physician, "she is fat, rugged, and rosy." Dr. Bowles, who is not a religionist, as that term is popularly understood, says that common[ly] called faith cures are not myths. In this case [it] was the woman's faith which made her whole but not supernatural power which Mrs. Woodworth invoked. It is a cure based upon physiological principles, by virtue of which the willpower of Mrs. Diltz, through implicit faith and fervent prayer and its efficacy, was aroused in its normal condition, and she became possessed of a desire and a determination to get well, and she did so.

Out of gratitude to Him who she believes has cured her, Mrs. Diltz has decided to enter the field as an evangelist. In preparatory to devoting her time and strength to this work, Mr. Diltz has decided to sell his personalty,[1] and assist her [in] the work. Mrs. Woodworth is to begin in one week a three-weeks' meeting, which is to be held in a large tent erected in a grove on the Diltz farm. Mrs. Diltz is to assist in this meeting and already the people in the vicinity are showing themselves not a little excited in anticipation of great results. This is in the vicinity in which Mrs. Woodworth created such excitement [last] winter by the use of her remarkable powers as a revivalist, and a repetition of the same is expected at this time.

[1] "personalty"—personal property (Webster's N.W. 1997).

September 21, 1885

The Indianapolis Times (IN)

Repentance Run Mad

MRS. WOODWORTH'S BIGGEST REVIVAL

Twenty Thousand Persons Under the Spell of the Trance Evangelist's Incantations—A Lively Day at Shelbyville—Ches Chambers on Trial.

MUNCIE, SEPT. 21.—

"The devil is mad, and I am glad. Oh my soul! Praise the Lord! Glory to God!"

The above quoted lines were chanted by twenty thousand people gathered in a small grove in the edge of Madison County yesterday. Perhaps never before was gathered together such an assemblage to hear and see Mrs. Woodworth, the great revivalist.

The tent where the meetings were held is in a ten-acre grove thirteen miles northwest of Muncie. Of this grove, fully half of it was so completely filled with wagons that walking about among them was impossible save by climbing over them.

In the woods stood a tent about forty feet by sixty feet, in the center of which was a platform raised about two feet, and upon this were two chairs, upon which Mrs. Woodworth stood. These chairs were held by two men, so there would be no danger of her toppling off. Around this were rude benches extending from the pulpit, or altar, about fifteen feet on two sides. On these benches sat the converts, contrite and submissive, as they said, before the power of the Holy Ghost.[1]

Mrs. Woodworth was dressed in black, sparingly trimmed with black lace. Her hair was braided, dressed high on her head, and confined with a conspicuous, old-fashioned, tortoiseshell-back comb. She began talking as the writer elbowed his way to the stand. She told her hearers that the Holy Ghost was about to knock at the heart of each one and might never come again, and if they did not heed the call, they would be damned irrevocably and irredeemably.

After several passionate appeals, there was weeping and wailing among the converts, piteous supplications from the repentant, and

[1] These benches were called the "mourners' bench" where people who mourned over their sin came to sit and pray for assurance from God of their salvation.

joyful, jubilant exclamations from the followers of the revivalist. When this spiritual manifestation had subsided, she continued her talk in a slightly different strain, always suiting her words to the thoughts, doubts, and fears of her hearers. By observing her listeners, she seemed to read what was passing in their minds and governed her language and gestures accordingly.

After she had finished her talk, which at times was singularly eloquent, she commenced singing, the audience joining in with a noise that was deafening. The tent seemed to swell and collapse as the thunderous manifestation increased in volume. As the singing died away, leaving oppressively near a low moaning that caused the most passive and indifferent to shudder, Mrs. Woodworth, throwing her head back, gazed aloft reverentially and earnestly, her hands supplicantly extended in the direction of her gaze and her whole frame quivering under intense excitement. As she majestically raised up to her fullest height, the manifestations of the audience would increase proportionately. Then as she crouched cringingly, as if in abject fear, the deafening voice would again die away into a moan. The demonstrations decreased as the distance increased from her, as though her violent agitations produced vibrations which lost intensity with distance. The most violent crowded on the stage, jumped up and down, wrestled, shook hands, hallooed, and pushed off the exhausted; and when worn out, their places were filled with fresh converts.

Words cannot describe the scene that confronted the writer as he stood on that platform and looked around at the confusion. Dozens lying around rigid and lifeless, as though in death. Strong men shouting till they were hoarse, then falling in a swoon. Women falling over benches and being trampled under foot. Children crying and weeping as though their parents were dead. Aged women gesticulating and hysterically sobbing, as though their sons and support had been murdered. It affected persons rods and rods[2] away. A big wagonload of people forty rods away were noticed who, hearing the evangelist's voice, stopped their team and commenced a wild demonstration of joy among themselves. People ran up and

[2] "rod"—A unit of linear measurement equivalent to 16 ½ feet or 5 ½ yards (5.03 meters) *(Webster's N. W.,* 1997).

gathered around the wagon and so they were surrounded with a concourse of people having a little meeting of their own, with all its wildest characteristics. A man heard the "hallelujah," jumped up, and holloed,[3] "Glory to God!" and fell down in a trance from which he did not wake for hours.

One fellow who went into the trance state during services, straightened upright and stood like a post. As he attracted much attention and there was not enough room to lay him down, three men took hold of him and doubled him up so he could be put on a seat.

In the afternoon, the meeting was held on a raised platform in the open air, where Mrs. Woodworth stationed herself with a woman beside her who held a hat for contributions. For forty minutes the people passed in front of the evangelist, two and three abreast, at the rate of fifty a minute, shaking hands with her and throwing in money literally by the hatful. The hat was emptied several times before the collection was finished.

[3] "holloed"—shouted, past tense of hollo *(Webster's N. W.,* 1997).

September 26, 1885

The Indianapolis Times (IN)

For One Night Only

Mrs. Woodworth's Local Revival

The Lord Calls Her to Louisville and She Cannot Tarry in This Wicked City—How She Talks and How She Acts—Her Thrilling Songs

rs. Maria Woodworth, the evangelist, who has during the past summer been throwing people into trances and creating great excitement at Tipton, Kokomo, and other places, held a meeting last night at the rooms of the Y.M.C.A. Mission School,[1] corner of Yandes Street and Home Avenue. A large audience assembled to hear her, entirely filling the rooms, blocking up the sidewalks in front and surrounding the windows outside.

Mrs. Woodworth is a peculiar speaker. It is difficult to believe that she is not in a measure sincere and yet there is a great deal of affectation about her. She says that she depends on the Lord to supply her with thoughts and rhetoric when she gets up to speak. It is very evident that she takes little thought previously as to what she will say, for her sermon last night was as rambling and disconnected as could well be imagined. She talks with such rapidity that she would probably paralyze the most accomplished shorthand reporter in the land. Her sentences are often ungrammatical, sometimes incoherent, and sometimes unintelligible from the chain-lightning style in which they are delivered. She talks in a conversational tone, occasionally raising her voice at an emphatic point, stamping her foot, and striking one hand upon the other or upon the table.

She held the attention of her audience well, and her emphatic sentences usually called forth an unctuous "Amen" from some good brother. It is difficult to understand the secret of her power. Of eloquence, she has none, of learning, very little. She has familiarized

[1] Young Men's Christian Association was originally founded as a Christian organization to help young men and focused on "saving souls, with saloon and street-corner preaching, lists of Christian boarding houses, lectures, libraries, and meeting halls, most of them in rented quarters." In the 1880s under the influence of D. L. Moody and others, the organization built many YMCA buildings and began using paid staff. — "About the YMCA," YMCA of USA, Webpage, Accessed: 7 March 2000, http://www.ymca.net/).

herself with a great many quotations from the Bible and has a way of weaving them into her talk that gives it a certain pointedness. She has also a good deal to say about the miraculous way in which she thinks she is engineered in making her addresses and in traveling from point to point. She said last night that out of the pulpit she could hardly speak so as to be heard, had almost no voice at all, that she was very weak and in ill health constantly; but when she came to preach, the Lord gave her strength and made her voice so strong that she could sometimes be heard a mile away. She does not look at all like an invalid but seems to be on the contrary, a fairly robust woman, both in and out of the pulpit.

The burden of her sermon was to urge the listeners to get hold of something she called "the anointing power." They must just get down and pray till they had gotten hold of it. In the past few weeks, she had seen thousands of sinners terror stricken. "Some of you," she said "may have had light here tonight." She told the sinners that she would meet them, as well as the Christians, at the judgment seat. She might never see them on earth again. She was going away, perhaps to a foreign land, wherever the Lord might take her. She hoped He would bring her back but didn't venture to oppose her will to His.

At the end of her sermon, she cast her eyes upward and began singing: "Oh, brothers will you meet me?" repeating the line three times and then adding, "on Canaan's happy shore." The audience joined in the singing. Several stanzas were sung with no change excepting that the words "sisters," "mother," "father," etc., were substituted for "brothers." During the singing she swung her hands around constantly and looked upward at the ceiling. She would occasionally rise on tiptoe and reach up as if she were grasping at something in the air. In conclusion she sang a solo, and it must be said that as a singer, she is not a success. Her methods could only be effective among people the majority of whom were ignorant. She had not put anybody into a trance last night and said very little about that part of her repertoire.

Mrs. Woodworth leaves this morning for Louisville, where she says the Lord has "called" her. He gave her only one night in this city.

September 26, 1885

Indianapolis Journal (IN)

The Trance Evangelist

Mrs. Maria Woodworth Holds a Single Gospel Meeting in Indianapolis

The Services Unmarked by Any Unusual Scenes or Incidents—The Substance and Character of Her Discourse

rs. Maria Woodworth, the trance evangelist, spoke last night at the W.C.T.O.[1] mission on Yandes Street. The room which is not large, was crowded, 350 persons being inside, many of them standing, while nearly half as many more were outside, trying to see and hear. Mrs. Woodworth's talk is not a sermon; it may be called an exhortation and is made up largely of gospel texts without logical arrangement, strung together with connecting threads of ungrammatical commonplaces, mixed metaphors, and faulty similes.

She gave out last night that her theme was "Conversion." She said that conversion was not, as many explain it, to cease to do evil and to do good.

> It is God's plan to change our hearts. It is to change us so that things we once loved we will hate. The moral man wants it. The inside must be changed so that we shall have spiritual discernment. This change takes place in all of us, and we receive God's nature. Even the moral man delights in singing and praising God. He thinks this enough, that he has received the pearl of great price. There are many who teach that salvation is merely to join the church. But, oh, my dear brothers and sisters, you may spend all your days in church and then go down and make your bed in hell. It is when we get into Christ that this change takes place. Thank the Lord! There is a time when we feel and know that we are born again. Yes, there is.

[1] Probably W. C. T. U., the Woman's Christian Temperance Union (begun in Ohio in 1873) or a similar organization. The YMCA is mentioned in the previous news article as the location for this same meeting and was also involved in temperance work and evangelism at this time. It was not uncommon for the WCTU to house its offices in the YMCA. The Illinois WCTU were also housed in the YMCA for a while in the 1880s.

Many speak of conversion as the happiest, holiest moment of their lives. I have heard people who have been Christians thirty, forty, or fifty years, look back to the time of their conversion and say this. Don't you think that this brings reproach upon a Christian life and upon the Christian religion? They ought to be happier and happier as they go on. It is like climbing Jacob's ladder, every day getting nearer and nearer to Christ—nearer and nearer to the pearly gates. We must have the Spirit of the living God in our hearts or we will never see heaven. You will never be permitted to pass the beautiful gates into the golden city unless you are born again, born of the Spirit. You cannot expect to be saved if you are merely drifting around in the church, depending upon the preacher.

The Holy Ghost is similar to the wind. Sometimes it tears up great forests. Sometimes it is the gentle breeze. Like the wind, you never see it. You feel it. If any man or woman have not the Spirit of God, he is not of Him. Many have a form of godliness yet deny the power of conversion. Blind leaders of the blind![2] Jesus says turn away from them; they are blind leaders, leading the blind down to hell. Every minister who denies this Spirit of God in the heart is a blind leader. When we feel the Spirit of Christ in us, we are converted. Then we step out in the faith of God's promise and expect Him to do the rest for us. Our sins are gone and the temple is cleansed. Then the Holy Ghost can go into the heart, for there is no sin there. We go to Christ; He pardons our sins and He sends His influence into our hearts, and then we love God. You must become personally acquainted with Christ before you can love Him.

Mrs. Woodworth continued:

We must be born of the Spirit, my dear friends and dying travelers upon the road with me. If we are not

[2] "Form of godliness," see 2 Timothy 3:5. "Blind leaders," see Matthew 15:14.

converted men and women, we will every last one go to hell. We may never commit a sin, and yet, if we neglect to have the love of God in our hearts, we shall be damned to all eternity. Arrange your hearts and not your garments. God does not see us as man sees us. God help us to look into our hearts. There are thousands in the church who were never converted. God help them. Oh, let us heed His call, or as sure as God lives, we shall be dashed to pieces as a potter's vessel. There are millions who will be—as the man who came to the marriage feast without the Bridegroom's raiment—cast into outer darkness where there will be weeping and wailing and gnashing of teeth. There was a time when God winked at the ignorance of the people, but today He calls upon all to repent and be converted, and woe to those who do not heed His call.

I feel God is leading me in every word I am saying. God help you to receive it. I expect in a short time to say farewell and go up and wear the robe and the crown. I will go up from the battlefield. I work for God even in my sleep. I know that I will not have a starless crown. Many I have saved will meet me on the other shore. We shall meet in heaven and strike glad hands in the gold paved streets, etc.

Mrs. Woodworth spoke of her ill health, whacked the churches and the ministers, and said she was going to Louisville in the morning. There were no trances.

May 12, 1886

Kokomo Gazette Tribune (IN)

Woodworth Meeting

etween four hundred and five hundred people of all grades and conditions in life attended the afternoon services at the pavilion spread near the poor farm in one of the most dismal and uninviting woods in Howard County. The services did not differ materially from many of her meetings held a year ago in this city. Her first move was to open up one broadside after another on the churches. She said her return to Kokomo had made the devil mad. Then she had the deck cleared for action, and the usual humdrum began around what was said to be an altar. During all this time her husband, who had an eating tent in front of the main entrance to the tent, was punching the fire in the cookstove, possibly in hopes of making the atmosphere in a condition to require the use of more red lemonade. Many people believe that Mrs. Woodworth is honest and laboring only for good, but they take but little stock in her avaricious husband and his moneymaking adjuncts. Monday they moved their tent and campground fixtures to Clark's grove, about two miles southeast of the city where she will begin a ten-day's crusade against the power of darkness.

June 29, 1886

Kokomo Gazette Tribune (IN)

[Cedar Lake's Gain]

e are informed that Mrs. Woodworth, who is rusticating at Tally's landing, has purchased thirteen acres of land on the east bank of Lake Manitou, of Mr. A. B. Sibert, which includes all the unsold lots in Manitou Park. Some say this noted evangelist will establish a campground for religious services that will be perpetual during the summer months. At her usual ratio of success, the entire population of Rochester Township would soon be converted and made members of the Daniel's Band. If Mrs. W. has made the purchase, we hope she will make a religious and financial success of it.

— ROCHESTER REPUBLICAN

This will spoil the fishing at Manitou. But Manitou's loss will be Cedar Lake's gain; while these meandering evangelists bait their hook for converts at Manitou, the disciples of old Isaac[1] will angle for bass at Cedar Lake.

[1] Walton, Izaak (1593-1683), English writer of one of the most famous books in the English language, *The Compleat Angler, or the Contemplative Man's Recreation* (1653), a book on fishing and pastoral life. "Walton, Izaak," *Encarta Deluxe Online Encyclopedia,* Website, Accessed: 7 March 2000, (Microsoft Corporation, 1997-2000), http://encarta.msn.com/index/conciseindex/20/02035000.htm

September 14, 1886

The Indianapolis Sentinel (IN)

Riotous Religion

The Cataleptic Outbreaks Produced by Mrs. Woodworth's Methods

A Wild Night at the Meridian Rink—People Driven Almost Stark Mad at the Converts Bench

ith Thatcher, Primrose, and West at the Grand, and Mrs. Woodworth's cataleptic combustion at the Meridian Rink, amusement lovers were abundantly provided for last night. The subject of Mrs. Woodworth's rambling remarks was "Cain." She preached a tirade against the churches.

"We mean business," one of the troupe said, "and if the preachers don't like our meetings, they had better go home and keep their mouths shut." She manifested great disgust for the church hymns such as "Prone to Wander."[1]

When testimonies were called for, an excited brother rushed forward announcing that his name was "not Cain, but McCain."

"I have always been tongue-tied until tonight," he shouted, and he seemed anxious to make up all in one evening for his life-long silence.

"Get your mouths open," he cried. "That is the secret of Christianity," and he proceeded to get his mouth very wide open. "Christ will do for you what He has done for me." But, strangely enough the sinners in the audience, whom Mrs. Woodworth had stigmatized as "people who would rather go to hell than come to the mourners' bench," did not seem very envious of what had been done for this man. "If you ain't got this kind of religion, come up and get it," but nobody seemed to want Mr. McCain's kind of religion.

---

[1] "Prone to Wander"— Robert Robinson wrote the lyrics to this hymn, entitled "Come, Thou Fount of Every Blessing" in 1858. The third verse has the phrase, "prone to wander":

O to grace how great a debtor
Daily I'm constrained to be!
Let Thy goodness, like a fetter,
Bind my wandering heart to Thee.
Prone to wander, Lord, I feel it,
Prone to leave the God I love;
Here's my heart, O take and seal it,
Seal it for Thy courts above.

The next witness was Mrs. John Haught, who told how yesterday afternoon her eyesight was restored after total blindness for many years. Her husband corroborated her story and recited several unnecessary and revolting details of his wife's medical treatment. He is another of those who had been unable to talk until they were converted and all of whom seemed blessed with seven tongues on this occasion.

Mrs. Woodworth told of several miraculous cures at Muncie and other places, which were corroborated by an old gentleman who had traveled all the way from Rushville and has used "his own money," to hear Mrs. Woodworth.

The evangelist announced that the praying would begin, and she wanted those who were not seeking Christ to keep away from the altar. Her grim spouse walked sullenly about ordering too-curious intruders back. After a sufficient crowd had gathered about the benches, the work of conversion began and the women were soon lying limp on the floor. As they gradually lost consciousness, the troupe grinned with increasing satisfaction.

The conversion is accomplished in this wise: All the brethren and sisters get their mouths open until such a din is raised as would shatter the nerves of the hardest sinner. Mrs. Woodworth and her satellites are all the time shaking their hands directly in the faces of the subjects for conversion, while others press the hands and foreheads of the sinners. By this magnetic or mesmeric process,[2] the willpower is entirely destroyed and the mind rendered passive. While in this condition, Mrs. Woodworth yields the subjects as she chooses. Such, at least, was the explanation of a medical gentleman present. After hysterical screeching the women sank into a faint from which they were invited to be declared converts. One poor man, too saturated with the spirits of frumenty[3] to be very susceptible to the Spirit of salvation, sank beside the bench and was soon being plied by the sisters. When the mesmeric stupor

[2] "magnetic or mesmeric process"—refers to the nineteenth-century theory that innate magnetism supplied the power to hypnotists over their subjects.

[3] "spirits of frumenty"—a sweet, spiced soup laced with alcohol.

had been added to his already stupefied condition, the two women lifted his arms heavenward and shouted, "another soul for Jesus."

The burlesque ended with an appeal for larger contributions and larger sales of Mrs. Woodworth's book.

September 24, 1886

Anderson Weekly Review (IN)

Communication

n last week's *Herald,* the Rev. Joseph Franklin makes an unwarranted attack upon Mrs. Woodworth and her meetings at this place. In that article he concedes the fact that Mrs. Woodworth is a good woman and has done a good work in Anderson, but he seeks to destroy her influence for good by an assault upon her manner of conducting services. Had that article been conceived in the *Herald* sanctum by the editor of that paper, the community could have forgiven it, believing it to have been but the expiring kick of infidelity. But when it is known that that paper has no religious belief, counts the Bible a hoax, and Christ an imposter, it sets candid people to doubting the soundness of the minister's Christianity who will make it the tool to drag down the sacred influences that he himself is not able to understand. We wonder he did not seek some paper to publish his views that at least itself has a decent respect for some form of religious worship.

But our wonder ceases when we come to that sentence in his article where he says, "It is out of the range of human experience to know even that God is"; for that is just what infidelity has always said. That is just the exclamation with which atheism has met Christianity for the last two thousand years. And had it not been for the heroism of some dear patient Job here and there along the course of time with enough moral courage to stand up and say, "I know that my Redeemer liveth,"[1] religion would be as dead in all the world today as it is in the hearts of those who malign the Woodworth worshippers.

[1] See Job 19:25.

But is it really beyond the reach of human experience to know that God is? If Mr. Franklin had said that it was beyond his experience to know that God is, I would not join issue with him but would at once cry out, "consent." I really believe that it is true that he, like many others who are professors, is living without the knowledge of God in the world. A thing may be contrary to our own experience and yet in strict conformity with the existence and knowledge of others. The king of Siam knew there was no such a thing in creation as ice because it was contrary to his experience to see water frozen.[2] But is [it] not a little strange that Mr. Franklin should continue to preach the great plan of salvation while he is not only out of the ark of safety himself, but living without the knowledge of God in the world.[3] The Christian man who has been born again knows as implicitly that God is, as he knows the air is. He can see neither, but the power of God is certainly not less convincing than that of the wind.

We are told by Mr. Franklin that all that is necessary is to believe and be baptized; and yet the man who does not believe is inferior to the devils in hell, for they believe and tremble.[4] "It is not of works lest any man should boast, but is the gift of God."[5]

"Verily I say unto you that unless you are born of the water and the Spirit, ye cannot enter into the kingdom of heaven."[6] And this being born of the Spirit is certainly a result of spiritual power that he who has been blest with it cannot be mistaken on the question.

Mr. Franklin thinks to array the enemies of Mrs. Woodworth on his side of his present political fight by saying a few days since the publication of his article, "to the dogs with politics if it must make a man a moral coward"; and we say, "amen." And we echo back, "to the dogs" with a man who is so bound up in the confines of his own creed that he is not even certain there is a God. "To the dogs" with

[2] This story was told in John Locke's (1632-1704) *Discourse of Miracles* and involved the king of Siam and the Dutch ambassador. It often appeared in the nineteenth century texts in various versions as an apologetic argument in defense of the existence of miracles.

[3] See Ephesians 2:12.

[4] James 2:19, paraphrased.

[5] Ephesians 2:8-9, paraphrased.

[6] John 3:5, paraphrased.

a minister who, under the sanction of his sacred calling, will thus attack other Christian people who he confesses are far more zealous than himself. "To the dogs" with a man, Christian, or otherwise who does not realize that different human organizations are but the workmanship of one great Creator and that the religion which will purify and sanctify one will not affect or reach another. We have no use for a man in the pulpit, in the legislature, nor in society who cannot hear above the clamor of his own creed the crying need of the fallen world for salvation and who is not ever ready to encourage and adopt as his own any means, whether it be exactly his own peculiar "faith" or not, that will make men happier, purer, and holier.

— One Who Knows God Is

July 24, 1887

The Champaign County Herald (IL)

The Camp Meeting

Mrs. Woodworth, the trance evangelist, is now in the fourth week of the camp meeting which is held in Kerr's grove, north of this city. Meetings are held each afternoon and evening and are attended by hundreds of people from this city and surrounding country. The methods of conducting the meetings are primitive and remind one of the camp meetings of many years ago. A number of conversions have been reported and good has been accomplished. Mrs. Woodworth is about 42 years of age, makes a pleasing appearance on the platform, and makes friends with all with whom she comes in contact. While the manner of conducting the meeting might be criticized in this day and age of the world, yet we remember that humanity is curiously constructed and it takes different ways to reach all people. It is to be hoped that still more good will be accomplished.

Flying reports are in circulation of wonderful cures of disease performed by Mrs. Woodworth. There is some truth in some of them, and much that is utterly unfounded. The lady has a wonderful magnetic power over those with whom she comes in contact, and by that means she has the power to relieve and sometimes cure those who are troubled with nervous diseases that are more imaginary than real, but that cures of diseases of a strictly physical or deep-seated character have taken place, we have no evidence and are not ready to so announce.

September 3, 1887

St. Louis Daily Globe-Democrat (MO)

Cancer Cured by Faith

Phenomenal Powers Possessed by a Woman Revivalist

MRS. MARIA WOODWORTH RESTORES LOST SIGHT AND HEARING AND CAUSES A PARALYTIC TO WALK

Special Correspondent of the *Globe-Democrat*

DECATUR, ILL., SEPTEMBER 2.—

Seven miles northwest of this busy county seat, at a place called "Boiling Springs," a great religious revival has just now been opened under the auspices of the disciples of "The Church of God."[1]

The moving spirit in this work of snatching brands from the fires of perdition is Mrs. Maria B. Woodworth, a woman whose intense enthusiasm, eloquent power of speech, and miraculous cures of the physically afflicted have occasioned more excitement among the people of Ohio, Indiana, and Illinois than has ever been known.

During the two weeks preceding her appearance at Boiling Springs, Mrs. Woodworth held forth under a mammoth tent pitched on the outskirts of the town of Urbana, some fifty miles to the northeast of this place. The excitement she aroused in that alleged cradle of infidelity has not yet subsided, and the most flattering offers have been made to encourage her to return. The residents of the conspicuous town of Champaign have also become aroused with the religious fever, and every facility has been offered Mrs. Woodworth if she will only return and continue the work of saving souls. The wealthy men of the town have even promised that if she will but promise to return, they will build a beautiful church for her exclusive use and vest in her the title to the property. These tempting offers Mrs. Woodworth has best constrained to decline, her reason being that she is as badly needed in many other parts of this wicked world as at Champaign, and she feels that it is telling evidence of the good she is doing that wherever she has been, they yearn for her.

[1] Maria Woodworth-Etter traveled under the auspices of this denomination until 1902 when she parted ways with them over the issue of healing.

The testimony concerning her doings in Urbana is certainly very astonishing. Her most extraordinary conversions have been among those who attended the revival to laugh and scoff. For example, she brought Lawyer Wright to his knees in thirty minutes after she began to work on his conscience.

A Converted Lawyer

Mr. Wright hadn't been inside of a church for twenty-five years, and his motive for attending the revival was mainly to gratify idle curiosity—perhaps to enjoy himself. Mrs. Woodworth had been advised of his coming, and when the rugged old counselor had seated himself, she pointed her batteries at him. She begged him as hard to confess his sins as if she were begging him for life, and when the old man began to get restless, she redoubled her efforts. Her magnetic[2] influence communicated itself mysteriously to her entire audience, and in less time than it takes to write it down, every one of her hearers was on his knees calling piteously upon heaven to incline the sinful lawyer's thoughts toward his soul's salvation. After a little the lawyer began to weep. Real tears coursed their pellucid way to the end of his nose and trickled down the furrows in his cheeks. Then he sprang to his feet, began waving his arms over his head and shouting with such vigor that his sonorous voice rose clearly above the exultation of the multitude. Such is the infection of religious excitement that as has been said, within thirty minutes of the lawyer's appearance under the tent, he was standing upon the platform by the side of Mrs. Woodworth calling upon those within "earshot" of his voice to cast aside the things of the world and seek a place in the kingdom.

Among the two thousand people present, very many were won to the revivalist's standard, and a circle of humanity, three and four deep, knelt at the altar during every service, wildly beseeching the Almighty to pardon them their sins and admit them to membership with the elect.

[2] The writer is describing what he sees in terms of popular nineteenth-century theories concerning personal magnetism as a hypnotic force in some people.

Conspicuous among these were Mr. Busey, the millionaire banker of Urbana; Barney Saulisbury, an old railroad conductor and a confirmed skeptic, who had come to look upon life as a failure and eternity a joke; and Lawyer White, like Lawyer Wright, whose case was such as to fill any ordinary revivalist with despair.

After two or three meetings, and when the people had been worked up to a degree of religious intensity, Mrs. Woodworth began her ministrations among the sick, the halt, and the blind. Eyewitnesses, residents of Urbana, describe the scenes, which then took place as the personification of frenzy. When the excitement was at its whitest heat, Mrs. Woodworth seemed ubiquitous. One moment she would face her shrieking auditors from the platform, wringing her hands, screaming to God for mercy in a voice that sounded high and shrill above the wailings of her congregation; the next, prostrate upon her face, tearing her hair, and writhing in the imaginary embrace of some demon from below; then flying about among the people, encouraging, arguing, commanding them to help her drive the fiend from their midst; again upon the stage, stamping her feet tragically upon the imaginary form of the "Old Boy" himself; and then, as the great climax to her exhausting efforts, shrieking, "Victory!" at the full power of her lungs.

A Frenzied Revivalist

In the midst of pandemonium thus engendered, she would call upon the afflicted to come forward and be healed. And with each demonstration of her certainly inexplicable power, the enthusiasm would break out anew, and men and women, overcome by their overwrought emotions, would hurl themselves upon the ground, bewailing their sins and invoking God to spare them from the endless torments of hell.

Under such circumstances "Farmer" Grover, of Warrensburg, was led to the altar. He had been deaf as a post for twenty-five years and suffered from a pain in his back caused by a fall from a horse that almost bent him double. There was no mistaking the physical agony in the old man's face. It was the agony of grim despair.

There was a moment of hush, painful in its suddenness, as the revivalist stepped forward with a quick, nervous movement and placed her hand upon the sufferer's head. Then she grabbed his ears and cried out at the top of her voice, "Brother, you are deaf no longer!"

The old man looked up, and a strange light shot from his aged eyes.

"Do you hear me?" shrieked the woman, "I tell you, you are cured!"

"Yes, I hear you," replied the old man, "but you needn't yell at me that way. I thought you were going to take the pain out of my back?"

Mrs. Woodworth, her face aglow with excitement, put her hands upon the old man's spine, and calling upon the Lord to help her, commanded him to stand erect.

Then followed a moment of nerve-straining intensity as the old man raised himself slowly to the perpendicular.

"The pain has left you!" shouted the woman.

"As God lives it has!" cried the old man, and he leaped into the air with an exultant whoop that touched as with an electric spark the pent up enthusiasm of the spectators. No whirlwind in all its unbridled fury could have surpassed the storm of voices that followed this marvelous manifestation of power. The old man was the liveliest of the lot and sprang over benches, clapped his withered hands.

"Don't imagine I did it," shouted the revivalist, when the excitement had in a measure abated. "It was the Lord's work, and you must give all the glory to Him!"

At the next meeting a Mrs. Harris of Urbana, was carried into the tent. She had been a helpless paralytic for twenty years. They placed her emaciated form on a cot before the rail, and the scenes already described were repeated.

A Desperate Cancer Instantly Cured

"The success of this crucial test should convince you all," said the revivalist, "that God's power is present among you."

She then approached the cot and laid her hands upon the body of the helpless sufferer.

"Do you believe in God?" she asked.

"I do," came faintly from the half-closed lips.

"And if God assumes your malady, will you devote your remaining years of life to his holy service?"

"I will," replied the sufferer.

"Then, in God's name, get up and walk!" cried the revivalist lifting up her hands and falling upon her knees.

Amid breathless silence and what seemed an eternity of suspense, the woman slowly raised her head and then put it back on the pillow, as though doubtful of her power to move it farther.

"The Lord of heaven commands you to rise!" cried the evangelist, her eyes distended with nervous anticipation and beads of perspiration standing upon her forehead.

Mrs. Harris raised her head again, then putting out her hands, caught hold of the sides of the cot and raised herself to a sitting posture. She stared about her wildly for a moment, and then as though unconscious of what she was doing, put her feet on the floor and stood erect before the multitude.

The people surged forward to convince themselves of the thoroughness of the cure, but the revivalist, her enthusiasm breaking out anew, lifted the woman in her arms and bore her in triumph to the platform, where she placed her again upon her feet.

"Now help me to convert these people to God's banner," said she, "and let them see that you are grateful to the Almighty for the great good He has just done you."

If a surprise were possible after the marvel just witnessed, it was certainly provided by the outburst of eloquence with which Mrs. Harris began an appeal in behalf of religion. Persons of culture in the audience said they had never listened to sentiments more elevating expressed with such a wealth of word coloring. And this from a woman who had been helpless from childhood, whose mind must have shared the paralysis of her body, and who had certainly never acquired more than the meanest rudiments of learning. And yet, carried away with the inspiration of her theme, while tears of gratitude for her deliverance flowed copiously down her cheeks, she awakened anew the fervor of the audience while the revivalist stood aside, regarding her with an expression of seraphic satisfaction.

Mrs. Harris returned to her home completely restored to health and vigor and gave proof of her condition on Wednesday last by doing a good day's washing and ironing.

Another Miracle

Under like conditions a woman was cured of a cancer of the breast at the next meeting. A huge tumor had grown around the sore, and physicians had long before confessed their inability to cope with the disease. Surrendered by sentence to death, the woman had made all her arrangements for the grave, even to the selection of her shroud and coffin and the purchase of a burial plot. She was induced with difficulty to attend Mrs. Woodworth's revival, and while there, it is claimed, the religious fire found its way into her heart. She was among those who worked their way to the altar; and while kneeling there, the attention of Mrs. Woodworth was directed to her condition.

"Will you promise me never to take any more medicine, except what the Lord is about to give you?" asked the revivalist, as she approached the prostrate sufferer.

"I will," was the reply.

"Then, as I place my hand upon your breast, pray to God that He may free you from this awful scourge."

So saying, the revivalist undid the top buttons of the woman's dress, exposing to those within range the horrible cancer that was slowly eating its way into the woman's lungs, and fearlessly placed her hand over the loathsome sore.

"God be praised!" shouted the revivalist. "I feel it going! See!" She cried, "The lump has already grown less and now—now it has disappeared, and the cancer is healed forever!"

She drew away her hand, and the woman rose to her feet, and all around her convinced themselves that the cancer had disappeared. Dr. Fugatt, or Urbana, who had attended the woman and gave up her as hopeless, proclaimed the completeness of the cure, which he claimed was nothing short of the miraculous.

That the daily recurrence of feats such as these should have turned Urbana well nigh topsy-turvy, it is not difficult to comprehend, and it is equally reasonable to believe that the town, and the country around it, are still stirred up over the advent of this modern wonder.

The revival already begun under the white oaks near Boiling Springs is likely to equal the one just concluded. And as the fame of Mrs. Woodworth has preceded her, the afflicted in body as well as the weary of heart are beginning their pilgrimages to her forest shrine.

Mrs. Woodworth's Appearance

In an unpretentious farm house, within 50 yards of her canvas church, Mrs. Woodworth was found by a *Globe-Democrat* reporter yesterday. She is a spry, everyday sort of body with a good face, and fine blue eyes that fairly speak with enthusiasm. While she is not an educated woman in the literal sense, she has evidently read a great deal that was worth reading, and her command of language is certainly phenomenal. She talks steadily and earnestly, the words flowing from her tongue with perfect freedom. There is nothing in her manner that suggests cant,[3] while there is much that impresses one with her possession of strong magnetic force, the best uses of which she seems thoroughly to understand.

She is of medium height, rather slender, but evidently a woman of strong constitution and vigorous frame. Her movements are quick, graceful, and wiry, and she has a habit of walking right up to you and looking into your eyes as though she were reading your very soul. Her forehead is lofty and is prominent in the regions of ideality and veneration.[4] Of her voice, which while naturally soft and musical, has grown a trifle hard throughout the severe tests to which her religious fervor puts it, she seems to have almost perfect control, and from the highest pitch she can modulate it surprisingly when effect demands it. She is just the woman to excite her hearers without seeming to try, and in this respect she is conspicuously superior to the young revivalist, Harrison, whose gymnastic antics and unnatural outbursts fall flat from over-straining.

[3] "cant"—insincerity or hypocrisy (Webster's N. W. 1997).

[4] The writer is describing the shape of her head using terminology from the popular nineteenth-century belief in phrenology in which the bumps on certain areas of the head were thought to indicate certain character qualities and intellectual strengths.

"I was born," said Mrs. Woodworth in response to the reporter's question, "in New Lisbon, Columbiana County, July 22, 1845,[5] and was the fourth daughter of quite a large family of children. My parents were not Christians; therefore, I was left without the religious teachings and influence with which so many homes are blessed. My father and mother joined the Disciples church one year before my father's death, which occurred in July 1858. The death of my father was the first great sorrow of my life. He had gone away to harvest in his usual health, and I will never forget the night he was brought home. Some neighbor children and I were out watching a terrible storm raging when we observed two strangers approaching our house, leading a wagon upon which was my father's dead body. My mother was left destitute with eight children to provide for. My eldest sister and I had to leave home and work by the week. It was a hard blow to my sensitive mother, for I was home sick, and above all, wanted to go to school, for I longed for an education. Still I obtained some books and used to study in the kitchen while cooking the meals or washing the dishes. At the age of 13, I was converted to Christ at a Methodist revival; and shortly afterward, I had a dream in which I beheld a vision of surprising beauty.

Her Vision of Heaven

"I thought an angel came to me where I lay in sleep and conducted me to the gates of a great and beautiful city. Before the angel's approach the gates swung open and a flood of brilliant light poured forth upon us. For an instant I was quite blinded, but all was well in a moment, and I found myself walking along a great street paved with gold, on either side of which the castellated dwellings towered loftily, and their turrets, piercing the golden azure above them, were lost to view. Everything and everywhere about suggested infinity. There seemed to be no end to what I saw and no end to my wonder and enjoyment. Delightful music filled the perfumed air, and a sense of perfect peace and comfort pervaded everything. Trees laden with the richest fruit abounded and as I turned from

[5] "1845"—Maria Woodworth-Etter gave the date of 1844 in her autobiography, *A Diary of Signs and Wonders.*

right to left, new beauties met my eyes and scenes extended before me to describe [for] which language is far too poor.

"As I floated along I became conscious that I would see whenever or whatever I might wish to see. I thought of my father and of my little brothers and sisters who had died, and instantly they were clustered about me. We went to the banks of a broad and beautiful river, whose windings were occasionally lost amid hills of coated green, only to creep forth again from their hiding and flow on forever in the vast expanse. Turning, I saw a Great White Throne, from which great rockets shot forth as from the sun. They were of endless variety and their colors prismatic. Presently I saw myriads of white winged angels approach the throne from every direction, and when they had reached it I saw the God of heaven, in his snow-white robes and crowned with glory's halo, step forth from the blaze of light and seat Himself. Then the angels began to sing, and I heard God, in great thunder tones that sounded loud and deep through the mighty chorus, proclaim His wish that I would go forth among the people of the earth and preach the Gospel of His dearly beloved Son. Then I awoke and found myself on my garret cot, but the music of the angels was still in my ears, and the voice of the Master reverberated through the room.

She Sees the Savior

"After this I dreamt frequently, and my dreams were nearly always accompanied with visions. Once I saw Christ as plainly as I see you now, and while He was near me I was conscious that it was only a dream. He said to me: 'You are chosen to preach My Word and must be up and at work. As My apostles did, so must you do, for I would have you heal the body of him whose soul you have already healed.'

"That was my last vision, and I have, since then, followed the Savior's command. It is through Him that I do whatever it is that I do. I am but a worm in His mighty hands."

Mrs. Woodworth said all this in a perfectly natural way that carried with it at least the conviction that she thoroughly believed all she was saying.

"Have you ever failed in your efforts to heal the afflicted?" asked the reporter.

"Never," she replies, confidently. "I cannot fail while God is with me. Personally, I could accomplish nothing, but to Him all things are possible; therefore, when I put my hands upon a sufferer and tell him or her to rise, I know that if the sufferer has faith in Christ, he will be cured. This is the plain truth, and it has ever been so since the night Christ commanded me to go forth and heal the sick."

"Will you visit St. Louis soon?"

"Such is my intention," replied Mrs. Woodworth, "and, by the way, I can tell you of a remarkable cure the Lord permitted me to bring about in the person of one of your townswomen. While in Indianapolis two years ago, a Mrs. Cobbs of St. Louis was brought to one of our meetings in a dying condition. Her trouble was cancer of the throat and lungs, and the doctors had given her up. She was not of a religious bent, and I told her I could do nothing for her unless she espoused the cause of Christ and promised to devote her remaining days to His exaltation. At the next meeting she professed religion and was so earnest that I concluded, if it were God's will, to help her. Placing my hands upon her troubled part, I told her to put her faith in God and that instantly the cancer would leave her.

A St. Louis Woman's Life Saved

"In a moment she raised her eyes, that were overflowing with tears, and, in a loud, clear voice, declared that the pain had left her and that she was cured. This was true, for upon examination, the cancer was found to have disappeared.

"Mrs. Cobbs had been quite a singer before the affliction came upon her and destroyed her voice, but now her voice returned in all its former beauty, and even at the meeting which brought her cure, she got upon the platform and sang several hymns in a manner that was certainly angelic. I have heard some lovely voices in my time, but no one could ever have sung so divinely. She kept her promise, too, and she and her husband are now engaged in earnest revival work."

The minister at Boiling Springs and the people thereabouts are firm in their conviction that Mrs. Woodworth is sincere in all her professions, that her cures are giant testimonials of her power, and that her interpretation of the Scriptures and wonderful facility of speech indicate the presence of inspiration.

September 14, 1887

The Church Advocate

From Urbana, Illinois

he *St. Louis Daily Globe-Democrat* published a dispatch dated August 30th, in which it was stated that the "faith-healer's camp-meeting here drew a vast crowd and created unusual interest today in the tabernacle. In the forenoon three prominent lawyers and eight well-known businessmen made addresses, one of them, Judge West, of Andersonville, Ind., affirming that he had been soundly cured of consumption by Mrs. Woodworth by prayer last winter.

"In the afternoon Mrs. Woodworth administered the ordinance of baptism by immersion to twenty-two converts, in Crystal Lake. The administration of baptism by a lady drew out over four thousand people to witness the impressive scenes. Great enthusiasm prevails in her meetings."

The Church Advocate was a Church of God publication.

September 14, 1887

The Church Advocate

Church Intelligence

From Urbana, Illinois

ne week ago Sister Woodworth finished a four weeks' meeting in our place. The first week but few attended her meetings, as the tongue of slander had been busy. Sister W. paid no attention to anything that was said. At the end of the second week, the tabernacle, which holds two thousand, was filled. At the end of her meetings, the crowd could not one-half get inside. Such an interest in religion was never known in this county. Nearly one hundred were converted to God. On Sabbath[1] before she left she baptized twenty-three in a stream near town. Three or four thousand witnessed the ceremony. Sister W. left many friends who can never forget her or to pray for her. The Woodworth converts, as we are all called, hold prayer meetings twice a week, and the house is crowded nightly. Even the old Christians of the place are crowding into these meetings, saying they are much better than their own prayer meetings.

God has done great work in sending Sister Woodworth and her helpers among us. We are praying for her return to our city and will not be comforted until our prayers are answered. I certainly have cause to rejoice, for I am one of the converts.

— S. I. Busey

Urbana, Ill., Sept. 7th

[1] "Sabbath"—Sunday.

November 25, 1887

Marion Chronicle (IN)

Repudiated by Her Church

rs. Maria B. Woodworth, the trance evangelist, has been stabbed in the house of her friends. Recently an official meeting of the Church of God, to which denomination she belongs, adopted the following, which is printed in the *Church Advocate,* of Harrisburg, Pa., the official organ of the sect:

> We regard sister M. B. Woodworth as an earnest worker; that souls have been converted under her labors, but that many of her interpretations of Scripture are misleading; that her manner of practicing the healing art is unscriptural and deceptive; that her act of allowing a deaf man to anoint her and kiss her feet in imitation of her Lord receiving divine honors is sacrilegious and without excuse; that hawking books and selling tobacco on the Sabbath day is injurious to Christianity; and on the whole that the work of Mrs. Woodworth is more detrimental than beneficial.

June 14, 1888

The Decatur Daily Republican (IL)

Mrs. Woodworth in a Trance

There were highly sensational features yesterday in connection with the faith-cure camp meeting at Oakland Park. After an exciting forenoon meeting, Mrs. Woodworth fell over in a trance in her living tent and remained in a prostrate condition with both arms above her head nearly the entire afternoon. Her condition excited no special alarm to her attendants, but the people at the afternoon meeting were greatly concerned about her and wondered if she would recover. She did and was at her post in the evening to deliver one of her earnest sermons.

Yesterday two aged ladies from the country were assisted to the tent, both suffering with a severe spinal disease. Both professed to be cured through faith and walked off without assistance.

M. G. Bear, from Shelby County, totally blind in one eye and nearly so in the other, professed to have had his sight restored.

A Polish woman, apparently a great sufferer, professed to have been made whole, soul and body, through faith. Her demonstrations created a great commotion.

Mrs. Woody, the wife of a prominent citizen of Champaign, was carried to the tent in a helpless condition, suffering with chronic rheumatism. She said she was cured instantly while the evangelist was invoking the divine blessing.

One of the ladies caused considerable merriment after being blessed at the altar. She declared joyfully: "Previous to today I have been obliged to sleep with my clothes on at night when no one was present to assist me to disrobe, but now, bless God, I expect to strip and go to bed like a human being."

July 12, 1888

Springfield Journal (IL)

At Oak Ridge

Continued Interest in the Faith Cure Meetings of Mrs. Woodworth

he meetings at Oak Ridge Park all day yesterday were of a grand and glorious character. A number of people from Jacksonville, Chicago, and from the southern part of the state, as well as a large number of Springfield people, were in attendance on (*sic*) the meeting. The interest in the meetings continues to increase, and many seekers for soul and bodily healing are to be seen at each meeting. Mrs. Woodworth spoke in the afternoon from a number of passages from the book of Luke. She cited many instances wherein Jesus rebuked devils and made whole the bodies of those possessed therewith. Satan afflicts the people, and God permits it because of our disobedience to His laws, and through lack of faith Satan hugs these [people] about and many times when driven from the heart takes refuge in the body. But his body can be cleansed as well as the soul if we come in God's way and give Him the glory. God gave the disciples, through Him, the power of healing the sick; and God's Word is the same today and forever.

The most remarkable cure of the day was that of the little 10-year-old daughter of Mrs. Hewit of Riverton, who was afflicted with a spinal disease. The child had taken no nourishment for the past four months, except a little milk and peanut candy, and had not been able to walk or even sit alone for that length of time. The little girl was after a short season of prayer able to walk around the tent, and instead of being carried out, as she came in, she walked by the side of her parents. Many other cures were affected. Mr. and Mrs. Woodworth are assisted in their meetings by Rev. Wm. Worley, from the eastern part of the state.

July 13, 1888

Daily Illinois State Journal

Cured by Faith

Persons at the Oak Ridge Meetings Testify to the Good Work of Mrs. Woodworth

he tent at Oak Ridge Park was crowded yesterday and very interesting and [earnest meetings?] were held, the earnestness increasing with each meeting. And Mrs. Woodworth feels very much encouraged from the support given her by the Christian workers of Springfield. The altar at every service is filled with seekers, most of whom are confident that through their faith, it is possible to be healed. Mrs. Woodworth talks to her congregations in an earnest manner, and that she impresses them is shown by their constant attendance upon the meetings.

The Mr. Rev. Silverson of Indianapolis, gave a very interesting and instructive talk and advised generally in the meeting. There were a large number of persons who claimed they were thoroughly healed and gave testimony to that effect. Among these were Francis F. Howard of West Springfield, who had been lame for years but who seemed to walk with perfect ease after an earnest prayer. A colored man from Jacksonville who had been partially blind declared that he could now read the Word of God, something he had not done for three years past. All manner of diseases are presented for healing, and much good work is being done by Mrs. Woodworth and assistants.

Maria Woodworth-Etter in a typical pose she often held in trances, pointing to heaven. Sometimes she was held for hours by The Holy Spirit with one hand pointing to heaven and one pointing down to hell, an unsettling, but persuasive, argument to her hearers about their need to make a choice.

July 25, 1888

Daily Illinois State Journal

Faith Cure

THE WOODWORTH MEETINGS AT OAK RIDGE PARK—MRS. WOODWORTH'S METHODS—ALLEGED CASES OF HEALING—STATEMENTS OF BELIEVERS AND NON-BELIEVERS

Mrs. Woodworth's meetings at Oak Ridge Park, continue to attract large crowds. Yesterday afternoon the *Journal* reporter was present. The number of horses and carriages standing just outside showed a very considerable attendance from a distance, and numbers went out on the streetcars. Mrs. Woodworth is a very pleasant speaker, quite demonstrative in her manner, graceful, too, in her gestures, easy and fluent in her style of address, and has excellent control of her audience.

After a short sermon, those who desired to be healed were requested to come forward. Quite a large number came out. Mrs. Woodworth passed down the line of invalids, talking to one after another, encouraging them to have faith, and assuring them that that alone was needed to ensure their being made well. She was assisted by a number of helpers, some of whom were said to have been healed at previous meetings. During all this time singing was continued, led by someone up on the platform, except that occasionally Mrs. Woodworth would call on one or more to pray.

After perhaps an hour of this work, the audience, who had gathered up as close as possible to see what was doing,[1] were requested to sit down, and testimony was called for from those who had been seeking to be healed. The first to respond was a man from the country who said he had a very severe pain in his leg, yesterday and this morning before coming here, and had been troubled for many years with rheumatism, but now he was healed. His knee felt numb and stiff, but the pain was all gone. Then a young lady, residing in or near the city, rose and said she had been afflicted with deafness and had been treated without success by specialists, but she was now healed and her hearing was good. Then an elderly lady, who

[1] "what was doing"—what was happening.

had long suffered from chronic rheumatism and whose hands and fingers were much misshapen from the effects of the disease and by no means as flexible as they might be, rose and told how much better she felt and how perfectly free from pain. And as she was phasing on from expressions of gratitude for her recovery to what seemed likely to be an extended exhortation, Mrs. Woodworth, who had been standing by her with an arm rather carelessly thrown around her, relieved the situation by starting a song in which the audience generally joined. After this there were more testimonies, and the meeting closed with the benediction, which was pronounced by Mrs. Brewington, a young colored woman who had taken quite a prominent part in the singing throughout the meeting.

Opinions are much divided as to the character of the work that is done. "A boy who lives near me," said one man to a reporter, "was brought here to be cured of lameness. He had one foot injured so that a piece of the bone was taken out. His limb was bent and he walked with a crutch, just touching the leg of the lame foot to the ground. He was taken forward, they talked and worked with him a while, and they told him to get up and walk and tell them that the Lord had healed him. He walked as before and hobbles on a crutch yet."

Another man living in Springfield said: "Yes, I believe it.[2] I went out without any confidence at all in the reports. I saw a man over 90 years old, who had not walked for 8 years on account of rheumatism, and was brought to the tent on a litter, got up and walked about. I had to believe."

A lady pointed to another in the front end of the car and said: "She was taken out there so crippled by rheumatism that she had to be helped on the car. She was cured, and now she goes about easily and gets off and on the car alone."

Another said: "There was a girl 11 years old, deaf and dumb from birth, taken to the meetings a few days ago and healed so that she got up and talked. She had never used her voice and didn't know how to use it properly, but she did talk."

---

[2] i.e., that the cures are real.

There is much interest felt in the meetings. Many are coming from a long distance. Some of these who testified yesterday to having been greatly benefited came from St. Louis, Waverly, Chatham, and other places.

July 26, 1888

Daily Illinois State Journal

The Faith Cure

The Oak Ridge Park Meetings — Incidents of Yesterday's Service

he crowd at Oak Ridge Park yesterday afternoon, notwithstanding the heat of the weather, seemed rather larger than the day before. Mrs. Woodworth preached a short sermon in which she insisted strongly that the sick could be healed now as they were in the apostolic age of the church, if they would only have faith. She took occasion to pay her respects to ministers and church members in Springfield who refused to believe the work that was being done at her meetings and expressed an earnest wish that they would come and see for themselves. When those who desired "to be healed, soul and body," were asked to come forward, quite a large number presented themselves at the mourners' bench. Mrs. Woodworth and her assistants passed among them exhorting, encouraging, and laboring with them. During this time there was almost constant singing by those on the platform and in the audience of some of the old-time revival songs such as:

> When I was a mourner, just like you,
> I mourned and prayed till I got through.
> Glory, hallelujah, etc.

And —

> I'm born of God, I know I am;
> Do you deny it if you can?
> Glory, hallelujah!
> When I passed by the gates of hell,

I bade old Satan a long farewell.
Glory, hallelujah, etc.[1]

There were several conversions reported of those who were not suffering from physical disease. Among those professing to receive healing was Thomas Terrell, son of a merchant of Easton, Mason County, 17 years of age, and fearfully crippled and enfeebled by chronic rheumatism. Mrs. Woodworth talked and worked with him for some time. The increasing color in his face showed a quickening circulation; he seemed to gain strength and, after a short time, rose and walked with a little aid, which he had long been entirely unable to do. He said that he felt much better and was confident that he would be entirely healed.

Mr. Thomas A. Ragsdale, a well-known citizen of Springfield, who has been suffering from a serious complication of chronic diseases, said he was much benefited.

A young lady said she had been healed of a tumor in her nose, from which she had suffered for seven years.

A Christian Scientist who was present believed the cures genuine and attributed them to the principles of Christian Science.

[1] Hymn and composer unknown.

December 7, 1888

Daily Illinois State Journal

Faith-Cure Folks

THE REMARKABLE MEETINGS IN PROGRESS AT ELECTRIC LIGHT HALL

here was a great crowd at Electric Light Hall at last night's faith-cure meeting. There were a large number of cases of conversions and ecstatic prostration and four cases of reported miraculous healing. One of the latter was a violent case of rheumatism. One of the remarkable recent cases of healing is this: On last election day, Oliver Hall, who lives on Miller Street, between Ninth and Tenth, had an arm broken in a difficulty at the polls. It is alleged that Tom Brewer broke it, and Hall has a suit now pending on that account against Brewer for damages. Tuesday night last, it is stated, Hall went to the faith-cure meeting carrying the broken arm in a sling. He was converted and the arm was healed. He took off the sling, threw it away, and swung the arm around recklessly showing the audience that it had been made whole as the other. The instances of overpowering are so numerous that the regular attendants think nothing of seeing a half-dozen laid out on the floor at a time, as stiff as pokers. Mrs. Woodworth is making things hum, and the hall is now too small for the crowds. There are constant additions to the band, and next Sunday, at 3 o'clock, there will be public immersion of new members, in the Sangamon River, at the classical spot known as Chincapin Hill.

July 1, 1889

Springfield Journal (IL)

The Faith Cure Band

How a Lady Told Her Experience of a Change of Heart

THE INAUGURATION OF OPEN-AIR MEETINGS IN OAK RIDGE PARK

A curious experience was brought to light yesterday afternoon at the first of the summer meetings of the faith-cure band. During an intermission, a group of attentive listeners gathered about a lady who was seated beneath one of the many large, white oak trees in the Oak Ridge Park, and she told them how she first experienced the power. She had been very anxious for it for days, she said, but had no idea of what it was to be. One day she went with her family to stay all day in the park, took a basket of provisions, and a number of bananas that she purchased the day before for the children. She was not fond of bananas herself and rarely ate them, but on this occasion her appetite was good and she tried one. The meeting was opened, and in a little while she began to have a very queer sensation in her stomach. She wondered what on earth she could have eaten, and presently she thought of the bananas and vowed she would never touch the "pesky things" again. Still she sat, thinking every minute she would have to leave, but she suddenly grew worse and to use her own words, "Sure as you live, I had the power and it wasn't the bananas at all." She had to acknowledge that at first symptoms, she "couldn't tell the difference between the bananas and the Holy Ghost," but she has been fond of the banana ever since.

Mrs. Woodworth's arrival in the city was the occasion for a stir among the leaders of the faith, but the Sunday announcement of the meeting seemed not to have reached the public, and the general attendance was not equal to the usual open-air gatherings. Mrs. Woodworth preached an earnest sermon of about an hour's length, during which Miss Annie Matthews, who lives with Engineer Darrah and is well-known here, went into a trance. In about 20 minutes she came out again and seemed perfectly happy. She is an intelligent young lady, very frank in her confessions in regard to the working of the power, and free in the expression of her belief. This is not the first time she has had the power. She attended Mrs. Woodworth's meetings in the hall last winter with friends who went with her from curiosity and had no belief whatever in the faith cure. On the night of January 16, she was overcome, and although she was brought up a Catholic, she has been a firm believer in Mrs. Woodworth's doctrine.

Something over a month ago, the child of a neighbor was sick, nigh unto death. Several physicians had given the child up and said that nothing more could be done. The ladies of the faith cure went one night and prayed for the child. The father, though he would give everything for his child, had no faith in their prayers. They told him he must believe if the child was to be saved, and he promised that he would, and the next morning the child got up and dressed itself. The man, however, has never repented. On the 28th of last month, Miss Matthews had a vision and was notified that she must fast. This she did and her mouth was as if sealed. She had been troubled with heart disease and often fell on the street with blood in her mouth. Until June 16 she neither spoke nor tasted food. At this time she was released from her fast, and since then she has not had a symptom of heart trouble. It has been revealed to her that, inasmuch as the father of the child above referred to has not repented, she expects that the child will be taken away some time soon.

After the sermon, a lady named Miss Atterbury, who lives in (*sic*) the family of Mr. W. P. Crafton, went into a trance. She stood rigid for three-quarters of an hour, with hands trembling and uplifted. It required the strength of two people to place her in a chair. After an hour she came out of the trance, opened her eyes, wiped her face, and looked around in a quiet, natural way, but was seized again and with one shaking hand uplifted, sat with closed eyes and the expression of death on her face.

In the evening the attendance was much larger. Mrs. Woodworth preached a very impressive sermon on "Weighed in the Balance and Found Wanting." She is a fluent speaker, continually walks from one side of the platform to the other, and keeps her arms in constant motion. When the meeting closed, a regular old-fashioned revival ensued and a number got the "power." The meetings will be continued during the week.

July 2, 1889

Daily Illinois State Journal

Annie Had the Power

And Made the Faith-Cure Meeting Rather Lively

SHE MONOPOLIZED MOST OF THE BUSINESS OF THE EVENING HERSELF

nnie Mathews monopolized the meeting in the faith-cure tent to such an extent last night that the effect almost made Mrs. Woodworth sick. The amateur performances of the young lady were quite startling and constituted the only redeeming feature of the performance for those who went to see a circus. Annie is punctual in attendance and a devoted adherent to the cause. Long before Mrs. Woodworth had finished her excellent sermon, Annie felt the power. While this was an encouraging symptom, it came near being disastrous. She has peculiar symptoms that differ from those of anyone else who has been affected by Mrs. Woodworth's magic influence.

Annie stood for a while near the platform with eyes and arms raised heavenward. Then she hurried through the crowd for a distance of fifteen feet and stopped. She seemed to gaze intently at something in the top of the tent as she swayed backward, forward, and sideways. Presently, she took another sudden start over chairs and the rough plank seats, the crowd giving way and scattering in every direction. Those behind watched intently lest she should step between the seats while she was looking upward and apparently giving no heed to her footsteps. The anxious spectators were not disappointed for before she reached the edge of the tent, she made a misstep and took a fearful fall among the rough board seats. Then the excitement increased; people gathered around her by the score to see if she had killed herself. Her clothing was of course disarranged, and she presented a pitiable aspect at which the ungodly giggled. A number of those present assisted in arranging her garments, placed two planks together, and got her laid out.

Suddenly, Annie sprang up again and made a start for the open air. Out she went into the darkness, men, women, and children fleeing as if she were some mad person. This nearly broke up the meeting, as fully three-fourths of the audience gathered around Annie to see what she would do next. The men folks were especially "leery" of her and were determined to keep out of her clutches. While she was out in the park, there was more hilarity than was becoming a religious body. Once she tried to sing, but as a songstress, it cannot be said that Annie is a sweet warbler.

After a brief hour of this greensward entertainment, during which Mrs. Woodworth had to labor hard to preserve the meeting, Annie took a spasmodic whirl and started back for the stand. Occasionally she would stop and with arms raised, would lean backward until her head came within a foot or two of the ground. After remaining in that position a full minute she would rise gracefully, with apparent ease, proving herself an accomplished contortionist as well as an expert powerist. Two young men, who seemed to have become satisfied that she was tame and harmless, accompanied her on the return trip through the benches, as a bodyguard. Occasionally, she whirled gracefully round and round proving that at some time in the sweet gone by, she had indulged in the wicked waltz. When she got back to the stand, the crowd was with her, but the hour had grown late. Mrs. Woodworth looked discouraged, probably from the fact that Annie had monopolized the meeting, and she dismissed the audience with the announcement that there will be services this afternoon and evening.

July 29, 1889

Daily Illinois State Journal

A Faith-Cure Dedication

THE BAND OF WORKERS SECURES A PLACE OF WORSHIP

The Result of a Remarkable Series of Peculiar Religious Meetings

The long season of earnest work by Mrs. Woodworth culminated last night in a time of rejoicing by the congregation of the "Church of God." It had been announced that the church would be dedicated yesterday morning at 10 o'clock, but it was found best that the indebtedness should be raised or provided for before the consecration of the building to holy worship. At the morning meeting Mrs. Woodworth preached a [strong?] sermon, taking her text from the fourteenth chapter of St. John, twenty-one and thirty-one verses. This was followed by a stirring address by Col. Felter, urging subscriptions for the liquidation of the balance due, which was about sixteen hundred dollars. A large collection was taken, but the Colonel said it was not enough. Then Mr. Thomas Lake, who has been very liberal in his donations, authorized the announcement that if ten persons would give ten dollars each, he would add one hundred dollars. This was done and nine hundred dollars was secured. It was then agreed to wait until three o'clock in the afternoon to proceed with the ceremony.

The audience gathered again in the afternoon and Mrs. Woodworth preached from the sixty-first Psalm, second verse. The dedication services were again postponed until evening. By eight o'clock the church was crowded and hundreds went away, not being able to find room inside the church. Meantime, several other amounts had been pledged; and the trustees agreed to take upon themselves the responsibility of raising the rest of the money, and the ceremony proceeded. Col. Felter made the address and Mrs. Woodworth offered the dedicatory prayer, which, in this society, is the principal feature.

The congregation is now happily located and is in a very thrifty condition. The meetings will be held regularly in the evenings, during the week, at Oak Ridge Park, to which all are invited. Mrs. Woodworth has declined an invitation to go to Chicago but will hold a series of meetings there next winter after her return from

California, to which place she will soon go to work up the interest on the Pacific coast.

Mrs. Woodworth's first work in this city was in June 1888. In the November following, she returned and held nightly meetings until the first of last February. Shortly before the close of this series, the subject of building a house of worship was first discussed. By the first of May, the plans for the building and for raising the funds were matured, and the work of erecting a building on Third and Dodge streets was commenced. Mr. Bechtel, in the absence of Mrs. Woodworth, had the congregation in charge and regular services were held. It was Mr. Bechtel who drew nearly all the plans and constructed the building, and to him is due great credit for the success of the society.

The building is forty feet in width by seventy-eight feet in length, including [a] vestibule and a recess for the pulpit, and will seat over six hundred persons. The auditorium is nicely carpeted and provided with chairs. The pulpit has a Brussels carpet and is furnished with a handsome sofa. The ceiling slopes to the center and the windows are of cathedral glass. Over the pulpit are the words: "Welcome, Church of God." The cost of the edifice is three thousand besides the lot, which cost about six hundred dollars. Mrs. Woodworth has been in the city since July 1, holding meetings in Oak Ridge Park. The services have been attended with an increasing interest, and all that Mrs. Woodworth has undertaken has been accomplished under very embarrassing circumstances.

November 21, 1889

Oakland Daily Evening Tribune (CA)

In a Tent

Cures by Faith, by Prayer, and by Science

The Belle Cured of White Swelling and the Cartridge That Exploded in the Stove

"The Lord did not come to the tent. The Lord was already there," said F. J. Wood, one of the ushers at the tent of the Union Camp Meeting, now in progress on San Pablo Avenue, near Twenty-sixth Street. Wood formerly was a member of the Salvation Army and for a time was a special police officer. A conflict of authority occurred between him and Special Officer Ross, and Wood's star was taken from him by the same power that gave him authority to wear it.

Wood was answering questions in the police court about the proceedings in the tent. On Sunday night last, the proceedings were not altogether orderly. During a solemn part of the services, straw about a stove was discovered to be on fire. A little while later a detonation sounded in another stove, and the stove doors were blown open. The noise sounded to the worshippers as though a cartridge had exploded in the stove. During a season of absolute quiet, devoted to silent prayer, whispering was heard, and giggling interrupted the petitions to the throne of grace. Usher Wood saw two boys, Lyle McKey and Noble Davis, and he believed they had some association with the mysterious fire in the straw, with the startling explosion in the stove, and that from their mouths had issued the sounds that disturbed the blessed season of silent prayer. He arrested them and gave them into the custody of Police Officer Turney.

Strange stories of healing by instruments other than potion and bandage and knife are not uncommon at this climacteric in the progress of intellectual development. Hiram P. Brown, an attorney at law of this city, a believer in the book of Mormon, but not a polygamist, is a zealous man and with deep emotion he tells of an event in Sacramento within his own experience. Once when addressing a congregation and about to end his discourse, a telegram handed him announced the illness unto death of a beloved member of the church in Virginia City. A strange feeling of enthusiasm and strength possessed him. With rigorous impression he exclaimed, "We can heal this brother. Let us pray that he may be healed," and they all prayed. "He will be here on this platform next Sunday night," said Mr. Brown after the prayer, as though relating a supernatural communication. The next Sunday evening the brother who had been ill unto death was on the platform at Sacramento well and thankful.

Mr. Brown also tells of faithful prayer restoring to strength and beauty a shriveled and wasted arm like that of the emperor of Germany.

Many people, among them many of intellect and heart, have implicit faith in cures accomplished by the means commonly called Christian Science treatment. A lady of this city, intelligent and earnest, a devout member of an evangelical religious association, the wife of a man of distinction, believes with all her devout heart that her beautiful young daughter, who recently made her debut in the best society here, was cured of the distressing malady, white swelling, by the Christian Science treatment. A story is told of a lady in San Francisco who recovered a lost eye by this treatment.

The boys, Lyle McKey and Noble Davis, were convicted by Judge Laidlaw of disturbing a meeting held for religious worship.

November 30, 1889

Oakland Daily Evening Tribune (CA)

A Timely Call

On the Authorities of the City of Oakland

To Suppress the Disgraceful Exhibitions of Voodooism in a Tent on Twelfth Street

EDITOR *TRIBUNE* —

Is it not high time that the authorities interfered to put an end to the disgraceful exhibition now going on in the tent on Twelfth and Webster streets under the cloak of religion? O religion, how many crimes are committed in thy name! These physical manifestations are of the same low order which characterizes the African voodoo, the frenzied leaps and gushings of the Mohammedan dervishes, and the delirium of the Indian medicine man. That they are superinduced by some hypnotic power on the part of the woman who is at the head of this show is altogether probable. By what right does she give such exhibitions for profit, without a license? The spectacle of a lot of cataleptic men and women howling and rolling about in physical excitement or lying rigid with nervous hysteria is sickening and debasing. Above all, the presence of 6-year-old babes in a fit, lying with glassy eyes and clenched muscles, is a sight to make heaven weep.

It should be put a stop to at once as not only harmful to the health of the community, but prejudicial to good morals and an insult to spiritual Christianity. Its continuance is a greater discredit to the fair fame of our city for intelligence and order than a score of opium joints and a hundred additional saloons. As a citizen of Oakland, I call upon Mayor Glascock, or whoever is charged with the duty, to suppress the nuisance.

CHARLES W. WENDTE

STUDY FIRST UNITARIAN CHURCH

OAKLAND, NOVEMBER 30, 1889

December 2, 1889

Oakland Daily Evening Tribune (CA)

He Disagrees

With Brother Wendte About the Tent Manifestations

The Early Methodist—Not an insult to Spiritual Christianity—What He Saw

EDITOR *TRIBUNE*—

I arise to protest against the spirit of an article in your paper of November 30th, by Rev. Mr. Wendte, asking the mayor of Oakland to suppress the religious exercises held in a tent on Twelfth and Webster streets. It is remarkable for its seeming uncharitableness, coming as it does from an eminent Unitarian divine, who represents a people of great religious liberality and unbounded charity. Is it possible that the mayor would at such a request trample upon religious liberty and violate the most sacred rights vouchsafed to the American people? These people are rather entitled to the protection of the law. These people who worship in that tent are citizens of Oakland, good and true, as well as neighbors of Brother Wendte, and have a legal right there. Their only crime seems to be that of having the jerks, nervous hysteria, etc., so extravagantly set forth as caused by the subtle powers of the woman, according to the brother. If there was a little more of this power which makes this tent resound with the shouts of "Glory to God for My Salvation," scattered around Oakland, there would be a grand religious revival in less than a week that would rival the outpouring of the Pentecost.

It is hard to get at the full meaning of Brother Wendte's saying: "O religion, how many crimes are committed in thy name!" The tent services are not a violation of civil law or morality. If he means this, the proof was not set forth to make a sure case. If all of these physical exhibitions in this tent are caused by the mesmeric power of this *"woman"* in charge, then what powerful hypnotists must have been the greatest evangelists of the early Methodist and other churches of America—under whose preaching, "Men and women have howled and rolled" and shouted and were entranced—had the power—and thousands brought to the light of truth and reformation. The persecutions of the early Methodists for what this brother would put out these tent folk has made them the strongest in America save one—the Catholics.

The subject of friend Wendte's last paragraph is astounding and teems with a spirit that is hardly becoming so really good a man. It is that these tent meetings are an "insult to spiritual Christianity," and greater, "a discredit to our fair city . . . than a score of opium joints or one hundred additional saloons." As if, forsooth, in a tent for worship where hundreds meet daily to breathe in spiritualistic truths instead of fumes of a poison drug and when prayer is substituted for profanity and the communion with the spirit of truth is substituted for the whisky and demoralization drained through a hundred extra saloons—is certainly a strongly drawn picture in favor of these saloons—against the hundreds of prayerful efforts for temperance and reformation.

I belong to no church—I have visited these meetings (Have you, brother Wendte?) and tried to be honest and fair. Last Friday, I sat in the midst of this prayerful and exceedingly noisy throng in the tent and listened to the testimony of converts; and while I confess that some might be pretending and all the rest of the hypnotizing by the preacher as claimed might come to naught, her influence over one man and his conversion and reformation, as told by himself, would hardly be less creditable to Oakland than the one hundred additional places of vice.

This man's own story was that for years he had been a drunken debaucher, driven from the home of wealthy and highly respectable parents in San Francisco, disowned and dishonored, that by an irresistible power he was drawn to this tent. The words of the preacher burned deep, and he came under this power and awoke to new life with appetite for whisky and tobacco all gone. It was a temperance lecture worth more than the condensed virtue of ten thousand saloons and opium joints, worth more to the cause of temperance and good order than all the prohibition laws the crankiest could make. Cure the appetite and we abolish the saloons.

W. C. Potter

516 Twentieth Street, Oakland

December 2, 1889

December 3, 1889

Oakland Daily Evening Tribune (CA)

The Blazing Signal Over Mrs. Woodworth

The Manifestations in the Tent

Four victims Overcome by the Alleged "Influence"—The Agent Says Mrs. Woodworth Must Leave

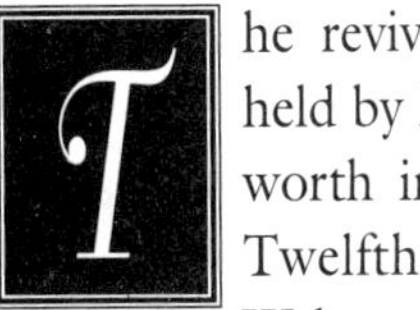

he revival meetings held by Mrs. Woodworth in a tent on Twelfth and Webster streets are attracting larger crowds than ever. Last evening the tent was crowded to the doors, and before the time for service arrived, crowds were turned away. The meeting last night was more exciting then usual. Mrs. Woodworth delivered a sermon on the "Power of the Holy Ghost." She dwelt at length on "Signs and Wonders" and told many remarkable stories. She related that on one occasion in the East while she was conducting a meeting, the ground beneath them shook in a fearful manner. The audience became so frightened that they fell upon their faces and cried aloud to God to save them. On another occasion a lady was talking to the audience when suddenly she fell to the floor and became unconscious. After she recovered she related that while she was talking, she saw the hand of God pointing out three men on one side of the house and two on the other. They were lost. The gate of heaven had been closed against them.

"A lady told me the other night," said Mrs. Woodworth, "that while I was preaching on this stand, she saw a sword of fire hanging over my head. Another lady told me that she had seen beautiful stars over my head. Oh, I tell you, my good people, the power of the Holy Ghost is with us. God is here and is going to make Himself felt. I expect every night to see some of these signs. While I am standing on this platform, I can see emissaries of the devil in the audience trying to stop me from telling the truth. But they can't do it. I have the power to overcome them. Glory to God. Hallelujah. Praise the Lord."

Mrs. Woodworth then invited all those who desired to be saved to kneel at the altar. About thirty people responded and fell upon their knees. Then the praying, crying, and yelling commenced. Men and women wrung their hands and yelled as if in the greatest agony. A crowd of people had gathered around them to see the extraordinary demonstrations. Pandemonium reigned. Presently a man who was praying fell to the straw, unconscious. The crowds pushed nearer. He had been overcome by the "influence." As if dead, he lay upon the cold ground, and with much difficulty kept his eyes closed under the glare of the electric light. Another chap pawed wildly at the air, as if in a vain endeavor to climb the golden stair. His contortions were pitiful to see. Finally he fell backward, a victim of the "influence."

Another man passed quietly under the "influence" while kneeling. Then a helper of Mrs. Woodworth led in prayer; and before she completed her little speech, she was under the "influence" and was laid out on the platform, her arms upstretched. The yelling of the saved ones sounded like the yells of a thousand wild men turned loose. The crowd laughed and joked, and Mrs. Woodworth suggested that she was not conducting a "circus." The praying was over, the sinners were saved, and quiet was once again restored. The "subjects" under the "influence" were raised from the ground and placed upon the platform. Mrs. Woodworth invited the audience to pass and look at them but admonished the people not to touch the "subjects," as it greatly disturbed them. No outsider was allowed to remain in the tent while the "subjects" came to.

G. G. Baker, the agent for the property, stepped up after the meeting and notified the people that they would have to move away. He was promptly fired out.[1] Collections are taken up every evening and books sold, and by this means the lady who has this great "influence" turns many a penny.

[1] "fired out"—escorted off the premises.

December 9, 1889

Oakland Daily Evening Tribune (CA)

Dr. Bothwell's Critic

Rev. D. E. Johnson on Mrs. Woodworth's Show

ev. D. E. Johnson, pastor of the African Methodist Church on Fifteenth Street, expressed himself freely and forcibly last night in criticizing Dr. Bothwell's recently published article entitled a "Pious Fraud."

The article referred to was a severe denunciation of Mrs. Woodworth and her meetings, calling upon the mayor to suppress them and the papers to cry them down.

Mr. Johnson said he had attended those meetings probably oftener (*sic*) than any other minister in town and had exerted his influence to encourage her. By so doing he supposed he had exposed himself to the doctor's ban and must be rated as one of the fools.

Nevertheless he regarded it ill befitting in Dr. Bothwell to criticize those meetings so sharply. His time and labor would be much better spent asking the mayor and the papers to cry down and suppress the numerous dens of infamy known to exist in Oakland.

It might be true, as Dr. Bothwell had said, that Mrs. Woodworth is ignorant of history, literature, doctrine, and Scripture. Notwithstanding this she has come to Oakland unannounced, has been opposed by the devil, some saloon keepers, and some divines—and yet draws greater audiences than any minister in town without the aid of a fine choir and organ.

"Either Mrs. Woodworth has given herself over body, soul, and spirit to the devil (which none believe who have seen her)," said Mr. Johnson, "or Dr. Bothwell has spoken against the Holy Ghost." It was not criticizing the doctrine, but the power, which was so sinful.

As to Dr. Bothwell's reference to Mrs. Woodworth's money-making, the speaker said it was a stab so mean that he hoped the doctor was ashamed of it when he saw it in print. The taking up of collections was but a poor reward, while every minister in this city had assurance of comfortable support or else he would go where pastures are greener.

December 24, 1889

Oakland Daily Evening Tribune (CA)

A Crumpled Heap

Is All That Remains Today of Mrs. Woodworth's Tent

A Breakdown with no Serious Mishaps—Immense Attendance—Future Arrangements

"It's a warning to sinners."

That was the opinion of an old lady who stood last night and watched the wreck of the Woodworth tent, from which she had just escaped. Whether it was a warning to sinners to keep away from a rotten tent in a storm, or an "act of God" designed to terrify the wicked, she was not at pains to explain. Meanwhile the soaked and ragged canvas slapped and whipped in the furious wind and rain. It was not a good night for a fire. The stoves were carried out and left to sizzle and have it out with the elements. The electric lights were put out by the breaking of the wires. The poles were cut down and today the tent is a crumpled heap forlorn.

Nobody was hurt. Mrs. Woodworth and the people with her on the platform acted with admirable self-control and quieted the people when the canvas first split. Notwithstanding the tremendous storm, which was in progress, there must have been [one thousand?] in the tent. They all got [out, going?] quietly, exactly, but without any broken bones.

The attendance at these meetings twice every day during the pouring rains of the past week is a phenomenon of remarkable interest. No matter how severe the storm, there are never less than one thousand people at the meetings. Since the tent was removed to Market Street, the meetings have been orderly, and although not exactly quiet in the ordinary sense of religious meetings, there has been nothing to afford the slightest [grounds?] for criticism. There is no doubt that Mrs. Woodworth is a revivalist of remarkable power, and the unfortunate impression created concerning the corner meetings was due to the presence of a gang of hoodlums who went there bun[g]ing a fight.[1]

[1] "bunging"—possibly, "spoiling for."

Mrs. Woodworth supplies an unexpected answer to the question, "Why don't the masses come to church?" They do come where they are wanted.

The new tent to accommodate six thousand people is expected to arrive on Friday, and in the meantime it is probable that the meetings will be suspended as the old tent is badly wrecked, and the season is not favorable for repairs. The Christmas entertainment for poor children, which was to have been given in the tent, will be held elsewhere.

January 9, 1890

Oakland Daily Evening Tribune (CA)

The Woodworth Manifestations

It is altogether useless and, in fact, injudicious to abuse Mrs. Woodworth and her methods. These are entirely within the law, so long as she confines her queer ministrations to grown people. There might be cause for interference were children worked upon or thrown into trances as described, but when a man chooses to allow himself to be made a subject, he does so at his own risk, which is perhaps not very great unless, in case, he is already more than half mad. A woman takes a greater risk, because her more highly organized and sensitive nervous system may very easily contract permanent epilepsy or hysteria from a single exposure. Yet there is no law against this, nor do we think that any such law is called for. If women are minded to undergo this liability to disease and take their chances, that is their affair. It is an interesting fact that more men than women appear to be affected by the "power," and some of the local physicians might make a valuable contribution to the pathology of nervous diseases if they would undertake the study of these phenomena. If the men are merely "fakers," they would be easily detected; and if the manifestations are real, the matter is worthy of scientific study.

January 9, 1890

Oakland Daily Evening Tribune (CA)

The Tent Rumpus

Almost a Riot at a Meeting Led by Mrs. Woodworth

MRS. MASSIE AND HER SON AT BAY

The Experience of the Girl Who Was Influenced on Tuesday Afternoon Last

Another riot took place at the Woodworth tent yesterday. In the afternoon Mrs. Woodworth told of a vision seen by one of her subjects, which she interpreted as meaning that in 1890 the world would come to an end. Mrs. Woodworth, "Dr." Smith, and the Rev. Mr. Johnson of the African Methodist Church delivered spirited addresses, and then all were called up around the platform. There amid tears, fervent ejaculations, and responses a little girl was overcome by the power and remained in an unconscious condition until night.

When Mrs. Woodworth opened her meeting last evening there were about 1500 or 2000 people in the audience, and on the stage stretched out like a corpse lay the little girl who had been unconscious since the afternoon meeting. Mrs. Woodworth took as her text "The Church of God" and went on to explain that there was no authority to be found in the Bible for the division of Christians into sects.

"There is no such thing as Methodists, Baptists, Presbyterians, and all the rest," said she. "All such distinctions are of men and woe unto them who try to enter the kingdom in any other way than the Church of God. All such are thieves," she cried. "Only those who enter through the Church of God are to be saved." In this way she continued until her audience was worked up to a high pitch, and the excitement began to tell upon the weaker ones. A man commenced trembling as if from cold, then rising to his feet he fixed vacant eyes upon space and clasped his hands, standing stiff and motionless.

"Behold the power of the Holy Ghost," she said. "Ministers don't know of such a power." Suddenly from the rear of the tent came the sound of a struggle, and a thousand people sprang to their feet as a man, refusing to be seated and completely breaking up the meeting. A riot was in progress, and Mrs. Woodworth's corps of special officers was being routed by the mob.

It seems that John Alexander Massie, the artist, had escorted his brother to the tent and had refused to sit down when ordered by the officers, who attempted to put him out. A row ensued, and the officers were roughly handled by the people; but the meeting had been broken up and the crowd dispersed.

People in the neighborhood of Mrs. Woodworth's tent are greatly excited over the episode of the young girl who was allowed to lie in the cold from 2 o'clock in the afternoon until 8 o'clock at night. The little girl was Flora Briggs, eleven years of age, a daughter of David Briggs, residing at the corner of Fifth Avenue and Twenty-seventh Street in East Oakland. She is still suffering from her strange experience and complains of a dull headache and nervous trembling, which confines her to her room. The little girl says she went to the tent with her little cousin, a boy about four years old; and while standing there a man came in front of her and made motions with his hands over her head just as he did to some of the others. She felt a tingling sensation in her head and arms and presently lost consciousness. Flora's uncle, who took the little girl from the tent by the aid of Chief of Police Tompkins, said that when he arrived at the tent the girl was lying on the altar, stretched out on her back with closed eyes, pale as death, and with rigid, marble-like features. Her hands were cold, her teeth set, and she presented in detail all the appearances of a corpse. The people at the tent would not allow him to touch the girl, and he had to appeal to Chief Tompkins for assistance.

Little Flora says she did not see any of the angels or heaven as she had been promised.

Mrs. Woodworth informed a *Tribune* reporter this morning that she had nothing to say for publication about the disturbances yesterday and refused to talk about the frequent series of turmoil at the tent.

January 10, 1890

Oakland Daily Evening Tribune (CA)

Devil in Them

Mrs. Woodworth Tells About Her "Subjects"

A STATEMENT FROM HER AT LAST

She Declines to Permit a Committee of Doctors or Clergy to Examine the Influenced

Tribune reporter called at the famous tent in the vacant square at the Market Street station this morning, and after using his persuasive powers to their full extent for about ten minutes, succeeded in gaining an interview with Mrs. Woodworth. She stated as her reason for at first refusing an interview with a reporter, that both Oakland and San Francisco reporters had called on her, and had never yet published the truth as told by her. She was asked if she would allow a committee of physicians or ministers to be at her meetings and examine those who receive the "power," from the moment they become under the influence till they recover their natural condition.

She stated that she would not allow this to be done, as the ministers would not tell the truth of the matter and the physicians would say nothing to conflict with public opinion in the matter.

Mrs. Woodworth said that Mrs. Dr. Kenny and Dr. Smith of Oakland and Dr. Bonten of San Francisco had examined these cases and that they acknowledged that they had never seen anything like it and that they did not understand it at all. They said that they had never met with such a power, "I have never said a harsh word against the newspapers or against the reporters," said Mrs. Woodworth, "and although they have persecuted me unmercifully and without cause, I have prayed for them that they might see the truth as it is. I have hardly spoken of myself since I have been in Oakland. I have not even told my experience.

"In regard to the Briggs girl that there has been so much talk about, I knew nothing about her till my daughter came and told me how the little girl's uncle had abused her, calling her everything but a lady. The girl received the power after I had left the tent. If people claim that these manifestations are through the power of mesmerism and I mesmerize them as people claim I do, who is it that mesmerizes me? Only yesterday I received the power and had no control over my actions. Isn't that enough to prove to the people that it is not mesmerism?

"There are a great many things occur in this tent that displeases (*sic*) me greatly, and that I have no power to control," she went on. "A great many of these manifestations are made by those who are possessed of the devil and have not the power of God, and to the unconverted all cases look alike. Then in regard to the disturbances the public hear so much about, we have all classes of people here. All the hoodlums of the city congregate here to raise a disturbance. This the churches have not to contend with, and the people ought to take all these things into consideration."

When asked if she didn't think it would be wise to allow a committee to examine those receiving the "power," she said that it would be a good thing for her, if they would give a truthful account of their examination; but with a whole city prejudiced against her, as Oakland is, she could not hope for a truthful statement.

January 11, 1890

The San Francisco Examiner (CA)

Break the Woman's Spell

Great Crowds Throng the Tent of the Woman Evangelist

PRECAUTIONS AGAINST ANOTHER RIOT

The Exhorters Moderate Their Zeal to Fit the Emergency, and "The Power" Does Not Overcome the Devotees—Prophesying the End of the World—A Picture of the Motley Assembly—Mrs. Woodworth's Record as a Revivalist in the Cities of Indiana

OAKLAND, JANUARY 10—

he usual motley throng of converts, idlers, church people, roughs, children, sailors, and artisans, athletes, and invalids assembled at Mrs. Woodworth's big tent this afternoon. The sight is always an interesting one. Wan mothers, with nursing babes in their arms, troop in by the dozens. The larger children laugh while the little ones cry or play promiscuously in the straw-littered aisles. Active tow-heads pull the curly wool of wee pickaninnies[1] and get their pudgy noses tweaked in return. Invalids with sunken eyes, narrow-chested consumptives, and men with all sorts of hurts and bruises are there to pass an afternoon, work being beyond their powers.

A Miscellaneous Gathering

Those who have evidently looked for labor without finding it, and tramps whose hope is that manual toil will be far from them, jostle the idle swells in box-top coats and silk hats circled by a wide felt band. Slouchy, unkempt matrons and slatternly creatures of the street sit side by side with dainty damosels in sealskins and fetching flat turbans. Nursemaids and haughty matrons crane their necks from positions on the same bench. Curious schoolboys just freed from their desks, troop in with grimy, nervous gamins, whose lives are a continual "playing hooky." These get as near to the front as possible, giggle during prayers, and fidget uneasily from seat to seat

[1] "pickaninnies"—a nineteenth-century colloquial, derogatory term for children of color.

until the meeting is dismissed. Hoodlums are there in bell-bottomed trousers, and solid men of business drop in on the way from the train to their homes.

On the benches near the altar where the converts most do congregate, the contrast of types is equally striking. Salvation Army vivandieres;[2] long-bearded patriarchs; old "mammies" whose life history takes them back to the slave cabins of the plantations; pallid young men with high, veined foreheads, big, set eyes and long, nervous fingers; bright-faced, rosy, sparkling girls with tears which start at the slightest provocation; hard-fisted working men; noticeable mothers, evidently well to do—all sorts, kinds, and conditions of people ready to shout or sing or pray, given to rigid conditions of body and mental ecstasy, making strange motions with their hands and uttering strange cries—all are under the spell of the pleasant-faced woman who walks her platform smiling and self-possessed.

The same faces are not seen every day, except in the case of a few of the most enthusiastic, but the converts come and go, their number constantly added to as the meetings progress and all apt to fall under the influence of "the power" at any moment.

Comforted by Police Protection

This afternoon those who went out to see "the circus" went away disappointed. There was little "hurrah" to the services and no prostrations. Mrs. Woodworth did not take a prominent part in the exercises, leaving most of the talking to be done by the Rev. Mr. Osgood and the Rev. Dr. Smith. All the speakers referred to the recent disturbances in the tent and expressed a belief that God would punish the rioters. Still they seemed comforted by the assurance that the police would protect them from further annoyance and denounced those who called upon the authorities to suppress the meetings.

Dr. Smith and Mrs. Woodworth both took occasion to contrast the reception tendered the revivalist in Oakland and in Indianapolis. In the latter city, Mrs. Woodworth said, the use of the big City Hall

[2] Spelled vivandiers or vivandieres. Originally a person who sold or provided provisions to armies (in Europe). In this case, a person in the Salvation Army who helps feed the poor.

was tendered her by the authorities, and the leading ministers of the place joined with her in her work.

"If you would all unite in prayer when one of these disturbances occurs," said the revivalist, "we would have no need of the police. God would strike the disturber to the floor where he stood. That is how we used to do in Indiana."

She then referred to the riots as a contest between the power of God and the power of the devil, telling in an unconventional way the story of how the staff of Moses was transformed into a serpent; of how the magicians, the adherents of the devil, duplicated the miracle with their staves; but how the serpent of Moses had swallowed all the other snakes. At this triumph of good over evil, the believers put up a shout and a chorus of amens was heard all over the tent.

"They want to drive me out of the town," continued the speaker, "but they have gone about it in the wrong way. I will never go as long as they treat me badly. If they had treated me well at the outset, I might have been gone long ago; but the worse they abuse me, the more I see the need of my work here. I never left a city yet where the people disliked me, and I intend to stay here until I win the citizens to my cause."

Cries, Moans, and Wails

In response to the usual request for those who wished the prayers of Christians to hold up their hands, a few palms were uplifted; and while the Rev. Mr. Osgood led, the converts dropped on their knees in silent supplication. This was the time when demonstrations were expected and the curious throng crowded toward the front and tiptoed to the full extent in order that nothing should be lost.

As the prayer progressed some of the converts began lifting their hands, twitching their faces, and otherwise exhibiting perfervid feelings. After Mr. Osgood had finished, two men began praying aloud at once and the excitement increased. The strained responses made up a singular piercing though muffled combination of sounds. Some cried; others shouted amens; a shriek was now and again heard; women moaned as if in more than mortal agony; the voices of the supplicators rose and fell in a dramatic minor intonation.

There is nothing which approaches this dissonance in intensity except that weird jumble of jangling voices which greets the ears of a visitor approaching the female wards of an insane asylum.

When the men ceased, the high voice of a woman took up the prayer. The voice alternated between a fierce ring and a half-[spirited?] wail. Two or three of the converts became worked up to the shouting pitch while others sobbed hysterically. The hands of one devotee were wildly shaken over his head as he groaned aloud.

All this time Mrs. Woodworth was [kneeling?] behind her pulpit, her hands [raised] but her eyes open and alert. She looked about the shouting, wailing company closely eyeing one after another. It was evident that the [remaining sentence unreadable]. As soon as the prayer of the woman [ ] with a [ ] invitation [unreadable phrase] motioned [ ] to [ ] and called [unreadable rest of paragraph].

Before dismissing the meeting, she requested all [Christians] attending [unreadable rest of paragraph].

Twenty or thirty colored people were in attendence, that race being [unreadable sentence]. A colored [woman?] the [ ] who had been [ ] of a revivalist but who had been incapacitated from work for a long time by disease, went to Mrs. Woodworth's meetings, said she had been entirely cured, and is now conducting revivals of her own among people of her color.

The End of the World

At tonight's meeting there was an immense crowd. It is said that the tent would seat six thousand people. If so, there were more than that number in the house. At the door a number of the special policemen scanned every face and turned away all small boys and [others] suspected of intentions to create a disturbance. As it was, there were indications of trouble several times.

During the singing of a hymn, a number of young men started to stamp, keeping time with the measure, but they received little support and were quickly suppressed. Then when Mrs. Woodworth rose to speak, some of those in the rear of the audience set up a concerted coughing, which seemed for a time infectious and threatened to drown out the speaker's voice. But Mrs. Woodworth kept right on talking, heedless of the interruption and the noise died away.

In view of the strained conditions prevailing, the exhorters moderated their zeal; their eloquence was [ ] , and their prayers less dramatic. None of the devotees suffered collapse, though the usual [sea?] of waving hands and [ ] faces occurred. "The power" was not potent.

The exhortation was principally directed to the immediate coming of the end of the world. A young man with a good voice and a rude, ungrammatical eloquence said that the last message had gone forth and that probably when the tent was pulled down, that message would never be [proclaimed?] again in Oakland.

Mrs. Woodworth solemnly affirmed that the end of the world was near at hand. [She] said she realized it in her soul and was convinced of it from her Bible reading. She was sure that the last generation was now living upon the earth. The wicked, she reaffirmed, would get worse, and only the wise would be saved. Likening those who laughed at her efforts to those who laughed at Noah when building the ark, she averred that the coming of the Lord would be with a great noise and the scoffers would be dumbfounded.

After the prayer for those that raised their hands requesting it, the meeting was quietly dismissed. A short, thickset man had his hat stolen and made some loud [ ] about it. When a special policeman approached, he grabbed up a billet of wood and the officer discreetly retreated. With this exception the exit was orderly.

It is said that Eli Denisen, the railroad man whose house is opposite the lot on which the big tent is located, is circulating a petition in the neighborhood asking that the meetings be abated as a public nuisance. This may create more trouble.

January 11, 1890

The San Francisco Examiner (CA)

"Pentecostal Power"

This Is What Mrs. Woodward (*sic*) Says She Has—Her Former Record

(Special to the *Examiner*)

INDIANAPOLIS (IND.), JANUARY 10.—

rs. Woodworth began to attract attention in the northern part of Indiana about five years ago. She felt called upon to preach the Gospel, as she understood it, and seemed to have notoriety as a "trance evangelist" very early in her career.

Her meetings were characterized by the most peculiar phenomena. Converts would be [ ] with a sort of trance; many of them would lie unconscious in all parts of the building where the evangelist preached, usually, however, near where the preacher stood. She declared that it was the "Pentecostal power" that was needed and that it was within the reach of all who sincerely desire it. She would pray with anyone who was willing to have her do so and frequently in the very mist of an exhortation, converts would swoon, some remaining in the state for a few moments only, others for several hours.

In several counties of northern Indiana, her success was wonderful and phenomenal. Hundreds and thousands gathered about her.

Those who watched the progress of the revival were divided in their views. Some insisted that she was endowed with a notable mesmeric power and that she mesmerized her converts, while others thought that they were so unstrung by her prayers and exhortations as to make unfortunate victims of some from catalepsy. Whatever it may be it was successful and thousands of people were converted, and it is claimed today that the large majority have stayed faithful to the promises and vows made at that time.

She herself claimed nothing beyond this "Pentecostal power" already alluded to. After she had left northern Indiana churches were organized in several cities, and each was called "The Church of God." These are still in existence and said to be doing good work. At Anderson there is one with a membership of one thousand members. Other smaller ones are located at Tipton, Oxenburg, and

Columbia City. The largest is at Springfield, Ohio, where last year it is claimed several hundred additions were made. She was not very successful at Indianapolis, although one of the churches was established here and is in existence today. It is not very strong owing to some factional disturbances in which Mrs. Woodworth had no part.

Her last meeting was held here on January 31st, three years ago. Her discourse was vehement and to some extent [abrasive?]. She was evidently worn down and out of sorts. She said that she was glad she would be at the judgment. Those who had been calling her followers a lot of cranks would wish they hadn't done so in this [life?].

"Ten thousand souls could have been saved had the Christians [from?] this city shown the proper friendship [and] put their shoulders to the wheel of trance evangelism."

[Remaining paragraph unreadable]

January 12, 1890

The San Francisco Examiner (CA)

Is Her Power Waning?

The Trance Evangelist's Tent Still Crowded Nightly

SHE DELIVERS AN ELOQUENT ADDRESS

Only a Few Fall Under the Influence of "The Power"—The Audience Greatly Disappointed—Great Preparations Made for Today's Meetings—The Regular Police on Duty at the Tent

OAKLAND, JANUARY 11.—

When Mrs. Woodworth opened her meeting tonight, there were two young girls—one about fifteen years of age and the other about nineteen years old—lying in the straw in a trance in front of the altar. On the long, narrow platform that runs from the rostrum into the audience lay another woman in a trance.

The audience numbered between one thousand five hundred and two thousand people, and it was a remarkably well behaved one. The special police were on duty but not nearly so officious as usual on account of the presence of a number of the regular police.

Chief Tompkins has evidently decided to reduce the chances for a disturbance at the tent to a minimum by placing a force of regulars on duty there each night.

Mrs. Woodworth took her text from the second chapter of Peter,[1] third verse: "How shall we escape, if we neglect so great a salvation."

Beyond question the sermon preached was one of the most earnest, eloquent, and impressive of the "trance evangelist's" series in Oakland. For almost two hours she alternately coaxed, pleaded, threatened, and denounced sinners. Her gestures and language showed that she was laboring under more excitement than usual.

The Audience Unmoved

Notwithstanding all this effort she failed to move the audience, and there was no undue excitement even among her converts. During her discourse the two young girls lying in the straw recovered from their trances and were taken away by friends. The woman on the platform at intervals mourned and cried aloud, raising her hands to heaven.

It was evident that Mrs. Woodworth was disappointed. She continually looked over the audience for someone whom her discourse had affected. As she drew near the close of her remarks, she began to talk of her children, Willie and Georgie, whom she said God had taken from her when young, in order that she might go forth and save the boys and girls.

The pathetic[2] is one of Mrs. Woodworth's most able arguments, and she was truly eloquent at times, especially in her description of the death of her own children, but even this eloquence failed to move her hearers.

At the close of her sermon, Mrs. Woodworth called for converts to come forward and one woman responded. Then she gathered all her converts around the altar, where prayer was held.

[1] The reporter is incorrect; Hebrews 2:3 is the reference Maria Woodworth used.

[2] "pathetic"—in other words, the reporter means that she uses stories which elicit sympathy from her listeners to persuade them. This use of *pathos* is considered a mode of argument in Aristotelian argumentation.

A Vision To Be Interpreted

The curious in the audience now expected to be repaid for their two hours waiting in the cold, but they were again disappointed. Only one man showed any signs of being under the influence of "the power," and he had been seen so often before that his actions had lost their grotesqueness for the spectators.

Several prayers were offered and the one by Dr. Smith, one of the evangelist's assistants, was indicative of the fact that Mrs. Woodworth was anxious for more startling conversions and trances among the people.

In his prayer he said: "Show the people that the power they have seen here manifested is not mesmerism or hypnotism but the Holy Spirit. Teach them not to be afraid of it. Oh! Let it take hold of more converts. Let it again take hold of those already converted. Let the people know that there is nothing to fear, no matter what the newspapers and doctors say."

Frequent and loud were the "amens" that greeted this prayer, Mrs. Woodworth being among the earnest.

Then Mrs. Woodworth announced that the thirteen-year-old girl had "seen a vision" in her trance and that it would be told tomorrow.

The audience was then dismissed with an urgent invitation to come to tomorrow's meetings, for which great preparations are being made.

January 13, 1890

Oakland Daily Evening Tribune (CA)

For Six Months

The Woodworth Meetings to Be Continued

How the Sather Lot Was Obtained

A Devil Gets Into the Stovepipe and the Wind Blows Through the Cordage of the Tent

stovepipe fell last evening in the tent in which Mrs. Woodworth holds her meetings.

"That's it," said Mrs. Woodworth. "The devil will get into the stovepipe if he can't get anywhere else."

The meetings yesterday afternoon and last evening were attended by hundreds of people, though the rain fell. In the evening, the rainstorm was furious and the wind blew fiercely. No one was sufficiently "influenced" to burrow his nose in the straw or become rigid. In the evening the fierce wind made the audience uneasy, and Mrs. Woodworth dismissed the people earlier than usual.

A new element of opposition has sprung up against the evangelist. Heretofore the colored people have been her most earnest adherents, led by Rev. Mr. Johnson of the African Methodist Church of Oakland, who has taken a prominent part in her meetings.

Some two months ago a colored woman by the name of Mrs. Rice, suffering from paralysis, attended Mrs. Woodworth's tent and went under the influence of the power, and when she came out of the trance she claimed to be cured.

The cure was not lasting, however, Mrs. Rice going to bed a day after her trance. She rapidly grew worse until yesterday when she died. The woman's relatives say that her death is due to the evangelist's influence, and the colored population is turning against the evangelist as rapidly as it flocked to her standard.

A resolution was recently passed by the City Council ordering the barbed-wire fence around the lot occupied by the tent removed. After the resolution was passed, the fence was removed within the property line. Councilman McAvoy criticized City Attorney Johnson in advising that it could not be removed.

"I think that there must have been some mistake," said City Attorney Johnson. "In regard to a published interview with Councilman McAvoy about the Woodworth wire fence, I explained the matter to him and he understood it thoroughly, and he is a man who is too fair-minded to make any such statement. At the time the resolution was passed, the barbed wire was in the street. Mr. Wall, the street superintendent, notified them to remove it and they moved it inside of the line of the fence, and therefore outside of Mr. Wall's jurisdiction, and nothing more could be done. The matter, however, is controlled by the statutes; and if is dangerous, I will give anyone a complaint and will prosecute the case vigorously."

There is no grounds for the rumor that Eli Denison has hired the block near the Market Street station upon which the tent is pitched and that Mrs. Woodworth will have to vacate it the first of next month. Mrs. Woodworth has a six months' lease of the property, and the second month has just begun.

William S. Dingee is the agent in this city for the trustees of the Sather estate. At his office the information is given that Mrs. Woodworth obtained permission from the trustees to use the lot for six months, paying therefore the nominal rental of $10 per month. The trustees did not understand the kind of meetings conducted by Mrs. Woodworth and believed that religious meetings of the usual orderly and peaceable kind were to be held on the property. The second month of the six months of occupation has been paid for.

January 28, 1890

Oakland Daily Evening Tribune (CA)

Flee to the Mountains

Mrs. Woodworth Prophesies Oakland's Destruction by Earthquake

The principals of the Woodworth revivalists have been the recipients of numerous revelations of late. On Sunday afternoon, a Mr. Overton of Santa Rosa, stated that while in San Francisco he had a revelation that three ministers of Oakland were giving evil counsel to the people of this city and that he was commanded by God to denounce them. Two of these men, he said, are well-known and of great importance in Oakland; the other is known but slightly. He referred to the first two as Rev. Dr. Bothwell of West Oakland and Dr. J. K. McLean of the First Congregational Church, and to the last one as J. Alexander Dowie. Dr. Bothwell he denounced as a liar and said that Dr. McLean and Mr. Dowie are but little better.

Last night Ms. Woodworth stated that God had revealed to her that the cities of Oakland, San Francisco, and Alameda would be destroyed by a mighty earthquake and a terrible tidal wave in just eighty days. In her dream she distinctly saw the waves rolling high over these cities and the words, "Flee to the mountains!"[1] came to her mind. She was so affected that she threw herself on the floor, prostrate before the Lord, and besought Him as Abraham did for Sodom, to spare these cities if ten righteous persons could be found in them.[2] In reply to her prayer, the Lord said that He would not spare them, that when the flood came there would not be ten righteous persons here as the righteous would take the warning and flee to the mountains. She also said that Milwaukee and Chicago would be destroyed at the same time by a tidal wave from the Great Lakes.

[1] See Matthew 24:16.

[2] See Genesis 18:17-33.

February 7, 1890

Oakland Daily Evening Tribune (CA)

Stolen His Mind

Effect of Visiting the Tent of Mrs. Woodworth

DAN CALLAGHAN'S SAD MENTAL STATE

A Young Victim of the Morphine Habit Says He Is Entirely Under Control of "The Power"

A pale-faced young man, shabbily dressed, answering to the name of Daniel Callaghan, called at the district attorney's office yesterday afternoon and announced that he was desirous of securing a warrant for the arrest of Mother Woodworth and her followers, asserting that he could have no peace because they had robbed him of his mind, and he, now, found himself a victim of "the power," and entirely under their control, being compelled to carry out their every wish and fearful lest he should commit some crime at their instigation. The story astounded District Attorney Reed, and he soon learned that his caller was evidently a lunatic.

Callaghan comes from an old family in this city. Many years ago his mother owned considerable property on Franklin Street, but the children squandered the estate soon after her decease. Callaghan admitted that he is a victim to the morphine habit, and the ravages of the drug plainly show on his pallid countenance. It is a case of Jekyll and Hyde[1]. When not under the influence of the drug, Callaghan is quiet and polite, but when under the influence of morphine he is a veritable Hyde, always seeking a fight and resorting to theft. The district attorney was interested in the strange case and therefore questioned the applicant for a warrant at length.

"You may believe me crazy," said Callaghan with a smile, "but you are fooled, I am not crazy; and I want you to understand that I know what I am talking about."

"Just explain to me how these people trouble you," said Mr. Reed.

[1] An allusion to *The Strange Case of Dr. Jeckyll and Mr. Hyde* (1886) by Robert Louis Stevenson (1850-1894).

"They seem to be working my mind," replied Callaghan. "I went down to the tent two or three times, thinking that I could work off the power; but it was no use. They only got greater control over me, I just got out of jail the other day for stealing a pair of boots. I could not help stealing the boots. Those people worked my mind and compelled me to steal them."

[Mr. R.] "What are your feelings?"

[Mr. C.] "They make me itch all over. It seems as if I am being cut to pieces. I try to throw the feeling off, but I am helpless."

[Mr. R.] "Do you have to do everything they tell you?"

[Mr. C.] "Why, certainly. If they should command me to kill a man I would have to do it. I could not help it, and it would not be my fault."

[Mr. R.] "Did they ever command you to do anyone any harm?"

[Mr. C.] "Not yet, but they may any day. If they should work my mind and tell me to slug somebody, I would have to do it. After they get me to do a thing, they take my strength away and leave me helpless. If I should attempt to whip a man, they would take my strength away, and I would get a beating because I would not be able to fight."

[Mr. R.] "How do you feel now?"

[Mr. C.] "They are working my mind at this very moment."

[Mr. R.] "What are they saying?"

[Mr. C.] "They are telling me, 'Dan, you can't get a warrant. There is no use in trying.' I would like to see all of them hung."

[Mr. R.] "Well, they are telling you about right this time about the warrant," said Mr. Reed.

[Mr. C.] "So you won't give me a warrant."

[Mr. R.] "Not today."

"Gentlemen, believe me, I am not crazy," said Callaghan as he left the office, still under the influence of "the power."

The fellow had evidently taken an overdose of morphine.

February 14, 1890

Oakland Daily Evening Tribune (CA)

He Was Moved to Speak

D. W. Thompson Had the "Power" and Got into Trouble

He Had Read of the Doom of Oakland and Was Preparing to Take His Family to the Hills

ustice Henshaw had to order the lobby of his courtroom cleared this morning. The case of *The People vs. D. W. Thompson,* charged with disturbing the peace by creating disorder in Mrs. Woodworth's tent on the night of the 3rd inst.,[1] was on trial and the evidence was, to say the least of it, funny. The mirth received its first impetus while the jury was being impaneled, for Attorney Chapman, who conducted the defense, interrogated them as to their object in visiting the revivalist's tent, one and all having admitted being present there on some occasion. In their replies all but one individual stated that religion had nothing to do with their patronage of Mrs. Woodworth's place of worship, some having gone there to see her, others because everyone else was going there, and still more because they wanted to ascertain further particulars about the destruction of Oakland.

But J. D. Strong, the prosecuting witness, when he was called to the stand by City Attorney Johnson, who conducted the prosecution in the absence of Assistant District Attorney Church, told a different story. Mr. Strong, who said that he had once been a minister, announced that he went to the canvas church for the sake of worship and to study and protect Mrs. Woodworth. He next described how the defendant had interrupted the services by rising and speaking to Mrs. Woodworth in what the witness said was incoherent language.

Then Mr. Strong fell into a trap set by Attorney Chapman.

"I suppose you heard a good deal that was incoherent at Mrs. Woodworth's meetings," was suggested, and a nod being given in

[1] "inst."—instant, meaning the 3rd of *this* month.

reply, the man of law continued, "Did you ever hear anything that was coherent?"

"I don't think I did," said Mr. Strong, and there was a general titter throughout the courtroom that made Justice Henshaw frown and Bailiff Mitchell cry for order.

In the course of his further evidence, Mr. Strong declined to admit that he had seen Mrs. Woodworth throw people into a state of temporary insanity. He said he had seen them under "the power" and was asked if that was the same "power" that was used when Thompson was dragged out of the tent. But Mr. Strong did not appreciate the joke and said that the power he referred to was a mysterious, unexplainable influence. He was capable of producing it himself: He had often done so when he was a preacher in the ranks of the Congregationalists.

Special Officer Miller was called to succeed Mr. Strong in the witness box and said that he had been employed by Mrs. Woodworth to keep order at the meetings. He had arrested Thompson because that individual had persisted in endeavoring to become the orator of the evening instead of the revivalist.

Then the defendant was called upon to speak in his own behalf and in doing so, developed a flow of language that the efforts of neither judge nor counsel could check. He not only told at a 150-word-a-minute rate everything that occurred the night of the trouble, but he further enlightened his audience as to every little detail in the chain of circumstances leading up to the complication. He had gone to the meeting, he said, for the benefit of himself and his family. He had previously heard of the fearful prediction that the streets of Oakland will soon be at the bottom of the sea, and he wanted to look out for his family and get them to the hills. As he listened to Mrs. Woodworth the mantle of greatness fell upon him, and the Spirit moved him to arise and speak.

This remark, leaving a doubt as [to] the nature of the spirit referred to, he was asked if he had been drinking, and he replied, "I met a friend downtown in the afternoon, and we had a couple of goes[2] of half-and-half apiece, that was all."

[2] "a couple of goes"—a couple of rounds.

Mr. Thompson then proceeded to explain to the jury what half-and-half[3] was, but there was a knowing smile on every face, so he was persuaded to forego his information by Justice Henshaw. He was expected then to go on with his story, but his ideas had been switched and to the surprise of all he pointed to Mr. Strong and said: "There's a man who's not very straight for a preacher."

The climax was capped. The lobbyites[4] did not attempt to restrain their feelings any longer and a roar of laughter went up, which resulted in a command from Justice Henshaw of "Clear the court," and out everybody but witnesses and officers had to go. Thompson's last shot had been fired, however, and he retired from the stand in favor of two witnesses who testified in his behalf, after which the case was submitted to the jury with short arguments by the counsel. The jurors walked into their little room, turned around, and walked back into the court again with a verdict of not guilty, whereupon Mr. Thompson was discharged from custody and left free to continue his arrangements for taking his family to the hills.

[3] "half-and-half"—possibly half porter and half stout.

[4] "lobbyites"—people in the audience of the court.

April 10, 1890

Oakland Daily Evening Tribune (CA)

Flee-to-the-Hillers

Congregating at Santa Rosa, St. Helena, and Vacaville

Mrs. Woodworth Has Flown and There Is a Split in Her Flock—Assorted Visionaries

otwithstanding the "hurrah" made over the matter by some of our contemporaries, the exodus from Oakland on account of the Ericksonian prophecy has not in any way affected business or property values. It is not even a foremost topic of discussion, except in the way of a joke. Probably more than half of the people who have gone to more elevated regions have gone from San Francisco, and yet the papers of that city seem desirous of spreading the impression that all are from this side of the bay. It is safe to say that not over two hundred people will be out of Oakland on the fourteenth inst. because of Erickson's scare, and it is quite probable that one hundred will cover the number.

A few continue to steal away. J. M. Russell of Fifth Avenue, East Oakland, with his two daughters, has gone. Mrs. Simons of Oak Street, Alameda, has gone into the hills near Redwood Peak with her children. Mrs. Furey and children and Fred Colburn, all of Alameda, are said to be on the road to the high places.

Mr. Ramsey, a hand on the creek boat, is said to have taken his family away, and Mr. and Mrs. Nelson, of A Street, North Oakland, are also reported as among the absent ones. Mr. and Mrs. Hall of Helen Street, left on Tuesday for Modesto, Mrs. Hall, an invalid, feeling timid about the flood, though neither herself nor her husband are believers.

A telegram from Santa Rosa is to the effect that Mrs. Woodworth has gone from there and that C. N. Carrington, a real estate dealer, is leading her flock and caring for the refugees. Carrington's wife is another who says she has had visions showing her the coming destruction of Oakland and San Francisco by means of the big wave. The Rev. Mr. Overton, leader of the Holiness Band of Santa Rosa, has rather split off from Mrs. Woodworth's crowd, on account of a belief in "Sanctification,"[1] but he believes in the wave and some of his people have seen it or heard of its coming during sleep. At Saint Helena it is said there are twenty-two Woodworthians gathered with W. H. Johnson, of this city, at their head. Johnson says that he, too, has seen the vision of destruction, but if it should not come he would be glad and consider it an evidence that God has changed his mind.

It is estimated that there are nearly fifty doom sealers huddled at Vacaville.

[1] "Sanctification" refers to the belief held in the nineteenth-century (and by some today) that there is a subsequent experience to salvation which results in power to live a righteous life. Maria Woodworth-Etter published a sermon by one of her associates which explains that this experience is not the same as the baptism of the Holy Spirit, an experience Holiness preachers in the 1890s called "the power." [Wayne Warner, *The Woman Evangelist: The Life and Times of Charismatic Evangelist Maria B. Woodworth-Etter* (Studies in Evangelicalism, No. 8),(Lanham, MD: Scarecrow Press, 1986), p. 143.]

April 14, 1890

Oakland Daily Evening Tribune (CA)

We Are Still Here

Erickson's Doom Wave Misses Connections

THE SIGNS-AND-WONDERS CROP FAILS

Some of the Things Which Might Have Happened to Take the Edge Off a Cataclysm

othing has happened yet!

The tidal wave has failed to keep its appointment with Erickson. The dust is still blowing in the streets. The courthouse tower is not waving in the green depths, like the wave-washed minarets of Savannah del Mar, which God smote in De Quincey's opium-induced dream.[1] San Francisco has not become Poe's "city in the sea."[2] And as for Alameda—well, Alameda is still Alameda. That is infliction enough.

Tomorrow, and the next day, and the next will see the return of the prodigal fool. He will come sneaking in, "as the flying come, in silence and in fear," after being out "shaking the depths of the desert gloom with their hymns of lofty cheer."[3] They will be the butt and jeer of their neighborhoods—these foolish followers of a crazy man.

Up to the time of going to press, there was nothing doing in signs and wonders on the street. A great deal had been expected, but even some of the phenomena ranked as possibilities did not get the cosmic lift or the necessary tumble.

It was hoped that Major McElrath would turn over to the secretary of the Committee of One Hundred that check for five hundred dollars which, in a tidal-wave condition of enthusiasm, he said had been given to him to help on the fight to oust the councilmen. It will be remembered that when the secretary eagerly reached for that check, the "Tiger of Temescal" suddenly withdrew into himself,

[1] Reference to the British romantic essayist, Thomas De Quincey (1785-1850) who wrote *Confessions of an Opium Eater*, (1821-2), a work which detailed the vivid dreams and nightmares induced by his habitual use of opium.

[2] A reference to a poem by Edgar Allen Poe (1809-1849), "City in the Sea," (1831), which describes ruins of a city that is underwater.

[3] Source of quote unknown.

quickly placed the check in his pocket, and said that he would place one of his own for a similar amount with it and then turn over both to the committee. The committee has ever since been looking for another tidal wave of enthusiasm to wash those checks out of the pocket of Major McElrath.

There have been some who felt that they could bear the horrors of the tidal wave if it would only cover that wee flag on the abnormal flagpole, which tells of the patriotism of Lincoln School but seems to carry with it a suggestion of penuriousness.

Bennett's bicycle was trundling about the streets today just as airily as if it had not been responsible for an exodus of those who could well be spared. Bennett himself is fleeing like a bird, but he no longer risks waving himself from the quarterdeck of the silent steed, for the bicycle hath more dangers than the sea in its wrath.

Mrs. M. B. Woodworth, the cause of all the mental cataclysms, has quietly stolen away for St. Louis, leaving her tent stored at Santa Rosa. In her mind's eye she sees the total destruction of all things mundane in 1896, even though she should have missed stays in sailing the April wave. She thinks that the waves will cover the just and unjust, if they are only given time. They were probably busy elsewhere today and forgot to come up and lay the dust where they were most expected.

From their lofty perches at St. Helena, Vacaville, and Santa Rosa, the believers lifted up their eyes today, expecting to see "the power" manifest itself in Sullivanesque[4] grandeur. But they lifted in vain. They will probably conclude that their prayers averted the awful cataclysm and will try to pose as the saviors of the cities of the plains. A. Victors of Alameda tells a singular story of how some of those who fled from the imaginary tidal wave ran afoul of an actual cyclone, greatly to their undoing. A few weeks ago he received letters from a Chicago relative, saying that a party of Chicagoans was coming here to settle in Oakland or Alameda. The emigrants reached here just as the Eriksonian prophecy was being most diligently exploited by Bennett and the other doom-sealers. They

[4] "Sullivanesque"—Possibly a reference to the style of Louis Sullivan (1856-1924). The architect designed big buildings which were known for their understated, neoclassical grandeur in Chicago from 1871, after the Chicago fire, to 1895.

became fearful lest they should be overtaken by the wave and fled for the East again before they had fairly settled themselves here. At Louisville they met the tornado, and two of them were killed.

Now that day of wrath has about spent itself as mildly as any sucking dove, the town will lose one of its most accepted subjects for jocularity, and "Oh, go flee to the hills," will no longer meet the requirements of the case, when a raconteur[5] is letting slip the tidal wave of his imagination, and "Go chase yerself" will be restored to the proud position in slang from which it had been temporarily deposed.

"Now is the time to plant sprinkling carts"[6] will be the advice of agricultural contemporaries, and not a wave of trouble shall roll over the peaceful breast of the landscape. Even the seismic disturbance at Mills College will probably pass away without shaking down the reputation of anyone, and the little hills will not clap their hands[7] for the disturbance of those seminarians who desire to sleep o' nights.

Later.

Nothing has happened yet.

[Missing portion of article]

. . . of negroes went to the summit of Mount St. Helena this morning.

Further than by their exodus to the mountains, the fanatics are not causing much commotion today. It is slowly dawning on them that their prophet of evil has failed them; and about tomorrow, it is thought the large majority will return to Oakland.

---

[5] "raconteur"—the French word for storyteller.

[6] "Now is the time to plant sprinkling carts"—It is April, and people will go on with the spring planting of their flowers and potted plants. This is another way to say, "Life will go on as usual."

[7] "the little hills will not clap their hands"—a mixed metaphor coined to refer to the hills being shaken by earthquakes, taken from Isaiah 55:12: "For ye shall go out with joy, and be led forth with peace: *the mountains and the hills shall break forth before you into singing*, and all the *trees of the field shall clap their hands.*"

April 14, 1890

Oakland Daily Tribune (CA)

Flight From Santa Rosa

About One Hundred People Praying on the Top of Taylor Mountain

Santa Rosa. April 14.—

reat excitement prevailed among the Woodworth followers this morning. At first it was supposed that Santa Rosa was in no danger, but since the Callaghan vision last week, the mountains were regarded as the only safe place.

Between seventy-five and one hundred people left this morning at an early hour for the top of Taylor Mountain, two miles south of this city. They were joined by a number of Salvation Army and Holiness Band people, who say they are going to have a picnic and spiritual festival, whether the wave comes or not.

They are now engaged in singing, praying, and many are laid out in trances. Many people are seen along the streets looking at the mountains with field glasses.

April 20, 1890

St. Louis Post-Dispatch (MO)

[Evangelist in the City]

Mrs. M. B. Woodworth, the evangelist, is in the city and will conduct gospel services at Union Church Hall, 940 North Third Street, everyday at 2 P.M. and 7 P.M. All are invited. The meeting will commence tonight at 7 P.M.

April 21, 1890

St. Louis Post-Dispatch (MO)

["The Vineyard of Christ"]

Mrs. Maria Woodworth preached yesterday evening to quite a good audience at No. 940 North Third St. The subject of her talk was "The Vineyard of Christ" and the labor that must be done by Christ's children. "Laboring in the vineyard" means service to God, a consecration which has its reward, for there is nothing so ennobling as laboring to save souls.

April 24, 1890

St. Louis Daily Globe-Democrat (MO)

[Meeting Unmarked by Frenzy]

ourscore people at Mrs. Maria B. Woodworth's fifth evening service at Union Mission Hall, 940 North Third Street. Last night Mrs. Woodworth gave a lucid talk on the Scriptures, unmarked by any display of the unnatural frenzy which has been attributed to her. The audiences have been increasing, but the rain of yesterday had a depressing effect on the attendance. Rev. David P. Stazman participates in Mrs. Woodworth's meetings every night.

April 28, 1890

St. Louis Daily Globe-Democrat (MO)

[An Attentive Congregation]

rs. Maria Woodworth, the lady evangelist, preached to an attentive congregation at 940 North Third Street last evening. Her discourse was of a biblical character and general application. She referred to mesmerism and kindred things and said that they were of Christian origin. About forty persons were present.

April 29, 1890

St. Louis Post-Dispatch (MO)

[Gospel Meetings]

rs. Maria B. Woodworth, the lady evangelist, is conducting gospel meetings at Union Church Hall, 940 North Third Street, every day at 2 and 7 P.M. The attendance at the meetings is very large.

June 8, 1890

St. Louis Post-Dispatch (MO)

[Gospel Services]

rs. M. B. Woodworth will conduct gospel services at the Union Market this afternoon at 2:30.

June 9, 1890

St. Louis Daily Globe-Democrat (MO)

Mrs. Maria B. Woodworth

rs. Maria B. Woodworth, who has gained considerable fame as a "divine healer," preached to a respectable-sized audience yesterday afternoon under one of the sheds at the Union Market. The audience was an average outdoor gathering, containing mostly white people, but a few well-dressed colored persons. Mrs. Woodworth, dressed very plainly, speaks readily and with much force and marches back and forth on the rostrum, beating time during songs. The singing, which is led by one male and two female voices, is quite entertaining. Mrs. Woodworth preached at the hall, No. 940 North Third Street, in the evening and will preach there each night during the week.

June 10, 1890

St. Louis Daily Globe-Democrat (MO)

Mrs. Woodworth's Tent

The friends of Mrs. Maria B. Woodworth, the famous evangelist, are looking for a suitable location upon which to erect a large tent in which it is proposed to hold services. This tent is 120x180 feet in dimensions and 60 feet high. It was donated to Mrs. Woodworth as a mark of appreciation by friends at Oakland, Cal. It will be erected sometime during this week.

June 11, 1890

St. Louis Post-Dispatch (MO)

Mrs. Woodworth's Mission

An effort is being made by the friends of Mrs. Maria Woodworth, the evangelist, to secure a portion of Washington Park for the purpose of erecting a tent to be used as a tabernacle, the tent having been presented to her by the residents of Oakland, Calif., to assist her in continuing the work.

If what they say of her is true, she is not only healing their spiritual ills, but their physical ailments as well. One of the attendants at her meetings, M. Douglas, formerly a minister of the Gospel but who has not been preaching for several years in consequence of chest trouble, claims to have been completely cured by the efficacy of her prayers. His voice has returned to him and his health is greatly improved. She has made many converts, and many drunkards have signed the pledge tendered by her. She works earnestly and with indomitable energy, and her meetings are well attended.

June 18, 1890

St. Louis Post-Dispatch (MO)

[Hoodlums Disturb Services]

rs. Maria B. Woodworth, the evangelist, is conducting camp meeting services in her tent at Cass and Jefferson Avenues. The tent is a large one and will accommodate five thousand persons. Services are held every afternoon and evening but are continually disturbed by a party of hoodlums who come in with their hats on, insist on smoking, and shout and scream in a most outrageous manner. There are generally a few patrolmen on the scene, but no effort is made by them to preserve order for the lady.

June 18, 1890

Missouri Republican

Mobbed Mrs. Woodworth

A Gang of Hoodlums Disturb the Services of the Female Evangelist and a Riot Ensues

Last week Mrs. M. B. Woodworth, the famous female evangelist who recently arrived here from California, had a tent erected at the corner of Howard Street and Jefferson Avenue for the purpose of holding religious meetings. She began the services in the tent last Sunday night. The congregation in attendance at the opening meeting was somewhat mixed. It was composed of the religiously inclined and hoodlums by the hundred. During the services Mrs. Woodworth was interrupted continuously by noisy behavior, and slang expressions were hurled at her by the gang, who are said to have disturbed the worship with impunity, notwithstanding the presence of police. Only one officer was on duty at the time; and when he was appealed to, he said he saw nothing which justified his making an arrest.

The conduct of the mob at the services Monday night was a disgrace to civilization. They joined in the singing, yelled at the top of their voices, and did everything imaginable to disturb the worshippers and even went so far as to throw clods of mud at the leaders of the services. That conduct was permitted within three blocks of a police station.

Last night the services were broken up, the participants mobbed, and the entire crowd—hoodlums, worshippers, and preachers—scattered by the police, acting under orders from Chief Harrigan. While the opening exercises were in progress, David P. Saltzman saw a hoodlum attempting to cut the ropes of the tent. He remonstrated with the fellow and was chased three blocks by a mob of boys and men. He took refuge in a drugstore and telephoned to the third district substation for an officer. One was sent to his rescue, but he was of no more use than a foghorn in clear weather. The hoodlums did not mind him a bit. The officer and Mr. Saltzman started for the substation; and on the way there, the gentleman was spattered with mud from his head to his heels by the gang, who followed behind.

The gang followed to the substation, and when, after the lapse of a half-hour, Mr. Saltzman started away in company with a reporter, the gang yelled and hooted like wild men.

It was Mrs. Woodworth's intention to remain in St. Louis during the summer, but last night a conference was held for the purpose of considering the condition of affairs and the feasibility of remaining longer.

No definite conclusion was reached, however, and another meeting of those interested in the tent meetings will be held today to further consider the matter.

Speaking of the conduct of the hoodlums last night, a police official said: "That conduct is an argument in favor of increasing the police force. Only one officer was sent to the tent meeting because no more could be spared for that duty. One officer could do nothing with a crowd like that; it would take fully a dozen to handle it properly. Chief Harrigan ordered the disbursement of the gang and officers had to be sent from their beats to do it. The crowd is a hard one, with respect for neither religion nor law; and had the officer who was on duty at the tent Sunday and Monday nights attempted an arrest, either he or some of the crowd, possibly an innocent person, would have been killed. The condemnation which will be heaped upon the head of that officer will be bitter and severe, but it will be unjust. The city officials should bear the condemnation for this disgrace, for the police force of this city is not large enough by one-half and this particular officer acted, in my opinion, with great wisdom and foresight."

Mrs. Woodworth is greatly discouraged in her work in this city. She claims that neither the press nor the people have given her the protection and encouragement her work deserves. If it is decided to continue the meetings in this city at the conference today, Mayor Noonan and the police department will be appealed to for police protection and several prominent citizens will act as a committee in Mrs. Woodworth's [behalf ?].

June 20, 1890

St. Louis Post-Dispatch (MO)

Religious Notes

rs. M. B. Woodworth, the evangelist, is now holding meetings in her tent at Twenty-sixth and Cass Avenues. The tent is a tremendous affair with a seating capacity of eight thousand and was presented to her by the people of Oakland, Cal.

June 29, 1890

St. Louis Post-Dispatch (MO)

[Still Conducting Services]

rs. Woodworth is still conducting services in the large tent at Cass and Jefferson Avenues. The difficulties under which the lady labored have to a great extent vanished, and the disturbances are less frequent and less distracting. Today there will be services morning, afternoon, and evening, at 10, 2:30, and 7:30. All are invited.

June 29, 1890

St. Louis Daily Globe-Democrat (MO)

[Public Thanks]

rs. M. B. Woodworth, the evangelist, who is now conducting revival meetings in a tent at Jefferson and Cass Avenues, desires to tender public thanks to the chief of police, Maj. Lawrence Harrigan, for the protection which he extended to her and her assistants. Mrs. Woodworth feels grateful, also, to the officers of the fourth police district for the cheerful spirit in which they executed Chief Harrigan's orders respecting the suppression of hoodlumism that threatened to break up the tent meetings. Services will be held today at 10:00 A.M. and at 2:30 and 7:30 P.M.

August 21, 1890

St. Louis Post-Dispatch (MO)

Strange Scenes

The Remarkable Manifestations at the Woodworth Revival Tent

MEN, WOMEN, AND CHILDREN GO INTO A TRANCE AND CLAIM TO SEE HEAVENLY VISIONS

People Testify That They Have Been Cured of Diseases From Which They Have Long Suffered and Which Baffled Physicians—Sights Which Are Astounding People of All Grades of Society—A Graphic Description of the Occurrences in the Tent Last Night

In the tent at the corner of Cass Avenue and Jefferson can be seen nightly some of the most weird and entirely inexplicable scenes ever witnessed in this or any other city—scenes which puzzle physicians, ministers of the Gospel, and cool-headed businessmen, and which seem like miracles to the ignorant. They cause the brain to whirl in wonder and cause those who have belief in the supernatural and in spiritualism to be more firmly impressed with the thought that wonderful things beyond the power of man are being performed before their eyes.

The readers of the *Post-Dispatch* will have an opportunity of judging for themselves as the scenes which took place in the gospel tent are described by the reporter just as they occurred. Perhaps believers in hypnotism may find an explanation of the occurrences in their science. Those who have strong religious beliefs may think that it was the work of a divine hand, while some will not attempt to explain it. But truly strange and wonderful things were seen in Mrs. Woodworth's gospel tent last night.

Two large electric lights and a couple of gasoline lamps lit up the interior and brought out the expressions on the faces of the interested listeners.

Mrs. Woodworth was speaking. Her utterances are probably more like those of the notorious Sam Jones than any other person. Her voice was rather hoarse, but it has a penetrating quality about it. She articulated rather indistinctly at times, but this seemed to be in a measure the fault of the cold.

A Strange Harangue

"O-O-O-h, why don't you come to the throne of grace? Come all of you; you want to be saved. Come and get salvation. Halleluja-a-a-h!"

She walked up and down the platform clapping her hands, while shouts of "amen" and groans of "God help us" sounded on either hand.

"It doesn't say the murderers and robbers and such shall go to hell, but it says those whose names are not in the Book of Life. The rich can be saved as well as the poor. I'd rather walk to heaven than ride to hell in a chariot."

Suddenly there was a bustle of excitement. Several people were seen to rise hurriedly, as though to make room for someone. The reporter changed his seat and saw a beautiful little girl about 10 years of age, supported in an apparently unconscious condition by a lady dressed in black. A strong, stoutly built man tenderly lifted her in his arms and laid her down on the bench, on which room was made for her by several who moved further toward the platform. The little girl had a smile of perfect peace on her face and seemed to be having some sweet dream. Her lips were parted in a half smile and her arms were stretched out as though to receive some loved one. There was no excitement and no one seemed to think the scene worthy of special interest. The man who had lifted her on [to] the seat calmly returned to close attention to the sermon. Behind her on another bench sat four women, two in mourning, and two younger ones, one quite pretty dressed in pink while the other, who was common-looking had a dress of some striped material. They looked interestedly at Mrs. Woodworth, and the child slept peacefully on in her trance.

Several hoarse voices in the rear of the tent could be heard calling: "More light!"

"Give us light!" etc.

The choir, on the platform behind Mrs. Woodworth, struck up a hymn to drown the noise, and after a couple of verses Mrs. Woodworth continued. The lights shone again and the audience attentively listened. Finally the little girl, who had been sleeping about a half-hour, made an attempt to rise. Her half-open eyes stared sightlessly as though in agony and her breathing was evidently painful. One of the women behind her placed an arm under her head and assisted her to rise to a sitting posture, but the girl fell back into her lap. The perspiration was wiped from her face and neck, and finally with a long drawn sigh, she opened her eyes, looked about her, and sat up. Her face was flushed as though from a deep sleep, and she perspired freely. No one paid any further attention to her and after wiping her eyes with her handkerchief, she began listening to the words of Mrs. Woodworth. Several old ladies who had watched the child in her trance, if such it could be called, wiped their eyes and whispered to each other that the child had just had a glimpse of heaven and responded more heartily with their "amens."

The sermon lasted about an hour and a half. Mrs. Woodworth became greatly enthused and worked the audience up to a state of nervous enthusiasm. Then a hymn was sung while time was kept by the beating of hands by some, while others waved their arms and stamped their feet. "Faster! Faster!" cried one singer, and the time increased, while the rapid cadence was kept by swaying bodies.

Becoming Enthused

"Just hold up your hands, right up, look up to God and give up everything. Just be willing to let everything go for God," said Wm. Franklin Upp, who was formerly employed at the Famous Shoe & Clothing [and?] who has recently left their employ.

He went from person to person touching each one by the wrist and giving a few encouraging words.

About two hundred swayed around the kneeling throng shaking hands with each other.

"Move right along, and to the left," said Mr. Upp with a wave of his hand. Everybody shook hands with everybody else.

"Praise the Lord!" exclaimed one old lady, as the tears streamed down her face and she grasped the hand of the reporter.

"Glad to see you here brother," said a fat man with a shiny bald head as he moved off a woman's dress on which he was standing.

"Glory to God! Hallelujah!" shouted a young woman whose hat hung down the back of her head while she excitedly waved her arms in the air. "Glory to the Lord!"

The choir struck up a slow chant while the people moved slowly along. On the outside of the moving throng stood a number of sightseers, who watched the proceedings with a great deal of interest and occasionally shook hands in a sheepish way with some enthusiastic singer.

"Faster, faster," cried Mrs. Woodworth clapping her hands, and the choir sang faster. The people moved quicker and the bodies of the [kneeling?] ones began to unconsciously sway to and fro.

"[Make?] way [for our?] brother," called out a voice from the platform, as a man was seen elbowing his way through the crowd. Of course everybody looked to see who was going to be saved, but the man came on unflinching through the sea of curious faces, and the moment he reached the moving circle, he was seized by the hand and pulled in amidst shouts of hallelujah as though he had just been pulled from the water while drowning. Then followed several others, who were quieted in a like manner while room was made for them to kneel by the "throne."

"Come up, come up. We are only going to occupy this old house of a body for a while. We'll get ready for a nice new mansion," shouted Mrs. Woodworth.

And they came up. They pushed and crowded and elbowed their way to the throne like persons fearful that the salvation would be exhausted before they could get there.

"Anyone who wants to be healed of any disease, just come right up, free of charge," called Mrs. Woodworth. "Crowd around the throne. It don't (*sic*) make no difference if you are two or three deep. It'll reach you just the same."

The moving, singing, band-shaking throng gave shouts of praise. Two or three red-shirted Salvation Army men were as active workers as the others and joined in appealing to the people to come to the throne and get salvation.

Suddenly a little girl was seen to throw up her arms and fall over backward, while her arms and hands fluttered convulsively. She was caught while falling by two women, who tenderly laid her down on the throne. Then another fell in the same way and was similarly served.

"I see Him, I see Him," gasped a girl about eighteen years of age, as her face took on a look of extreme delight. She pointed upwards with her finger and slowly started to walk away. The crowd made way for her while a benignant old lady with spectacles followed holding her hands out as though she expected the girl to fall. Suddenly she stopped, half turned, and fell into the arms of the old lady, who had a struggle to keep from also falling. A sturdy young man sprang to her assistance and the girl was laid on a bench.

Then those kneeling at the throne began dropping over, and the corps of assistants, numbering about twenty-five, was kept busy carrying them to the large platform. Soon this was crowded, however; and the benches in the vicinity of the throne were covered with unconscious people.

Falling in All Directions

There were strong men, women, and boys and girls of all ages. One man, who was kneeling in the sawdust, kept calling continuously: "Dear Father, help me. O, Father! Father!" in such an agonized tone as to cause the tears to start from many an eye. One boy was seen walking aimlessly about with closed eyes, while his hands were held out as though in expectancy of clasping someone. A man, evidently an acquaintance or a relative, made a move as though to seize the boy, when someone said:

"Let the boy alone, the end will take care of him." The boy finally succumbed and was tenderly laid on a bench.

At one time there were as many as forty people lying in an unconscious condition on the platform and benches. They lay on their backs, some with their arms stretched out as though in entreaty, others lying peacefully, while some had their hands clasped and their lips moved occasionally as though in prayer. Several little girls lay as though they were peacefully sleeping. One little boy who was lying on a bench seemed to be sleeping as quietly as though he were in his own bed at home. The reporter touched his wrist to find out how his pulse was and found it beating very rapidly, but the boy impatiently jerked his hand away before it had been held for more than four or five seconds.

One thing, which was rather annoying, delighted a crowd of young fellows and caused a policeman who was present to go out into the night and laugh.

Two young fellows, apparently of the kind called toughs, went to the altar "just for fun" and knelt down. One of them began to quietly laugh at the others but was suddenly transformed with horror on seeing the eyes of his chum become glassy and observe him finally fall over in a swoon.

"Dat boy's got 'er fit. Just trow some cold water in his face an' he'll be all right," said the skeptical one.

"He's in the hands of the Lord and is all right," indignantly responded an old lady who was kneeling beside them. The young man got up and sat down on a bench.

"Will Bro. Greenwood lead us in prayer?" asked Mrs. Woodworth, and in response a slightly built, elderly man stepped to the front of the platform. He was E. S. Greenwood of the Liberty Evangelical Mission.

The prayer lasted fully a quarter of an hour and when it came to an end, the colored woman humbly remained kneeling. Then followed more singing, and at about 11 o'clock the people began to move out. The friends of those who were still in an unconscious state remained waiting for them.

Slowly they revived, one by one, and after taking their hats or bonnets, etc., went home with their friends. It was fully an hour after the meeting closed before some of them got away from the tent, as the influence seemed to be stronger with some than with others.

Some Who Saw Visions

Lying on a bench near the altar was stretched an athletic young man, his face showing traces of dissipation, while his general make-up showed him to be a rather rough young fellow. His hands were clasped and his face wore a look of peaceful repose. Occasionally his lips moved and he seemed to be talking with someone.

Sitting on a bench beside him was a young man who in dress and appearance denoted a common interest.

"Bill's got 'em bad," he said, in response to a *Post-Dispatch* reporter's inquiry.

"I never seen him like this before. He ain't full I know, an' he never had a fit in his life," he disconsolately said, as he surreptitiously took a chaw of tobacco from a black plug of generous proportions.

"Don't want them people to see me chaw," he said as he sat on the ground and carefully covered the spot over with loose sawdust. "Ef Bill's goin' to be like this, I don't know what I'll do, but he's got 'em bad, got 'em bad."

On the altar lay a little girl apparently about eleven years old. She was dressed in a sailor dress of blue cloth, while a little trinket was tied around her neck. She was a pretty little brunette, and as she lay with her hands crossed on her breast, she seemed like a sweet child at rest on her bier.

"That little girl hasn't got no one to go home with," said a manly little fellow named Willie Malone. "She came here with another little girl. That one (pointing to one who was being led around by two men), but now she hasn't no one to go home with. That's why I'm waitin'," he said, as he picked the little girl's hat up and laid it on the altar beside her. "I'm goin' to see that she gets home all right," he said, as he manfully expanded his chest and seemed to grow a little bigger.

On the sawdust away from the others, lay a man whose gray hair was covered with the sawdust. His arms were thrown out in an attitude of carelessness and he was breathing regularly, while the expression on his face denoted that his thoughts were pleasant ones. His hat lay on a bench and he had evidently rolled off. He was left sleeping calmly with his thoughts alone for companionship.

James Nash, a bright-looking boy about thirteen years of age, laid half an hour on a bench and then recovered consciousness. He lives at 3002 North Market and was getting ready to go home alone.

"What did you see in your vision?" the reporter asked.

"Oh, it was lovely," he replied while his eyes brightened with the recollection. "I thought that I was taken away up in the air someplace where there was sweet music all the time. There were angels flying all around. They had big white wings and had on long white gowns. Their faces shone bright and like gold, and in the middle of them stood Jesus. His face and form were so bright that it would hurt your eyes to look at Him. Way down below, in what looked like a big city, full of church spires, there was a big crowd of people on the streets, a whole multitude of them and they seemed to be waiting for the world to come to an end. They looked so bright and happy and the angels seemed to be so glad all the time. I want to see it again."

"Did you know where you were all the time?"

"Oh, yes; people kept punching against me as I lay there and of course that broke the thing once in awhile, but it was just grand while it lasted."

Wanted to Climb to Heaven

"Look there," suddenly exclaimed someone. A little girl, Josie Keller, was seen trying to climb one of the ropes leading to the top of the tent. She had climbed about five feet when her father and another man caught her and pulled her down. Then she walked over to the side of the tent and tried to climb up the canvas by seizing it with her hands.

"She wants to climb to heaven," whispered one lady to another.

A little girl in a white dress, with her hands stretched out as though asking someone above to take her, lay Maud Hinmen. She was moving her lips as though in prayer; and occasionally, endearing words addressed to some unseen person could be heard.

Seated by the side of the altar, with one hand caressingly laid on the head of a little girl, sat a pleasant-faced German woman.

"Whose little girl is that?" asked the reporter.

"That's my little girl. Her name is Minnie Breckerbonna."

"Is this the first time she has been here?"

"Oh, no, she's been here seven or eight times, and she says she sees such pretty things that she wants to come every night. She sees angels and Jesus and everything in heaven. I have never been in that state yet."

Saw Her Sister

Pretty little Addie Otto, the girl whose trance is above described, was asked by the reporter about her vision and she rather hesitantly complied.

"The first vision I had," she said, "was the other night. I dreamt that I was going to heaven, and I climbed up a long ladder to get there. I saw Jesus leading the flocks of people around, and it was all so beautiful. I saw among those people there my sister, who has been dead several years, and also my little niece. They seemed so happy.

"Tonight I had another beautiful vision. I dreamed that I saw heaven again. The roof of the tent seemed to whirl around and round, and all of a sudden it seemed to whirl into a beautiful fountain with the water all the color of diamonds and other bright things. Then it seemed to change until it was all as red as blood, and a voice seemed to tell me that it was the blood of Christ washing away the sins of the people. It was a beautiful sight and I want to see it again."

"Why are the children given a sight into these things, Mrs. Woodworth?" asked the reporter. "Isn't it all merely caused by excitement?"

"The children are old enough to give themselves to God and therefore are permitted to do so. I don't know how it is. People are cured here every night of different diseases by the power of God. I have faith and that helps them.

"I was in a little church one day and prayed to be given the power of faith. Suddenly I felt that it had been given me, and I became strong and have since worked for the Lord. Here are some that have been cured:

"Mr. Douglas, who is now one of my active assistants, lives at 1215 North Tenth Street. He was cured of a number of diseases which baffled the efforts of the doctors.

"Mrs. Alley of 4928 Lorraine Ave. was cured of dropsy which had troubled her for fifteen years, while her husband has been cured of head trouble caused by a sunstroke.

"Frank Hardy of 4217 Cottage Avenue was cured of Neuralgia which had [troubled ?] him for forty years; and Lizzie Hammond, who lives at 1858 South Thirteenth Street, was cured of nervous prostration and St. Vitus dance[1] after having been in the hospital two years."

A Physician's Opinion

Dr. King of 2726 St. Louis Avenue, a practicing physician, was watching his little girl who was in a trance and waiting to take her home.

"I had attended several meetings here, and Saturday night I came near being brought under this influence. I went home but was restless all night; and when I went to take my bath Sunday morning, I fell into a trance, if such you might call it. I saw wonderful things."

"Don't you think that it is injurious to your little daughter to go into such a state?"

"No, I do not. She feels better afterwards and likes to see the beautiful things. She seems stronger afterwards even. I do not think that it has a debilitating effect."

A Minister's Opinion

Rev. E. M. C. Botterill, who at present is filling the pulpit of Rev. Dr. Brooks of Compton Avenue Church, was an interested spectator at the meeting. He is the state evangelist for the Y. M. C. A. and is used to attending such meetings.

"But I will admit," he said, "that I never saw anything like it, and it is beyond my comprehension. It must be that the people who go into that state are led into it by their imagination and the force of will stronger than their own. You know that eighty-five per cent of the people can be controlled by the others, and this undoubtedly

[1] "St. Vitus dance"—"Chorea," which is any of various nervous disorders of infectious or organic origin in man and dogs having as common features involuntary, uncontrollable purposeless movements of body and face and marked incoordination of limbs. [*Webster's Third New International Dictionary of the English Language: Unabridged*, Springfield, MA: Merriam-Webster, Inc. (1993)].

illustrates the fact to a certain extent. But I will admit that I never saw its equal."

Rev. Wm. Smith

A colored pastor of North St. Louis, stated that he had seen such things in his church, but they were indulged in only by the more ignorant. He says the younger generation is not so subject to the influence of the leaders. A prominent physician claims that it is nothing more or less than hypnotism, and that it is practiced by those who are leading the meetings.

The reporter shook hands with a few of those remaining and started away, thoroughly mystified. Near the door, on a bench, lay Josie Keller, who had tried to climb to heaven but failed practically. Her father, a butcher, who lives at 2627 Sullivan Avenue, was waiting for her. Her face wore a beatific smile, and she seemed more like an ethereal spirit in the uncertain flickering of the electric light than like a human being.

August 22, 1890

St. Louis Daily Globe-Democrat (MO)

Wanted to See Wonders

An Enormous Crowd at the Woodworth Tent

SEVERAL VISITORS FROM BEYOND THE CITY LIMITS—THE POWER WHICH IS EXERCISED OVER CONVERTS DESCRIBED—WHY IT CANNOT BE REGARDED AS HYPNOTISM OR MESMERISM—FEELING AMONG THE NEIGHBORS

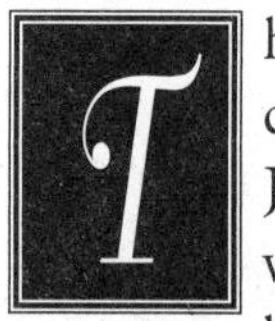

he gospel tent at the corner of Cass and Jefferson Avenues was crowded early last night by worshippers and by readers of the *Post-Dispatch* who were anxious to see "strange scenes" similar to those described and illustrated yesterday. The Cass Avenue cars, going west, carried unusually heavy loads as far as Jefferson Avenue, including among the passengers a large number of persons living in the Southern part, with several from East St. Louis. The Jefferson Avenue cars coming from both directions were uncomfortably crowded; and before the usual hour for commencing service, every seat was occupied and the aisles were crowded.

The arrivals, however, were still numerous and there was a crowd all around the outside of the tent at least ten or twelve deep. These took in the service very contentedly; and the wave of excitement was so far-reaching in its influence that one of the number, a well-dressed mechanic, fell down and was carried into the tent and to the platform with his arms straight in front of him and his hands pointing upwards. The best of order prevailed after the service commenced, although there were some manifestations of impatience on the part of those who, in their eagerness to secure good seats, had come very early in the evening.

Mr. E. S. Greenwood led in prayer and sang "Nearer My God to Thee" with great power and expression. Mrs. Woodworth's discourse was listened to very attentively by the crowd, which could not have numbered less than 8,500, keeping perfect order and evincing—some profound reverence, and others a determination to investigate the matter fairly and to treat the lady with all respect. After the address Mr. Greenwood again prayed. He invoked special

Maria Woodworth-Etter (far right) rarely took time off from ministering. She often preached twice a day for months during revivals. Her diligence and the many conversions which resulted often gained Etter the respect of even her enemies. The other two women might possibly be her associates, Emma Isenberg and Ollie Daggett.

blessings on the press and alluding to the report in yesterday's *Post-Dispatch* offered thanks for the spirit of fairness that had been displayed by the writers and for the assistance given to the movement by the increased publicity given to it. He also solicited divine blessings on the press not only of the city and the state, but also on the press of the whole land.

The number who came forward to the platform was even larger than usual, and between twenty and twenty-five passed into the trance condition described in yesterday's *Post-Dispatch*. The majority were young girls, but there were three or four grown-up men and four colored people. The excitement was intense, and several penitents professed conversion and great happiness. The services were concluded shortly after 11 and the immense crowd dispersed. The number of visitors from a distance was so large that the streetcar accommodation proved entirely inadequate; and there were large crowds on the corners until close upon midnight, although several parties walked over to the Northern Central road. The crowd was of a perfectly orderly character, and the rough element was so poorly represented that the patrolmen on duty had little or nothing to do.

Not Hypnotism

Speaking to a *Post-Dispatch* reporter this morning, Mr. Greenwood said:

"I cannot account for the falling down and the apparent trance condition. I don't think it can be accounted for by hypnotism, and I will tell you why. Years ago, when I was in the East, I knew a laboring man who accidentally discovered that he had an immense willpower and that he could influence men with whom he came in contact. He gave up his work and took to giving exhibitions of what he called mesmerism, but which was identical with what is now called hypnotism. He could call up the best citizens from among the audience and compel them to do the most childish things on the stage. If Mrs. Woodworth were a mesmerist, she could compel these people to obey her will and make them do anything she desired while they were in a trance. But she cannot do anything of the kind and does not profess to be able to do it. I repeat I cannot explain the phenomena which occur at the tent nightly. Those who fall invariably seem to strain upwards, holding their hands aloft, and sometimes even trying to climb up. It is a wonderful thing certainly, but it is not hypnotism or mesmerism."

"You mentioned the *Post-Dispatch* in prayer last night?"

"I did and the prayer was a very sincere one. I assured Mrs. Woodworth that if the *Post-Dispatch* wrote up the services, they would do so in a spirit of fairness. Directly [after], I read the report in yesterday's paper, I knew we should have an enormous crowd; and I got to the tent half an hour earlier than usual in consequence. Everyone on the street car was discussing the article; and when I got to the tent I found the discussion general, and it ought to have made you feel proud to see the number of copies of the *Post-Dispatch* in people's hands. Our work will be aided immensely by the increased publicity that has been given to it."

Volunteering Aid

"How did you become connected with the work?"

"I volunteered my services. As the churches went west and left the 125,000 people in the downtown districts practically unprovided for, I commenced to work among them and am thankful for the mission established at Sixth and Spruce and on Franklin Avenue. When I saw that a petition had been gotten up to have Mrs. Woodworth silenced, I determined to offer her my aid. Before she went to the corner of Cass and Jefferson, there used to be Sunday baseball and general Sabbath desecration on the lot, but I never heard of a petition for relief from the nuisance or I would have promptly signed it. I know no creed in evangelistic work; and being satisfied that Mrs. Woodworth is doing good work, I am willing to help. But I can't explain what takes place. Last night I saw ex-Mayor Brown in the tent and asked his opinion, but like myself he could offer no explanation."

"Have you seen much faith-healing in the tent?"

"Not much. One night a lady came up to the platform walking with crutches. Mrs. Woodworth told her to walk away unaided and she obeyed her. Then the lady who sings so sweetly was suffering badly from consumption when she joined Mrs. Woodworth. She doesn't look much a consumptive now, nor sing like one either."

Inquiries made in the neighborhood show that the opposition to the mission has largely died out, and it is doubtful whether many signatures could be obtained now to an adverse petition. There is little or no disturbance, and the bulk of the attendance seems to be from a distance.

August 24, 1890

St. Louis Post-Dispatch (MO)

The Woodworth Wonders

The Public Becoming Interested in Them—Peter Cartwright's Work

he Woodworth revival tent at Jefferson and Cass Avenues was packed last night. A large number were unable to obtain admission. Mrs. Woodworth preached one of her characteristic sermons, after which those who had been moved by her words came forward to receive the "power." The scenes, which have been taking place every evening for some time, were repeated to the intense interest of the large audience which became considerably excited, although perfect order prevailed. A large number were influenced and returned to consciousness again to tell stories of marvelous sights and strange scenes.

A large number of people came to the tent this morning to attend the meeting which they thought was to be held, but they were disappointed, as the only meetings held in the morning are on Sundays.

Considerable discussion has been aroused in consequence of the strange actions of those who are overcome by the "power." Similar scenes were enacted years ago by Peter Cartwright, the famous evangelist, and his associates, who traveled through several states and gave meetings at which the same strange manifestations occurred.

They called it the "power" and the state in which the person went was called the "jerks," in consequence of the convulsive movements of the hands and arms. Cartwright and his followers would pray for the power, sometimes for ten or twelve hours, until it came and then they would go into the trance which was supposed to be the result of their prayers. Cartwright, it is said, was the founder of a number of the Methodist churches in Missouri and Illinois.

Mrs. Woodworth firmly believes in the efficacy of prayer and newspapers. She tells the following story:

> At last night's meeting a man got up and told his experience. He said he was reading the article which appeared in last Wednesday's *Post-Dispatch* when he suddenly realized that the hand of God was in it. He began to tremble and finally fell under the influence of the power. His wife, who was not a believer in religion, also came under the influence and they were converted. They told their story at our meeting.

The lease for the tenting ground expires September 10, and the evangelists will travel through Illinois and Indiana visiting the churches which they have established. They will establish a mission here before their departure. It will be called the Church of God, and will be non sectarian.[1]

[1] Maria Woodworth-Etter traveled under the auspices of the Church of God (a name used by many nondenominational groups of her day), which at the time did not consider itself a denomination but a fellowship that avoided denominational ties with this simple title.

August 26, 1890

St. Louis Daily Globe-Democrat (MO)

Miraculous Cures

Some of the Marvelous Effects of Mrs. Woodworth's Ministrations

What Some of the Subjects Say About Their Diseases and Their Recovery—Dropsy, Rheumatism, Neuralgia, Etc., Cured

rs. Maria B. Woodworth, the evangelist who has been holding revival services for some weeks past at Jefferson and Cass Avenues, is fast becoming famous for her cures of bodily ailments as well as her healing of wounded souls.

Mrs. Woodworth maintains that her cures are strictly the work of faith in the power of God. Mesmerism and hypnotism, says she, are [the] devil's words and manifestations of the devil's power. Her strength owes nothing to either of these but in faith pure and simple. In order to be cured of any bodily ailment, no matter how virulent or of how long standing, she claims, all that is necessary to do is to come to her with one's heart ready to be converted. At the same instant that the conversion is effected, the worldly disease falls off like a useless garment and never returns as long as the heart is purged of sin and full of the belief in God and Christ.

At nearly every meeting poor diseased beings come to her simple service in the tent, and in many cases really wonderful rejuvenations are effected.

Yesterday afternoon, though no cures effected, several persons who had before been subject to Mrs. Woodworth's ministrations were seen by a *Globe-Democrat* reporter and willingly gave their experience.

Had Dropsy for Ten Years

"For ten years," said Mrs. Wm. A. Allen of No. 4928 Lorentz Avenue, "I was afflicted with dropsy. My whole body was swollen so that I resembled a big tub. I could not move. My husband on going away to work would put me in a chair and upon his return home would find me in the same position. If I attempted to leave the chair in his absence, I would fall upon the floor and be obliged to lie there till he came home again."

"I was in an awful state. The neighbors came in to see me every day [and] expected to find me burst open like a great bag of water. I was given up to die by the best doctors in town after spending a great amount of money on them. At length I heard of Mrs. Woodworth and felt a longing to get to her and ask to be cured. But my husband, who was a drunkard—bless God that he isn't now—would not hear of my going to the tent. 'It is all a cheat,' he said."

"At length I begged to go so much that he gave in and said, 'Go if you can; I'll go with you.' The neighbors helped to get me here, and then I went to the side of the altar on my hands and knees. I had faith in Mrs. Woodworth and the Holy Father. Almost before I knew it, I was cured but could not believe it. I felt the disease leave me like water does after being poured on your head."

"Now walk!" says Mrs. Woodworth.

"I can't," says I.

"You must," answers she. And I did.

"I slipped my feet along carefully at first, expecting to fall down in awful pain, but went ahead all right. I threw away my crutches and refused the neighbors' help to get onto the cars. I got off the cars all safe and have been well ever since. My husband was cured of the liquor habit and blood trouble at the same time, last Thursday night."

Cured of Drunkenness

"At once!" said Mr. Allen at the conclusion of his wife's story. "For a long time I had been a victim of that devil's curse—drink. Sometimes I would not be very bad, but often I would be blind and roaring drunk. Nothing could cure me. I had besides the drink habit something the matter with the blood in my head. I would seem to stop up, and I couldn't move. When I went to the gospel tent, I made fun of the idea of getting well. But when I had been there a little while, I became convinced and went up to the altar like my wife did. There, as if by magic, the craving for whisky left me and also that awful head trouble. Neither has come back since, and I could sing for joy. My home is a perfect heaven compared with its condition before and I am happy."

[Partial Blindness Healed]

Mrs. Joseph Funtz of No. 5325 McKissick Avenue, was cured of partial blindness last Friday night. "For eight years," she said, "my eyes have been growing weaker and weaker. They had got so at last that I could hardly see across the room in broad daylight. Last Friday, I went to the tent but not to get cured, for I thought that out of the question. When I got there, however, the way seemed so bright that I went and knelt before Mrs. Woodworth and begged to be cured of my affliction. Hardly had I expressed the wish when I felt that my sight was saved. A mist seemed to fall from before me and I looked at the electric light in the tent without feeling pain. I went home and took up my Bible and found that I could read as well as I ever could. I am cured, and my eyes are as good as anybody's."

Pneumonia and Bronchitis

"I had a severe case of pneumonia and bronchitis," said Mr. Joseph Christman of No. 2237 Dickson Street, "and could hardly reach the tent I was so exhausted. I could only breathe with the most fearful pain and difficulty, and one of my lungs was affected. After going to the tent and worshiping only a little while, I was cured. Before I could not talk. Now I can shout and sing with anyone in the city."

[No Longer Crippled]

"I was completely crippled," said Thomas Peakes of Springfield, Ill. "My right leg was a wreck from an accident, and no doctor could cure it. I was obliged to use crutches continually, and had the most fearful pains in the injured limb. I visited Mrs. Woodworth, and so had scarcely completed a prayer for my deliverance when I was as well as I ever was. My leg is all right and I am going to start for home tonight."

Other Cures Effected

Briefly stated, Mrs. Woodworth gives the following list of remarkable cures effected during the last months:

"Little Lizzie Hammond of No. 1858 South Thirteenth Street, was suffering from a number of ailments. She had nervous prostrating paralysis of the right side, her breastbone protruded far out of the proper position, and, moreover, she had St. Vitus dance. She could not move when brought to Mrs. Woodworth and had been discharged from the hospital as a hopeless case. She went away by herself completely saved. Her mother could not believe it but was convinced. The child is all right now, her breastbone has returned to its proper place, and she does not suffer from any of the other diseases.

Theresa Raymond of No. 127 Lombard Street was made well after suffering ten years with rheumatism. She left her crutches in the tent and now does all her own work.

Frank Hardy of No. 4217 Cottage Avenue, after suffering from neuralgia forty years, was cured of his sufferings.

Eliza Harris, who lives at No. 1828 Market Street, was cured of rheumatism of four years' standing. She left her crutches at the tent.

Lizzie Gerdel, 2217 Howard Street, had suffered seventeen years with asthma. She could hardly get her breath and was in a pitiable condition. She left the tent well and can now breathe as freely as anyone."

A letter reached Mrs. Woodworth from Reddick, Ill., two hundred miles from here, asking that Mrs. Dr. Petry, of that place, be prayed for. She had neuralgia and paralysis. A service of prayer was held for her and she was cured.

C. W. Brown, of No. 2901 Rauschenback Avenue, was cured of a bad case of bronchitis.

These and a great number of others just as wonderful, Mrs. Woodworth says, have been cured by the power of God. She does not claim to have effected the cures. God and Christ did it all.

August 30, 1890

Weekly Medical Review
(St. Louis, MO)

"The Peculiar People"

mong the English this expression will be found in common use, which appears to be applied to "Faith-Curists," "Salvationists," and other sects of that ilk, as a mild token of the general contempt or want of esteem in which they are held. It is an appropriate way of designating such bands of fakirs, although their methods would justify one in using infinitely stronger expressions without doing violence to truth.

There is at present sojourning in this city a band of "converters," led on by Mrs. Maria B. Woodworth, a self-styled "evangelist," whose methods would well entitle them to be called "peculiar people," if nothing worse. We hesitate whether to class them among the "fools" or the "knaves," and candidly confess that we regret that our choice of terms is so limited. Lest we may be deemed harsh, we will at once proceed to explain.

These people are using hypnotism in their performances and yet assert that the scenes to be witnessed nightly in their tent are nothing more nor less than visible manifestations of the divine power, brought about through their own humble intervention. We can place them in one of the two above-named categories only after deciding for ourselves whether they do or do not really believe what they say. A brief description of their methods might prove interesting. The speaker, generally Mrs. Woodworth, delivers a long address, during which she continually makes use of suggestion and in a most effective manner. Quotations are given from the Bible, relating instances where people have been thrown into trances by the divine will, and statements are made that similar manifestations have been given on previous nights and will probably be vouchsafed on that particular evening.

After these points have been dilated upon and repeatedly dinned into the ears of the listeners, a general invitation is extended to come nearer to the platform so as to be more accessible to the influence, an invitation that is immediately accepted by the more susceptible hearers, mostly young women and all probably intellectually handicapped to some degree. A glaring electric light suspended before the audience may be presumed to be a prominent factor in the proceedings. After assembling about the platform, prayers and songs are next in order, and during this time the workers or operators pick out and endeavor to influence the more promising subjects before them, usually with great success; the subjects succumb almost by the dozen.

Some may say, "Granted that this be hypnotism, does not the end justify the means?" In reply we can only say that it remains to be proven that one or repeated hypnotizations can permanently reverse the moral tendencies of an individual. Certain it is that such exhibitions are reprehensible and highly demoralizing in their general effects, even though conducted in the name of religion. While this is undoubtedly the case, it is extremely improbable that anything can or will be done to check the performances unless some very positively harmful results are shown, as, for example, in the case of the faith healers recently punished in New York. In the meantime the medical profession can stand back and marvel at the wonderful cures which Mrs. Woodworth and her followers are performing, cures of organic diseases which physicians have treated in vain.

One in particular, published in a daily paper, is that of "a young man who was suffering from an abscess in his side which had cost him hundreds of dollars. He was living on tonics and stimulants, but just living and no more. Preparations were being made for a surgical operation which contemplated the removal of two of his ribs which were rapidly disappearing before the inroads of the disease. He went to two meetings and before he had been in the presence an hour, he came under the influence; and now he is cured, ready to testify to the wonderful and inexplicable powers of the faith."

After this nothing more need be said.

September 1, 1890

St. Louis Republic (MO)

By Wholesale

Fifty-Four of Mrs. Woodworth's Converts "Dipped"

AN IRREVERENT CROWD
OF TEN THOUSAND PEOPLE
TURNS THE SOLEMN
CEREMONY INTO A HOWLING
FARCE—
SENSATIONAL INCIDENTS

One of the most remarkable events in the history of St. Louis occurred on the Levee yesterday at the foot of Locust Street. Fifty-four persons, the converts of the famous revivalist Mrs. Woodworth, were baptized in the Mississippi River in the presence of more than ten thousand people. Never has such a spectacle been witnessed before in St. Louis. The whole affair, however, was on a par with the methods of Mrs. Woodworth, and it is her reputation for dramatic and sensational effect that undoubtedly drew such an immense audience to her great exhibition yesterday. Such a ceremony as baptism is, from its nature, one of the most solemn sacraments of the Christian religion, but yesterday it was transformed into a howling blasphemy by the raving, roaring, ungodly crowd that lined the river's front. If it was the intention of the promoters of the affair to impress the crowd with the beauties of religion by such an ultra-public exhibition, they defeated their own ends most lamentably. But if it was the purpose of Mrs. Woodworth to add to her own notoriety, she certainly met with abundant success.

The Crowd Gathering

It had been announced that the ceremony would begin at 2 o'clock. Long before that hour, the streets leading to that part of the Levee were thronged with a holiday crowd bent upon seeing and enjoying a novel exhibition. The usual Sunday river excursions, which leave about the same hour, also added to the crowd. A rough pier of planks had been built into the river, a distance of thirty or forty feet between Locust and St. Charles Streets, and this was the center of attraction for the crowds. Long before 2 o'clock the Levee, from Olive Street to the big bridge, was crowded with a motley mass of people of all ages, conditions, and colors. Every coign of vantage[1] was occupied. Over all a swaying mass of umbrellas and parasols added confusion to the scene and disaster to eyes and hats.

One of the big excursion boats was almost abreast of the little pier, and her forward decks and gangplank were crowded with humanity surveying the scene and "guying" the less fortunate humans on the stones below, while the band boisterously played extremely secular tunes, which the crowd occasionally took up and sang in unison. Just above and below the scene of action were two wharf barges, that of the Cape Girardeau and Clarksville Packet Line and the Alton Packet Line. These were captured with a rush by the crowd and loaded flat with pleasure seekers who joked each other cheerily or swore earnestly at the barge master, according to their good fortune in securing front seats for the show. The big bridge was lined with a vast crowd and the roofs of all the buildings in the vicinity wore a fringe of humanity, while every window was an eruption of heads.

And still the crowds came until the Levee, from the water's edge to the railroad tracks, was a solid mass of people, while the whole river-front above was blockaded with all manner of vehicles, from the stylish West End coach to the huckster wagon.

The "barefooted boy with legs of 'tan'" was also there, also all the rest of his species including Little Paul Fauntleroy,[2] who got right into the push and the river, clear up over his knees, and never minded the immaculate toilet. In fact, the small boy had the best of it. He just simply waded right out up to his waist and saw it all — whole droves of him did. But he wasn't the only one who got wet. Never in the history of St. Louis has there been a more elaborate and varied exposure of hosiery than was seen at the water's edge yesterday. For the ladies—without regard to age or color—would see the proceedings. And when the pressure from behind forced them forward, they daintily gathered up their drapery and with a magnificent disdain of shoe leather and the proprieties, waded in.

[1] "coign of vantage"—advantageous position for observation *(Webster's N. W.,* 1997).

[2] "barefooted boy with legs of 'tan'"—source unknown; "Little Paul Fauntleroy"—the hero of the book, *Little Lord Fauntleroy* (1886) by Francis Hodgson Burnett, who would have been dressed in a suit.

There was one dainty little blonde in a ravishing lilac toilet[3] who came with an escort, and who, after 15 minutes hard work, succeeded in reaching the water's edge. But even then she couldn't see. The gallant escort stepped into the water, regardless of his varnished shoes, waded out nearly to his knees, and then lifted his fair companion to a big rock, an inch or two above the current, where she perched as daintily as a bird. But presently a big steamer came by, and the surges rolled in and beat upon that rock—and it canted over and spilled the little maid into the water. With a shrill shriek she snatched her lilac skirts above the muddy flood and fled afar while certain cynical and unfeeling males criticized her. This is but one of scores of similar incidents that distinguished Mrs. Woodworth's service.

The Chief Actors

At 2:40 o'clock three enormous closed furniture vans came from Locust Street upon the Levee and headed for the water. They were followed by the hoodlum wagon with a detail of police. They had a severe struggle with the crowd which greeted them with wild and irreverent acclaim. They were even likened unto circus vans.

At 2:55 the doors of the first van were opened. A man in a blue jacket leaped out, sized up the howling, limitless mob, and retired to the seclusion of its interior again. The crowd yelled some more and demanded that "de performers get action on demselves."

At 3 o'clock Mrs. Woodworth headed a procession of the elect from Locust Street down to the water amid deafening cheers. About that time an Italian appeared with a big bunch of red balloons. A shrill voice from the stones suggested that these were to be used by way of illustration—one after each immersion.

At 3:15 the Rev. Charles Bulion of Kansas City, the minister who had been engaged to officiate, waded out with a long pole and took soundings. He was a short, stout man with a gray beard and determined, self-assured manner.

At 3:18 a mighty yell up rose from the crowd and a moment later two little girls in white appeared at the river's brink, led by Mrs.

[3] "toilet"—outfit.

Woodworth and a gentleman in a silk hat. The officiating clergyman received them; Mrs. Woodworth raised her hands, the choir sang "Nearer My God to Thee," the solemn words were said, and the great father of waters received them into his bosom.

Then the crowd raised an approving shout and another hymn was sung.

Rapid Dipping

After that there was no delay. The next candidate was a fleshy woman in white. Instantly the crowd fired a volley of advice at the clergyman, which was no wise relevant or reverent. Her reappearance was received with a tremendous encore, which had not died away until another woman and a little girl had passed through the ceremony. Next followed a woman who lost her presence of mind and struggled violently as the water closed over her. But Mrs. Woodworth came to the rescue with a towel, and she was brought safely ashore amid the plaudits[4] of the audience while the choir sang "Shall We Gather at the River."[5]

Two other young women followed peaceably, and then came a prepossessing brunette in white. The instant she was lifted from the water she got the "power" and left the river with arms wildly waving in air, shouting praises and hosannas. She received enthusiastic encouragement from the crowd. The next candidate was a fleshy woman in blue, who went through the ordeal calmly and got a splendid round of applause in which the preacher was included. Three young women and a little girl followed without incident.

Then the preacher solemnly led forth a tall, very bald, old man in a long black coat. He got a tremendous ovation all the way from the big bridge to the uttermost confines of the crowd. He came out wildly hysterical, while the irreverent crowd yelled something about McGinty.[6]

[4] "plaudits"—applause, expressions of approval or praise *(Webster's N. W.,* 1997).

[5] "Shall We Gather At the River?"—(1864), music and lyrics by Robert Lowry (1826-1899).

[6] "McGinty"—an allusion to an Irish drinking song, "Down Went McGinty," in which McGinty drowns himself in the sea from grief.

A Corpulent Convert

Three young women followed the old man. And then came an exceedingly corpulent convert in a very voluminous dress. Her debut was received with shrieks of approval and a storm of jeers and advice to the minister. She was very calm, however, and walked bravely into the water. The preacher held her firmly and gave her the immersion. But when he attempted to raise her, there was a hitch. Then the desperate man braced his shoulder beneath her, and with a mighty effort heaved her up. As one man the vast crowd screamed: "Saved! Saved!! Saved!!!" Then such a shout went up as was never heard before on the riverfront, and the choir sang "Safe in the Arms of Jesus."[6]

Next came a man in jean pants, a hickory shirt, and a very meek manner. He received many indelicate little attentions from the crowd but came up calm and smiling. Then came a girl in white, followed by another bald-headed man in black. He went in like a lion and came out like a lamb, and the choir sang, "Trim Your Lamp, My Brother."[7]

A young man with a linen duster and a frightened smile was the next candidate. He was followed by another man in black, a youth in a white shirt, and a man in a long frock coat.

At this stage of the proceedings, one of the six oared barges of the St. Louis Rowing Club created a diversion by shooting into the bank and nearly colliding with the officiating clergyman. He waved them solemnly back and the crew exchanged some language that could not possibly be heard in polite society, while the crowd calmly but acrimoniously criticized their "form." It seemed for a few minutes as though things were getting mixed up[8] and somebody was going to get hurt. But the boat backed out and business proceeded.

Three young men in white shirts and a little boy, followed by a fat man with gray hair and black clothes, next passed through the ordeal. Then another very tall man with a full suit of clothes came

[6] "Safe in the Arms of Jesus"—(1868) Lyrics: Fanny J. Crosby (1820-1915), Music: William Howard Doane (1832-1915).

[7] "Trim Your Lamp, My Brother"—source unknown.

[8] "getting mixed up"—escalating to a fight. A "mix up" is a fight.

out with a violent case of the "power." In the midst of the excitement, a small boy who had been indulging in some very extraordinary "monkey business" on a hawser[9] stretched from a barge to the shore, fell into the drink. He was hauled out by a grim man in a skiff and the choir sang "Pull for the Shore, Sailor."[10] Then came a little boy, followed by a man in a white shirt, another wearing a vest, and a gentleman in what appeared to be a bathing suit. Another man in a hickory shirt was succeeded by a companion in misery. Then followed a very tall young man who came out fairly frantic to the intense and vociferous gratification of the crowd. Next came a little girl, a young man, three young women, and a girl with a Stanley sash. They were succeeded by two women in black, a girl in white, a tall woman in muslin, a little boy, and another woman in white.

The exhibition closed with the immersion of a bald-headed man in black who also arose from the deep with a well-developed case of "power."

Then the officiating clergyman delivered a short address to the newly baptized members and a word of warning to the crowd, and the congregation was dismissed.

The converts returned to the furniture cars where they exchanged their wet clothing for everyday habiliments,[11] and the great crowd slowly dispersed.

The police had a hard time of it and worked like Trojans to preserve a semblance of order. No arrests were made, however, and singularly enough, there were no serious accidents.

---

[9] "hawser"—rope.

[10] "Pull for the Shore, Sailor"—(1873) by Phili Paul Bliss (1838-1876).

[11] "habiliments"—clothing.

September 1, 1890

St. Louis Daily Globe-Democrat (MO)

Baptized From the Levee

SOME OF MRS. WOODWORTH'S CONVERTS SUBMIT TO IMMERSION

The Solemn Rite Celebrated in the Presence of an Unsympathetic Crowd—Furniture Vans Used as Dressing Rooms—Irreverent Remarks by Spectators

The Levee, from the foot of Locust Street to the bridge, was lined yesterday afternoon with thousands to witness the baptism of converts made under the preaching of Mrs. Maria B. Woodworth, the evangelist who has labored with the sinful all summer long, in the big tent on the old Union baseball grounds at Jefferson Avenue and Mullanphy Street.

The ceremony of baptism had been announced to take place at 2 o'clock sharp, but long before that hour, thousands of people stood along the Levee, swarmed over the wharf boats of the Clarksville and Alton Packet Companies, and lined the big bridge as far as the middle piers. The people crowded to the water's edge with the omnipresent mad boy in the van[1] and the ladies pressing closely behind. About 2:30 o'clock considerable diversion was created by the departure of the Oliver Beirne and Grand Republic on excursion. The waves from the departing boats gave hundreds of spectators a realistic imitation of the ocean surf, and hundreds of drenched people of all ages, conditions, and colors attested the novelty of the sensation. The display of hosiery of variegated hues during this episode was decidedly interesting, albeit somewhat alarming.

After the boats had backed out of the way, the crowd proceeded to capture the Eagle Packet Company's wharf boat; the watchman who endeavored to stem the tide speedily discovered that he "wasn't in it." A good view was to be obtained from these boats, the central point of attraction being a narrow platform extending out some twelve feet into the river, which bore a startling resemblance to the crude springboard from which juveniles dive in surreptitious swimming excursions.

[1] "van"—short for vanguard, i.e., the leading portion of the crowd.

The Furniture Vans Arrive

Fully five thousand people had assembled and were beginning to manifest their impatience by crowding, pushing, and an altogether uncalled-for indulgence in cat calls and slang. Three furniture vans[2] were moved in solemn procession down the Levee, and their appearance was greeted with cheers and shouts of laughter, and such remarks as these:

"Here come the animals," "New museum in town," etc. With the utmost difficulty the vans were forced through the crowd and drawn up near the water's edge, but not before a large squad of police had driven the crowd back by a liberal display of their clubs. The crowd evidently thought the candidates for baptism were ensconced in the furniture vans and manifested a most unreasonable desire to surround them and take possession. This idea was dissipated at 3 o'clock sharp by the appearance of Mrs. Woodworth and a large number of followers on the Levee. The police again wrestled with the crowd and finally succeeded in clearing a path by which the worshippers could make their way to the front.

The following fifteen minutes were full of anxious suspense, which told heavily upon the assembled thousands. A clerical-looking gentleman took on a position at the end of the plank, and a sturdy individual in bare arms and gray undershirt waded out some 5 feet from the platform and set a stake. It was now 3:10 o'clock and the spectators were becoming decidedly hilarious and were recklessly indulging in all sorts of promiscuous expressions not calculated to arouse an exalted spirit of piety in the breasts of the listeners.

The minister who performed the baptismal service waded out into the water with a long pole and took various soundings. The irrepressible small boys took this as a signal for the opening of the exercises and promptly set up a yell. When evicted from their perches at the water's edge, they proceeded to execute a flank move by wading out for twelve feet or more. Several skiffs loaded to their fullest capacity also drew up as near the shore as they dared come and, while the services were being held, had to be warned back repeatedly.

[2] "vans"—In this case these are horse-drawn furniture wagons.

Beginning of the Baptisms

At precisely 3:16 o'clock Mrs. Woodworth stepped down on the platform leading a little girl dressed in pure white. The clerical individual who had kept watch on the platform before the arrival of the furniture vans now assumed his former position, while the officiating minister waded out to where the water was about waist deep. The first candidate submitted to the plunge without resistance, and her reappearance was the signal for tremendous cheers from the unregenerate spectators on the wharf boats.

The modus operandi for the succeeding forty-nine candidates was as follows: The minister waded to the shore and seized the left hand of each candidate, while Mrs. Woodworth from her position on the plank took the right. The minister took all the candidates with a few exceptions, about five feet out from the end of the plank where the baptismal formula was repeated, and the candidate was duly plunged beneath the water.

Candidate No. two was a very fleshy[3] woman dressed in white. When the crowd saw her a loud cheer went up from the wharf boats and cries of, "Let her go!" were heard. Other ladies in white were dipped in quick succession. The sixth candidate showed evidences of weakening; for after entering the water, she stood and listened to Mrs. Woodworth's persuasive arguments for fully a minute before she would consent to baptism. Some vile wretch in the crowd, whose sense of humor was abnormally developed, seeing her predicament, shouted, "The spirit is willin', but the flesh is weak,"[4] and his sally was greeted with uproarious laughter.

A Bald-Headed Male Convert

Female candidates in white came forward and were plunged under with clockwork regularity, when finally a woman clad in a blue dress appeared. Three girls in white went through the ordeal, and then the first male candidate appeared. His baldhead glistened in the sun, and he manifested a great deal of nervousness at first, but came up smiling.

---

[3] "fleshy"—obese.

[4] Matthew 26:41, paraphrased.

More women in white followed and then a very large fleshy lady in somber black was baptized. Her appearance was the occasion of much unseemly laughter and ribald jests from the spectators.

A man dressed in a hickory shirt and jean pantaloons submitted gracefully to immersion and came up like a practiced diver.

Another bald-headed man was followed by seven males in the borderline between adolescence and mature years. The crowd had more fun with a man clad in a spotless white shirt and generous pantaloons, which encased his portly frame. As he disappeared the crowd sang, "Down went McGinty."[5]

Eight other men and several women were baptized without any special notice being given them by the crowd, which had evidently begun to weary of the spectacle.

Mrs. Woodworth addressed the people briefly, a hymn was sung, and then the officiating minister ascended the plank and discoursed briefly on the nature of baptism and its spiritual symbolism. The crowd slowly dispersed, a way being made for the furniture vans which had been converted into temporary dressing rooms for the use of the candidates.

The crowd was unsympathetic to a remarkable degree and treated the services in the light of a circus or a free outdoor entertainment given by harlequins,[6] unmindful of the evident sincerity of the converts or the rite itself.

The baptismal service was rendered by Rev. C. S. Bolton of Clay City, Kan., a regularly ordained minister of the Church of God and its missionary for Missouri.

[5] "Down went McGinty"—Joseph Flynn (n.d.); An Irish drinking song in the end of which McGinty jumps into the sea an sinks to the bottom. Each verse has an ending line which begins, "Down went McGinty to the bottom of the . . . "

[6] "harlequins"—clowns or mimes.

September 2, 1890

St. Louis Daily Globe-Democrat (MO)

Mrs. Woodworth's Mind

Two Physicians Declare They Believe It to Be Unsound

AFFIDAVITS READY TO BE PRESENTED TO THE PROBATE COURT ASKING FOR AN INQUIRY AS TO HER SANITY—HER MEETINGS

rs. Wellington Adams and Theodore Diller will today make application to the probate court to hold an inquiry into the mental condition of Mrs. Maria B. Woodworth, the evangelist. They claim to have the affidavit in readiness and say that the papers will be served at once. Under the law the respondent will have five day's time in which to summon her witnesses and prepare her defense. This course was determined upon by the two physicians, after a consultation with Dr. Dudley, the health commissioner.

Dr. Theodore Diller was seen in his office at 500 N. Jefferson Avenue, last night relative to the course which he and Dr. Wellington Adams are taking in this matter. Dr. Diller said, "We thought that the performances in that tent ought to be stopped, either by abatement as a nuisance or by an inquiry into the mental condition of Mrs. Woodworth, whom we regard as undoubtedly insane. Then again the tent is made a rendezvous for clandestine meetings of young people, and it is a place where a perfect pandemonium of disorder and chaos prevails, between the woman's weak-minded followers and those who attend to sit in the seats of the scornful. Now I don't mean this to apply to all, but I do not think the really intelligent portion of the crowds who attend believe in the methods employed or in the manifestation of 'power' so called, to be witnesses there night after night."

"What are your reasons for believing Mrs. Woodworth insane?" was asked.

"Well, in the first place, she has had 'visions' both in the hypnotic state and during the waking state. She believes firmly in the reality of these 'visions' and that she receives direct commands from the Deity.

As is frequently the case in her type of insanity, she has diverse visions. She has penetrated the depths of hell, and she has been exalted into the seventh heaven. She states that she was troubled in mind during her youth and was personally tempted of the devil who ridiculed her call to preach and urged her to commit suicide. She declares that she has talked face-to-face with Deity and has pleaded her extreme ignorance as an excuse for not wanting to preach. No doubt she was, and is, ignorant. Mrs. Woodworth says she preached for some time before she was taken under the influence of the 'power' or knew of its existence. I call this 'power' hypnotism.

"Mrs. Woodworth evinces another symptom of insanity in her intense egotism: She compares herself to the prophets of old, and does not in any way speak of being called to the ministry in the ordinary sense that ministers use the expression. She claims that her call came directly from the Lord, with whom she spoke in person. The woman claims that when under the 'power,' a halo encircles her head which may be seen by others. She states that she was alarmed at first by the manifestations of the 'power,' but that the Lord appeared unto her in a vision and told her it was the power of God. I do not regard the person as being endowed with any special degree of personal magnetism and think the effects she produces are due to her peculiar method of preaching and to the surroundings.

Her Visions and Dreams

"According to Mrs. Woodworth's own statements, she will sit in a room and talk aloud with the Deity and with the prophets. Unto her these visions and dreams are realities. She imagines that she has been sent into the world, perhaps like Mahomet,[1] as a divinely appointed leader. She says she seldom sees the Deity, except when under the 'power,' and she claims to hear voices. This latter is classified as hallucination, while her false and unreasonable beliefs are insane delusions."

Dr. Wellington Adams entered the office at this juncture and took up the thread of conversation.

[1] "Mahomet"—Mohammad, founder of Islam.

"We are instituting these proceedings against Mrs. Woodworth in the interest of public health. The public does not appreciate the injury this woman is doing. We, as medical practitioners, can see her influence for harm, and therefore purpose to stop it to prevent the spread of disease as well as to cure. She is exerting a most injurious influence upon the people who flock to hear her—a subtle, insidious, contagious disease. Her pernicious influence is exerted principally upon a class of people known to the medical profession as neurotics, or people who are by nature peculiarly subject to nervous diseases. If Mrs. Woodworth either consciously or unconsciously exerts hypnotic influence upon her deluded followers, and suggests that they are inhabited by the Holy Ghost, and the subjects believing it neglect their business and the common affairs of life, is not great harm wrought? Nor will it end here. Take away the stimulus of these meetings and there will come a reaction more deplorable than the first excited condition.

"The woman is densely ignorant. I view with alarm the idea of such a woman exerting hypnotic powers promiscuously. Mark you, it is not simple hypnotism, but is induced under and combined with religious fanaticism. I think it's time to call a halt upon such people, the Salvation Army ranters and the followers of Schweinfurth[2] who use religion as a cloak for the most disgusting practices. This woman and her followers believe that all other denominations are not blessed with the superabundance of 'power' bestowed upon them."

The Motives of the Doctors

Both gentlemen strenuously asserted that they had not taken action against Mrs. Woodworth from any other motive than a desire to put a stop from what they seem to regard as a menace and an injury to a considerable portion of the public. They disclaimed any intention of acting in the interest of any particular denomination, or at the suggestion of any resident in the neighborhood of the gospel tent, who may have been annoyed at the scenes of disorder in that vicinity. The names of Drs. Theodore Diller and

[2] "Schweinfurth"—Meaning of reference unknown. The September 1890 article, "Claim to be Cured" by *The St. Louis Post* (MO) mentions him briefly as "making Holy Ghost babies."

Wellington Adams do not appear in the city directory, which the former gentleman explains by stating that he was not practicing in St. Louis when that valuable volume was published. By a singular coincidence the name of "Theodore Diller, machinist," residing at No. 2243 Howard Street, is duly recorded in the city directory. Dr. Adams states that he has lived and practiced in St. Louis for the last six years, and he is, therefore, at a loss to understand why his name does not appear in the directory.

Dr. Dudley was seen but declined to express an opinion upon the merits of Mrs. Woodworth's alleged insanity. He said he had merely counseled Drs. Diller and Adams how to proceed in order to have the matter authoritatively settled.

She Refused to Be Interviewed

A *Globe-Democrat* reporter called on Mrs. Woodworth last evening to attempt to interview her and secure a statement from her in regard to the proceedings now being taken against her. Mrs. Woodworth had been absent from her tent all afternoon, attending to some business, and sent word to the reporter that she would not see him, as she was too weary to give an interview, and also required the time to rest herself, preparatory to holding her nightly service. It appears that Mrs. Woodworth considers that she has been grossly misrepresented by the press, and she sent a message to the reporter to the effect that she did not desire to have any discussion with any newspaper man.

The reporter made repeated attempts to see her, but she has so surrounded herself with assistants that it was impossible to get to see her. One of the assistants informed the reporter that she would make a statement during the meeting and that the press would be forced to remain content with that. Her companion, or as someone informed the reporter, her daughter, stated that when the two physicians were introduced to Mrs. Woodworth as being reporters that she and Mrs. Woodworth both discovered that they were physicians before they had been there five minutes, and that the charge about her being of unsound mind was all bosh. But the main point which she wished to make was that since the press had so deceived them, they were afraid to trust it further.

The Evening Meeting

Shortly after this conversation the lights in the tent were lit and the crowd began to pour in until every seat in the large tent was occupied, and rows of people, three, four, and five deep, surrounded the seats. Mrs. Woodworth soon appeared upon the platform. Her face was lighted up by a pleasant smile. The weariness which she had complained of seemed to have disappeared and her eyes were unusually bright. She gave out the hymn, and in singing her voice was clearly distinguishable above the others who were singing. Three hymns were sung, during which she walked backward and forward on the platform, lifting her hand in a graceful, waving gesture and appeared every now and then letting it rest when halfway down, as though she were pointing to some particular person in the audience.

Brother Bolton delivered the sermon on the subject of regeneration, and Mrs. Woodworth took the same subject for a few closing remarks. At first she seemed to speak with an effort, as though the words would not come. There was no diffidence. She appeared to be waiting for something, and presently her manner changed, her eyes lightened up, and the words flowed rapidly from her mouth. There was no attempt at elocution, but she appeared to be the subject of an intense nervous enthusiasm. Her hands would clasp each other convulsively; she would brush one of them across her forehead as though attempting to drive some thought away, and finally it was noticed that as she became more under the influence of the enthusiasm that she leaned forward, appearing to be unable to control herself at all, and eventually her forehead almost touched the floor of the platform.

The reporter waited until the close of the meeting, but Mrs. Woodworth failed to make any statement in regard to the insanity proceedings.

September 2, 1890

St. Louis Post-Dispatch (MO)

She Has No Fears

Mrs. Maria B. Woodworth Willing to Stand a Test of Her Mental Condition

SHE SAYS SHE HAS RECEIVED MANY OFFERS OF ASSISTANCE FROM LAWYERS, PHYSICIANS, AND MINISTERS

Rev. Dr. Boswell of the First Methodist Church, Dr. A. N. Thompson of the Glasgow Avenue Presbyterian Church, and Father Powers of the Immaculate Conception Church in Favor of a Public Inquiry into the Power Used by the Evangelist—Mrs. Woodworth Promises Some Remarkable Evidences of Cure—What Drs. Diller and Adams Say

Mrs. Woodworth is not in her usual health and spirits today. The hard work she has undergone added to the intense mental worry of the last few days has had a marked effect on her personal appearance, and when a *Post-Dispatch* representative called on her this morning in her tent, which forms her home, she looked careworn and weary. Instructions had been given to refuse admission to all callers, but the lady finally consented to make an exception in favor of the *Post-Dispatch* and to answer a few questions. Her manner was subdued and earnest, and if the lady is mad, then there must certainly be an immense amount of method in her madness. Her answers were given in a quiet and very decided manner, and when a question was put that she did not feel disposed to answer, the refusal was so emphatic and ladylike as to put any attempt at persuasion out of the question.

"You must excuse my giving any information that might be used by these two jealous individuals to further their persecution" was the reply to the question as to how the proceedings by Drs. Adams and Diller would be met.

[P. D.] "Have you any knowledge of these proceedings?"

[M. B. W.] "None whatever, except what I have read in the *Post-Dispatch*. I have not been served with papers of any kind."

[P. D.] "Have you retained an attorney to represent you?" was next asked.

Mrs. Woodworth smiled and replied, "I have received offers of assistance from a large number of attorneys and also from several physicians who are not afraid of having their living taken away from them by one woman."

[P. D.] "But have you accepted any of these offers and authorized an attorney to act for you?"

[M. B. W.] "I really cannot say as to that. I shall do as the Lord directs me, have no fear whatever as to the result."

A Distinct Denial

[P. D.] "It has been stated that your sanity has been called into question on previous occasions. Is that correct?"

[M. B. W.] "Certainly not. No one has ever suggested that I was insane, and everyone has always remarked on how strong-minded I was and how very easily I managed my business."

[P. D.] "Was there not some trouble at Springfield, Ill.?"

[M. B. W.] "Oh, yes, but that was as to my orthodoxy and no question of sanity raised. Dr. Brinie, a well-known theologian and a great debater, stood up one night to prove that the power of God did not exist today and that I was a false teacher. His three arguments were: First, that women have no right to get up and preach at all; second, that the healing power has been done away with; and, third, that I had no single proof that I had been called to preach. I took no notice of these arguments for a time, but several of the leading [newspapermen?] of the city asked me to reply to them so I finally did so. At their request I charged an admission fee, and in spite of that, over [?] persons were unable to secure admission. I summed up every point and used the same passages of Scripture to argue from as the doctor had quoted with the result that I thoroughly disposed of the contention. The doctor made a very brief reply but it was generally admitted that I had held my own."

[P. D.] "How do you explain the power that is exercised over converts at your services?"

[M. B. W.] "I argue that 'Jesus Christ is the same yesterday, today and forever.'[1] All Christians believe that, and I say that if He is the same now as He always was, He can exert His power just as He did when Martin Luther, Wesley, Whitefield, and Cartwright preached. Hypnotism was never charged against any of these, and I don't suppose any of them knew anything whatever about it. I am quite sure I don't."

[P. D.] "And you say the 'power' is just the same as was exercised when these men preached?"

[M. B. W.] "I do. It is just the same. I don't explain what makes people fall down and hold up their hands, but I know it is no personal influence of mine. If it were, how is it that some converts feel the power at home, as I can prove they do and have done. It isn't supposed I can hypnotize people I cannot see, is it?"

[P. D.] "But you say it is nothing akin to hypnotism?"

The Power of God

[M. B. W.] "No more it is. It is simply the power of God exercised on the converts. But all the converts do not go into these trances by any means. Only a comparatively small number do so. The power of God is exercised in more ways than one. What I cannot understand is how these physicians can justify their position. First they said I was practicing hypnotism and doing injury to people even when I cured them, and now they want to say I am insane. Yet they admit there are cures, but they don't seem to have any explanation to adduce since abandoning the hypnotism theory. If this matter goes on there will be some very remarkable evidences of cure, though I have never claimed to cure anybody. I merely pray, and unless the sick person has faith in God's power, no cure can be effected, except in the case of little children who are too young to understand."

[P. D.] "What class of cases do you hold can be cured by faith?"

[M. B. W.] "We don't expect the Lord to make new limbs or to exercise His creative power, but in all other respects the body can be as quickly healed as the soul saved. God is no respecter of persons."[2]

[P. D.] "You do not make a specialty of faith curing?"

[1] See Hebrews 13:8.

[2] Acts 10:34.

[M. B. W.] "No, I was preaching for over five years before I ever prayed for anyone to be healed or before I realized that it was my duty to do so."

[P. D.] "What part do you take?"

[M. B. W.] "None whatever. My presence is not even needed."

Cured at Home

[P. D.] "Do not all the cures take place in the tent and in your presence?"

[M. B. W.] "Not all. A notable exception was in the case of Sister Cobb, a Christian lady who was lying in what her physicians declared was her death bed. They had said she could not live [past?] midnight, and a messenger came to me and asked me to pray for her cure. I arranged to do so and sent word to the sick lady to pray at the same time we prayed. She did this and in the morning everyone was astonished to see her well. She was in the tent here last night, a striking instance of God's power. The lady has testified to these facts, again and again and will do so again.

"Another lady, whose cure was very remarkable, was in the tent at the time. Her name is Tame and she lives at [8015] Market Street [?] lifted off, and even helped into the tent. She was the victim of an immense number of diseases, and as she received salvation, she said she could feel the disease going from her just like water running off her back. She finally got up and walked away. Here is one of the crutches she held that night. She has never required it since, and she frequently attends our services.

"The case of Sister Allen was just as miraculous. She had for years been afflicted with dropsy, and life was a burden to her as well as everyone with whom she lived. She was perfectly helpless at times and was attended by as many as five doctors at once. One night a few weeks ago she was brought here, and although there was no visible effect of the power on her, she was immediately healed. Her husband was so astonished that he came and was at once converted. He says he has been a drunkard and a victim to disease, but that when converted he was absolutely cured. The whole family was baptized last Sabbath. These are only a few of the incidences of miraculous cures, but a good many more might be given."

Over a Thousand Converts

[P. D.] "Do you know how many you have cured here?"

[M. B. W.] "I don't know how many have been cured by the power. There have been over one thousand conversions, including a large number of visitors from a distance. God's power for the salvation of souls has been manifested to a marvelous extent."

[P. D.] "With regard to the visions you are said to see, do you admit seeing them?"

[M. B. W.] "I shall certainly never deny the fact."

[P. D.] "You know this is one of the delusions on which the doctors rely to prove your insanity?"

[M. B. W.] "Yes, I understand so. But if I am insane because I see visions, how is it with regard to the apostles? You remember that Paul saw visions and on one notable occasion heard a voice from on high? Was he adjudged insane in consequence? Then there was Peter who saw the vision which resulted in the mission among the Gentiles. Who has ever said that Peter was insane? Then there was the apostle John, who saw any number of visions, but there is no suggestion that John was a lunatic, unable to look after his business affairs, and a source of danger to the community at large."

[P. D.] "The answer to that argument will probably be that these men lived a long time ago and that the conditions are not the same now as then."

[M. B. W.] "Well, John Wesley did not live in the remote ages, and anyone who has read his life knows that he saw visions. You remember that on one occasion he thought he saw the devil and threw an inkstand at it, the ink stains on the wallpaper giving evidence of the act.[3] You can't lock up everyone who sees or has seen visions, and I may say at once that I dispute the accuracy of the doctors' statements as to the visions I am reported to have told them I saw. What hurts me most is the statement that I am incompetent to attend to my business affairs. I am at a loss to see how that can be. Between September and April last, I paid over fourteen hundred dollars for

[3] This event occurred in Martin Luther's life, not Wesley's.

freight and transportation, to say nothing of other expenses. I have no means of my own at all and I simply rely on the Lord's promise to provide. He always does so, and hence I am enabled to carry on the work He has mapped out for me."

Arrangements for Future

[P. D.] "Do you think of leaving here, as reported?"

[M. B. W.] "My lease is up at the end of this week, but I can get it renewed if I wish. A great many people have asked me to remain and have promised to relieve me of all responsibility so far as the rent is concerned. But I have not decided what I shall do. I shall be directed to do what is right. These proceedings have disturbed the quiet we have been enjoying. For over two months we have had perfect quiet and order so far as the crowd was concerned, but the last two nights a rougher class have been attracted to see and hear one who is described as a crazy woman. It is long since we had so much disorder as last night."

[P. D.] "What is your own idea as to the cause of the proceedings?"

[M. B. W.] "I think spite and jealousy are at the bottom of the proceedings, nor do I think physicians of good practice or intelligent men who understand their business will care to have anything to do with them."

[P. D.] "What are your plans after leaving here?"

[M. B. W.] "I go first to Springfield, Ill., and then to several towns in Indiana. I hope to get back to St. Louis in about a year but may not be able to do so, as there is a difficulty in getting away too soon from a town after the work has been got well in hand."

Ministers Oppose the Meetings

A *Post-Dispatch* reporter called on the Rev. Dr. Boswell this morning. Dr. Thompson of the Glasgow Avenue Presbyterian Church was calling on Dr. Boswell at the time; and when the reporter was introduced, Dr. Thompson said:

"I had just dropped in to ask Dr. Boswell about these meetings myself, and we were just talking about them."

"Will you give your opinion for publication?" asked the reporter.

"You give yours first, doctor," said Mr. Thompson, "you are the oldest and ought to speak first."

"Very well," said Dr. Boswell, "now you put it down just as I tell it: While I think that Mrs. Woodworth may be perfectly sincere in her convictions, I regard the movement as exceedingly dangerous to the Church and to religion."

Dr. Thompson said: "I have no hesitation in saying that in my opinion Mrs. Woodworth and her followers are sadly deluded. I will say further that I fear the physical phenomena which are encouraged at the tent meetings are working harm, morally as well. I will say they are fraught with the greatest dangers and may result in great injury both morally and spiritually. So far as I can judge Mrs. Woodworth, she is in deeply earnest in her work. I simply think her greatly deluded."

Will Speak Against the Meetings

Father Powers of the Church of the Immaculate Conception was seen by a *Post-Dispatch* man, and in response to an inquiry as to his impressions of the Woodworth meetings said:

"There are two things under discussion, only one of which I can deal with. One is her sanity, which the medical profession should deal with, and the other is the character of the meetings, which interests the exponents of religion.

"As to Mrs. Woodworth personally, I think that she is perfectly sincere, but I believe her to be unconsciously the medium of hypnotism. Our church is, or course, strongly opposed to such exhibitions, and it has taken steps in some countries to endeavor to have them stopped. I shall mention the meetings incidentally from the pulpit next Sunday and advise my people not to attend the meetings."

The father thoroughly believes in the endeavors of the physicians to inquire into the sanity of Mrs. Woodworth.

The Doctors Chagrined

Drs. Diller and Adams express the greatest surprise and chagrin at the sentiment which has been shown towards their action in attempting to demonstrate to the people the result of hypnotism as practiced by an ignorant person and to endeavor to cause a cessation of it in the Woodworth case. They say they expected that when they took up the matter, sentiment would be the other way and their sole object in doing it was for the general good of the public. If the public declares itself unwilling to be shown where certain wrongs exist, they declare themselves as being no candidates for martyrdom, and that their interest in it is at an end.

Dr. Adams said: "When I first went to the tent and saw the scenes which were being enacted nightly, I was filled with the thought that here was a great evil in existence of which the public was not cognizant. I discussed the matter with a number of physicians and ministers and was led to believe that if an attempt was made to eradicate the evil, I would receive the assistance of the people. I have no interest in it whatever, otherwise than that. If the people would merely remain neutral until I had been given a chance to prove my assertions, they would then see who was right and who was wrong. If I was mistaken, then let them denounce me thoroughly."

Almost a Riot

At last night's meeting two respectably dressed young ladies stood upon a bench to see the manifestations on the platform more distinctly. They were told to sit down by a man who is supposed to have been connected with the mission. When they neglected to obey the order, he pushed them off the seat rather roughly. Fifteen or twenty men who saw this attacked the man and were proceeding to mob him when the police came in and interfered. For a few minutes the disturbance was very great and a general riot seemed imminent.

September 3, 1890

St. Louis Republic (MO)

Quackery and Emotional Religion

ne of the most meddlesome and mischievous pieces of quackery which St. Louis has seen in many a day is the attempt of Doctors *Clyster* and *Jalap*[1] to have Mrs. Woodworth, "the Pentecost evangelist," committed as insane. The proceedings which these busybodies have begun are at the expense of the public. A great many witnesses are likely to be summoned and a heavy bill of costs made for the taxpayers for no other purpose than of filling the newspapers with the names of Doctors *Clyster* and *Jalap*.

The country is full of "medical colleges" which from year to year are turning out hundreds and thousands of doctors—good, bad, and indifferent—on the community. As long as the bad and indifferent have their diplomas and are "regular," the public is defenseless against them. They are free to pursue their course of quackery, virtually unchecked. The attempt of the better class of physicians to hold them within bounds by the "code of ethics" is a mournful failure. They make up in fertility of expedience what they lack in other directions. If the code says, as it does, that they shall not advertise—they interpret it to mean that they shall not pay for their advertisement, and they at once set their brain to work to find ways of deadbeating the newspapers.

Ordinarily this may be treated as a jest, but when the effort to obtain free advertising takes the form of cowardly annoyance to a defenseless woman, who, however ignorant and unconventional she may be, is certainly trying to do what good she can, it deserves the unqualified condemnation of all who love fair play.

It is asserted that Health Commissioner Dudley is an accessory to the proceedings brought against Mrs. Woodworth. We are loath to believe this, because it is none of the health commissioner's business.

[1] Dr. Theodore Diller and Dr. Wellington Adams, the men who tried to bring charges against Woodworth. The pseudonym "Clyster" is a term meaning "enema," and "Jalap" refers to a powder made from the dried root of a Mexican vine used to cause the bowels to evacuate ("enema" and "jalap," *Webster's N. W.*, 1997). The writer is using these terms to express his disgust for these two.

If he thinks that excess of religious fervor is dangerous to health, it cannot possibly be an *ex sepias*[2] judgment. Nor can he allege experience as a basis for it. It is a mere *a priori*[3] theory. The facts are all against it. The so-called "trances" and other forms of religious exaltation are of frequent occurrence wherever "old-fashioned revivals" are held. At any genuine camp meeting in the backwoods, it is still common enough to see these "trances," and all the learned talk of hypnotism is stuff and nonsense—mere quackery. But even if people chose to mix hypnotism with their religion, it is no more the affair of the health department than it is the affair of

other people what is the exact mental, physical, and spiritual effects produced on an attaché of the health department by his morning cocktail. In this free country the health department can best earn its salary by seeing that the watermelon rinds are kept out of the alleys. If Dr. Dudley will attend to that, he will have his hands full.

As for Doctors *Clyster* and *Jalap, The Republic* advises them to let Mrs. Woodworth alone. She is a woman and apparently easy game, but they may find it otherwise. However that may be, we are fixed in the opinion that any mental trouble to which she may be subject is far less liable to be dangerous to public health then their own mental and spiritual imbecilities. She has been concerned in no deaths thus far. An examination of the burial certificates outstanding at the health department against Doctors *Clyster* and *Jalap* might show that public health has been suffering from causes of which they are more or less cognizant, though instead of attempting to remove them, they are meddling with what is no affair of theirs. If they worry and oppress this unprotected woman, it will be right and fitting that every death certificate on record against them, now or filed hereafter, shall be dangerous to public health. "Truth is not always on the side of probability," and they could very possibly explain that their patients die in spite of them rather than on account of them, but if they continue in the course they have marked out, and insist on making public nuisances of themselves, the burden of proof is on them—in every graveyard transaction with which they have been connected.

[2] "ex sepias"—meaning unknown; possibly "an in print" or "published" judgment. In other words, no authority has published anything supporting this statement.

[3] "a priori"—based on theory without examination of the evidence.

September 3, 1890

St. Louis Daily Globe-Democrat (MO)

The Gospel Tent

Mrs. Woodworth Makes a Statement—A Businessman's Protest

A crowd which assembled at Mrs. Woodworth's evangelical tent last evening was even larger than the night before. The place was packed with a hot, restless, and perspiring mass of humanity, many being attracted thither by the account of the proceedings against her published in the papers. The service was one of prayer and song. The meeting was one of the most disorderly that has even been witnessed under the tent, for no sooner would someone throw up his or her hands in a religious "trance," than the crowd would stand up on the seats, push forward, and do everything but literally climb over each other to see the person. Mrs. Woodworth's face had a harassed or troubled look, but she still possessed the same pleasant welcoming smile which she always wears; and she walked up and down the platform making the same graceful curving gestures which many claim to be her method of hypnotizing her followers. Toward the close of the services, Mr. Greenwood, one of the most enthusiastic of Mrs. Woodworth's followers, walked out on the platform and as soon as he could secure silence from the throng, read the following, which he stated was a copy of a letter received by Judge Woerner from a prominent businessman who stands high in church circles.

> St. Louis, September 2, 1890
> Judge J.C. Woerner, Judge of the Probate Court,
> St. Louis, Missouri:

Dear Sir—The enclosed clipping explains itself:

> To the Hon. J.C. Woerner, judge of the probate court of the city of St. Louis—The undersigned hereby gives information, and alleges the facts to be, that one Maria B. Woodworth, of the city of St. Louis aforesaid, is a person of unsound mind and incapable of managing her

affairs, and pray that an inquiry herein be had according to the statues in such case made and provided.

Wellington Adams, M.D.
Theodore Diller, M.D.

I desire to make a written protest against the proceedings. I have attended, out of curiosity, and with a critical spirit, two of Mrs. Woodworth's evening tent meetings recently, but I heard nothing from her lips that was irreverent or reprehensible. Those proposed proceedings are an outrage and an insult, not only to Mrs. Woodworth, but the vast body of evangelical Christians in this city who believe in allowing any reputable person to preach the Gospel of Jesus Christ. . . . Before you render a decision, I would respectfully ask that you personally attend one of her evening services and judge for yourself from an observation that will be far more reliable than the testimony of men who may be prompted either by malice or by a false religious bigotry.

Mrs. Woodworth is already very much exhausted by her protracted labors, and is, or was, about to discontinue them. If her work is not of the Lord, it will speedily come to naught, and all the sooner if let alone.

Yours, etc.

Mr. Greenwood did not give the name of the writer, as he was under promise not to divulge it. When he finished his reading, he spoke on the subject for a few moments and made frequent allusion to the fact that the name of neither of the physicians was in the city directory. He then read the following clipping from a morning paper:

"The petition to be filed in the probate court for an inquiry into the sanity of Mrs. Maria B. Woodworth, the evangelist, will show conclusively that there are two doctors so insanely meddlesome that they ought to be locked up."

The reading was greeted with a round of cheers from the congregation. He then made a long prayer for the falsifying press, the editors, and especially the reporters. At the conclusion of this, Mrs. Woodworth spoke for some minutes in regard to the proceedings.

She said that she regretted to see the tough or hoodlum element that had been attracted to the tent last night by two men, who had introduced themselves under the disguise of reporters, but that she was not afraid to stay in St. Louis; that she had been warned frequently not to pitch her tent where it now stands, as the class of people who inhabited that neighborhood would not allow her to remain in peace, but that she had stayed there and would stay until the Lord told her to go. She was not at all afraid of persecution, inasmuch as she would be willing to die at any moment if only to bring people to Jesus. Mrs. Woodworth broke down last night for the first time, and the tears streamed down her face. The throng who have night after night seen her carry on her services under the most auspicious circumstances were subdued and silenced by the sight of tears on the brave woman's face, and when dismissed went in an unusually quiet manner.

September 4, 1890

St. Louis Post-Dispatch (MO)

Claim to Be Cured

Stories of the People Alleged to Have Been Benefited by the "Power"

DR. WELLINGTON ADAMS MAKES REPLY TO THE CRITICISM HEAPED ON HIM

He and Dr. Diller Are Not Threatening Mrs. Woodworth With Incarceration in an Asylum but Simply Want a Public Inquiry as to the Power She Is Using—Dr. Messick of St. John's Methodist Church Speaks of the Woodworth Meetings to His Congregation—Some Marvelous Tales Told by Persons Relieved of Disease

Dr. Adams has received a number of letters, threatening in their tone and warning him to stop proceedings against Mrs. Woodworth. The letters hint that if he does not stop, divine providence will be called into requisition. A number of letters have been received from out of the city. He has also received a number of letters from ministers and physicians congratulating him on the stand which he has taken in this matter. He was called on this morning by a *Post-Dispatch* reporter to ask him what he contemplated doing.

Dr. Adams said:

"I am somewhat surprised at the attitude that many people have assumed in this Woodworth matter. Prior to the investigation instituted by Dr. Diller and myself, nearly every paper in the city was poking fun at those meetings and giving humorous accounts of the outlandish scenes to be witnessed there. No sooner do we come out with our statement regarding the character of the 'physical phenomena' nightly manifested there than lo and behold there is a complete change of heart. It is possible that those who criticize us have all received the 'power' and been attacked by the 'spells.' The most amusing part of the whole thing consists in the fact that the personal view of many persons now violent in their opposition are known to be diametrically opposed to the sentiments they express.

"People who upbraid us should be sure that their pretensions bear no unfortunate [d]isproportion to their actions. As abuses naturally arise in this as in all other departments of everyday life, the law should, when possible, afford ample and thorough redress. We undertook this investigation not in a spirit of scoffing, and we should not have been met by this rude clamor of rebuke and ridicule. That is not the honest and fair way to treat a matter of such seriousness to the health, lives, and social condition of the community.

"Dr. Diller and myself are firm believers in true religion, holding the most liberal views and having the utmost respect for all religious sects. But we believe there is a regularly ordained ministry and theology which represents true religious doctrine and also a species of religious quackery, just as there is a regular medical profession and science of medicine which represents the accumulative teachings of science and a class of medical quacks, who, because they find it impossible to enter the profession through the legitimate portals, stand upon the outside holding sideshows and denouncing the regular profession.

"Mr. Schweinfurth, who is engaged in making Holy Ghost babies, the Salvation Army, Mrs. Woodworth, and others of this class represent the religious quacks who stand on the outside of the regular church and hold sideshows because they find it impossible to enter through the straight and narrow gate that marks the entrance to the legitimate church of God. These people and their methods are in no wise in accord with the sentiments of the church proper, and a large part of their time is taken up in denouncing regularly ordained ministers of the Gospel and in claiming that they themselves are the only regularly anointed representatives of the Deity and His divine will.

"In support of this, they are continually citing the fact that their ministers cannot draw the crowds that they can nor produce the manifestation of the 'power' like themselves. I have heard these expressions time and again and [early ?] today received a letter from one of Mrs. W.'s followers, in which this statement is made. I hand it to you for publication. We are assured from our experience and the expressions of a majority of the ministry, that such people and their practices work immeasurable mischief to the cause of true religion. From our knowledge of medicine, which is simply a reflex of the opinion of the whole medical profession, we knew that the psychical, physical, and moral results of the abnormal manifestations attending the meetings of Mrs. Woodworth are in a very high degree harmful, not only to the present, but to future generations.

We, therefore, have a right as representatives of a noble profession, which has to do not only with the treatment, but also with the prevention of disease and the conservation of the public health, to honestly inquire into a mischief which is so widespread and which we believe to be of such vital importance to the health and homes of the people. This is a subject which should interest every man of family who has loved ones to care for besides himself.

"The injury which is being inflicted is not a palpable one—that is manifest to all, a physical wound or injury that all can see, but it is a subtle, insidious, and highly diffusible injury that is not apparent upon the surface, although well-known to the profession. Therefore, it cannot be reached by ordinary processes of law. If Mrs. W. is of unsound mind; [and] as a result is conducting meetings that are harmful and discordant with the views of the church of God, then her meeting can and should be stopped—and this without any interference of the State with religion. We certainly ought to have a right to honestly and by regular process of law to inquire into this as a commendable measure for the public good, without receiving maledictions and vituperations. We are prompted by the purest and most charitable of motives, and we are moved as much by respect for true religion and an abhorrence of the blasphemous and sacrilegious as by a desire to subserve the good of the public health."

Her "Cures"

Mrs. Woodworth and her adherents claim that one of the results of the meetings which they have been holding is the absolute cure of a number of persons afflicted with all sorts of incurable diseases and who had spent all the money that they could raise on doctors and medicines. Mrs. Woodworth claims that these people have been made whole by the power of God and that this proves her assertion that genuine miracles are being performed at the present day. The following are some of the cases, the stories of which are told by the people who claim to have been cured by the "power of God":

Mrs. Yates' Wonderful Tale

Mrs. Emma Yates, who lives at 1016 Market Street, is one of the principal witnesses on whom Mrs. Woodworth relies to prove the healing properties of "the power." A *Post-Dispatch* reporter called at the residence of Mrs. Yates this morning for the purpose of getting her story.

A tall man, about 60 years of age, but still strong and robust, came to the door in answer to the reporter's knock. He was dressed in a pair of light blue overalls and was evidently ready for work. "You can't get a thing from us about my wife's cure," he said very forcibly.

Then Mrs. Yates came to the door. She is a large woman weighing probably three hundred pounds and seemed strong and healthy. There was no indication of weakness about her. She invited the reporter to step inside.

In the window was a large wooden cage containing a pretty pair of pigeons which cooed to [?] and were evidently well [?]. On the floor were the pieces of a homemade rug, the process of manufacture having just been interrupted. The reporter was given a chair and Mr. Yates began the story of his wife's illness.

"Emma was taken with rheumatism in '86," he said, "and it got worse and worse right along. First she had to get a cane, then a crutch, and finally two crutches. She got worse and worse, and I began buying medicine for her and paying doctors. I expect I've paid out nigh onto twenty-five hundred dollars. I've earned about five or six hundred dollars a year and paid out all it didn't cost us to live. I had a regular drugstore in the house, bottles of every kind; but Emma kept getting worse and worse. Finally she made up her mind that she'd die a natural death and so we quit paying out money to the doctors. She said [they ?] picked our pockets for the last time.

"People commenced telling us about those meetings and wanted her to go out and see if she couldn't get cured. So finally we just thought we'd go out there and see what they done."

"It was on the evening of July 11," said Mrs. Yates, as she took up the story. "It took two, besides the old man, to get me to the car, and to get me into the meeting. When I stepped into the tent, it was just as bright as if the sun was shining.

"'It is just as light as day,' I said to the old man.

"'No, there's only one little jet burning and it seems as though there ought to be more light,' he said. Then Mrs. Woodworth and her followers came in."

"She knew her the minute she set eyes on her," said Mr. Yates in a tone of awe.

"Yes, I'd never seen her, but it all went right over me in a wink that it was her when she came in. I hadn't thought that I could get cured, but when I knew that it was her, it kind of gave me faith. She came up and they began singing.

"'All those who want to be healed come up, too,' she said.

"Then they helped me to the altar. I just rested with my crutch under my left arm and my right hand on the platform. She came up and put one hand on my forehead and the other on my hip. Then I felt the disease begin to creep right down from off me, just like as though a pail of water had been poured over my head. I felt the disease go right away as she moved her hand down. I had catarrh, rheumatism, dropsy, lung trouble, and trouble with my heart besides eczema. My face was covered with blotches and I had a big ridge right across my forehead. It just slipped off, just like when you pull one hand through the other. My knee was swelled (*sic*) as big as a bucket and I felt it just go right down.

"'Put your foot down on the floor,' she said to me.

"Now before this, if there had been a big rope waiting to be put around my neck if I hadn't put my foot down, they'd a-had to put it around; but when she rubbed her hand on my ankle, I felt it fall right off—all the disease."

"It went right into the ground," said Mr. Yates.

"I just stamped my foot right down hard; and I felt as though if a big stake had been there, I could have driven it right into the ground. Then I walked off all cured; and I haven't used a crutch since, but I walk around all right."

"She left the crutch out there; and if you don't believe that she was cured, you can see the crutch; that'll prove it," said Mr. Yates, nodding his head conclusively.

Mr. and Mrs. Yates have been in St. Louis about thirty years, Mrs. Yates being the woman who slept fourteen days at a time and narrowly escaped being buried.

Worthy of Consideration

Dr. Hermann, in speaking about Mrs. Woodworth and the demonstrations at the gospel tent, said today:

"I have not attended any of the meetings and therefore cannot personally give any opinion, but the opinions of Dr. Adams are worthy of the most careful consideration, and should be received with the respect which is due his standing as a physician."

Dr. Messick Discountenances Them

The Rev. B. M. Messick, pastor of the St. John's Methodist Church, was asked for his opinion on the Woodworth meetings, as he mentioned them in last Sunday's sermon in no encouraging manner. He said:

"I desire to be entirely noncommittal on the subject, but I will say that I do not think that the church should be held responsible for such things. It has nothing to do with them at all. I do not desire to get mixed up in this thing, but that is my opinion."

A Widow Cured

Among the cures claimed by Mrs. Woodworth and her friends, the case of Mrs. Elizabeth Hammell is a very remarkable one. Mrs. Hammell is a widow in very poor circumstances and occupies one room in the frame building known as 1858 South Thirteenth Street. Her husband died eight years ago, leaving her with four children and no money. The oldest of these is now working for Jacobs Bros. on Seventh Street and Lucas Avenue, the youngest is at home, and the other two have been inmates of the Orphans' Home at Warrenton, Mo. Mrs. Hammell has earned a livelihood for herself and child by washing and has a reputation in the neighborhood in which she resides of being industrious and honest. A *Post-Dispatch* reporter called at 1858 South Thirteenth Street, this morning and found her hard at work washing in the little room on the second floor which is her home. When questioned about her case, she said:

"Yes, I was cured by divine power at one of Mrs. Woodworth's meetings after I had been under medical treatment and got no benefit at all."

[D.P.] "What was the trouble?"

[E. H.] "It was my right arm. Since my husband died I had to earn my own living by washing and ironing and never had any trouble with my arm till last [month ?]. Then I lost much of the [use?] of it; the nerve power seemed suspended, and I suffered intense pain, the skin being as hot sometimes as a furnace. It got so bad at last that I was compelled to get medical advice. I went to the Clinic Hospital on Jefferson and Lucas Avenues, and the doctors told me the nerves were badly affected and I must undergo a course of electrical treatment. I did this and was treated three times a week for over a month but got no better. The electricity seemed to drive the disease up my arm and left it so helpless that I could do no work and began to get into debt. The pain was so intense that I lost my rest at night and became a very sick woman. Four weeks ago last Tuesday, I decided to ask Sister Woodworth to help me. I had been to one of her meetings and seen her save people and I had faith in God's power to cure me. I have been a Methodist Church member for several years, but I got a fresh awakening under Mrs. Woodworth's teaching. I went up to the platform believing in God's power to cure me, and while they were praying I suddenly felt the pain vanish."

How the Cure Comes

[D.P.] "What was the sensation when the cure was effected?"

[E. H.] "It just went; that was all there was to it."

[D.P.] "Were you entranced or under the influence of the power?"

[E. H.] "No, I have never been. It was just this way: One instant my arm was burning hot, just as if it was being held close to a fire; the next it was cool and comfortable and absolutely free from pain. Then I heard a small voice within me saying:

"'You have got no pain. Stand up and testify for God.'"

[D.P.] "Did you do so?"

[E. H.] "No, not then. I first asked Sister Woodworth if I was to regard it as a regular cure or merely a temporary relief. She advised me to go back to my work and I should have no trouble, and I found she was correct."

A bright, cheerful-looking girl about eighteen years of age, having the appearance of being slightly overgrown and rather thin, but otherwise healthy, was busy ironing clothes in the same room. This was the girl Eliza Hammell, who was cured of St. Vitus dance and other complaints after having been prayed over by Mrs. Woodworth for nearly two days. Explaining her case, Mrs. Hammell said:

Cured of St. Vitus' Dance

"Eliza was at the Warrenton Orphans' Home and had nervous complaint, some call it St. Vitus' dance. The poor child had been treated before for erysipelas[1] and cured by the doctors. She went back to the Home, but this spring the principal notified me that she must come home, although by the agreement she was to remain until she was 18. But he complained that he had no use for her, as she was so sick she could not even wash dishes up. When she came home she was suffering from an enlargement of the breastbone and also from what seemed like paralysis of the right arm, which she could not raise above her head. Her nerves was (*sic*) also so bad that the whole right side seemed lame, and the bone I spoke of kept growing out rapidly.

"The Saturday morning after I was cured, I took her to Mrs. Woodworth and told her about the trouble. The sister prayed over her that morning and afternoon and evening and on the next day. She passed her hands over her and repeated the words 'Evil spirit, get out of her,' and then Sunday evening she was cured. Instead of having to drag her right leg after her, she could walk as quickly and actively as anyone and has never had a day of sickness since. The enlarged bone didn't recede. God doesn't work miracles that way, but it has not grown anymore. Now she will either go back to the Home or get work at one of the large stores downtown."

[1] "erysipelas"—an acute infectious disease of the skin or mucous membranes caused by a streptococcus and characterized by local inflammation and fever *(Webster's N. W.*, 1997).

The little girl, who is intelligent and bright, confirmed her mother's statement and said she [felt the quivering go?] all at once and strength come back to her. Mrs. [six words illegible] shoemaker on the ground floor of the same house and several neighbors were questioned, and all confirmed Mrs. Hammell's statement as to the cures.

In Favor of an Inquiry

The *Post-Dispatch* has received numerous communications in every mail concerning the now-celebrated Woodworth case which has attracted so much attention; and among them is one of special interest from a well-known German citizen, who requests that his name be withheld, because he does not wish it to be associated with so public a matter. He writes:

"A short time before I left Germany, about fifteen years ago, there was a strange case a few miles from Esson, which attracted the attention of the Imperial government and aroused intense interest all over the empire. Two little girls came home one day and they had seen the image of the Virgin Mary appearing just above a cluster of bushes. They were not believed at first and even monetary inducements were held out to them to 'tell the truth,' but they persisted in their story and said they could take their parents and friends to where the vision appeared. They led the way, a crowd followed; and when they arrived at the spot, the whole crowd witnessed the vision. An altar was erected there and the most miraculous cures were performed. It was represented that the cures were performed miraculously.

"The German government thought the people were being duped and spent a great deal of money in a vain attempt to solve the mystery. The only agency there was the supernatural power which Mrs. Woodworth claims, but when it was 'manifested' there were none of those awful trances which, at least, are revolting to see if they are not horrible to endure. Why then should it not be proper to institute a legal inquiry in this case when it is evident to every thinking man that Mrs. Woodworth is using some power which produces peculiar, perhaps dreadful results?

"I have been somewhat surprised to see that many people criticize Drs. Diller and Adams, and Mrs. Woodworth and her friends speak of them as persecutors who are trying to drag her into any asylum. I think even Mrs. Woodworth, with many others, misunderstands the nature of their action. There is no question of an asylum in it. No one wants to lock her up. Mrs. Woodworth may be a religious fanatic, otherwise known as a monomaniac, but there is no need to lock her up. The question is simply this: Mrs. Woodworth claims to be curing people by the power of God. A few people may believe her. Thousands do not. Physicians say that they can explain the power, that it is hypnotism. Certainly none of the laymen who have been so free with their opinions know what the power is; none who have been subjected to it know. But two physicians say they do, that they can prove that Mrs. Woodworth is using hypnotism and in her ignorance is attributing its effects to God. They further say that this indiscriminate use of hypnotism is very harmful.

"Dr. Bremer, the neurologist, in a paper read before the Medical Society, declared that hypnotism was almost epidemic here and that it was something to beware of, as it led directly to epilepsy and other forms of insanity. He further said that hypnotism should only be resorted to in the most extreme cases and then only by the most careful and learned scientists. Yet Mrs. Woodworth, it is claimed, is hypnotizing thirty and forty people a night in the crudest and most unscientific manner. If hypnotism is the power she uses, no sane person will deny that she ought to be stopped, for certainly science has proved the harm of indiscriminate hypnotism both to mind and body. And surely religion must suffer if a power known to science is used and attributed to the Almighty.

"Therefore, if Mrs. Woodworth is practicing hypnotism, though she may be utterly unconscious that she is exercising any such influence, she is doing harm and should be stopped. If she is the medium through which God is manifesting His greatness, she need fear no inquiry. The doctors have proceeded in the method prescribed by law for just such cases. Their conduct has been fair. There is no more reason for attributing selfish motives to them than to Mrs. Woodworth. They have spoken in behalf of the community; they deserve the thanks of the community. Mrs. Woodworth ought not to object to going into court or anywhere else she may be called to show the power that she claims to exercise. The public wants to know what that power is, that is all, and the attempt to smother that question by talking of insane asylums is away from the point of the controversy."

September 5, 1890

St. Louis Post-Dispatch (MO)

The Woodworth Case

Judge Woerner Considers the Proposal to Investigate Her Sanity

THE LAW UNDER WHICH THE INQUIRY IS [?]—THE MEETING LAST NIGHT—BRO. BOLTEN'S APPEAL FOR MONEY MEETS WITH QUITE A LIBERAL RESPONSE—DR. DALTON OF THE CITY HOSPITAL GIVES AN OPINION

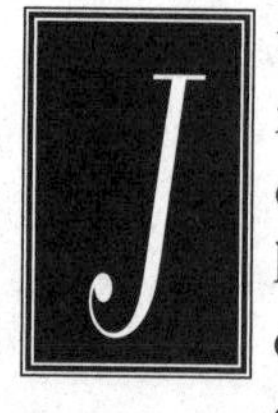udge Gabriel Woerner of the probate court returned home last night, but he did not visit the courtroom this morning, so nothing was done in the matter of the application of Drs. Adams and Diller for a jury *lunatico de inquirendo*[1] in the case of Mrs. Woodworth. The application will be considered by Judge Woerner, however, without delay though it may be a day or two before the order for the inquiry is made or refused. The judge will not proceed in the matter until he has had personal interviews with Drs. Adams and Diller.

As careful as that venerable jurist always is, he will be even more cautious on this case because of its very peculiar nature. Usually applications of this character are made by relatives or near friends of some unfortunate person in private life, and even then great care is exercised before the sanity of anyone is subjected to a legal doubt.

The presentment of a person in public life is something novel at least, and Judge Woerner will approach it with care. If he decides to issue the order, Mrs. Woodworth will be notified and she will then have five days in which to prepare her case for trial, so the hearing will not take place before the latter part of next week, and it may be laid over until the following week.

The Law of Inquiry

The law under which the proceedings have been begun is very explicit. Sec. 5.513. Revised Statutes, provides for all such inquiries, and says: "If information in writing be given to the probate court that any person in its county is an idiot, lunatic, or person of unsound mind, and incapable of managing his affairs, and praying

[1] "lunatico de inquirendo"—inquiry of insanity.

that an inquiry thereinto be had, the court, if satisfied that there is good cause for the exercise of its jurisdiction, shall cause the fact to be inquired into by a jury."

The matter is therefore in the discretion of the court, which is a provision against the continual cry of "motive! motive!" in all such cases, for while anyone is at liberty to present suggestions to the court, the court may say whether an investigation shall be held. Judge Woerner will of course exercise this discretion, and if he orders the inquiry, it will be a sufficient answer to all questions of justification and motive.

Another section provides that the alleged insane person shall be given five days' notice, or the court shall spread upon its minutes the reasons why such notice was not given. It is the invariable custom to give the notice unless the insane person is a raving maniac or his reason is so entirely dethroned that he is incapable of understanding.

There are two other sections, which, in view of the question of motive, it is well to understand. Sec.5.518 says:

"When any person shall be found to be insane, according to the preceding provisions, the cost of the proceedings shall be paid out of his estate, or, if that be insufficient, by the county."

Sec. 5.519 says: "If the person alleged to be insane shall be discharged, the cost shall be paid by the person at whose instance the proceeding is had unless said person be an officer acting officially according to the provisions of this chapter, in which case the costs shall be paid by the county."

Drs. Adams and Diller, therefore, are not acting with responsibility, for if the investigation takes place and Mrs. Woodworth is declared to be a person of sound mind, they will have costs to the amount of several hundred dollars, perhaps, to pay.

Last Night's Meeting

The usual meeting was held at the tent last night, but the routine was varied somewhat by an appeal which Rev. Mr. Bolton made for money. He began the appeal by saying that he made it of his own motion and not at the request of Mrs. Woodworth. On the contrary, when he informed her that he intended asking for money, she opposed it; and it was with difficulty that he persuaded her to consent to it. She had been working there for five months and the collection during that time, he said, only amounted to $75. He wanted the congregation to understand that the people who do the work of the Lord have to eat just as other people do; and if anybody supposed that they hadn't been eating regularly, they were mistaken. Mrs. Woodworth was not working for money, he said, but for the Lord. She was not like the ministers of churches who will not preach unless they get big salaries. She didn't take summer vacations and draw a salary all the time she was away, and she did not stay idly at home while there was work to do for the Lord. She was in the tent every day working, carrying on the meetings, and trying to save souls. Yet there was not a minister in the city [illegible phrase] were less than five hundred dollars [3 lines illegible] tent which cost one thousand five hundred dollars and money to live on. He did not suppose that the people of this city wanted it said that they sent Mrs. Woodworth away without money enough to live on or that they wanted her to pay the expenses of the meetings out of her own pocket. Many good people had come to her and said they hoped she would continue this good work, but they didn't bring any money with them and the work could not [go] on without money.

Someone in the audience cried out, "I thought the Lord supported her."

Mr. Bolton's remarks frequently elicited comment from the audience, but he paid no attention to what was said.

He proceeded with his call for money.

"There is money in this congregation, and I know it," he said, "and I want some of those who want to see this work go on to contribute. Those who will give a $10 bill, send it right up. Just pass it up; don't be backward.[2] It won't stop anywhere; it will go right to Mrs. Woodworth."

"Where did you get your nerve?" came from several parts of the audience, and the unmannerly ones laughed and were noisy.

"Come on, now, those who will give $10 send it up," said Mr. Bolton. "I know some people don't bring their pocketbooks here,

[2] "backward"—shy or reluctant.

because we have a pretty rough crowd at the meetings and they are afraid, but if they will write their names and addresses on a piece of paper and give it to the ushers, we will collect it."

Nobody responded, and Mr. Bolton said: "Well, those who have Vs[3] to give Mrs. Woodworth, give them to the ushers. The ushers won't keep them. Don't be backward. We have to have money to carry on this work and we have to eat just like other people."

Three five-dollar bills were handed the ushers and Mr. Bolton thanked the givers, and when it was apparent that the Vs were all in, Mr. Bolton called for the dollars. A number of them went up and the baskets were then passed around for the small change. While the baskets were going around, Mr. Bolton said, "I want to say that if there is any grocer here who does not want to give money, he can send groceries. We need them to eat; and if he wants to send $25 worth of groceries, the wagon can come right around to the back of the tent. He needn't be at all backward."

When the money was collected, the prayers were resumed and the meeting progressed as usual. The interest in the meeting has not lessened and the publicity given to the peculiar work in the papers has caused the attendance of hundreds of people who go to see those who fall into the trances.

Dr. Dalton Thinks It Harmful

Dr. Dalton, superintendent of the city hospital, was asked by a *Post-Dispatch* reporter what he thought was the effect on the children at Mrs. Woodworth's tent when they went into the trances or hypnotic state.

"It cannot help but be harmful," he said. "The effect on the nervous system must be extremely deleterious. Then I do not think the influence is good from a moral standpoint. I do not think any beneficial results can be attained by these trances."

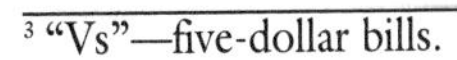

[3] "Vs"—five-dollar bills.

September 6, 1890

St. Louis Globe-Democrat (MO)

The Civil Courts

The Proceedings Against Mrs. Woodworth Virtually Dismissed

JUDGE WOERNER THINKS THE SHOWING DOES NOT WARRANT HIS INTERFERENCE—THE BOSLEY SLANDER SUIT—OTHER CASES IN COURT

The proceedings begun in the probate court not long since by Dr. Wellington Adams and Dr. Theodore Diller to have Mrs. M. B. Woodworth, the evangelist, declared insane, were virtually dismissed by Judge Woerner of the probate court in chambers yesterday. The judge appeared in the courthouse for the first time since his return to the city from his summer vacation and proceeded to dispose of some minor matters pertaining to his numerous duties, when Dr. Wellington Adams put in an appearance for the purpose of making a preliminary statement of the character of the proceedings against Mrs. Woodworth and the motives that actuated him in the premises and to procure the official sanction of the court to begin them. He explained the character of Mrs. Woodworth's religious services at her gospel tent on Jefferson Avenue, the motley crowd that went there, and the bad effects produced upon the community. He said that the meetings were sacrilegious and described in a very interesting manner what he denominated delusions, Mrs. Woodworth's influences over her deluded followers, and the pernicious effects caused by her generally. He also said that the whole religious community recognized that her influence was bad and demoralizing, and in substance, that she was recognized as a nuisance and ought to be suppressed.

Judge Woerner replied that he agreed with the doctor that the result of Mrs. Woodworth's work might be of a pernicious character—that is, if the published reports about her were true—and that it was damaging to religion, but with the showing made, he did not think that he would be justified in entertaining a proposition to have her declared insane. It was true she might be a regular nuisance, but his court was not the proper tribunal in which to try nuisance cases. A different kind of tribunal would have to be appealed

Much of Maria Woodworth-Etter's ministry took place under the shelter of tents like this one. No matter how big the tent was, she soon filled it to overflowing with people.

to for that purpose and a different kind of proceeding begun. He advised the doctor to change the nature of the actions—at any rate, to consult a lawyer. He did not absolutely dismiss the proceeding, but in effect did so. In speaking of Dr. Adams, he said the doctor was undoubtedly an intelligent gentleman with honest motives, but that he had undertaken a somewhat complicated task.

September 6, 1890

St. Louis Post-Dispatch (MO)

The Doctors Satisfied

Hypnotism Discontinued at the Woodworth Tent

DR. WELLINGTON ADAMS SAYS THAT WHAT HE AND DR. DILLER WERE AIMING AT IN THE INSANITY PROCEEDINGS HAS BEEN ACCOMPLISHED—HE WILL BRING THE CASE BEFORE THE MEDICAL SOCIETY

Judge Woerner has decided that the probate court has no authority to inquire into the sanity of Mrs. M. B. Woodworth. The court is authorized only to take care of the property of insane persons and of the persons themselves only so far as the care of their property may demand.

Dr. Wellington Adams was found in his office this morning; and when asked about his interview with the Judge, he said:

"Judge Woerner asked me what my motive was in instituting the proceedings against Mrs. Woodworth. My reply to him was that Mrs. Woodworth was a person of unsound mind who was exercising a physical power upon others which was harmful to those subjected to it and harmful to future generations. I did not wish to attack her religion or to say anything whatever about that, but I wished to prove that her mind was unsound and to restrain her from exercising a harmful power.

Had No Jurisdiction

"Judge Woerner said that the probate court had no jurisdiction over such cases. That it had power only to appoint guardians for those who were incapable of attending to their own business affairs, and the inquiry into their sanity was only an investigation of the necessity for appointing a guardian. He told me that the only course open was to prosecute Mrs. Woodworth as a public nuisance, but that, of course, I will not do. I do not mean to let the matter drop, however. Hypnotism is a power with which, of late, we have become somewhat familiar, and we can fully appreciate the danger of it and the harmful results which follow its indiscriminate practice. It is being legislated against in Europe, where it is best understood, and I intend to send to the next legislature a bill prohibiting all exhibitions of hypnotism and its use in public. There is a need for it which is appreciated by all medical men.

"I intend also to prepare some articles on this case for the medical journals, and I will present Mrs. Woodworth's case to the medical society at the first meeting after the vacation is over. I am interested in this matter solely because of its influence on the public health and not only in St. Louis, but elsewhere. She has been in California; she will go elsewhere and probably others who are similarly afflicted will follow in her footsteps. There ought to be some way of preventing the exercise of these harmful influences on the weak and nervous people in the community.

"I want to say, however, that I have accomplished my object. I attended Mrs. Woodworth's meeting last night and saw that the use of hypnotism in the meetings has been discontinued and that is all I wanted. There was not a solitary case of hypnosis or catalepsy. There were some of the old-fashioned revival manifestations, shouting and clapping of the hands, but no hypnosis; and that is what I wanted to stop. Before this matter was given publicity, Mrs. Woodworth and those who assist her called the people closely about them and told them to 'look up for the coming of the Holy Ghost, to raise their hands to the Lord,' and placed them in attitudes which subjected them to the exercise of the hypnotic power. There was none of that last night. There was no 'suggestion' and consequently there were no trances. Now I insist still that Mrs. Woodworth is of unsound mind, but two causes have led to the discontinuance of hypnotism—those about her who control her have thought it advisable to stop it, and those who attend the meetings have been informed of the nature of the power exercised.

What He Has Aimed At

"They have gone to the meeting with doubts in their minds and they have not been so fully convinced of the miraculous nature of these manifestations that they could be easily controlled or influenced. This is what I have aimed at and all I sought to accomplish. Mrs. Woodworth is a religious monomaniac, but if people enjoy her preaching, well and good. So long as she does not use this harmful influence and so endanger the health of people of today and future generations, I haven't a word to say.

"I will present the case to the Medical Society, however, and it can be discussed there by men who have given the subject study. The society can then speak and say whether hypnotic trances are or are not harmful to health. The medical journals have so spoken repeatedly and so have the ablest scientists."

Mrs. Hammill's Case

The case of Mrs. Eliza Hammill, who was cured by the "power," was cited as one of the proofs that God was miraculously curing people and that hypnotism played no part. A full account of the case was given in Thursday's *Post-Dispatch*. Mrs. Hammill is a poor washing woman who has to support herself and four children by hard work. She said that last winter she was attacked by rheumatism, which had so afflicted her that she had lost the use of her right arm almost entirely. Medical treatment had not relieved her, though she went to the Polyclinic on Jefferson and Lucas Avenues, three times a week for more than a month. She had seen people cure (*sic*) by the power of God and believing that she could so be cured, she applied to Mrs. Woodworth for assistance. She went up to the platform; and while she was standing there, she felt the disease leave her, and she had been well ever since.

The chief of the nervous clinic at the Polyclinic was seen this morning and asked if he remembered Mrs. Hammill's case. He did, and consented to talk about it, but only on condition that his name be withheld. "I do not like the notoriety which has been given to everyone connected with this case," he said, "and I want to stay out of it. If people are fools enough to go there to be injured, I suppose it is all right. It is against the law of the college to show our books; but since Mrs. Hammill has given her own case to the public and referred to the college, it is not improper for us to tell what her complaint was. He then brought the book and showed the entry. "Name, Eliza Hammill; diagnosis, hysteria." It was not rheumatism, but hysteria.

"Now," said the doctor, "when she came to me and told me she had lost the power of her arm and told me how she lived, I thought it was the result of overwork, poor food, and bad air, but I recognized her trouble when she described the symptoms. She said that in one place it burned like it was on fire. That is a well-known and well-recognized symptom of hysteria. The trouble is with the vaso-motor nervous system, which controls the circulation. Then she said that the fingers tingled and she was afraid she was going to be paralyzed. I soon saw that she was simply suffering from hysteria, and I convinced myself by suggestion. She bared her arm and then I placed my thumb upon a spot which is not very sensitive to pain because it is not a 'nerve point.' I told her that I was going to press upon it and it would hurt her, but she would have to bear the pain. I pressed lightly and she screamed with pain. I then selected the nerve points, told her that pressure upon those spots would not hurt her at all; and though I pressed hard upon them, she declared that she felt no power whatever.

"Finally she complained of globus hysteria; that is, she felt as if she had a heavy pressure on her body, a heavy and suffocating sensation. That is plain hysteria and nothing else. Mrs. Hammill came here three times and then ceased her visits. That was her condition. She had no rheumatism. She was simply hysterical and any great excitement might have cured her. A big fire, anything which would have aroused her mind, would probably have done it. Or if she had made up her mind firmly that she was going to get well, she would have gotten well. Such cases of hysteria are common. Physicians see them every day and treat them by treating the imagination. Hundreds of people are so afflicted, and if people generally knew half as much about it as physicians, they would laugh at the absurdity of the whole thing.

September 11, 1890

St. Louis Post-Dispatch (MO)

Her Husband Writes

Dr. Wellington Adams Receives a Letter from Mr. Woodworth

HE HAS A VERY PATHETIC TALE TO TELL—ALTHOUGH HIS WIFE, HE CLAIMS, ABANDONED HIM AND LEFT HIM SICK AND IN DISTRESS, HE STILL LOVES HER—MRS. DIEDRICKSON'S EXPERIENCE

Several weeks ago Rev. Dr. Boswell of the First Methodist Church of this city received a letter from a man purporting to be the husband of Mrs. Woodworth, the evangelist, who has been conducting revival meetings for a number of months in a tent at Jefferson and Cass Avenues. Dr. Boswell declined to make known to any person the contents of the letter but intimated that its contents were a severe reflection on Mrs. Woodworth and her followers.

Yesterday Dr. Wellington Adams received a letter from the same source and a portion of the communication is here given. The letter, while written in a rough and uncouth style, devoid of grammar, correct spelling, etc., is nevertheless rather a pathetic appeal for the sympathy and love of a, perhaps, forgetful wife.

The Letter:

> Rochester, Ind.,[1]
> Sept. 7, 1890
>
> I have seen your name in the *Post-Dispatch* about how you believe my wife is crazy. In regard as to me being in the asilum I will say at present I am at home. I was compelled to leave my wife Maria B Woodworth at Oakland Cal on the 15 day of last Dec by the request of Mrs. Woodworth. . . . My wife left me alone in the camp ground not able to be on my feet only part of the time. . . . After dark 2 of Mrs. W friends came to me found me [?] sick in my tent they said to me [we have a ?] propostin

[1] The letter is printed as it appeared in the news article with brackets around illegible phrases.

to make to you; [leave?] to-mory morning at 8 o'clock [or we will have?] you arrested for threts of murder [. She is?] my wife and after all [which we ?] has [?] to have past through I would give [up the?] last cent I have if She stood in need [I spent?] all night in agony. I made up [my mind that ?] before I would ezspose her I would [attempt?] to start home. God only noes what I suffered on the way home and have suffered—everything but death.

All the aid I have received in supplying my wants sence the 15 day of Dec. is 20 dolars. I am broken down, total wreck amung strangers I need medical aid, but I hav not one cent of income. Often when I was down to a crust of bread and a cup of water I wonder whether Mrs. Woodworth when she is using money to support persons, setting them down to a well filed tabel on money witch I chould of had wheather iff she thinks of the person she promest God to nerish and cherish through sickness and death that sollem vow she has broken, yes she has. The Lord Have Mercy on her is my prayers. The only thing I desire is fer her to repent and make Heaven Her Home. God save my wife from a burning Hell is my prayers.

P. H. Woodworth

The hypnotic séances which have been a feature of the gospel meetings have been to a great extent abated. This was the object for which the doctors were working, and they consider their object as having been accomplished.

Mrs. Diedrickson's Story

The stories of cures performed at the gospel tent have acted as a considerable factor in attracting attention to the work of Mrs. Woodworth. Some of the stories as told by persons who claim to have been cured at the tent are marvelous and seem hard to explain, except to those who are familiar with hypnotism, and these claim to account for the strange occurrences through hypnotism as the following story as told to a *Post-Dispatch* reporter this morning by Mrs. Diedrickson, explains itself. Mrs. Diedrickson went to Mrs.

Woodworth's tent to get cured of a complication of diseases and tells how it was done. This morning a *Post-Dispatch* reporter went to the home of Mrs. Diedrickson, on St. Louis Avenue near Leffingwell. The entrance to her dwelling was through a saloon and up a flight of stairs. The reporter knocked at the door, which was opened by a slender woman. That she was not in good health could be seen at a glance, and she was evidently very feeble. The reporter explained his errand and was invited to stop into a neat little kitchen.

"I went out to the tent three or four times to get cured," said Mrs. Diedrickson, "and you see how I look now. I have been sick since last April and my neighbors came in to persuade me to go and be cured by the power of God as demonstrated by Mrs. Woodworth.

"I was too sick to walk at all, but my son got a carriage and I went one afternoon. They helped me into the tent and I sat on a bench and they prayed for me. We all got down on our knees in the sawdust and I began to feel better. I just thought that if the power was going to come to me, it would come anyway.

"When I got up I felt better, the pain had all left me, and when I tried to walk, it seemed as though I was all right.

"'You needn't to ride home in the carriage,' said Mrs. Woodworth, 'you can walk all right.'

"I started to walk home feeling good and strong. It is only a few blocks but before I got halfway, my feet began to feel heavy and I finally had to give it up. My friends then helped me the rest of the way and I felt much worse. It seemed as though I had been under a kind of stimulant and that it had all been worked out.

"They got me to go other evenings, but it only seemed to make me get worse. I sat on the hard benches and it made me so sore that I could hardly lie down in my bed. Then besides, I guess I caught cold from kneeling so long on the damp ground. I had to go to bed again.

"When some of my neighbors came to me and said that I was really not sick, but that the devil had got into me, and that I was acting that way—you can see whether I seem sick or not."

Mrs. Diedrickson evidently had no more confidence in Mrs. Woodworth being able to cure her and will not make any further attempt to be made well in that way.

September 12, 1890

St. Louis Post-Dispatch (MO)

Why She Left Him

Mrs. Maria B. Woodworth Makes a Reply to Her Husband's Attack

HIS OWN BAD CONDUCT SAID TO BE THE SOLE CAUSE OF THE SEPARATION—A CALIFORNIA PHYSICIAN ON THE "POWER" AND HYPNOTISM—LETTER OF INDORSEMENT (*SIC*) FROM INDIANA—EXTRAORDINARY SCENE AT THE TENT

he letter from the husband of Mrs. Woodworth, published in the *Post-Dispatch,* has been read with considerable interest by that lady's supporters who say that the allegations contained in it are totally groundless and that the whole fault of the separation rests with the husband. Parties who were in Oakland, Cal., during the Woodworth stay there say the man's conduct was so bad that he was expelled from the vicinity of the tent, and some people even went so far as to suggest that he should be driven out of the town. He was accused by Miss Emma Isenberg and Miss Ollie Daggett, two of Mrs. Woodworth's attendants, with having made improper overtures to them and other very serious charges were brought against him. His wife was advised to sue for a divorce on the ground of infidelity, but she declined to take this extreme step. It is said that she has always been willing to help her husband to reclaim but that his conduct has rendered a reconciliation impossible.

Among those who testify to Mrs. Woodworth's respectability and innocence of the offences insinuated against her are, Dr. A. Troy of Milner Corner, Hancock County, Cal.; Judge W. R. West of Henderson, Ill., and Elder H. H. Spiher of Muncie, Ind. Dr. Troy was an atheist prior to Mrs. Woodworth's work in California. He attended her meetings, became quite an enthusiast, and professed conversion. Quite recently he was in St. Louis, and while here he attended one of the services at the tent and addressed the congregation. Besides testifying to the lady's respectability, he spoke at some length as to the difference between hypnotism and the "power." Among the point of dissimilarity mentioned by him was the way people recovered, or came to. Speaking as a medical man and a student of hypnotism, he said that when a subject was hypnotized, he had to be brought out of the trance condition by the person who induced it. In the cases at the tent, people were sometimes affected outside the tent and they came round gradually and without assistance. Whatever the "power" was, it was not hypnotism. The address was listened to attentively and the arguments carefully followed.

A Letter From Indiana

Elder H. H. Spiher's letter, dated Sept. 8, and written from Muncie, Delaware County, Ind., is a strong indorsement (*sic*) of the "evangelist now laboring in evangelist work, corner Cass and Jefferson Avenues, St. Louis, Mo." The writer says:

"I, Elder H. H. Spiher, pastor of Muncie and Anderson (Ind.) Churches of God, representing five hundred members and chairman of the standing committee of the Southern Indiana eldership of the Church of God, of which Sister M. B. Woodworth holds license to preach the Gospel and practice the ordinances of said church and body [as] an ordained minister of the same, do testify that her name is beyond successful reproach; and further, she is perfectly sane. I have known her for eleven years personally, and she is worthy of your best support in all respects. And further, her husband, T. H. Woodworth, has proved himself unworthy of Christian support and that his name has been erased from said eldership and church and is, I believe, trying to injure his wife's good name and work, and advise you and all good men to abstain from him."

In a postscript Elder Spiher expresses a willingness to produce twenty-five ministers and hundreds of doctors, lawyers, and businessmen to back up his statement.

An Extraordinary Case

There was a very exciting scene in and around the tent yesterday afternoon when Thomas Farley of Carondolet came to be cured of paralysis. Mr. Farley resides at 7120 Minnesota Avenue, and is forty-six years of age. For nineteen years he was a member of the police force but had to resign two-and-a-half years ago in consequence of a severe attack of rheumatism, supposed to have been induced by sunstroke. He has spent altogether one thousand dollars of his savings in vain attempts to get cured or at least relieved. At various times Drs. Robinson, Starkloff, Volker, and Brebach have attended him, and he has also visited Sulphur Springs in search of relief. But all his efforts have proved unavailing, and yesterday he visited Mrs. Woodworth.

He was so helpless that he had to be taken to the tent in a furniture car into which he had to be lifted. When the car arrived at the tent, Mr. Farley was taken out and assisted up to the platform, his arms hanging at his side, and his general condition was very feeble. Mrs. Woodworth spoke very earnestly to the sick man and asked him if he had faith in Christ's power to work miracles in the flesh now as in the past. He responded in the affirmative, and after prayer and singing, the evangelist said:

"Rise up and walk."

Mr. Farley at once arose and leaving his cane behind him, walked out of the tent evidently greatly relieved. His arms were uplifted and he praised God in a loud tone of voice. When he reached the car, he set on his chair still holding his hands on high and calling for praise for the Almighty. There were a large number of persons on the street and the [illegible last line].

September 18, 1890

St. Louis Daily Globe-Democrat (MO)

Healed by Faith

Thomas F. Farley, who has for nineteen years been a member of the St. Louis police force and who retired three years ago because he was prostrated by three paralytic strokes, has been cured of his affliction by Miss Maria B. Woodworth, the evangelist. Farley was brought to the gospel tent on a cot in a furniture car, and after a half hour's praying by about six hundred of the congregation, he walked from the platform cured. The excitement in the meantime was intense and dozens fell into trances. Farley is a member of the Carondolet Methodist Church South, is forty-six years old, and has been drawing a pension from the Police Relief Fund on account of his disability.

September 22, 1890

St. Louis Daily Globe-Democrat (MO)

Her Last Week

The Woodworth Revival Meeting to Close for the Year

THE MOVEMENT TO BUILD A TABERNACLE TAKES SUBSTANTIAL SHAPE—MRS. WOODWORTH TO RETURN—THE SUBSCRIPTIONS—YESTERDAY'S SERVICE

bout seven thousand persons—young, middle aged, and old—jostled one another yesterday at the services in the gospel tent of Mrs. Maria B. Woodworth on Jefferson near Cass Avenue. When this week has ended, Mrs. Woodworth will be compelled by the demand of her services in other quarters to leave St. Louis until early in 1892, when she expects to reopen in a substantial temple or tabernacle, which will in all probability have been constructed for her here by friends. If the project succeeds, Mrs. Woodworth said last night to a *Globe-Democrat* reporter that she will make St. Louis her headquarters and will begin a systematic evangelization of Missouri, as already arrangements have been made whereby she will hold meetings in various parts of the state.

A Woodworth Tabernacle

A select audience, in which the female sex was in the ascendant, greeted the lady evangelist at the afternoon meeting yesterday. The seating capacity of the tent was put to quite a test to afford accommodations to the worshippers. A. D. Rutledge, a businessman of St. Louis, addressed the congregation, suggesting that the offers of aid in continuing the Woodworth meetings, which have been made by hundreds, be put in definite shape. Mr. Rutledge briefly outlined the tabernacle enterprise which had been proposed. The idea is to erect a large structure, which shall be comfortable in all seasons, one story high, of brick or wood, about 80 X 120 feet, or to accommodate about seven thousand people, that it have an inclined floor converging from all points to the base of an altar in the center of the building, and lastly, that it be built at once and the occupancy, management, and control be put in charge of Mrs. Woodworth, and the title be vested in five trustees, or their successors, to the end that it may never be diverted from its intended uses. Mr. Rutledge spoke at some length, reviewing the work accomplished by Mrs. Woodworth.

After Mr. Rutledge delivered his address, all those in favor of furthering the evangelistic work were asked to raise their hands. Thousands were uplifted in response. Afterward the usual altar services were held, at which many converts knelt at the platform.

Evening Services

The evening attendance ranged from six thousand five hundred to seven thousand. Seating room was at a premium. The multitude was a most orderly one, and quiet was maintained throughout the meeting. Quite a number of colored persons attended, a few of whom fell into trances. Mrs. Woodworth spoke for one hour, taking "eternity" as her text. After the sermon Mr. Rutledge repeated the plan for building a mission. After a list of subscribers had been secured, the customary altar services were held. The space reserved for seekers after salvation was thickly crowded with persons in kneeling attitudes. Only a few instances of persons becoming rigid and cataleptic were observed. It was 11 o'clock before the worshippers departed from the spacious tent. Much enthusiasm prevailed among Mrs. Woodworth's followers at the prospect of permanent quarters in this city.

The Sermon

Mrs. Woodworth spoke substantially as follows:

> The word "eternity" occurs but once in the Word of God. It concerns us as individuals more than any other word. We have had a beginning, but as to our ending, a few people try to believe that we die like beasts and that there is no future life. It is grand and glorious to the Christians, though, because Christians know that they live forever. Eternal life is the gift of God. The unbeliever's future is a fearful thought. God has placed men and women on this earth but for a short period. Life is

only a drop in the great ocean of eternity. This dying, judgment-bound congregation was placed here that we may give our hearts to our Creator. We belong to the royal line; we are children of the King. God is no respecter of persons; He will receive all in [to] His family who accept His teachings. His love is everlasting, but His wrath will soon burst in awful fury on this sin-cursed earth. God made us stewards of our attainments. Many accept the bountiful blessings He offers yet do not take a decisive step toward eternal life. Only the pure in heart will step heavenward. Many on their deathbeds moan: "Oh, give me a seat in the kingdom!" But it is only the cowards who wait till the eleventh hour. Old Christians have repeated oftentimes: "I am glad I started when I was young."

Everlasting Life

It is a Christian's privilege to work for eternal life; God has given us the opportunity. Remember salvation is free—when we pay a penny, it is not a gift. It is a soul-inspiring thought that the more earnestness with which Christianity is spread, the better are Christians capable of enjoying everlasting life. "Get ready for heaven now—tonight."

The lady preacher then drew a forcible comparison between the gospel ship and the ship of destruction, both laden with human beings. One is sailing to eternity, the other, over the falls to perdition.

"The gospel ship is stopping here tonight. Oh, won't you all embark? There is no neutral ground. Choose one side—the shelter of God's banner—before it is too late."

Tabernacle Subscriptions

When the time came to figure on how large a fund could be raised for the new Woodworth Mission, many volunteers stepped forward. A lady headed the list with one hundred dollars and stated that she had authority to subscribe five hundred dollars more for a friend who wished to be unknown. Several hundred dollars had been secured in a few moments. Owing to the lack of time, subscribers were asked to put their names, addresses, and amounts on slips of paper, which were sent to the platform. An old married couple who came from Tennessee to be healed and were successful, contributed largely. A rough estimate of last night's subscriptions footed up nearly fifteen hundred dollars. A businessman has promised five thousand dollars conditionally, while numerous church workers will contribute largely. All moneys will be received and credited by Mrs. Woodworth or Rev. Alexander Douglass at the gospel tent.

October 13, 1890

St. Louis Post-Dispatch (MO)

The "Power" Was In

Unusual Demonstration in Trinity M. E. Church Last Night

A Number of the Congregation Give Such Manifestations of Enthusiasm as Shocked Both Pastor and People—The Methodist Episcopal Ministers Furnished With a Live Topic for Discussion

hen the Methodist Episcopal ministers met this morning in their regular Monday meeting at the Methodist book concern on Fifteenth Street and Lucas Place, the question was what caused the congregation of Trinity Church on Tenth and North Market Streets to be seized by the power. Dr. Mariatt, the pastor, could not really explain the occurrence, nor could any of the other ministers, but they all agreed that it was simply religious enthusiasm which had taken hold of the people.

Yesterday during the evening service for young folks, held in the basement, and again during the later service upstairs, members of the congregation were suddenly taken with attacks very much like those which affect the enthusiasts at the Woodworth revivals. They shrieked and prayed and yelled and sang, making a great deal of noise and confusion.

Children Seized First

The first to be seized were the children at the early meeting, which was held at 7:30 o'clock. About a dozen of them were taken. One little girl who was just beginning a prayer was seized and fell in a heap on the floor, as if she had been shot. Others followed, some singing and some praying. The services were immediately stopped and the children quieted and order restored.

A few minutes later the services in the church were commenced. A few hymns were sang (*sic*) and some prayers were said, when Dr. Mariatt began his sermon on the "Childhood of Christ." He had not progressed far when one of the congregation rose and began to pray out loud in the church while the sermon was being delivered. Others followed rapidly, some jumping to them felt[1] with loud cries

[1] "them felt"—possible error. Could be "some jumping to their feet with loud cries" or "some jumping to their feet fell with loud cries".

and others dropping as if in a faint. The confusion for a few moments was very great and services completely stopped. Dr. Mariatt stopped his sermon and tried to quiet his excited audience and succeeded in doing so after some little time, but it was nearly an hour before the regular service could be resumed with any degree of certainty that the same outbursts of enthusiasm would not reoccur. About 11 o'clock the last of the congregation went home quieted. There were about fifteen people in the congregation who were violently attacked with the "power," and nearly all of them had been to the Woodworth meetings and had heard and seen what was done there.

The Pastor Displeased

Dr. Mariatt was seen and asked about the occurrence and said: "I cannot explain the matter in any way. I am sure I would not encourage anything of the kind and am completely at a loss to understand why it should have occurred last night.

"The condition into which they lapsed was not exactly like that of the converts of Mrs. Woodworth. They did not become rigid, but some of them dropped as if they had been hit with an ax. All who were so attacked are good people in the congregation and undoubted honestly (*sic*) in their convictions. There was nothing unusual in the services yesterday and nothing to cause any excess of religious enthusiasm.

"I would not permit services to continue while any of them were in that excited condition but just stopped everything and waited for them to come round. We had them all quieted after a little and then went on with the services. Nearly all of them had been at some time or other to the Woodworth meetings, but I do not think that could have had any serious effect, as the doings resembled very much one of the old-fashioned Methodist meetings. We intend holding a protracted meeting next week but feel a little nervous about the outcome of it."

The occurrences of yesterday are very unusual and it is the first time in the history of the Trinity church that such things have occurred.

No explanation but a religious enthusiasm has been advanced as a reason for the strange conduct of the congregation.

January 3, 1891

St. Louis Post-Dispatch (MO)

Mrs. Woodworth's Flock

It Seems to be Much in Need of the Shepherdess

MESSRS. AHLE AND WHEELDON WRITE A CARD TO THE CHRISTIANS OF THE CITY DENYING THE RIGHT OF THE PASTOR TO EXPEL THEM FROM THE FLOCK

hen Mrs. Woodworth, the evangelist, went away from St. Louis some months ago, she left her spiritual flock enjoying a harmonious feeling, but when she returns next week she will find things turned topsy-turvy. The trouble amongst the workers of her temple has now reached a white heat, and so it will doubtless remain until her return. Messrs. Wheeldon and Ahle, two former associates with Rev. A. Douglas in the management of the affairs, but who were suspended by the reverend gentleman, have thrown before the scrutinizing gaze of the public the following card, which intimates very decidedly that the two gentlemen possess a mine of information which they will spring in the near future:

> To the Christian People of St. Louis and to All Whom it May Concern—Informing them that we hold our respective positions as appointed us by Mrs. M. B. Woodworth, previous to her leaving St. Louis for Indiana, and that we are in receipt of letters of recent date telling us to hold the same until her return, as no one has the authority or was delegated with power to remove us.
>
> We, therefore, ask the public to kindly suspend their judgment for a few days. Yours respectfully,
>
> F. Wheeldon
> J. F. Ahle

Wait a Few Days

Mr. Ahle was asked what his new information was but refused to say anything very interesting on the subject.

[P. D.] "Will you not show your letters from Mrs. Woodworth?" was asked.

[A.] "Not for the present."

[P. D.] "To whom does your information refer?"

[A.] "To the people now in charge of the Woodworth congregation. There is gross mismanagement in the affairs."

[P. D.] "In what way?"

[A.] "This is not the proper time to speak. We are expecting Mrs. Woodworth here at the present, and when she comes there will be a good old-fashioned shaking up of dry bones in the skeleton closet up on Fourteenth and Lucas."

[P. D.] "What will you charge?"

[A.] "As the papers are not ready for submission, I will not say anything at present. But I will say that I have been in St. Louis for the past twenty years and do not intend to be bulldozed out of standing in the community by a man like Douglas. There is going to be trouble—no end of trouble. My friends have been aiding me, and the result is that a mass of evidence has been collected that will astonish the congregation when they are read" (*sic*).

[P. D.] "What does Mrs. Woodworth say in her letters?"

[A.] "That will be made public at the same time the other information is given. When this mine is sprung there will certainly be weeping, wailing, and gnashing of teeth. The pastor, as he well knows, had no power to oust Mr. Wheeldon and myself, and he did it more through personal spite than from any other motive. When the whole case is made public, the Christian people will be more able to judge more knowingly as to who is to blame and that someone must take the consequences, and they are not far away. Rev. Douglas and Messrs. Floyd and Rutledge are running things with a high hand. Just wait until after the explosion."

Mr. Ahle would under no circumstances make any direct assertions but depended upon general accusations of mismanagement, especially in regard to the building fund. He said that from the tenor of Mrs. Woodworth's letters, he would be replaced in his former good standing when she returns.

"But should I not be," said he, "I will take my own action. Mr. Wheeldon and myself have many supporters and friends among the workers," which is supposed to mean that a revolt will take place.

They Are Bad, Bad Men

At his study in the church at Fourteenth and Lucas Place, Rev. A. Douglas, who suspended the young men, was seen, and when shown the card, his small black eyes snapped fire, his lips twitched nervously, as though excited. He retained his composure, however, and talked calmly and collectedly over the matter.

[D.] "This matter is growing personal," said he, "and I am sorry of it. But when it comes to such a pass, these young men will find that they have started out in the worst way possible for themselves. There is not one iota of doubt in my mind that these selfsame young men have been trying in every way to get charge of the congregation. Mr. Ahle wants my present position, while Mr. Wheeldon desires the management of the financial affairs. They commenced this crusade against the management almost as soon as Mrs. Woodworth left for Indiana. They have waged a constant warfare, doing everything in their power to make members of the congregation dissatisfied. Their whole object from beginning to end has been to undermine the work that has been accomplished."

[P. D.] "What course do you propose to pursue?" he was asked.

[D.] "I intend to calmly await the arrival of my chief, and I am sure that when she makes her decision, it will be just and right. These men are growing desperate in their desire for promotion and power. They attempt to throw mud at me because I stand in their way. I have had constant trouble with these fellows, and if they shoot the first gun, I will feel justified in shooting back. When the case is given to the public, I will be ready with my defense. Let me show you a letter from Mrs. Woodworth in regard to the matter."

The letter referred to contains this passage:

"We all send our regards to Sister Bissell (a coworker of Rev. Douglas), who is standing so nobly by you and the work. God bless you both. Hold the reins in your hands."

"This," continued Mr. Douglas, "was written to me before I had communicated with Mrs. Woodworth regarding the trouble. Mr. W. J. Floyd wrote to Mrs. Woodworth and received a letter endorsing my course in this matter. This letter was read to the congregation. One of the champions of the opposition grossly insulted me during the meeting New Year evening, (*sic*) but I did not notice it. His speech was uncalled for and very much out of place during the presentation."

The quarrel promises to develop some very interesting features.

January 15, 1891

Rochester Weekly Republican

The Truth of It

A statement from the "Manitou Musings" Man

EDITOR *REPUBLICAN:*

Your extracts from the *Anderson Bulletin* and other papers contain some statements about the Woodworth difficulties so at variance with the truth and so shamefully and cruelly unjust to Mrs. Woodworth that I deem it my duty to offer a correction.

I sold the property known as Manitou Park to the Woodworths and have the statements of both as to the means of payment. My residence is near theirs and the property is generally left in my charge in their absence. I have been consulted in the difficulties that separate them, have seen a portion of the correspondence that passed and been made conversant with the remainder, and have endeavored to act the mutual friend in effecting the best possible settlement for both. These circumstances enable me to speak from personal knowledge of the facts and to reveal a real state of affairs of which the newspaper world is utterly uninformed or else ignorantly and maliciously blind.

Manitou Park was deeded jointly to Philo H. and Maria B. Woodworth and was paid for wholly from the proceeds of the sale of Mrs. Woodworth's books and the other receipts of her meetings. Since the separation Mr. Woodworth has had the entire use of, and receipts from, the Park property, while his wife, in addition to supporting herself, has paid the taxes on the Park and sent a considerable sum of money to pay a store bill and other obligations that Mr. Woodworth was unable to meet.

A short time ago, in answer to several letters asking further assistance, Mrs. Woodworth replied through her attorney, Judge West, of Anderson, in substance as follows:

> All attempts at reconciliation, after what has occurred, are useless. An application for divorce will be made in the Fulton Circuit Court. If you are in such an urgent need, we will purchase your interest in the property, paying a sufficient sum down for immediate requirements and the remainder, as you need it. If this suits you make trustee's deed, and payment will be made immediately.

With the unimportant details of this letter, the general public has no business, but I will say in further explanation that the price offered therein was all that Mr. Woodworth has been asking and probably $250 more than he could get from anyone else at this time.

Instead of trying to effect a settlement on the lines laid down in the letter, Mr. Woodworth made another effort for a personal meeting with his wife; but receiving no reply to his letter to her and believing that no divorce proceedings would be instituted, he arranged for such institution on his own part in order to secure a division of the property.

Before these proceedings were perfected, however, Judge West, not having been informed of Mr. Woodworth's intentions, placed on file the wife's application with its sensational charges.

Since then Mr. Woodworth, accompanied by his attorney, went to Anderson to accept the terms of sale and to secure if possible a modification of the charges. The result of that visit I will give in Mr. Woodworth's own words:

"I did not see Mrs. Woodworth. All the business was transacted through Judge West. I sold on the terms offered in Judge West's letter, and the charges for divorce will be changed to abandonment and failure to provide. In addition to this I was told to continue using the property until it is needed and will be given sufficient furniture to set up housekeeping. I could not ask Mrs. Woodworth to be more generous than she has been in this matter, and I will say to you candidly that she is not to blame for the difficulties that have arisen between us."

I might say much more to prove that Mrs. Woodworth is not "trying to rob the old man of his property and drive him into the poorhouse," but hope this is sufficient at present, and I feel that under existing circumstances I could not be true to myself were I to remain silent or say less.

I am an utter disbeliever in many of the doctrines that Mrs. Woodworth is teaching and do not approve of some methods she is using to convert the heathen, but I believe her to be honest and sincere; and when I see churches arising on every hand and thousands being turned from their evil ways through her, I cannot help but feel an admiration of the zeal and willpower that enables her to overcome difficulties not one woman in a million would grapple with.

We owe it to justice to be fair and impartial in such matters and we owe it to our mothers, wives, and daughters that we display a little of our much-boasted manhood by refuting such unkind, ungenerous, and cruel slanders as are now being used against Mrs. Woodworth. Let us be manly at least, but if we can't be manly, let us be as manly as we can.

—A. B. Sibert.

January 15, 1891

Rochester Weekly Republican

Maria's Miracles

The "Power" Gets in Its Work on Prominent Andersonians

Speaking of the trance revival which "Dr." Maria Woodworth is now holding at Anderson, the *Bulletin* says that some 1891 years ago "little feats, such as raising the dead, healing the sick, causing the blind to see, the deaf to hear, and the lame to leap for joy, were recorded as marvelous happenings and the credit given to a supernatural power. What was then considered and believed to be the workings of supernatural forces is now performed by natural power, outside the cabinent (*sic*), in full view of the audience, and beneath the uninterrupted glare of natural gas light. . . . When Maria simply confined herself to pulpit exhortations, punctuated with an occasional trance, she was regarded as a most marvelous woman by the generality of people. But her new specialty of healing the sick, raising the dead, and so on, has made her fame and reputation that she had never hoped to gain. In her new line of business, she stands without a peer and to all intents and purposes has letters of patent upon her remedies. Nobody else can use them with any degree of success."

"Four years ago, Lafe Burr was caught in a bear trap, while sneaking through Bob Grimes' backyard one dark night. Both legs were taken off just above the knee and since then he has been a helpless cripple. Day before yesterday he was taken down to the Church of God, and Mrs. Woodworth noticed his helpless condition. The evangelist walked out in the audience to where he was, uttered a fervent prayer, and then placed her hand gently upon the sawed-off members. Almost instantly a pair of shinbones began to put in an appearance, the calves to develop, and finally two Number-ten feet, just the original size, grew on the stubs. The result of the treatment is that Mr. Burr is a stout, healthy man, in full possession of his lower limbs, and only this morning kicked Bert Gedge out of the third story of the club building for having defeated him at a game of billiards."

"Gene Brickley has for some time been suffering from a fractured bank account. Do his best, nothing seemed to have the desired effect, and in a fit of despair, he set out to wander aimlessly about wherever fate should lead him. Whether accidentally or led by some unseen power, he dropped into the church where services were being held. He took a seat well back toward the door and for quite a while was an interested looker on. Finally he felt that he must say something and arising told the story of his affliction in plain, simple terms. The story was related in such an earnest, childlike manner as to impress those about him that he was telling the truth. Mrs. Woodworth left the platform and advanced toward the distressed speaker. After singing nine verses of "Let Me in the Life Boat," in which Mr. Brickley joined, she passed her hand gently over his inside pocket. The effect was magical. Mr. Brickley drew his check then and there for one hundred thousand dollars and has the check today to show for itself."

January 23, 1891

St. Louis Post-Dispatch (MO)

The Woodworth Church

rs. Woodworth is expected to arrive in St. Louis Monday. Her church at Fourteenth and Lucas Place is being thoroughly renovated for the appearance of the great spiritual worker. The old chairs are being dusted, the seats are being patched up, and the broken windows are being stopped up with new pasteboard. Rev. A. Douglas, the pastor, is anxiously awaiting the arrival of his chieftess, who will immediately upon her arrival settle the factional quarrel that is now raging in her flock.

February 2, 1891

St. Louis Post-Dispatch (MO)

Back Once Again

Mrs. Woodworth Returns to Look After Her Divided Flock

SHE REFUSES TO DISCUSS THE CHARGES AGAINST PASTOR DOUGLAS

Rev. Douglas and Messrs. Ahle and Wheeldon, the Men Who Made the Charges Against Him, Summoned Before Their Chief—The Pastor Will Demand a Public Trial

Shortly after 12 o'clock this afternoon, an ordinary cab, driven by an ordinary driver, drew up at the Woodworth church, Fourteenth and Lucas Place; and a not uncomely lady jumped lightly from the vehicle. The lady in question was Mrs. Woodworth, the spiritual healer of national renown. A *Post-Dispatch* reporter was expecting the arrival and was present to have a chat with the lady. Mrs. Woodworth was looking tired and worried, but by an effort she was enabled to talk in a light and cheerful vein. When the trouble in her St. Louis mission was mentioned, she grew thoughtful for few moments and then said that she did not care to discuss the subject. But notwithstanding this reluctance to speak, she invited the reporter in, talking all the while of the work she had done since she left this city and her plans for the future.

Has No Opinion in the Case

[P. D.] "Mrs. Woodworth, what is your opinion of the Douglas case?" she was asked.

[M. B. W.] "Please, now, don't ask me. I am tired and do not want to think, as I must appear before my critics tonight. It is a matter that is painful to me to even hear mentioned."

[P. D.] "What charges have been preferred against Rev. Douglas?"

[M. B. W.] "That is a matter of which I am not prepared to talk. I will say, however, that I will attempt to instill into all my followers the Christian spirit of forgiveness. The absence of such a spirit will bring disaster upon any congregation."

[P. D.] "Will you see any of the gentlemen affected this afternoon?"

[M. B. W.] "As to that I am not sure. I can tell more about it after I have taken a nap. Please serve my dinner," said Mrs. Woodworth to Mrs. Colliers.

The dinner was accordingly served, but satisfied appetite did not make the lady any more communicative. She talked of everything except the Douglas-Ahle and Wheeldon squabble, of which it was impossible to get her to express an opinion. She said she was determined to make the proposed new tabernacle here a success while in the city this time.

"I have been at work almost continually since I left St. Louis," said she, "yet, God being with me, I will fill this mission with penitent souls within a week."

The Parties Summoned

Hardly had the reporter left the building when a messenger was dispatched for Rev. Douglas with an imperative command for his immediate presence. He answered the call promptly and was in conference with Mrs. Woodworth for some time, when both Messrs. Ahle and Wheeldon were sent for. They also arrived and went into consultation. The result will not be known until tonight, but the temporary decision is said to have been in favor of the pastor. The doors leading to the consultation room were locked, but this fact was gathered from the attendants, who could not hold their tongues so well as Mrs. Woodworth. The four were still together at a late hour this afternoon.

Brushing Up

Great preparations were made for the arrival of Mrs. Woodworth. All forenoon the windows at her church were open and the main room given a thorough airing. The seats were dusted and a dainty carpet was put on the stage. The entire building echoed with the sound of the hammer and the constant tramp of the people who were doing the work. On the second floor in the northwest corner of the building, a room has been furnished for the accommodation of Mrs. Woodworth. A carpet, not new, but bright, adorns the floor; and a few nondescript pictures, commonly framed, decorate the walls.

Rev. Douglas' Absence

While Mrs. Wilson and Mrs. Collier were preparing the dinner for Mrs. Woodworth, Rev. Douglas did not appear. His study was formerly on the third floor of the old church building at Fourteenth Street and Lucas Place; but he has, for reasons unknown, taken up his residence with his brother at Tenth and Biddle Streets. The ladies preparing the dinner said that the reverend gentleman had deserted his study from his own choosing and flatly contradicted the story being circulated that he received a telegram last night from Mrs. Woodworth suspending him from duty until after her arrival.

Last evening at the services, Rev. Douglas denounced his accusers from the pulpit and in an animated address called upon those present to look upon him, think of his work, his sacrifices, and his worries, how all these things had kept him busy by day and by night, and then judge whether he was guilty of the immoralities that had been charged against him. He declared that at times this winter he had actually suffered for the necessaries of life because the collections made at the mission meetings were not sufficient to cover the expenses. This statement is verified by both Mesdames Wilson and Collier, who assert that their pastor was wanting for absolute necessities, yet he said nothing—never once complained of his lot. Several members, however, discovered the true state of affairs and relieved the gentleman's distress.

In the Opposition Camp

The opposition camp is not without its flutterings of excitement. Messrs. Ahle and Wheeldon are preparing for the production of their boasted witnesses. It is from this source that the information of Rev. Douglas' suspension came, the truth of which is so vehemently denied by Rev. Douglas and his adherents. They[1] assert that Mrs. Woodworth has looked over the documentary evidence introduced and has seen fit to suspend the pastor, for the present at least, which they insist indicates what her future action may be. These two

[1] "They"—Ahle and Wheeldon.

men making the charges will, it is understood, ask that the trial be secret, but the pastor, on the other hand, will ask that the doors be thrown wide open to the press and others who may desire to attend.

February 4, 1891

St. Louis Post-Dispatch (MO)

The Douglas Scandal

Mrs. Woodworth Hearing the Evidence in the Case

Mrs. Woodworth keeps the doors leading to her private rooms in the old church at Fourteenth and Lucas Place carefully guarded and also locked. The Douglas-Ahle and Wheeldon case is being heard, but not one word of what is going on reaches the world outside. Rev. Douglas continues to occupy his position as pastor but is said to have partially asked to be relieved temporarily or until the charges preferred against him have been proven true or false. In the latter case he of course expects reinstatement. Mr. Ahle attended Mrs. Woodworth's first services Monday evening but did not appear on the rostrum last night. While this is regarded as significant by Rev. Douglas' many friends, the opposition say there is nothing in this fact more than Mr. Ahle missed one service.

The hearing of the case will most probably occupy all week as Mrs. Woodworth has announced from the pulpit, giving reasons that she will not, as is her custom, hold her afternoon services. Her decision will, therefore, probably be announced at next Sunday's services, unless she makes up her mind before that time.

This morning a large number of witnesses, nearly all members of the congregation, were before the lady, but what testimony they gave can only be a matter of surmise. Rev. Douglas looks much worn and worried and has lost all his old-time fire and repartee. The case is thus shown to at least be a serious worry to him.

February 5, 1891

St. Louis Republic (MO)

Mrs. Woodworth's Power

It Still Affects Worshippers With a Koch Lymph Potency[1]

he Woodworth meeting last evening in the old church at Fourteenth Street and Lucas Place was attended by the usual crowd of curious persons. "The power" has not ceased to work, and every now and then the ranks of the worshippers are thinned by the conversion of some of those present.[2] The meeting last evening was not as enthusiastic as the meetings usually are. There were, however, six persons who felt the power in a greater or lesser degree. The power in these instances was manifested in the usual way, the converts going into a regular trance. Mrs. Woodworth herself preached. She went over the life of Christ briefly, dwelling especially on His healing power and on His mission to the afflicted, both in body and spirit.

At the close of her discourse, which was extremely plain, she invited those of her audience who wanted to be healed in body or spirit to come forward to the mourners' bench. The remainder of the program was more in the nature of an old-fashioned revival. Prayers were offered by first one then another of Mrs. Woodworth's aides and then by them all in concert. After this there was more singing, during which the power was manifested. The singing seemed to have considerable to do with the manifestation of the power, as it was noticed that while the congregation sang:

> At the cross, at the cross, where I first saw the light,
> And my burden of sin rolled away;

[1] "Koch Lymph Potency"— Robert Koch (1843-1910) discovered something called tuberculin in the late nineteenth century, which he thought would be a cure for tuberculosis and also a vaccine against it. For a number of years he was famous for having found the cure for tuberculosis. It was found later that tuberculin didn't work for either a cure or vaccine. The headline is basically emphasizing that Maria Woodworth's power is still working the way an effective vaccine or wonder drug works.

[2] The reporter means that people leave the worshippers in the pews and go up front to the mourners' bench where they pray for personal assurance of salvation.

'Twas there by faith I received my sight.
And now I'm happy all the day.[3]

The burden of sin seemed to drop from many of the penitents; and they began to sway back and forth to the music, their hands were slowly raised above their heads, and they finally fell over into the arms of friends and were laid upon the mourners' bench until the trance passed off. One young lady, a girl of about fourteen years of age, seemed to have received a greater portion of the power of the Spirit than the others. She was one of the first to be affected, and it was not until almost three-quarters of an hour after the close of the meeting that she came out of her trance and could be taken home. This young lady has been affected by the power every evening for a week or more and on one occasion did not recover until 1 o'clock in the morning.

[3] Isaac Watts, "At the Cross," (1707). The refrain above was written by Ralph E. Hudson in 1885 to sing with the verses to the hymn by this name written by Watts.

February 12, 1891

St. Louis Post-Dispatch (MO)

Mrs. Woodworth's Decision

She Acquits Pastor Douglas on the Charge of Immorality

ev. Alexander Douglas has been partially exonerated. Mrs. Woodworth this morning announced that the charges of immorality had not been sustained and that she would, therefore, decide in favor of her former pastor. This case is a peculiar one. Some time ago Rev. Douglas suspended from the Woodworth mission at Fourteenth and Lucas Place, two members [Messrs.?] Wheeldon and Ahle. These gentlemen brought charges against the pastor before Mrs. Woodworth, included in which was [a?] specified case of immorality. Upon Mrs. Woodworth's return, Messrs. Wheeldon and Ahle were summoned to her presence to prove the charges they had made. This they have not done, at least to her satisfaction, and today Rev. Douglas was declared innocent of this charge. This does not affect the other charges that are pending, all of which will be investigated.

One Reason for the Decision

Besides the fact that dates and places were not given in a suitable way by Messrs. Wheeldon and Ahle, another fact influenced the lady evangelist in making her decision. This was the appointment of Joseph H. Goodman as watchman by the police board two weeks ago. Messrs. Wheeldon and Ahle appeared before the board at that time and filed affidavits, which charged that Mr. Goodman had registered at three precincts and attempted to vote a like number of times. It happened, however, that Mr. Goodman upon the occasion named was acting as a judge of election and could hardly, under the circumstances, have attempted to vote three times. These facts were presented to Mrs. Woodworth and she immediately decided one of the charges against Rev. Douglas in that gentleman's favor.

The Mission Torn Asunder

Notwithstanding this decision the mission is torn asunder and the trouble is not yet at an end. The attendance since Mrs. Woodworth's arrival has been poor, and at present an unsatisfied debt of some four hundred dollars is hanging over the congregation [part of article was missing].

July 3, 1891

Topeka Daily Capital (KS)

Mrs. Woodworth's Work

Where She Has Labored During the Last Ten Years and What She Has Done

rs. M. B. Woodworth, the lady evangelist, held another intensely interesting and highly spiritual meeting last night in her tent at the city park.

Mrs. Woodworth is about forty-six years of age and has been working in the evangelical[1] field for the past ten years, during which time thousands of people under the influence of her words have been brought to see the error of their ways.

Mrs. Woodworth is not an educated lady as her father died when she was quite young and left her mother almost destitute with a large family of children to care for. She was therefore under the necessity of working for her living and had no time to devote to study.

Mrs. Woodworth conducted a meeting about a year and a half ago in Oakland, California, at which nine hundred people were converted. From California she went last April to St. Louis where she held a meeting at which hundreds of people were converted. She went from St. Louis to Canton, Ohio, and from Canton to Topeka. She has held meetings from Pennsylvania to California but has given most of her time to Ohio and Illinois. In Ohio she has established thirteen churches. She is accompanied by two young ladies, Miss Ollie Daggett and Miss Eunice Isonhart,[2] who have been her companions and coworkers for six years.

[1] "working in the evangelical field"—working as an evangelist.

[2] Possible misprint: The second companion in other articles is designated Miss Emma Isenberg.

July 8, 1891

Topeka Daily Capital (KS)

Mrs. Woodworth's Meetings

The Interest Increasing With Each Meeting and Large Crowds Coming Out

he meetings at the city park, under the leadership of Mrs. Woodworth, that grand and courageous Christian worker, are steadily growing in interest; and great crowds are coming out to every service to hear her wonderful words and witness the strange manifestations of "power" such as is said to have been common in the days of the fathers.

Great earnestness pervades all who take part; and while in such meetings there are always found many emotional people who are apt to give way to the tides of feeling, yet Mrs. Woodworth has a peculiar tact in controlling every tendency towards undue excitement and in every respect displays a wonderful power as a leader.

On Sabbath last, at all the services but especially in the afternoon and evening, a special interest prevailed. A multitude were present at each service including what are known as the best people—thinking cultured men and women of the city—and the earnest attention and deep solemnity shown upon every face in these vast assemblies were remarkable. The people are coming to see and investigate for themselves; and it is becoming more and more evident that, notwithstanding the slanderous report given out by sensational newspapers and other enemies of Mrs. Woodworth and her work, the truth is being found out and her good work is growing in the confidence of the best people of the community. And it is said that even certain church people who at first condemned this work as "irregular," "unauthorized," etc., are now coming to see for themselves so that the influence of the meetings is growing and widening the spirit of the opposition.

The new tabernacle is now being made at Chicago and is expected here in a few days, and when put upon the grounds, additional seating will be provided and everything done to make the people comfortable and thus induce them to come and hear this wonderful woman.

July 9, 1891

The Kansas Democrat (Topeka, KS)

Mrs. Woodworth's Meeting

Immense Gatherings of People—Great Interest at All the Services

At the meetings yesterday and last night, immense crowds gathered at city park to hear the wonderful preacher, and many presented themselves at the altar of prayer at both services and declared they were healed in body and soul. Evidently there is a strange and peculiar influence present.

Mrs. Woodworth took for her text last night Ecclesiastics 12:3, (*sic*) "In the day when the keepers of the house shall tremble, and the strong men shall bow themselves, and the grinders cease because they are few, and those that look out of the windows shall be darkened," from which she first warned the young to turn to God before old age came on and the fearful consequences of delay and that God would surely bring them into judgment. Her sermon, however, was more particularly directed to the old—those who had neglected salvation until now they were bowed with age and tremulous with the weight of years and sins.

It was an earnest, eloquent appeal and many hearts were moved; and as they rushed forward to the place of prayer and their cries went up for mercy and salvation, the multitude stood in awe and wondered.

Many leading citizens were seen in the audience, and evidently the people generally are becoming interested. The public services are held every week day at 2 and 8 P.M. and on Sundays at 10 A.M. and 2 and 8 P.M.

July 10, 1891

The Kansas Democrat
(Topeka, KS)

Mrs. Wentworth's (*sic*) Meetings

A Vast Concourse Present at Last Night's Services

he meetings at the city park continue with increasing interest. The audience on yesterday afternoon was not so large as expected, but last night the vast seating capacity of the tabernacle was occupied, and many stood up in the rear and at the entrances.

As usual, the preaching was pointed and powerful. The line of thought pursued by the speaker was intended to show that all along the ages, when the pure truth was withheld from the people or in any manner perverted, the result was always death and destruction to God's people. Her subject was based on Proverbs 19:18 from which she assumed and argued that in all the history of the church down to the present time, where the power of God was not poured out in such effusion as to cause "visions," there was no salvation; and the people perished from lack of the pure wheat of the Gospel. The speaker was listened to with marked attention; and at the close of her address, a number went forward for prayers.

July 19, 1891

The Kansas Democrat
(Topeka, KS)

The Woodworth Meetings

An Exciting Time Last Evening—An Amusing Incident

A *Democrat* reporter went down to one of Mrs. M. B. Woodworth's meetings in city park last evening, more from motives of curiosity than duty, and found an audience of about two hundred in every sense mixed—the masculine and feminine, white and colored, good, bad, and indifferent.

Mrs. Woodworth herself is a pleasant appearing lady, a fair talker, and refined. Her meetings appear to be rather of the Salvation Army sort, but this is due more to her class of converts than from her own teachings.

At the close of her address she asked, as usual, any who so desired to come to the "mercy seat" and kneel, and about a dozen did so. They gradually grew noisy, and more noisy, until they wrought themselves into a sort of hysterical joy—dancing, swinging their arms, and shouting, their ecstasy knowing no bounds. One rather ridiculous incident occurred when the excitement was at its height. One lady who was more hilarious than the rest had the misfortune to have her hair undone. It was done up in a sort of Grecian knot on her head and came down. Immediately those around her ceased their gestures and noise for a few moments and very kindly took out the hairpins, one by one, that they might not be lost. The absurd contrast between the spiritual and the temporal was very evident.

Mrs. Woodworth has visited a host of the great cities of America and is very much pleased with Topeka and is encouraged by the results of her labor here. She has been an evangelist for eleven years and is out on her own responsibility and is getting no salary and having no organization back of her. The tent which she brought here was a very large and fine one, but the heavy storms here have torn the northern end of it into shreds. She has ordered another one from Chicago costing $1,385, which is smaller and more easily managed. Mrs. Woodworth will remain for some time.

AN ENTHUSIASTIC ADMIRER OF MRS. WOODWORTH SAYS:

July 24, 1891

The Kansas Democrat (Topeka, KS)

Not a Crank

An Outside Opinion on Mrs. Woodworth and Her Methods

"To those who have not heard her, I wish to say that she is not that kind of an evangelist who depends upon stories to make the people cry or laugh. Her theory is that of faith and repentance, a new heart and a correct life. Her motto is 'Holiness to the Lord.'

"Her meetings have been well attended; and, she informs me, with a few exceptions, perfect good order has been observed. This speaks well for our city. There have been many conversions, and the friendly churches and preachers in the city will enjoy the ingathering.

"Mrs. Woodworth is without doubt a worthy woman and deserves more help from the resident ministers than she has been getting. She is not a crank found dabbling with private opinions. Her work is to oppose actual and all sin and advocate a free and a full salvation in the name of Jesus and that He is able to save to the uttermost all who will call upon Him.

"Her new tent is up, and everything is in good order. She expects to have it dedicated next Sunday. I hope to see many ministers present."

July 27, 1891

The Topeka State Journal (KS)

The Tent Dedicated

A LARGE CROWD PRESENT AT MRS. WOODWORTH'S MEETING YESTERDAY

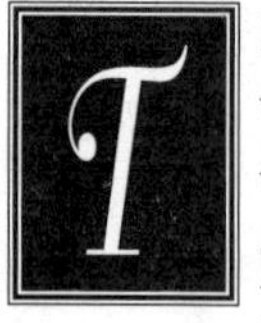he dedicatory services at Mrs. Woodworth's tent in city park Sunday afternoon were largely attended, all the seats being occupied and many standing on the outside. The behavior was very good and there was a solemnity discernable indicating the deep interest felt by those present. Mrs. Woodworth took for her text 1 Peter 4:18, "And if the righteous shall scarcely be saved, where shall the ungodly and sinner appear?" After dwelling at some length on the saving of the righteous persons, she said that the ungodly were those who are upright, try to do right, and generally termed good or moral men or women. While they are better than the sinner so far as this life is concerned, they can no more enter heaven than the latter for they must be born again—lo, made like God, and have the Spirit of Christ. Close attention was given the sermon and the subject made so plain that no one present could say they did not understand.

Rev. Freeman, at the close of the sermon, stepped forward and pointed out the glorious condition our city would be in if every man, woman, and child was converted. He said this might be brought about in a degree by helping to pay for the tent under which souls are brought to Christ and made to rejoice in the blood of the Lamb. Several collectors were appointed and they canvassed the congregation for money and subscriptions, while Rev. Freeman kept everyone in a good humor by his good-natured manner.

The cost of the tent and freight was $106.38 and the sum yet to be raised was $196.38. The indebtedness was not wholly lifted by the audience but Mrs. Woodworth assumed the balance, the committee agreeing to reimburse her by outside subscriptions.

The dedicatory service was conducted by Rev. Rudisill; and Mrs. Woodworth and Misses Emma Isenberg and Ollie Daggett, her coworkers, were made trustees for the Lord to whom the tent was dedicated.

Another large crowd assembled at the evening service and great power was demonstrated. Several sinners were at the altar and made happy by setting their back upon the world. Four ladies it is said lay in trances, and one of them remained under the power until yesterday noon, when she arose, happy in the Lord. It is reported that another of these stricken down was a young lady standing in the audience making fun of the power and remarked that nothing could strike her down. She had no more than spoken the words when she fell and as she revived pled with Jesus to save her soul.

July 27, 1891

The Kansas Democrat (Topeka, KS)

The Woodworth Tent

IT WAS DEDICATED YESTERDAY IN THE PRESENCE OF A LARGE AUDIENCE

he Woodworth tent was dedicated yesterday afternoon at 2 o'clock. The attendance was very large and many were unable to find seats. The dedicatory service was conducted by Rev. Rudisill; and Mrs. Woodworth and her coworkers, Misses Emma Isenberg and Ollie Daggett, [were] placed in charge as trustees for the Lord. The total indebtedness was $406.38, and $210 of this had been previously raised. Though the balance was not obtained in the meeting yesterday, Mrs. Woodworth made good the deficiency, and she will be reimbursed by the committee having the matter in charge.

There were four in trances at the meeting last night. One of these was a young lady who made no profession but was making light of those under the power when she was stricken down and lay as a dead person.

July 31, 1891

The Kansas Democrat (Topeka, KS)

The Woodworth Meetings

To the Editor of the Democrat:

It is a source of gratification to the friends of this good work to note the revolution in public sentiment in reference to Mrs. Woodworth and the revival meetings at the city park. It has been well known that the most stubborn opposition to the work in this city has come from influential church members, persons who without proper investigation, having read lying reports concerning her meetings in other places, have allowed their prejudices to blind them and keep them aloft from this work, and also to use their influence to prejudice others. Many of these people are now coming out and are confessing that they were mistaken and that this is surely the work of God.

The meetings are growing in interest wonderfully. The audiences are composed of intelligent, thoughtful people, and great numbers are daily persuaded to begin a new and better life. And it is the hope of all that this revival power and influence may reach every family in this city and be the means of stirring up dead churches and formal professors to real spiritual life and inaugurate in every church an old-fashioned zeal for the salvation of precious souls.

Those of our friends who are still clinging to their prejudices, we earnestly invite to come to the meetings and see whether these things be true. And you cannot fairly judge of the character of the work by coming once only, but come out to several consecutive services and then you can determine whether the work is of God or whether it is a delusion.

August 14, 1891

Topeka Daily Capital (KS)

People Indignant

The Attack on Mrs. Woodworth's Meetings Denounced

An Uncalled-for Attempt of an Evening Paper to Cast Reflections on Hundreds of Persons Who Worship After a Time-Honored Custom—Mrs. Woodworth Says She Is Accustomed to Such Sensations

he meetings conducted by Mrs. Woodworth at the city park have been drawing steadily increasing numbers. Last night's services were attended by at least fifteen hundred persons, including some of the best-known professionals and businessmen of the city.

Mrs. Woodworth has had erected for her use in these meetings a tent capable of holding at least one thousand persons. The tent is provided with benches, and Mrs. Woodworth speaks from a raised platform at one side of the tent. The singing is lead by a choir of men and women, with a number of well-known men acting as ushers.

These meetings begin generally at 8 o'clock and continue for several hours, sometimes as late as 11. The large number who attend, with but few exceptions, enter into the spirit of the exercises devoutly. Mrs. Woodworth always takes charge and proves herself a woman of great power over people who believe in this kind of worship. Her voice is clear and easily heard at all points in the tent and beyond. Her style is exhortative, but she is far from being boisterous. In manner she is pleasing and winning. Her sermons are neither logical nor eloquent, but very earnest and always receive the closest attention from her audience.

That Mrs. Woodworth is doing good work in Topeka no person possessing a respect for all kinds of worship and who has taken the trouble to investigate the results of the meetings so far held will deny. About three hundred individuals have been converted, and the number is growing nightly. Those converts come from all classes of people and their manifestations of faith appear to be as sincere as they are outspoken. Mrs. Woodworth claims to exercise no wonderful power by which she puts different ones in a trance; she claims this power comes direct from God.

At the close of last night's exercises, Mrs. Woodworth kindly accorded a representative of this paper a short conversation concerning the attempt of an evening paper to work up a situation at the expense of the religious beliefs of a large portion of the city's people.

"I have not read the article very closely," said Mrs. Woodworth, "but I noticed it was another attempt to revile our manner of worshiping. At many of the places that I have conducted these meetings, the papers have resorted to similar attacks on the meetings in an attempt to work up a sensation. In every case the paper has brought upon itself the disfavor of fair-minded people, and today hundreds of my congregation have come to me and assured me of their contempt of such an unprovoked attack upon our earnest efforts to accomplish a good work. I see a doctor says the power which acts on the people is mesmerism. This is false. A committee of the leading doctors of St. Louis investigated the matter thoroughly and their report was that there was no mesmerism about it. I tell you it's a power direct from God. This is our manner of worship, we are not ashamed of it, and the evening paper can't harm us."

Mrs. Woodworth is thinking of closing her meeting next Sunday evening. It is possible, however, that she may prolong her stay many months.

August 14, 1891

Topeka Daily Capital (KS)

Concerning Religious Liberty

rs. Maria B. Woodworth of Rochester, Ind., an evangelist, has been holding religious meetings in a large tent in the city park since June 4. Her audiences have varied from three hundred to fifteen hundred, the interest apparently increasing. Mrs. Woodworth has been engaged in evangelical work for years. She preaches one and two sermons per day for weeks without exhaustion and is unquestionably a very sincere and unselfish Christian woman, devoting her life to bringing men and women to the faith of Christ. She claims no unusual power for herself. Her addresses are plain, forcible, and earnest, reaching the hearts of common people. The "power," which has thrown a number of converts into fits or trances, she claims to be the manifestation of the divine Spirit.

An evening paper published on last Friday an attack upon Mrs. Woodworth's methods of securing converts and supported its opposition to the continuance of the meetings by a number of interviews with prominent physicians who claimed that this religious "zeal" or "ecstasy" or manifestation of "power," leads to cataleptic fits, and on (in various stages) to insanity. The discussion has created a great deal of interest throughout the community. There is no power to interfere with the progress of public meetings except municipal authority and the higher courts, and these can only be exercised for the protection of the peace, good order, and rights of citizens infringed; and such gatherings as menace by mob law the city or state governments may be dispersed by the strong hand of the law. To talk of suppressing a meeting where a minister preaches the doctrines of Christ and urges men and women to better lives is sheerest nonsense. Religious tolerance for the believer of every shade of opinion and for that large and intelligent body of citizens who have no religious creeds is the plea the *Capital* makes this morning. This same liberty, demanded of papacy centuries since and conceded grudgingly by kings in past ages, is today in this republic dear to every citizen.

The real question which all liberal, intelligent, and fair-minded people will ask is not whether this form of religious education taught by Mrs. Woodworth is according to the opposing individuals' idea of propriety, but whether Mrs. Woodworth and those who daily and nightly go to those meetings are sincere and honest. If they are, then the principle of religious liberty guaranteed by the constitution of the country gives to them the right to continue their meetings and to worship God according to the dictates of their own conscience. The doctors' certificates of possible grave results to weak-minded persons who may be drawn into these meetings do not reach the point. These results are merely incidental, and few, very few, of the number who claim to be benefited by these meetings are thus affected, and the medical certificates exaggerate the probable results.

The position of the *Capital* is not a captious one. We believe in religious freedom. This is a country where every form of modern worship claims tolerance under the laws and from public opinion, so long as the rights of others are not disturbed. To whom shall be given the right to draw the line? And under what rule shall it be determined that only established religious forms, ceremonies, and meetings shall be continued? In this great republic the American Indian dances to the Great Spirit, the Mormon worships through Joseph Smith, the Jew, the Catholic, the Protestant of many and varying beliefs and ceremonies, each and all express in their own way their religious convictions.

The *Capital* has had occasion heretofore to say kind words for the great work of the much-abused Salvation Army. Why? Not because of its outlandish noise, of its drum beating and blundering attempts at sermonizing, but because it was sincere and deeply in earnest to reach men and women beyond the churches. Not one-half of the people of this or any other country are reached by any kind of religious teaching. There is a mass of humanity in every city against whom the church doors of all fashionable churches are practically closed. Not in fact, not by decree of the deacons, but because there is so great a social gulf to span, because the poverty of the one and the riches of the other do not mix satisfactorily to either party.

If there are organizations in halls or in tents or in the open air, as Christ talked, where people of every condition may go for religious instruction or "zeal" or "ecstasy," men and women resolve for any reason or any influence to try to be better for the Lord's sake and the sake of the liberty of the republic, place no petty hide-bound sectarian or bigoted prejudices in the way.

The clanging of the church bells may not be pleasant to some nervous unbelievers, and the band of the Salvation Army and the shouting at Mrs. Woodworth's tent may not be the highest manifestations of religious culture, but over all this and under it is the great principle of religious toleration and liberty that brought the pilgrims to Plymouth Rock.

August 15, 1891

The Topeka State Journal (KS)

Cooling Down

ONLY TWO TRANCES AT MRS. WOODWORTH'S MEETING LAST NIGHT

here were only two trances at Mrs. Woodworth's city park meeting last night. This seems to indicate that most of the people who have allowed themselves to be carried away by excitement are realizing the danger they are undergoing and are exercising their common sense. The crowd last night was fully as large as at any time during the season, but the excitement was held in check and there was not much uproar.

Mrs. Jake Stitt and Fred Menker were the persons overcome by the "power." Jake Stitt made an excited effort to frighten a boy apparently not more than seven or eight years old into making a profession of religion but failed.

Mrs. Woodworth said she had expected the devil to howl; and sure enough, he was howling now through an evening paper.

The meeting was brought to a close at 10:15, and the audience was told to go home at once.

"Don't let anyone handle those who are down," said Mrs. Woodworth, "and then go away and make light of it as was done last night."

A crowd of men gathered around those who had the "power," apparently intending to protect them. The women of the crowd were sent home. Tom Archer and Jake Stitt gathered a crowd of men around them and stood near the altar. "There is going to be a row here," Archer said, "and I am going to see it through." His suspicions were vain as no effort was made to create disorder of the crowd who stood around the altar.

The crowd did not disperse rapidly enough and Mrs. Woodworth called out, "Clear the tent, clear the tent; let no one but the relatives of those stricken down remain." The police, who had been silent before now, stepped in and in five minutes drove the crowd of two or three hundred people out of the tent leaving no one behind but Jake Stitt and half a dozen children besides the two who were lying on their backs in the trance state.

Dr. Saxton put in an appearance while the tent was being released and wanted to be admitted as a medical man, but a policeman prevented him. There were six policemen on the grounds. It is said that Mrs. Woodworth expected trouble.

Two doctors had declared their intentions of taking an electric battery to the grounds and experimenting on those affected.

August 16, 1891

Topeka Daily Capital (KS)

Concerning Mrs. Woodworth

C. E. Kalb, Formerly Editor of the Thomas County "Cat," Writes of Her Work in Illinois and Other Places

TO THE EDITOR OF THE *CAPITAL:*

I would like to say a few words in regard to the work of Mrs. Woodworth. When she held her meetings at Springfield, Ill., I was city editor of the *Daily Monitor.* I visited her meetings; and though not a Christian myself, but a church member, I felt that she was preaching the true Gospel. And I commenced to report her meetings from day to day and not only assisted in this way to do a great deal of good, but the people flocked to the support of the *Monitor,* while the other city papers were afraid to be honest and stand up for these things which have a tendency to better the morals of a city.

The people there had trances and many would shout. I have seen them falling in trances faster than I could count them and in all parts of the audience. That was three years ago and not one of them has gone crazy, but instead they have become intelligent, sober, and industrious and are still filled with the Holy Ghost.

A church was organized and built in a very short time. Each meeting is a revival and souls are converted, and at present they have no pastor either.

Instead of a fight being made there by any of the papers, it was made by the ministers association because they were losing many of their members who wished to go and hear the true, simple Gospel as preached by the apostles. They selected their most eloquent divine, Rev. J. F. Briney, to expose the whole business. He went at it just as the physicians did here and had medical books and scientific works piled up all about the altar. Mrs. Woodworth answered the speech some three days after, taking the Bible for her foundation. The members of the legislature and other talented gentlemen were interested in hearing both discussions and were not unanimous in saying that Rev. Briney was wound up, hauled over, and torn to pieces. I reported both discussions, and Rev. Briney as good as acknowledged his defeat. From that time on the work progressed more rapidly than before, and Mrs. Woodworth had gained a grand and glorious victory as she has everywhere. Ask anyone in Springfield which is the live church and they will answer the "Church of God." No one there now says the members are crazy or are weak-minded, for some of the brightest people in the city belong to this church.

What has become of Rev. Briney? He is almost a total wreck, had to cease preaching, and afflictions, one after another, have been visited upon him. His congregation, which was one of the largest in the city, has diminished over half and those who left the church united with the Church of God.

Take the advice of Gamaliel of old and take heed lest ye be found fighting against God.[1]

—C. E. Kalb

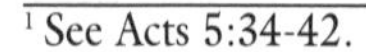

[1] See Acts 5:34-42.

August 18, 1891

Topeka Daily Capital (KS)

The Church of God

Mrs. Woodworth Organizes a Church Composed of Her Converts

he meetings at the city park on Sunday were largely attended and especially in the afternoon and evening. The morning service consisted of singing, prayer, and testimony, at the close of which Mrs. Woodworth organized a church to be known as the Church of God. She said that when she came here it was with the hope that the ministers of the city would take hold in the work and then let the converts unite with the church of their choice.

She did not feel that the Lord wanted her to turn the lambs loose, hence the organization was necessary that the converts may stand firmly together. The Church of God is a chartered organization of the United States and Mrs. Woodworth is one of the leading officers. She stated that the Bible spoke only of one church or religious organization, and that was the Church of God. They have no creed or church discipline except the Bible, which contains all the rules and regulations for God's people. They believe in baptism by immersion and washing of the saints' feet, though these are not obligatory to membership nor doors to the Church. Christ is the door and you must be born into the Church.

During the day there were 148 taken into membership by the right hand of fellowship and there will probably be at least fifty more before the week closes. This is without doubt the largest membership any church ever started out with in this city.

A hall will be rented when Mrs. Woodworth leaves and a minister sent to take charge of the flock.

The stand taken by the *Capital* Sunday morning is being heartily endorsed by the great mass of churchgoers, and the consequence was that the audience in the afternoon fully numbered two thousand. In the evening it was yet larger, but the best of order prevailed and the crowded throng listened attentively to the preaching of the Word of God.

August 20, 1891

The Kansas Democrat (Topeka, KS)

The Churches and Mrs. Woodworth

peaking of Mrs. Woodworth's meetings, a prominent citizen said to us yesterday that he had quit going to church and was attending Mrs. Woodworth's meetings, because she taught Christianity, not "creeds."

The gentleman also said that the preachers in Kansas, for the past ten years, had done little else than talk republicanism pure and simple from the pulpit, even going so far as to tell their congregations what candidates to vote for.

The spectacle, continued the gentleman, of ministers like Bernard Kelly, Dr. Milner, Dr. Krohn, Dr. Campbell, and Dr. McCabe, standing for republicanism in a free country, proves to what base uses the church may descend when preachers get the idea in their heads that the world must be ruled by the elect and that they are the elect.

Verily, there is work for such as Mrs. Woodworth and the churches are in a panic.

August 20, 1891

The Kansas Democrat (Topeka, KS)

A New Church

Mrs. Woodworth Organizes Her Converts into the Church of God

rs. Woodworth has organized a church to be known as the Church of God. She says when she came here it was with the hope that the ministers of the city would take hold in the work and then let the converts unite with the church of their choice.

She did not feel that the Lord wanted her to turn the lambs loose, hence the organization was necessary that the converts may stand firmly together. The Church of God is a chartered organization of the United States, and Mrs. Woodworth is one of the leading officers. She stated that the Bible spoke only of one church or religious organization and that was the church of God. They have no creed or church discipline except the Bible, which contains all the rules and regulations for God's people. They believe in baptism by immersion and washing of the saints' feet, though these are not obligatory to membership nor a door to the church. Christ is the door and you must be born into the church.

There are 148 members. A hall will be rented when Mrs. Woodworth leaves and a minister sent to take charge of the flock.

August 20, 1891

The Kansas Democrat
(Topeka, KS)

Miss (*sic*) Woodworth's Meetings

Spirituality Versus Materialism

Several medical gentlemen of this city have recently ventured to make a scientific diagnosis of the spiritual phenomena so often manifested at Mrs. Woodworth's meetings in the city park and have given their individual opinions of the nature and effects of such experiences.

But how long any intelligent doctor, who has ever read his Testament halfway through and did not find out before this that none but those who are "spiritually minded," can understand spiritual things, I cannot conceive (*sic*).

"For the natural man receiveth not the things of the Spirit of God: for they are *foolishness* unto him: neither can he know them, for they are spiritually discerned. But he that is spiritual judgeth all things, yet he himself is judged of no man" (1 Corinthians 2:14-15 [paraphrased]). Hence it is plain to be seen that every doctor, who has given an opinion through the *Journal* recently that the spiritual phenomena attending the marvelously pure gospel teachings of Mrs. Woodworth are harmful, has shown a total lack of spirituality in himself and has unwittingly declared to the world that genuine spiritual things are positive "foolishness to him" and that he himself is in perishing need of a personal Savior.

And it furthermore teaches all genuine Bible Christians that a doctor, or any other man of science who does not carry the conscious love and Spirit of God in soul "every day and every hour," is no more competent to pass judgment on spiritual teachings and spiritual experiences than a mustang pony on the plains of Mexico.

He who undertakes to analyze and define the nature and effects of the spiritual inflowing of divine life, love, and glory into a human soul or body by the use of his chemical retort, microscope, or galvanic battery will come as far short of his undertaking and will show as much ignorance of his subject as the little boy who should attempt to explain and illustrate planetary speed and planetary distances by the speed of his kite and the length of his kite string.

I will now quote from the *Journal* of last week a few words from our esteemed Dr. Roby: "Speaking seriously," he said, "exhibitions of 'ecstasy' are not new in the world. The thing is as old as the hills."

[Many doctors share the?] same general opinion as Dr. Roby. But, respected doctors, you are all on dangerous ground—exceedingly dangerous to yourselves and to all who listen to your materialistic teachings. Such poor human materialism would overthrow the whole Bible. Ezekiel, Paul, and John were holy men of old, who spake as they were moved by the Holy Ghost. Through them, while in states of trance, vision, or "ecstasy," God gave us a large part of the Bible.

Mrs. Woodworth and her converts, as well as all other Christians, want no better company than such men as old (*sic*). And furthermore, we are all very thankful to God for such heaven-gifted visions, trances, and reasons of "ecstasy" as in divine mercy were given to Ezekiel the prophet, to Paul the apostle, and to John the beloved disciple.

Now, if you doctors and all others who condemn or make light of visions, trances, and ecstasies could only be laid out awhile yourselves and be held still long enough to give you a chance to think rationally about spiritual things and long enough to let the Lord God talk to you personally awhile, it might be the best thing that ever happened to you. It might possibly open your eyes.

As for myself, I have never been in a trance where I was held silent and immovable. But during the last ten years, I have been filled and flooded hundreds, yes, thousands of times with a spiritual baptism of divine love, glory, and celestial "ecstasy," peculiar to the third heaven. And the "rapturous height of this holy delight" is so intense at these times that I would not be moved or disturbed for the world, lest I should lose some of the inflowing divine sweetness and celestial bliss of heaven.

No mortal can form any possible conception of this angelic bliss without personal experience. I never pray for these ecstasies, but they come as a free gift as I do the will of the Lord from day to day, and they always tend to enlighten my mind, purify my heart, and strengthen my body. And I know positively that during one of these spiritual experiences, I receive and enjoy more of the unalloyed bliss of heaven than any unspiritual man can receive in a lifetime. And it always seems to me as if they were free to everyone who lives fully up to his own highest ideas of personal purity and spiritual righteousness. Neither the man of the world nor the ordinary church member has any more conception of the heavenly possibilities of this present earth life than that round-faced old gentleman who dwells in the moon.

Mrs. Edwards, wife of the great Jonathan Edwards, once described a celestial experience in the following beautiful language:

"I think," she says, "what I felt each minute during the continuance of the whole time worth more than all the outward comfort and pleasure which I had enjoyed in my whole life put together. It was a pure delight which fed and satisfied my soul. It was a sweetness which my soul was lost in. My soul was filled and overwhelmed with light and love and joy in the Holy Ghost."[1]

O, you materialistic doctors and others who are vainly trying to satisfy your lean souls on the dry bones of materialism, what do you think of such spiritual ecstasy as this?

Was ever a woman more highly favored with "outward comforts and pleasures" than Mrs. Jonathan Edwards? Yet one single minute of this sweet divine "ecstasy" was of more value in her estimation than all the happiness that earth could give in a lifetime.

Have any of you a brighter intellect or better judgment than she?

How many such materialists would it take to make one giant intellect like that of Jonathan Edwards, her husband, who also had similar experiences?

O, may "God turn the light in" upon your withered souls until you, too, can think and talk rationally on these deep spiritual things. You all know your duty, but you do it not. You know very well that you are feeding on nothing but such husks as the swine eat.

Every man not spiritually minded, be he a church member or not, can easily manufacture objections to the ideas and experiences of

[1] Sarah Edwards (1710-1758), wife of Jonathan Edwards, a New England theologian, pastor and past president of Princeton, (text source of quotation unknown).

those who are "spiritually minded." And why does he do this? First, because he wishes to ease his own conscience for not being what he knows he might and ought to be; second, because he wishes to pull everybody down to his own level; third, because it makes him miserable to believe that others are purer and happier than himself.

You who object to the way God is manifesting His presence and power in connection with Mrs. Woodworth's efforts to lift men out of sin and wretchedness, go and have a private talk with God Himself about it. Get down upon your knees and suggest to the Infinite some of your better methods, if you have any. Don't be bashful in the presence of Him who seems to be your inferior in wisdom, or if it seems inconsistent with your personal dignity to kneel down before Him, stand upright and present your superior methods of manifestation with all the eloquence and skill you possess. Then calmly retire with a dignity becoming your wisdom.

O, the wretchedness and insanity of your self-righteousness! There is no class of beings on the face of the earth so insane as those who ignore and make light of spiritual things. You are living in an inverted order of life. Your souls are like a bowl bottom side up, open to all that is false below and closed to all that is true above.

"May God turn the light in" and lead you all out of spiritual insanity into spiritual wisdom and its attendant blessedness.

Truly the preaching of the Cross is to them that perish foolishness; but unto us who are saved it is the power of God.[2]

Mrs. Woodworth's theology and methods of work do not always harmonize with my own ideas; but I am willing to let every man and every woman work in their own way, especially when they are doing such a stupendously good work as she is doing.

—C. E. Pond

[2] 1 Corinthians 1:18, paraphrased.

August 22, 1891

The Topeka State Journal (KS)

Emma Shammed

So Says Mrs. Woodsworth (*sic*) in Court This Morning

THE MCCALL GIRL DIDN'T HAVE THE POWER OF GOD

She Merely Lay on the Altar and Monkeyed

A sample case

John Long and Charles Goheen were discharged at their hearing before Justice Marple this morning. They were charged with being criminally intimate with Emma McCall, a girl thirteen years of age, but the girl testified positively that no such relations had ever existed between them, and there was no evidence pointing to any criminal conduct on the part of either of them, except that the girl charged Long with placing a bitter powder on her tongue, causing her to go into hysterics.

The girl was sick for several days and a number of witnesses were examined to ascertain the cause.

Dr. Mitchell said that he was called in on Wednesday of last week and found the girl suffering from nervous excitement. He was informed that she had attended the meetings conducted at the park by Mrs. Woodworth and had been in a trance twice. He attributed her trouble to the excitement and the trances. Her trance was simply a form of hysterics.

Mrs. Woodworth, the evangelist, was placed on the stand. Most of her statements were made without hesitation and in a positive manner.

She had seen the girl at the meeting twice. The first night she pretended to have a trance and acted very foolishly.

Deputy County Attorney Wagener asked her: "Did you think from her conduct that she was sincere?"

Mrs. Woodworth—"No, she was not sincere. She was simply shamming, and when I discovered it I was very indignant. That girl was not under the power of God at any time."

"Where did you first see her?"

"When I went into the evening meeting, I saw her lying on the altar and at first supposed that she had been converted and was under the power, but I soon saw that she was shamming. She lay on her back and kept moving around pointing with her hands and sometimes raising her body a little. She looked at me and laughed. I did not want to expose her in public but waited until the services were over and then told some of the brethren to send her home. There was a man with her—that was the man, (pointing to Long).

"The next time I saw her, she was standing on the seat, I think, and holding up her hands. The young man had his arm around her as though he meant to protect her, but I called to him to let her alone, that she would not fall, and if she did it would not hurt her. His conduct was altogether improper; there were plenty of ladies there to take care of her."

"Did you think that she had been converted?"

"She pretended to be. The girl was conscious all the time and looked at me occasionally and laughed. I was thoroughly disgusted with her behavior."

Jake Stitt was called as a witness. He had seen both Long and the girl pretending to be under the power, but they swung their arms and showed that they were only making fun. They lay on the altar; he lay in such a shape that her feet touched his side and whenever he tried to get up, she would reach over and pull him down. Someone said to me 'they are just monkeyin'; make 'em get up. I told Long to get out, and he said he was taking care of the girl. She was a relation of his. When I got close to her, she reached out her hand and shook hands with me. She did it again before the meeting broke up.

"Next night, she got a trance as soon as she got into the tent. She just threw up her hands and keeled over flat on her back. He kept feelin' of her until the sister said to stop."

The girl said that she had been sick two or three days after her second trance and did not remember what had happened during that time. She had not known either of the defendants long and denied ever having had improper relations with either of them.

She repeated the story told while she was sick about Long giving her a bitter powder that made her sick a few minutes after she went into the tent, but as this was contradicted by other testimony and was not a part of the offense charged, the case was dismissed.

To the Editor of the State Journal:

August 24, 1891

State Journal (KS)

A Question of Doctrine

When Mrs. Woodworth began her meetings, several of us ministers visited her at her tent and had a conversation with her as to her soundness of doctrine on the Word of God, especially that part that teaches that men and women are to be sanctified after they are justified, or converted.[1] As she said this was to be a union meeting and desired all of the ministers in the city to take part, I thought it very necessary to have a talk with her as to her soundness of doctrine in the beginning of the meeting. So I had the following conversation with her before several witnesses:

> I said to her: "Do you teach that men and women are sanctified at conversion?"
>
> She said, "No, I don't teach that."
>
> "Then you teach that they are first converted, then after this, receive the blessing of holiness as a separate work done after justification?"
>
> "Yes, this is what I teach."

Then said I with the rest of the ministers (three or four in number), "We can go into the meeting with you on these promises." I want to say, there was no clash between any of us in the conversation as to our doctrinal views on the blessings of holiness, not in the least. With these understandings, I went into the meeting with all my

[1] "sanctified"—During the nineteenth century there were many different beliefs about spiritual experiences or stages which were supposed to come after conversion. Some Christian groups made these a matter of doctrine.

mind and soul, yes, and money, too, as many in this city know, but when I saw her go square back on what she had told us in the conversation as to the work of holiness, I felt that I, with the rest of the brethren, could go with her no farther in the meeting as I am no Zinzindorfian.[2] Furthermore, we were completely shut off from testifying to the work of holiness, the very thing that we had agreed upon at the beginning.

I now see her design in not telling us the truth in the beginning. She was aiming to get all the influence we have or in other words, use us for scaffolding until the meeting was under good headway to build up her own at the expense of all the other churches in the city. Then it was clearly seen by all that she was bound to shut all from the meeting that did not agree with her, if she had to insult them, which she did do more than once. I am satisfied that she is "a wolf in sheep's clothing."[3] I also feel that what I have written is due to the ministers and good people of Topeka, whom she has abused and denounced again and again. My motive in writing is to clear myself and all of our ministers of any sympathy with such doings. "With malice toward none and charity for all."[4]

—ELDER WM. HACKETT,

CONFERENCE EVANGELIST OF THE WESLEYAN METHODIST KANSAS CONFERENCE

[2] "Zinzindorfian"—Count Nicholas Zinzindorf was the leader of a group of Christians in 1727 who found shelter on his land. This group began a twenty-four-hour prayer chain that lasted one hundred years and also heavily influenced John and Charles Wesley. Zinzindorf believed in dropping denominational differences before a unity in Christ could be made possible by the Holy Spirit.

[3] The writer is calling Maria Woodworth a false prophet: "Beware of false prophets, which come to you in sheep's clothing, but inwardly they are ravening wolves." (Matthew 7:15).

[4] The concluding sentence from Abraham Lincoln's second inaugural address. The complete sentence is "With malice toward none, with charity for all, with firmness in the right as God gives us to see the right, let us strive on to finish the work we are in, to bind up the nation's wounds, to care for him who shall have borne the battle and for his widow and his orphan, to do all which may achieve and cherish a just and lasting peace among ourselves and with all nations."

August 25, 1891

The Kansas Democrat (Topeka, KS)

The Church of God

Ninety-One Woodworth Converts Immersed in the Kaw River

inety-one of the two hundred members of the Church of God lately organized by Mrs. Woodworth were baptized in the Kansas River[1] below the Rock Island Bridge yesterday afternoon.

There were about five thousand persons present to witness the ordinance fulfilled by those who deemed immersion the true and proper mode of baptism.

There was a brief meeting held at the tent, and then the members and congregation, led by Mrs. Woodworth and other ministers of the Gospel, went to the place selected for the rite to be performed. Arriving there, "Shall We Gather at the River?"[2] was sung, and Rev. H. C. Wykert of Troy, Kan., offered prayer and asked that divine blessing rest upon the services.

The candidates for baptism were led to the water by Mrs. Woodworth and there immersed by Elder Bolton, pastor of the Church of God. So far as possible, the ladies were dressed in white, and the gentlemen appeared with white shirts and dark pants, without shoes, coat, or hat. Many of them came up happy and shouted praises unto the Lord. It only required thirty-four minutes to perform the ceremony.

When all had been baptized, Rev. J. M. Harrington, pastor of the Baptist church, offered prayer. "God be with us till we meet again,"[3] was sung in a plaintive tone, and the benediction was pronounced by Elder Bolton.

The meetings will continue over next Sabbath, and Mrs. Woodworth and her co-workers will conduct the services.

---

[1] "Kansas River"—The headline uses "Kaw River". "Kaw" refers to the American Indian tribel also known as Kanza, from which Kansas takes its name. In this article Kaw and Kansas are used interchangeably.

[2] "Shall We Gather at the River"(1864), music and lyrics by Robert Lowry (1826-1899).

[3] "God Be With You" (1880). Lyrics by Jeremiah Eames Rankin (1828-1904), music (1882) by William Gould Tomer

August 25, 1891

The Topeka State Journal (KS)

Watery Rites

Baptism of Ninety-One Converts in the Kansas River

THOUSANDS OF SPECTATORS WITNESS THE CEREMONY

Elder Bolton Makes Quick Work of It

In the Flowing Tide

he most interesting perhaps of all religious observances is the ordinance of Christian baptism.

The baptism of the Woodworth converts at the city park yesterday afternoon was witnessed by thousands.

For hours before the time appointed, crowds of people were moving toward the park; and by eight o'clock there were between four thousand and five thousand people on the grounds. They were a very orderly and quiet crowd.

At the tent there was a short meeting, after which Mrs. Woodworth led the procession to the place of baptizing, some one hundred yards up the river. The place selected was in a little indented point on the river, with a knoll rising above some ten or twelve feet. A big flat boat was anchored at the head of the little bay, and planks were laid across to the bank from the lower end of the boat, making a complete triangle with the bank as a base and enclosing a space twenty by thirty feet on the inside.

Here the converts were immersed. Mrs. Woodworth stood on the bank and handed them down one at a time, while Elder Bolton performed the ceremony. He made rapid work of it and kept two or three standing in the water waiting their turn. He averaged three a minute. Some went into the water with their arms outstretched, shouting or singing. Others went down silently and smilingly. They came up blowing water from their mouths or clapping their hands and shouting, "Praise the Lord."

Whenever anyone came out happy, the others joined their voices in the general acclamation.

Some went in with their feet bare, and all the men took off their coats. Billy Williams stood on the bank and checked off the names as one after another went down into the water.

After the exercises were over, they sang "God be with you till we meet again" and marched back to the tent where Rev. J. M. Harrington gave some instruction as to how a Christian should conduct himself. Not more than a third of the people who went to the park were able to see the exercises of baptism. Hundreds sat on the Rock Island Bridge with their feet hanging down over the water, and others paraded back and forth along the Avenue Bridge. Some hired boats and paddled up and down the river near the bank. Half a dozen little darkies[1] waded out into the river and stood in water up to their waists, watching with eyes and mouths wide open.

The total number baptized was ninety-one. They were:

George Wheeler; William Boyle; Emma Tyler; Peter Shafer; Catharine Wiley; George McCany; Mary Vantrey; G. E. Dunn; Henry Lamb; Thomas Vickey; E. M. Dolland; J. A. Crowdry; Sarah E. Allen; S. L. McJimpsey; A. A. Kirby; George Engalls; C. W. Housenecht; R. V. Wells; J. E. M. Church; Wilson Shookley; Mathew Stewart; Eunice Carter; Susan Anderson; and Meredith Shookley; Hiram; S. E., H. H., G. G., and Minnie Coffman; Lizzie King; Minnie Milton; Charlie Carper; K. Warick; Mary A. Rounder; Sarah E. Shoaf; Mary A. Vogt; Irene and W. M. Churlepher; Matthew and Mary McDaniel; Maggie Shafer; Maggie Ulen; Annie Wilke; Nelli Schwahn; J. L. Witherhold; Charles E. Cordon; C. W. Housenecht; Otto and Emma Sleg; Daniel Smith; W. A. Johnson; Ellen Sillix; Fred L. Samy; N. S., C. J., and M. Theakston; Delbe Carter; Benjamin Knight; Edna Shaffer; Carrie Laseem; J. L. Tabgor; Elizabeth Richardson; Pearl Theakston; Frank Allen; B. E. Park; Mary T. Gordon; Ida M. Lamb; Rose B. Lamb; Mary M. Miller; L. Gill; P. W. Nelson; W. L. Browner; Ida Pierce; Maggie Redding; Sarah Wenborn; Minnie Archer; Harriet McElroy; George E. Smith; Annie Scott; Virgie Gullian; Thomas Archer; James G. Kline; and Mr. Swinaster.

Mrs. Woodworth will remain in Topeka another week and "unless the Lord says to stay longer," will start for Florida next week. She will camp in an orange grove next winter and besiege the devil in the land of the alligator and pineapple.

[1] "Darkies"—a nineteenth-century colloquial, derogatory term for persons of color, in this case some children of color.

August 27, 1891

The Kansas Democrat (Topeka, KS)

The Park Meetings

Mrs. Woodworth Will Close Sunday—Announcements

There was another large audience at the Woodworth meeting last night and a much deeper interest manifested than has been for some days past. Rev. Bolton, of Cameron, Mo., who arrived yesterday, preached a splendid sermon and made a very favorable impression with his hearers. There were some eight or ten seekers at the altar and two or three professed conversion. Five were added to the church, making the total membership about 165.

Announcements were made that services would be held every afternoon and evening this week and Sunday at 9 A.M., 2 P.M., and 8 o'clock. Those attending the morning service are invited to bring their lunch baskets and stay all day.

Some thirty-five have handed in their names [requesting] to be baptized. This rite will be administered probably on Monday by Rev. Bolton, assisted by Mrs. Woodworth.

Mrs. Woodworth will close her meetings Sunday night and soon afterward take her departure for the South.

August 31, 1891

The Topeka State Journal (KS)

Farewell Mrs. Woodworth

The Evangelist Ends Her Meetings at the city park

rs. Woodworth has packed her tent, shaken the dust of this wicked city from her feet,[1] and started for the sunny South.

She preached her farewell sermon last night and after it was over shook hands with all the brethren and sisters and bade them an affecting farewell. She assured the public that she bore no ill will toward any one and told the new members of her church to stand firm in the faith and press on toward the mark of their high calling.[2] There were probably two thousand people on the grounds last night.

The services were quiet, and there were only two or three trances. The later meetings, since the trances have been held in check and the crowd has been kept in some kind of order, have been more successful than those during the period when there was a general rivalry to see who could have a trance first.

[1] See Matthew 10:14-15, Mark 6:11, or Luke 9:5.

[2] See Philippians 3:14.

September 1, 1891

The Topeka State Journal (KS)

Baptized at Sunset

Thirty-five More Converts Dipped in the Kansas River Last Night

Just at sunset last night, about three hundred people, most of them members of Mrs. Woodworth's new church or sympathizers with her, met at the city park and led by Elder Bolton, marched to the place of baptizing, just below the Rock Island Bridge.

Elder Bolton stood in the river within the triangle between the boat, the bank, and the long plank between them and baptized thirty-five converts in a very short [amount] of time. The ceremony was quietly performed and the crowd dispersed in a few minutes after it was over. This makes 126 converts who have been baptized and taken into the church. A number were admitted who had been baptized in infancy and Mrs. Woodworth told them a second baptism was not necessary.

September 2, 1891

Topeka Daily Capital (KS)

A Card of Thanks

Through the medium of the *Capital*, we desire to return thanks to the council committee on public grounds for the use of the city park, where we held meetings for the past three months. They were very kind and gave us the privilege of having it as long as we desired to stay. May God bless them.

To the citizens of Topeka, for their liberality in replacing my old tent with a new one: I appreciate the gift for the sake of my Lord and Master, and I pray that each one who shared in lifting its cost may be prospered a hundredfold.

To the city officers who offered their services if required and to swear in special officers to maintain good order: But we desired to rule by kindness and with but a few exceptions, it was done. I am thankful that no special officers had to be sworn in, but we appreciate the kindness of the city marshal.

To the many friends who gave us their fruits, vegetables, etc., and in this way lightened our expenses: We believe it was freely given and we accepted it in that spirit.

To the *Topeka Capital* and *Kansas Democrat* for writing us and the meetings up and the *Journal* for writing us down: May God bless the editors and reporters of Topeka, and I trust all persons who love the right will give their support to these papers who stood by the right.

The ministers and Christians of other churches who assisted and labored so faithfully in bringing souls to Christ, I sincerely thank, and they have added many jewels to their crown awaiting them in that blessed home above.

The ushers and those engaged in maintaining good order will receive a reward when they pass into heaven for the faithful manner in which they performed their duties.

To the many of those out of Christ who aided us with good wishes and financially, we feel very grateful and trust that God will permit them to live a little longer and be brought into the kingdom before it is too late.

We have nothing but the kindest feelings for our persecutors in this city and believe that now they are convinced that we are sent by God to present the Gospel as taught by the apostles.

—M. B. Woodworth

Emma Isenberg

Ollie Daggett

May 14, 1892

Daily Statesman (Salem, OR)

Mrs. Woodworth's Meeting

It Opened at 7:30 Last Night in Yew Park with a Large Attendance

rs. M. B. Woodworth, the celebrated evangelist, opened her meetings in her tent in Yew Park last night with a large attendance for the first night.

Mrs. Woodworth was assisted by Miss Emma Eisenberg[1] and Miss Ollie Daggett, who led the singing. She talked over an hour on the subject of repentance and salvation, teaching, "Ye must be born again."

The revivalist is a kindly faced woman, something past middle age, and one who possesses a great deal of personal magnetism. Her whole attention is centered in the work of spreading the Gospel, and she appears to be perfectly happy when she can talk to a gathering of people. She receives no salary for her service though she says she has been offered large remuneration in a number of cities, though she prefers to work with the people all over the United States, "the laboring class preferred." Her influence is potent, and she is confident that she will have many converts ere she leaves the Capital City.

Services will be held today at 2:30 and at 7:30 P.M. Tomorrow there will be services at 10:30 A.M. and 2:30 and 7:30 P.M.

[1] "Eisenberg"—A misspelling of Isenberg.

May 27, 1892

Daily Statesman (Salem, OR)

The Evangelist's Work

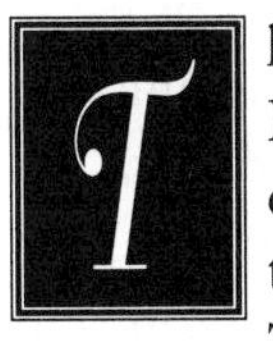

he meeting in Yew Park opened yesterday afternoon with the song, "Drifting Towards the Lee,"[1] followed by an earnest and effectual prayer by F. Kundret, who said we must bear the cross if we would wear the crown. Mrs. Woodworth

[1] Composer of hymn unknown.

spoke from 1 Timothy 2:8, "I will therefore that men pray every where, lifting up holy hands, without wrath and doubting." This shows the true Christian character in a nutshell. The condition of a true child of God is to live in an attitude of prayer all the time. Even our silent thoughts are written in a book.

We have a great work to do here on earth, and women have as great a part of it to do as men. If we are led by the Spirit of God, our work is blessed. We are all one in Christ. We should all work together. We can glorify God in the kitchen as well as in the church. Our religion should show in our business. Do we live what we preach? If our religion will not bear inspection here—what will it be in the Day of Judgment? Do good everywhere and let your religion shine forth in your business. The world is watching you. Pray without ceasing. Prayer strengthens. Walk by faith and see with spiritual eyes. If we are constant in prayer, we will never backslide, and if we live as we ought, we will be rewarded. If we walk in the light of Christ, we will keep His commandments. And by this we shall know we are His disciples—if we love one another and have true fellowship.[2]

Prayer with doubt is unavailing and does not rise higher than our heads. There is no mutual ground. If our hearts are pure, we have no condemnation. Our home is not here; let us lay up treasures in heaven.[3] Glorify God with the body as well as with the spirit. If our hearts are pure and our hands clean, we will not be afraid or ashamed to speak. If we are born of God, we have no fear for He is our own Father, and we trust implicitly in Him. What a glorious experience to know we have a clear title to heaven!

Only by a complete consecration to God do we receive great blessings. If we are ashamed to own Christ here, He will be ashamed to own us on the portals of eternity. The apostles were persecuted, but their persecution only served to make them stronger. Christ has the same power today as in the days of the apostles, but we lack in faith and purity of heart. A fearful thing to defy the God of heaven! Take the world but give me Christ—heaven. Let us rise, shine, and give

---

[2] See John 13:35.

[3] See Matthew 6:20.

God the glory.[4] All must bow the knee. True Christian life [is] not by sight but by faith. If we fail to use aright the powers we are endowed with, we will fall short of the glory of God. Necessity for a more complete consecration. Let us press forward to the mark of our high calling, which is in Christ. There will one day be a reckoning. How do you stand? Meetings at 2:30 and 7:30 every day.

[4] See Isaiah 60:1.

May 29, 1892

Daily Statesman (Salem, OR)

Evangelist Mrs. Woodworth

Who She Is, Where She Came From, and What She Is Doing at Salem

The accompanying engraving[1] is quite an accurate likeness of Mrs. M. B. Woodworth, the evangelist, who is conducting daily meetings at her tent in Yew Park. She has been here two weeks and has already succeeded in creating quite an interest in her work. Mrs. Woodworth is making her home in a little cottage near the tent. She receives no salary, but voluntary collections are taken to defray the running expenses of the meetings. The evangelist is the publisher and proprietor of *The Bible Truth*—as preached by the apostles—of St. Louis. This is a monthly publication now in its third volume. She is a disciple of the Church of God but preaches to all denominations and extends cordial invitations to the poor.

A correspondent in the *Statesman* yesterday morning having stated that Mrs. Woodworth was a dangerous woman and imbued with powers of hypnotism, she yesterday afternoon devoted her talk to her own defense and loudly called for proofs. Mrs. Woodworth will preach three times today—at 10:30, 2:30, and 7:30.

[1] "engraving"—The writer refers to a 2 ½- by 2 ½-inch, head and shoulders engraving of Maria Woodworth which rests in the center of the column where the article appears.

July 4, 1894

Columbus Gazette (Columbus Junction, IA)

The Work Goes On

Crowds Still Flocking to Columbus Junction

THE PREACHING TENT CROWDED DAY AND NIGHT—MANY CLAIMING TO BE HEALED IN BODY AND SOUL—DISEASES OF ALL KINDS SAID TO BE CURED

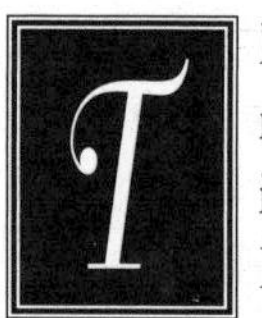he excitement in regard to the meetings of Mrs. Maria B. Woodworth has greatly increased during the past week, and vast numbers of people crowd the tent where the services are held, day and night. People who are afflicted with all manner of diseases come in hopes of being relieved, and many go away professing to be healed. Cancers, tumors, bad cases of rheumatism, Bright's disease,[1] heart trouble, everything and anything that can be mentioned in the catalogue of ills that flesh is heir to, have been brought to this wonderful woman, and she claims and the patients assert that they are entirely healed.

It is only fair to state that many people have grave doubts in regard to this healing, and especially do they doubt its being divine healing. They attribute the work done to mesmerism or hypnotism on the part of Mrs. Woodworth or to the manner in which the emotions of the imagination are affected. The assertion is made that only nervous or excitable people are healed. But others are just as firm in the belief that it is all miraculous, that she is endowed with divine power and that through prayer and the laying on of hands all these wonderful works are wrought.

One young lady [missing line(s)] she could scarcely speak or walk and given up by the physicians to die, came to the meeting and claims to be healed. She is now able to eat and walk about and converse and ride out and sends word that her strength is returning and that she is all right. One old lady, whose hands were drawn out of shape terribly with rheumatism and who could not raise her hands

[1] "Bright's disease"—a term once used for nephritis (inflamed kidneys) in general (Webster's N.W. 1997).

to her head, came and was healed; and her hands it is said are all right, and she can use them as well as ever. People come from long distances and claim to be healed of the worst forms of diseases in the last stages. One woman healed of cancer of the stomach, who had been given up to die by fifteen doctors, could not eat nor sit up; after she was healed could eat heartily and walked to the tent to the meetings.

Scores of cases might be cited of perfect healing, the authority being Mrs. Woodworth and the persons healed, and this authority would seem to be sufficient. One thing all must acknowledge who meet Mrs. Woodworth or who hear her talk and that is, as was suggested last week, her intense earnestness. She certainly believes her doctrine, and it is earnestness that gives success to any teacher. She has written a book called *The Life, Work, and Experience of Mrs. Maria B. Woodworth.* This will appear in a very short time and will no doubt be of much interest. To those who wish to know more of this matter, we would say: Come and see. This is not done in a corner. It is open and public and all can see it. Come to Columbus Junction and see and hear Mrs. Woodworth.

July 18, 1894

Columbus Gazette (Columbus Junction, IA)

Mrs. Woodworth Closes Her Work Here and Goes to Muscatine

Mrs. Maria Beulah Woodworth closed her meetings here last Sunday evening and began work in Muscatine Tuesday evening, having transported her tent thither in the meantime. Her meetings here will long be remembered both by her adherents and by those who differ with her. Columbus Junction was for a time profoundly altered by her work, and interest in the meetings kept up to the vast, immense crowds attending all three of the services on Sunday, many coming long distances. The general belief in the divine healing seemed to grow less and less as the meetings went on, though many people were benefited bodily and consider her work miraculous. She evidently thinks so herself, but amongst the better educated and more thoughtful people there are comparatively few who agree with her. These are disposed to attribute all her healing power to magnetism or hypnotism or the influence of the mind upon the body. How much permanent good has been done remains to be seen.

August 31, 1894

Leaves of Healing, Vol. 1 (Zion, IL)

Trance Evangelism

mong the many strange things, too numerous to mention, which we have seen in this strange land, one of the strangest and most absurd and yet most dangerous forms of anti-Christian error is that of "trance evangelism."

A Mrs. Woodworth, calling herself "an eldress of the Church of God of Indiana," has appeared on this coast and is at present preaching in the city where we are writing, Oakland, California. Many Christians, and especially those who have received the doctrine of healing through faith in Jesus, have been attracted to her meetings by the widely-published statements which she has made that the Lord is using her in the ministry of divine healing, and our attention was first directed to her by some of those who had been blessed under our own ministry. Rejoicing, as we heartily do, in hearing of any whom the Lord is thus using, we visited her tent and have given much attention to her work. We know of not a single case of divine healing in this city through her agency and have asked again and again concerning those whom she publicly alleged were healed and in every case have found that they were not healed. Some are dead, some are dying, and, so far as we have been able to ascertain, we say before the Lord that we do not know of one case of healing and we have made close inquiry. Recently little claim has

Leaves of Healing is a publication of John Alexander Dowie who at first supported Maria Woodworth and then turned against her and denounced her publicly through newspaper interviews and his own publication.

been made and little attention seems to have been given, in her mission, to divine healing.

Reading her own writings and listening to her own words, we say emphatically that she is ignorant of the very first principles of the truth of God concerning the doctrine of divine healing, neither understanding the teaching of God's Word concerning the nature and origin of disease, nor the remedy for this, as for all other evil, to be found in Christ our Lord. We also say that reading closely what she has written and listening earnestly to what she has said, we have failed to recognize that she is teaching the doctrine of salvation by faith through grace in Christ. The work of true repentance for sin in the heart of the sinner and the setting forth of the atoning sacrifice of Jesus as Savior and justification by grace through faith in Him alone are manifestly untaught by her. She quotes in her biography with approval reports of her own meetings, which must be shocking to every true Christian who reads them. At page 376 of her *Life and Experience*, in large type, she quotes the words in giving a description of a baptism at Anderson: "WASHING AWAY SIN. The turbid waters of White River as the soul-cleansing element. Singly, and in pairs, and in bunches, men, women, and children are made pure. One hundred and five persons received the rites of baptism by immersion." And further on, at page 381, under the appropriate heading of "Bubbles," she quotes these words: "The load of sin, floating down the river, jarred the foundation of the Moss Island Mill."

Any true Christian will at once perceive that such statements as these indicate, not salvation by faith in Christ and regeneration by the inward work of the Holy Spirit, but cleansing through the mere outward ordinance of baptism, which, however important in itself it may be and is, can only be an outward act of obedience without in itself possessing any spiritual cleansing power. Indeed, the Gospel of salvation and of healing plays little part in the work in this "trance evangelist," for everything is subordinated to the continuous craving, croaking cry for *"power,"* and to a declaration over and over again that that "power" is present, *"the very same power that came on Pentecost!"* Hence she is continuously declaring that men and women must come up within reach of her touch and influence to there confess their sins and receive the "power." She declares this "power" is the power of the Holy Ghost and is in accordance with Joel 2:28-29 and Acts 2:16-18; and women of all ages and children and young people of both sexes have come under "the influence," as she calls it, and trances, dreams, visions, and revelations *"from the Lord"* are alleged to have been given to these, but in not one single case are the allegations supported by the facts.

Knowing the facts intimately, as we do, and having in our ministry given much attention to this subject, we say unhesitatingly that these so-called "divine revelations" are but shameful diabolical delusions. And it is painful in the extreme to see how many of God's children are being led away into darkness by this "eldress," whom we can only compare fitly with one spoken of in the message of the church at Thyatira, in the second chapter of the book of the Revelation, twentieth verse, who is referred to as "that woman Jezebel, *who calleth herself a prophetess.*"

On two occasions we tested the nature of these alleged divine trances. In one we found a woman extended upon a bench, called by them "the altar," who was said to be "under the power," and truly she was under the power of the devil, for when we laid our hands upon her in the name of the Lord Jesus and lifted up her hands, we found that she was perfectly sensible and conscious of surrounding things. Accordingly, we whispered in her ear, "You are in no trance. In the name of the Lord Jesus get up," which in a few seconds she did.

The following day, in another case, we saw an aged lady extended upon her back on the damp straw of the tent, surrounded by a crowd of merely curious people for the most part, in a state of apparent unconsciousness, yet struggling, writhing, and screaming petitions to God for unconverted friends. This we were told was another manifestation of the "power." But, as we looked at that aged sister of Christ, with her nerves wrought up to the highest point of tension, and the veins standing like whipcords upon her brow, perspiring in her agony, we felt once more that this was the power of the devil. Accordingly, quietly entering into the midst, we asked those who were holding the struggling victim to let her go and, breathing first an unspoken prayer to God that He would give us power in Jesus' name to cast out the evil spirit that was possessing her, we bent down. Quietly placing our right hand upon her brow, and seizing her extended left hand with our left hand, we said audibly: "In the name of the Lord Jesus Christ be perfectly still," and in a moment she was still and lay without movement of any kind. We then caused her at once to be lifted up and seated in a chair. In a few moments she regained consciousness, and then, exhorting her in a few words to remember that to rest in the Lord for her dear ones, we left her perfectly calm and composed and have heard that she has remained so ever since. Not more than a minute had elapsed after this incident when an impertinent message reached us from one of the female helpers who travel with the "trance evangelist" requesting us to keep our "hands off God's work." Quietly saying it was the devil's work, which in Jesus' name we had been destroying, we left the tent.

Subsequent visits and many other facts coming to our knowledge have convinced us more deeply that this is indeed the only right verdict and that we are face to face on this coast with one of the most dangerous forms of anti-Christian error coming in the guise of Christian teaching. We therefore give warning to all the members of the American Divine Healing Association throughout this coast and to all to whom our words may come, that, having fully considered the importance of the statement, we say, *Beware of this false prophetess,* who, in the name of Jesus is, like her of Thyatira, teaching and seducing God's servants. She is, we believe, leading many into paths where they will drink the cup of devils and find themselves at last to be in company with others who also speak lies in the name of Jesus, such as Christian Scientists, spiritualists, free lovers, papalists,[1] and others, "led captive by Satan at his will."[2]

It is our purpose to deliver lectures on this subject on Thursday, January 23d, in Hamilton Hall, Oakland, and on Lord's day, January 26th, in the large Saratoga Hall, Geary Street between

[1] "Papalists"—papists.

[2] 2 Timothy 2:26, paraphrased.

Hyde and Larkin, San Francisco. But these words of warning we have felt it our duty to place on record so that God's children shall take heed. "Blessed is he that watcheth, and keepeth his garments, lest he walk naked and they see his shame" (Revelation 16:15).

January 14, 1896

Syracuse Register (IN)

Revival Meeting

he series of revival meetings under the auspices of M. B. Woodworth, the famous evangelist, still continues with undiminished interest. Immense crowds throng the house to overflowing. Mrs. Woodworth's sermons are very powerful, she being filled with the Holy Ghost. Every word pierces the hearts of the unsaved, bringing them the Christ she so greatly loves. Some two hundred precious souls have been brightly converted.

Many persons of integrity testify to the power of divine healing. Amid the poison arrows of the enemies of God, with her pure character which so sweetly resists every effort of the powers of darkness, and in the strength of Almighty God, she fails not to preach the old apostolic doctrine in all its purity and truth. Christ our Lord sets the royal seal upon her labors. "I the Lord have called thee in righteousness, . . . to open the blind eyes, to bring out the prisoners from the prison, and them that sit in darkness out of the prison house."[1]

ISABELLA J. CALLANDER

[1] Isaiah 42:6-7.

February 24, 1897

The Church Advocate

Church Intelligence

From Trinity Chapel, Wells County, Ind.

Our meetings, which began January 21, conducted by Sister M. B. Woodworth, have grown rapidly in interest from the first, notwithstanding the extremely cold and stormy weather. Many have come more than twenty miles to hear the "glorious" Gospel of the Son of God preached in its primitive purity, to be saved from sin and healed of bodily afflictions. So great are the crowds of people that many are turned away for want of room, while others, coming from a distance, remain and build fires on the outside by which to keep warm, so determined are they to see and hear the noted evangelist. Perhaps also the usual number of Satan's agents come out of curiosity, and to oppose God's messengers, and to reject the message. Yet, blessed be God, the cries of the penitent, the shouts of the redeemed arise above it all, and a great shout of victory is going up out of Israel, for we know "the King is in the camp," and, bless the Lord, He is "just the same today."[1]

At this date about one hundred have professed having faith in Christ, and probably forty or fifty have been healed of divers bodily diseases. One lady, well-known in this community, who had not walked without crutches for eleven years, came and laid all at "Jesus' feet," by faith touched the "hem of his garment,"[2] and was made whole, and the wooden staves that were her support throughout these years were left and still remain in the church house. She now walks perfectly, leaning on the "everlasting arms."[3] Oh! We have a wonderful Savior. Another lady upward of seventy years of age, who had walked only by the aid of crutches for ten years, was healed and has had no need of them since. A lady, who was afflicted with what the doctors pronounced consumption and had been given up to die by four different physicians, came and gave it all to

[1] See 1 Samuel 4:5-6 and Hebrews 13:8.

[2] See Acts 4:34-35 and Matthew 9:20-21.

[3] Deuteronomy 33:27.

the Lord and to the great surprise of many bore testimony in a clear, ringing voice, that was heard distinctly in all parts of the house, that she was healed, not by mesmeric or hypnotic power, but by the power of God, carrying conviction to many minds who had heretofore been skeptical in regard to divine healing.

The church at Trinity and the community for miles around feel that they are highly favored of heaven to have Sister Woodworth with us. Her sermons are not composed of borrowed matter, but are messages fresh from the throne. She wields the sword of the Spirit with a strong arm, boldly and fearlessly defying the world to prove that the gifts and power of the Holy Ghost are not with the church today as in apostolic times. Sister Emma, the lady singer, is a power in song, in prayer, and in exhortation, and is wielding a great influence for good. Eternity alone will reveal the great good that has been accomplished in these meetings. One thing, of which we are sure, is that the servants of the great God are with us, and they have cleared their hands of the blood of all men. May the Lord continue to bless them abundantly and spare them yet many years to do His blessed will [final part of news article missing].

January 23, 1901

Topeka Daily Capital (KS)

[Revival Meetings Open]

The revival meetings of Mrs. Woodworth in North Topeka were successfully opened last night. The attendance was not large. Mrs. Woodworth before coming to Topeka held revivals in Pratt County and other places in Kansas. For the past three weeks, she has been conducting revival services in Oakland. She expects to continue here for several weeks after which she will probably answer a call to go to St. Louis. Assisting in her work are the Rev. Mr. Wyler of Troy and a young lady and a man who are traveling with her. Mrs. Woodworth, who is a pleasant lady and an enthusiastic revivalist, has been engaged in this work for a number of years, having held a series of revivals here nine years ago.

Her meetings will be open every afternoon and evening at 1904 North Kansas Avenue.

EDITOR'S DISPATCH:

July 27, 1903

The Moline Daily Dispatch (IL)

Thinks Word Should Be Said of Etter Meetings

ermit me through the columns of your paper to call attention to the evangelistic meetings of Mrs. Woodworth-Etter, now being held at Twenty-fourth Street and Fifth Avenue, Rock Island.

I do not ask you to endorse a single act of conversion or divine healing by the publication of this communication, but through your kindness of heart, you ought to be as willing to publish acts which are vouched for by eyewitnesses as you are to publish other happenings in the vicinity which are no more [illegible word].

Many people declare that they have been cured of various diseases and are perfectly sound today. Afflicted children have been cured and made to walk for the first time in their lives, which is certainly a blessing to them; severe cases of rheumatism, cross-eyes, cancer, deafness, and one of blood poisoning are some of the results of this woman's preaching. But as great as the above are, they are no more wonderful than the changing of a cursing, swearing, drinking infidel to a sober, praying Christian; and this has been done in Moline.

In private conversation with one of the prominent pastors, he said, "Anything that would benefit the people ought to be encouraged"; and still he could not speak of these meetings from his pulpit.

People are coming for hundreds of miles to her meetings and from all classes, from the poor of the three cities to a bank president out of town.

Whether you believe in the methods used or not, you ought to allow suffering humanity to receive any benefit they may be able to do; and they will thank you for telling them of the chance. Thanking you for the publishing of this letter, which I believe you will not refuse to do, I am,

—Yours in Behalf of the Afflicted

September 4, 1904

The Indianapolis Star (IN)

Evangelist to Try to Enact Miracles

Church of God Worker Says She Can Exert Divine Influence

n a large circular tent having a seating capacity of several hundred persons, Mrs. M. B. Woodworth-Etter, an evangelist of the Church of God, opened a series of revival meetings last night, which she announces will last for several weeks and perhaps months. The tent is pitched at Shelby Street and Bryan Avenue.

Besides being an evangelist, Mrs. Etter professes to be a divine healer, and within the next few days, she says she will begin that branch of her work and promises to give some remarkable demonstrations of divine healing during her stay in Indianapolis.

Although she is a young-looking woman, Mrs. Etter has been an evangelist for more than twenty-five years. Twenty years ago she held a long series of meetings in this city and has held them here at intervals since.

Mrs. Etter and her husband, S. P. Etter, to whom she was married little more than two years ago, came to Indianapolis from St. Louis, where they held meetings lasting six months.

In a circular distributed in St. Louis, Mrs. Etter tells of a meeting she held there fourteen years ago in the famous Kerry Patch, at which she claims that sight was restored to the blind, hearing restored to the deaf, the dumb made to speak, and that paralytics were healed.

Only a few persons were at the meeting last night, which Mrs. Etter said was merely a keynote to the meetings to be held every evening this week. Beginning next week, afternoon meetings will be held at 2 o'clock each day.

Mr. and Mrs. Etter will be assisted in their meetings here by the Rev. and Mrs. John Vinson of the Church of God, Le Grande Avenue and Hamburg Street.

September 10, 1904

The Indianapolis Star (IN)

Spiritual Life Must Precede Her Cures

ALLEGED DIVINE HEALER SAYS THAT HER SUCCESSES ARE DUE TO SPIRIT OF THE LORD WORKING THROUGH HER

here was no divine healing at the tent revival meeting of Mrs. M. B. Woodworth-Etter at Shelby Street and Bryan Avenue last night, and those in the crowd who had expected to see demonstrations of the evangelist's power went away disappointed.

The meeting was a very successful one, but the subject of divine healing was not mentioned until after the services had closed. Then Mrs. Woodworth-Etter, surrounded by a small circle of friends, explained the nature of the divine healing that she proposed to do while in Indianapolis.

"I do not claim to be a divine healer," she said. "It is only the Spirit of the Lord manifesting Itself through me that enables me by laying my hands upon the sick or crippled to effect complete cures.

"Those persons who may come to my meeting expecting me to heal them when they are unprepared spiritually will be disappointed. They cannot hope to be healed until they have accepted Christ and believe in His saving power. The moment that that faith comes, I can help them."

The evangelist said that during her six month's stay in St. Louis that she healed hundreds.

"My most remarkable cure was in restoring sight to a little blind girl. She was also helpless from paralysis and had to be carried into the tent. She became converted after a glorious outburst of religious enthusiasm; and when I placed my hands on her, she was healed instantly. She could see plainly and was able to walk. Today she romps and plays like other little girls."

"Yes, and she has healed hundreds of consumptives," said Mr. Etter, the husband who was in the group [and?] was listening to his wife. "Some of them could hardly speak above a whisper; when healed you could hear their praises for a square away."

"I healed myself through divine faith many years ago," said the Rev. John Vinson of Indianapolis, who took an active part in last night's meeting. "I had catarrh[1] so badly that it was affecting my memory. In prayer one morning I promised to enter the ministry if God would heal me. Instantly the catarrh left me. That was more than twenty-five years ago, and I've been in the ministry ever since.

[1] "catarrh"—inflammation of a mucous membrane, especially of the nose or throat causing an increased flow of mucous *(Webster's N. W.,* 1997).

September 11, 1904

The Indianapolis Star (IN)

Sells Books at Meeting

Mrs. Woodworth-Etter Has Way of Mixing Business with Religion

At her services last night, Mrs. M. B. Woodworth-Etter, who is holding a series of meetings at Shelby Street and Bryan Avenue under the auspices of the Church of God, sold many of her books which she has written herself. Her books include one on her experiences, a book of sermons, and a book containing a collection of hymns.

One aged man, who was on his way to Danville, Ill., and who was so poor as to require a charity ticket, was among those eager for one of the books. Because of his misfortune Mrs. Etter's husband very kindly let him have a book for a quarter.

One book relates her experiences in twenty years' work as a traveling evangelist, and her stories of divine healing are so remarkable as to arouse the incredulity of many.

Today there will be three services in the tent beginning at 10:30 o'clock this morning. Other meetings will be held at 2 o'clock and in the evening. Mrs. Etter has not begun divine healing in Indianapolis yet and says she must wait until she gets the people in the right spiritual condition.

September 16, 1904

The Indianapolis Star (IN)

Waves Arms to Show She Has Been Cured

PEOPLE "GET RELIGION" AND SAY THEY ARE HEALED BY DIVINE POWER AT TENT MEETINGS—GIVE THEIR EXPERIENCE LATER

Muffled in heavy overcoats and wraps, several score of not overenthusiastic people sat and shivered through the tent meeting of Mrs. Woodworth-Etter, the evangelist, at Shelby Street and Bryan Avenue last night.

After a brief exhortation, Mrs. Etter announced that she was going to ask for money. "We can't get along without money," she declared. "If the meetings continue we must have money contributed freely."

After the contribution had been finished, she said: "Now, if there are any who want to be healed, the power is here."

Evidently the people were too busy trying to keep warm to think of being healed and the service soon concluded.

Wednesday night Mrs. Anna Robinson, 320 North Capitol Avenue, after being touched by the evangelist, arose and went to another part of the tent and waited until the experience meeting began. Then she said: "For six months I have been crippled in my left knee. It was rheumatism, the doctors told me. When I came here tonight, I limped at every step. But now I am cured. Watch me." To show that she had been cured, Mrs. Robinson walked past the platform several times.

"I have been a believer in divine healing for many years," said Mrs. Robinson after the services had closed. "However, I always lacked the faith necessary to be cured. Mrs. Woodworth-Etter has helped me to get that faith. I feel that I am completely cured."

A Mrs. Hicks claimed to have been healed of rheumatism in her left arm last night. To convince the crowd, she waved her arms above her head a number of times.

Mrs. Woodworth-Etter's book treating of divine healing continues to sell well.

September 18, 1904

The Indianapolis Star (IN)

Gray-Haired Man Hears His Convert

Woman Evangelist Finds in Audience the One Who Led Her to Accept Christianity

TOURED WHOLE COUNTRY IN THE LAST 25 YEARS

George Hitz, Former Mayoralty Candidate, Pronounces Benediction for "Divine Healer"

Persons who attended Mrs. M. B. Woodworth-Etter's revival services in her big tent at Shelby Street and Bryan Avenue Friday evening looked on with open-eyed curiosity when the evangelist stopped short in her exhortations and stepped from the platform to wring the hand of a gray-haired, dignified man, who had come in late and was edging his way through the crowd to the front part of the tent.

Their interest increased further when Mrs. Etter led him to the platform and introduced him to her husband. Then she resumed her speaking.

"This is the man who first led me to Christ," she said to her audience, at the same time turning toward the stranger. "He is Mr. Charles Stratton, now a manufacturer at Muncie.

"Just twenty-five years ago, I was visiting at Damascus, O[hio]. A wonderful religious revival was on. Everyone was excited. Hundreds were being converted. But I held aloof from the meetings. I could not convince myself that I ought to accept Christ. Finally this man here, who was taking an active part in the meetings, earnestly solicited me to attend just one meeting. I might see things in a different light, he told me.

"I went to the meeting. Within an hour I was converted. That was twenty-five years ago, and I have wandered over the United States ever since. I owe much to this man."

After leaving Damascus Mrs. Etter never saw Mr. Stratton again until Friday evening. She recognized him instantly, however. Since taking up evangelistic work, Mrs. Etter has preached in nearly every state in the union. Nearly all her meetings have been held in tents. Fifteen years ago a wealthy Californian who was converted in one of her meetings presented her with a tent that comfortably seated eight thousand persons. Within the last ten years Virgil Roberts of Knoxville, Iowa, has given her two tents.

At last night's meeting George Hitz, a former mayoralty candidate, in pronouncing the benediction, took occasion to criticize worldly amusements. His reference to theaters as the "work and creation of the devil" brought forth "amens" from all over the tent.

September 19, 1904

The Indianapolis Star (IN)

"Deafness Cured" but Keeps Her Trumpet

WOMAN SAYS EVANGELIST RESTORED HER HEARING—DOCTOR TESTIFIES PRAYER RAISED DEAD SON

rofessing to have been completely cured of deafness which had afflicted her for twenty-five years, Mrs. Rhoda Shaffer of Morgan County yesterday afternoon, at the tent revival service of Mrs. M. B. Woodworth-Etter at Shelby Street and Bryan Avenue, flung into the midst of the big crowd the ear trumpet that had done her service for the last ten years.

However, before leaving the tent at the conclusion of the service, she hunted up the trumpet that she had thrown away while her religious enthusiasm was at its height and carefully deposited it in a handbag that she carried.

"I shall probably never need it again, but there's no use throwing it away," she said to one who asked her in a surprised sort of way why she was taking it home with her after she had been cured.

When she came back to the evening service, she did not bring the trumpet with her. There was no need of it she said. She could hear as well as she did twenty-five years ago, before her sickness had rendered her totally deaf in one ear and partially so in the other, she said.

Mrs. Shaffer explained that she had stopped off in Indianapolis yesterday in the hope of being healed by Mrs. Woodworth-Etter. She was en route from her home in Morgan County to the northern part of the state to visit a sister. She had read of the evangelist in the newspapers.

Dr. David M. Bye, a physician at 316 North Illinois Street, at Saturday night's meeting in speaking to the audience concerning the possibilities of divine healing, testified that his own son had once been raised from the dead by prayer.

"My boy was dead; there was no doubt about it," declared the doctor. "Those who had watched over him with me and my wife were also convinced that life was extinct, and several of them had left the house. The undertaker had been sent for.

"I alone was certain that the child would come to life again. The Lord told me so. I had gone to a shed in the rear of our house for some wood and as I entered a voice seemed to me to say, 'Thy child shall live.' When I returned to the house, the child was dead. I did not weep. I knew that he would come to life again.

"After awhile the child's body suddenly grew warm, his eyes opened, and he raised up in bed. From that moment he was well. There was not the slightest sign of disease after that. The Lord had restored him."

Dr. Bye said that this had happened thirty-five years ago. It was many years after this that the son died.

September 25, 1904

The Indianapolis Star (IN)

Storm Blows Down Evangelist's Tent

M. B. Etter, the Husband, Buried Under the Canvas, but Is Rescued by Watchman

Even prayers did not save Mrs. M. B. Woodworth-Etter's big tent at Shelby Street and Bryan Avenue from being blown down yesterday.

About 1:30 o'clock when the wind was blowing the hardest and rain was falling in torrents, the tent went down burying under it Mr. M. B. Etter, husband of the evangelist. He had gone to the tent early to put things in readiness for the afternoon meeting and was standing on the raised platform when the center pole gave way.

For fifteen minutes "Jim" Barby, the colored watchman at the tent, hustled trying to extricate the evangelist's husband from the fold upon fold of twisted and flapping canvas. Finally he crawled under and led him to the light. Then the rescued man shouted a loud "amen."

Less than a week ago after a heavy storm had visited Indianapolis, Mrs. Woodworth-Etter, in commenting on miracles, observed to her audience that her tent no doubt had been saved from the storm's fury through divine intervention.

With her tent down and flapping in the winds, Mrs. Woodworth-Etter will preach this morning at the Church of God, La Grande Avenue and Hamburg Street. If the tent can be raised during the morning, she will preach in it this afternoon and evening.

September 28, 1904

The Indianapolis Star (IN)

Paralyzed Negro Becomes Athlete

Moses Foreford Takes Treatment of Mrs. Woodworth-Etter at Revival Meeting

ore supposed miraculous demonstrations of divine healing were gazed upon by a curious crowd at the tent meeting of Mrs. Woodworth-Etter at Shelby Street and Bryan Avenue last night.

A mother brought in a little boy, hobbling along as she held him by the hand. She said that he had been afflicted with spinal meningitis and had been unable to walk. When he wanted to get about the room, she said, he "scooted on the floor."

After loud shouting and prayer and many amens and hallelujahs, the little fellow was told to stand up and run. As he wriggled his little body in an attempt to run, there was an uproar of laughter in the tent.

A young woman, who had lost her hearing years ago during sickness, communicated with Mrs. Woodworth-Etter by means of writing on paper. After a few sentences had been written, the young woman's friends were sure that she gave evidence of hearing the songs.

Moses Foreford, a Negro who was paralyzed three years ago by being hit in the head with a rock, came to the tent last night at the request of James Barbee, another colored man who said he had been healed of rheumatism. Moses walked in leaning on the arm of his wife, but before the meeting was over he gave an exhibition of running—hop, step, and jump; and broad jump—shouting until he could be heard all over the neighborhood.

After the meeting Mrs. Woodworth-Etter was very tired, and wrapping herself in a shawl, said: "There are people from all over the state attending my meetings. I am tired, but it is His power that keeps me up."

October 2, 1904

The Indianapolis Star (IN)

Woodworth-Etter Goes into a Trance

Falls into Husband's Arms After Thirty Minutes of Rigidity

rs. Woodworth-Etter went into a trance at her revival meeting in the tent at Shelby Street and Bryan Avenue last night and remained so more than forty-five minutes. Then she talked awhile and went into another of shorter duration.

She had been praying and preaching for the conversion of a gray-haired deaf man who had come and knelt in the straw before her. She stood in front of him, raised her hands, and waved them as though trying to fly. She rose on her toes a number of times and her eyes assumed a glassy stare, wide open. She remained in this position half an hour.

Some snickered, while her husband warned them not to laugh at the presence of the Holy Ghost among them.

After a time all was deathly still. All waited to see what she would do. She fell into her husband's arms and was laid on some chairs.

When she rose the first time, she opened her eyes and stared awhile, then said: "God has had possession of my body. He is giving you a warning. I am not God, but He is here. The gates of heaven will soon be shut. Christ is coming again, while many of you here are living. You will see Him."

She sank again and was laid on the floor. When she roused the second time, she told everybody present to bring baskets of dinner and stay at the tent all day today. Services will be held at 9 this morning, at 2 this afternoon, and at 7:30 this evening.

October 3, 1904

The Indianapolis Star (IN)

Shouting Converts on City Street Car

PART OF MRS. WOODWORTH-ETTER'S CONGREGATION CONTINUE SERVICE ON WAY HOME

rs. M. B. Woodworth-Etter's meeting did not end in her tent last night with the benediction but was continued on a street car by some of her converts on their way downtown.

About sixty of her congregation boarded Shelby street car No. 802 at Bryan Avenue after the service. The car had hardly gone a square before William Howard of Summitville, who was converted in one of Mrs. Etter's meetings twenty-five years ago, started the words of a church song.

At first the passengers on the car looked amazed and then as the song progressed, one or two and then practically every passenger on the car took it up. When it was finished, other songs were sung and persons along the street stopped and others came rushing from their homes to watch the car.

Men and women on the car clapped their hands and screamed and shouted and all of the enthusiasm displayed at the tent meetings was shown on the car until it reached Washington Street.

Several hundred persons attended the meetings yesterday, and about fifty from the surrounding country took baskets of lunch at the morning services and stayed all day, eating their dinner and supper in the tent.

Mrs. Etter, the "divine healer," is showing the strain of the meetings she has been conducting in the city and last night was troubled with [a] severe cold.

October 16, 1904

The Indianapolis Star (IN)

Totters but at Last Walks Without Aid

Thomas Wayt Healed by Mrs. Etter After Illness of Two Years

aken from a sick bed by neighbors and half carried to the church, Thomas Wayt of 910 Concord Street arose from the altar at Peniel Temple last night, declaring he had been healed of partial paralysis and stomach trouble by Mrs. M. B. Woodworth-Etter.

Wayt's "healing" caused no little curiosity and interest among the people who had seen him taken to the altar, and as he arose the entire congregation crowded about him. As he stood up under the direction of Mrs. Etter, he almost fell but was supported by other converts.

Although he tottered and almost fell several times, Mrs. Etter insisted on his keeping his feet and holding his hands compelled him to walk but apparently with great difficulty. Finally an aisle was cleared and the man walked alone although he staggered. After the meeting he walked to a streetcar and went home.

Wayt related that he had been ill nearly two years, had not worked since February 13, and had not been out of bed more than half a day at a time since. Last night, he said was the first time in months he had been out alone.

Mrs. Etter is continuing to draw large crowds at Senate Avenue and 11th Street. At the meeting last night was Charles Ault of Brown County who said he had been here a week and had been cured of partial blindness by Mrs. Etter.

October 24, 1904

The Indianapolis Star (IN)

Remains in Trance for Over an Hour

GIRL AT WOODWORTH-ETTER MEETING SAYS SHE SAW VISION OF HEAVEN—EDITOR AFFECTED

or more than an hour at the meeting of Mrs. Woodworth-Etter, in Peniel Hall, 11th Street and Senate Avenue last night, Miss Pearl May, 1124 Arsenal Avenue, stood in a trance. The audience lingered after the meeting had been dismissed to see what the girl would do. She waved her hands and smiled and stared without blinking until tears ran down her cheeks. Mrs. Etter appointed three women to remain with her and prepared to leave her there when the girl came to and said she had seen a vision of heaven.

Eugene Boyden of Greenfield, editor of the *Greenfield Evening Star,* fell on the floor in a trance and rose shouting. He said that he was healed of catarrh and was not going to take any more medicine.

A woman, who said she had been almost totally deaf, prayed loudly and shouted. She said she could hear better and ran from the church leaping and shouting.

Miss May will tell of her vision of heaven at tonight's meeting, according to the request of Mrs. Woodworth-Etter.

Dearly Beloved in the Lord,

1912

Victory

The Dallas Revival

Texas, U.S.A.

bout three months ago, a few of us sat round a tea table in England and read the account of the wonderful revival in Dallas, Texas; and as we read the account, the power of God fell on us; and we could do nothing but praise our heavenly Father, who is so wonderfully pouring out His Spirit in the last days. The dear Lord put the desire in our hearts to visit these scenes of heavenly visitation, and He has graciously allowed the desire to be gratified. Before leaving England, a brother asked us especially to enquire as to how the revival began, what were the causes of revival, and how such a revival may be repeated in other centers, and we have made special inquiries on this line.

During the sixteen days we have been here, we have been witnesses of many mighty manifestations of the power of God. On our way to Dallas from Winnipeg, we stayed off a day at St. Paul, Minnesota, and there we met a Swedish sister who had been sick for over two years with serious internal troubles. The night previous to our arrival, she had been awake praying for the Lord to open the way for her to get to Dallas. She was so weak that it was with difficulty she could get from her bed to a chair; and so she knew she could not undertake the forty-eight hour journey unaccompanied, and her husband could not afford the time or the money to accompany her. Imagine her delight when the day after her all night of prayer, she heard there was a company of thirteen people in St. Paul who were on their way to Dallas by the evening train. Her husband consented to her joining the company; but at the end of the journey, she was in a very weak condition. She was taken in a cab to a room and stayed in bed the next day, but on the second day she came to the meeting. Sister Etter laid her hands on her in the name of Jesus. She felt nothing at the moment, but almost immediately afterwards she sprang up, and impelled by the new inflow of divine life, she ran up and down the building like a young schoolgirl. All the organs that had been wrong were put right and remain right, and every day she is stronger and able to take more exercise. All glory be to Jesus.

A brother from Missouri came down to Dallas on Saturday [this] week, very far gone in consumption. For five months he has been disabled, during which time he has only been able to work about 15 days. Latterly he had been confined to his bed. Whilst there the Lord told him to come to Dallas. The undertaking of a journey of over five hundred miles was no light one; but he rose in the name of the Lord, and God gave him the strength for the journey. The Lord healed him whilst hands were laid on him the night of his arrival. From the clear, ringing testimony he gave on the Sunday morning, one could tell that not only his lungs were repaired, but that he had a fresh touch of fire from the Lord. He went back on the Monday believing the Lord would make him a real blessing to his friends on his return.

Another night a man came in looking like death, suffering with appendicitis. He came for healing, and the Lord not only healed his body, but saved his soul. Another sister, who came from Chicago, was healed of appendicitis on the day of her arrival. Every case of sickness and disease is healed of the Lord here when the sick ones come in faith. And even when the sick ones appear to have no faith, they seem to be either inspired with faith through the preaching of the Word or they catch a little of the overflow of faith from the One who deals with them. And God always honors faith, even though it may be small, and when He inspires faith there is always victory.

This morning a boy came to the meeting on crutches with a poisoned foot. He was prayed with, and he was able to walk away without his crutches, walking as well as anyone in the building.

It is inspiring to hear the testimonies of those who have been healed, one of twenty cancers and epilepsy, one of pellagra (an incurable deathly disease akin to leprosy), another of asthma, another of deafness, another of rheumatism, another of consumption, another of broken limbs. One young lad came with a broken arm; this arm was put right and at the same time his other arm, which was paralyzed, was healed. He waves both his arms as an indication of how perfect the Lord has made him. He was only a street urchin, but someone looks after him now; and he has a shining face and a bright testimony for Jesus. At this morning's service, it was wonderful to see a sister who has been deaf and dumb and is now blessedly healed, mightily under the power of the Spirit of God, doing her best to show what great things God has done for her. We have a wonderful God, and as they say here, "He has not gone out of business yet."

Every day souls are being saved and baptized in the Holy Ghost, speaking with other tongues as the Spirit gives them utterance. The leaders here teach everyone that is saved to seek immediately the baptism of the Holy Ghost and they usually receive the same night.

Sometimes a number of sinners have come to the "altar," as they call the front bench in this country, and there have not been enough workers to attend to them. They weep their way into the kingdom, and when the workers come to attend to them an hour or so later, they find them speaking in other tongues. Having been baptized by the Holy Ghost, one Catholic girl came one night and was saved and baptized in the Spirit; immediately, she had the desire for the salvation of two of her friends. She took away two anointed handkerchiefs and they were placed under their pillows. The next night these girls came to the meeting and were saved and baptized in the Spirit as at Pentecost—hallelujah!

A great number of spiritual songs have been given in the meeting, enough for a hymn book. Many of these came through tongues and interpretations, but many in pure English. Sometimes the Lord has given a beautiful poem of a hundred verses, all in the most beautiful language. One brother stood up to preach one night and the Lord gave him a poem of about forty verses, running right through the Bible from the Fall to the marriage supper. It came just as he stood up, without any premeditation. This same brother has had the most marvelous visions and revelations. The Lord is continually giving visions and dreams here according to the promise in Joel.

Brother Bosworth, the pastor here, his wife and Brother Bindsall, came to this town in September, 1910, and when they arrived it was as dead and cold and hard a place as any that can be found. But they purposed in their hearts there should be a revival here, and they prayed and believed to this end. They would get down to prayer after they had had their breakfast, and it would frequently be late in the afternoon before they got up from their knees. Bro. Bosworth says that if you purpose anything in your heart, God will supply you with the faith for that thing. God gave them faith for a mighty revival here; and moved by that faith, they worked to that end.

But humanly speaking everything was against them. They had no money, no influence, no helpers, and no friends. They put up a tent but the cold and wet and the mud, which is phenomenal in this city, kept the people away. Some nights Bro. Bosworth and Bro. Bindsall were the only ones at the meeting, but they had faith in their hearts and the Lord gave them a good time. In February of 1911, after praying for five months, the fire fell in a Methodist Church in an outlying district; and from that time the revival has stayed, and we believe the revival will go on until Jesus comes. Bro. Bosworth is sure the best part of the revival has yet to come. He was saying last night that the men of faith of old asked for things from God for which there was no precedent and we should do the same. Joshua commanded the sun and moon to stand still, and God caused them to obey the voice of His faithful servant. Elisha asked the Lord to bring blindness on a whole army, and God honored his faith and let it come. Then when he had brought them to the place he wanted them, he asked for a wholesale healing; and a whole army of blind people received sight in a moment. And should we limit God in our petitions? It is the privilege of every child of God to enter into the holiest place every day of his life and make a definite request and receive a definite answer from God. "Keep prayed up," he frequently exhorts the people. The Lord has laid soul travail[1] on many of the workers here and Bro. Bosworth always encourages this, for "when Zion travails she brings forth."[2] We have seen young children of ten years of age in soul travail in the meeting.

After the revival began, the enemy soon stirred up persecution and it was not safe to hold meetings long in one place. But every time they made a move, the Lord set His seal on the move by baptizing a soul in the Holy Spirit the first night. They found it was a wise

[1] Some readers may not be familiar with the term "soul travail," which can also be referred to as "travailing in the Spirit." The biblical reference is Romans 8:26. The Holy Spirit fills the intercessor with an overwhelming burden to pray for a person or situation. Praying may involve groanings, diverse tongues, weeping, crying out to God, or declaring God's Word. The person praying may not know what the situation is or even for whom they are praying, but they are moved to pray until the burden "lifts" and peace fills their soul. This indicates they have accomplished what the Holy Spirit wanted accomplished in prayer.

thing to move their tent occasionally (about half a mile from the place it was last pitched), for they could take their old friends and they would soon get a new crowd in. The present tabernacle is in South Dallas; but Bro. Bosworth says that immediately [when] the warm weather comes in, he is going to pitch his tent in North Dallas, and he believes for a greater revival than they have ever seen. Anyone will come to a tent, he says, and our own experience during the past summer in England confirms the truth of this statement. Nowhere in the New Testament do we find the apostles getting subscriptions for the erection of buildings or spending their time in the building of sanctuaries. The manifestation of the power of God in the healing of the sick and the working of miracles bring the crowd more than a comfortable building.

God has confirmed His words all the way along by many miracles of healing. In the first two months, 125 received the baptism of the Holy Ghost with the scriptural evidence of the new tongue; and all the way along this present truth has been preached, and about twelve hundred have received the baptism of the Holy Ghost as at Pentecost. Over three hundred have received during the last three months; fifty were baptized in one week.

Sister Etter's book, *The Acts of the Holy Ghost,* has always been a great inspiration to Bro. Bosworth and Bro. Birdsall, and oftentimes when they were praying for this revival, they used to get it down continually and read it, and the story of the wonderful revivals God gave this dear child of His spurred them on to larger petitions. It was an inspiration to read of five hundred souls being saved in a week in some services of hers, of hundreds being healed of all kinds of incurable disease, of the blind seeing, of the deaf hearing, of the dumb speaking, and of other miracles which God wrought in response to the faith of this servant of His.

In July, Bro. Bosworth went down to see Sister Etter and persuaded her to come down to Dallas. She came, and immediately God began to use her very wonderfully in healing. During the first meetings, three deaf and three dumb people were healed. The news of what God was doing soon spread all over the country, and the sick and

[2] See Isaiah 66:8.

dying have been brought from practically every state in the union, and the power of the Lord has been present to heal.

Since Sister Etter commenced her ministry in Dallas, more than a dozen deaf and dumb people have been healed in addition to many deaf people having their ears unstopped.

What strikes an outsider most when they come to the meetings is the amount of *life*. "Jesus came that we might have *life*, and have it more abundantly."[3] The testimonies are full of life and the joy of those who give them recommends the "gospel goods" to the sinner. The worldling is shown by the very faces of those who testify that God has got something a thousand times better for them than anything the world can give. There is no need to "preach at" the sinner; unless he is utterly foolish, he wants the best in this life and in the world to come; and when he sees the child of God is really having the best of it, he wants to obey the conditions by which he can come into these blessings. That is why the "altar" is continually flocked with sinners, and the sick ones come and get both saved and healed. The saints come up to the altar too every night, not only to help the seekers, but to seek more of God for themselves. Sister Etter, although God has probably given her as much as He gave any of the apostles, is always seeking for more of God and exhorting others to do the same. We need more power, we need more love, we need more wisdom, we need more faith, we need more of the gifts of the Spirit. She continually says, "Let every saint come up to the altar and seek for more," and there would be invariably a response.

There is so much love here there is no room for division. There is no fight for terms—*Jesus is the theme*—and they are not looking for another. Some who sometimes take up time with long experiences are reminded in a loving way to "talk about Jesus." Praise is called for more than testimony. There is no check to manifestations, but rather an encouragement to those who are under the power of the Spirit to let Him have His way. They trust the Lord to keep out fleshly manifestations and He does.

Well, we all praise the Lord for bringing us. It was worthwhile coming from England to America to get the stimulus to faith the

[3] John 10:10, paraphrased.

Lord has given us here. What He has done here, He can do everywhere. There is no reason why there should not be a similar revival in every Pentecostal center, if the saints will pray and believe and work to that end. And above all "talk about Jesus."

—Yours in the boundless grace of Jesus Christ,

Stanley H. Frodsham

1912

Victory

Dallas, Texas, U.S.A.

I would like to tell you a little of the work in Dallas, Texas, and the way it's carried on. The meetings are at present being held in a large wooden tabernacle put up for the occasion; it holds over a thousand people, has wooden seats with a rail for the back to rest against, and a platform which holds about eighty to one hundred. Here the choir is seated and the organ and table placed. I will tell you of this morning's meeting, which was very beautiful and powerful.

At 10:30 the people began to come in, and from that time till 11:15, they were all down on the sawdust-covered earth praying to God for blessing on the meeting. Then as the place fills up with visitors, strangers, and regulars, the leader says, "Take your seats and we'll sing something." Those who sit in the choir take their places and a hymn is called out. The choir leads the singing with some very bright, lively, full, salvation hymns, in which everybody joins.

To look at the choir singing is a tonic to start with, as their whole bodies sing as well as their voices, and they go up and down on their toes and heels. Then [there are] some definite remarks about what the hymns really mean.

After singing, Mrs. Etter said, "Now we will have some definite testimonies from those whom God has blessed lately, but before doing so, everybody who knows their names are written in heaven (not on the church register), stand up on your feet." Hundreds stand up. "Now then, everybody who has been healed by Jesus raise your hand"; again they go up. "Now then, everybody who has been baptized with the

Holy Ghost and He has spoken through you in other tongues or a tongue, put your hands up." And again, hundreds raise their hands.

Then, after a few inspiring remarks, we all sit down or stand perfectly still for a few minutes, and she says, "Now let's hear what the Lord has done for some of you".

Then some wonderful soul-stirring testimonies are given. This morning it was wonderful how the power of God swept over the place from time to time, as dear ones, full of the joy of the Lord, spake out of full hearts of what Jesus had done for them. It thrills me as I write it, and the love of Jesus courses through every part of my being. Glory! Glory! Oh, glory to our Jesus; everything in me tells me He is coming so soon, as one African said recently in his broken English, "Jesus is plenty near." This is what I saw in the meeting today. A dear woman, born deaf and dumb, fifty-four years of age, so drunk with the power and love of the Spirit of God that she could not stand straight, and her whole being shaking, and her tongue and lips and mouth moving at the control of the Spirit, and her face radiant as she praised God.

Another man who had been healed of an awful incurable disease called pellagria[1] (a form of leprosy), praising and magnifying God with his body perfectly healed and as he gave his testimony and extolled Jesus, the power fell all over the meeting and Jesus had such a good time with many of us. Hallelujah!

A boy, one arm broken, the other paralyzed, both healed at once, was there singing in the choir.

A poor consumptive man, who had traveled three thousand miles to get to Dallas, gave a beautiful testimony as to the power of God.

An architect from New York gave a marvelous testimony as to his conversion, baptism, and healing. Others gave visions they had had, and others praised and sang in the new tongue, and Jesus had all the glory. Then Mrs. Etter got up to give a talk to the saints, which lasted an hour or more, then an appeal to all those who wanted more of God to tarry, and we got home at 2:30. One thing strikes

[1] "pellagria"—a misspelling of "pellagra," a chronic disease caused by a deficiency of nicotinic acid in the diet and characterized by gastrointestinal disturbances, skin eruptions, and mental disorders *(Webster's N. W.,* 1997).

us here, that when the meeting really begins, there is no prayer; they have it before and after, but no time of waiting during the evangelistic part of the service, and the interest of the sinner is held all the time, and numbers flock to the front at the close of the address, and at every meeting something definite is done. Everybody expects to see God work and of course He answers their expectations. Jesus is the one theme and so many are running over with the blessing He has given them that they love to praise Him.

These are very wonderful days to us all, as we really see with our eyes that the greater works are being done. One case Mrs. Etter told us of was more wonderful than any story in the Bible.

A little boy was brought to one of her meetings deaf, dumb, blind, and insane. God healed him completely, and today he is a bright, intelligent child, and a mind able to comprehend; and [he] can learn also.

I would advise everybody to buy her book which gives the story of her life; it is the most wonderful I have ever read and is all true.

Mrs. Etter is sixty-eight years old, has hardly a grey hair, is nimble on her feet, and a very lovely, humble woman, rarely speaks of herself, is full of power and of faith and the Holy Spirit, an intensely practical woman, and full of the Word of God. Mr. Etter is at every meeting but rarely speaks. She never visits anyone or sees anyone outside the meetings for healing as her time is taken up with correspondence and doing her own work while in apartments.

We are busy each day helping at the meetings and doing a little visiting among the dear ones who come to be healed and encouraging those who are being tested, etc., and the days are flying by, and we are expecting to meet Jesus any day.

Oh! If I could only tell Him as I know Him. He gets more wonderful every day, and the last two days have been the best of all as He has revealed His love to me.

We pray for you all and love you all; tell them God has no favorites, and they with us can have all God is giving away these days to all who will take.

I hope you will understand this letter, but I am so full of glory it is difficult to write. His name is Wonderful!

Glory! Glory! Glory! "He is altogether lovely."

"O come let us adore Him."

September 7, 1912

The Dallas Daily Times Herald (TX)

Acts of the Holy Ghost in Dallas

Continues

very night at the Woodworth-Etter meetings, God continues to display His power, bearing witness to the preaching of the Gospel "both with signs and wonders, and with divers miracles, and gifts of the Holy Ghost" (Hebrews 2:4).

Hundreds in Dallas and all over Texas and many other states have already been healed in this meeting of all manner of diseases and afflictions by the power of God in answer to "the prayer of faith." Many have been brought over one thousand miles and have been wonderfully saved and healed. The lame, the blind, many deaf and dumb, the palsied, the paralytics, consumptives, those suffering with cancers, tumors, fistulas, pellagra, operations, many with epilepsy, and invalids for years are praising God for healing for soul and body.

Perhaps never before was there such a scene as that witnessed by the great audience Monday night when three deaf and dumb mutes, 54, 34, and 17 years old, all strangers to each other, hugged, kissed, wept, shouted, and praised God for perhaps twenty minutes because He had opened all their ears, gave them their voices, and saved their souls. Sinners look on and weep and make their way to the altar. Sunday, God came in slaying power and twenty-one, like Saul, were struck down by the power of God and lay from one to eleven hours. They had wonderful visions of heaven and of Jesus and all got up with shining faces, filled with the love of God. The tent looked like a battlefield for "the slain of the Lord were many."

This power has continued all the week, and sinners have been struck down in their homes several miles from the tent. Hundreds in Dallas have been filled with the Holy Ghost as at Pentecost. Perhaps in no other place in the world is God so wonderfully displaying His power at the present time.

The meetings will continue indefinitely.

Come and see the wonderful works of God. Tent corner Perry and Fletcher, one block east of Coliseum.

—F. F. BOSWORTH

[1] Isaiah 66:16, paraphrased.

September 9, 1912

Triumphs of Faith

Miracles in Texas

The following letter was written by Brother Fred Bosworth to his brother, but knowing our deep interest in the marvelous meetings which are now being held in Dallas, Texas, he sent us a copy of this letter. We are glad to pass it on to our readers. Praise God for His mighty working in these last days!—EDITOR.[1]

I am sending you under separate cover a picture of the crowd in and around the tent. This was taken at night by artificial light and is not very plain, but it will give you a little idea of the immense crowds that gather to hear the Gospel and to see the works of God. This picture does not show a third of the crowd. On the end of the tent, they stood clear across the street, and twelve hundred who were sitting are all hid by those who stood in front of the camera. The meetings are increasing in interest and power, and people are coming from many states. A man got here yesterday morning from Minneapolis, Minn., on purpose to attend this meeting. Another from the Pacific Coast, some from Illinois, Michigan, and other states. Many drive forty and fifty miles and they were there yesterday from Galveston, Houston, and many other towns in Texas.

[1] Carrie Judd Montgomery.

On August 12th, three men brought a man dying with consumption and fistula two hundred miles in a baggage car on a cot. He came from Mercury, Texas, and looked like a dead man when they carried him into the tent on the cot in the very last stages of tuberculosis and nothing much but bones. When prayed for, the power came, and he jumped from the cot and ran up and down before the people praising God. He returned home and is gaining four pounds a week, and the fistula[2] was healed over the next morning and never had to be dressed again. The country was stirred and about twenty-five more have come from that vicinity.

Night before last a delegation from that county came with two deaf and dumb mutes. One was thirty-four years old and the other a beautiful looking young lady of seventeen years. God opened the ears of both. The young lady has attended the Deaf and Dumb Institute at Atlanta for the past seven years. She was saved and healed at the same time and is very happy. They were both in our home this morning and I played on the organ for them. Many others have been healed of deafness. Yesterday was the most wonderful day I ever saw in this work. God came with the melting and slaying power. Twenty-one like Paul were struck down by the power of God and lay from one to ten hours. They had wonderful visions of heaven and of Jesus and all came out with shining faces and filled with the love of God. Twelve of them received the Holy Spirit and spoke in tongues for the first time. The people said they never saw such power displayed. It looked like a battlefield to see them fall and lay as dead. God said, "The slain of the Lord shall be many."[3] Sinners look on and weep as they see the wonderful works of God.

Saturday night a boy fourteen years old was brought forty miles in a wagon. He had a paralyzed leg; could not raise his foot off the ground but had to push it along as you have seen paralyzed people walk. God instantly healed him and he could raise his leg and foot just as perfectly as I can. He was brought from Wiley, Texas. Some of the worst cases of epilepsy have been healed in the last three

[2] "fistula"—an abnormal passage from an abscess, cavity, or hollow organ to the skin or to another abscess, cavity, or organ.

[3] Isaiah 66:16.

weeks. One epileptic was brought over one hundred miles from Bells, Texas. She has had these fits nearly all her life. She has had as many as forty-two in twenty-four hours and would be almost dead for days—had one or more nearly every day. God's power struck her the very moment she knelt at the altar, and she was delivered and filled with the glory of God; and I wish you could see her face shine. She has been on fire for God ever since. Her girl was cross-eyed, both eyes turning in toward her nose. God instantly straightened her eyes.

A woman seventy-five years old, suffering from rheumatism twenty years, was brought 250 miles and was healed in the first service. She came through the healing of the consumptive above referred to.

A boy totally deaf from birth was brought by his father from Mattingburg, Texas. God healed him perfectly, and his parents have written to us that his hearing is perfect and he is learning to talk. A woman from Palmer, Texas, was healed of pellagra and filled with the Spirit at the same time. She was given up by the physicians. She is still here in the meeting and is well. A man from Blue Ridge, Texas, sixty miles from Dallas, had suffered ten years with a cancer all over one side of his face and neck, suffered so he had to be taken from the meeting, could not talk on account of the awful suffering from moving his jaw. When Sister Etter prayed for him, the power came and he was healed. The pain and all the burning and stiffness left instantly and he could turn his head in any direction without any pain. He got up on the altar and preached to the people. His friends told me yesterday that the cancer was healing up and he is getting well. A minister's daughter was brought by her father from Austin, Texas, suffering with fistula, could hardly stand the pain. She was saved and healed and has returned to Austin. One old lady from Streetman, Texas, with rheumatism all over her body for twenty years was instantly healed about two weeks ago and her niece testified yesterday she was well.

An invalid woman was carried into the tent from Elim, Texas. She had rheumatism all over her body for four years, was instantly healed, walked and leaped and praised God, was back again yesterday and testified.

One fifteen-year-old boy with his right arm paralyzed ever since he was one year old was instantly healed and is in the meeting every night. Can use his arm perfectly and for the first time he can remember, he raises his hand straight over his head. An old lady living in Dallas, with rheumatism for eight years, a great sufferer, seventy-four years old, was healed the other night.

Mrs. Hess, living in Dallas, a Catholic lady, with scrofula eighteen years, also [a] running sore on her limb, totally deaf in one ear and the other very poor, was healed of all these things. The sore and scrofula have completely disappeared. She was struck down by the power of God and had a vision of the marriage supper, was baptized in the Spirit, and is in the meeting every night with a shining face. Night before last a Catholic lady came into the meeting for the first time. She was deaf in both ears and could not hear a sound as the choir sang. She was instantly healed and could hear an ordinary conversation. Saturday night a lady was brought from Beaumont, Texas, dying with tumor. The doctors said she could not live forty-eight hours. She was instantly saved, healed, and baptized in the Spirit and leaped and praised God before the people. Sinners look on and weep and then make their way to the altar.

Pages like this could be written, but I have not the time. I am receiving many letters from all over the United States and Canada inquiring about the meeting. The best citizens in Dallas are cooperating in the meeting. They say they never saw anything like it. We expect to begin to build a large tabernacle one hundred by one hundred fifty feet this week. The lumber firms are going to give the lumber. This will be built in sight of six car lines. We are expecting great things during the coming weeks. . . .

There is so much to write that I hardly know where to stop. It is impossible to describe the wonderful works of God. They want to be seen and experienced to be appreciated. Sometimes there are a hundred seekers at the altar at one time. Give my love to all inquiring friends.

—YOUR BROTHER,

F. F. BOSWORTH

Maria Woodworth-Etter stands on the right with friends and associates in a photo taken around 1920. August Feick, her associate pastor, is sitting on the car.

P.S. I did not get your letter off last night, so will add a little. I said that Sunday was the most wonderful day I had ever seen. I now want to say that last night was still more wonderful. No tongue or pen could describe that meeting. Three deaf and dumb mutes, fifty-four, thirty-four, and seventeen years old, all strangers to each other, hugged, kissed, wept, and shouted for about a half hour because God had opened all their ears and gave them their voices and saved them all. The great audience looked on and wept, and as many as could crowd into the vacant space at the front of the tent sought God for salvation, healing, and the baptism. Many were struck down by the power of God and had wonderful visions of Jesus, and many received the baptism in the Holy Ghost as at Pentecost. Some are stricken down in their homes. It surely looks like a battlefield to see the slain of the Lord lying in the tent. I wish you could see how those deaf and dumb mutes looked at the choir, making signs to each other that they enjoyed the singing and the instruments. The delegation that came with the deaf and dumb mutes returned with them this morning, saying that they were going to bring another mute and perhaps other afflicted ones. A preacher last night, that came up with them, got up and told how he had known the deaf and dumb young lady from birth and loved her as his own daughter. It was wonderful how the power of God fell on the audience during the services last night.

It was impossible for anyone to doubt. We expect the power to increase more and more as the people are taught and see the displays of God's power. I never heard such preaching as that done by Sister [Etter] under anointings of the Spirit.

November, 1912

Triumphs of Faith

The Meetings in Dallas, Texas

The following is an extract from a letter received from our dear Mrs. Nuzum, who has for several weeks been attending the meetings in Dallas, Tex., held by Mrs. Etter and by Mr. Bosworth. She adds in another letter just at hand that she has received great personal blessing in these meetings, and she hopes to return to her missionary work in Mexico with a new enduement of power.

> Dallas, Texas.
>
> The meetings are marvelous, cannot describe them. They are full of power and the presence of God. Persons get messages in tongues from God and others interpret; oh, such precious loving messages! Jesus is seen walking in the midst; angels are seen; firelights are seen by saints and sinners. Very little preaching; volumes of praise, much prayer, and some testimony. People here from twenty states, letters from over the ocean. I have never seen so much simplicity, love, and unity. Nobody looks at others but all look to Jesus. Meetings sometimes last all day. Mrs. Etter and Mr. Bosworth are so simple. It is sweet to be among these saints. God spoke through Brother Miers[1] in tones of thunder and a sister interpreted it as "Woe to the rejectors of God." About fifty were baptized and spoke in tongues last week. Mrs. Etter is strong in ignoring all Satan does and lauding Jesus.
>
> —C. Nuzum

[1] "Miers"—possible misspelling of H. C. Mears' last name, who appears in the next article.

December, 1912

Triumphs of Faith

The Mighty Power of God at Dallas, Texas

BY THE EDITOR[1]

y husband and myself are just leaving Dallas, Texas, after a most interesting time at the meetings which are being held here in this city at the large tabernacle (recently built to take the place of the tent) on Grand and Fourth Avenues. This Pentecostal mission is in [the] charge of Mr. F. Bosworth and Mr. Birdsall, but Mrs. Etter has been assisting them for about three months and will remain until the first of the year, when she goes to San Antonio, Texas, for a series of meetings. Mrs. Etter is an old-time friend of ours. When we first knew her, she was in the midst of a very remarkable revival work on the Pacific Coast, where many thousands were saved and many were healed. We were delighted to meet each other again, after the lapse of many years. She extended to us a most loving welcome and gave us seats on the platform by her side.

We have already published reports of these Dallas meetings, which we knew were reliable, but it has been a joy to attend them for ourselves and to witness the mighty power of God convicting and converting sinners, healing sick bodies, and baptizing saints with the Holy Ghost. We could only make it possible to remain for a few days, but in that length of time we saw much that we shall never forget. As we entered the tabernacle on Saturday evening, we saw a crowd of rejoicing ones at the front, and we learned later that a deaf and dumb man, about sixty years of age, had just been instantly healed by the power of God through Mrs. Etter's command of faith, as she bade the deaf and dumb demons to depart in Jesus' name. Another man who had been healed of deafness was pointed out to us; and as he was singing a hymn in unison with the others with his eyes closed, it was evident how well he could hear.

[1] Carrie Judd Montgomery

We saw one lady who had been stone deaf; but after prayer was offered, the ears, which had been dead, began to have life in them and she could hear loud sounds near her. Some people are healed at once and others gradually, but Mrs. Etter feels that if they have been receptive, as she has prayed "the prayer of faith" for them, that they have only to hold on in faith and continue to praise God on the authority of His Word and the symptoms will surely pass away. There really are so many healings day by day that only the more remarkable ones attract much attention. Mrs. Etter's greatest concern is to have people "get right with God" in their souls and then she tells them they will be healed.

When they come to her with more desire for physical healing than for the spiritual healing, she refuses to pray for the healing of their bodies until their souls come into right relations with God. This undoubtedly is one great reason for her success, and another reason is that she believes in working for the unifying of all the members of the body of Christ, and therefore, she does not preach mere theories, but holds up a living Christ, receiving all who are honest in their hearts and purposes toward Him, even if they do not yet see the truth just as she teaches it. She also avoids laying stress upon certain words or expressions with which the enemy is trying to cause divisions in the body of Christ. Therefore there is no contention or strife in these meetings, but love and unity. Dear Brother Bosworth and Brother Birdsall are of the same mind with Mrs. Etter in these things, and their precious Pentecostal work will go on even when Mrs. Etter goes elsewhere.

It is interesting to note that Mrs. Etter teaches healing in the atonement[2] (in the same way that we were taught by the Holy Spirit Himself many years ago). She also encourages all the saints to press on for more power from God to do the miraculous works which Jesus said believers should do in His name.

Mrs. Etter is one that speaks with no uncertain sound, and we have never seen anyone else rebuke demons and disease with such heaven-sent authority and power. It brought a new wave of spiritual

[2] "healing in the atonement"—the belief that physical healing, in addition to spiritual healing, for all believers occurred when Christ died for sin and that it is a finished work that the believer receives by faith.

joy to our own heart to hear the way in which these "cruel demons" were ordered to depart. Perhaps it is needless to say here that when people get their eyes on the instrument that God uses, instead of upon Himself, they do not receive healing; while, on the other hand, those whose gaze of faith is upon the Savior alone often receive healing through the application in faith of the anointed handkerchiefs or tracts sent out from these meetings. Some periodicals have ridiculed these means of reaching the sick, but God is wonderfully using them just the same, and as He wrought "special miracles" by the hands of Paul (see Acts 19:11-12), He seems to be doing the same now through those who trust Him, for so many of God's children are sick everywhere that the need is most urgent; and the unbelief is so great that often in isolated places these suffering saints cannot get one near at hand to offer for them the "prayer of faith."

Mrs. Etter preaches the Gospel in great simplicity and power, backing up all her remarks by quotations from the Word of God. The altar services are very remarkable, as saints and sinners gather around in deep earnestness, seeking God for their individual needs. The power of God falls upon them, and it is wonderful to note the changes that come over the faces of the seeking ones as the light dawns upon their souls. The power of God often prostrates them and even little children are seen "under the power," apparently unconscious to all but God and with their little faces shining like angels.

There seemed to be people present from many different states in the union, but the attendance is not as great as it has been, owing to cold and rainy weather at this time of year. On Sunday nights, however, the large tabernacle is crowded to its fullest capacity.

The night we left there were three remarkable cases of healing, one of goiter, one of cancer, and one of deafness. The lady with goiter was suffering very much with the choking or suffocating sensation occasioned by it. Mrs. Etter commanded the enemy to depart in Jesus' name and soon we saw her turning her head freely from side to side, while the swelling seemed mostly, if not entirely, gone. The pain and swelling of the man's cancer were also taken away in a few minutes.

It is stated by Pastor Bosworth that since Mrs. Etter came to assist him, about three hundred and fifty have received the Pentecostal baptism with the sign of speaking with "new tongues."

There is usually a great solemnity in the meetings and the faces of the people are very earnest. With the exception of the altar service, where many are often praising or praying at once, the meetings are conducted very quietly. All tendency to wildfire or fanaticism is entirely discountenanced.

Perhaps the explanation for the solemnity of these meetings is that there is continual teaching about the soon coming of the Lord for His bride and exhortations to get ready. One dear brother, Rev. H. C. Mears, who has preached the Gospel for over forty years, came to fight the work but became convinced that it was of God. He received the baptism of the Holy Spirit with the sign of tongues, and afterwards God gave him the most wonderful visions of heaven and of what the Lord is preparing for His people and also visions of the coming of the Lord. It was most inspiring to listen to the revelations of the coming of the Lord which have been vouchsafed to this dear brother. His spirit is so loving and gentle that he reminded us of what the Lord Jesus said about Nathaniel, "Behold an Israelite indeed, in whom is no guile!"[3]

[3] John 1:47

March, 1913

Triumphs of Faith

Mrs. Etter's Meetings in Oakland

BY THE EDITOR CARRIE JUDD MONTGOMERY

e had the privilege of attending all of Mrs. Etter's meetings in Oakland, during her six-days' stay in this city. The meetings were held in Castle Hall, 387 Twelfth Street, a comfortable, well-ventilated hall, seating several hundred. The services were well attended. Mrs. Etter gave Bible addresses on the subjects of the new birth, a victorious life in Christ, the double cure or healing for soul and body, the coming of the Lord, and kindred topics. Often for more than an hour at a time she gave teaching from the Word of God, and the power of God would so hold the audience from beginning to end that scarcely a person would leave before the close.

The altar services were remarkable, large numbers crowding forward for spiritual blessing and healing of the body. So many desired healing that it was impossible for Mrs. Etter to pray personally with each one, but she laid her hands on a large number at nearly every altar service and prayed the prayer of faith for them. Many of these seemed very ill and we often noticed a great change in their outward appearance after prayer had been offered for them. We also heard many say that they had been wonderfully relieved from suffering. It was quite marvelous at times to note the different expression on the face, as the light of God came into the soul through some teaching given at the moment by Mrs. Etter. Quite a number of these suffering came from a distance, returning home after prayer had been offered, and so we did not see these again.

We conversed with a young woman who was instantly healed of deafness. She said she had been deaf for fifteen years and very deaf for three years. She heard me as I conversed with her in an ordinary tone, and she seemed very happy and full of praise. Mrs. Etter had commanded the deaf demons to come out of her ears in the name of Jesus. A man whom we knew was healed of deafness with which he had been afflicted for more than fifty years. He thought I must be shouting at him when I talked in an ordinary tone. He was delighted that he could hear people conversing as he passed them on the street. One little boy who was afflicted with a cleft palate and could not talk intelligibly was prayed with and could talk clearly afterwards, greatly to his delight.

There were many other deaf workers at the altar, and the sick ones who could not get near Mrs. Etter were often prayed with by these brothers and sisters, and many testified that they were healed. The power of God was so manifest in the altar services that it seemed very easy to lead souls to Christ and to see them receive Him in great simplicity. Others received the Pentecostal baptism. The young daughter of a friend of ours, sixteen years old, was converted during the meetings and received the baptism of the Holy Spirit in one of the missions after the meetings had closed. Sometimes a wonderful wave of praise and joy would strike the audience, and many faces would shine with heavenly rapture. On one occasion, there was a marvelous heavenly anthem in which many voices joined. One lady who is herself quite a musician, who had never heard anything of the kind, said afterwards to me with surprise and pleasure: "I think some angels must have been helping."

Since I began to write this article, a lady (almost a stranger to me) said over the phone: "I never expect to be as near heaven again while on earth as I was in those meetings." And then she added about Mrs. Etter, "How wonderful she was in always pointing us to Jesus and never letting anyone get their eyes upon her." Yes, praise God that was true. She begged the Christians to hold her up in prayer while she preached.

I believe that people received in those meetings what they came for, and if they came to criticize (and I fear there were some of those even among God's children) and they stayed coldly at the back and did not come up to even try to help the many seekers at the altar, then I do not wonder that they went out of those meetings with less blessing than when they came in.

Mr. and Mrs. Etter went from Oakland to San Jose, and they are there at this writing. She expected to remain there until April 1st, and perhaps longer. We were not successful in getting complete notes of Mrs. Etter's addresses, so we are printing one of her sermons from her new book, *Acts of the Holy Ghost.*

February 20, 1913

Word and Witness (Malvern, AR)

God Visiting San Antonio With Mighty Power

It has pleased our heavenly Father to grant us a gracious time of refreshing in this city during the past six weeks. Sister Etter has preached the old-time Gospel, not with enticing words of man's wisdom, but in the power and demonstration of the Spirit. She has utterly ignored the "creeds, theories, and dogmas of men," and held high "The Bloodstained Banner of King Emmanuel," pointing to the bleeding victim of Golgotha as *the only hope of the race.*[1]

From the first, God set His seal on her work, "confirming the word with signs and wonders in the name of Jesus."[2] Sinners have been gloriously saved, the sick have been healed, the deaf have received hearing, the lame have been made to walk, and many have received the gift of the Holy Ghost, speaking with tongues as the Spirit gave them utterance.

Some Healing Miracles

A Spanish lady, a Catholic, seventy-nine years of age, all crippled up with paralysis, came into the meeting, was saved, healed, and filled with the glory of God, her face shining like an angel as she stood on the altar with uplifted hands praising God for saving her soul and healing her body. A man eighty years old, his form all bent with rheumatism for years, a great sinner and a Catholic, came into the meeting, heard the singing, saw the shining faces, felt the mighty power of God, fell down at the altar under awful conviction, got saved and healed, threw down his stick, and ran up and down the aisle shouting the praises of God. Three deaf mutes came into the meeting, came to the altar, were converted; and two of them declared they could hear the saints praising God, and their tongues were loosed to such a degree that they could say, "glory" and "praise God" with a loud voice.

[1] Source of two quotations unknown.

[2] See Mark 16:20.

Another man came into town, heard about the meeting, came out, heard, saw, and felt the mighty power of God; had faith to be healed, came to the altar dragging a leg that had been stiff for twelve years. Sister Etter prayed for him, commanding him [to] stretch out the lame limb in Jesus' name, and like the lame man at "the Beautiful gate," he instantly obeyed, "leaping up,"[3] hopping, and skipping like a school boy. He climbed upon the altar, clapping his hands, shouting, "I'm healed, I'm healed." Leaping down he ran through the aisle giving glory to God before all the people. One aged man, a precious saint of God, living in this city, who for years has been an invalid, suffering from a fall, unable to come to the meeting, but was brought in a buggy, was prayed for and God touched him. Now, using his own terms, he "can walk like a man again."

Many miracles have been performed in Jesus' name. People have been healed of cancer, tumor, catarrh, rheumatism, diabetes, consumption, sore eyes, and eating sores. Lame limbs have been made whole and deaf ears have been opened. One lady, dying from all appearances with heart failure, was snatched from the very jaws of death. Her form was cold and limp, her eyes glassy, and the death damp stood on her brow. She had bidden all good-bye and was sinking fast when Sister Etter reached her. But, glory be to God, when our sister rebuked "the grim monster," commanding him to loose his grip and calling to the departing one to come back, she rallied and came forth in the strength of Israel's God. Now more than a week she has been in the meeting, shouting the praises of God.

Other Signs and Wonders

Beside the mighty miracles of healing, God has shown many other signs of His mighty presence and the soon coming of the Lord. In many ways the Holy Ghost has signified that we were near the end. Sometimes during the preaching, God's power would settle down on the saints till some were melted to tears, others saw wonderful visions of His coming glory. Sometimes "the handmaiden of the Lord" was held like a statue, unable to utter a word. Other times

[3] See Acts 3:6-11.

she stood weeping over the people, while the power of God swept over all like the tide of the great ocean.

Around the altar souls saw visions of Him who is walking today among the "candlesticks, holding the stars in His right hand." Numbers seemed to hear that voice as the sounding of "great waters" and like John "fell at his feet as dead."[4] Oh glory! The unsaved, beholding the shining faces of those lying as dead men in the presence of God, wept and said, "These are strange things."

Many saw visions of Jesus coming in the clouds of heaven with power and great glory. Sometimes the Spirit would move like the gentle breeze, fanning every soul with the breath of heaven, then send torrents of weeping over the lost till it seemed to some that the very shades of the dark "tribulation" cloud was casting a shadow all around us. One morning while the Spirit was dealing with the saints in a marvelous way, suddenly a sister began to speak in a tongue unknown to anyone present but seemed to be calling us forth to battle. At this same time, several in the Spirit were hearing the "tramp, tramp" of a mighty army, and two saw the mighty armies of heaven riding forth on white horses. Then the lady who had been speaking in tongues began giving a shout of victory—and victory was felt in many hearts—which was taken up by the saints, while the power and Spirit of God settled down upon us until it seemed the whole place was lighted up with the glory and presence of God. The Spirit has been revealing in many ways that God is sifting out a people from among all the factions, tribes, and kindreds of earth whom He will send forth in love, clothed with power and might to do exploits and wonders in the name of Jesus, giving to the household of faith their portion in this God's due season.

Sister Etter left us February 17th to hold meetings in San Jose, Cal., Mar. 1 to April 14, in Los Angeles, April 15th to May 15th. Then she goes to Mount Moriah, Conn., for another camp meeting June 1, 1913. Saints join us in prayer for these meetings. God is wonderfully using our sister in gathering together the saints in unity, shedding forth the mighty truths of the Pentecostal baptism, showing

[4] See Revelation 1:10-17.

forth the mighty power of God in this end of the age, helping the bride to make herself ready for the coming of the Bridegroom. "Behold he cometh."[5] Arouse, ye sleeping virgins, the day draweth near; yea, it hasteth greatly. The Bridegroom is at the door.[6]

YOURS LOOKING FOR THE RAPTURE,

FRED LOHMANN

3323 S. FLORES ST.

SAN ANTONIO, TEXAS

P. S. Our meetings will continue in San Antonio, for some time at least, in the same building. M. M. Pinson will assist us.

The new book by Mrs. Etter called *Acts of the Holy Ghost* is meeting with favor everywhere. One thousand have gone out and the second one thousand has been ordered from the press. $1.65 postpaid anywhere in the world. Send all orders to E. N. Bell, Malvern, Ark.

[5] Revelation 1:7.

[6] See Matthew 25:88-13.

February 20, 1913

Word and Witness (Malvern, AR)

Mrs. Etter to San Jose, Cal., March 1, 1913

rs. Woodworth-Etter, who has been in Dallas and San Antonio, is to begin meetings in San Jose, Cal., on March 1 and continue, the Lord willing, for six weeks. She is then to go to Los Angeles on April 15th for one month.

The meeting at Dallas is going on with God's blessings upon it. Also at San Antonio the meetings are to continue.

For further information about the San Jose meeting, address Pastor W. E. Moody, 545 S. 11th St., San Jose, Calif. Will all the saints pray for this meeting?

March 20, 1913

Word and Witness (Malvern, AR)

God Doing Wonders at San Jose, Cal., in Etter Meetings

San Jose is admitted to be a hard field, and we believe God sent Sister Etter here in direct answer to the prayers of His saints who have been calling on God for a mighty visitation on this most wicked city. While pitching the battle in full confidence in the God of victories, still we all felt a mighty conflict was before us. Sure enough, for the first few days it seemed all the hosts of hell were arrayed against us, but as in the name of God we continued to shout for victory, the walls began to tumble and the power and glory of God settled down upon us. The Lord has stretched forth His hand to save, heal, and to do wonders through the name of Jesus. The signs are following the preaching of the Word.

Before the meeting began and before Sister Etter arrived, God began to heal in answer to her prayers. A sister here, in bed suffering with kidneys, heart, and liver troubles, indigestion and tumors, testified she wrote for an anointed handkerchief as in Acts 19:12 and that the moment the handkerchief touched her body, she was instantly healed of all her diseases and the same night walked out to the mission. The Spirit fell on her in the meeting, and the same night she was baptized and spoke with other tongues as in Acts 2:4. Since Sister Etter came, this same sister, in a vision, saw above the platform a group of angels, each with a trumpet in his hand ready to sound.

Another sister was healed of muscular rheumatism and testifies she is now able to walk without difficulty twenty-seven blocks to and from the meetings.

A brother deaf in one ear and suffering with liver and kidney troubles was instantly healed. His wife, who suffered so severely for a long time with internal troubles that life was a burden to her, was wonderfully healed and now feels the quickening life of Jesus in her mortal body as promised in Romans 8:12.[1] While at home she had a vision of Jesus in His glory, as in Revelation 1:12-17.

[1] The reference should be Romans 8:11.

One old man testified that when Sister Etter laid hands on him in Jesus' name, his [missing line] healing power of God go throughout his body like electric waves and that he was at the same moment healed of catarrh in the head and stomach and of liver trouble. He also had a vision of Jesus standing with wounded side.

One night a sister brought to meeting in a wheelchair, when commanded in the mighty name of Jesus to rise and walk, to the astonishment of the spectators [?] who had disbelieved, rose and walked up and down the [platform?].

Several Roman Catholics have been healed and saved.

A number have been slain under the mighty power of God. At one morning meeting the glory cloud swept down upon us from heaven. Many were prostrated, some wept, and others shouted for joy and some wonderful messages were given in tongues with the interpretation.

One man who came in from the country to the meeting was healed of chronic stomach trouble of many years standing, and in the same service both his boys were saved. Another testified to being healed of rupture[2] he had had for years.

While slain under the power of God, a sister had a vision of a great army of horsemen rushing to battle; and a brother saw and heard the tramp, tramp, tramp of mighty armies marching to battle, and this was followed by a great earthquake which shook the whole earth. Truly, as Jesus promised, the Spirit is showing the saints in these last days things soon to come.

The meeting is just getting under headway. Already God has confounded the doubting and unbelieving by healing before their eyes and by giving visible manifestations of His power and glory.

The tide is rising higher and higher, and we are looking for and praising God for the still greater things we believe are coming during the next few weeks to this beautiful California city. On April 15th Sister Etter goes to Los Angeles.

—W. E. MOODY

PASTOR

[2] "rupture"—possibly a hernia.

August 19, 1913

Unknown Source

Woman "Healer" Is Arrested at Revival Service

Mrs. M. B. Woodworth-Etter Taken on Charge of False Pretence (*sic*)

SOUTH FRAMINGHAM, AUG. 18—

he revival meeting conducted at Mount Wait[1] this afternoon by Mrs. M. B. Woodworth-Etter was interrupted when Chief of Police William M. Holbrook arose from the audience in the middle of the session and, advancing to the pulpit, arrested Mrs. Woodworth-Etter.

Within the last week great numbers of sick and crippled have been attracted to Mount Wait by alleged assertions by Mrs. Etter that she could cure all manner of disease through hypnotism inspired by reading of the Bible. In the district court tomorrow morning Chief Holbrook will charge Mrs. Etter with obtaining one hundred dollars by misrepresentation and false pretences (*sic*).

Mrs. Woodworth-Etter came to town three weeks ago. She leased the land at Mount Wait owned by the New England Chautaqua Association and began holding meetings. Within a few days her fame spread to such an extent that hundreds were attracted to the gatherings—persons coming from far distant towns.

Day after day those who attended her services watched her seeming miracles. Sometimes more than fifty advanced to the pulpit from which she spoke, held converse with her, and then passed into a stage of unconsciousness. After awakening they told of experiences while under the influence of the woman and asserted their belief that their diseases had been wiped away.

Hundreds of converts were gathered to her standard and were willing to rally to her support when skeptics doubted the truth of the wonders performed before them.

This is probably from the *Boston Herald*.

[1] "Mount Wait"—This article spells the name of the city as two words. Subsequent articles print the name as one word. The name is as found in the originals.

Certain of the doubting ones made known their skepticism to Chief of Police Holbrook, and this afternoon he interrupted the proceedings and notified Mrs. Woodworth-Etter that she was under arrest. She submitted without the slightest argument, and her followers made no attempt to prevent the chief from taking her.

She will be arraigned before Judge W. A. Kingsbury in the district court tomorrow.

August 20, 1913

Word and Witness (Malvern, AR)

God's Deeds of Mercy and Power in Chicago

he meetings here are progressing nicely. Among those healed was a woman who had been blind fifteen years and had several children whom she had never seen. She was perfectly healed, so she could see as good as ever.

A man who was paralyzed and whose joints were ossified was brought to the church in a chair. He had no use of his muscles at all, could not move his head or any of his limbs. His speech was almost gone and he had to be fed on liquid food with a spoon. When he was prayed for, he jumped up and ran out of the church, down the steps and a half block down the street. The next day he was back to testify to his healing and to glorify God. This man had been in this sickness eight years.

A young lady who was totally deaf in one ear, the drum being destroyed, and was almost deaf in the other ear, having also a terrible abscess behind one of her ears, was prayed for. She has been back several times and testified to her complete healing and the restoration of her hearing. She can hear a watch tick when placed to the ear that had the drum destroyed.

Perhaps fifty people were prayed for today, among whom was a girl who was totally blind in both eyes. One eyeball was very large and

This article refers to meetings which occurred before the Mountwait meetings and the arrest.

apparently bulged out, and the other one seemed as if the white and colored parts had run together. When she was prayed for and the Lord began to restore her sight, she became "excited" and jumped and screamed until she fell, and when she recovered herself and opened her eyes again and could see the light and distinguish the windows, she started in again and was almost guilty of disturbing public worship. But such scenes are so common in these meetings that we are not disturbed by them.

—F. A. Hale

S. D. Kinne Writes:

Several days ago a lady was brought to the platform in a big chair. She said she could not bear to be moved into the chair that others were being prayed for in. After prayer and some effort with her, which did not appear to be doing much good, Mrs. Etter, with authority in the name of Jesus, commanded her to rise and walk. She did so and was soon walking very well. She testifies in the meetings and goes about apparently as supple as others.

An old lady was afflicted with two cancerous or poisonous sores. One of these was near the size of a silver dollar located above the right temple in the edge of the hair, the other on her side near the heart. Several days after she was prayed for, neither of them was sore nor had run a particle, though they often run so badly as to fill several handkerchiefs at a time. The first night she went to bed forgetting to bandage her head as she always did, but there was no blood.

Monday morning at the beginning of the meeting, soon after they began singing, Mrs. Etter said to an old lady sitting on the front seat who had not walked without crutches for three years, having been hurt in a street car fall and afterwards fell again and broke the ligaments. Mrs. Etter said to her, "You can walk in Jesus' name." She said she could not, but again she was told she could. She made the attempt and was soon walking all over the church.

Sitting beside her was an old gentleman who said he had been crippled so he had to use a cane. Sixty years ago when a boy of ten, he had been crippled with rheumatism. She spoke to him and soon he was walking beautifully too.

A young lady soon got up and began walking and was beautifully healed who said she had been crippled for five years with a disease in her foot.

Then a young girl of ten who had been crippled for seven years was healed. Something had been broken in her knee. All four were walking around at the same time.

The Blessed Close

The attendance was large and increasing. Many Pentecost[al] ministers and workers were present. At two morning services Mrs. Etter, assisted by brethren, laid hands on more than one hundred ministers and workers for a deeper enduement and the reception of gifts of the Spirit. These were two of the most powerful services in the series. The imposition of hands was preceded by instructive teaching as to being sound and sensible and avoiding foolish and fanatical extremes and the preaching of hobbies and doctrines that tend to division. They were told to preach Christ and the resurrection. To leave such questions as forbidding to eat meats and abstinence from marriage alone. If you have faith that you ought not to eat meats, have it to thyself. Marriage is honorable. Do not be personal and single out this church or that lodge, but hold up Jesus and people will drop those things which are wrong, for the Spirit will show them. It was asserted we are not yet up to the fullness of the *former rain*, and that when the *latter rain* comes, it will far exceed anything we have seen. This was confirmed by powerful messages of prophetic interpretation. The plaintive notes of the dove were heard as a warning that the storm of wrath and the tribulation is soon to break on this poor sin-cursed earth. We were warned under the Spirit of prophecy to *awake* and seek for shelter from the storm.

I was told that there were many crooked and wrong spirits [that] came to the meeting. A brother said to his wife, "They are all here." But they were silent, chained down by the power of the Spirit. The croak of the frog and chatter of the raven could not join in the heavenly chorus and the notes of the dove.

In the last service of prayer for ministers and workers, about fifty were prayed for, most of whom were prostrated under the power of the Spirit. Some testified to having been very greatly helped and anointed. One of the best testimonies was the fact that numbers of ministers and workers were praying for the sick of all classes with gracious success. The numbers were far too many for one to pray for. Sometimes nearly two hundred were prayed for in a single service.

After having laid hands on as many as she could at this ministerial service, there were still perhaps one hundred and fifty waiting. She had them stand before the platform and requested the ministers to join with her, stretching their hands over the people while she prayed for them all together. She then requested some of the brethren to lay hands on the people. Most of those who were touched by the hand fell to the floor. It seemed like taking a sword and cutting them down, the power of God was so mighty upon us.

Every Pentecostal convention has its distinguishing features. The one thing that stood out most prominent in this one was this impartation of gifts of healings and faith for their exercise. This was accomplished through teaching, practical demonstration by example before the whole congregation, through prayer and laying on of hands. They were then put to work praying for the sick on the platform. As many as four or six groups of workers praying for as many sick ones at the same time. It is much to be able to do the mighty works by faith but a still more blessed ministry to succeed in stirring up the gifts in others and arousing them to battle. Many will, we feel sure, go forth from this meeting to cast out demons, heal the sick, and work the mighty works of the coming King.

There has been for some time a prophecy in the hearts of many of the more spiritual of God's saints that a greater and mightier revival than the world has yet seen is soon coming. May it not be that this has been a decided step in that direction? As each went his way to scatter the fire, hearts burned with a deeper love and worship of the King and with a stronger zeal and courage to press the battle with vigor and faith.

"And this gospel of the kingdom shall be preached in all the world for a witness unto all nations; and then shall the end come" (Matthew 24:14).

—Seeley D. Kinne

824 E. Monroe St.

Bloomington, Ill.

August 27, 1913

The Boston Globe (MA)

Aver[1] They Are Cured

One Threw Her Brace Away

HOLY ROLLERS FAIL TO HELP BLIND BOY

Hypnotism Practiced, Say Doctors at Trial

One Saw Pile of Money "Nearly a Foot High"

SOUTH FRAMINGHAM, AUG 26—

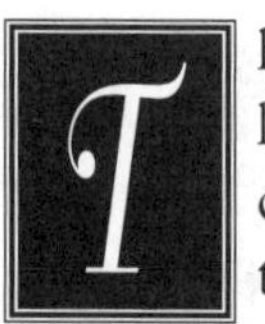

That a Miss McKinley, claimed to be a cousin of the martyred President, asserted that she had been healed of an infirmity after treatment from Mrs. M. B. Woodworth Ettor (*sic*) at Montwait campground in this town; that another young woman, attended by an "array of physicians," had come all the way from Pennsylvania for a cure at the hands of Sister Ettor (*sic*); and that a blind boy of Saxonville failed to get his sight restored, these were among the interesting bits of testimony in the South Middlesex District Court today before Judge W. A. Kingsbury.

Mrs. Ettor (*sic*) and Cyrus B. Fockler and Earl W. Clark, two of her staff, were arrested August 15 at Montwait by Chief of Police W. W. Holbrook on a charge of obtaining money under false pretenses, after complaint had been made that the colony that had leased Montwait for the month was making disturbances far into the night. The evangelists are known variously as "The Pentecostal Disciples of the Latter Reign," "The Pentecostal Society," "Christian Workers Union," and "Holy Rollers."

Told to Give His Mind to Them

The case came up for trial today after two continuances. M. E. Nash is attorney for the defendants and D. C. Ahearn for the prosecution. The courtroom was filled with Mrs. Ettor's (*sic*) followers and the doors were closed long before court opened.

Probably the most dramatic incident of the day occurred when Joseph Walton Tuttle, a boy of eighteen, who is totally blind, gave his testimony. Young Tuttle's home is in Saxonville. He has not had the use of his eyes since [1900?].

[1] "Aver"—to assert or allege to be true.

Tuttle said he attended five of the meetings at Montwait Campground, on August fifth, sixth, seventh, and ninth, attending two services on one of the days.

"I had heard a lot of talk of what had been accomplished there," said the blind witness, "and two of the members urged me to go, telling me it was not hypnotism. I went to the camp meeting the night of Aug. 6 and following instructions, brought a card which I had filled out. A foreigner, who said he had been cured of drunkenness, told me to kneel and pray and my turn would come. I did as I was bid. Someone else told me to give my mind up to them and not let reason get the better of me.

Shouted "Come Out, Devil"

"My turn did come. Mrs. Etter came over to me on the platform. Some men then rubbed my forehead, my eyes, my abdomen, and my legs—it was just like osteopathy. Then they told me to clap my hands. Someone else got close to my ear and shouted, 'Come out, devil, come out,' and 'Hallelujah.'

"Mrs. Etter was over me once. She said, 'Have faith,' and 'Can't you see?'"

"What happened to you?" counsel asked.

"Nothing special," was the answer of the blind witness.

Continuing, Tuttle said, "The treatment immediately stopped. I got up, was assisted down from the platform and told to come again. I was told also that I must have faith.

"I went again August 7, but I could not get a chance to go on the platform. Saturday night I went again, and they told me that I had better come up and study. I derived no benefit whatever."

Attorney Nash asked if the phrase "spiritual sight" was not used by the evangelist, but witness said "No." He said it was understood, however, that God did the healing: that was emphasized. He said also that there was no suggestion to him that he should contribute at collections. He thought that the people at Montwait believed thoroughly that his sight could be restored.

Woman Said She Was Cured

It was during the testimony of Fred L. Train of Montwait that reference was made to Miss McKinley as cousin of the president. Mr. Train testified that Miss McKinley appeared at the camp meeting with her side wired. She said she had not been able to walk for a long time. She was carried onto the platform by two men. According to [the] witness, Sister Etter then went through her "performances," and after this was over Miss McKinley arose and walked around the platform telling the believers that she was healed.

Mr. Train told of seeing one large collection made at a camp meeting. He said: "On my way home I came upon two men counting a big pile of bills and coins. There was a pile pretty nearly a foot high. It looked like a lot of money to me."

Asked whether Mrs. Etter had urged that money be given, [the] witness said he had heard her mention at meetings how people who were sick paid lots of money to physicians or to hospitals and also say that the camp-meeting expenses were heavy, but the collections were small.

"Did you ever hear Sister Etter say, 'Dig Down'?"

"It sounds familiar."

"Healed of Burns in Forty-five Minutes"

Since August 15, when the arrests occurred, [the] witness said that more emphasis has been laid on the fact that God did the healing. According to his account Mrs. Etter even asked in meeting, "Is there anybody here that I have cured?" There was no answer. When she asked, "How many has the Lord cured?" all the believers stood up in response.

I. S. Roberts of Nashville, Tenn., who has been at Montwait about a week, said he had heard of Mrs. Etter and her work when he was in California and also when he was in the South. He told of investigating while at Montwait and said a boy lying in the straw beside the platform—where those patients who have been treated and who are unconscious are laid—had told him that he was lying down in the straw simply because he was tired of standing up. He thought, however, that older people are really put under hypnotic influence.

Witness further testified: "Last Monday afternoon a cook at the campground had his arms and face badly burned. He went to Sister Etter and she laid her hands on him. The cook said that forty-five minutes thereafter he did not know he was burned. He went back to work and his arms and face were badly blistered from the heat of the kitchen. He said that he took that as a command from the Lord to get out of the kitchen. In the evening, at meeting, he testified to all but the part where the Lord had commanded him to get out."

Had Men Collect the Money

Chief of Police Holbrook told of the complaints made to him and the resulting arrests, saying that there had been many complaints from neighbors of noise late at night. He had talks with the campground people and they had agreed to close at 10 o'clock.

Describing the nature of the meetings, Chief Holbrook said: "Mrs. Etter conducted most of the time. There were singing and prayer. Then Mrs. Etter would call for testimony regarding cures. Different ones would stand up and say they had been cured of such and such a disease. One lady said that for six years she could not see, but through the work of Mrs. Etter, she now could see."

Asked to tell of collections at the meetings, the chief said that he had seen Mr. Fockler stand on the platform and lay the Bible down. Mrs. Etter then told the people to "come up for the Lord's good." They did not come up, the chief said, so Mrs. Etter had men pass through the audience to gather the money. Witness also declared that he had heard Mrs. Etter tell her flock that travel expenses were large and that she hoped the people would contribute freely.

Two nights ago the chief testified of a sick woman who was brought to South Framingham on a train from Pennsylvania. She had been in an accident and had injured her back, spine, and hip. The best doctors and hospitals could not help her. Ten days before coming she received Sister Etter's book.

Medical Examiner's Testimony

She had an array of doctors all the way from Pennsylvania to South Framingham, [the] witness said. When she reached here she could not go to Montwait for several hours. According to testimony,

Sister Etter took charge of her, and the woman asserted at the meeting that through the work of the Lord she had been able to throw her brace away and was as well as anyone there. The chief admitted that he did not investigate her story.

Dr. L. M. Palmer of Framingham, medical examiner, was a witness for the prosecution. He told of the nature of the camp meetings.

"The first time I went there," he testified, "I arrived at about 9 A.M. The speaker was nearly through with his sermon, the people were singing songs, very catchy songs, and they were not always in tune. Then some of the people walked up to the platform and took chairs. A woman and two men helped them to be seated.

"Then occurred what I call manipulations. The leader placed hands on the head and breast of the candidate and sometimes stroked his legs, shouting all the while. Then the patient raised his hands in the attitude of prayer and sometimes his legs would dance. Some of the people had to be lifted and carried off the platform, but others were able to walk themselves.

"Unconscious, but With a Tremor"

"I went around to the left of the platform and found ten people lying in the straw, apparently unconscious. Others were in a mental state that was purely hysterical."

Dr. Palmer said he did not believe cancer, tuberculosis, leprosy, blindness, or deafness could be cured by hypnotic influence.

"Take the last case I saw," said the witness. "The lights were nearly out. I came upon a man of about thirty lying on the ground entirely unconscious but with a violent tremor. That case was entirely injurious."

"What is the difference between enthusiasm and excitement at a football or baseball game and the state of mind at the Montwait services?" asked Mr. Nash.

"Well, I never saw anybody laid out as these people at Montwait were, except those at the bottom of the scrimmage," witness answered.

Dr. L. W. Jessaman of this town told of witnessing services at which Mrs. Etter presided. He said he had talked with one of the persons alleged to have been cured and found him neurotic and of an hysterical nature. Dr. Jessaman said he was not at the meetings when collections were taken and he had never heard of money being asked for healings.

Dr. Roy J. Boynton of South Framingham was asked concerning the condition of the rigid persons who were carried off the platform. He said they were in a condition which resembled hypnotism.

"Screeching" Broke His Sleep

Rev. Henry E. Bray, a Congregational minister at Sherborn, also told of attending the Montwait meetings. He testified that a number of the Montwait colony had said they had been healed, the cases being chiefly deafness or muscular troubles. They had mentioned the name of Mrs. Etter but she herself had said it was "the power of Christ." Witness added that a list of diseases was frequently read from the platform.

Rev. T. F. Gambill testified that he had heard the Lord given credit for the alleged cures and had heard many testify that they were cured. In his judgment hypnotism was practiced.

Arthur Green of Montwait testified that he had not had a good night's sleep since the meeting started. He described the noises as "wailing, hollering, and screeching." He testified that he had heard Mrs. Etter claim to have cured cancer and that he had also heard Mr. Fockler say the "wrath of God would be visited upon anyone who appeared as a witness against the defendants."

At the close of the day's session, the prosecution rested its case and tomorrow the defense will begin. It is expected that Mrs. Etter will take the stand. Judge Kingsbury decided to open court at 9 A.M., as the courtroom is very hot in the afternoon.

August 28, 1913

The Boston Herald (MA)

Maim and Halt Tell Wonders of "Faith Cure"

Followers from Far and Near Sing Praises of "Sister" Etter at Trial—Case Goes on Tomorrow

(Special Dispatch to the Herald.)

SOUTH FRAMINGHAM, AUG. 27—

After hearing more than a dozen witnesses testify that they had been miraculously cured or relieved of long standing ills through the laying on of hands of the Pentecostal disciples, Judge Kingsbury today continued until tomorrow the trial of Mrs. M. C. Woodsworth-Etter (*sic*) and C. B. Fockler and Earl W. Clark, her co-leaders in the religious sect which has been holding meetings at Montwait.

Perhaps the most remarkable story told in court today was that unfolded by Jessie Van Husen of Knoxville, Pa. In describing her "cure at the hands of God through Mrs. Etter," she said: "I came here with my nurse, Florence Cargil, after suffering for many years from the result of a railroad accident. All the physicians and surgeons who attended me were unable to help me. I was operated on twice at the Williamsport Hospital but never was free from pain until I was treated at Montwait.

"I submitted to a third operation but was barely able to walk. Again I went to the hospital, this time to Philadelphia, where the best surgeons attended me. I suffered untold agony and had to be carried in and out of my house because of weakness. I was delirious and a helpless cripple. I read Mrs. Etter's book and the scripture quotation: 'Lay hands on the sick and they shall be healed.'[1] I was penniless from my sickness, and I prayed the Lord to furnish me carfare to Montwait.

Carried to Train

"I finally got enough money to pay transportation. I was carried to the train. The physicians said that I would not be able to go six

[1] Mark 16:18, paraphrased.

miles. I arrived in South Framingham exhausted and was carried from my wheelchair to the platform at the meeting grounds, and God quickened my mortal flesh. For the first time in years, my pains left me following my treatment on the platform, my spine and hip are now well, my heart and stomach troubles have left me, and God has given me a spiritual uplift."

Mrs. Van Husen walked to the witness stand without assistance and to all appearances was in perfect health.

Florence Cargill, the nurse referred to, corroborated Mrs. Van Husen's testimony.

Mrs. Frederick A. Peck, whose husband is pastor of the Baptist church at Petersburg, N. Y., testified that she had been cured of an illness of seventeen years' standing as the result of attending the Montwait meetings. She said she had never heard any of the defendants ask for money in exchange for cures.

The Rev. Mr. Peck testified that he came to Montwait "for divine guidance and to get in closer touch with God." He described the condition of patients while being worked on by the leaders as "passive." He admitted he had been a subject on the platform, but he had never been hypnotized by the leaders. He never heard any of the defendants ask for collections for healing people.

Mrs. Lila T. Magwood of Dorchester testified that "all the glory for the cures was given to God."

Outsiders Caused Trouble

Robert H. Magwood of Dorchester, secretary of the Massachusetts No-License League, also vice-president of the association which owns the campgrounds at Montwait, testified that the disturbances at the camp meetings were caused by outsiders, who came there for the purpose of creating trouble. He also said there was insufficient police protection.

"I heard a denial from the platform," he said, "that leprosy had been cured, and I also heard it said from the platform that persons with contagious diseases would not be allowed on the ground[s]."

Mrs. Eva Norris of Albion, N. Y., testified: "I believe in the work going on at Montwait. I came for spiritual instruction and because

I have a daughter who was troubled with epilepsy. I brought my daughter along and she is now a changed child. A wonderful change has been worked in her. I never heard the defendants claim credit for cures. This first night I visited Montwait, I heard a girl say that she had been cured of blindness."

Was Physical Wreck

Mrs. Carrie F. Braigin of 583 Chestnut Street, Lynn, testified: "I have been in evangelistic work many years and have been cured at Montwait of heart trouble, tumors, rheumatism, kidney, and bladder trouble. I was a physical wreck when I came here and had not been able to wear corsets for years. Mrs. Etter said when she cured me: 'I smite this tumor and may it wilt like the fig tree of old.' I did not even tell Mrs. Etter what ailed me. I am positive the nature of my disease was never communicated to Mrs. Etter before she helped me. The Lord has been my only physician."

Robert G. Lake of New York City said: "I am an undertaker, director of the First National Bank in my home city, and have been a member of the Methodist church for the past twenty-eight years. I have been a mental sufferer for the past three months. My wife and I came to Montwait out of curiosity, and I have been wonderfully cured of mental depression and my wife has been relieved of a physical ailment of twenty years' standing. For twenty years she suffered from varicose veins and had to wear an elastic stocking, but now I believe she has been miraculously healed by God since coming to Montwait. If this is hypnotism, I would like to be hypnotized all my life. I would be a coward not to stand up and say what God has done in my case."

Cross-examined regarding the cause of his mental depression, he replied, "It was caused by the realization of my limitations as a Sunday school teacher." He added, "My mental state was such that my heartbroken wife thought I had ceased to love her and was about to separate from me, yet the sky above seemed of hard brass and I could get no help until I came to Montwait."

Robert J. Jameson, who was a machinist but is now a religious healer, testified that he assists Mrs. Etter in her work but gets no salary. He said the daily offerings at Montwait averaged twenty dollars and that they were equally divided between Mrs. Etter and the superintendent of the grounds. He said he first met Mrs. Etter at Long Hill, Ct.,[2] in June.

[2] "Ct."—Connecticutt.

August [30,] 1913

Unknown Source

Saved Through Fire, "Healing" Priestess Says

Thrills Curious Throng at Trial With Story of Fiery Whirlwind Bringing Salvation

COURT RESERVES DECISION

SOUTH FRAMINGHAM, AUG. 29—

Judge W. A. Kingsbury today reserved decision after hearing the testimony of Mrs. Marie (*sic*) Beulah Woodworth-Etter and arguments of the lawyers who are prosecuting and defending her and her fellow-workers at the Pentecostal Society meetings at Montwait on the charge that they received money under false pretences in accepting payment for "cures" or relief afforded physical sufferers. Mrs. Etter held the audience in the courtroom spellbound while she told the story of her conversion to the Pentecostal cult, which, she said, took place in Salem, O[hio].

Cyrus B. Fockler, the principal associate of Mrs. Etter, also testified today, but the lawyers for the defense did not call on Earl Clark, her other assistant.

Mrs. Etter testified that she is sixty-nine years old, that she was born in Lisbon, O[hio]., began to preach at the age of thirty-five, and that she has a husband and six children. She said she was "converted" when eighteen years old, and when she made this statement, appeared to be making an effort to check sobs. Led by the inquiries of her counsel she said:

"In Salem, O[hio]., I was given up by physicians and was lifted from a bed of sickness by prayer. I was a poor orphan girl and promised God then that I would go where He directed. I have never had the advantage of education, but have received daily strength to do my work.

"I was so afraid to go before the public that I nearly lost my soul and thought of taking my life. But the Lord knew His business and I promised Him to go to the ends of the world if I could bring one soul out of darkness.

"Finally I went to a meeting and was asked to kneel in prayer. The baptism permeated my whole frame. I stood up and could not sit down. God held me there before the audience and I heard a minister say, 'God bless that sister.'

"I was lifted off my feet and whirled around in liquid fire. I fell, finally, under the power. I don't know how long I lay still.

"I held meetings near home for some time, preaching in twenty-eight different churches. Everywhere it was agreed that I was chosen by God. The Lord showed me I must leave all and go out into His work."

Here Mrs. Etter enumerated the places where she has held meetings, and they were in nearly every corner of the country.

"Hundreds Struck Down"

"The same power has fallen on me," she went on, "when I have been unassisted. The power has also fallen on the audience. At St. Louis I had a tent filled with eight thousand people, and hundreds were struck down by the Lord.

"People have been struck down five[?] miles away from my tent."

Mrs. Etter denied the practice of hypnotism. "The most noted hypnotists have come from all over Europe and the United States to see the power," she declared. "I have stood fixed before an audience for an hour before preaching a sermon."

"Have you ever claimed credit for these cures?" she was asked.

"No," was the reply.

Q.—Do you believe you have any special power? A.—No.

Q.—Do you believe any people have been helped by you? A.—Yes, thousands.

Q.—What is the matter with your husband? A.—Rheumatism.

Never Arrested Before

Q.—Have you ever had trouble with the authorities before? A.—I was never arrested until I came here.

This concluded Mrs. Etter's testimony.

She was preceded on the witness stand by Cyrus B. Fockler, her associate, who testified he had a wife and several children in Indiana, that he attended Mt. Union College in Ohio and began life as a salesman in a hardware store. Later, he said, he was a carpenter and builder, remaining in that business until his "sick mother was made well at a Christian meeting." He then gave up his business, he testified, and has known Mrs. Etter since that time. He told of being with Mrs. Etter at meetings in Chicago, Indianapolis, Montwait, and elsewhere, describing the meetings as consisting of singing, prayer, preaching, and the invitation to those who desire baptism and "healing."

"People are generally asked if they are right with God," he said, "and as to the nature of their diseases. In some cases the diseases are commanded to depart. I never practice hypnotism, nor do I know whether I could. I have no power to heal diseases, nor have I ever claimed to have such power. I have never asked for financial contributions because of Mrs. Etter's healings."

Asked how he lived, he replied: "I have been on the faith line and have no stipulated salary. I receive money whenever I need it. Perhaps I have received fifteen dollars over expenses in the last three weeks."

Under cross-examination, Fockler said he had studied nerve anatomy in a general way, had never studied hypnotism, but had seen an exhibition of it.

"I believe that back of all diseases is the devil," testified the witness. "I believe that the demon is the cause of cancerous growths. It is not true that cures of leprosy have been claimed at Montwait. We make no physical examination of clients on the platform; we only take a statement. I place my hands on the patient's head and pray. Sometimes I place my hands on the affected parts of the body. We command the clapping of hands and the tapping of feet by the patients and sometimes assist them in doing it."

Questioned further, Fockler said his salary might reach fifteen dollars a week and repeated that neither he, Mrs. Etter, nor Clark practiced hypnotism on their clients.

"Often people are prostrated here," he said, "but they are in a calm, peaceful, sweet communion with God, as distinguished from a wholly different state under hypnotism. We have stated that if hypnotists would come forward in the name of God, we would put them out of business."

August 29, 1913

The Topeka Daily Capital (KS)

Minors Take Part in Holy-Roller Services

Great Crowd Sees Girl, 13, Lying on Ground

NO EFFORT MADE TO STOP PARTICIPATION OF CHILDREN IN MEETING LAST NIGHT IN NORTH TOPEKA

Despite warnings from Probate Judge Hugh MacFarland given two weeks ago that minors must not be allowed to participate in the excitement incident with their meetings, a girl about thirteen years old was in attendance at two meetings yesterday. During both the afternoon and evening meetings, she lay on the straw-covered ground in front of the altar with her shaking hands extended in the air or quiet at her sides from exhaustion.

Two other girls, apparently minors, were at the converts' bench in front of the platform on which the evangelists and choir members stand. Both were waving their hands in the air and were visibly excited.

If any officer was present, no attempt was made to interfere with the meeting or the minors who participated in it.

Mrs. Woodworth-Etter, evangelist in charge of the holy-rollers meeting, was kept busy throughout the evening meeting treating persons with ailments who sought her assistance. Many of them, after receiving her help, declared they were cured of diseases or infirmities and gave audible thanks.

The tent in which the evening meeting was held was crowded to the walls. People were packed along the seats and many stood in the aisles. The platform about the altar was filled with excited singers; and along the converts' bench, aged and young knelt side by side.

Although swayed by a high excitement that caused them to dance and shout "Glory to God," the meeting was not unusually noisy and there was no rolling about on the ground. A spirit of courtesy and goodwill was apparent among the members of the audience who welcomed visitors drawn there by curiosity as they welcomed those who belonged to their sect.

September 6, 1913

The Christian Evangel

Report of Woodworth-Etter Camp Meeting

S. FRAMINGHAM, MASS.

e are having fine meetings. I never saw so many perfect healings out of the total number as here. God certainly has marvelously worked—all manner of diseases. The enemy is stirred and tried to stop us. Had us arrested. We appeared today at 9 A.M. with a great crowd of witnesses, but they postponed it until next Tuesday. Now we are thronged with reporters. When we came we tried to pay for an ad in the *Boston Herald* but they would not accept it: now they are printing columns. Praise God!

People [are] here from many states—way from the South; Ohio; Indiana; Illinois; New York; Pennsylvania; Washington, D. C.—a good body of good preachers to help us. Praise Him! Our next meeting is at Hot Springs, Ark., commencing September 22, lasting from thirty to sixty days. Love to Brother Myland and all the saints. Salute all in your paper in my name.

YOUR BROTHER WITH LOVE,

—EARL W. CLARK

April 4, 1914

The Atlanta Journal, Saturday Evening (GA)

Faithful Believe She Can Cure All Ills

Mrs. Etter, at Old Tabernacle, Treats Her Hearers by "Laying On of Hands"—They Believe in Her

aturday at the old Baptist Tabernacle. On chairs, benches, and floor, all over the dim-lit room people are praying, praying noisily and with tears, shouting, and calling on the Lord. Most of them are women, many old, many young, a few gray-haired men, rough fellows in working clothes! Up and down the rostrum strides a little woman all in white, white hair, white dress, a white knit shawl over her shoulders!

"Praise the Lord, sisters!" she shouts. "Believe in Him and be healed!" She is Mrs. M. B. Worthington-Etter, (*sic*) "divine healer."

From the kneeling people all around come shouts and amens. But most of them moan in a weird swelling sound like some Arabian desert song that rises and falls and swells again.

A woman kneeling in the center of the rostrum begins to sway back and forth and shout. The others cease all but the low crooning noise, while she cries aloud on the name of Jesus. Gradually she works herself into a frenzy of prayer, her body rocking to and fro to the accompaniment of the moaning all around, her hands raised to heaven, her face streaked with tears.

She breaks off with a loud sob and there is momentary quiet. Mrs. Etter walks to the front and tells all who are in need to come forward.

Waiting for the "Healer"

The men and women crowd around the platform and kneel. A window is raised on a back room. Here a wan-faced woman lies listless in bed. The lame, the halt, the blind, struggle toward the platform. The healing is about to begin.

On one side of the platform, a number of converts gather around a piano and begin to sing. On the other a mother advances leading a little girl by the hand. The girl is totally blind. She sits down in a chair. Below the rostrum a woman holds a baby in her arms, the child's mouth covered with sores, a deaf mute, a crippled boy on crutches crowd together around the woman [i]n white.

While the singing increased in fervor on one side, Mrs. Etter motioned to the first subject. She was an old lady, deaf for thirty-six years. She sat down in a chair.

Mrs. Etter placed her hands on her face and rubbed them back and forth. Then she placed her mouth close to the old lady's ear and shouted. One could hardly hear what she said for the storm of singing, the clapping of hands, the stamping of feet on the rostrum, the moans and prayers.

The old lady said both drums had been destroyed. "Praise the Lord!" yelled Mrs. Etter in one ear. "Praise Him!" she yelled in the other, rubbing fiercely with her hands.

The smile on the old lady's face was very wistful and she looked up with a pitiful light in her brown eyes. Mrs. Etter and her man assistant worked like Trojans, shouting and rubbing with their hands.

The old lady clapped her hands after while and rose, a puzzled expression on her face. She could hear, she told Mrs. Etter, but couldn't distinguish the sounds. But she could hear the shouts and the music.

[Missing line] the healing waters flow," shouted the singers. "Where the hea-ea-ling waters flow."

The young man in the chair leaned back with his hands raised while Mrs. Etter laid seemingly violent hands on his shoulder, his throat, his face. She called to him to believe on the Lord, to have faith. She rubbed his chest.

Pretty soon the young man arose, waving his arms. The singing stopped as he stumbled off the platform, with tears of joy streaming from his eyes. A woman advanced half-running down the aisle to meet him. She was crying in long sobs. At the first row of benches, the young man leaped to the top of them and fell into her arms. They sobbed and wept crying, "Thanks to Jesus! Glory to God!"

Believes He Is Healed

Afterward a reporter asked Bowie if he was really healed. He said that when Mrs. Etter was treating him, he could feel a shiver pass through his lungs, that he believed he was healed, but time alone would show.

Mrs. Etter applied the same treatment to a woman who said she suffered from catarrh. All the time the singing continued and the men and women below the rostrum prayed loudly. This woman stated that she, who had been able to breathe through but one nostril for years, could now breathe freely through her whole nose.

The most pitiful spectacle of the morning was that of a deaf mute. While Mrs. Etter shouted into his ear and forced his mouth open, his friend, a young man, stood in front of him, shaking all over with hope, while tears streamed down his cheeks and his whole face twitched convulsively. This boy declared that his friend had been unable to utter a sound for years. Under Mrs. Etter's treatment he made noises in his throat but could not speak or hear.

These daily services of Mrs. Etter's take up the healing as the last part. She opens with song and then come testimonies from those who said they had been healed. Among those who testified Saturday morning was Mrs. K. E. More, of Chapel, S. C., who said she had paralysis of the arm so badly she couldn't raise it but that Mrs. Etter could cure her. She illustrated by waving her arms back and forth above her head.

Mrs. Sarah Puckett, of 99 Dargan Street, Atlanta, said she had leakage of the heart but was cured.

John M. Rosser, a Confederate veteran at the soldiers' home, said he was cured of catarrh of twenty-five years' standing, partial blindness of two years' standing, and deafness since he was a baby.

Mrs. Rushie Ramsey, of Eatonton, Ga., said she had broken her hips and had to walk on crutches but that she was now able to walk about the house without any assistance at all.

Mrs. J. L. Gossett, of East Point, said she was cured of painful heart trouble.

J. M. Bennett, whose daughter, Mrs. W. W. Wooten, of 12 Baltimore Block, testified that Mrs. Etter had healed him of dumbness.

A. L. A. Bridge, of Cottageville, S. C., came all the way through the country to see Mrs. Etter and testified that Mrs. Etter had cured him of lameness that confined him to his bed.

Rev. Arnoa Smith, of Gainesville, testified that Mrs. Etter had healed him of mental confusion.

For her alleged cures Mrs. Etter claims no credit, only divine inspiration. As she walks about the platform and calls on those who are in trouble, she asks them first if they are Christians and then tells them to believe on the Lord, to pray hard enough, and He will heal them.

April 13, 1914

The Atlanta Journal (GA)

Divine Healer Tells Why Husband's Ills Defy Her Treatment

"He Lacks Faith and God Has Purpose in Keeping Him Sick," Declares Mrs. Woodworth-Etter

HAS TRIED TO CURE HIM BUT FAILS EVERY TIME

Woman Says Weather Aggravates Attack of Rheumatism, but Blames Absence of Faith for Its Continuance

itting in the parlor of her boarding house at 69 Luckis Street, Monday morning, Mrs. M. B. Woodworth-Etter, who claims to have worked a number of marvelous cures though the power of God at the old Baptist Tabernacle, explained to the *Journal* reporter exactly why she has not cured her husband, who has been confined to the house ever since Mrs. Etter came to Atlanta, suffering from rheumatism and forced to walk on crutches.

"He lacks faith," said Mrs. Etter. "God has a purpose in it."

Her voice was cracked and strained from a cold she said, brought on by the varied heat and cold of the tabernacle meetings and by the vigorous shouting she employed in working over the lame, the halt, and the blind.

"He is more than seventy years old," she said, "and has been sick about a year. He has rheumatism and used to have great swellings on his legs.

Has Kept Him Alive

"Traveling as we do from coast to coast, he is constantly exposed to the weather and this, I think, has brought it on. Yes, I have tried to give him faith, and I think I have kept him alive by working over him and have kept his mind clean.

"No, he has not been to any meetings since we came to Atlanta, hasn't been out of the house. He is lying down now, lying down most of the time, and he's always in the house.

"Why hasn't he been cured? Well, God works in mysterious ways, His wonders to perform; and He must have some purpose in keeping my husband sick. I can't attempt to say why God does some things.

[unreadable sentence]

"He doesn't believe in cures all at once, but thinks they come gradually. When the weather gets brighter, I think he will be much better."

Doctors Have Seen Him

"Doctors? Yes. I've had doctors see him. He takes medicine. I don't tell people not to see doctors, you know, but I do tell them when doctors have failed to cure them: 'Come to the Lord.'

"Did you see last night's meeting?" she continued. "The building was packed. All back to the doors and up on the sides around the windows, like Zacheus (*sic*), you know, and against the back walls like sardines.

"My voice was clear as a bell. You could hear me outside just as easy as in. And the people were silent as death, not making fun or laughing."

Mrs. Etter says she does not know how long she will continue her meetings, maybe all summer. She says when she leaves Atlanta she is going to her home in Indianapolis to give her husband a long rest.

April 13, 1914

The Atlanta Constitution (GA)

On "Divine Healing" Dr. Holderby Preaches

Pastor Says Mrs. Etter Is Supported by Authority of the Bible

uring his services Sunday morning at Moore Memorial Church, Dr. Holderby referred to Mrs. Etter, who is conducting what she calls "divine healing" services at the old Broughton Tabernacle.

"Having been asked by a number of people, both in and out of the church, to express my opinion of the teaching and methods of Mrs. Etter, who claims that God can heal the sick, I have no hesitancy in giving my views," said Dr. Holderby.

"I have not attended any of Mrs. Etter's services—but from what I am told as to her doctrine in the matter of God's power to heal the sick, she certainly has behind her the authority of the Bible and is, therefore, right. I never criticize anyone whose object is to do good, although I may not endorse all of their ideas and methods.

"The doctrine of divine healing or healing by faith is certainly taught by Jesus Himself and He gave command to His early Church to 'preach the Gospel of the kingdom and to heal the sick.'[1] And this, the disciples did by the power of Christ. But the Church seems to have lost that power because she repudiates the doctrine. The doctrine has become a 'dead letter.'

"Will the Church ever regain her lost power? Yes—when she has faith. But this question of 'divine healing' is very unpopular with the Church today. The man who preaches it is regarded as a fanatic or an idiot. If the preacher is not prepared to lose his job, he had better not preach the doctrine of divine healing."

[1] See Mark 16:15-18.

July 7, 1914

Petoskey Evening News (MI)

Pentecostal Camp Meetings

Many Are Being Healed by Mrs. Etter

MEETINGS ARE BEING HELD THREE TIMES EACH DAY AT THE BIG TENT ON EMMET STREET

The Pentecostal meetings being conducted by Mrs. Etter at the big tent on Emmet Street seem to be attracting a great deal of attention, and according to reports several persons have been marvelously healed.

Among these reported healed are Joseph Walker, a farmer living near Niles, Mich., who some time ago suffered a stroke of paralysis and who has been unable to work since. He was healed Monday night through the ministration of Mrs. Etter and is now able to walk and run as he was used to doing before the stroke. Mrs. J. B. Callahan, of Battle Creek, was healed of stomach and bowel trouble Saturday.

T. B. Howell, of Los Angeles, Cal., one of the workers assisting at the meetings, is reported to have given a message in various languages, and there are many other evidences of the wonderful power through the ministration of Mrs. Etter.

Mrs. M. Everett of Atlanta, Ga., has arrived in Petoskey to assist in the meetings and will be there at each of the three daily meetings.

July 24, 1914

Petoskey Evening News (MI)

[Seventieth Birthday Celebrated]

The seventieth birthday anniversary of Mrs. Woodworth-Etter was celebrated Wednesday at the Pentecostal tent. Before the morning meeting many of her friends gathered at the tent and under the leadership of Mrs. P. J. Howard decorated the platform prettily with flowers. As Mrs. Etter approached, the people sang a hymn as a birthday greeting, afterward presenting her with a purse of about twenty-five dollars.

"Do the healings received in these meetings last, or do they relapse as soon as her influence is withdrawn?" is a question often asked. There are several witnesses here that have attended her meetings at different times during the past twenty-four years who testify to the permanence of their healings and in addition to these, she has testimonials from ministers and prominent church workers attesting to complete and full recoveries following her ministrations. Mrs. Etter will be here but a short time, leaving next week for Philadelphia.

July 25, 1914

The Christian Evangel

God's Wonderful Work Through Mrs. Etter

We, the undersigned members of the executive committee and workers in charge of the Woodworth-Etter meetings, held in the city of Atlanta, Ga., from March 8th to May 10th, 1914, conducted by Mrs. M. B. Woodworth-Etter, of Indianapolis, Ind., wish to, unsolicited, put our unqualified endorsement upon her work while here. Many were saved; many hundreds were most marvelously healed of nearly every disease known to science. Many that had been declared hopeless and sent back from sanitariums to their homes were brought to these meetings and were healed by the laying on of hands and the prayer of faith, in many cases instantly.

Atlanta has never been so wonderfully blessed in her history. Thousands were lifted to a higher plain and their faith increased by seeing such wonderful miracles performed. Indeed it was a most wonderful visitation of God.

Though we have purposely delayed this report in order to test the healings, we can now say that we do not know, out of the many hundreds that were healed in Atlanta, of a single one that has not only retained their healing, but many have also increased in health ever since; and we have heard from many that have come from other cities and towns all over the U. S. to Atlanta to get healed and went away healed and are still healed.

We were forced to enlarge the buildings in which the meetings were held twice, and then many nights we had to turn hundreds away who were clamoring for admittance.

It is the desire of the many thousands that were saved or healed in these meeting to have Sister Etter come back in October and hold meetings indefinitely. The work is going on in her absence under the leadership of Brother C. B. Fockler.

(SIGNED)

—E. H. BURGE

—STELLA MURRAY

—THOS. BEDFORD

—MRS. J. P. EVE

—CHAS. D. BOSE

—M. P. ASKEW

—C. W. HATCHE

August 29, 1914

The Christian Evangel

Mr. Etter at Rest

Notice has come to us of the death of Mr. Samuel P. Etter, husband of Mrs. Woodworth-Etter. Both are well known over the country, from East to West, having ministered to many in conventions, camp meetings, and revival services. May the Lord strengthen our dear sister and continue to make her a great blessing to others and give her the comfort of the Holy Ghost.

January 16, 1915

The Christian Evangel

Mrs. Etter Wonderfully Recovered

God Answers Prayer After Gates of Death Have Been Reached

or the last three years my burdens and cares have been heavy. I traveled over eleven thousand miles, carrying and caring for my invalid husband. I carried him from the Atlantic to the Pacific, holding meetings three times a day in many of the large cities, and stayed at each city for a month or longer.

With all the burdens that are connected with the work of the Lord, standing alone at times; caring for my husband day and night, then adding to all this the sorrow and bereavement of laying my husband to rest last August, while I was in the midst of a large campaign in Philadelphia, Pa., he urging me to go forward with the work to the very last; passing through this heavy strain and laboring continually, I finally got very weak in my body. I only kept going through divine life and strength.

When I left home for our meeting in Chicago, they had to take me to the depot in an auto. I went, believing that God called me and that He would hold me up through the meeting, which was to continue for one month or longer. D.V.[1] The Lord wonderfully sustained me through the time that I had promised. In my weakened condition I contracted a severe cold one day, which soon developed into pneumonia. My co-laborers and friends at once decided to take me away from the meeting, home to Indianapolis where I could rest. Following you will find the testimony of a skilled medical brother, Dr. Green, of the Martinsville sanitarium, Martinsville, Ind., about my condition at this time:

Martinsville, Ind., Dec. 24, 1914
Mrs. M. B. W. Etter
Indianapolis, Ind.

[1] "D. V."—*Deo Volente* or God willing *(Webster's N. W.,* 1997).

My Dear Mrs. Etter:

I wish to testify that on the 20th of November, on 63rd Street in Chicago at 10 A.M. in the morning, I saw you in your room at a temperature of 102,[2] pulse rate 100 and irregular, with prune-juice expectoration, making a germ cell pneumonia, and an engorged entire lower lobe of left lung. Upon my advice you were removed to a drawing room in Indianapolis on Wednesday evening, Nov. 11. (*sic*).[3] On the following Friday evening at 5:30, I visited you in your home, found a temperature of 100_, pulse rate 84, respiration 28, complete consolidation of whole lower lobe of left lung with tubular building. I again visited you on Tuesday morning, found temperature 100, pulse rate 84, expectorating with great difficulty great quantities of prune juice loaded with pneumonococci. I again visited you on a Friday afternoon, found temperature normal, pulse rate 84 and regular, lower lobe of lung clearing nicely, tongue clean, taking a sufficient quantity of milk and eggs and having slept soundly during the night before. I again visited you on Monday following and found a complete crisis had been passed, lower lobe clearing up nicely, respiration 24, excessive sweating for two days, appetite good, sleeping well.

This result came to you through implicit faith in God's power to heal you. You took nothing but air, milk, and eggs and passed through what is ordinarily fatal in sixty per cent of persons seventy-two years of age.

Sincerely Yours,
E. V. Green

When I was told of my condition, I began to praise the Lord. Soon the Lord appeared to me in a vision in a cloud of glory, sitting on a

[2] "102"—degrees Fahrenheit. All subsequent temperature and also stated in degrees Fahrenheit.

[3] "Nov. 11"—probably a misprint for November 21.

great white horse with a sword in His hand, showing me that He had conquered death and disease and that I should go forth again in great power and that He would be with me.

I praise God, through the prayers of the saints that have gone up in my behalf, my life has been spared. Now He is calling me out in the work again. The Lord willing, I shall commence my next meeting in Tampa, Florida, sometime between now and the beginning of February.

January 16, 1915

The Christian Evangel

Etter Meeting in Tampa, Fla.

A New Date Has Been Set Since Sister Etter Has Been Healed in Answer to Prayer

he meeting which had been announced for Tampa, Fla., was indefinitely postponed on account of the illness of Sister Woodworth-Etter. Since God has so wonderfully answered prayer in her behalf and raised her to His glory, Sister Etter feels led of the Lord to proceed to Tampa after a short rest and commence the meeting January 23rd, 1915. These services will continue for one month or longer, D.V. All who wish further information about this meeting can address J. L. Webb, Secretary, R. R. 3, Box 272, Tampa, Fla.

January 23, 1915

The Christian Evangel

Dropsy Twice Divinely Healed

SISTER HAD HARD FIGHT WITH ENEMY WHICH RESULTED IN SALVATION OF HER FAMILY AND COMPLETE HEALING OF HER BODY

n gratitude to God my Savior for what He has done for me, I desire to write my testimony to the glory of God.

Over three years ago I injured my spine through lifting, which resulted in kidney trouble. I kept on my feet, doing what work I could, and soon noticed that I had difficulty in walking. At this time my limbs began to swell and my heart cried to God for help. Nineteen years ago I had been healed by the Lord through the ministry and teaching of Dr. Dowie, and I knew where my only hope would be found. I do praise God. He is our all in all.

Shortly after, my limbs began to swell and I turned saffron. As I was about to get up one morning, I was unable to rise; and for four weeks I could not get out of bed. My stomach, also, was in a terrible condition. I could scarcely eat without vomiting and could not stop until someone bathed my face in cold water.

We kept holding on to God and looking into our lives. God is so patient with us. Different ones came and prayed for me during my illness. In four weeks I was able to get out of bed, but the cough still bothered me. I could not talk without coughing.

This was in 1912. In the spring of 1913, my blood turned to water. We knew then that I had dropsy.[1] I could not walk or help myself in any way and only grew worse and worse. Someone had to sit at my bedside all the time to fan and care for me.

Then we heard of Mrs. Etter's meetings at the Stone Church in Chicago and of the wonderful work she was doing. It seemed impossible for me to go as I was so weak, but, praise God, He always opens up the way. A lady friend of mine called and persuaded

[1] "dropsy"—edema, a condition in which the body retains fluids for such causes as kidney or heart failure.

Mr. Dolan to let me go. We went on a Sunday morning. They put me on a wheeled chair and placed me in the baggage car.

The next morning I was taken to the meeting, and Mrs. Etter prayed for me and God heard and answered prayer. Glory to His name! I was carried to the platform and when God touched my body, I was enabled to walk off. The trouble with my stomach disappeared and the following Sunday, God healed my cough. I had not been able to sing for over a year, and you can imagine my joy in being able to join in singing the dear hymns again.

I noticed how happy the people were who were baptized in the Holy Spirit, and a longing came into my soul for such an experience. Although God had already put a peace, joy, and love into my heart, it made me hungry for more.

There were seekers' meetings in the church every afternoon. I attended them and the third afternoon, God baptized me in His Holy Spirit. How He did fill my soul with His glory! I do praise His holy name!

We sent the wheeled chair home by freight and I returned home on the train. I cannot begin to tell the joy in getting home again and seeing my loved ones. To think that I had been taken out of bed and helped down to Chicago and that I had come back able to walk. It seemed wonderful, and I was very happy.

The Second Healing

All went well until the threshers were here in the fall. We could not get help and I overworked. Then came a severe cold. We intended going to the meeting on Saturday night but Mr. Dolan thought I had better stay at home. I was very happy and just longed to go, but agreed to stay at home. Whether we made a mistake in staying home or not, we do not know. I was all right until I went to bed, when I became very sick. My suffering was terrible, the folks remaining up all night with me. The pain left in the morning, but my blood had turned to water again. I was very weak, and oh the anguish of my soul as I did not want to bring shame on the cause. But God is very merciful—He did not let me lose my spiritual experience.

My limbs began swelling again and the cough was worse than ever, but to my delight, the trouble with my stomach did not return. During this time many dear friends came and prayed for me, and oh the blessings that I received from God! It was wonderful how He would fill me with His Spirit until my heart overflowed with praises and the healing seemed a small thing compared to this great love. Still, at times, I would ask God to give me another chance.

But I could see that I was growing worse, and one evening at family worship, I told the children that they would have to help us or they would not have a mother very long. Bless their dear hearts; they knew the first thing to do would be to give themselves to God. Praise His name! He wondrously saved five of them. Charley, the one that was saved first, came from meeting one night and told me he was saved. We were very thankful. He said, "Now Mamma, if you had not taken sick again, I would not have been saved." After he had left the room, it was literally filled with the glory of God. As He revealed some things to me, I knew I had to suffer a little longer, as each dear one was saved, it seemed like new props were holding me up to God.

Still I continued to grow worse but was sure that I would get better in God's own time. I continued to swell and at times had to open my mouth to get my breath. I had to sit in a chair night and day and could not even feed myself. But we were not tempted to use means and continued to look to God for deliverance.

To avoid any trouble, Mr. Dolan called in a doctor. Before he left, I asked him what I could expect. He said there was only one hope for me and that was a miracle, that I could not go through in the condition my heart was in. I sat there and faced death awhile and thought, "Have I really got to die?" Several things passed through my mind as I sat there. I thought of my loved ones and how lonely they would be. All at once, the thought came to me, "No, I don't have to die. God is the healer, and if I meet the conditions He will heal me." A deep peace and rest came into my soul.

A few days later, in the evening, I seemed to be passing away. I could not swallow a drop of water and my whole body quivered. But God heard the cry of our hearts and I could feel my heart start up again. I began to get better at once. We noticed the swelling was going down, and in two or three days the flesh opened at both ankles and the water left my body. I was very thankful to be comfortable again.

I am determined to live to please God every day. The half has not been told of how God held us up. It is now over a year since He healed me. I have been able to do my own work ever since last spring and I am well all the time. We give God all the glory.

—Mrs. Jas. Dolan
R. R. 1, Box 41
Zion City, Ill.

February 27, 1915

The Christian Evangel

Mrs. Etter in Florida

Tampa

e are in the midst of the work here. God is with us in power. Saints have come in from many states. God has saved, healed, and baptized already. A number of Cubans are being reached and getting the baptism. Last night it was raining all evening, but God saved two and baptized one. The night before, two received the baptism and others were saved. One Cuban came out speaking in other tongues.

After this campaign, which will end Feb. 23rd, D.V., we are to continue our work which we started in Atlanta, Ga., about a year ago. The saints are rejoicing over the fact that we will be able to help them again. Let all the saints pray for both the work at Tampa and Atlanta.

—Mrs. M. B. W. Etter

March 6, 1915

The Christian Evangel

Etter Meeting Closed

Tampa, Fla.

od met us the first night and set His approval on the meeting. We praise God for the way He did bless in the meeting. Many were healed and saved, also a number filled. A man was kicked in the breast by a horse and was not able to do anything for months. He came to the meeting and Sister Etter prayed for him, and God healed him and he went to work the next morning and has been working ever since.

We could tell of many just such cases as the above. The last day was the best of all. The power of God came down. My wife began to play on the piano under the power of God and continued for about an hour and a half. We had a melting time. Sister Etter has gone to Atlanta, Ga., for a meeting. We pray God to bless her labors there. Baptism service will follow Sunday at 3 P.M. Let all who read this pray for the work in South Florida. There were twelve or more states represented at this meeting. Some came who knew Sister Etter thirty-eight years ago and told of the work of God in Indiana.

—Pastor J. M. Rowe

March 27, 1915

The Weekly Evangel

God Again Visits Atlanta

ETTER MEETING REPORTS BLESSING OF GOD IN CONVERSIONS, HEALINGS, BAPTISMS, AND WONDERFUL WORKS OF GRACE AND POWER

 am in the midst of a big work here in Atlanta. God is here in power. From the first, He worked mightily. The second night (nearly two weeks ago) a lady was healed of cancer. She went down under the power of God. Later, in a half-raised condition, she prophesied, speaking under the inspiration of the Lord. It was marvelous. This sister was in a critical condition, given up by doctors. Last night she testified again (pounding the place of the cancer with

her fist as hard as she could) saying that all pain was gone. She soon went to the altar, prayed for a sister to receive salvation. As she prayed, the power struck the sister, and she jumped to her feet and began to dance and praise the Lord. Soon the fire struck another one and she, too, was saved and began to dance and later, under the power of God, saw a marvelous vision of Jesus.

All kinds of diseases have been healed—among them consumption, pellagra, tumors, etc., and cripples have been healed. One night a lady was carried to the rostrum by several persons. She was unsaved and had previously made fun of the meetings, saying it was all of the enemy. God convicted her, and when she was prayed for she jumped out of her chair and began to praise God and shout, "Glory to Jesus! Glory to Jesus!" The power of God struck her and she walked back and forth alone crying for joy and giving praise to God. After the service she proved to the people that her case was genuine by running in their sight. These sinners said that if a person did not believe this was of God, he would not believe though a person arose from the dead.[1]

The house is packed to the utmost and people are being awakened all around. Daily people come and give their hearts to God and are saved and baptized. Some of the young converts God is using to give messages in tongues and interpretation. People all over the house testify that they were prayed for last year, and today they are still well. Consumptives who were carried into the meeting last year are strong today and have been all summer in the work of saving souls. One of Atlanta's leading physicians and surgeons who was healed last year is still well and praising God. Her case was a hopeless one from a medical standpoint. All the physicians had given her up.

So we praise God for His wonderful works to the children of men[2] these days. Greetings to all the saints.

[1] An allusion to Luke 16:20-31, especially verse 31.

[2] Psalm 107:15.

June 26, 1915

The Weekly Evangel

Sister Etter Now in St. Louis

After Closing a Successful Meeting in Chicago Found Time for a Ten-Days' Meeting in St. Louis Before Going to Topeka Camp

ister Etter has come to St. Louis and we are indeed glad to have her with us. The meeting, which had been widely announced in Chicago at the Tabernacle, a red stone church on the corner of Ashland Blvd. and Ogden Ave., with Brother L. C. Hall as pastor, was closed a week ahead of time on account of the streetcar strike which hindered the people from getting out to meetings. The church has also been closed and Brother Hall is expecting to spend the summer in evangelistic work, leaving for the Berlin, Ontario camp meeting within a few days. The reason for this is that the Baptists who own the church objected to Pentecostal meetings being held in it and particularly as the meetings attracted larger and more enthusiastic crowds than had formerly attended the church.

To Be in St. Louis All Week

Sister Etter planned to be with the saints in St. Louis this week, until June 26th, and possibly a few days longer. The Assembly on Easton Ave., joined in with the Assembly on Olive St., and the two assemblies are now cooperating to the best of their ability in helping on the cause of God and in upholding Sister Etter's hands as she preaches the Word and prays for the sick.[1] There are many obstacles to be overcome, and this meeting is only a forerunner of another greater and longer meeting which we trust will be held in St. Louis sometime in the future.

Already we have seen some good results as the sick have been prayed for and as sinners have wept their way through to Calvary. Some needed instruction has also been given which is going far to help the people in their desire to obey God and let the Holy Spirit

[1] An allusion to Exodus 17:8-14, especially verse 12 in which Aaron and Hur hold up Moses' hands in order to win a battle.

have His way with them. Sister Etter is fearlessly declaring a full Gospel, and the Lord is graciously confirming the Word with signs following.[2]

Blessed Reports From Chicago

We received some blessed reports from the Chicago meeting. One brother wrote us that God was present in great power, saving, healing, and baptizing in the Holy Ghost. Brother Feick wrote that "a number of helpless invalids, who came to the meeting in wheelchairs, are now walking by themselves." It was reported that twenty states were represented and that the power of God was prostrating many of the saints daily, some of whom received marvelous visions.

Healed of Gunshot Wound

It was reported that a sister in attendance at the meeting received word that her sister in Battle Creek, Michigan, had been shot by a burglar in the lung. The doctors had taken her to the hospital and reported that she could not live. Her sister and the rest of the saints immediately had special prayer offered for her. Soon, a special delivery letter was received stating that the crisis had passed, and she was sent home from the hospital, considered well.

Brother Hall's Testimony

Brother Hall sent a short, but stirring report which we publish intact:

> God is in the midst of His people! Great joy is upon His redeemed! There is a shout in the camp. The Lord is here! Visions of glory! Revelations of truth! Manifestations of power! Great joy—dancing—leaping—shouting—praise Him! Great interest! Devil stirred and fighting! His time is short to harass the saints who are going into the rapture. Hallelujah!

Brother Hall also enclosed a few testimonies which were taken down in shorthand just as they were given, which we cannot print in full now, but which we will mention briefly.

A man healed of rheumatism, asthma, and bronchitis—says it is all gone and he now sleeps like a baby, whereas he used to have to get up four or five times every night. Feels like praising Him day and night.

[2] Mark 16:20.

J. W. Gordon, 1106 Monroe St., Chicago, Ill., testified that he had been healed of Bright's disease, dropsy, and kidney trouble, after he was dying, having fallen off thirty-eight pounds in weight. This testimony was confirmed by a brother who arose and said he had known brother Gordon for seven years.

A woman who was brought into the meeting in a wheeled chair testified to healing of palpitation of the heart and an injury to her back which she received in a runaway nine weeks before.[3] She said it was all gone now, including a severe stomach trouble, and that she hardly knew she had a stomach now.

Some stirring messages in tongues were also given and interpreted which called upon the people to come to the Lamb of God and accept of the feast which had been spread. Also a solemn warning of the soon coming of the wrath of God was given, also comfort for those who look for Him.

After a brief rest at her home in Indianapolis at the close of her meeting in St. Louis, Sister Etter will go to the camp meeting announced elsewhere in this paper, at Topeka, Kans., commencing July 31, and continuing to August 31st.

[3] "runaway"—She refers to an injury caused when she lost control of her horse(s).

August 9, 1915

Topeka Daily Capital (KS)

Bring Man on Cot for Cure at Camp Meeting

Audience at Garfield Park Sees Two Do Frenzied Dance

MOVED BY SPIRIT, DANCERS SPEAK IN STRANGE TONGUE—LEADER A WOMAN OF 72

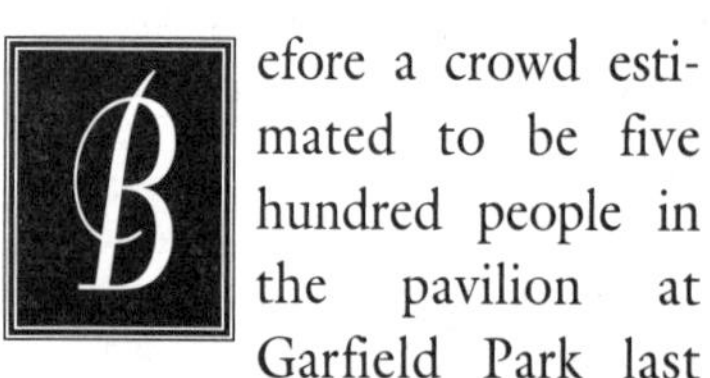

Before a crowd estimated to be five hundred people in the pavilion at Garfield Park last night, a score of singers stood on a platform with upraised hands and singing religious songs. At the front of the platform, two persons—a man and a woman, both under twenty-five years old—were dancing backward and forward as fast as their feet could carry them and with their eyes closed. Out in the audience nearly a hundred people were standing, many of them with hands raised and looking upward. Frequently there were fervent exclamations of religious adoration and praise from the members of the congregation.

The meeting was a religious service held by the Pentecostal assembly that has been holding an evangelistic service in Garfield Park for the past week. Mrs. M. B. Woodworth-Etter of Indianapolis, Ind., a woman seventy-two years old, is conducting the meeting.

"The Spirit of God"

As the two young people danced frenziedly back and forth on the stage, Mrs. Woodworth-Etter smiled at them approvingly.

"The Spirit of God," she frequently exclaimed.

As they danced the young woman's hair had become loosened and hung below her waist. She frequently brushed aside the locks that fell over her face. The two danced unceasingly for twenty-two minutes. As they paused, the young woman stretched out her arms toward the audience and began uttering unintelligible words, mostly made up of sibilant sounds and ending in vowels.

"God speaking through lips and tongues of clay," exclaimed Mrs. Woodworth-Etter.

The young woman continued and spoke rapidly. Occasionally her words could be distinguished. Her eyes were closed as she spoke. Finally she stopped and retired to a nearby seat.

Wailing Follows Cries

The young man who had stood by with his hands covering his face suddenly stepped forward and began talking in the same manner that his companion had, but his words were more inarticulate, though louder. After speaking for several moments, he stopped abruptly and put his hands over his face. He was silent a moment and then began groaning in a wailing tone, not unlike a patient first recovering consciousness after an anesthetic.

"Heed the Spirit's warning," said Mrs. Woodworth-Etter.

"Amen," shouted a dozen others.

The groaning took a higher but softer tone and finally died away. Then the young man began talking again in the same unintelligible sounds as before, but evidently pleading with the audience, who listened reverently.

Mrs. Woodworth-Etter explained that the two converts had received the gift of tongues. She said that they spoke in different languages and could be understood by a linguist or parts of their speech could be understood by those familiar with the language in which it was spoken.

Bring Man on Cot

Mrs. Woodworth-Etter preached for nearly an hour. At the close of her sermon, a man seriously ill with an intestinal disorder was brought to the platform on a cot. Mrs. Woodworth-Etter and the others prayed fervently for him, asking that his infirmities might be healed.

Those who are affiliated with the Pentecostal faith believe that healing is done by prayer and tell of many interesting cases in which persons seriously or believed to be incurably ill, were made well through their prayers.

The meeting will continue for three weeks more. Nearly four hundred persons are attending the meeting—many of them camping in Garfield Park.

August 12, 1915

Topeka Daily Capital (KS)

Boy Cured by Miracle Is Taken From Meeting

Lewis Romer, 10, Removed Before Baptism

Probate Judge Orders Children Be Kept From Participating in Holiness Services at Garfield Park

are, wriggling toes were all the officers could see of the person about whom a crowd was gathered at the camp meeting of the Holiness Association last night at Garfield Park. The feet belonged to Lewis[1] Romer, a ten-year-old boy of Allen, Kan., and he was kneeling at the altar to receive the baptism.

In the afternoon Judge Hugh MacFarland, of the probate court, had sent word to Mrs. Woodworth-Etter, who is conducting the meetings, that children under sixteen years were not to participate in the meetings. Her answer to him was: "God made us to conduct our meetings this way and we shall keep right on—interfere if you wish."

Boy Taken From Altar

Detective Tom Morgan and Probation Officer Edward Rooney made their way through the crowd to the side of the boy. He was crying. There was a storm of protest when Morgan picked the boy up to take him out of the meeting, and the believers crowded around, cheering, singing, clapping their hands, and dancing. The mother, Mrs. C. H. W. Romer, tried to hold the boy, but she released her hold when she felt herself going into the officer's arms with the boy. The mother and son were taken to the detention home by order of Judge MacFarland and will be sent home today if the mother does not promise to keep the boy out of the meetings.

The boy cried as Detective Morgan carried him out of the pavilion where the meetings are being held.

"I'll give you fifteen cents if you'll let me go," was the tempting offer the boy made between sobs.

[1] The Topeka Daily Capital prints Romer's name as Lewis, but a 1981 paper publishes his name as Louis. Both spellings are quoted as they appear in the originals.

Cruel Treatment, MacFarland

Official interference with the meeting last night resulted from a visit which Judge MacFarland made to the meeting Tuesday night, when he found a ten-year-old daughter of Chester McCarter, 1215 Lime Street, in an hysterical condition following what the judge said was inhuman treatment.

Before interfering, Judge MacFarland asked the opinions of a number of Topeka doctors, who told him that children subjected to the nervous strain of a conversion at such meetings frequently lose their minds. An old statute was found that made the parents responsible in such cases, and the court made the order prohibiting the participation of children.

City Wants Its "Bit"

Today, Commissioner W. L. Porter will have the grocer who is handling supplies on the grounds come to his office for a conference. Meek, the grocer, will have to pay the city a percentage for what he has sold and will sell on the grounds at Garfield Park.

In order to make the case clear, Porter bought a loaf of bread from Meek, who was in charge of the provision tent.

Mrs. Woodworth-Etter paid her respects to the peace officers in her three-hour sermon before the baptism was given. She said doctors, generally, knew that the religion she and her followers taught was good for sick persons and she had cured many men, women, and children who had been given up by physicians.

Cured of Saint Vitus' Dance

Mrs. Romer said Lewis was cured of Saint Vitus' Dance at the morning meeting yesterday.[2]

"You could hear his shoulders crack twenty feet away," Mrs. Romer said, "and the pain and sickness was all gone when the meeting was over.

"Lewis asked me tonight to take him to the altar so he could be baptized, and we were waiting for the blessing when the officers took us away."

Mrs. Romer came to Topeka [on] Tuesday from Allen, where her husband is in the hardware business.

[2] Wayne Warner interviewed Louis Romer about this incident (Wayne Warner, "Stormy Topeka Camp Meeting 66 Years Ago Recalled," [*Topeka Capital Journal*, (8 August 1981) pp.9, 12.]

[Romer] was afflicted with what was known as Saint Vitus' Dance. Today the disease is known as chorea, a nervous disease closely associated with rheumatic fever. Children who are afflicted with the disease often lose control of their movements, stumble and fall easily. . . .

The illness affected Louis' feet so that his toes drew under preventing him from wearing shoes. Frequently he would lose control of his hands and fingers. The boy's condition got so bad that he could no longer feed himself with table utensils. And because there was no effective treatment in those days, doctors had little hope that he would live beyond age thirteen. . . .

Romer, who is now seventy-five and living in Lowell, Ore., remembers the events as if they happened just yesterday:

"Mrs. Etter came over to our quarters and talked to us. She asked me if I thought God would heal me, and I said I did. Then in the afternoon meeting she prayed for me. I was standing by my mother who had me by the hand. Sister Etter laid her hands on my head and I felt a cooling of my nerves as a tingling warmth went through my body. My hands straightened out, my shoulders and neck felt good, my feet and toes straightened out, and I felt so good I cried. I felt fine. All of this happened in less time than it takes to tell it. . . .

After Louis was healed, he asked his mother if she would take him to the camp meeting altar so he could receive the Pentecostal blessing. Despite the ban on children praying at the altar, Mary Romer honored her son's request after the evening sermon. Other worshippers had heard Louis' testimony of healing and gathered around him at the altar to pray that he would receive the blessing.

That's when two police officers left their seats in the pavilion and made their way toward the kneeling Louis. . . .

Romer says today that he never had any further trouble with St. Vitus' dance after he left Garfield Park. He said his doctors were amazed at the instant recovery.

August 13, 1915

Topeka Daily Capital (KS)

Took Her Child to See Christ, She Tells Judge

MRS. MARY ROMER SHOUTS PRAISES IN PROBATE COURT—TRIES TO EXPLAIN HER RELIGION—HUSBAND COMES TO TAKE HER AND BOY HOME

"Judge I took my child to see Jesus. Glory to God, I found Him two years ago, and you or anyone else can't take Him away from me. And I wanted my child to find Jesus, and that is why I took him. Glory! Glory!"

A slight-built woman, plainly attired and wearing her hair in a tightly rolled knot at the back of her head, stood before Judge Hugh MacFarland in the probate court yesterday afternoon explaining why she had taken her ten-year-old son, Lewis, to the Pentecostal meeting Wednesday night in Garfield Park.

Judge MacFarland had visited the meeting and had seen the intense nervous strain the men and women were under. The children apparently suffered even worse than the men and women and a patrolman was ordered to remove the child and place Mrs. Mary Romer, the mother, under arrest. She was charged with being a delinquent parent. The boy was taken to the detention home.

Not Proper Place for Child

Yesterday afternoon Mrs. Romer, whose home is in Allen, was brought into court to answer the charges. Judge MacFarland read the charge to Mrs. Romer and explained carefully what the offense was.

"What have you to say, Mrs. Romer, in reply to the charge?" the probate judge asked. Mrs. Romer's first reply was as quoted above. She then started to explain in detail to Judge MacFarland how her faith had cured her of a serious illness but he interrupted.

"I am sorry, Mrs. Romer, but that has no bearing on the subject. You are here because you permitted your child to attend that meeting. I have nothing to say about your faith or whether or not you may attend, nor would not for a moment think of keeping you from attending the meetings if you desire; however, I am convinced that such meetings are not a proper place for a child, and I must require you to promise me that you will not take him there anymore."

Mrs. Romer then asserted that she would have to stay away from the meetings herself if she could not take her son with her. She asked permission to return with her son to her tent in Garfield Park and offered to return home today.

Under Nervous Strain

Judge MacFarland refused to let the boy be taken back to the park and said that he could be kept in the detention home. Mrs. Romer finally agreed, but not until she had spent several minutes in talking of her religion. As she talked, her nervousness seemed to increase, and she spoke fervently with frequent exclamations of "Glory to God!" Finally she finished and was released on her promise that she would not take her son to the meetings. She remained with her son last night in the detention home. As she left the courtroom, Mrs. Romer exclaimed:

"The boy is under the law, but thank God, I'm not. I'm under Jesus. Glory! Glory!"

C. H. Romer, husband of Mrs. Romer, who is a hardware merchant in Allen, came to Topeka yesterday afternoon and will return with them to their home today.

August 13, 1915

Topeka Daily Capital (KS)

House Bars "Holy Rolls" and Breaks Up Meeting

Subdued Meeting Fails to Satisfy Mayor

EVANGELISTS TOLD THEY CAN HOLD ORDERLY MEETINGS, WORSHIPPING QUIETLY, BUT NO MORE "SPECTACLES"

"Holy rolls" went under the ban of the city officials last night and Mayor Jay E. House, in an ultimatum to Mrs. Woodworth-Etter, evangelist, and her two assistants, who are conducting revivals in Garfield Park, North Topeka, informed them that their meetings would be closed if any further spectacles were staged.

The appearance of Mayor House, Chief of Police Harvey Parsons, Judge Hugh MacFarland, and several police officers, broke up the Holiness meeting last night. Warned in the afternoon by Mayor House that the frenzied actions of converts must be eliminated from their services, the leaders held a subdued meeting last night and at no time did the excitement reach the point it has on several nights recently.

When the officers were noticed in one corner of the pavilion being used as a meeting place, Mrs. Woodworth-Etter dismissed the audience and urged the people to leave. Then she disappeared, leaving her two assistants and several of the audience to work over a man who was in a trance.

They Make No Promises

Before the two men who assist the evangelist were able to leave, Mayor House stopped them and delivered his ultimatum. He told them that as long as they wished to worship quietly and orderly, they would not be disturbed; but if they allowed converts to roll around on the floor and go into excited trances at any future meeting, they would be forced to close the revival.

No promises were made by the leaders of the sect in answer to the mayor's declaration.

After his trip to Garfield Park last night, Mayor House said that the first intimation of further wild performances would result in the immediate closing of the pavilion and the ousting of the colony from the park. They will also be prohibited from holding their meetings in any other part of the city, he said.

City Officials Visit Leaders

The visit of the city officials last night followed an inspection of the meeting yesterday by Mayor House, W. L. Porter, and George F. Hayden, city attorney. While in the park, Mayor House was interviewed by two women members of the congregation regarding what action the city officers expected to take.

After Mayor House had told them that he would insist on the elimination of the frenzied dances and contortions at the meetings, one of the women prayed fervently in an unintelligible jargon, ending in a request spoken in English, that he think before he took any action.

Knowing that their meeting would be watched last night, the leaders kept the excitement of the audience at a low pitch.

August 30, 1915

Topeka Daily Capital (KS)

Holy Rollers Break Benches From Fervor

MEETINGS NEAR GARFIELD PARK CLOSE FOLLOWING DAY OF "CURES" AND ENTHUSIASM

The evangelistic meeting that has been held in Garfield Park and later in the tract across the street from Garfield Park, by the Pentecostal Association, closed last night with an unusual manifestation of religious fervor. Before the crowd that packed the tent to its capacity left, several benches were broken down, and fourteen persons asserted that they had been healed of chronic afflictions. One young woman, said to be eighteen years old, early in the evening underwent what the members of the creed called "the power of God" and laid in a stupor except when she "received the power of tongues" and she made unintelligible sounds that some of the members said they could translate. The young woman remained in this condition until after the close of the meeting and was taken away from the tent in a cot.

Mrs. M. B. Woodworth-Etter, who has been conducting the meetings, will this morning leave Topeka for Colorado Springs, where she will conduct a series of meetings.

The meeting in Topeka will be resumed next Sunday in a tent at Seward and Elliott Street and will continue indefinitely, Pastor C. E. Foster says. Excepting Sunday, only night meetings will be held. On Sunday, Sunday school will be held at 2:30 o'clock in the afternoon and church services at 3:30 and 8 o'clock.

The meeting that closed last night was attended by persons from nineteen states and from Canada.

November 13, 1915

The Weekly Evangel

The Deaf Hear and the Dumb Speak

God Owns and Blesses Sister Etter's Meetings in Colo. Springs, Colo.

God anointed His servant with mighty power to preach the Word and proclaim deliverance to those bound. Many received with gladness. One man was nearly dead of miner's consumption—was not saved and could not live but a short time. He heard and believed and when prayer was offered for him, Jesus touched him and saved his soul and healed his body. This was a mighty miracle, as the man was partially paralyzed and the bones of his neck ossified until he could not raise his head. But Jesus broke the chains and set him free. He walked up and down the platform praising and glorifying God and preaching to the people—said he would work for the Lord the rest of his days.

A woman of forty years, born deaf and dumb, was prayed for and Jesus opened the deaf ears and she heard the songs for the first time in her life. It was like heaven to her. Then Sister Etter told her to speak. At first she could only squeak, then a word, and she said "Praise the Lord"—the first words that had ever passed her lips.

From Colorado Springs Mrs. Etter went to Pueblo, Colo. and held a ten-days meeting. The people were stirred and blessed of God so that they desired to continue the meetings under her. One woman afflicted with two tumors in the bowels and other diseases, so that she could not sleep for pain, was raised up in answer to the prayer of faith. All pain left. "O" she said, "now I can sleep." She went home rejoicing in deliverance and praising God.

Let the people pray that God will do a mighty work here in Los Angeles and save and baptize many souls.

—F. Langdon
1604 Griffith Ave.
Los Angeles, Cal.

November 20, 1915

The Weekly Evangel

Sister Etter Has Success in Los Angeles, Calif.

Meetings will continue to Nov. 30th

We have received a number of good reports from Sister Etter's meetings which have been held with Brother Garr's Assembly in Los Angeles, Calif. Brother William Black sent in an account of wonderful healings and of the special blessing of the Lord upon the services. He said, "We have been greatly refreshed by the visit of our sister to this city, so much so that she has decided to stay another month with us. A great number have been with us from other parts, from the East and South as well as from along the coast. The interest seems to be increasing and great numbers of our city people seem to be attracted. The singing at times is wonderful, accompanied by our fourteen-piece orchestra, led by Brother Benham, cornet soloist. Our Brother F. F. Bosworth of Dallas, Texas, a converted bandmaster, and his brother Burt, have been a great blessing to the people. Sister Etter's sermons have been powerful and faith-inspiring, and great numbers have been healed as well as saved and filled with the Spirit."

Brother Black stated that he has personally investigated and witnessed the following cases:

A sister, seventy-seven years old, was brought directly from the hospital (in her hospital attire) and claims to have been perfectly healed when prayed for. She had been given up by five doctors.

Mrs. Rosa Lopez, a Mexican preacher's wife, who had been afflicted for seven years with a stone tumor, was healed. During the past four years, she had suffered much and was continually getting worse, being almost at the point of death. She was brought to the meeting and prayed for on Sunday afternoon, and at 3:30 Sunday morning, the tumor passed completely away. This woman testifies with great power. Her husband desires the saints to pray that the way will open up for them in Mexico to preach. He can be addressed as follows: Abundio L. Lopez, 130 N. Vignes St., Los Angeles, Calif.

Jessie Ehmann, aged twenty-three, was brought to the meeting a born invalid, absolutely helpless. She had been in the hospital five times and could not turn in bed or dress herself. She had to eat with a spoon and her voice had almost gone. She was severely afflicted with bowel and kidney trouble. She knew nothing about church or religion. She has been saved and filled with the Holy Ghost. Her voice was restored when prayer was offered for her, and she turned in bed for the first time. When she found that she could turn, she turned over in bed six times. She can now eat with knife and fork and dress herself and lift her arms. The day she was prayed for she took some steps alone for the first time, and she says she is daily rapidly improving.

Mrs. Parker of this city (Los Angeles) was prayed for and healed of a tumor, which later passed away and weighed three-fourths of a pound. Her little daughter, five years old, was prayed for and healed of epilepsy. She had been having from two to five spasms a day. The mother says there is a remarkable change in the child.

It is reported that a good spirit has been manifested all through the meeting. The big, long altar is daily filled with seekers and many break through to God getting saved, healed, and baptized in the

Holy Spirit, coming out speaking in other tongues and magnifying the Lord.

Among other things related was that of a visit of angels. Brother Edward Leroy Wiley of Gonzales, Monterey Co., Calif., came four hundred miles to get the baptism in the Holy Ghost. Three weeks before he had been reclaimed from a backslidden condition and had been filled with a hunger and thirst for more of God. He came to Los Angeles and tried to get the baptism with his head bowed down in quietness. Finally he held up his head and praised God with all his might for what had already been done for him, and the power of God came upon him and he spoke in two languages, giving one special message for these last days in a language which was understood to be Turkish. He tried to tell them in English but could not. He cried out to the sinner to come to God and be filled with the Holy Ghost. Then he took hold of his sister and told her to get down on her knees and ask God to baptize her; and she obeyed and received her baptism, speaking in other tongues. Brother John Reese understood every word that was spoken. Brother Reese is an educated young man, born of Italian parents, educated to be a Roman Catholic priest. He was converted through reading the Word of God. He speaks seven languages, having served three years during the Italian-Turkish war. He came to America on a sightseeing trip, but God baptized him with the Holy Ghost and fire and keeps him here and uses him for His glory. He gave the message spoken through Brother Wiley to thousands.

That night Brother Reese went home and went to bed. He was awakened by hearing a voice and opened his eyes and saw two angels standing by his bed. A light filled the room, as the angels were bright and shone like the sun. They had long golden hair and beautiful wings, and each carried a golden palm. Even their feet, finger nails, and toe nails were all shining with the same brightness, and their feet never touched the floor, but they stood on a level with his bed. Brother Reese thought Jesus was coming sure and he tried to awaken the brother who slept with him, but he slept on.

The angel spoke to him in a tender voice of sweetness and said in English, "Go and warn God's people to watch and pray, for the time is at hand for the coming of the Lord. Tell them to warn the American people that God is preaching to Europe at the cannon's mouth because He spread His hands all day long to a rebellious people, speaking to them by the Spirit and they would not hear.[1] Each nation is claiming that its god is the greatest, yet in reality they are all mocking God. A man will soon conquer Europe and then God will preach to this nation with the mouth of the cannon; and those who are asleep (deceived) will remain asleep, and those whose eyes are on man will remain with man; and this country will be conquered. Then Jesus will catch away His bride and God will take away His Spirit from the earth; and those who are not filled with the Spirit, whose lamps are not trimmed and burning,[2] will fall on that day. The time is at hand."

The angels then disappeared. Brother Reese said that all strength left him and he seemed so small and helpless before these ministering servants sent from God.

This is certainly a warning to come to God and to be filled with the Holy Spirit and be ready before it is too late. Truly the time is short when God will send His angels down to earth to warn the people.

The above account of an angel visit was reported by Grace Cochran Thomson of 3029 Sixth Ave., Los Angeles, Calif. Whether the message is correct as to detail or not matters little, the fact remains that visions are being received in many places which emphasize the fact that Jesus is coming soon.

---

[1] See Romans 10:21.

[2] See Matthew 25:7, Revelation 1:3; 22:10.

July 19, 1916

Petoskey Evening News (MI)

Have You Heard That

Miracles and gifts of Bible times are here today. Mrs. M. B. Woodworth-Etter is holding meetings in Petoskey at the Pentecostal campground at 1038 Emmet Street with great success. They have been in session for two weeks, will continue four weeks longer. Over thirty years Sister Etter has been one of the most successful evangelists of this country. The signs that the Bible says shall follow the believers, *vis-à-vis*[1], "In my name shall they cast out devils"; they shall speak with new tongues . . . they shall lay hands on the sick, and they shall recover (Mark 16:17-18), have followed Sister Etter's ministry during all those years. Especially is this true in the healing of the sick; many thousands having been healed of all manner of diseases and many after being given up by the best physicians as hopeless.

Recently Mrs. Etter held meetings in Los Angeles; San Diego; San Francisco; and Houston, Tex., all of which were highly successful, especially on the coast where rheumatism, tumors, cancers, fevers, lameness, deafness, and many other diseases yielded to the prayer of faith. We have already seen similar results during the last two weeks in this city. Every person in Northern Michigan should attend these meetings; come and bring the sick and afflicted to be healed. Public sessions will be held daily at 10 A.M., 2:30, and 7:30 P.M. Come and see the power of God being manifested as in times of old. "Jesus Christ the same yesterday, and to day, and for ever" Hebrews 13:8.

[1] "*vis-à-vis*"—over and against, toward; compared with (Webster's Third N.I. 1997). Not quite correct usage of this term. The reporter means "that is to say," or "i.e."

July 29, 1916

The Weekly Evangel

Mrs. Etter in Petoskey, Mich.

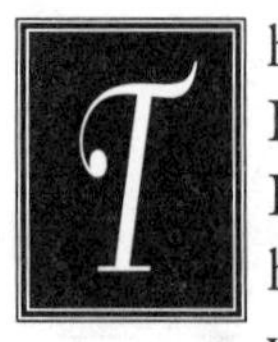he Woodworth-Etter meetings in Petoskey, Michigan, have begun with wonderful interest and power. The interest and attendance are rapidly increasing. People have come and are coming from far and near. A minister from the state of New York writes, "I am coming to get Pentecostal power in my life." We are looking for an unusual outpouring of God's Spirit in these meetings. The "signs of the times," as they are being manifested among the warring nations this summer, almost demand that God's people have corresponding signs and demonstrations of His power in their camps. Let us pray that this may be so.

Last night, the third night of the meeting, the power of God fell like large drops of rain all over the tent. Saints were praying, weeping, shouting all over the congregation as the power fell upon them. A woman back in the audience came hastily forward with her friend to the altar and began to weep and pray her way through to God. In just a few minutes the power fell on her. She rose and almost ran up onto the platform to Sister Etter and asked her to forgive her for speaking evil against her and of the power of God, saying that she thought it was hypnotic power and that she prayed for God to smite her if it was not His power. God's smiting power came, but it fell on her so that with heavy tears and prayer she asked God to forgive her for speaking evil of His power.

Already quite a number have been saved, healed, and baptized with the Spirit, having the evidence of tongues. Some wonderful testimonies on healing of two years ago are being given. These souls do demonstrate that the work that the Spirit wrought in their bodies two years ago has been permanent. The shout of victory is all over the camp. Let all the saints pray that this whole northern peninsula may become enlightened with Pentecostal truth and power.

—August Feick, Secretary

Note: Mrs. Etter's address while in Petoskey is 214 Washington Street.

August 5, 1916

The Weekly Evangel

Further Report of Mrs. Etter's Petoskey Meeting

he Woodworth-Etter revival, which began July 1st, continues to grow in interest and power. The Lord is coming forth in a marvelous way, confirming His Word with the signs following, and signs and wonders are done in the name of the Holy child Jesus. People from the various states are still continually coming in. People are flocking to the altar by scores. Many are being prostrated by the mighty power of God and see wonderful visions.

There are many marvelous cases of healing. A sister came from a distance who had not walked without a cane for three years, [she] got healed while sitting in her chair, without the laying on of hands. Another one, while caught away in the Spirit, saw a mighty angel descending and hovering over the tent; also [she saw] the power of God coming and filling the place, making it shine like glittering jewels. She was shown that the Spirit was gathering together the elect and binding them together in bundles. Surely the Lord is working "His acts, His strange acts"[1] in these last days, confirming His Word with the signs following. Glory to Jesus!

Cancers and various diseases are healed through the prayer of faith. A deaf-mute was healed and immediately she heard the music and began to dance, keeping perfect time with it. It was a beautiful sight.

A sister from Detroit, who several physicians said could not get well even if she did have an operation, was instantly healed of her internal troubles. She had worn spectacles for twelve or fourteen years and could not stand the light at all. Now she can see distinctly without them. Her husband also was healed of a double rupture.[2] When the power of God came upon, him he leaped and danced as if nothing had ever been the matter with him. They both received the baptism of the Holy Ghost.

---

[1] See Isaiah 28:21.

[2] "double rupture"—double hernia.

Many stirring messages are given in tongues, with interpretation, about the soon coming of the Lord, also about the wrath of God to be soon poured out upon the earth, warning people to be hidden away under the blood of Jesus, the only place of safety.

The heavenly choir, with the swelling notes from the invisible instruments of music, is heard in a wonderful way and then music as sweet and soft as the sighing of the summer breezes; also sounds as of the warbling of birds. No words can describe these things.

One sister had a vision of the Lord bursting the clouds with all the angels, catching up the saints to meet Him in the air. Another one saw the glory of God like tongues of fire come down and rest upon the heads of the saints; and as she continued to pray for yet greater power, she saw the whole place so filled with the glory that she could not distinguish one from the other.[1]

Surely the Lord is pouring out His Spirit in a wonderful way. The time is short and He that is to come will come and will not tarry, and that which is done must be done quickly. "Even so, come, Lord Jesus."[2]

—Mrs. Susie Woods

[1] See Acts 2:3 and 1 Kings 8:10-12.

[2] See Hebrews 10:37, John 13:27, and Revelation 22:20.

September 2, 1916

The Weekly Evangel

Mrs. Etter's Petoskey Meeting Closed

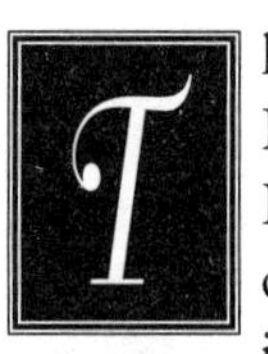

The Woodworth-Etter meetings at Petoskey, Mich., closed with great interest and power. The last day, one hundred and fifty or more were anointed for service in the master's vineyard. Reports have come back already from some of these in which they say they have received new gifts. One reported that the power of God falls and the saints dance in the Spirit in the assembly for the first time. God has also given us one of the worst women in the city.

For September, Sister Etter is billed for Sidney, Iowa. The report comes that over one hundred tents are spoken for already. Come and join us in this feast.

From October 6th to 30th, she is billed for Salt Lake City, Utah, and then from November 4th and indefinitely for San Francisco, Calif., where God so marvelously worked last winter. The pastor there has written, "Ever since your campaign last winter, we have had afternoon meetings daily." They moved from their little hall to one that holds about eight hundred people. The way it looks now, San Jose, Calif., will be next, and then (D.V.) Los Angeles, Calif.

Next summer it seems the Lord will have Sister Etter hold a large campaign in Indianapolis, Indiana. Let all the saints pray for God's handmaiden and for the work.

—August Feick, Secretary

***

We have been unable as yet to publish the report received from Sister Etter a short time ago in which further accounts of the revival at Petoskey were given. We will give the substance of it as follows:

> The Spirit of God has melted the various Pentecostal factions into one spirit of unity so that a deep conviction is settling upon scores of people.
>
> A Catholic family living close by bitterly opposed us when the meetings started. As the meetings progressed, a deep conviction settled upon them. One night the Spirit brought text after text of Scripture to her, which she quoted to her husband, but did not know herself where they were, not having a scriptural knowledge. The next night the husband came forward and soon was saved and baptized with the Spirit. He got up on the altar and asked the audience not to speak evil against this work as he had done, saying it was of God. He asked Sister Etter and all the saints to forgive him for what he said.
>
> Another family came up from Indiana and stayed as long as they could. Their daughter was healed of tuberculosis,

spinal trouble, and a goiter [. . .} (*sic*)[1] in arrangements and moved temporarily up here so that they could be in the balance of the meetings. All the symptoms of the disease in their child are gone and the goiter also totally disappeared.

Another sister of Boyne City, Mich., was perfectly healed, her sense of smell (which had been completely lost) being perfectly restored. She was so rejoiced to find she could smell a rose and is now praising God for her healing.

All the saints in this northern peninsula received great inspiration. More than half a dozen from one community came here and received their baptism and healing and went back home happy and praising God.

—August Feick, Sec.

[1] The article was apparently misprinted, leaving something out.

November 4, 1916

The Weekly Evangel

The Etter Meeting at Salt Lake City

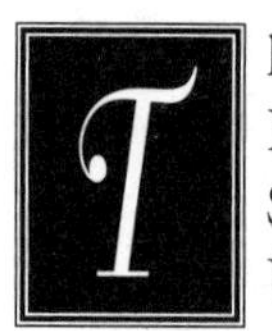

The Woodworth-Etter meetings at Salt Lake City, Utah, are at the time of this writing causing much interest over a good part of this city. Many people are under deep conviction and people surrender daily to God and are saved. Others again get healed and baptized with the Spirit. Last night two came through with the Bible evidence.

On the same mat, where prize fights are staged—stained with blood—sinners weep their way through to God and saints receive their baptism. This piece of canvas certainly will be witness for and against some people in the Day of Judgment.

Last night the glory of God filled the theater mostly all through the meeting. Sister Etter was held like a statute (*sic*)[1] a good part of the time by the power of God. At the close of the meeting,

[1] "statute"—incorrect; statue is meant here.

about a half-dozen of the most spiritual young saints made inquiries about the peculiar mist in the building. They did not know that it was God's glory or that anyone else saw and felt it. Jesus was seen on the platform. A report just came to me through a sister saying she knows of outside people who testify that they saw angels while the meeting was going on.

Marvelous messages in tongues with interpretations come continually. Some Mormons have received their baptism already; others are seeking. The work that God does in the way of healing is drawing many people. People get proofs that God heals which cannot be gainsaid.

Just one little instance. About two years ago a woman fell and fractured her wrist. It healed up, leaving her fingers cold and stiff. The blood would not circulate properly through them. She could not close them or move them. When she was prayed for they limbered up, and now they are perfectly natural. The natural life has come back again. She was also healed of chronic rheumatism of forty years standing. She testifies continually, "I would not take a thousand dollars for what God has done for me. Oh! I am so glad; so happy, etc."

The work is in such a condition here now that if carried on in the same spirit, there is no reason why a strong mission will not be established in a short time. This city is so centrally located that there is need of a strong center here. Let all the saints pray for the work in this part of the vineyard.

—August Feick

December 9, 1916

The Weekly Evangel

Sister Etter at San Francisco, California

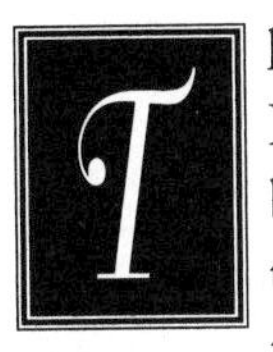

he Woodworth-Etter meetings have been going on at this place for over two weeks now and much has been accomplished for God. In a very unusual way, God seems to be laying a foundation for a deep work which He is going to carry on till Jesus comes.

The saints of various beliefs and missions are being brought together and bound together by the one Spirit.

It is the belief of many of the saints that God wants to start a deep revival here, much like He did at Azusa Street, Los Angeles, that will sweep over the whole country and bring all the saints back into the deeper things of the Spirit. Messages in tongues and interpretations come forth daily to this effect. The glory of God is seen time and time again in the house. Sinners are getting saved and saints baptized, also wonderful healings take place daily and a deep conviction is over the whole audience.

The pastor, R. J. Craig, and the saints, feel that God does not want us to leave this city for some time to come, so I expect to be here at least all of December. We expect and look for a mighty outpouring during this month, one that will shake the whole city.

Unless God changes us otherwise, in January we will be in San Jose, Cal. Then beginning about February 10th at Los Angeles for six weeks. Beginning about the 1st of April, we expect to be at Omaha, Neb., for a month. Then from June 1st, we expect to begin an indefinite campaign at Indianapolis, Ind. Let all the saints pray for the work.

For Mrs. Etter,
—August Feick

December 16, 1916

The Weekly Evangel

The San Francisco Etter Meeting

Sister Woodworth-Etter and her assistants, Brother Feick and Sister Susie Wood, arrived in San Francisco a month ago fresh and vigorous after a number of battles in the East and Middle West. Sister Etter is a monument of the sustaining power of God. After forty years of the most strenuous and trying work in which one could engage, her force and power are comparatively unabated. If the Pentecostal ministry would study her life and count on God, expecting the supernatural to be revealed in each meeting, what a mighty agency ours would be in the hands of God. Sister Etter is simply brokenhearted if the Lord does not work in each meeting. For this reason God does not disappoint her. She has discovered through her long years of evangelistic work that, if the people come together in unity and love, yielding to the will of God, He never fails to come forth, so that in reality the responsibility for a spiritual revival is placed upon the saints.

Many hindrances are in the way of great awakening on the Pacific Coast. Doctrinal strife, which has been rampant for some years, has caused saints to be suspicious of one another. All divisional differences had to be laid aside, that the various "factions" might flow together in love. This is no small task, as Satan contests every inch of advance in this direction. God adheres strictly to His own divine law for a spiritual awakening. He is doing so in San Francisco. Victory is in the Commander!

In less than one month a great work has been accomplished in blending, melting prejudices, in the salvation of sinners and the restoration of backsliders. Not a few have been healed and many baptized in the Holy Ghost. This meeting, in the mind of God, is to be an epoch-making one, judging from many encouraging messages that have come forth in the Spirit. God is striving to bring the latter-day Pentecostal saints into the white-heated love of the early Pentecostal church, where no one called anything that he had his own—where great grace was upon all the church.[1] This program should girdle the whole world, and getting all who will ready for the great world event, the coming of our dear Elder Brother.

—ROBERT J. CRAIG, PASTOR

[1] See Acts 52:44-47 and 4:32-33.

January 6, 1917

The Weekly Evangel

Miraculous Healing of a Child

uring the month of November, 1916, my baby, who will be two years old in February, 1917, was in the Children's Hospital affected with pus in the bladder and continued to get worse and worse until she was not expected to live; and while waiting for her to pass away, I came to Mrs. M. B. Woodworth-Etter's meetings and had her pray over a handkerchief. Leaving the meeting for home, the telephone rang; and the hospital asked me to take the first taxicab and come immediately to the hospital, as [the] baby was very low and might not be alive unless I made haste. Arriving at the bedside around which the house physician and nurses were standing awaiting the end, I placed the handkerchief on [the] baby's stomach, and she at once commenced to quiver and shake under God's power and within four minutes sat up and said, "Take me home, Mamma."

"What did you do to the child?" asked the doctor as the nurses stood amazed.

"I did not do anything; the Lord did it all," I replied. The next morning she got up and was playing around. I give God the glory for her life."

—Inez Broberg, San Francisco, Cal.

March, 1917

The Pentecostal Herald

Woodworth-Etter Meetings at Los Angeles, California

he meetings have at the time of this writing been going on for nearly one week. Prospects look very good for a "mighty revival to break out in this city." The saints are in a remarkable way all of one mind and are praying and working to this end. Doctrinal differences are all laid to one side for which we are very glad. God has also given us a fine hall in a new location to hold our meetings in. Both the business and the spiritual part of this meeting are entirely in the hands of Sister Etter. This has been done to make the people absolutely free to come and partake of the feast and help to push the battle against the "powers of darkness."[1]

The saints are coming in from many outside places, some from a long distance. One brother and sister, who have been writing us of late from Scotland, made their appearance and are being greatly used in the meeting. About twelve or more got saved already, others reclaimed, and quite a number received the baptism. Last night after the message came forth, the Spirit took possession of the meeting, so that it never was dismissed. People fell under the mighty power on the right hand and on the left. Some danced, others sang in the Spirit. Others again got a spirit of intercession and plead[ed] with sinners. It truly was a solemn time.

One young man of the Y. M. C. A., a worker, came into the meeting. He had just heard of Pentecost a few days before. The power came on him and stretched him out on the seats. Shortly afterwards he made a rush for the altar and fell prostrated by the saints who worked around the altar. He had a great conflict before he yielded wholly to the Spirit. The saints prayed for him and soon he came out with a bright baptism, "praising and magnifying God"[2] in another language, just as Christ said they should if they believe (Mark 16:17). Another sister got marvelously healed when the power came on her and she laid her hands on the afflicted part of her body. Some others got saved. Sinners are asking, "What does all this mean?" The answer is plain and simple. God has many people these days who are sitting and learning at the feet of Jesus: By faith they see Him on the right hand of God. They are partaking of His Spirit daily so that a transformation takes place in their lives. Like it was said of His disciples of old, so it is today, "they take knowledge that these people have the Spirit of Jesus."[3]

[1] See Colossians 1:13.

[2] See Acts 10:41.

[3] See Acts 4:13.

Yesterday a number got saved and baptized with the Holy Spirit. A few days before, a message was given in tongues and interpreted in English. A young man who has studied for the priesthood said a good part of it he understood, that it was in Latin and that it was correctly interpreted. These are just a few things that we mention. We pray that God will shake this city before this campaign closes. If you have friends close by, invite them to the hall, 1121 S. Los Angeles Street, "The People's Auditorium." We hope to be here all of March. Pray much for this campaign.

Just a few words about our arrest at San Jose, Cal., since many saints are anxious to know. We were arrested, Sister Etter and Brother Kline, the third night of our campaign, for disturbing the peace of the neighborhood and lewd conduct. The disturbance of the peace and the supposed lewd conduct took place on Sunday evening, the second night of our meeting, when between ten and eleven o'clock a young woman came out "praising God in another language," or in other words, when she received her baptism. The glory of God filled her soul and body and she, giving vent to her feelings a little, disturbed the peace (or conscience) of a neighbor. Sister Etter had left the meeting that night at twenty minutes to ten. Brother Kline, who is a pastor, did not have charge of the meeting. The warrant was made out for these two, so they were arrested and taken to the police station. Some of the officers testified that it was a shame to have to make the arrests but that they were obliged to do it. People outside of the work at once offered us bail so that we had them bailed out in a short time. We all appeared in court the next morning, when the judge put the trial off for two weeks. When the two weeks were up, Sister Etter was told that she need not appear. It was then put off for one more week and then dismissed for good without Sister Etter appearing at all. The enemy had no case and I guess he knew it. God got some glory out of it.

God greatly blesses *Signs and Wonders.* Very encouraging reports come in almost daily. The following is part of one letter that came today: "I have always been a good church worker and supposed I was good until I picked up your book." This is what it will do for many others if it can only be placed in their hands. Why not help us to scatter them? We are making a great sacrifice on this book. Write us and see how many books we will have the factory ship you direct for $25. These are the days to scatter the truth. If you can, God will greatly bless your efforts.

AUGUST FEICK
210 E. 11TH ST.

March 10, 1917

The Weekly Evangel

Woodworth-Etter Meetings at Los Angeles, Cal.

e have at this time of writing been holding meetings in this city for about ten days. Prospects look very good for a great outpouring of God's Spirit. The saints are turning out in large numbers. On Sunday, the hall would not accommodate the people. We have been very much impressed with the sweet spirit that is manifest among the saints: a spirit of love and unity. It appears as if God is preparing His people here for another Azusa revival. For this we are all praying and working. Many have been saved already, others reclaimed, and lately each day two or three received the baptism. Also some wonderful cases of healings have taken place—some got healed while sitting in their seats.

A few days ago a message came forth in another language by a brother who can only speak German and English. A young man who is educated for the Catholic priesthood sat back in the audience, testified later on that he understood a good part of the message, which was spoken in the Latin language. He further stated that the sister who gave the interpretation gave the correct interpretation in English. Many such workings in the Spirit might be mentioned. The saints testify on all sides about the sweet unity of the Spirit that prevails in this campaign. We expect a great revival before we close, which may be after a few months.

I wish to say that God greatly blesses our new book *Signs and Wonders*. It pays to make some effort to circulate this book. The following is just a little sample. This came in yesterday's mail from a pastor of the M. E.[1] Church of the Central Illinois Conference. "Mrs. Woodworth-Etter, Dear Madam, and sister in Christ: I came as I have fully supposed into the experience of the baptism of the Holy Ghost thirty-one years ago. I have been a preacher and teacher of the Pentecostal baptism ever since. However, since reading your new book, *Signs and Wonders,* according to your teaching, I have never received the real Pentecostal baptism. Now, I want, yea, I covet the best gifts and am absolutely in God's hands to be, to do, to forego, or to suffer anything, in any way, at any time, and in any place. I want your prayers and the anointing of this handkerchief, first that I may receive the divine anointing to speak with tongues, to lay hands on the sick and pray for them, or to do anything God has for me to do." Surely God is blessing the book. Let us pray for this pastor.

Beginning about June 1st, we expect to hold meetings at Indianapolis, Ind.

—August Feick.

Sister Etter's new book can be obtained from the Evangel office, $1.15 postpaid.

[1] "M. E."—Methodist Episcopal.

March 17, 1917

The Weekly Evangel

The Etter Meetings at Los Angeles, Cal.

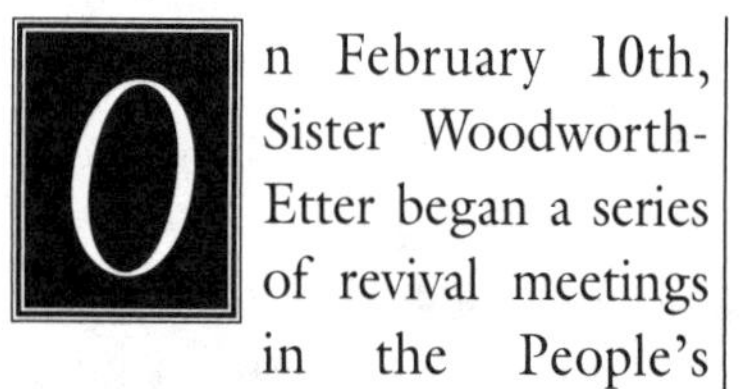

On February 10th, Sister Woodworth-Etter began a series of revival meetings in the People's Auditorium, 1121 South Los Angeles St., Los Angeles, Cal. From the first meeting, which was on Saturday night, to the present writing, it has been one wave of glory and power after another, each succeeding wave rising higher than the former.

The result has been that many who were far out on the sea of life without chart or compass have been brought ashore and anchored in the haven of eternal life through Jesus Christ our Lord. Many backsliders have been reclaimed, many believers baptized in the Holy Ghost, and many sick ones healed. The love, the unity, and the sweet fellowship is deep beyond description. Many of the most remarkable messages in tongues and interpretations that we have ever heard have been coming forth almost daily.

Wonderful visions have been seen by many. A man who served on the police force of Los Angeles for five years, and who has been saved, is seeking his baptism and is just at the point of receiving it. A few nights ago, while under the power, God showed him one thing in his life which he had to make right. Then He gave him a vision of the whole earth, taking him from one continent to another and letting him see the conditions of the world and the final closing of the age.

He saw Satan sitting, and back of him great clouds of darkness enveloping multitudes of peoples, held in darkness by his satanic power, waiting for the last sound of the trumpet. Then the bride was caught away and the darkness covered the earth, and the multitudes went forth destroying and to destroy. Others have seen Christ in the audience, standing among His saints. One sister saw the Holy Spirit in the form of a white dove flying about over the people. On all sides saints are heard saying, "This is the greatest meeting I was ever in." People are here from all parts of the United States and Canada. Frequently the glory of God fills the place so the priests cannot minister.[1]

Sister Etter's new book, *Signs and Wonders,* is being read eagerly by the people. I suppose the same is in your section of the country by your recent "rush order" for fifty additional copies.

—YOUR BROTHER IN CHRIST

W. M. COLLINS.

[1] See 2 Chronicles 5:13-14.

March 24, 1917

The Weekly Evangel

The Etter Meetings in Los Angeles, Cal.

Brother William H. Giles sends us a good report of the meeting that has been proceeding during the past month in Los Angeles. There are many manifestations of the Spirit's presence. He writes, "A lady, coming with four others from Maryland, had a cancer on the tongue. She had lost the use of that member completely, so that she could not speak. Her doctors had told her that the only hope for her life was to have her tongue cut out. After listening to the messages at a few meetings, she was convinced her time for action had arrived. She was assisted onto the long platform and was prayed for, the cancer was rebuked in the name of Jesus, and by the power vested in the name, it underwent a surgical operation. Last evening she arose and told the vast audience that Jesus had not only completely healed the cancer, but had given her a new tongue and a new voice with which to praise Him. Another old lady was cured of what seemed to be diseases without number and while under the mighty slaying power of God, received the baptism of the Holy Spirit.

"On Sunday evening, March 4th, a lady brought a handkerchief to be prayed over, stating that it was for her child who was badly afflicted with eczema, his face being badly broken out and swollen. The following Wednesday the same lady rose in the meeting and said, 'Praise God, my child is completely delivered, and all traces of the swelling have disappeared.' Many testified during the same meeting that while the power was falling, and the "heavenly chorus" was being sung,[1] the Lord reached down and completely healed their bodies."

[1] "heavenly chorus"—possibly a reference to singing in the Spirit, that is, singing spontaneously created tunes in their own language and in tongues.

April 7, 1917

The Weekly Evangel

The Etter Meetings in Los Angeles, Cal.

he meetings in "The People's Auditorium," 1121 South Los Angeles St., conducted by Sister Etter are still in progress and will continue until some time in the early part of April under her supervision. She will then leave for her home in Indianapolis, where she begins another campaign June 1st.

We are arranging for other help so that our meetings here will continue right on without ceasing, probably through the entire summer.

We are utterly at a loss for words to express the depth and sweetness as well as the power in these meetings. It is truly wonderful. Souls are coming through at almost every service. The singing of the heavenly choir is characterized by a harmony surpassing that of the most skillfully trained voices. And then in a low, sweet voice, like the dove answering one another from the branches of different trees, the Spirit speaks back and forth from one to another over the audience, reminding one of the words in the Song of Solomon: "The voice of the turtle is heard in the land."[1]

Another pleasing feature of the meeting is, there have been no doctrinal issues brought forward. Christ has been held up with a joy and gladness surpassingly beautiful. If this were done everywhere, a revival would sweep the country, and soon from the crest of the wave we would rise to meet our Lord in the air. The Lord hasten the day when it shall be so!

Tonight after Sister Etter had given a very effective message on the "signs of the times," fourteen Armenian brethren, who had come in from their mission, sang a song in their own language. Sister Woods, who goes with Sister Etter as interpreter, gave the interpretation and the Armenian brethren confirmed it as correct.[2] They sang a second time and again the interpretation came forth and they confirmed it. The effect on the audience was marvelous to the last degree. The altar is now full of seekers at this writing.

—W. M. Collins

[1] Song of Solomon 2:12, paraphrased.

[2] Sister Woods is not a linguist. She has the gift of interpretation as mentioned in 1 Corinthians 12:10. She does not understand Armenian, but the Holy Spirit gives her the English translation in a supernatural way. Audience recognizes this interpretation as a miracle.

August 18, 1917

The Weekly Evangel

Sister Etter Closes at Indianapolis, Ind.

he Woodworth-Etter meetings at her home city, which have been going on in June and July, turned out to be a great success. Scores of people have come in from various states and have received what they came for and went back rejoicing.

Already mail comes in telling us how the fire kindled in the hearts of saints while here is spreading in their homes and mission fields. A letter came a few days ago, which stated that on their way home a meeting was held by some of the saints at a station with marvelous results. Surely the results of this campaign in the light of eternity will be seen to have been marvelous. Many saints, who came prepared to stay only a few days, went back and made arrangements to come and stay to the end of the campaign. These proved a great blessing.

I do not believe that I ever witnessed a campaign where so many people were disappointed when we closed. The interest and power were on the increase through the whole campaign. Yesterday a woman stopped me on the street and with tears streaming down her eyes remarked, "When are you starting up again? I live here and now believe this is of God and the baptism is for me."

A vegetable peddler came to the house and said, "My wife wants to know when you folks start up again. We both believe your work is of God." Many such instances might be mentioned.

One night Sister Etter and a few of the saints were held like statues for nearly half an hour. It seems like as if we could never dismiss the meeting, the power of God was so great. The night following, the power fell on a young woman back in the audience who was in the meeting for the first time, not saved, so that she ran forward back and forth around the altar, then got on top of it; later on she got on the platform and began to plead with sinners. The Spirit took the meeting so that a message by a preacher could not come forth.

Some marvelous cases of healing took place daily. A woman was so marvelously delivered of a snaky, shaking spirit which she had for forty years, that she at once sent for her sister in Florida to come.

Her sister came and got healed of her diseases, too. Now they are both well and happy.

Because Sister Etter and her workers needed rest so bad (*sic*), it was thought best to close. The work begun will, when God opens the way, be carried on in a tabernacle and made permanent. Let all the saints pray for it. Thus far no other meeting is announced yet.

—August Feick

February, 1918

The Pentecostal Herald

Report of Mrs. Etter's Work

2114 Miller St.
Indianapolis, Ind.

ear Brother Brinkman:

Following is a little report for your next issue:

Many calls come in and many inquiries are made about our meetings. The saints are anxious to find out when and where the next meeting will be held, but so far as we can see now, the Lord is going to help us here all winter. It is a great privilege to be at home and learn at the feet of Jesus.

He has made us intercessors for many people. So many people write for help and send handkerchiefs, which we anoint and send back; and we receive testimonies continually where people get the victory for either their body or spirit life.

God also sends people in from other states. Yesterday a young preacher came in from Watertown, New York. The day before a sister came in to tell us that she and her husband got the victory from a mad dog bite. They came in from near Evansville, Indiana, a few weeks ago and said their little dog acted strange for some time and later bit her and her husband and then died. They had the head sent to medical authorities in this city, who notified them that it died with hydrophobia and that they had to come in at once for examination and treatment. They came in; but before they went to the authorities, they came in the home and we all prayed for them. We had a glorious time. The power fell in the meeting and prostrated the husband on the floor. They both got the witness that they were healed. When the authorities examined them, they found no sign of hydrophobia in their blood. Nevertheless they made them stay in confinement in this city for eighteen days; all this time no trace of hydrophobia could be found. Their whole neighborhood nearly drove them out when they got the word that the dog's head was bad with the disease. The man was bitten on the finger and the woman in the arm. Today they have gone home, rejoicing in the victory.

Last week a young man for whom many prayers had been offered came in the home and said: "Sister Etter, I want you all to pray for me. Oh, I feel so miserable. Won't you all pray for me. I want to give my heart to God. I have been a bad man, an infidel to a large extent; I read all kinds of infidel literature—Tom Paine,[1] etc. I feel so bad. Oh, I feel like as if God won't hear me, I did so many things." Such like came from his heart, tears streaming down his eyes and humbly confessing his sins. We prayed for him and he soon received the light. In our next meeting he came in with his wife and is now determined to go on with God.

We have two meetings a week, Saturday and Sunday evening, in the home. Any of the saints coming into the city and desiring to see Sister Etter should arrange to come to these meetings. I desire to say just a few words about *Signs and Wonders.* God is truly blessing this book. So many wonderful reports come in daily that it makes our hearts leap for joy and praise God. The following testimonies are little instances:

A book, *Signs and Wonders,* found its way into the household of a prominent engineer of London, England—one that has a M.A.A.M.I.C.E. attached to his name. He took a great interest in it and soon felt impressed that its contents should be scattered all over the British Isles. He therefore wrote us about getting out an abridged edition that would appeal to his people and asked how we

[1] Thomas Paine (1737-1809) A seventeenth-century deist who wrote books during The American Revolutionary War and afterwards. Many of his works questioned the Bible and orthodox Christianity.

felt about it, as he did not want to take a step in the wrong direction. Later on, when he received our letter of prayers, counsel, and advice, he wrote back these words:

"My wife and I and our children's nurse were having evening prayers as usual on October 27, and as we were singing a hymn, nurse fell over on the floor in a trance. My wife thought she had fainted, but when she spoke a few words every now and then in a language neither of us knew, we saw that it was God's answer to our prayer, that He would fulfill Joel 2:28 to us. She remained in a trance two hours: Saw the crucifixion in detail and the Second Coming of the Lord in glory; saw her mother come out of her grave and go up to meet Him; saw our youngest boy, (2½ years old) follow, looking exactly as he does now. The telling of the vision in detail has already brought five people to Christ, to my knowledge, and many more are gloriously uncomfortable."

The Spirit impressed this man to go ahead with this work, but he was a little fearful. God soon put His approval on it, so that now he knows it is of God.

We are living in the very last days; what we do must be done quickly. A sacrifice was made to get this large edition out so that we can get it in the hands of the people (postpaid) for $1.15. About five thousand have already been sent out all over the country, including many [sent to] foreign countries. Will not the dear saints who have means and can't go out themselves, make some effort to get some of the books scattered in their neighborhood? If you do God will greatly bless you, and you will find that they will win souls for Christ and especially get honest people into Pentecost and the deeper things of God.

Write for prices of books in quantities. We will make every sacrifice we possibly can to assist you and pray over them as they go out. Let us sacrifice, work, and pray. The last days are right upon us. "For yet a little while, and He that shall come will come, and will not tarry."[2]

—August Feick, Secretary

[2] Hebrews 10:37.

March 9, 1918

The Weekly Evangel

Woodworth-Etter Tabernacle Going Up in Indianapolis

In the name of God our Father and of our Lord and Savior Jesus Christ, greetings to the saints, the beloved of the Lord who in every place are waiting and watching for the glorious appearing of our blessed Lord when we shall be caught away in the rapture to be forever with the Lord. Hallelujah! I think that you all will rejoice when I tell you that the Lord has shown me and many of the saints that we ought to build a house for the Lord on the west side of Indianapolis. Oh! Praise His name. He has made it very plain to me to arise and build at once, that whatever we do, must be done quickly for the time is very near when no man can work.[1] I have secured a lot next to my house (2114 Miller St.) and will start laying the foundation for a tabernacle at once.

For years the heart cry of the saints over the country has been for me to establish a permanent central work somewhere, where they can come at all times and receive the help they need for spirit, soul, and body. California and other places wanted this established work; but the Lord has shown me to build at Indianapolis, which is very centrally located, where the saints can gather together from all parts, in one spirit and have unity and liberty.

The Lord will surely make this a lighthouse and prepare His children to go out as flames of fire in all directions to get His people ready for His coming. Many already are talking of coming to stay and live in the city and help the work and get what they need from the Lord.

Now beloved, this is a great undertaking for me, stepping out on faith; but Jesus says, "Go forward, I will not fail you." The cattle upon a thousands are the Lord's (*sic*).[2] Many of you have been blessed in many ways in my meetings. You know what the work is, the Holy

[1] An allusion to John 9:4.

[2] Misprint in original, which should read "The cattle upon a thousand hills . . ." See Psalm 50:10.

Ghost bearing witness with signs and wonders that God is pleased with it. Now pray for this work. Moreover I would love to hear from every old friend. Tell us what the Lord shows you to do. We need workers on the building. Any can help on that line. I desire earnestly that you pray to God to help us build this tabernacle for His glory and when you pray, obey what the Lord tells you to do also.

This is to be a place where souls will weep their way into the kingdom. If all obey God, this building will go up without a jar, will be unitedly put together, and turn out to be a shining temple for the Lord in this eleventh hour. Souls will receive Pentecostal power and fire and go out and herald the Gospel unto all nations. This is the burden of my heart. May God put a hearty amen in all your hearts. Address me as follows:

Mrs. Woodworth-Etter
2114 Miller Street
Indianapolis, Ind.

June 1, 1918

The Christian Evangel

Woodworth-Etter Campaign in Indianapolis

he first general public opening of the Woodworth-Etter Tabernacle took place on Sunday, May 19th, and marks the beginning of a great work for God. Though the meetings had not been very widely announced, it was gratifying to see parties from distant towns and cities present; and quite a representation of Christian workers came, including a number prominently known throughout Pentecost. But more excellent than all was the manifest presence of God in the midst of His people to save, to bless, and to heal. A celestial golden, light-like mist filled the Tabernacle, a glorious symbol of the outpouring of the latter rain, which melted the audience and created in them a desire to be more like Christ. The weight of God's glory was on the people in every service. One sister testified that she saw the blaze of God's glory round about Sister Etter; and from behind, the everlasting arms were passed through her arms, lifting her up in the strength and power of the Anointed One, a sign of the omnipotent power of God with her to do the work that God has called her to.

Evangelist A. H. Argue delivered a powerful message in the afternoon on setting the church in order so that all the gifts of the Spirit could be manifested through the body. At the evening service, the power of God was most notably manifested when Sister Etter prayed for the sick. One brother, coming from Toledo, O[hio], had from his birth, upwards of forty years ago, his eyes so twisted that no oculist could fit glasses to them and his sight was very defective. He was prayed for, and the twist was almost instantly taken out of his eyes and his sight was restored. Another man, who had his face all bandaged up and had suffered two years with a cancer, was gloriously healed. A lady, whose eyes were sunken and almost dried up, said the eye specialist told her there was no hope for her. She was prayed for, her eyes filled out, and she was able to see all over the house. A number of others were prayed for who testified that they were healed.

A big all-summer convention is inaugurated, and a fine crowd of God's chosen workers are gathering; and God is pouring out His Spirit in mighty fullness of power.—M. W. B.

Brother A. H. Argue writes, "Mrs. Etter's new tabernacle was dedicated Sunday, May 19th, and God's power was present in a very marked way in every service. This week one young lady was carried as it were into the third heaven for about twelve hours. She was perfectly dead to the world and it was wonderful what she saw. A special invitation is extended (to all who will attend) to a great rally, commencing June 16th, for one month and as much longer as the Lord leads. All friends and those in need of help and healing for their bodies are specially invited. Board and room can be obtained at a very reasonable rate near the tabernacle. All visiting friends should come prepared to bear their part of the expense. Workers invited. For further particulars write: Mrs. Etter, 2114 Miller St., Indianapolis, Ind.

2114 Miller St., Indianapolis, Ind., July 17, 1918

August, 1918

The Pentecostal Herald

Sister Etter's Meetings

ear Brother Brinkman: I want to thank you first of all for your kindness to my daughter and I while at your place, as I did not see you before leaving; we enjoyed your good tent meeting which Brother A. H. Argue is conducting for you and the way God was manifesting Himself in your meetings.

We arrived here at Sister Etter's Friday evening, July 5, and our hearts were made to rejoice with that overflowing joy to see how God is working in such a wonderful way in saving, baptizing, and healing power. Six were baptized in the Holy Spirit one night. I think as near as I can remember there have been about twenty-five the last twelve days. There have been some wonderful healings as Sister Etter prayed for sick. They are coming from nearly every state and also Canada. God is drawing them, as the eagles are drawing the carcass,[1] so it makes me feel like shouting hallelujah. It just seems that night after night as the heavenly choir comes forth, heaven and earth come together and the heavenly birds come down and sing as they did to the shepherds on the hills of Galilee. Neighbors are coming in and crowds are increasing all the time. God is saving and baptizing many of them. In the last six or seven weeks, the address book showed over one hundred and fifty have come from all parts to be prayed for, most of them for the healing of their body, but nearly all get the double portion, the fire of God in their souls as well as healing for body.

A lady from Linten, Ind., came to the meeting almost in a dying condition. She was afflicted with cancer of the womb and was given up to die by the doctors. She had been in bed several weeks. The day before she came she had only been able to sit up a few minutes at a time and could scarcely eat any food. She felt her life swiftly ebbing away, but she looked to the Lord, and the next morning she got up to the astonishment of her husband and took the train for

[1] Misquoted allusion to Matthew 24:28, "For wheresoever the carcase is, there will the eagles be gathered together." The writer means that God is drawing them as a carcase draws eagles.

Indianapolis. The next morning, after reaching this city, she came to the meeting, and Sister Etter laid hands on her and she rebuked the disease in Jesus' name; immediately she jumped to her feet and ran across the platform leaping and shouting for joy, bending her body in various ways which she had not been able to do before. She was a woman of fifty-five or sixty years old. She said she felt like a girl of sixteen. The next morning at the boarding house she received the baptism of the Holy Spirit and saw a wonderful vision while under the power. She returned home on fire for God and her daughter was also healed of a broken arm, so they both went home shouting victory for what God had done for them.

A brother from West Virginia, through an anointed handkerchief, was wonderfully healed of hemorrhage of the lungs; later he came to the meetings and was prayed for for tuberculosis and was instantly healed. He ran across the platform shouting and praising God, throwing his arms up in the air and striking his chest which if he had done before would have caused him to have a hemorrhage. He went back home shouting the victory.

A lady from Beloit, Wis., was wonderfully healed of varicose veins. It was very hard for her to walk when she first came to the meetings, but God wonderfully touched her body; and after she was prayed for she was able to walk as well as anyone and is praising God for His wonderful healing.

Brother H. O. Scott is preaching every night for Sister Etter in the tabernacle. He has improved wonderfully since I last saw him. He sure has the full gospel message for the people of today: full salvation, and the near coming of Jesus, and other great Bible themes.

Quite a number of ministering brethren have been coming in from other places and getting greatly blessed, refilled with the Spirit, etc., and are going greatly encouraged to preach this glorious Gospel.

YOURS FOR LOST SOULS TILL HE COMES,

HOME ADDRESS, HYENS, CAL.

EVANGELIST J. C. TIMMONS

September 7, 1918

The Christian Evangel

Woodworth-Etter Revival

he revival which began at the dedication of the tabernacle last spring is still going on with unabated interest and power. Souls are daily finding their way through to God. People are coming from all the surrounding states, get[ting] on fire for God, and then go[ing] back home and start[ing] to work for God in their neighborhood.

About sixty have thus far received the baptism of the Holy Spirit with speaking in tongues as the evidence. A much larger number have followed the Lord Jesus in the ordinance of water baptism.

Some people are being wonderfully healed each day. A few days ago a woman came in from Missouri with tuberculosis of the bones. She has been on crutches for four years. When she was prayed for, she threw away her crutches and has never used them since.

A young woman from this city came to the meeting for the first time. After she was in just a little while, she felt a peculiar power come on her. She got up, walked out, and said to herself, "These people ought to be prosecuted for worshipping God the way they do." In her heart she longed to have the same experience. Going home on the car she felt the same power come down on her again. It scared her. She got off the streetcar, got on the next one, and continued her journey home. Three or four nights later she came back, and at the close of the meeting came forward to join the church. She was told she had to be born into it. She got down at the altar and sought God and soon received salvation and her baptism. Now she is out and out for God and has had visions of Jesus.

This revival is to go on indefinitely. A hearty invitation is given the dear saints to come and partake of the feast.

—August Feick

2114 Miller St.

Indianapolis, Ind.

October, 1918

The Pentecostal Herald

Woodworth-Etter Meetings

e are glad that we can report victory for the Lord's host in the camp, or Tabernacle, in West Indianapolis, Indiana The power of God is seen and felt daily as we come together and pour out our hearts to Him in supplication and prayer. The Lord is ever ready to heal, save, and baptize people with His Spirit, if we only come in childlike faith and meet the conditions laid down in His Word. Last night a dear brother came through with a marvelous baptism as quick as the meeting was dismissed. He had been seeking his baptism for years but never got absolutely free. When God baptized him, he spoke in tongues a long time. Whenever he tried to express himself in English to his wife, he would always break out anew in the other tongue that the Spirit gave him. The Spirit fell on all the saints who witnessed the scene. All felt that the language he spoke or praised God in was an Indian dialect. The night before, while the Lord went forth, a sister who had been seeking for over a year felt impressed to go into the prayer room and tarry for her baptism. In a short time, the power of God came upon her and baptized her. She exclaimed with joy and tear[s]: "I never felt the power of God come upon me like this before."

A short time ago a colored woman was brought in in a dying condition with dropsy, rheumatism, and other troubles. She had been in an absolutely helpless condition for years and confined to her bed a long time. When the prayer of faith was offered for her, she got up and demonstrated, something she was unable to do for years. Her husband had held for some time that this work was of the enemy; but when he saw what God did for his wife, he went to the altar and in a short time God baptized him with the Spirit. Others were moved to tears.

A great miracle was performed on a child about three years old that was brought in from Illinois. This child was a natural-born imbecile. It could not see, nor walk, took numerous spells at times which were of such a nature that it screamed more like an animal than a human being. Shortly after prayer the child gazed a long time at the nurse as if it was saying in its heart, "Where did you come from?" Its nerves began to get calm, too, so that the nurse thought it was most wonderful. Before it was prayed for, it was impossible to keep it in church while the meeting was going on but since prayer was offered its nurse kept it with her during service without making any disturbance whatever.

A young man came in from Union City, Ind., who was born with his feet and legs helpless and crippled. After being here a few days, God baptized him with the Spirit. His face shined with the infilling of God's glory in his body. This brother began to mend gradually. When he left he could stand on his feet alone and he has also walked some by himself. May God help the dear ones who are afflicted in body and help them to trust Him fully, lean wholly upon His promises, and receive healing.

We have a nice Sunday school every Sunday morning. God has greatly put His seal on this branch of the work thus far. The saints of God, when passing through this city, are cordially invited to stop off and worship God with us.

Sister Etter is billed for Ainsworth, Neb., Sept. 28 to Oct. 13, or longer. After this campaign she expects to come back to Indianapolis again. While she is gone the work in the Tabernacle will go right on without intermission.

Let us labor together and do all we can for the Master while we have the opportunity. Surely the day is far spent, the evening is upon us. What we do must be done quickly.[2] May God's blessing be with each one of His little children is my prayer.

—August Feick

[1] Allusion to Romans 13:12.

November, 1918

The Pentecostal Herald

Ainsworth, Neb.

Sister Woodworth-Etter arrived here from Indianapolis, Ind., Sept. 27, and opened the convention in the opera house the next night. She was accompanied by two workers, Brother J. C. Timmons and Sister Hardister. Brother W. B. Oaks and [his] wife of Lemmon, S. D., also came to assist in the meeting.

The convention was advertised to continue until Oct 13; and Sister Etter had extended the time until the 17th when on Oct. 9 all public meetings were ordered closed on account of the influenza.[1] The meeting was just getting well underway when the closing order came. We thank God for what was already accomplished. Had the work been allowed to go on, we believe it would have been one of the greatest meetings Sister Etter has ever had. Great good has been done as it is. The work has come to be looked upon with great favor in this new field. The large audiences were held with a wonderful grip and gave the closest attention to the strong messages of our dear sister now more than seventy-four years old. The singing of the "heavenly choir"[2] impressed the people deeply, and the hush upon the entire audience as Sister Etter was held motionless for some time by the Spirit was wonderful.

The power of God was clearly manifested from the first. In the second meeting a Free Methodist minister's wife fell to the floor under the power of the Holy Spirit while quietly standing by her husband in the audience. She was not a seeker for the baptism, and we saw no more of them. Others were nearly overcome at the same time to prove the mighty presence of God in the place. In the afternoon of the third day, a bright light was seen by several in the audience as it hovered over the platform. There have been conversions,

[1] This is at the height of the 1918 worldwide influenza epidemic which scientists estimate killed twenty million people and may have killed closer to fifty million. America lost an estimated 675,000 people from this flu. Many WWI American soldiers died of it while overseas.

[2] "heavenly choir"—an allusion to a time of singing in the spirit.

baptisms in the Holy Spirit, and healings of incurable diseases: we do not know how many.

The last night was the most wonderful of all. The sick flocked to the platform to be prayed for. Some very remarkable cases were two women with inward goiters, a young woman with heart disease, and a trained nurse from Kansas with an incurable case of Bright's disease. All of these were immediately healed when hands were laid on them by Sister Etter and her workers; and their faces, their testimonies, and their demonstrations of new life and freedom from soreness and pain were wonderful. The women with the goiters threw back their heads and twisted their necks in a way impossible before being prayed for. The young woman with heart trouble paced the platform, shouted and praised God for her healing, wept and laughed for joy, and after embracing her weeping husband, went to her sister who quickly came to the altar and was saved. The trained nurse told how she had been examined in the best hospitals in the land by the best physicians and was given up as a hopeless case, but now after the prayer of faith had been offered for her, not a symptom of the dreadful disease remained.

The number attending the convention from different states was large and increasing when the meeting so suddenly closed. We had rented and fitted up a large hotel a half block from the opera house for the convention. More than forty double beds were furnished and meals for all who came. No one was charged anything and all expenses were met by the freewill offerings with never a mention of money. We are sure God is pleased with the "faith method" of providing for the people at these conventions.

—Hermon L. Harvey, Pastor

April 19, 1919

The Christian Evangel

Woodworth-Etter Revival

e all believe that a mighty revival is coming to the tabernacle here in West Indianapolis, Ind., this spring and summer. Already large drops of spiritual rain are falling; and saints are coming in from far and near, bringing in the sick and afflicted and going back rejoicing in the Spirit.

These last few weeks the Lord gave us quite a number of souls and baptized in the Holy Ghost numbers of others. Sunday afternoon three received the baptism of the Holy Ghost. One of them was a young man, a Hebrew. This man has a burden for his people and desires to go out into the ministry. Last night a large man who has been in the Holiness work for years, lay prostrated under the power of God and soon came through speaking in other tongues. He came to be healed of high blood pressure and apoplexy.[1] The doctors told him he was in no condition to make the trip to Indianapolis and that the least little excitement would put an end to him. He was prayed for and healed. He demonstrates that God has completely given him the victory.

A professor of Bible ethics, etc., of a large Holiness university of this state heard about the work that God was doing in the tabernacle here. He decided to come and see for himself. What his eyes beheld left such an impression on him that he cannot get away from it. He gazed in awe and wonder at some of the manifestations of the Spirit which put him under deep conviction, for away down in his heart he knew that it was God. Yesterday we had word from him that he was coming the second time and says he wants all God has for him.

Meetings are going on; and as quick as the weather permits, we expect to have a special campaign, so that all the hungry souls that desire to come from far and near may receive the help for body and spirit that they are crying for. Pray that God will greatly bless all special revival campaigns this coming summer.

—August Feick

[1] "apoplexy"—formerly used to indicate cerebral accident or stroke (Webster's N.W. 1997).

June 14, 1919

The Christian Evangel

Special Campaign at Woodworth-Etter Tabernacle

he summer's revival campaign will be held in the new tabernacle from June 1 to July 31. A heavenly banquet is anticipated, and God's people are especially invited to come at that time and partake of the honey and wine. Manifestations of His presence are already being manifested here. Sister Woodworth-Etter, who has been in the work for over forty years, still takes an active part in the meetings; and God is greatly using her to His name's honor and glory.

A girl from Richmond, Indiana, came to the meeting, who only slept about two hours out of twenty-four. A nervous, restless spirit had taken possession of her. Her cheeks were sunken and she ate but little. She was prayed for by Sister Etter and helpers. The nervous spirit was cast out, and she lay down and slept nine hours. This was something she had not done for nine years. Since then she has been sleeping like a little child. She is now working steadily, eats more, and has gained nine pounds in four weeks. Many other cases of healing might be given showing what God is doing. Testimonies are also coming in, telling how God is healing through the anointed cloth. An evangelist, who sent a handkerchief here to be prayed over, writes: "I was so nervous and my heart was so weak that I could not assist in the meetings, but since applying the handkerchief to my body over the disease, the Lord has healed me and I am in the meetings every night telling the wonderful story of Jesus."

There has been such a demand lately for information on healing that Sister Etter felt led to get out a booklet on divine healing, which is just coming off the press. If you wish light on divine healing, send for the new booklet, fifteen cents postpaid. God is giving sweet fellowship among the saints who come to worship here. Accommodations can be had near the meetings. For information write Mrs. Woodworth-Etter, 2114 Miller Street, Indianapolis, Ind.

—Lillian P. Hardister

August 9, 1919

The Christian Evangel

Woodworth-Etter Revival

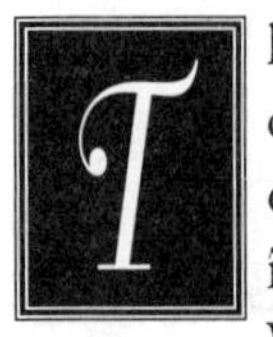

he special revival campaign is going on with increasing interest and glory. When the saints assemble, the Lord pours out His Spirit in a wonderful way; a wave of glory sweeps over the house, young and old dance under the Spirit's power. Big, stout men fall under the mighty power of God.

The Lord is using the little ones in a wonderful way. The most of them have received the baptism of the Holy Ghost and spoken in tongues as the Spirit gave utterance. It is certainly wonderful the way they dance under the power with little outstretched arms before the Lord. A message in tongues came out the other night with the following interpretation:

Interpretation of Tongues

Surely the Lord is in our midst. We will rejoice and be glad and we will praise Him in the dance.

I say unto you I am showing you signs and wonders.... I am putting My Spirit upon these little ones. If they hold their peace, the rocks and mountains would cry out.[1]

God is also proving by signs and wonders in our midst that He still dwells in Zion. Sick are being healed, devils cast out, the lame walk, the deaf hear, the blind see, and the poor have the Gospel preached to them, without money and without price.

People are coming in from the different states who have been healed in Sister Etter's meetings years ago and again receiving healing for soul and body. God is meeting the people in a wonderful way, and they are going back to their homes on fire for God.

Calls for help are continually coming from the sick and afflicted, and wonderful testimonies are coming in telling of deliverance after receiving the anointed cloth.

God is sending out His Word through Sister Etter's books and testimonies are coming in of what God is doing through them. She has

[1] See Luke 19:40.

Maria Woodworth-Etter with Cherokee Evangelist Watt Walker (c.1920). Unusual in her time, Etter often ministered with and to people of color and native Americans.

a new book called *Questions and Answers on Divine Healing*, which sells for fifteen cents.

The Word is being preached here with signs following. Come and see the wonderful works of God. The regular meetings are to continue after the special campaign closes.

—LILLIAN HARDISTER.

Mrs. Woodworth-Etter's address is 2114 Miller St., Indianapolis, Ind.

November 1, 1919

The Pentecostal Evangel

Sister Etter at Muncie, Ind.

Sister Woodworth-Etter has for the past number of weeks held a wonderful Pentecostal revival campaign at Muncie, Ind. Thousands of people attended these meetings. It is estimated that the average evening audience numbered from one to two thousand people.

People attended in large numbers. The old people remembered her by her large campaign held in Muncie some thirty years ago in which scores of people were healed and wonderfully saved. These old converts were very eager to see their spiritual mother again and again hear from her lips the old story of the Cross. They came from miles around and told in this campaign of the wonderful works of God in her meeting then. They listened for the first time to the latter-day truth that Jesus is about to come again and take His people away; that God is now filling His people as He did on the day of Pentecost with the same signs following: devils being cast out, people speaking in new tongues, and the sick healed. God gave her great inspiration and liberty in giving the message. Her voice was strong and could be heard for blocks. People said it sounded just as it did thirty years ago. The messages came forth with power and conviction and a hunger for deep things of God followed.

One night an old grey-haired man who was an infidel was at the meeting. He had just lately buried a son. His attitude was that if there was a God in heaven and had put his son in hell, he did not wish to worship Him. During the services the power struck him and he came to the front and began to praise the Lord in a wonderful way. A lady, who was a Baptist, was also in the audience. The power fell on her in the meeting. She ran forward and around the altar praising and giving glory to God.

A Jew, who was a merchant in the city and who was a backslider, came and surrendered his life, his business, and all to Jesus. God honored his sacrifice, met him in a wonderful way, poured out of His Spirit, and baptized him and his wife in the Holy Ghost; and they were among the number who lay under the power in the meeting one night. During the campaign he opened up his store and helped conduct the meeting, with food. He lost about forty dollars each week in his business in order to attend. For many years he has worn double glasses. His eyeball had been split with a hot glass. After he was prayed for for healing in the meeting, he never wore glasses again. He wishes to sell out his business and he and his wife go right out into the Lord's work.

God poured out His Spirit in a wonderful way upon the children. They fell at the altar and cried; and [they] prayed and cried out to God with their baby voices for pardon and forgiveness of sin; and the power fell, and they lay prostrate at the altar. The blood of Jesus was applied to their souls and the joy in their faces spoke of peace and joy within. Some of them had wonderful visions and many danced under the power.

One night a spiritualist medium came to the altar, got converted, got up praising the Lord, and told the people spiritualism was of the devil.

The Lord blessed soul and body in this wonderful campaign. People were taken off their crutches who had walked on them for years, and many diseases of various kinds were healed by the wonderful power of God.

A woman who had a large tumor on her back came to the meeting. Sister Etter prayed for her and the tumor left that night. The next night she was back to the meeting and testified to her healing. There was no sign of the tumor there.

A boy about eleven years old, who had been deaf and dumb since infancy, received hearing and began to talk after prayer was offered for him in the meeting.

A man was brought to the meeting almost blind. The doctor said there was no hope for his eyes. He was not able to work. He was not able to distinguish anyone on the platform when he was brought up for prayer. After he was prayed for, he could distinguish people out in the audience from the platform. The next morning he went to work and worked all day and came to meeting that night and testified to what the Lord had done. All traces of eye trouble were gone.

The last Sunday of the campaign was a remarkable day. God poured out His Spirit in a wonderful way. So many fell under the power, and four received the baptism of the Holy Ghost.

God is blessing in a wonderful way the work in Indianapolis. People are receiving the baptism of the Holy Spirit, souls are being saved, and wonderful healings are taking place

—Lillian Hardister

(The following books by Sister Etter can be gotten from the Gospel Publishing House, Springfield, Mo.: *Signs and Wonders,* which gives the story of Sister Etter's life of ministry, $1.65 post paid; *Holy Ghost Sermons,* a book of Sister Etter's latest messages, $.54 post paid; *Questions and Answers on Divine Healing,* $.15 post paid.)

August 7, 1920

The Pentecostal Evangel

Great Visitation of God to Alexandria, Minn.

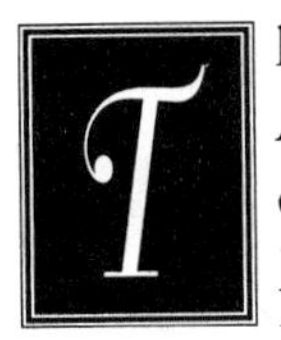

he meetings at Alexandria, Minn., conducted by Mrs. M. B. Woodworth-Etter and coworkers, assisted by the Cherokee Indian Evangelist, Watt Walker, commenced with a good attendance and interest, a number of states and cities being represented.

The first service was a dedication service. It was very impressive and solemn. The large tent, estimated to hold sixteen hundred, was dedicated to the Lord, also the small tents, and prayer that the power of God would go out from there in convicting power throughout the town of Alexandria. Then the glory of the Lord came down and filled the place. The altar was filled with hungry seekers desiring to go deeper in the Lord by seeking the baptism in the Holy Ghost. Several were healed in answer to prayer.

The Lord has demonstrated in this meeting that He is the same "yesterday, today, and forever,"[1] and came forth in mighty power, confirming the Word with signs following.

Many of the people I have talked with personally have said that Sister Etter is the greatest miracle in the meeting. Seventy-six years old, attending all three meetings a day, preaching the Word sometimes over an hour, and then praying for the sick, also encouraging and superintending the altar work. The Scripture is fulfilled in her. "They shall still bring forth fruit in old age; they shall be fat and flourishing."[2]

The plain, simple message of the hour, salvation for the soul and body, the coming of the Lord, the outpouring of the latter rain, the preparation of the bride to go forth to meet the Bridegroom (for "She shall be brought unto the king in raiment of needlework"[3]), is preached in a clear, forceful way by Sister Etter so "that wayfaring men, though fools, shall not err therein,"[4] nor fail to discern that we are living right in the last days, near to the coming of the Lord, and that we must "earnestly contend for the faith once delivered to the saints,"[5] looking for the promised signs to follow the preaching of the Word. The Lord wonderfully blessed Brother Walker in preaching the truth. He will continue the meetings until August 1st, assisted by the saints and other workers.

Night after night the altar (the full length of the tent) was crowded with seekers. Many were saved, others reclaimed, and numbers were baptized in the Holy Ghost.

[1] Hebrews 13:8, paraphrased.

[2] Psalm 92:14.

[3] Psalm 45:14.

[4] Isaiah 35:8, paraphrased.

[5] Jude 3, paraphrased.

The healing services were wonderful; so many received the healing touch that we could not enumerate them. Some were real miracles. Messages in tongues, prophecy, etc., were in evidence.

Among the many interesting things that occurred was the case of a Catholic family where the father was seeking the baptism; and his nine-years-old daughter, who had been baptized, together with her little four-years-old brother, tried with hands lifted in prayer to help the father, the little girl speaking in tongues over her father and interpreting the same. A great shout went up and doubters were convinced.

A Methodist minister from Nebraska, who with his wife attended the meetings, testified that he came because his wife needed healing but that he did not have any faith. But before he left he said he was seeking the baptism of the Holy Ghost; and he was now convinced that Pentecostal power was for this age, as well as for the apostles in their days.

The local assembly will commence to build a tabernacle right away, quite a fund having already been raised.

—S. Ione Woods

September 4, 1920

The Pentecostal Evangel

Warren, Ill.

he tent meeting at Warren, Ill., conducted by Mrs. Woodworth-Etter and coworkers, closed with a great victory for the Lord. There were only a few baptized saints in this part of the country, and Pentecost was practically new. God put His seal on the messages given with many visible signs as in healing the sick, saving hungry souls, and baptizing believers in the Holy Ghost.

An old soldier and his wife came three hundred and fifty miles to give the testimony of their daughter's healing, who had been healed in the meeting at Alexandria, Minn., of tumors and cancer. Also they wanted to be saved. They were converted and went to tell others what great things the Lord had done for them.

A lady from Iron Mountain, Mich., came to be healed of ulcers of the stomach from which she had been suffering many years. Her condition was so serious that her husband feared to let her come lest she should die on the way. The Lord wonderfully healed her. She went back to her home rejoicing.

A man came from Arizona for salvation and healing. God met him and now he has dedicated his life to the service of the Lord.

Interest and attendance increased daily until the last night of the meeting. The tent was filled and hundreds were standing outside. Warren had never before seen such crowds and interest as were manifested in these meetings.

—L.V.O.

September 23, 1920

Fremont Evening Tribune (NE)

Performing Miracles

he wonderful happenings in this city under the ministrations of Mrs. Woodworth-Etter are startling to a [illegible word]. For an invalid to feel the refreshing flow of blood and a renewed vigor, and [for] the victim of some deformity to see and realize that deformity righted is an experience bordering on nothing short of a miracle; and a miracle is accepted only as an act of Almighty God. This woman who secures such a strange result modestly makes no claims for herself but attributes the physical healing to divine power exercised through her intercessors. She claims a call from God to go out and do this work. She acts on faith in her revelation and asserts the answers to her prayers are but the fulfillment of God's promises to her.

After all, are these transformations in the physical life of a person any more of a miracle than the conversion of a soul as commonly witnessed? Every one of us have known men of dissolute habits, that practiced all the vices men are heir to and even ran them to wild excesses, who were completely transformed and lived an entirely new life. The removal of the old and degrading desires and their replacement with an aspiration and an intense longing for nobler and better things is as great and a far more important event in the life of that individual than restored vision, unstopped ears, a straightened limb, or the cure of any other physical ailment, because the cured soul is not only benefited for life in this world but for all eternity to follow.

The favored ones who come under Mrs. Woodworth-Etter's treatment testify to the peculiar feeling they have while the healing process is on, in the same way the Christian convert experiences a feeling indescribable but real, which is the work of the Holy Spirit in making the change in the spiritual life of the individual.

If the suffering unfortunates who are restored to a reasonable degree of normal condition prove to be permanently healed, this woman's visit to Fremont will give spiritual ideas a mighty uplift among our people and strengthen belief in omnipotence.

September 24, 1920

Fremont Evening Tribune (NE)

Hundreds Crowd Tent of the "Divine Healer"

TRAGEDIES ENACTED BY THOSE WHO HOPE FOR RELIEF FROM SUFFERING

Hundreds of people of Fremont and hundreds more from territory surrounding this city have been attending the services at Second and D Streets, where Mrs. M. D. Woodworth-Etter, so-called "divine healer," has been ministering to the sick, the blind, the deaf, and the crippled.

Tragedy has been found in that tent each service. Scores of people have crowded to the platform in the hope of relief from their ills, and their faces have borne the look of despair. Some of them have said they have been benefited; others have admitted that no cure has been effected.

While the crowd in the tent has looked on and a choir has chorused its hymns repeatedly, Mrs. Etter (with her two assistants) has exhorted the suffering to "praise God"; and in an ecstasy of hope they have cast their eyes toward heaven and prayed for relief. No more touching scenes have been witnessed in Fremont than at the tent of the "healer" when those who have despaired of cures have made this new effort to seek freedom from their pain.

Mrs. Etter has won an even more enthusiastic and a larger following than Warhoochee Aryerno, the Hindu-Cherokee herb doctor, who practiced medicine near Snyder until arrested for her lack of license. Warhoochee, however, charged huge fees, while Mrs. Etter makes no charge to those she treats, only taking up collections as at any religious meeting. Nor does Mrs. Etter use medicines as did Warhoochee; but at all times she insists that whatever benefits are derived from her treatments, they come from God.

Long Preliminary Service

The services at the tent are tediously long. Hymns sung and sung again, choruses repeated and repeated, prayers lengthened interminably, and a sermon have preceded the demonstrations of "healing." Then has come the collection and while men who will testify to good that has been done them are passing the hat, the silver flows freely into the treasury of the workers. Each night the hats are emptied into a large bag that Mrs. Etter holds, and the weight of the coins has proved impressive. She herself, holding a hat in one hand, accepts offerings from those who crowd forward to shake her hand.

A woman with a face that shows much strength, perhaps the most impressive thing about Mrs. Etter is her hands. While the singing is going on, she walks up and down the platform, waving her hands, raising them above the crowd, almost caressing the people. When she goes about her healings, her hands are once more the prominent thing as she passes them over the sick and draws them across the foreheads of those who take their turns before her.

Assistants to Help

Assisting Mrs. Etter are two men, who work as she does with those who come to the platform. They shout, they bend back and forth the bodies of the ailing, and then they send them up and down the platform in a frenzy of hope for cures.

Yesterday the tent that was first raised for the meetings was replaced by a larger one, because the crowds have been increasing with each session. Mrs. Etter plans to remain until Monday.

September 30, 1920

Fremont Evening Tribune (NE)

Healer Bound Over to District Court Under Heavy Bonds

EVANGELIST LEAVES FREMONT AFTER ARREST BY OFFICIALS OF COUNTY

Local Men Sign Bond

Mrs. Woodworth-Etter, John Saunders, Clyde T. Miller, and August Feick, members of the evangelist party holding services at the corner of Second and Union Streets, were arrested yesterday afternoon on the charge of practicing medicine and surgery without a license and unlawfully treating and professing to heal. The four evangelists were placed under five hundred dollars bond each, furnished by Otis Gardner and Wallace Smith of this city.

The arrest is a result of a complaint lodged against the party by County Attorney J. C. Cook, who is much embittered at the "healers" and has been attacking them and their meetings for the past week. He asked for an opportunity to speak from the platform in their tent to the congregation, to prove his convictions to them. This privilege was refused. Mr. Cook offered a sum of one hundred dollars reward for one case of goiter that the evangelist alleges to have cured. He later raised this amount to five hundred dollars but no one came to claim the reward.

Yesterday afternoon was the climax of his attack. He lodged a complaint with Justice of the Peace Stone against Mrs. Etter; August Feick; John S. Saunders; Clyde Miller; and Mr. John Cheatham, colored. All appeared yesterday afternoon, following the midday service, except Mr. Cheatham, who is alleged to have gone to Sioux City before the party were aware of any action to be taken against them. Deputy William Lowry served the notice to the evangelist and her companions at the home of Wallace Smith where they are staying during the visit in Fremont.

The case was bound over to district court and each one was placed under five hundred dollars bond, furnished by two members of the committee responsible for inducing the party to come to this city.

Services were held as usual last evening, and people still continued to ascend the platform seeking to be cured, regardless of the charges pending. Mrs. Etter had no statement to make in regard to the arrest. Many people in the audience testified to the rest of the congregation of cures effected and cases that were on the road to recovery. The entire audience yesterday afternoon seemed convinced of Mrs. Etter's power and made statements to that effect.

Mrs. Etter and the party left for Omaha this morning. Services will be conducted at a tent at Twenty-second and Paul Streets. Omaha is looking forward to the arrival of the evangelist and have been following eagerly the reports of cures and alleged recoveries.

October 1, 1920

The Fremont Herald (NE)

The Longing for Spiritual Life

hatever one may think regarding the ability of the "miracle healers" who have attracted such crowds in Fremont, one cannot deny the eagerness of the thousands of people who attended their meetings to believe that spiritual aid could be invoked to alleviate temporal suffering. The crowds at the meetings again demonstrated that longing in nearly every human soul for some communion with the infinite. The crowds demonstrated more; they showed that besides longing there is faith—the substance of things hoped for, the evidence of things unseen.[1]

The great moral revival that came with the prosecution of the war[2] has had, observers tell us, a slump. People grew tired of being unselfish and the rebound brought on an overemphasis upon selfishness. This may be true, and the prosperity and prevalence of the profiteer indicate that it is true; but there has been no diminution of the eager interest of all peoples in things spiritual.

We have seen this in our own town. Fremont people became as engrossed in the ouija board as those of any other community. A modest "fortune teller", whose coming was unheralded, has been visited by hundreds of women and girls of the city, and her popularity has not waned. Then came the so-called "divine healer"; and again the crowds responded, although in the last instance there was added an outpouring of religious fervor.

Medical authorities tell us that such waves are always experienced after periods of great stress, such as the war, and that in time they recede; and normal, common sense reigns supreme.

Regardless of the merits in the pretensions of the "divine" healer, none can observe, without quick sympathy, the response of her audience to the simple hymns of faith in God. The great danger is that those who have expected cures of dread diseases and who are disappointed may lose their faith in divine power. This would be a pity and in this lies the danger of such gatherings as Fremont has been host to the past week.

[1] Hebrews 11:1, paraphrased.

[2] "war"—World War I.

October 2, 1920

The Omaha Daily Bee (NE)

Fremont Leads in Infidels, Says Healer's Aide

Asserts There Are More Unbelievers in Town Where Mrs. Etter Was Arrested Than Other Places

"I don't believe that there are so many infidels in any one place as there are at Fremont," exclaimed P. L. Robinson of Fremont, Sunday school worker, from the platform at the tent meeting of Mrs. M. B. Woodworth-Etter, divine healer, yesterday afternoon at Twenty-first and Paul Streets.

This hot shot, from one of the followers of Mrs. Etter at the town in which she and her assistants were arrested Wednesday on charges of practicing medicine without knowledge of it, was one of several made at the afternoon meetings. Robinson declared that he had witnessed many wonderful cures at Fremont despite the five-hundred-dollar offer of the county attorney there for testimonial of just one. Robinson later softened the blow at his native hearth by declaring that he knew of no place where there were so many saints.

William Craig of Union arose and declared that he had recovered the sight of one blind eye following treatment by Mrs. Etter at Winnebago recently.

Says He Is Recovering

Carl Larson, 2215 Mason Street, declared that he is recovering rapidly from tuberculosis following treatment by Mrs. Etter at Fremont.

In the morning six persons, Fred Elphlin (Randolph, Nebraska); Vera Eaton (15 Union); Mrs. Herman Steckelberg (Osmond, Nebraska); and three others who refused to give their names said that they had been cured of various ailments.

Assistants and converts of Mrs. Etter started the afternoon session with more than an hour of hymn singing. Then Mrs. Etter took another hour for her sermon.

"Hell's loose!" she shouted. "Heaven's looking down on the fight of the army of the Lord against the hosts of hell. . . . He will not force you to join His army in the fight with the hosts of hell," she declared.

Rev. Savidge Agrees

"Amen," cried several in the audience.

"God says that to him that overcomes shall be given that he shall sit with Me on My throne,"[1] continued Mrs. Etter.

"Hallelujah!" shouted August Feick, her chief assistant.

"It's true!" exclaimed the Rev. Charles W. Savidge of the People's Church, who is sponsoring the meeting.

"Jesus is coming to this earth again soon," exclaimed Mrs. Etter. "Such things as the persecution in Fremont convince me of this. We must overcome, the time is drawing short. To him that overcomes will be given the right to sit with Him on His throne and to walk that city with the streets of gold. I am going to walk those streets."

"I believe it!" exclaimed Rev. Savidge.

Many Spiritual Cripples

"I see men coming in here on crutches," said Mrs. Etter. "There are a lot more on spiritual crutches. I would rather be on wooden crutches than on spiritual crutches. My mission for forty-five years has been to cure in the body as well as in the soul."

"That's true," exclaimed one of the assistants from the back of the audience.

"Jesus left hundreds in a city who were sick and crippled because they would not come to Him, would not have faith. So it is today." Mrs. Etter intimated that she also must leave many because they would not have faith.

By this time many women were wiping their eyes and groans and excited shouts of "Amen" and "Hallelujah" were coming from all parts of the audience.

"Can't you almost hear the angels singing," exclaimed Mrs. Etter, gazing at the top of the tent.

Several Testify

"I have seen as great things as the miracles of the Bible at some of my meetings," declared Mrs. Etter.

---

[1] Revelation 3:21, paraphrased.

Following her address, members of the audience were called on to recount their experiences in faith cures and many were told.

After one man had told of the benefit he had received, the assistants struck up a hymn, singing, "A little talk with Jesus makes it right, all right."[2]

Next, those desiring to be healed were asked to come up and kneel before the "altar," a long bench in front of the platform.

"Get under the blood of Jesus!" Mrs. Etter exhorted them.

Mrs. Etter then went along, aided by her assistants, and punched and massaged the bodies and limbs of the paralytic and crippled, thrust her fingers into and shouted into the ears of the deaf. The other assistants and converts chanted a hymn. Many of those being treated cried. Several declared after it was all over that they felt better.

[2] "A little talk with Jesus makes it right, all right"—composer of hymn unknown.

October 3, 1920

The Omaha Daily Bee (NE)

Healing by Faith

nd Jesus rebuked the devil; and he departed out of him: and the child was cured from that very hour.

> Then came the disciples to Jesus apart, and said, Why could not we cast him out?
>
> And Jesus said unto them, Because of your unbelief: for verily I say unto you, If ye have faith as a grain of mustard seed, ye shall say unto this mountain, Remove hence to yonder place; and it shall remove; and nothing shall be impossible unto you.[1]

This is the language of Saint Matthew, telling how Christ cast out a devil that had possessed a child, after His disciples had failed to do it. It is the basis of the claim of every "faith" healer, and the refuge,

[1] Matthew 17:18-20.

as well, for those who are not healed must be left to suffer and endure on account of their unfaith.

If credulity be a crime, as is often charged by the cynical, it is also a comfort, as will be testified by the devout. "Though he slay me, yet will I trust Him."[2] On that rock rests the everlasting belief of the mind and soul that looks through simple faith up to the Almighty and by that trust hopes for the things that are to come in the better world beyond. The wise and sophisticated are confounded by this, for they have not yet become "as a little child."[3]

To be sure, these trusting souls are cruelly deceived by charlatans, frauds, and fakes who practice upon them all sorts of miserable deceit, yet who is there would deny them the solace of their faith? Happiness is not always bought by erudition. Content dwells as frequently with those who do not know as with those who do. While those who can see with the eyes of faith view things that are hidden from those who look only through the eyes of material things, very few have the faith to believe in healing through laying on of hands; yet none are the worse because it has been tried. And there is quite as much reason to think that a living woman can do the things that are needed to work a miracle of healing as to accept, as millions do, the accounts of cures wrought at the shrine of a saint long dead and gone.

[2] Job 13:15, paraphrased.

[3] See Mark 10:15, Luke 18:17.

October 4, 1920

The Omaha Daily Bee (NE)

Healing Power of Mrs. Etter Is Avowed by Many

HUNDREDS FLOCK TO TENT MEETING IN HOPE OF BEING CURED—REV. MR. SAVIDGE TESTIFIES

Many people, afflicted with various maladies, testified to the healing power of Evangelist Mrs. M. B. Woodworth-Etter Saturday afternoon at the "divine" healing meeting being conducted by Mrs. Etter at Twenty-second and Paul

Streets. The afternoon and evening sessions were better attended than those on Thursday and Friday.

The large tent packed from end to end, reverberated with murmurs of "Glory to God; let us pray. Thanks be to God for what He has done for me."

A choir of thirty male and female voices started the ceremonies. After a few hymns were sung, books were passed among the people who came to seek spiritual and temporal strength. After the singing, Mrs. Etter made a few remarks as to the futility of her efforts if those seeking "healing" did not dismiss all doubt from their minds and have faith in God's miraculous power.

Many Want Aid

When questions were asked as to how many wanted the Lord God to heal their body, hundreds rose to their feet and others raised their hands. At this juncture the entire audience fell on bended knees and prayed.

"Get a shock from heaven," was Mrs. Etter's way of expressing herself when she exhorted her followers to get on their knees and pray for faith in God. Standing on her tiptoes, with both arms outstretched to heaven and eyes gazing upward, she asked the blessing of grace and confidence upon these who sought relief. "Unload your souls with the rubbish of this world," she exhorted. "Take time to think of God in heaven; make Him a part of your business. I do not profess to be supernatural or to be able to lay hands upon anyone and cure them. It is your faith in God, God's almighty goodness that cures you."

Invited to Testify

After Mrs. Etter's sermon, the audience was invited to tell of their shortcomings and testify as to the "great things the Lord had done for them."

An old lady who appeared to be fifty years old was the first on her feet. "Early in my life I suffered from a rupture and floating kidneys," she said. "Doctors pronounced me incurable. I attended a meeting such as this in Sioux City five years ago where I learned that God was my only hope. I placed my faith in Him. I am here now with my little boy, who was blind in one eye, who now leaps for joy with his eyesight gradually coming back."

Rev. Mr. Savidge then took the stand. "I joined the church and was a seeker after complete rest for twenty years," he explained. "I can truthfully say that in the course of my efforts in this behalf, I never had a meeting inspire me to work harder in my chosen calling. I am thankful more and more that I took up the work of God."

The meeting will continue Sunday and close Monday night.

October 6, 1920

The Omaha Daily Bee (NE)

Healer Denies That Miracle Age Has Passed

MANY OF THOSE ANOINTED BY MRS. ETTER REPORT THAT THEY ARE NOW PHYSICALLY PERFECT

he opinion that the day of miracles is a thing of the past was flatly denied by Mrs. M. B. Etter in her final "divine healing" sermon at the tent meeting at Twenty-second and Paul Streets last evening.

Since the opening of the meetings last Thursday, approximately 365 people, who have applied for "treatment," reported that their physical defects had been corrected. Many told how futile it was to consult surgeons.

"Miracles have been wrought in this tent," declared Mrs. Etter. The congregation imposed implicit faith in Mrs. Etter's statements, as was indicated by their remarks that the lame could walk, the blind could see, and the deaf hear only through her divine intercession.

Those who were partially or wholly cured of their ailments were called upon to relate their experiences. The final report showed that of 1,500 who have been anointed and prayed for, 365 have been rendered "physically perfect."

Many thousand other people who came out of curiosity marveled at the mysteries which had been performed before their eyes.

Mrs. Etter bases her power to work good among the afflicted on her faith in the almighty power of God. "If you have this," she says, "and your prayers are in earnest, they will be properly answered."

Services will be continued after Mrs. Etter and her party leave for Indianapolis tonight for those who have been converted to her faith at Rev. M. B. Long's church, 4004 North Twenty-fourth Street.

October 6, 1920

The Omaha Daily Bee (NE)

The Bee's Letter Box

A WORD FOR FAITH HEALING

BELLEVUE, NEB., OCT 2—TO THE EDITOR OF THE BEE.

Permit a few words concerning the coming to Omaha of this old lady engaged in faith healing and the reception accorded her by some Omaha citizens.

Is it not amusing, to say the least, with what a paternal interest these critics regard the possible money receipts of this venerable lady? I hold no brief for her, but as a layman feel rather annoyed at the manner in which our would-be legal and clerical protectors(?)—save the mark[1]—would invoke the law to shield us poor simpletons from possible loss. The childish, absurd suggestion to prosecute for the illegal practicing of medicine where there is no medicine used, is, to my mind, prima facie[2] evidence of unfitness of anyone so prosecuting to hold office of city or county attorney.

As to the regular practitioners, it is an old dog-in-manger[3] policy, hoary with age; but the allopathic growl has time and again been all lanced as the people demanded the recognition of other -pathies: So homeopathy, hydropathy, and other systems have succeeded in winning their place in the field of human struggle against disease.

---

[1] "save the mark"—i.e., leave the question mark in the sentence.

[2] *"prima facie"*—at first glance; on first examination *(Webster's N. W.,* 1997).

[3] "dog-in-manger"—the expression is "dog-in-the-manager," a person who keeps other from using something which he is not using himself *(Webster's N. W.,* 1997).

In recent years osteopathy, chiropractic, and Christian Science have had to run the gauntlet of the same growl only to succeed in gaining recognition. The best of those old regulars are free to admit their weakness and the faultiness of their system. As to the reverend opponents, is it not passing strange that they have no knowledge of healing by or through faith when the Master's commission included "healing the sick" with preaching the Gospel?[4] I am glad to be able to bear testimony to the fact that God heals today when approached in the name of Christ. As already stated, I bear no brief for this lady, but would venture the opinion that she should not be interfered with, except it be shown that she uses other than proper methods; and I very much fear that the critics quoted in your recent issue are not competent to judge.

—H. R. Baldwin

[4] See Mark 16:15-18.

October 8, 1920

Fremont Evening Tribune (NE)

"Divine Healer" Returns to Indianapolis Home

rs. M. B. Woodworth-Etter, over whose "miracle healing" meetings in Fremont a fierce controversy raged a week ago, and who went from here to Omaha, where she continued her ministrations, has completed her services there and returned to her home in Indianapolis.

In Omaha, with the publicity that attended her arrest preceding her, Mrs. Etter did not enjoy the crowds that flocked to her tent here. Many there were, however, who had her lay her hands upon them, and many pronounced themselves cured of ills of long standing. Rev. Charles W. Savidge, the "People's minister" and the famed "marrying parson" of Omaha, was sponsor for her meetings there and declared that they did much to revive a flagging spiritual faith in the metropolis.

Denunciations of Fremont and Fremonters for the opposition there to the faith healing were frequent at Omaha. Presley L. Robinson, Sunday school missionary for Dodge County, was quoted as saying that there were more infidels in Fremont than most any place he knew about, and then he admitted that he thought the town hosted an equal number of saints. August Feick, Mrs. Etter's secretary, made numerous references to the lack of faith among Fremonters in the power of the divine healing.

Fremont may get another glimpse of Mrs. Etter and her party at the January term of the district court, when they are supposed to appear for trial on the charges brought by County Attorney Cook: that being without knowledge of medicine or surgery, they nevertheless professed to heal.

June 20, 1921

Des Moines Evening Tribune (IA)

Will Faith Heal Dying Girl Whom Doctors Cannot Save?

thel Zellner of Kensal, N. D., lies in a tent at Chautauqua Park, deathly ill with tuberculosis. At her side sits her father, ever ready to carry out her slightest wish, always watching for the change for the better. Occasionally Sister Woodworth-Etter, faith healer, walks into the tent and speaks words of good cheer and faith in God. "I am getting better already. I have faith and will soon be able to walk and have a good time once more," says this twenty-year-old girl whom doctors have declared beyond human help.

She Has Faith

"Sister Woodworth-Etter and other members of the party have prayed for me; they have faith, my father has faith, and so have I. So, you see, I cannot fail to get well."

Des Moines persons who live near Chautauqua Park are skeptical. They are doubting Thomases. But, they go back to each meeting conducted by Mrs. Etter and each time their faith grows stronger.

Sunday night no one went forward to be healed, but after the meetings, a *Tribune* reporter began making inquiries and finally located the Zellners in their tent.

Father Believes

"I am superintendent of schools at Kensal," said the father. "I am going to stay here a week or two at the end of which time I have faith my daughter will be better. I am not easily excited or led by mob psychology to believe in such things as this. So, you see, I have really thought this thing out by cold reasoning and have faith. My daughter insisted on coming here. She had heard of Mrs. Etter, and when we arrived Saturday afternoon, I had to carry Ethel up to the platform. Sunday afternoon she walked around a little, the first time she has done this in months."

Temperature Lower

"She also took an automobile ride and here's another thing, her temperature has dropped from 102 to 100 since Saturday, when faith began to heal her. Her pulse is not so rapid and she and I have faith that she will soon be well." Mrs. Etter has been healing for forty years. At Chautauqua Park with her is a party of members of the Pentecostal Assemblies of God. They hold meetings every afternoon and evening.

To get to Chautauqua Park, one should take a West Ninth streetcar.

June 23, 1921

Des Moines Evening Tribune (IA)

Prayers Save Girl Thought to be Dying

RISES FROM SICKBED AND WALKS INTO MEETING OF HEALERS

thel Zelner,[1] the little girl who was brought Sunday from Kensal, N. D., almost dead of tuberculosis, walked unassisted into the meeting Wednesday night of the Pentecostal faith healers who are in session for the next four weeks at Chautauqua Park.

On Sunday she was prayed for by the congregation after Mrs. M. B. Woodworth-Etter had laid hands upon her as she lay on a stretcher, apparently at the verge of death.

Pray for Mannassa

Several new sufferers were prayed for Wednesday night. Ralph Mannassa, 2720 High Street, who has tried unavailingly to rid himself of what Mrs. Etter says is locomotion ataxia,[2] sat in the altar chair and received the laying on of hands.

The Mannassa boy was treated by Evangelist Smithson at Council Bluffs a year ago.

Mrs. Fence of Centerville, Ia., shows marked improvement, she says, after her treatment for a tumor and gallstones.

Claims Healing

William Blood of Des Moines declares a complete healing of his dropsy.

Mary Bain of Des Moines reported in meeting that she had been healed of an inward goiter and a crooked vertebra.

The Pentecostals are in session under the guidance of Mrs. Etter of Indianapolis, president of the denomination. She speaks three times daily and at each meeting performs the faith healing, which causes many broken-down sufferers to seek her for aid.

[1] "Zelner"—This name is published as "Zellner" in a previous article by the same paper. Both articles are published as printed.

[2] "locomotion ataxia"—a chronic disease of the nervous system, usually caused by syphilis and characterized by disturbances of sensations, loss of reflexes and of muscular coordination, functional disorders of organs, etc. (Webster's N.W. 1997).

Woman Takes It Up

Mrs. Sadie Kress of Hartford, Ia., formerly of Des Moines, who was Wednesday night ordained into the ministry of the Pentecostal denomination, said: "I couldn't see without glasses even to cook for twenty years, and now I can read the tiny text of this Bible," indicating a small edition she held. "Seven years ago I was cured of cancer, too, and I believe so thoroughly in faith healing that I am going to devote the rest of my life to the work."

The minister of the local Pentecostals is C. W. Waters, who has a small church on the East Side, with a congregation of about 150.

Joseph A. Darner, 1439 Thirty-second Street, a graduate of Grinnell College, is local manager of the camp meeting.

June 24, 1921

Des Moines Evening Tribune (IA)

Lame, Blind, and Halt Flock to Tent of Woman Faith Healer

The maimed, the blind, and the halt continue to flock to the Pentecostal faith healer meetings at Chautauqua Park, where Mrs. M. B. Woodworth-Etter of Indianapolis works wonders upon them, according to their own testimony.

Thursday evening, Mrs. G. S. Hayden (935 Twenty-seventh Street, Omaha, Neb.), who came here to Mrs. Etter in the last hours of the thirty days the doctors had given her to live, said Thursday night:

Says She Is Healed

"Now at last I am healed. I had a tumor and swelling of my heart and was in such a condition that the doctors in Omaha were afraid to operate, giving me only until July first to live. I had been trying everything, and hearing that Mrs. Etter saved many others, I was brought here unable to walk, but Monday night in the meeting the tumor left me all at once, and now I feel cured and thankful to the Lord."

Throws Away Crutches

A huge, stoop-shouldered stranger, bent almost double and leaning upon a pair of heavy canes, painfully hobbled into the big tent Thursday night and sat in the front row.

When Mrs. Etter called for penitent cripples to come up to be healed, the paralytic laboredly arose but almost fell in his attempt to stand straight. After the old evangelist had stroked with her hands the unfortunate man's trembling back a few times, he finally straightened up, threw aside his canes, and though still very weak, he walked unassisted from the tabernacle.

His name was given as John Davis (1056 Fourth Street Place).

Regains Hearing

Donald Smalley (3404 Second Street) was prayed for by the Pentecostals Thursday night and asserts that he regained his hearing, having been deaf for many years.

After being unable to talk aloud, on account of having drunk strong whisky while a very young man, David King (612 School Street), Thursday night shouted his joy and praise for all to hear as he came off the platform where Mrs. Etter had healed him.

No Hypnotism

The Rev. Samuel E. Waters of Sioux City, brother of the local Pentecostal pastor, gave an inspiring sermon at the meeting yesterday, assuring the several hundred people congregated that there is no hypnotism in the work of his church. He said:

"Unbelievers and hypocrites who are feeble in the faith of the Lord so accuse us, but we know it is the coming in of the Holy Spirit today just as it used to come in the days of Paul."

Mrs. Etter will conduct services in Des Moines until July 10, when she will leave for Sioux City.

June 29, 1921

Des Moines Evening Tribune (IA)

Pentecostals Flee Their Tent When Wind Storm Breaks

he Pentecostals were forced to adjourn last night before their healing services, when the storm threatened the big tent at Chautauqua Park. The lights went out, and the wind flapped the high canvas tabernacle till the worshippers feared its collapse.

The afternoon session resulted in the mending of several crippled unfortunates. One man, deaf and dumb since a baby of three years, was able to converse in good English. The man, Emmet Fisher (620 Southwest Eleventh Street) had not heard a human voice for forty-one years.

Marie McLaughlin (4220 West Grand Avenue), who had Saint Vitus' Dance, testified she was relieved. Her mother, Mrs. Bartley (of the same address) asserts that she was cured of a goiter at Tuesday's camp meeting.

Minnie Taylor (1745 Walker Street) was relieved of misery in the shoulders, she says.

A double rupture apparently was taken away from E. Visser of Harvey, Ia., who leaped and danced about the platform in praise after Mrs. Etter had laid hands upon him.

"The doctors said I was too fleshy to operate on and remove two stones from my kidney and a tumor which has been back of my right eye for nine years," said Mrs. T. A. Burgess (1437 East Delaware Street). "The Lord healed me."

May 27, 1922

The Pentecostal Evangel

Easter Meeting in Woodworth-Etter Tabernacle

he recent Easter revival in Woodworth-Etter Tabernacle was a blessing to all who came; and although in the first part of the meetings we had stormy weather, the latter part was bright and fair. People came from every direction, and the power of God was powerfully felt in our midst.

Mrs. Etter was assisted by Brother and Sister Earl W. Clark, traveling evangelists. Mrs. Clark is Mrs. Etter's granddaughter and Mr. Clark was a missionary for several years in South America. They ministered to the people in song and giving out the Word, and many hearts were touched so that a goodly number were saved and baptized in the Holy Ghost. Many strangers and ministers came in to see and investigate, and all were impressed with the solemnity of the service and the manifestations of the Spirit. Easter Sunday was a blessed day for all. It started with a sunrise meeting—people came as early as 5:15 in the morning. All sought the altar, and about fifty souls were wonderfully blessed in this early morning meeting. The afternoon and evening meetings were largely attended and a good spirit was manifested throughout the assembly. The afternoon service was followed by a baptismal service, and a number were buried with Christ in the likeness of His death.

Many bad and extreme cases came to this meeting for healing, and God touched them one and all. The ringing testimonies of those who had been healed in Mrs. Etter's meetings, cheered and blessed all who heard; and many afflicted ones took on fresh courage for their own needs.

Mrs. Etter has been kept by the Lord in a marvelous way and has again gone forth to minister in other places. She is now in Dallas, Texas, holding a three-weeks meeting there. She goes to Ft. Worth, Texas, and expects to hold meetings in Sikeston, Mo.; Ottumwa, Iowa; and Osborne, Kansas.

Her new books are now ready and all who read them will be blessed in body and soul. Those who are in need of anything from the Lord will do well to read them. You could do good missionary work getting these books into the hands of those who are in need, as they speak for themselves. *Marvels and Miracles* $1.65, prepaid. *Spirit-Filled Sermons* $.65, and *Questions and Answers on Divine Healing* (revised and enlarged) $.25, both prepaid. All these together for $2.50. All these can be gotten from the Gospel Publishing House, Springfield, Missouri.

—Helen V. Gorton

June 22, 1922

The Sikeston Herald (MO)

Revival Meetings Attract Thousands

MANY SEEK EVANGELIST TO BE HEALED OF DISEASES

Pentecostal Churches of Many States Represented—Services Held Both Morning and Evening

The Pentecostal meeting now in progress here is drawing very large crowds. Not only are many local people attending these meetings, but people of that faith are here from many other southeast Missouri towns and from several surrounding states. Among the states represented are Illinois, Kentucky, Arkansas, Indiana, and Tennessee.

This meeting, which is under the auspices of the local Pentecostal church, of which Rev. Shoemaker is pastor, is being conducted by Mrs. Woodworth-Etter, of national fame in that church. The evangelist has with her three helpers: P. F. Kruse, of Glen Ellyn, Illinois; Mrs. J. F. Ormsby;[1] and Miss Orendorf, daughter of Mrs. Woodworth-Etter.

This meeting, which began last Thursday and will last until July 2d, is being held in the Dorris Theatre building. It is drawing a capacity house every night.

[1] Mrs. J. F. Ormsby is Mrs. Woodworth-Etter's daughter, Lizzie.

The evangelist, Mrs. Woodworth-Etter, is said to be a divine healer of national repute. Many people each night go to her meetings here to be healed of physical ailments, some of whom claim to have been greatly benefited.

Mrs. Woodworth-Etter does the principal part of the preaching. A large choir and several musical instruments lead the congregational singing, which is a feature of the meetings. Services are held every morning and evening.

July 6, 1922

The Sikeston Herald (MO)

Pentecostal Revival Closed Last Sunday

After two weeks of strenuous work, both personal and public, the Pentecostal revival, which attracted thousands daily, closed here last Sunday night. Mrs. M. B. Woodworth-Etter, the principal evangelist, and her helpers left Tuesday for Ottumwa, Iowa, where they will open a similar meeting.

Much interest seemed to be shown in the meeting, many hundreds attending daily, not only from this locality, but from the outlying districts. There were four hundred sick who came to be healed, an average of nearly thirty each day. There were over ninety persons claiming salvation, who never heretofore had done so. Of this number nine were baptized in the first ditch east of town last Sunday afternoon. Twenty more local people are yet to be baptized. This number does not include the many out-of-town people who are to be baptized at their home churches.

Local Pentecostal workers consider the meeting one of the greatest of its kind ever held in this section.

July 22, 1922

The Pentecostal Evangel

Woodworth-Etter Meeting,

Fort Worth, Texas

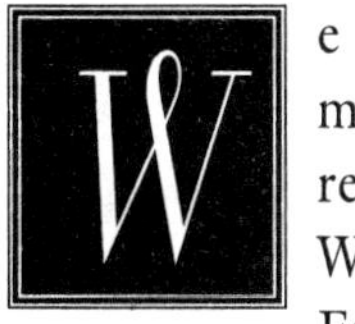e are glad to make a good report of the Woodworth-Etter meeting in Fort Worth, Tex. The power of God came down and many were saved and great numbers received the baptism in the Holy Ghost.

This was a real Pentecostal meeting in which the manifestations of the Spirit were welcome; and the Lord came forth in tongues and interpretations; and at times the heavenly choir was heard with great spiritual uplift.

Another outstanding feature of the meeting was the many miraculous healings. Sister Etter has been strong along this line during the twenty years of the writer's acquaintance with her; and we can say that, although she is almost seventy-eight years old, she is just as strong in faith; and God is using her mightily in the ministry of healing and in preaching the deep mysteries of the kingdom of God.

Among those healed were

S. L. Houston of Skiatook, Okla., who was deaf in one ear from birth, and M. Robles, a Mexican preacher of Fort Worth, who was deaf in one ear for twenty-five years; both testified to being perfectly healed.

Eugene Enequer was suffering from an eating sore on his leg for eight years so that the bone was exposed; after being prayed for, [he] said the sore was drying up and new skin growing over the bone.

Mrs. N. A. Hazelwood of Hollis, Okla., was suffering from goiter and testified to immediate relief in throat and heart.

Mrs. A. I. Anderson, seventy-two years old, testified to being healed of stomach trouble of four years' standing.

Mrs. Alice Stracener, Breckenridge, Tex., was healed of a paralyzed arm.

Mrs. Lula Harrison, Delphine, Okla., brought her seven-year-old girl who was born with a diseased and deformed spine and paralyzed legs. After prayer the back was found to be healed and straightened and the legs healed so she could stand and walk.

These are only a few of the wonderful manifestations of God's love and power, for great numbers were prayed for every day and most of them were touched of God and went away rejoicing.

Sunday, June 4, was a great day for the church in this district. In the afternoon Sister Etter addressed the church, reviewing the Bible teaching on spiritual gifts and their uses, which was very helpful and instructive. After the sermon about fifty workers were prayed for that the gifts might be manifested in their lives more than ever before. The power of God came down upon them in a wonderful way.

We are praising God for what He is doing in Fort Worth and are looking for greater things.

—F. A. Hale

September 30, 1922

The Pentecostal Evangel

District Council Camp Meeting

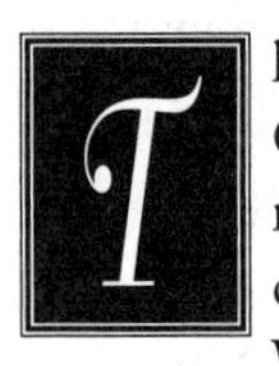

he District Council Camp Meeting for northwest Kansas, conducted by Sister Woodworth-Etter, was a most wonderful success. The Spirit fell in torrents; the Spirit-filled praises and shouts of glory sounded like the voice of many waters.[1] About forty souls were saved and fifty received the baptism in the Holy Spirit and came through so beautifully. Hallelujah! The healings were wonderful. Many were prayed for each day. God surely blessed Sister Etter in preaching twice almost every day and praying for so many people, some of almost every disease.

One woman, who had had a goiter for years, causing heart trouble and a stiff neck, was instantaneously healed. The stiffness and pains in her neck left, heart trouble ceased, and she stayed to the end of

[1] See Psalm 93:4, Ezekiel 43:2, and Revelation 1:15.

the camp (*sic*) praising God for the complete work. One man brought in on a cot was prayed for for dropsy. The next morning the swelling was gone down, pains leaving. Many said they never saw it on that fashion. The wonderful healings by the hand of God were many. Truly God wrought special miracles by the hand of Sister Etter. People came from all parts of the state and from several adjoining states. Many times there were fifteen hundred people on the grounds. Sixty living tents were full; some slept under the large gospel tent, and room had to be made under the cook tent. Several were ordained into the full ministry; some were licensed; and many were prayed for that the gifts of the Spirit might be stirred up. This truly was a blessed service.

June 16, 1923

The Pentecostal Evangel

Cincinnati, Ohio

rs. M. B. Woodworth-Etter and her co-workers, Brother Robert Benjamin and Brother Thomas Paine, have just closed a most successful campaign at the Pentecostal Assembly, 9th and Plumb Streets. It was a remarkable meeting—an old-time revival full of the Holy Spirit and of power. The interest deepened as the meeting progressed, the crowd increased, and the tide rose higher and higher up to the very last meeting. Hundreds of sick people were prayed for and there were many remarkable cases of healing. Miracles of healing were wrought before the eyes of the people, some of whom no doubt came to scoff but went away convinced, as they could not deny what they saw with their own eyes. I will mention just one of these. Mrs. John Theis, 700 Carlisle St., Cincinnati, Ohio, had been in a wheelchair for three years and was brought to the meeting in a wheelchair. Sister Etter prayed for her, and she stood up and walked across the platform back and forth. A few nights ago she came back without any chair and is now doing her work without its assistance. The Lord willing, we are to have another campaign in a few weeks.

—J. W. THOMPSON, PASTOR

October, 1923

Word and Work

A Great Revival at Wynnburg, Tenn.

ister Woodworth-Etter conducted an old-time revival at Wynnburg which stirred that part of the country. Thousands attended these meetings and heard the full Gospel of salvation, divine healing, and the baptism of the Holy Ghost.

Sister Etter showed the people that we are living in the very last days and the coming of the Lord is near at hand, by the Word of God and the signs of the times and the fulfillment of prophecy. The Lord confirmed the Word with many signs and wonders. Numbers were saved and healed; also many received the baptism of the Holy Ghost as on the day of Pentecost.

The people came from many states and from all the surrounding towns. The last night of the meeting there were about four thousand people on the campground.

A man brought his wife to the meeting. She had tuberculosis of the lungs. She had not been out of bed for three months. Sister Etter prayed for her and the Lord wonderfully touched her, and she attended the meetings about a week. She testified many times how all the doctors gave her up, could not do anything for her. She would go back and forth on the platform, her face shining with the glory of God, praising the Lord.

A young man was brought to the meeting. He was unsaved and suffering with a large carbuncle on his limb. He could hardly walk at all. While Sister Etter was praying for him, the power of God fell on him; and he leaped from the chair, shouting and praising the Lord for salvation and healing.

A sister came from Arkansas suffering with asthma for four years. The Lord wonderfully healed her. She testified many times that all the symptoms of disease were gone. She also received the baptism of the Holy Ghost.

A lady was healed of a cancer on her arm. She said the Lord told her to come to the meeting and He would heal her. She testified how the pain was all gone and she could move her arm any way.

A little girl was brought to the meeting partially blind since she was six years old. She was prayed for; and when she found she could see without her glasses, she began laughing and praising God. A week later her mother came to the meeting and told what the Lord had done for her daughter.

A mother brought her two children to the meeting who were born dumb. The one was nine years old and the other four years. Sister Etter prayed for them and commanded the dumb spirit to come out. Instantly they began to speak and say "Praise the Lord" plain so that everyone could hear them. There was great rejoicing when the people heard them speak.

An elderly man received his hearing who was almost deaf for six years. A lady was healed of pellagra. She had it for four years. Doctors could not do anything for her. A week after she was prayed for, the scabs dried up and dropped off.

The altar was crowded with hungry souls seeking God. Quite a number were slain under the power of God and some had visions. Brother Robert Benjamin assisted Sister Etter in this meeting. The Lord greatly blessed him in giving forth the Word and in the altar service. The people marveled to see Sister Etter in her eightieth year preaching, singing, and praying for the many sick. They looked on in amazement and said it is the power of God.

They had three services daily. Sister Etter was in on the afternoon and night services. They had two baptismal services at the lake. Forty-one were baptized in water. The glory of God overshadowed the scene.

—Verne Orendorf

November 17, 1923

The Pentecostal Evangel

Louisville, KY

ister Woodworth-Etter conducted an old-time revival at Louisville, Oct. 14 to 28. Several attended these meetings and heard the full Gospel preached; quite a number were healed, saved; and some received the Holy Spirit as in Acts 2:4. The deaf were made to hear and the lame to walk; it was truly wonderful to sit and see God work. Mr. J. M. Broomback of Frankfort, Ky., was healed of a very sore leg; he had a running sore, could hardly walk. After he was prayed for, it began to dry up and go away. A sister who brought her little boy, paralyzed in his hands, Sister Etter prayed for him; and he used his hands, something he had not done for eight years. His mother testified he was healed. A sister had a very bad cancer; had had it for years, could not walk, and could not ride on the streetcars. Someone brought her to the meetings and she was prayed for. She was at the next meeting and had come on the streetcars, had been out visiting, stayed for the night service, shouted all over the platform, [and] testified she was healed. A sister who came in on a crutch had not walked for a year. After prayer she threw her crutch away and walked; every one in the house shouted—even the sinners threw up their hands and praised God. There were many other cases healed, such as rheumatism, tumors, blood-poison, tuberculosis; surely the Lord was there in power.

—Mrs. L. A. Sappington

January 12, 1924

The Pentecostal Evangel

Toledo, Ohio

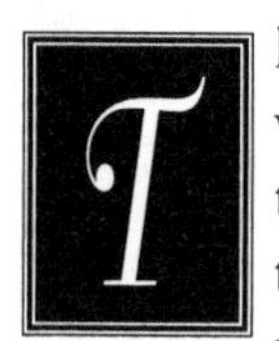he Lord worked in a wonderful way. Sister Etter preached the Word with power and the Lord confirmed it with many signs and wonders. Quite a number were saved and healed. Some received the baptism in the Holy Spirit as

in Acts 2:4. A lady came to the meeting who had had a broken hip for nine years. She was prayed for and the Lord healed her. She threw away her crutches. A week later she came back and told what the Lord had done for her. She had no need of any crutches. She said her limb was one inch longer since she was prayed for. She belonged to the Salvation Army. She had given her testimony there of what the Lord had done for her.

A Catholic lady, Mrs. E. B. Huerd, 1638 Wayne St., Toledo, Ohio, gave a testimony as follows:

> I suffered from a tumor on the back of my neck for twenty years. I have had some of the best surgeons in the U. S. A. examine it, and they all told me that it would be impossible to remove it as it was right on the jugular vein. For the last five years, my arm has been paralyzed. I also had hardening of the arteries. Sister Etter prayed for me; and thank God, Jesus healed me. The tumor is gone and I can use my arm. I always believed in Jesus, but I believe in Him more now.

A sister testified that she was instantly healed of neuritis. She had had an operation but did not receive any help. The Lord instantly healed her. A mother testified that her little son, who was almost blind, received his sight. A Catholic priest attended some of the meetings and was very much interested. It was remarkable how the Lord used Sister Etter and gave her strength and power to preach the Word and pray for the sick.

—A Worker

June 21, 1924

The Pentecostal Evangel

Easter Revival at Woodworth-Etter Tabernacle

he annual Easter revival at Woodworth-Etter Tabernacle closed April 27, after fifteen days of blessed praise and worship and drinking in the Spirit-filled messages as they were given forth by those empowered from on high.

A few weeks before the meetings began, the tabernacle was remodeled and the seating capacity enlarged. This makes it convenient for people who come for the all-day meeting to spend the day here. It also helps to take care of the overflow of our big meetings during revivals.

Sister Woodworth-Etter attended the meetings, giving counsel and encouragement and urging the people of God to stand fast, hold steady, and press the battle to the gates. We praise God for raising her up and for the divine strength He gives her to go on hour after hour as she labors among the needy ones who come here for her ministrations. No one could come to the meetings and look on these two faithful warriors[1] and listen to their words of triumph without being lifted in body, soul, and spirit.

Some wonderful healings took place, the following being but a sample of what God did in our midst. Mrs. Henrietta Maag of Peoria, Illinois, says,

> I cannot praise God enough for all He has done for me. He has healed my body in a wonderful way. I never knew anything about this wonderful healing until one of my near neighbors was healed after the doctors had given her up to die. I had been watching her ever since; and I knew that what God did for her, He could do for me. I had a nervous breakdown, kidney and bowel trouble, high blood pressure, and a stroke of paralysis. The doctor told my husband that I could never get well, that he could only relieve the pain, and not to be surprised if I were found dead anytime. I could not sleep at night for smothering and coughing. But praise God I came to Indianapolis, and Sister Etter prayed for me, and I am healed. I sleep all night without awakening, and I eat anything I want. I just feel fine. Glory to God.

Mrs. Etter intends to stay in Indianapolis this season and take charge of the meetings. She is therefore inviting all those who wish

[1] The other warrior may be August Feick who usually ministered with her.

to attend her meetings or wish her to minister to them to come and attend the summer campaign, which will start June 14, and continue indefinitely. A large tent will be pitched in a vacant lot next to the Tabernacle—the same as was done last year. There will be rooms or room and board to be had in the neighborhood at reasonable rates. A restaurant for those wishing lunches or single meals will be near the tent.

Come to this summer revival and spend your vacation in these meetings. It will be a time well spent and profitable for body as well as soul.

—HELEN V. GORTON
2114 MILLER ST.
INDIANAPOLIS, IND.

September 27, 1924

The Pentecostal Evangel

Sister Etter With the Lord

e just received the following telegram:

Indianapolis, Ind., Sept. 16—
Mrs. Etter died at 4 A.M.
Funeral Friday. September 19—
August Feick.

Our precious sister has fought a good fight and, we are sure, was glad to finish her course.[1] She has been the means of blessing to hundreds of thousands, and many will rise up and call her blessed.[2] We desire at this time to express our warmest sympathy for the loved ones that she leaves behind, who will surely miss her godly presence and counsel.

[1] See 2 Timothy 4:7.

[2] See Proverbs 31:28.

October 18, 1924

The Pentecostal Evangel

Sister Etter's Homegoing

rother August Feick writes us from Indianapolis a further word concerning the homegoing of Sister Etter after her fifty years of ministry. When she passed away on September 16, she had reached the age of eighty years, one month, and twenty-five days. Brother Feick tells us that one time during the last three weeks, the fire of God came upon her, and she was a long time praising and magnifying God in another tongue. A number of times she came under the anointing of the Spirit and preached a regular sermon to those who were in her room. She passed away without a struggle.

There was a wonderful funeral service when a number yielded to the Lord. Brethren Earl Clark (son-in-law of Sister Etter's daughter), Cyrus Fockler, Miller, J. S. Saunders, and a number of others assisted. The procession was one of the largest ever held in that section of Indianapolis. Brother Feick tells us that he is expecting to get out a new booklet, about the beginning of the year, completing the biography of Sister Etter's life. It was the will of Sister Etter that Brother Feick carry on the work, which she had begun, as faithfully as he could. This Brother Feick is doing, and at present there is a real spirit of revival in the midst of the church in Indianapolis.

Maria Woodworth-Etter lying in state in her living room in Indianapolis, Indiana, September 1924.

SECTION FOUR

What Maria Woodworth-Etter Taught

(SERMONS, ARRANGED TOPICALLY)

Salvation

Gift of God, or Eternal Life

esus answered and said unto her, If thou knewest the gift of God, and who it is that saith to thee, Give me to drink; thou wouldest have asked of him, and he would have given thee living water. . . . But whosoever drinketh of the water that I shall give him shall never thirst; but the water that I shall give him shall be in him a well of water springing up into everlasting life.

John 4:10,14

The gift of God is the most important question in the world for every individual to understand and know that we have it beyond a doubt. It is the only thing that will keep us out of hell and pass us through the pearly gates of heaven. Jesus said, "If thou knewest the gift of God and who it was that was talking to thee, thou wouldest have asked him for the gift, and he would have given thee living water, and this water would be a well of living water, gushing up and springing up into everlasting life."[1]

Very few know by experience what this gift of God is or how to obtain it. If they did, they would take the poor sinner the nearest way to the bleeding Lamb of Calvary—to the fountainhead.

Jesus said, "And ye will not come to me, that ye might have life."[2] He has power to give life to everyone that cometh to him. Some will say, "Here is Christ," or "There is Christ," "Come join the church," "Come and be baptized," or "Break off from your habits," or "Visit the sick, clothe the naked, build churches or charitable institutions, attend all the church doings, and if you do these things you will be all right."

[1] See John 4:10,14.

[2] John 5:40.

> Not by works of righteousness which we have done, but according to his mercy he saved us, by the washing of regeneration, and renewing of the Holy Ghost; Which he shed on us abundantly through Jesus Christ our Saviour.
>
> Titus 3:5-6

You see, the Father, Son, and Holy Ghost unite in saving us by the washing out of our sins through regeneration and giving us the Holy Ghost; it is the gift of God which He sheds on us abundantly. The Jews wanted to know how they might work the works of God. Their religion was all work—outward show. They wanted to get eternal life by something they could do. Jesus said to work the works of God is to believe on Him that God sent.[3] When we exercise saving faith, fervent faith, we meet all conditions; and we are saved through faith, met by faith. Faith touches God and He honors that faith and comes and saves us by His grace and power. To "as many as received him, to them gave he power to become the sons of God."[4]

Thousands all over our land are being taught to trust for salvation to what they do—good works. When they do good they feel better, but this is not salvation. The worst sinner, when he does a good act feels better. Being good and godly are different things. The ungodly and the sinner will be cast into hell together. These people are honest and by false teaching they are deceived, being rocked to eternal sleep in carnal security. If they do not awaken from their sleep of death and call upon God for light and receive the gift of God, eternal life, they will awaken up in hell when it will be too late.

"The gift of God is eternal life."[5]

It is a gift from Jesus to the seeking soul. If you work for it, it is not a gift. If you pay a penny, it is not a gift. Oh! If anyone thirst, come and drink of the waters of life freely.[6] If you have money, come. If you have no money, come and drink wine and milk.

---

[3] See John 6:28-29.

[4] John 1:12.

[5] Romans 6:23.

[6] See John 7:37.

He that hath the Son hath the witness in himself, and "He that hath not the Son of God hath not life."[7]

This eternal life, this gift of God, this well of living water Jesus said He would give, is in the Son. He that hath the life hath the Son abiding in him, for if He hath given us His Son to abide in us and with us, will He not with Him also freely give us all things, as He has promised?[8]

Jesus said to the scribes and Pharisees and hypocrites who made a great profession and outward show of works and solemn faith, who boasted of their knowledge of the Scriptures, "Ye think ye have eternal life. I know you, you have not the love of God within you. You profess to keep the law and follow Moses' teachings. You do not. If you did they would lead you to Me, the fountainhead of living waters, but you will not come unto Me that you might have life."[9]

There are many, whole multitudes, who belong to this class who think they have, or will have, eternal life when they die. They are building on the sand, and the whirlwind of God's wrath will soon sweep them away, and great will be the fall of their house.

And this is life eternal: To know the only true God and Jesus Christ whom God hath sent.[10] We must know, not only by the hearing or reading about Him; the Spirit must bear witness within us that we have this new life, that we are born of the Spirit, that we are now the children of God.

The woman came out to Jacob's well with her pitcher to draw water. Jesus talked to her about her lost condition. He drew her attention to the need of salvation. He showed her she was living in sin, in adultery, and told her if she would get the well in her soul, she would never thirst again.[11]

Not that she would never thirst for the natural water, but she would not want to live in sin. The thirst or desire for sinful things would be taken away; she would hate the sin that she once loved. All this thirst

---

[7] 1 John 5:12.

[8] See Romans 8:32.

[9] John 5:39-42, paraphrased.

[10] John 17:3, paraphrased.

[11] See John 4:6-26.

for sin would be gone. She would love the Lord. Her thirst would be for heavenly knowledge and to please God. All things become new.[12]

Jesus said, "I am the bread of life: he that cometh to me shall never hunger; and he that believeth on me shall never thirst" (John 6:35). When we get this living water, this well down in our souls, the pipe of faith reaches to the river of life, flowing from beneath the throne of God, from the great heart of the Lord Jesus Christ. Keep the pipe open and the connection right. Keep out doubts, sin, and unbelief and the well will never go dry, but will continue to spring up and overflow, leading others to the same fountain.

This woman gladly accepted the gift and left her sins behind her. She left her old self and the pitcher and took the well with her, back to the city. She began to preach Christ; she became a street preacher, shouting out, "I have found the Christ, the Messiah of the Jews. He told me all the things ever I did and all the sins I ever did. Come with me and see the Christ."[13]

When we receive the Spirit of Christ, we speak with a new tongue; we begin to tell of the Savior we have found and try to lead others to the living Christ.

No doubt the people who knew this woman who had been living in sin had no use for her, would not be seen in her company, but there was a great change. She commanded respect and attention.

"The righteous are as bold as a lion,"[14] not the boldness of sin, but a holy, gentle boldness. We are not afraid of what the people will say or do unto us. We love their souls; we have found the Lord, have tasted of "the powers of the world to come."[15] We see their danger while they are living in sin and the awful doom that awaiteth the sinner. We know the day is far spent,[16] the night of death will soon overtake them. If we would save them we must be up and doing.

As this woman lifted Christ up on the street, men and women came from their business places and gathered round to hear the wonderful news of the Savior she had found. As the words fell from her lips,

[12]See 2 Corinthians 5:17.

[13]John 4:29, paraphrased.

[14]Proverbs 28:1.

[15]Hebrews 6:5.

[16]See Romans 13:12.

many believed in Christ. A great crowd followed her. She knew the way and she led them to the well where they saw Jesus and talked with Him, and many of the Samaritans of that city believed on Him for the sayings of this woman who testified, saying, "He told me all things ever I did."[17]

And many more believed because of His own words and said to the woman, "Now we believe, not because of thy saying: for we have heard him ourselves, and know that this is indeed the Christ, the Saviour of the world."[18]

See what a great revival, what success, followed this woman (that Christ had picked up out of the filth of sin) by her earnestness and positive testimonies. It is one thing to know the Christ by hearing of Him and another thing to hear and know Him yourself. Faith is one thing and knowledge is another. Those in the city had faith that it was the Christ but those who came to Him said, "We have seen him and know indeed this is the Christ, the Saviour of the world."

Praise God for such ringing testimonies. "We know that we have passed from death unto life."[20] "His spirit beareth witness that we are the children of God."[21] Those who received Him were like the woman; they wanted all their friends to know Him. They begged Jesus to go into the city. He heard their pleadings and went and stayed two days.[22]

May the dear ones who read this sermon, who are not drinking from the fountain of life, ask Jesus for the gift of God and receive the well of water and then lead other poor thirsty souls to the Lord, that they, too, may receive of this water; that they may never thirst again.

Taken from *Acts of the Holy Ghost*.

---

[17] See John 4:29.

[18] John 4:42.

[19] John 4:42, paraphrased.

[20] 1 John 3:14.

[21] Romans 8:16, paraphrased.

[22] See John 4:43.

THE GREAT COMMISSION

Proclaim Freedom from Satan's Power—God Confirms Our Message

And he said unto them, Go ye into all the world, and preach the gospel to every creature. He that believeth and is baptized shall be saved: but he that believeth not shall be damned. And these signs shall follow them that believe; In my name shall they cast out devils; they shall speak with new tongues; They shall take up serpents; and if they drink any deadly thing, it shall not hurt them; they shall lay hands on the sick, and they shall recover.

Mark 16:15-18

I will show, by the help of God and the enlightening and leading of the Holy Ghost, that the last Commission was not given to the apostles alone, but to all who would believe through their immediate preaching and for all who would believe through their written word until Jesus the Lord of Glory comes again in the clouds for His Church.[1]

Observe, He said, "Go ye into all the world and preach the gospel. And, lo, I am with you alway, even unto the end of the world. Amen" (See Matthew 28:20).[2]

The Gospel was to be preached all over the world and until the end of the age, with all the Pentecost[al] power and gifts. The signs were especially promised to those that would believe and be saved after the Day of Pentecost, or in the future, even to the end. This is the Commission Jesus gave to His Church to preach. The Word with all its power and glory was to be preached by His Church to a lost and sin-cursed world. And He said, "These signs shall follow

[1] See John 17:20 and Matthew 24:30.

[2] A paraphrase of Mark 16:15 and Matthew 28:20.

them that believe,"[3] that He might be glorified in His Church throughout all ages. Amen and amen.

Jesus Claimed All Power—Do We Believe Him?

Perhaps we doubt His love for us, or His willingness to use His power. Jesus was and is the head of the Church and all power in heaven and earth was given to Him.

If we do not speak and act as if we believe Him, we make Him a liar. He had the highest authority to choose His apostles and commission them to go and to give them the greatest commission that was ever given to angels or men. "All power is given unto me in heaven and in earth."[4]

"Go ye, therefore, into all the world and preach the gospel to every creature"[5] because all power is given unto Me, and I am able and willing to deliver all men from every power that can harm, injure, or hurt them in any way. Go and proclaim this Good News everywhere to everyone that whosoever will may benefit by My atoning death and victory over the kingdom of Satan and share in My triumph, that now they may enjoy freedom from satanic supremacy and power, that now they may receive and exercise the rights and privileges of citizens of the kingdom of heaven and enjoy the security and protection of the bloodstained banner of King Emmanuel.

Jesus did not say, "All power is given Me in heaven and earth, but I will keep it a secret and never manifest any of it in any way that anyone can notice."

The Commission Universal

The Commission was broad. It was to reach around and across the world. It was universal; it was to every class and condition of people and tongues. "Of a truth I perceive that God is no respecter of persons: But in every nation he that feareth him, and worketh righteousness, is accepted with him" (Acts 10:34-35). Praise the Lord! It was not only to be preached all over the world, but to the end of the world. His presence and power were promised to those living in the end, just the same as to the disciples.

[3] Mark 16:17.

[4] Matthew 28:18.

[5] Mark 16:15, paraphrased.

He said the Father would send the Holy Ghost, and He, the Holy Ghost, should be with the Church forever: not a limited influence with a degree of power, but as the agent and representative of Christ who has all power in heaven and earth. He was to remain forever, with all the power to save and work as a wonder-working God, to convince the world of sin, of righteousness, and of judgment, to save and to keep us saved by the power of Christ, and to heal us of all our diseases: "Himself took our infirmities, and bare our sicknesses."[6]

He has anointed us with power and especial gifts to demonstrate the power and presence of Christ in a visible manner: "As he is, so are we in this world" (1 John 4:17); God also bearing us witness, "both with signs and wonders, and with divers miracles, and gifts of the Holy Ghost" (Hebrews 2:4). "For he shall not speak of himself; but whatsoever he shall hear, that shall he speak: and he will shew you things to come" (John 16:13). "All things that the Father hath are mine: therefore said I, that he shall take of mine, and shall shew it unto you."[7]

Revelations Are Made to Us

Paul, speaking of the deep things of God, says: "But God hath revealed them unto us by his Spirit: for the Spirit searcheth all things, yea, the deep things of God. . . . We have received the Spirit of God, that we might know things that are freely given us of God, which things we speak not in the words that man's wisdom teaches, but which the Holy Ghost teaches."[8]

God help us to honor the Holy Ghost and let Him work the mighty works of God through us. To preach the Gospel is to preach a living Christ and the power He obtained by His resurrection working in us: the resurrection of the soul in this life, in spirit and oneness with Christ, the resurrection of the body, to tell the world all the Good News Christ has brought from heaven, with all the benefits He purchased on the Cross and left in His last Will and Testament for all the heirs of God and joint-heirs with Christ.

---

[6] Matthew 8:17.

[7] John 16:15.

[8] 1 Corinthians 2:10,12-13, paraphrased.

Baptism

"He that believeth and is baptized shall be saved."[9]

Thousands of teachers teach that this is water baptism, and tens of thousands believe the same and trust in water baptism for salvation and think they cannot be saved until they are immersed.

Water baptism is all right in the right place. Peter said, "Can any man forbid water, that these should not be baptized, which have received the Holy Ghost as well as we?" (Acts 10:47).

They were then baptized in the name of the Lord. There are thousands of professors all over the land who believe by the hearing, but have not had saving faith that brings the knowledge, the witness from God, that they are saved beyond a doubt. Without this saving knowledge, the wrath of God abideth on them.

"He that believeth and is baptized shall be saved," then and there.

"For by one Spirit are we all baptized into one body, whether we be Jews or Gentiles, whether we be bond or free; and have been all made to drink into one Spirit" (1 Corinthians 12:13). God help us all who read these lines to know what this is and what it means to be saved. This is the meaning of the text, "He that believeth and is baptized shall be saved."

Saving Faith

"But he that believeth not shall be damned."[10] No matter what your faith is, until you come to Christ with saving faith that brings the Holy Ghost and brings you into Christ, you are lost. The Word says, "Ye are damned."

The damning sin is unbelief! Until you believe in Christ in a way that brings eternal life and you have the witness within you, you make God a liar.

We do not hear much in these last days of the judgment of God, of the future punishment of the wicked, and they have almost done away with hell, but Jesus says: "The wicked shall be turned into hell, and all the nations that forget God."[11]

---

[9] Mark 16:16.

[10] Mark 16:16.

[11] Psalm 9:17.

All whose names were not written in the Book of Life were cast into the lake that burns with fire and brimstone.[12] God help us to preach and live the truth! Tell one and all, if they are not saved by the power of God, they will be lost forever.

Handling Serpents

Some, in antagonizing divine healing in these days, say: "If you can heal the sick, why don't you raise the dead?" A so-called doctor of divinity in writing several articles against me, trying to prove that divine healing and other demonstrations or visible manifestations of the Spirit were done away with and that they died out with the early church, said: "If the sick are healed, we ought to do everything else that the apostles did."

He said, "No one could be an apostle unless he would raise up the dead, take up serpents, and drink deadly poison." If this is true then there was not an apostle among the twelve. He makes God a liar and a fraud, also the holy apostles. Peter is the only one in the New Testament record that raised the dead. He did not take up serpents or drink deadly poison.

According to his argument, Peter was not an apostle. Paul is the only one who took up a serpent. He did not dare to tempt God or charm the serpent, but took it up by accident: "And when Paul had gathered a bundle of sticks, and laid them on the fire, there came a viper out of the heat, and fastened on his hand. . . . And he shook off the beast into the fire, and felt no harm" (Acts 28:3-6,12)[13] No doubt when Paul saw the poisonous viper on his hand, he knew unless God came to his rescue he would fall dead, and he remembered the promise: "You shall take up serpents and they shall not hurt you."[14]

He exercised faith in God and shook off the serpent and felt no harm. He did not drink poison or raise the dead. According to this learned man, he could not be an apostle. Some say he raised the man who fell out of the window from the dead. This man was not dead:

[12]See Revelation 20:10 and 21:8.

[13]The actual verses from the passage quoted are 3 and 5.

[14]Paraphrase of Mark 16:18.

"Paul went down, and fell on him, and embracing him said, Trouble not yourselves; for his life is in him" (Acts 20:10).

God did not command them to drink deadly poison, but if by accident they drank any deadly thing and then they would remember the promise and look to God in faith, it would not hurt them.

The First Commission of the Twelve

"Heal the sick, cleanse the lepers, raise the dead, cast out devils" (Matthew 10:8). You will see a report of their work in Mark 6:13: "And they cast out many devils, and anointed with oil many that were sick, and healed them." [And also,] "He called his twelve disciples together, and gave them power and authority over all devils, and to cure diseases. And he sent them to preach the kingdom of God, and to heal the sick. . . . And they departed, and went through the towns, preaching the gospel, and healing every where" (Luke 9:1-2, 6).

He sent the seventy out: "Into whatsoever city ye enter. . . . heal the sick that are therein" (Luke 10:8-9). He gave them power over all the works of the enemy that nothing should hurt them, provided they trusted God. The apostles were all noted for teaching healing of the body, for casting out devils, and healing the sick. The power of God was with them to do these things when it was needed for the glory of God. Their main work was to preach the Gospel for soul and body.

Jesus reached the masses by casting out devils and healing afflicted humanity. The disciples did the same, and we should do so also; many, otherwise, will never be saved.

The Commission was Given to Us Also

Matthew gives us the Commission in a few words. The apostles were to preach the Gospel all over the world as far as their voices could be heard, bringing all classes to Christ and to teach all that were saved to understand and to observe and to do all things whatsoever Christ had commanded them. The apostles were not only to reach the people by their voices, or presence, but with their written word.

Jesus prayed not only for the disciples, but for all that shall in all ages believe on Him through the Word, that they all might be one: "As thou, Father, art in me, and I in thee, that they also may be one in us: that the world may believe that thou has[t] sent me. And the glory which thou gavest me I have given them; that they may be one, even as we are one . . . that the world may know that thou hast sent me, and hast loved them, as thou hast loved me."[15] This prayer was for those that would accept Christ through their (the apostles') word, through all ages.

All the mighty works Christ did were done through the Holy Ghost, and He sent the Holy Ghost to be with the Church forever. He says: "And the glory which thou gavest me I have given them."[16]

God Confirms Our Message

He prayed that all the glory and mighty, wonder-working power might be with His followers to the end. This is what He meant when He said, "Lo, I am with you always."[17] It would be strange indeed if the Most Mighty and Most High never manifest[ed] His presence by any visible display of His power.

Oh, hear Him pray that we may be one in Christ. One with Christ and God in the great work of bringing souls from the darkness into the glorious light of the Gospel; that we may be united to each other and to the Lord as the members of His body, drawing all life and strength and God-given intelligence from the great heart and brain of Christ, our living head.

Men Are Saved by Seeing God Work

Jesus did not convince the world that the Father sent Him so much by what He said as what He did: "That ye may know that the Son of man hath power on earth to forgive sins, (then saith he to the sick of the palsy,) Arise, take up thy bed, and go into thine house" (Matthew 9:6 [paraphrased]).

The people blasphemed when He was preaching, but now they were convinced and gave glory to God.

Jesus said, "The words that I speak unto you I speak not of myself: but the Father that dwelleth in me, he doeth the works" (John 14:10).

[15]John 17:21-23.

[16]John 17:22.

[17]Matthew 28:20, paraphrased.

But they would not believe it; then He said [to] believe it for the very works' sake. He said if I had not done the mighty works they would have had a cloak for their sins, but now they had no cloak, or excuse.[18] We should be able to say this, too.

Jesus left all His glory and power to do the works with the children of God that the world might believe that the Father sent Christ into the world and that God loves us as He loved His Son.

We, Too, May Have Signs and Wonders

Don't you see that the Lord wants to confirm His Word through us with signs and wonders, to convince the world that the wonderful Gospel of Christ is true and that they may know that God hath sent us; that He loves us as He did Christ? They were to believe the message for the very works' sake: "And they went forth, and preached every where, the Lord working with them, and confirming the word with signs following. Amen" (Mark 16:20). As they told the wonderful story, the Lord was by their side and in the midst of the people, working with them by visible signs and wonderful demonstrations.

Christ could not convince the world that He came from God by His mighty eloquence and He does not expect that of His followers; but He wants to work with us and show to the world, by His mighty signs, His invisible presence: "In my name shall they cast out devils . . . they shall lay hands on the sick, and they shall recover" (Mark 16:17-18).

God Must Save People—Preaching Alone Cannot

Men and women are the same today that they were in the days of Christ. It takes as much power to save the soul and keep it saved, it takes as much power to cast out devils and heal the sick, as it did then.

All sickness is from sin; all sin is of the devil. Diseases are evil spirits in the body. Jesus said, "Thou deaf, thou lame, thou unclean spirit, come out of him."[19] He came out at once. The lame walked, the dumb spake.

[18]See Matthew 11:21,23.

[19]See Mark 9:25.

When devils were cast out, the disease or cause was gone and the effects soon left. He said, "Behold, I give unto you power . . . over all the power of the enemy" (Luke 10:19).

I praise God, all the gifts and signs are scattered through the Church and thousands of devils are being cast out, and all manner of diseases are being healed through the children of God by the power of the Holy Ghost.

A Stupendous Error That the Days of Miracles Are Past

Why will intelligent people believe, through false teaching, that the days of miracles are past and the power of the Holy Ghost was taken away? Why do they? I ask.

There is no excuse for it, only that they want a more popular, man-pleasing way. There is not a man in any church, or in the world, that can show by the Word of God where and when these things were taken away.

Paul says, "But though we, or an angel from heaven, preach any other gospel unto you than that which we have preached unto you, let him be accursed."[20] Those who preach another gospel today are highly honored and praised, while those who preach the true Gospel are despised. Many do not choose to do anything they think so wicked as to detest such hateful teachers (that is what "accursed" means), but they look up to honor and listen to them instead: "As we said before, so say I now again, If any man preach any other gospel unto you than that ye have received, let him be accursed" (Galatians 1:9).

God have mercy on those who are sinning against light, fighting and denying God's Word, "Having a form of godliness, but denying the power thereof." Paul says, "From such turn away."[21]

Moody and Talmage

Mr. Moody,[22] when preaching in New York, said, "Some people thought the promises of God were too good to be true, but," he

[20] Galatians 1:8.

[21] 2 Timothy 3:5.

[22] Dwight Lyman Moody (1837-1899) was a well-known American evangelist who founded Moody Bible Institute.

said, "they were all for us on conditions and if we met these conditions the Lord would blot out the sun rather than go back on His promises or fail in bringing it to pass." We say, amen!

Mr. Moody, in speaking of Elijah and Elisha, said: "Elijah had great faith. Elisha had a double portion and did just twice as many miracles as Elijah." And [he said] that we ought to have a hundred times as much faith as these men of God had.

The noted Talmage[23] said, in one of his sermons: "Instead of looking back to a dead Pentecost, we ought to have ten thousand Pentecosts all along the way. We all ought to have that Pentecost anointing." He said, "Some men and women in all ages have had this faith and power."

You see, these noted men who stood so high in the work of God both declared, in a few words, that the power of God and the Holy Ghost is for us today in all the blazing glory of Pentecost and ought to be greater, for the Pentecost storm was only a sample of what would follow.

Trust and Obey

If we would obey Christ and go forward as He commanded, He would work with us, confirming the words with signs and wonders everywhere. The Father, Son, and Holy Ghost witness that this is all true. Then how will teachers who deny these things (who are reprobates concerning the faith, having a form of godliness but denying the power[24]), how, oh, how, will they stand before God in the great Day of Judgment?

I am a witness. I set my seal this day that God is true. In the work He has called me to do, He has sent all the signs of the apostles, all the gifts and operations and manifestations of the Spirit, even raising the dead. Several have been raised after being pronounced dead so that none could doubt—in two or three cases, in the midst of mobs that gathered around with violent threatening to arrest or

[23]Thomas Dewitt Talmage (1832-1902), an American pastor and evangelist of D. L. Moody's time.

[24]See 2 Timothy 3:5.

kill some of the workers. But through faith and courage, God raised them up, healed, so that they stood, walked, and praised the Lord.

Greater Works Shall Ye Do

The time is now here when God will seal His work in many places by raising the dead, and many more and greater signs will follow His true work. He will show His power as never before. He says He will work as He did with Joshua, who commanded the sun and moon to stand still. Yes, God hearkened to the voice of man, that even the sun obeyed and stood still so that the fear of God fell on the armies.[25]

He says He will rise up with us and do the same, and greater things, "His strange acts." (See Isaiah 28:21.) Now, in the close, or consummation of this dispensation, to show His power through His bride, it must be so. This mighty power must be scattered and seen as never in the history of the world, through the overcomers, who will soon sit with Christ on His throne, judging the nations.

Praise the Lord! He is just the same yesterday, today, and forever. His promises are "Yea" and "Amen" forever.[26] Amen.

Taken from *Spirit-Filled Sermons.*

[25]See Joshua 10:12-14.

[26]See Hebrews 13:8 and 2 Corinthians 1:20.

The Acts of the Holy Ghost

The Glory of the Lord Abode Upon Mount Sinai

We May Now Come Within the Veil, Into the Most Holy Place—He Writes His Laws Upon the Fleshy Tables of Our Hearts—Summary in Conclusion

nd the glory of the Lord abode upon mount Sinai, and the cloud covered it six days: and the seventh day he called unto Moses out of the midst of the cloud. And the sight of the glory of the Lord was like the devouring fire on the top of the mount in the eyes of the children of Israel.

Exodus 24:16-17

We read with wonder the supernatural displays of God's power and glory, but how many comprehend that we, too, may behold them? The people seem to think that these manifestations were for the early followers. We do not find any such teachings in the Word of God.

Lord, help us to know that our God is the same forever. God would ever dwell with His people. He does not want to live apart from them. His delight and pleasure are to ever be with them. He would walk with them; and wherever the footsteps of God have been among His people, He has left a beautiful pathway of light and glory. God delights to reveal His arm of power; He rejoices to show forth His glory. He "maketh a way in the sea, and a path in the mighty waters."[1]

His glory is for His people. He wants to bestow it upon them. O that His people should reject it! O that He should come unto His own and His own receive Him not! God has ever desired to manifest

[1] Isaiah 43:16.

Himself unto His children. In the ancient days He made Himself known in various manifestations of His power. He descended upon Mount Sinai in fire and smoke and a cloud of glory covered the mount. His voice was heard in the thunder; He revealed Himself in the lightning. He went before Israel in a cloudy pillar by day and hovered over them in a pillar of fire by night, and the glory of His presence was with them.[2]

In the apostolic days God revealed Himself, through the blessed Holy Ghost, in many miraculous ways. He came to Saul of Tarsus in the brightness of the noonday sun and changed him from a bold persecutor to a bold preacher.[3] He came to the amazed disciples upon the transfiguration mount, and the old dispensation and the new held heavenly converse.[4] He came upon the Church with such magnifying power that she presented, not simply one of the phenomena, but the grand phenomena of history.[5]

In all these exhibitions of His power, the people recognized the presence of God and gave Him the glory. That there came a time when there was an interruption of the communication of God with His people was not due to God's plan. God has told the people that if they would hearken unto His voice, He would give them counsel.[6] But they apostatized, and God withdrew Himself. God will never dwell with an apostate people, nor will His voice be heard in their midst. God never speaks in the heart where the whispers of Satan are heard. It is only the pure in heart who shall see the manifestations of God.[7]

We are living in the last days, and the glorious times of the early Pentecost are for us. If, as in the days of Samuel, there could be a return of the "open vision" and the interrupted communication of God with His people restored, the great decline of the power of the

---

[2] See Exodus 13:21.

[3] See Acts 9.

[4] See Matthew 17:2 and Mark 9:2.

[5] See Acts 2:1-4.

[6] See Exodus 18:19.

[7] See Matthew 5:8.

Church would be arrested. The Holy Ghost is no longer with us in primitive Pentecostal power. Instances of marked faith-power, of unction in preaching, of wondrous displays of the Holy Ghost are painfully inconspicuous and exceptional. The Church is merely a negative barrier in restraining the floods of wickedness, when she should be a positive, aggressive force in driving back evil. Sorrowfully we must acknowledge that the glory of the former days has departed.

Now, there is a reason why we do not see the wonderful displays of God's power among the people. There is a hindrance. The trouble with the people today is that they believe that this power was for the early Church only, and we have taken the views of our ancestors and abided by them. We have not tested God and met His conditions and seen whether He would pour down His Spirit. We have not met the conditions such as would ask God to display His power. We have believed that God has taken His power from the Church; and when one does put forth the faith and believes these days may be for us now, such a one is called a crank, a hypnotic, etc.

The glory of God was withdrawn from the temple because they had abandoned Him. He told them that so long as they would obey His laws He would be with them; but it was because they forsook God that He withdrew His presence from them. The Lord is always ready to do His part. Though His true believers may be few, He will be to them a mighty host. "Fear not, thou worm Jacob, and ye men of Israel; I will help thee, saith the Lord."[8] God's people are in the minority. Wherever God's people were engaged in warfare, the numbers of the Lord were the smallest. But whenever the battle was fought in the strength of the Lord, then God fought the battles for them and delivered them. God will make the minority victorious when the fight is in the strength of the Lord.

The masses of the people are not looking for signs and wonders today. They do not want to see them. The preaching of God is foolishness to them that believe not.[9] We preach the Gospel as the Lord gives it to us. Bless God, His people obey the Spirit; and where the Spirit is, they recognize it. Where you see these manifestations—the

[8] Isaiah 41:14.

[9] See 1 Corinthians 1:21.

lame leap[ing] as an hart, the sick healed, people stricken down with the power, etc.—it is a visible sign of God's wonderful presence.

Jesus said: "I will send you the Holy Ghost and He shall abide with you for ever!"[10] But oh, how many of God's professed people despise the Holy Ghost! In many places where the people profess to follow God, the Holy Ghost has been driven out; and there are thousands to whom the Holy Ghost has come for the last time. We are not going to stay here very long. We are bound for judgment, and the time has come for us to get out from the traditions of men. The Holy Ghost is our leader and teacher.[11] We must depend upon Him for our teachings.

The glory of the Lord covered the mountain for those six days, and the people saw it and believed it. They saw the visible power of God. Do we look for the visible power in our midst today? Moses lived with God forty days and forty nights, shut up with God without nourishment.[12] Now, you don't believe that. I believe it. I believe the whole Bible. God help us to believe the whole Bible or throw it away.

Now, they had to do something. They made a consecration—repented of their sins and shortcomings. They made a new consecration to God, and then they were ready for duty and then expected the glory and the visible signs and wonders.

It was just the same at the time of Pentecost. The one hundred and twenty came together, forsaking everything, and tarried in earnest prayer and consecration for ten days, waiting for the enduement of power to fit them for life's service. And they didn't wait in vain, for while they were yet praying the Holy Ghost came upon them in wondrous power, the city was shaken, and three thousand souls were converted in a single day.[13]

If we were ready to meet God's conditions, we would have the same results and a mighty revival would break out that would shake the

[10]John 14:16, paraphrased.

[11]See John 14:26 and 16:13.

[12]See Exodus 24:16,18.

[13]See Acts 2.

world and thousands of souls would be saved. The displays of God's power on the Day of Pentecost were only a sample of what God designed should follow all through the ages. Instead of looking back to Pentecost, let us always be expecting it to come, especially in these last days. God help us to get into line and come together as one man.

In the nineteenth chapter [of Exodus], God came again in the bright cloud. In the fourteenth verse, Moses came down from the mountain and the people washed their clothing. This was the emblem of purity. This was the sign of the inward cleansing. We must be sure we have a pure heart. We can never expect to have these visible manifestations of God unless we are children of God. The people were in a condition to meet God—clean bodies, clean garments. God help us to get the cleansing power.

The people trembled when they heard the sound of the trumpet, and the mountain quaked because the Lord descended into the mount.[14] The people prayed for the power to be stayed. That's the way today. They were not right, some of them. And so it is now. People pray for these demonstrations of God to be stopped. They do not want a visible sign of God's presence. The cloud of glory hung over them. God help us to pray for the cloud of glory to hang over us. The cloud over them by night, that had the appearance of fire, and the pillar of a cloud by day, were visible signs of God's presence with them.

I will turn to the third chapter of Second Corinthians. I want the dear people to know why we preach the power and believe in these visible signs: "Forasmuch as ye are manifestly declared to be the epistle of Christ ministered by us, written not with ink, but with the Spirit of the living God; not in tables of stone, but in fleshy tables of the heart" (2 Corinthians 3:3).

Oh, God, help us to know whom this means. The fleshy tables of our hearts. Praise God for the new covenant. We may now come within the veil, into the most holy place. The apostle wants us to understand that we can come so much nearer to God. He writes His law on the fleshy tables of our hearts. God wants us to be walking Bibles! He wants us to be a living ark, bearing about the glory of

[14]See Exodus 19:16.

God! Our body is the temple. He lights our lamp and it becomes brighter. Then we have the epistle written in our hearts. Brother Paul says we have treasure in an earthen vessel.[15]

> But if the ministration of death, written and engraven in stones, was glorious, so that the children of Israel could not steadfastly behold the face of Moses for the glory of his countenance; which glory was to be done away: How shall not the ministration of the spirit be rather glorious? For if the ministration of condemnation be glory, much more doth the ministration of righteousness exceed in glory. . . . For if that which is done away was glorious, much more that which remaineth is glorious.
>
> 2 Corinthians 3:7-9,11

Well, if the glory of God was displayed in [such a] wonderful manner in the old dispensation, how much brighter should it burn in the temple of our bodies today? Brother Paul says the letter killeth: it is the Spirit that giveth light.[16] God gives us light today! God gives us light! Paul says the old was done away when the middle wall of the partition was broken down, but that which is more glorious has come to stay.[17] Christ said: "I will send you the Comforter."[18]

Those who have the courage to stand up and tell the truth will be persecuted. But we must go on and preach the truth; we've got no time to listen to the howling of devils. Let us boldly dare, like Hezekiah, to strike for a reformation! Let us purge the priesthood, the temple courts, our own hearts and lives of every unclean and defiling thing and bring all to the storehouse, putting God to the proof, whether He will not open the windows of heaven and pour us out a blessing that there shall not be room enough to receive it.[19] Whenever the beauty of holiness is found in God's temples, the Shekinah will flood them with the glory of the Lord!

Taken from *Life, Work, and Experience of Maria Beulah Woodworth.*

[15]See 1 Corinthians 6:19 and 2 Corinthians 4:7.

[16]See 2 Corinthians 3:6, paraphrased.

[17]See Ephesians 2:14.

[18]John 15:26, paraphrased.

[19]See Malachi 3:10.

The Fire and Glory of God Filling the Temple

A Symbol of the Outpouring of the Holy Ghost on the Day of Pentecost

(Abbreviated)

[Let's look at] Second Chronicles 5:11-14:

> And it came to pass, when the priests were come out of the holy place: [(for all the priests that were present were sanctified, and did not then wait by course: Also the Levites which were the singers, all of them of Asaph, of Heman, of Jeduthun, with their sons and their brethren, being arrayed in white linen, having cymbals and psalteries and harps, stood at the east end of the altar, and with them an hundred and twenty priests sounding with trumpets:) It came even to pass, as the trumpeters and singers were as one, to make one sound to be heard in praising and thanking the Lord; and when they lifted up their voice with the trumpets and cymbals and instruments of musick, and praised the Lord, saying, For he is good; for his mercy endureth for ever: that then the house was filled with a cloud, even the house of the Lord; So that the priests could not stand to minister by reason of the cloud: for the glory of the Lord had filled the house of God.]

I want you to see how they came—one hundred and twenty of them with different instruments, yet all making the same sound; the Levites arrayed in white linen, emblematic of purity. "It came even to pass, as the trumpeters and singers were as one, to make one sound to be heard in praising and thanking the Lord; and when they lifted up their voice with the trumpets and cymbals and instruments of musick, and praised the Lord."[1]

[1] 2 Chronicles 5:13.

There were one hundred and twenty priests blowing trumpets; there were singers and instruments of music, but they were as one, to make one sound. "For he is good; for his mercy endureth for ever: that then the house was filled with a cloud, even the house of the Lord; So that the priests could not stand to minister by reason of the cloud: for the glory of the Lord had filled the house of God."

The one hundred and twenty priests who were supposed to minister stood like statues and the Holy Ghost took the meeting. The entire building was filled with the glory of God. All this demonstration, the house filled with the glory of God, was brought about by the one hundred and twenty priests blowing the trumpets. The sounding of the different instruments mingled with the voice of the great company of singers, the whole object being to glorify God, and all making one sound.

God wants perfect harmony—no one criticizing, no one finding fault, but all sounding forth His praise; and in white—purity. If we go out to meet God clothed in white, washed in the blood of the Lamb; if we go out, all making the same sound; if we go out to glorify God, God will honor all the noise.

It is not excitement. God comes down to acknowledge the praise. They pressed the button and the power of God came down. That same power will either save or destroy us someday. The house was filled with the power and glory of the Lord.

There was no preaching then; but singing, shouting, praising the Lord and all that praise glorified God. The house was filled with His glory. The people were still standing, Solomon ready to dedicate the temple. The temple represents the Church of Jesus; it also represents our bodies. "Know ye not your body is the temple of the living God?"[2]

Two or three verses from the seventh chapter.[3] It is like Pentecost; it represents Pentecost. "When Solomon had made an end of

[2] 1 Corinthians 6:19, paraphrased.

[3] Now when Solomon had made an end of praying, the fire came down from heaven, and consumed the burnt offering and the sacrifices; and the glory of the Lord filled the house. And the priests could not enter into the house of the Lord, because the glory of the Lord had filled the Lord's house. And when all the children of Israel saw how the fire came down, and the glory of the Lord upon the house, they bowed themselves with their faces to the ground upon the pavement, and worshipped, and praised the Lord, saying, For he is good; for his mercy endureth for ever.

2 Chronicles 7:1-3.

praying." So many people never look to God to answer. They would be frightened if He did. Solomon stretched out his hands and prayed to God, and God heard him.

When he had made an end of praying something happened. God will come forth if you are not afraid of the power, if you are ready to stand for God with all there is of you. As Pentecostal people we should always be "prayed up," so we can get hold of God quickly and be sure it is for the glory of God.

"The fire came down from heaven, and consumed the burnt offering and the sacrifices; and the glory of the Lord filled the house." Some people talk as if God never had any glory, as though the glory of God was never seen at any time.

Paul said, "If the ministration of death, written and engraven on stones, was glorious . . . shall not the ministration of the spirit be rather glorious?"[4] The glory under the Law did not last, but the Holy Ghost came at Pentecost to stay, and the manifestations under the ministry of the Holy Ghost are to be with much greater glory, to "exceed in glory."[5] The power under the Law was only a shadow of what we ought to have under grace. This was the ministry of life, not death.

The house was filled with the glory of the Lord; they saw and felt it; it was not a shadow. I am glad the glory of God has been seen here a number of times. Many times in our ministry the glory of God has been seen over us. God is here. This you see and hear; "this is that"; that is the promise of the Father; this is the Holy Ghost.[6]

The priests could not enter into the house. They could not get in at all, because the glory of the Lord had filled the Lord's house. "When all the children of Israel saw how the fire came down, and the glory of the Lord upon the house, they bowed themselves with their faces to the ground upon the pavement, and worshipped, and praised the Lord, saying, For he is good; for his mercy endureth for ever."[7]

Everything connected with this represents this glorious age. The apostle says God can reveal His doctrine, which was hidden from all

---

[4] 2 Corinthians 3:7-8, paraphrased.

[5] 2 Corinthians 3:9.

[6] See Acts 2:16 and 33.

[7] 2 Chronicles 7:3.

ages.[8] Those who crucified the Lord did not know about the mystical body of Christ. This divine life in us, they did not know it or they would not have crucified Him.[9]

It could be revealed only when the Holy Ghost came down from God to make men understand the new covenant. The glory that belongs to the ministration of death did not come to stay. The glory came from the ark of the covenant, containing the tables of stone on which the Law was written, the Ten Commandments.

There were the cherubim, two angels, facing each other with wings outspread over the ark and mercy seat where God dwells in His temple. In His tabernacle nothing is supposed to be in the heart but God's Word, the new and everlasting covenant, written on the fleshy tables of the heart, not on stone, but with the finger of God Almighty.[10]

If when the people obeyed, the glory of God came down and the people fell prostrate, how much glory ought there to be today? There was just one tabernacle and two tables of stone. Today your body is the temple of the living God. Our bodies are the temple of the Holy Ghost, and God with His own finger writes His Word in our hearts.[11]

The ancient temple in all its glory represents each one of our bodies. If we are filled with the Holy Ghost, as we ought to be, the body will be flooded with rivers of water flowing out to others; and it will be on fire for God.

The glory of the Lord was seen over the ark. Inside the tabernacle the lamp was always burning, being kept supplied with oil; it never went out.[12] In the temple of the body, God puts His love in our hearts, and He wants us to keep the light always burning, never to let it go out.

By keeping all obstructions out of the channel of faith, we get a supply of oil continually; and the light shall shine through the tabernacle always. If the oracle written on stone was glorious, how much more glorious under grace! The Holy Ghost shall abide with you always.

[8] See Ephesians 3:5.

[9] See 1 Corinthians 2:8.

[10] See 2 Corinthians 3:3.

[11] See 1 Corinthians 6:19, Exodus 31:18, and Jeremiah 31:33.

[12] See Leviticus 24:2 and Exodus 27:20.

Jesus said if we keep His commandments, the Father and He would both take up their abode with us.[13] They dwell with us and we are flooded with the Holy Ghost—people to be wondered at. "Here am I, and the children Thou hast given me."[14] There should be perfect fellowship and harmony; we should all make one sound. The glory came down at Solomon's prayer. At a glimpse of that glory, they lost their strength and the whole multitude went down.

When we are praying for people to get saved or healed, some shout, some praise, some pray, but all are making the same sound. We put on the blood by faith and get a glimpse of His glory. Is it any wonder people lose their strength and fall prostrate under the new life that comes to them?

Is it strange we are people to be wondered at? You have seen all this here: singing, playing, making the same sound. Is it any wonder these people who come here (especially to get under the blood as never before), when they get a glimpse of Jesus, is it any wonder they fall prostrate?

You must prove God has changed, has taken His power away, before you condemn us. His gifts and callings are "without repentance."[15] He never changes; He is "the same yesterday, and to day, and for ever."[16]

No one has any right to condemn us, to say the people are hypnotized, crazy, have lost their minds, or I have put a spell on them. Great God! Awaken the people before the thunders of judgment shall arouse them! You must throw the Bible away or you must prove the gifts and callings have been taken from the Church before you reject us.

We are going the Bible route, and you have no business to teach anything else; you must stick to the Word of God. We do not hold anything up but the Word of God. It is good enough for me. I am not ashamed of the Gospel of Christ or of His power.[17]

[13]See John 15:10.

[14]See Isaiah 8:18.

[15]Romans 11:29.

[16]Hebrews 13:8.

[17]See Romans 1:16.

What a wonderful people we are in our privileges! Today everyone may be God's priest. If we abide in Him and His words abide in us, we may ask what we will and it shall be done.[18] We indeed have wonderful privileges. The power of the Lord shines forth a hundred times greater than under the law; the power then was typical of Pentecost.

Get your Bibles and search out these things. You are getting the light of God, and He expects you to walk in the light, even if you get it from a little, weak woman. In His name we tell you these things are true. What do you care for man's opinion when you stand before God? Dried opinions and traditions of men all go to destruction, but it is the living Word that we are preaching to you.

When John was in prison he began to doubt a little whether Jesus was the Christ and he sent his disciples to ask, "Art thou he that should come?"[19] Jesus did not say, "I belong to the church or I belong to a college." He said, "Go and tell John the things you have seen here; the lame walk, the blind see, different diseases are healed, and the poor have the gospel preached to them. Blessed is he whosoever shall not be offended."[20] Men get mad at the signs of the Holy Ghost—jealous, spitting out hatred, trying to tear down God's work.

If John did not believe in Christ through the signs, no eloquence would be of value. If he did not believe what the witnesses told him, he would not believe anything; neither will you! There is a devil's counterfeit and there is a genuine, as sure as you live.

If you only look on, it will seem foolishness to you as we praise God and as people get filled with the Holy Ghost and get gifts, but it is Jesus first, last, and all the time. We hold up Jesus and praise His name. We see bright, happy faces; we see pain go out of bodies; and we go home rejoicing, feeling we have heaven here below.

Resist the devil in the name of the Lord. Sometimes when I am standing up preaching, the devil would make me drop dead if I

---

[18]See John 15:7.

[19]See John 11:3.

[20]Matthew 11:4-6 and Luke 7:22-23, paraphrased.

would listen to him. I resist in the name of the Lord and he has to go.[21] We have such a wonderful Savior!

"You shall lay hands on the sick"; it does not say where. He commissioned me and I obey God rather than man. Neither the deadly serpent nor any poison shall harm you. "Ye shall cast out devils."[22] I believe every bit of it, and I have seen it all. Hallelujah!

I got my commission from the Lord, and I did not go until He called me or until I was baptized and qualified. I get my message from heaven. I do not know what I am going to talk about; but God knows everyone here and just what everyone needs, and He will give you something.

The power Jesus promised His disciples, when He told them to tarry at Jerusalem, was to change their lives and qualify them to transact the business of heaven. After they were baptized with the Holy Ghost, they would be true to their master and be witnesses for Him.[23]

They went down from that mountain praising the Lord. They were filled with a great joy as they went back to Jerusalem to await the fulfillment of the promise. They had confidence in God; He said so, and they began to praise.

Are you full of joy, having not a doubt about Jesus being your Lord and Savior? You want power to do the work of God; you want to be clothed with power. God says He will baptize with fire, bestowing wisdom, knowledge, and gifts. He will make you to understand the deep things of God and as you teach them and live them, God will be with you.

You must believe you are going to get this blessing. They were "with one accord."[24] God help us to get to that place. God wants us of one accord, hearts running together like drops of water.

A little company like that could shake a city in a day. We are not of one accord when one is pulling one way and one another; when we hear "maybe this" and "maybe that." Do you suppose God will bless you in that?

[21] James 4:7.

[22] See Mark 16:15-18.

[23] See Acts 1:8.

[24] Acts 2:1.

You cannot understand the first principles. Once you have the newborn joy in your heart, when you see it in someone else, you know it is of God. Be of one mind. No matter how much you have to praise God for, we always want more.

At Pentecost, suddenly they heard a sound like a mighty, rushing wind. This Holy Ghost we are holding up is a mighty power. He came from heaven like a windstorm—like floods of water filling the vessels and as fire upon the heads of the one hundred and twenty people. As it were, cloven tongues of fire sat upon their heads. Then the Holy Ghost went in and took possession of the temple; took full possession of the machinery, wound it up, and set it running for God. They staggered like drunken people and fell. This mighty power took possession of their tongues and spoke through them in other languages.[24]

It said away back in the prophets: "With men of stammering lips and another tongue will I speak to this people."[25] Think of that! God doing such a mighty thing! But some do not want to believe. That is the way the Holy Ghost came and comes today, and people say it is some other power.

They did not lose their minds; they had just found it! They got the spirit of love and a sound mind. We never have a sound mind until we get the mind of Christ. People who cannot understand it say these things are foolishness. We are told the wisdom of this world is foolishness with God.[26] This is the power of God and the wisdom of God, not the work of the devil. People saying so doesn't make it so.

God had complete control. He came in and took possession. The Holy Ghost is in the world today. You must prove He has been taken away, and also the gifts and callings, before you have a right to lay hands on God's people.

The things called foolishness today are the power of God unto salvation. Step out in the deep with God. Paul tells us the Lord ascended into heaven and sent down gifts, for the work of the ministry, the perfecting of the saints, the edifying of the body of Christ.[27]

[24]See Acts 2:2-4.

[25]Isaiah 28:11, paraphrased.

[26]See 1 Corinthians 3:19.

[27]See Ephesians 4:8 and 11-12.

The ministry does not want the gifts today. Saints, that is, Christians, are baptized with the Holy Ghost that the whole body may be edified, no matter how much you have got. When God is working, every one of His children is edified. If God works through someone else, I am edified and encouraged, and I rejoice.

The working of the Holy Ghost is the visible sign of the presence of Jesus. They went from Jerusalem to preach the Gospel everywhere and the Lord was with them. I love that word. He is in heaven? Yes, but He is with us also.

The Lord was with them, confirming the Word. How? With signs and wonders following.[28] Amen. Wherever they went they saw faces shine, someone healed, someone speaking in tongues. This you see and hear; it is the Holy Ghost and it is for the work of the ministry.[29]

If I did not know Jesus was by my side and His loving arms around me, I could not stand here today. I should not have the strength if I did not know that He dwells in this body. If I did not know by experience that these things are true, I could not stand here.

I have tested the truth; I know it is of God. How can we help talking of the things we have seen? I have seen things by the Spirit and in visions. I have seen Jesus, the heavens open, the marriage supper, hosts of angels, the glory of God. I have seen them, glory to God! I know what I am telling you. I know Jesus lives and is standing by my side more truly than I know you are here. These things are verities.

I am not ashamed of the Gospel of Christ. Glory to God! When a weak woman comes here to tell you what strong men ought to have told you, what are you going to think about it? I say these things are true, and when people say they are foolishness and fanaticism, dare they attempt to prove it by the Word? I dare them to do it.

When they can prove the Holy Ghost has been taken out of the world, away from God's people, I am ready to go to prison, not before.

---

[28]See Acts 5:12 and 14:3.

[29]See Acts 2:33.

"Open the Pearly Gates"

We are marching upon the King's highway,
We'll shout and sing, and we'll watch and pray;
No time to idle, no time to wait,
But hasten on to the golden gate.
Chorus
Open, open the pearly gates,
Open, open the pearly gates;
Open, open the pearly gates,
And let the redeemed pass in.

With joy and gladness upon each head,
We're marching up where the feast is spread;
For a royal banquet will there be giv'n
To all who enter the gates of heav'n.

No unclean thing shall go up thereon,
No lion there, O no, not one;
But those arrayed in pure garments white,
With souls prepared for the mansions bright.

With our battles fought and our victories won,
Our warfare weapons all laid down,
We'll strike our golden harps and sing,
And crown our Christ as a conq'ring King.[24]

Taken from *Signs and Wonders God Wrought in the Ministry of M. B. Woodworth-Etter.*

[24] Miller, "Open the Pearly Gates," (n. d., Possibly the 1920s).

Christ's Great Revival on the Plains Our Example

Fasting—Jesus Empowers His Disciples

And it came to pass in those days, that he went out into a mountain to pray, and continued all night in prayer to God.

And when it was day, he called unto him his disciples: and of them he chose twelve, whom also he named apostles. . . .

And he came down with them, and stood in the plain, and the company of his disciples, and a great multitude of people out of all Judea and Jerusalem, and from the sea coast of Tyre and Sidon, which came to hear him, and to be healed of their diseases; And they that were vexed with unclean spirits: and they were healed. And the whole multitude sought to touch him: for there went virtue out of him, and healed them all.

Luke 6:12-13,17-19

This is one of the greatest revivals that Jesus Christ ever held, with great and wonderful results. We find much preceding these verses: where the Son of God had healed a lame man who had a withered arm; the time the devil got up in the people and they tried to kill the Son of God, but He slipped away from the crowd and went into the mountains and prayed all night alone with God.[1]

Fasting

If the Son of God found it necessary to pray all night alone with God, don't you think we ought to spend some time alone with

[1] See Luke 6:6-12.

God? He was probably fasting. When Jesus Christ fasted something happened afterwards, and if God puts a fast upon you and you go in God's way, something will happen afterwards. (Besides afflicting your body and being all out of sorts when you are through and making everybody miserable around you. That is not God's fast.) Always when Jesus went out and fasted and prayed, some great miracle took place afterwards.

When Jesus got His baptism at the Jordan, the Holy Ghost came upon Him to stay; and He was led away into the wilderness where He was alone with God forty days, fasting all that time. After the forty days the fast[ing] communication[s] with God were over. He was hungry, but He was not hungry all the time He was fasting. Afterwards, we are told, He was hungry.

The devil is always at hand, so the devil tempted Him in a wonderful way by asking Him to make bread out of stones. Of course He could have done it, but you see He got power, while fasting with God and communing with the Spirit, to meet the devil. He came with all his satanic force and even the wild beasts came out of the forests and joined with the devil against the Son of God. But He had won the victory while in prayer alone with God and was enabled to drive the devil back.[2]

Another time after He had been alone in the mountains praying, a great storm came and the disciples thought the ship was about to go down. He calmed the tempest and the sea became as glass.[3]

And in this lesson during this fast in the mountain, He was alone with God all night in prayer. He was not talking to the wind, but in the ears of His father, the God of heaven. He was about to undertake to do something requiring great wisdom and mighty power from God. He was about to select the pillars that were going to establish the Church of Christ—the Church of the living God.

Jesus Chooses His Twelve Disciples

So, Jesus Christ could not be hid. If you are filled with God like you ought to be, you cannot be hid either. He could not be hid, and

[2] See Matthew 4:1-11.

[3] See Matthew 14:22-33.

when He came out of His place of prayer, He saw the disciples and a great multitude that were watching and waiting for Him. He called the disciples together to do a mighty work. He had many thousands following who had been healed and wonderfully blessed and who knew a great deal about the Son of God, so He had a mighty responsibility to choose the right ones. So He selected twelve and ordained them.

He clothed them with power. He gave them license from heaven—God-given authority. He filled them with the Holy Ghost. He loaned them the same power that He had over all devils and all unclean spirits and told them to go out two by two and preach the same Gospel He was preaching, in the same way, and exercise the same faith He had exercised with God—cast out devils, heal the sick. He qualified them and ordained them with power from on high to go forth to accomplish the same results that He had. This was wonderful, and all the disciples went down further into the plains.

The Multitudes Follow Jesus

We are told that great multitudes followed Him from Judea (a multitude is not less than five hundred people), and multitudes came out of all Judea and Jerusalem and from the sea coast of Tyre and Sidon and all along the sea coast out of towns and from every direction. There must have been many thousands out there in the hot sun. What did they come for? They came to hear Jesus, not just to get healed like some of you. They came to hear about Jesus, to get acquainted with Him, to see Him whom to know is life eternal. They came to hear the Word that He brought from heaven, to find out the way that they might be saved and healed.

They had a wonderful meeting there. Remember, they came to hear the Word and to see. "Faith cometh by hearing and hearing the word of God."[4] How can they hear the Word of God without a preacher and how can he preach the Word of God unless God has sent him?

Oh, you preachers, how are people to get faith today to be healed when you preach against it? How will they get faith about the

[4] Romans 10:17, paraphrased.

coming of the Son of God when you don't talk about it? Faith cometh by hearing the Word of God. No man can get down into the mysteries without the enlightening power of the Holy Ghost. If the Bible is sealed, it is sealed to those that are lost—who are blinded by the god of this world.[5] But this glorious Gospel brings you into communication with Jesus—God Almighty's dear Son—and with the Father that sent Him.

A Divine-Healing Meeting

So these people were gathered there to hear and get acquainted with Jesus and to find the way to be healed. He took these disciples, the first thing after they were ordained for the ministry, into the greatest revival He ever held and gave them a start for the great work they had to do. It was a divine-healing meeting from start to finish. Jesus Christ preached the glad tidings, salvation for the soul and healing for the body and redemption for the body.

He preached the double cure—otherwise His fame never would have gone out over that country. They heard of the Great Physician, of His mighty love and power. No case was too hard for Him. No one too poor nor too rich. If they came in God's way, He healed every one and not only healed, but also saved, for He gave them the double cure. Himself took our infirmities and bare our sicknesses, by His stripes we are healed today.[6]

"Which is easier to say, Thy sins are forgiven thee, or to say to this paralytic, get up and walk?"[7] One is as easy as the other. Both miracles—God's power being demonstrated—the same power saves the soul and heals the body and will take us up to glory. Make us so light we will rise without wings. Hallelujah!

So the Lord preached the Word to these people and they were healed, every one. "Son, thy sins are forgiven thee—go and sin no more lest a worse thing come upon thee. Go and tell your friends, every one, what great things the Lord hath done."[8] Don't forget it. Don't be so forgetful of His benefits. Serve God, give glory to God

[5] See 2 Corinthians 4:3-4.

[6] See Matthew 8:17, 1 Peter 2:24, and Isaiah 53:5.

[7] See Matthew 9:5, Mark 2:9, and Luke 5:23.

[8] John 5:14 and Mark 5:19, paraphrased.

and that disease will never come back anymore. Go—thou art whole. Go and sin no more lest it comes back and you die or something worse comes. Glory to God. You must see how much glory God is to get out of this. Hallelujah! So when He healed the body, He saved the soul.

So all classes gathered in the plains, they came out to see Jesus. Did you come here to see Jesus, or did you come here out of curiosity? I hope if you came through curiosity you are satisfied by this time. They came to see Jesus, get acquainted, and hear the blessed doctrine He was preaching; came to learn the way and to get this great salvation. It cost such an awful price, but God is offering it to you without money. Glory to God—accept it.

Shocks from the Heavenly Battery

These disciples were initiated in a great revival. Jesus preached as never man preached. He preached the glad tidings, salvation from sin and healing from their diseases. He preached the Word and made it plain and gave them to understand that whosoever will may come.[9]

O you nervous people, you who are going to have an operation. God can keep you from all these things. "I am the God of all flesh."[10] Is there anything too hard for Jesus? No. He can move the mountain or tumor in a minute, move the cancer, soothe your nerves. You who are afraid the excitement will make you nervous, get a shock from the battery of heaven and you will sleep like a baby. He is the very same Jesus, the wonder-working Jesus, the same yesterday, today and forever.[11] Glory! I am a witness.

So He went out to preach, and He did not have a lot of music, no pianos, but the power of God was there. It is not so much music, not so much singing, not such long prayers, not so much preaching, but *the Spirit of the living God*. So as He opened His mouth, He spake as never man spake, because there was something back of it.[12]

[9] See Matthew 10:32, Luke 6:47, and Acts 2:21.

[10] Jeremiah 32:27, paraphrased.

[11] See Hebrews 13:8.

[12] See Mark 1:27 and Luke 4:36.

He said, "My Word is like the hammer that breaks the hard rock—like coals of fire on the brain lodged in the heart, arrows dipped in the blood of Jesus and shot out by the lightning of God's power, striking men in the forehead and they fall like dead men."

The City of Destruction

Move out of the City of Destruction,[13] move to the cross. Get out of the plains and start for glory tonight. They had a wonderful meeting there. So He preached the Word, showed them it was for them, showed them how to come, showed them what they had to do, and they met the condition. Every last one of them had to believe on Jesus and get close enough to touch Him.

"Someone touched me"—glory. How do you know? "I felt the virtue going out."[14] You touch Jesus Christ with faith and God will come if He has to bring heaven down. It isn't the long prayer, nor the flowery prayer, but the prayer of faith—faith that touches God and brings heaven down. Hallelujah!

The preaching was over, the altar call given, and they began to make their way to Jesus, and they stood on the watch. Faith comes by watching, faith comes by hearing the wonderful testimonies they hear right here. We see them trying to come, trying to get there first, and everyone that came received; and if they had faith it did not take two or three hours for the light and power to come from heaven.

These people accepted it. They did not carry their sick back over those plains in the hot sun, but they touched Him, and the diseases went out and the demons went out like whipped dogs obedient to their master's orders; and the healing virtue of Jesus went in and their bodies were healed, and they went out to bring in others. Is that what you are doing? Or are you sitting down and waiting for your sickness to come back? Bless the Lord.

---

[13] "City of Destruction"—From *The Pilgrim's Progress* (1678, 1685) by John Bunyan (1628-1688): The City which Christian, the pilgrim, left in order to go to the heavenly city. The City of Destruction stood for those living without the faith in Jesus Christ that brings salvation.

[14] See Mark 5:30 and Luke 8:46.

A Great Work Done

So faith grew into knowledge. When they went they listened and heard, but now they saw and knew it was so. They saw it before their eyes—saw them running, leaping, and skipping in every direction. And the excitement, as you call it, ran high and everyone got in the battle. When you begin to get your eyes on Jesus Christ, you will do it. So their faith grew and pretty soon they said we will just all rush there and the whole congregation—thousands of people—made a rush to try to touch the Son of God, and everyone that touched Him was made whole. He cast out devils—"You deaf spirit, you dumb spirit—come out."[15]

Jesus Christ came to destroy the works of the devil. So the multitude tried to touch Him, and everyone got the double cure, salvation for the soul and body—got joy in their hearts. Don't you believe it? Praise the Lord! So this was a great revival. He cast out the demons, and those possessed with devils will do all kinds of foolish, devilish things to torment everyone. But when Jesus came they knew they had to go out, and they will have to go out if you come right. You have just as much power to cast out devils in the name of Jesus Christ. The devils will run like a lot of dogs. "Resist the devil, and he will flee from you."[16] But you have to keep them out or they will try to get in again. You keep them out.

The maniac represents the tribulation. The man had these devils all his life. Jesus says, "You come out of him and don't you ever come in any more." But He will cast the devils out of you, and you have to keep them out yourself. Get the house full of glory of God and give the Lord the key, and you will not be bothered any more.[17]

The Double Cure

This was a glorious meeting. And Jesus initiated His disciples there to give them courage, and they went out with gladness, filled with the Spirit of mighty power, and they went into the villages and cities and preached the Gospel—the double cure. They had never heard it before, but they preached the Gospel and healed the sick

[15]See Mark 9:25.

[16]James 4:7.

[17]See Matthew 12:43-45.

everywhere. Wherever they preached the double cure, somebody believed and was healed. If they had not preached it, no one would have known anything about it. Glory to God! You find this all through the Word of God. The greatest work that Jesus ever did was the healing of sick and the casting out of devils.

Demonstrate God Is With You by Healing the Sick

We are told that Jesus Christ was anointed by the Lord and began to preach and heal the sick of all kinds of diseases, for God was with Him.[18] He was anointed of God to do this. Preach the Gospel and demonstrate it and prove it to be from God by healing the sick. Wherever He went He did that. The greatest revivals in the New Testament after Pentecost were the direct result of one or more divine healings of the body. It was used more than anything else in the Word of God to draw the people to Christ.

Nearly all the great revivals were brought about by divine healing and sometimes only one was healed. The man at the Beautiful Gate was healed and got the double cure.[19] They were just going to preach. The result was five thousand men were converted that day, and Peter and John were thrown into prison.[20] If you are all right, you are going to be persecuted. But they began to shout and rejoice; they had results and were willing to lie in prison when they thought of the souls saved. Hallelujah!

Hundreds have been healed here. Look how hard your hearts are! You would not believe God if He walked over the platform. May God sweep away this damning sin of unbelief.

Jesus Empowers His Disciples

We find that the same power Jesus had He gave to His disciples. He ordained seventy and sent them out.[21] He first chose twelve and a few days later He chose seventy and gave them power over all kinds of devils. They went out and had great success, and as soon as they believed Jesus

[18] See Acts 10:38.

[19] See Acts 3:1-12.

[20] See Acts 4:1-4.

[21] See Luke 10:1.

Christ, they had power. The Word was demonstrated by signs and wonders following and so must God's Word be demonstrated today.

All through the Word, from Genesis to Revelations (*sic*), whenever God gave a message to one or two, the message looked very foolish from the human standpoint. It took wonderful faith to go out and carry the message, but they knew God, and whenever they went out and carried a message in God's way, something happened. The Lord God came in a visible way, with signs from heaven that all the people could see. God demonstrated that message. So these visible signs of the Spirit are the Word demonstrated.

Demons of Witchcraft and Sorcery

The working of God's Spirit is foolishness to man. You go to some mesmerist or spiritualist[22] and let them call up the dead, and they can pull the wool over your eyes, and you would rather believe that than believe Jesus Christ. They always try to counterfeit the real, don't they? God works today and the devil works. Back then there were witches and sorcerers, but God's people knew God. And all through the Old Testament, God demonstrated His Word. They acted like crazy people, but God was with them. He always came to the rescue, and those that laugh last laugh best. The result was the fire of God fell on the people. They thought these men must be connected with heaven.

So the working of the Holy Ghost is foolishness to the natural mind. He is not discerned by the natural man; but you go to God and get the oil of heaven, and you will have light on the blessed Word of God. God will talk to your heart, and Christ will be real and salvation will be real and heaven will be real because the Spirit of God will let you down into the deep things of God. Glory to God!

It was so on the Day of Pentecost when the Holy Ghost came. They said these are drunk.[23] They lied about the Holy Ghost and they have been lying ever since, but the work went on just the same.

[22] "spiritualist"—Seances and attempts to speak to the dead were popular as a result of a crisis of faith that haunted nineteenth-century Americans and Europeans. Because of an atmosphere of skepticism people doubted the afterlife and sought to know through seances that their loved ones were safe. Maria Woodworth is addressing a vital issue of her day.

[23] See Acts 2:13.

Glory to God! They have always persecuted the work of God and grieved the Holy Ghost and treated the blood as something unholy.

Does My Neighbor Think It Is God's Work?

If you don't know, if you don't believe, if you don't understand, ask God about these things. Don't go to some old infidel. Go to God. But you say as they did then: What do you think of it? Have any of the scribes believed? Does our preacher approve of it? That is what they said before. Have any of our smart men believed yet?

You had better believe in Christ, seek the wisdom that comes from above. He will make you wise in spiritual things. They are foolishness in the sight of man, but the wisdom of God, the things of God, are eternal; and they are what will take us to heaven.

I praise God for this wonderful salvation. I want to say a few words more about the work I know about. I have been standing before the public for forty-five years, and God has given me grace and courage to stand. I have preached the Gospel in nearly every denomination. Thousands have gone out as ministers and workers. Many saints have gone home to glory.

We have been praying for the sick. If you have read my book, you will remember when I started out I did not know I would have to pray for the sick; but I was sick, and God healed me and raised me from a deathbed. My friends said, "Somehow, I believe God is going to raise you up." I did not look like it, but I knew inside God wanted me to do something. I promised God if He would raise me up and show me His way, I would do it.

I started out after God baptized me in the Holy Ghost. I knew God was calling me for public service. I knew I would die unless God came to me like He did to the fishermen. I told the Lord if He would baptize me with power and knowledge that I would undertake the work. I would go to the ends of the earth and live a thousand years if I might take one soul to heaven. So the Lord wonderfully baptized me and sent me out.

God Does the Healing

I did not try to heal then—don't now. God does the healing. But after a while, God showed me I must pray for the sick. I had a big battle—nearly lost my soul before I would consent. He had to give me power. Bless God, He did. After that I began to pray for the sick. The devil kept telling me, "O you go to praying for the sick and they will bring wagon loads and nobody will be saved, and that is what you started out for." And I felt that was so. When God comes, the devil comes. I fought about three nights, and I was holding meetings in a big skating rink. About three nights I lay awake, but I thought God knew His own business so I said, "Lord, if You want me to pray, You send them to me; and by the grace of God I will do it."

Since that time thousands and thousands have been saved through the healing that never would have been saved—they might have died in their sins. Dear friends, the people came, got convinced and saved and healed. I have been in Chicago three times and some of you know they came by hundreds, rushing down the balconies, sides, and aisles. The altar was full from one side to another. Everyone trying to get there first. The whole place was crowded and people tried to get in the back way.

The Biggest Cripple There

The first meeting in the big stone church, many hundreds came to be healed and saved. And they came so thick and fast I could not stand it, so I told the preachers they had to commence. I called a brother and said, you take this chair and pray for the sick. He said, "O I can't pray for the sick."

I said, "Yes you can. I will pray for you."

He said, "Give me an easy one." I gave him the biggest cripple I could find. Never mind, God can heal that cripple as easy as any. They thought they were in for it. We had five chairs standing on the great platform and two or three ministers to pray for the sick, but you would be surprised to see how many were healed.

It is Jesus that does the healing. When a few were healed, they had faith for the next one. And it is wonderful how those people jumped and ran, shouting and praising God. Soon we had five rows of chairs, and I would go back and forth and encourage them. God did mighty works. The next place we go we expect to see them

coming by hundreds. Sometimes the power is so great when the saints are in one accord.

People who are afflicted come from Saint Louis, California, Alabama, and all over; and some come bringing their grave clothes along, but never one died yet that we know of. Jesus is a mighty Savior. Sometimes the power has been so great that I would go along great long altars telling them—I have no time to talk much. "You know what to expect. The power of God is here. You give everything to God." In a few minutes they would be leaping and running in all directions.

The power of God will go out like rivers of water, and if you are looking to God in faith, you can get your baptism without waiting two or three weeks. It is not man or woman, but God that does the work. Jesus Christ is the divine healer and baptizer. God gave Him power to give life to everyone that will come in God's way.

In one meeting they came by hundreds and we never could get around; and the power of God was so great, but we sprinkled the blood on them by faith and looked to God; and we only had two or three minutes and fifty or one hundred trying to come up. It was so late I said, "The power of God will come if you believe." I said, "By faith Moses took the blood of lambs and sprinkled the people and I take the blood of the real lamb, Calvary's Lamb, by faith, and sprinkle it over the people."[21] I asked God to rebuke these diseases and take away their sins, and right there the power of God fell in every direction. God did the work. Oh! Glory to God, who has given such wonderful powers to His Church, through Jesus Christ, our Lord.

Taken from *Spirit-Filled Sermons.*

[21]See Exodus 24:8.

The Promise of the Father—Life, Power, and Gifts to Men

God's Gift Eternal Life—The "Gifts" of the Spirit

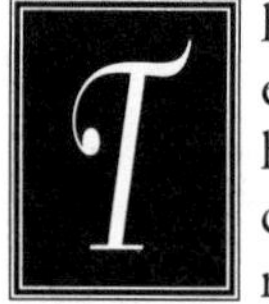

Thou hast ascended on high, thou hast led captivity captive: thou hast received gifts for men; yea, for the rebellious also, that the Lord God might dwell among them.

Psalm 68:18

If Christ had stopped short at Calvary or at going down into the cold grave, His work would have been a failure. Men would not have been able to receive pardon or salvation. Many people look at the dead Savior. They have only a dead religion of form! And of works. (They don't know His resurrection life!) They have no life or power. Remember, Jesus brought life and immortality to light, to us, through resurrection. No, the grave could not hold Him, though all hell was up in arms to hold Him cold in death. A hundred or more armed soldiers stood around His grave, for fear that His disciples would steal His lifeless body away. They also sealed the sepulcher with the governor's seal, and it was death to break the seal.[1]

Jesus, the Mighty Conqueror

A mighty battle was fought. All the armies of heaven were engaged with the hosts of hell in fierce array around the rock casket, or tomb, where the body of Jesus, our crucified Lord, lay cold in death. Hear the demons, "We have got Him, and we will hold Him captive. Where is your Prince? Where is your King?" But hark,

This sermon is the same as the one entitled, "Gifts for Men" in *Diary of Signs and Wonders.*

[1] See Matthew 27:62-66. Note: The exact number of soldiers at the tomb is unknown, but the Jews had several companies of soldiers available for their use by Pilates' permission.

listen! The battle turns, victory is near, help is coming. The Lord God Almighty is coming Himself, with His great angel, who rolls back the stone from the sepulcher and sits upon it. His countenance was like lightning, His raiment white as snow, and for fear of Him the keepers did quake. They fell, and lay as dead men.

God, with His mighty presence, sent a great earthquake, and with a great shout over death and hell and the grave, we see the conqueror come forth, holding the keys to unlock the prison house of the dead.

No, dear reader, He is not dead. The Lord is risen indeed. Oh! Praise God for a living Christ, a living Church, and soon-coming King and Lord. Praise Him for the great marriage supper of the Lamb that will soon take place in the air (1 Thessalonians 4:16-17).

God's Gift Is Eternal Life

He ascended on high and gave gifts to men.[2] Yea, to the rebels also. Jesus did not have all power until God raised Him from the dead. No one could have the gift of God, eternal life until after He was born of the Spirit.

Jesus has all power. He was raised up with all power. The Holy Ghost was with the disciples, but Jesus said, "He shall be in you."[3] When they were all together Jesus met with them, and He opened their spiritual minds. He breathed on them and said, "Receive ye the Holy Ghost."[4] They received Him and became partakers of the divine nature. They received the gift of God, were enlightened, and cried out, "My Lord and my God."[5] No one ever had that experience before that time. They were sons of God, by the new birth. It was the gift of God, eternal life, "Yea, for the rebellious also."[6] This is the most important of all gifts. For without this gift, you can never get inside the pearly gates.

When the sinner stops his rebellion and repents, God gives him faith to accept Christ. God gives him power to become a son of

[2] Ephesians 4:8, paraphrased.

[3] John 14:17, paraphrased.

[4] John 20:22.

[5] John 20:28.

[6] Psalm 68:18, paraphrased.

God, who are born, not of man nor of the will of men, nor of flesh and blood, but by the power of God.[7] He is then no longer a rebel, but a son, for he has received the gift of God and has been born of the spiritual family of God. His name has been written in the family record by the finger of God, and it has been said, "This man was born in Zion."[8] He has received the benefit of the finished work on Calvary for cleansing from sin and uncleanness. And he is now a child of God, ready for any or all of the gifts of the Pentecostal baptism and power. He is God's man.

Jesus received gifts for men. When Jesus was giving His last blessing, on the mountain, before going up to heaven, He said to them, "Tarry at Jerusalem, until ye be endued with power from on high.[9] Ye shall receive power after that the Holy Ghost has come upon you. Ye shall then be witnesses of me.[10] All power is given unto me in heaven and earth.[11] Go ye into all the world and preach the Gospel to every creature. These signs shall follow them that believe (all that believe on Me). These are some of the gifts that I will give to men, in my name shall they cast out devils, they shall speak with new tongues, they shall take up serpents, and if they drink any deadly poison it shall not hurt them, they shall lay hands on the sick and they shall recover."[12]

These were the last words our Savior spake on earth, before He was taken up in a visible manner out of their sight. After that, they got the promised baptism and greatest gift; they went forth preaching the Word everywhere, the Lord working with them, confirming the Word with the signs following.

They could not see the Lord in person like in days past, but saw the visible signs of His invisible presence.[13]

These signs and gifts could be seen and heard with the natural eye and ear. Jesus was with them, with all gifts and signs and miracles

[7] John 1:13 paraphrased.

[8] Psalm 87:5.

[9] Luke 24:49, paraphrased.

[10] Acts 1:8, paraphrased.

[11] Matthew 28:18, Paraphrased.

[12] Mark 16:15, 17-18, paraphrased.

[13] See Mark 16:20.

and diverse operations of the Spirit. With these He confirmed and put His seal on the truth and on their preaching.[14]

Sat Like Cloven Tongues of Fire

At Pentecost He sent the promise of the Father. The Holy Ghost came as a rushing wind and sat on all their heads, as cloven tongues of fire. For they were all filled with the Spirit and began to speak as the Spirit gave them utterance.[15]

It was the time of the great Jewish feast and all the Jewish nations under heaven were gathered there, and they saw and heard the wonderful display of the Holy Ghost and the gifts and the glory of God.[16]

They were amazed, saying, "What meaneth this, and how hear we every man in our own tongue wherein we were born?"[17] Jesus had sent gifts down for men and women. The Holy Ghost had come to stay. He was given now without measure.

God sent Peter down to Caesarea to hold a revival amongst the Gentiles; and while He was preaching the Holy Ghost fell on them that heard the Word, for they spake with tongues, and magnified God.[18]

The Holy Ghost was poured out with all the gifts on the Gentile nations, just the same as at Pentecost on the Jews. "For the promise is unto you, and to your children, and to all that are afar off, even as many as the Lord our God shall call."[19] Oh! Praise God, beloved brethren, that takes in you and me.

The "Gifts" of the Spirit

Jesus sent these gifts with all the Pentecostal power and glory. He put them in His Church to stay. Our bodies are God's powerhouse, they are the channels for the Holy Ghost to flow out of like rivers of living water.

---

[14]See Acts 4:30-33.

[15]See Acts 2:2-4.

[16]See Acts 2.

[17]See Acts 2:7-8.

[18]See Acts 10.

[19]Acts 2:39.

"Gifts for men that the Lord might dwell amongst them."[20] These gifts are the sign to the lost world, that God is with us, that He dwells among us—the signs of His invisible presence. We are a people to be wondered at. We are for signs and wonders in Israel from the Lord of Hosts that dwells in Zion—down here, not in heaven.

"He led captivity captive, and gave gifts unto men. . . . And he gave some, apostles; and some, prophets; and some, evangelists; and some, pastors and teachers" (Ephesians 4:8,11). These imply and include all the gifts and workings of the Holy Ghost.

Why did He send this power and gifts to men, to His brethren, and to the Church? He says, "For the perfecting of the saints, for the work of the ministry, for the edifying of the body of Christ."[21] To make the saints, God's men, perfect and like Christ; to lead them in the same Pentecostal power and gifts.

The ministers need it, and they must have the seal of the Holy Ghost with all these signs and gifts to encourage and empower them. The gifts are the visible signs to the world and seals to them that God is working together with them, confirming the Word.[22]

When the disciples were put into prison and their lives were threatened on account of the great power with them in healing and miracles, they were forbidden to preach in the name of Jesus; for their accusers saw the power come through His name.[23]

The disciples came together and they knew it was the power of God that caused all their persecution. *They knew if they had a form of religion and denied the power, that they would have no more trouble.* But, beloved, they said, "We will be true to God. We will preach the Word if we die." Then they prayed to the Lord, saying, "Lord, behold their threatenings: and grant to Thy servants, boldness to preach Thy Word, by stretching forth Thy hand to heal, and grant that signs and wonders may be done in the name of thy Holy Child Jesus."[24]

---

[20] Psalm 68:18, paraphrased.

[21] Ephesians 4:12.

[22] See Hebrews 2:4.

[23] See Acts 4:18 and 5:40.

[24] Acts 4:29-30, paraphrased.

You see, these ministers needed power to give them boldness to stand up for Jesus, to preach all the words of this life.

His Presence and Power Miraculous

When they preached, they knew they must see the signs in the meeting of the presence of the invisible Christ, who said He would be present to confirm the Word and their message. Jesus had said, "I will be with you all the way, even to the end of the world."[25] Then like Peter they could say to those present, "This that you see and hear and feel, it is the promise of the Father, it is the Holy Ghost."[26]

The Son was pleased with their prayer and with their faith and courage, and the place was shaken—the building where they were assembled—and they were all filled with the Holy Ghost and spake the Word with boldness.[27]

Beloved, see, this was a greater baptism. They needed it to prepare them for the work they had to do. After this they had greater success. God did mighty signs and wonders at the hands of the apostles; great fear fell on all the Church and on all that heard and saw these things. Multitudes of men and women came flocking to Christ and were added to the Lord.[28]

A "multitude" means thousands. They came from Jerusalem and all the cities round about, bringing their sick folk in beds and cots; placing them along the streets, that the shadow of Peter passing by might overshadow them.[29] You see, the power went forth from their bodies like when Paul laid handkerchiefs on his body and sent them to the sick, and the devils or disease went out, and they were healed.[30]

Oh! Praise God, I am likewise a witness to these things. We see the same thing today, the living Christ manifesting His presence and power; some of the greatest miracles of healing and salvation ever seen have been done in the same way. He gave gifts to men.

---

[25] Matthew 28:20, paraphrased.

[26] Acts 2:33, paraphrased.

[27] See Acts 4:31.

[28] See Acts 5:5,11.

[29] See Acts 5:15.

[30] See Acts 19:11-12.

Read carefully the twelfth chapter of the first epistle to the Corinthians. Paul shows that the Church is in possession of all the gifts, power, calling, and work of the Holy Ghost; [he shows] that they are in the body of Christ, His Church.

Quality for the Gifts

Oh! Beloved, we ought to come up to this in all places in these last days when the bride is making herself ready. He says He does not want us to be ignorant concerning spiritual gifts, "Covet earnestly the best gifts," "Follow after charity," or love. "Desire spiritual gifts," for God has set them in the Church.[31] "Gifts for the rebellious also."[32]

Thank God, the sinner need no longer be rebellious, but fall at His feet and settle the old account. He says He has a gift for you. Oh, "The gift of God is eternal life,"[33] and then you are God's man. No longer a stranger or foreigner, you have been brought near by the blood of Christ. Through Him we will have access by one Spirit unto the Father. You are a citizen with the saints and of the household of God; you are lively stones in the building that is being fitly framed together, a holy temple in the Lord.[34]

Brother, you are a son and an heir to all the Pentecostal blessings, gifts, and power. Press your claims at the court of heaven.

Seek the baptism and power of the Holy Ghost. You can be a pillar in the temple of God—in, to go out no more. Be among the wise that shall know of the Lord's coming—among the wise that shall shine as the brightness of the firmament.

Let all that read this sermon take warning. "He that knoweth My will and doeth it not shall be beaten with many stripes."[35]

Taken from *Spirit-Filled Sermons.*

[31] 1 Corinthians 12:1,31, and 14:1.

[32] Psalm 68:18, paraphrased.

[33] Romans 6:23.

[34] A paraphrase mixing parts of Ephesians 2:13,18-19 and 1 Peter 2:5.

[35] Luke 12:47, paraphrased.

THE TWO GREATEST RELIGIOUS MOVEMENTS IN HISTORY

The Two Outpourings of God's Spirit: The Early and the Latter Rain

"And it shall come to pass in the last days, saith God, I will pour out of my Spirit upon all flesh" and great signs will follow just "before that great and notable day of the Lord's coming" (See Acts 2:17-20).

The first great outpouring was at Pentecost when Christ set up His Church in great power and glory with visible signs of His presence, with special demonstrations, and with great signs and wonders and "gifts" of the Holy Ghost.

"The last days" signifies the last two thousand years, which is the time of the Gentiles. God made the world in six days and rested on the seventh day. Each day stands for one thousand years. At the close of this sixth day, or six thousandth, the seventh day will be the day of rest when Satan will be bound, and the saints will reign with Jesus in the millennial day—one thousand years.

All the prophets show plainly that the six thousand years would wind up with the Rapture, the resurrection of the dead in Christ, the translation of those then alive, and the manifestation or revelation of Christ and the sons of God.

The translation, Rapture, or catching away of the bride will be followed by the Great Tribulation and will wind up with the Battle of Armageddon, the binding of Satan, and the setting up of the glorious Millennium of [a] thousand years.

Notice that God promised these two outpourings in the last two days, or two thousand years: one in the beginning of the last two days—the early rain—and one in the close. The latter rain, or outpouring of His Spirit, is to prepare the people for His coming; it is called "the preparation time."

The disciples had been with the Lord for three years. They had seen all His mighty works, had heard His wonderful sermon right from the mouth of God. "Behold the man"; "Never man spake like this man"; "They marvelled at him"; "His word was with power."[1]

He sent His disciples out to preach and gave, loaned, or transmitted power to them to do the same things that He did. He gave them power over all devils and sicknesses. They went out preaching in all the towns and villages, healing the sick everywhere.[2]

Tarry Ye Until Ye Be Endued with Power

Yet just before He ascended up on high, He stopped all their work and told them all to wait for the promise of the Father, to wait for the enduement of power, to wait till they were baptized with the Holy Ghost and fire.[3]

Then they would be qualified to be true witnesses, to be flaming heralds of the great redemption plan of His wonderful salvation of which the hosts of angels sang "Glory to God in the highest."[4] "Behold, I bring you glad tidings of great joy which shall be to all people . . . a Saviour which is Christ the Lord."[5] The Lord could not trust them with this great work to be true witnesses without the baptism with the Holy Ghost.

The time of the early rain had come. See the wisdom of God in calling all the Jewish nations to Jerusalem at this time to the feast, so that they could be present as witnesses of the wonderful work of God.

They were all together, waiting and expecting to meet God, when suddenly, they heard a great noise coming from heaven like a windstorm. The house was filled with the glory of God, then the fire fell, like tongues of fire. They were all filled with fire and the Holy Ghost and began to speak with other tongues as the Spirit gave them utterance.[6]

[1] John 19:5, John 7:46, Mark 12:17, and Luke 4:32.
[2] See Matthew 10:1, Mark 6:7, or Luke 9:1.
[3] See Acts 1:4-5.
[4] Luke 2:14, paraphrased.
[5] Luke 2:10-11.
[6] See Acts 2:4.

Now when this was noised abroad the multitude came together, composed of Jews, devout men out of every nation under heaven. A multitude came together, they were confounded and amazed and marvelled because they heard them speak every man in his own tongue or language. They said to one another, "Behold are not all these which speak Galileans? And how hear we every man in our own tongue, wherein we were born? What meaneth this?"[7]

Others mocking said, "These men are full of new wine."[8]

Peter said, "They are not drunken, it is the Holy Ghost, the promise of the Father."[9] They began to lie about the Holy Ghost, and they are doing the same today.

Jesus said, "When the Holy Ghost is come, he will testify of me; then you also shall bear witness."[10]

They said, "We do hear them speak in our own language, telling the wonderful works of God."[11]

The Devout Jews Received the Same as the Apostles

Now these wise men present, these devout Jews, had all heard and knew of Jesus and His mighty works; yet they had crucified Him. But now, when they saw the mighty works of God and heard these unlearned men and women speaking with the tongue of the learned and educated linguist, as with the pen of a great scholar, explaining the Scriptures and the deep things of God, they were convinced that Jesus was the Christ, the Messiah, the Son of God. They cried out for mercy. *Is there any hope for us? We have killed our Prince. We have crucified our Messiah.* "Men and brethren, what shall we do? Then Peter said unto them, Repent, and be baptized every one of you in the name of Jesus Christ for the remission of sins, and ye shall receive the gift of the Holy Ghost."[12]

[7] Acts 2:6-8, paraphrased.

[8] Acts 2:13.

[9] See Acts 2:14-17.

[10] See John 15:26.

[11] Acts 2:11, paraphrased.

[12] Acts 2:37-38.

They were all Jews, and they had to humble themselves to be baptized in the name of the despised Nazarene, who had just recently been put to a criminal's death by the government.

It does not say [that] when they were baptized, the name of the Father and Holy Ghost were left out (they obeyed the command of Jesus in Matthew 28:19); but it was specially mentioned and emphasized that when they were baptized, they could on no account omit the name of Jesus, which brought persecution, reproach, disgrace, and rejection by the rest of the Jewish nation.[13]

They said, "This that you see and hear is that spoken by the prophet Joel."[14] Yes, they saw and heard and felt the Holy Ghost. And were told it is the promise of the Father, it is for you and your children, and to all that are far off, even as many as the Lord our God shall call.[15] It was not for them in a limited measure, just forgiveness for their guilt, but was for them in all its fullness, just as they saw it working in and through the apostles.

To those poor, guilty men who had killed their Lord, it was glad tidings of great joy to know that not only could they be saved, but that they could receive this great baptism of power with all its wisdom and gifts. They could go back to all these different nations as flames of fire, telling the Good News that Jesus was the Messiah, that Christ had come, and that the Lord would be working with them, proving or confirming the glad tidings with the signs of His presence and power.

The Worldwide Revival

Then they that gladly received the Word were saved and baptized and received the gift of the Holy Ghost, having received the promise of the Father. They were baptized into the body and added to them, with all the wisdom and doctrine of the apostles. The revival continued in the temple and also throughout the city. Men and women went from house to house telling the Good News,

---

[13] Maria Woodworth makes this statement in response to the Jesus Only movement which began in Los Angeles where she ministered at the Worldwide Camp Meeting.

[14] Acts 2:16, paraphrased.

[15] See Acts 2:39.

praising God, and getting souls saved everywhere. All the signs of God's presence and power followed all the believers in general as Jesus had said they should.

These devout Jews mentioned were from every nation under heaven, just visiting Jerusalem at the feast, and therefore, no doubt every church in the land was represented in this great revival. Paul wrote, "I thank my God through Jesus Christ for you all, that your faith is spoken of throughout the whole world" (Romans 1:8). Paul said he had received apostleship among all nations to preach that Jesus was the Son of God. Praise God, this great Pentecostal movement spread over the world in a few years.

The Second Outpouring

Praise God! Pentecost has come again and is shaking the world once more. The latter rain is falling, "The flowers appear on the earth; the time of the singing of birds is come, and the voice of the turtle is heard in our land."[16] And the roses of Sharon and the lilies of the valley are sending their notes of praise and their sweet incense to heaven.

Oh! Dear reader, hear the voice of Jesus saying, "Ask ye of the Lord rain in the time of the latter rain; so the Lord shall make bright clouds, and give them showers of rain, to every one grass in the field" (Zechariah 10:1). He says He will give us the early and latter rains, double what it was at first.

Jesus set up and organized His Church in power, but in this outpouring the Church will be taken up in a blaze of glory, for all the wise will shine brighter than the sun. God is calling you to the marriage supper of His Son, but there must be no delay in putting on the wedding garments.

The Second Pentecost

For forty years or more there have been many showers in different parts of the world. Nearly twenty years ago the great outpouring, or Pentecost, came. Many of God's saints knew the time had come and were meeting in different places and tarrying and waiting for

[16]Song of Solomon 2:12.

the promise. And suddenly, the Holy Ghost came on a band of saints in Los Angeles. The fire fell and there were many signs of the presence of the Lord. They were all filled with the Holy Ghost and began to speak with other tongues as the Spirit gave utterance. When it was interpreted it was known that they were all telling the wonderful works of God.

It was noised abroad and the waiting saints in the city and over the state and from other states flocked as hungry doves to the place. They were amazed and filled with joy and soon received the baptism of the Holy Ghost and fire that Jesus promised. The Word was given and great was the multitude who published it. The news flashed everywhere over the wire and over the seas. Ministers and evangelists from every state and from many nations left their homes and came in haste to Los Angeles to see and hear the wonderful works of God and started at once to tell the glad tidings.

Oh! Praise the Lord. The Pentecostal fire began to cover the land and sea till today it is no local affair but encircles the world. Men and women out of every station and class in life, out of every tongue and nation and people, have received the baptism with the Holy Ghost and are speaking in other tongues, telling the world that Jesus is coming soon.

Like the early and first outpouring at Pentecost, there has never been any religious movement that has grown or spread over the world so quickly or done so much for the salvation of souls and the glory of God.

Words of Admonition and Teaching

In closing, I would like to give some needed notes of warning and admonition. Spiritualism is flooding the land; a great part of the world will soon be controlled. And especially, the evil spirits are trying to counterfeit the power of the Holy Ghost. They will be the greatest factor in the antichrist army. Always try the spirits, see whether they are of God.[17] We must at all times speak and prophesy in the demonstration of the Spirit. It must always be done under the anointing of the Holy Ghost, or it is done in our own

[17] 1 John 4:1.

spirit or some false spirit. We might speak with tongues in any or all languages, the language of heaven and the angels, and yet be led of the devil and be as sounding brass in the sight of God.[18]

You may lose your experience and a wrong spirit come in almost unnoticed, and yet retain your "gifts." Then the devil will use you in bringing a reproach on the real power and demonstration of the Holy Ghost. These people with these spirits talk from their heads and their minds instead of from hearts filled with the love of God. There are lying and deceiving spirits who many times condemn the minister or someone else, or perhaps the whole church. These are unteachable and you cannot control them; they will rule or ruin if possible. These things ought not to be allowed. It has, and still is hurting this movement, and keeping many of the best people away who judge by these loud and unruly ones. Beloved, try the spirits for many spirits have gone out into the world that are not of God. If they were of God, they would hear us and be teachable, loving, kind.

If we have the "gifts" and are used of God, we will also have the fruit of the Spirit (See Galatians 5:22-23). Everything will be done and we will be led and controlled by and through the Spirit of God; and it will edify, build up, strengthen, and help God's children. It is the Spirit of the Good Shepherd whose concern is for the sheep; and not the spirit of the "stranger" which harms, destroys, and scatters.

Let All Things Be Done to Edification

Dear little children, especially you who have the baptism of the Holy Ghost, or think you have, when you feel or think the Spirit is on you and that you think you ought to do something in the assembly or any place, stop a minute and try the spirit and see if it is of God. Ask yourself, would the congregation be edified? If God is leading you, whatever you say or demonstrate will be a blessing to all who hear you.

Oh! If we would all wait a minute and test the spirits, many things we say and do would not be said or done. Oh! I warn you to be watchful and careful! How you cause precious hungry souls to be disgusted with the counterfeit work of Satan and turn away from

[18]See 1 Corinthians 13:1.

the genuine, concluding and thinking that we are all alike and cause them to say hard things against this wonderful outpouring of the Holy Ghost that God is offering to all flesh who will receive it. Some imitate the workings of God's Spirit and act as if God's power was working with them. Souls are too precious to be trifled with. As Jannes and Jambres withstood Moses, so these try to counterfeit and destroy the effect of God's great works.[19]

God's people never have to be ashamed of anything that God does through any of His children.

The Word of God and the Spirit always agree. One confirms the other. Watch closely and note that if they do not agree, it is not of God.

We will not permit demonstrations or tongues or doctrines that cannot be justified and backed up with a "Thus saith the Lord." We deal with these gently; try to show and teach them, to lead them in the doctrine of the apostles and the true Word of God and Spirit. If they are of God or have any desire to be, they will hear us (See 1 John 4:6). If they are not of God, they will show a fighting, arguing, resisting spirit; will either rule or ruin you, and do you all the harm they can. Oh! Beloved let us be true to God and His Word if we have to stand alone. But we must be very gentle, rule and lead with love, and keep these trials from the congregation as much as possible. Keep off the judgment seat. Do not lay hands on anyone suddenly or unkindly; they have had wrong teaching, so try to show them the right way.[20]

Though I speak with the tongues of men and angels and have not the love and anointing from God, I am become as sounding brass.[21]

Taken from *Spirit-Filled Sermons.*

---

[19] 2 Timothy 3:8.

[20] See 1 Timothy 5:22.

[21] 1 Corinthians 13:1, paraphrased.

The Great Revival in Jerusalem

(Sermon Preached at Montwait)

And great fear came upon all the church, and upon as many as heard these things. And by the hands of the apostles were many signs and wonders wrought among the people; (and they were all with one accord in Solomon's porch).

Acts 5:11-12

This was the greatest revival given in the New Testament, greater in many ways than Pentecost. Then they were all with one accord in one place, waiting the outpouring of the Spirit. They all made the same sound. You get there and God will shake the country.

"Signs and wonders were wrought . . . and of the rest durst no man join himself unto them."[1] They were so full of fire no one dared to say falsely, "I am one of you." They were afraid God would strike them dead. God wants to get a people so full of power—His power—that others full of wildfire will not say, "God sent me."

What was the result? Believers were added to the church? No, to the Lord—multitudes both of men and women.[2] Some say that this excitement, this fanaticism, is good enough for women, but there was a multitude of strong-minded men there.

They brought the sick into the street and laid them on beds and couches that Peter's shadow might overshadow some of them.[3] See what a cranky set they were! I wish we were just like that. Excitement rose higher and higher.

The whole country was stirred. There came a multitude out of the city about Jerusalem, bringing the sick and they were healed, every one.[4] Healed because they came right. A wonderful revival was it not?

[1] Acts 5:12-13, paraphrased.

[2] See Acts 5:14.

[3] See Acts 5:15.

[4] See Acts 5:16.

In the midst of it [all], it was broken up. The high priest and Sadducees arrested them and put them in prison. Bless God; they did not stay there long. God sent His angel down and brought them out and told them to go into the temple and preach to the people.[5]

It took some grace to do that, did it not? To go right back there and preach all the Word, not leaving out divine healing, but showing all the signs and wonders. In the morning they sent to bring them out. They found the prison locked but no one there; those they sought were out preaching.[6]

It is better to obey God. We are determined to obey God, let the result be what it may. God's people must meet persecution. People say this work is not of God. That is the kind of talk the devil likes to hear. All the devil has to do is to blow his whistle and his army runs to do his work.

God has to blow and blow before He can get His people to do His work; yet we have the promise, "One shall chase a thousand."[7] The devil hates holiness and power; he persecutes, and persecution is all that makes men fit for heaven.

This was a great revival. Every one of the apostles seemed to be there and God gave them wonderful power. Many mighty signs and miracles were done by them because they were of one accord, preaching and believing. Because of this, the fire of God fell upon the Church and sinners began to tremble.

I believe in preaching in such a way that the power of God will make people tremble and come up to the front to do His will. "The fear of the Lord is the beginning of wisdom."[8] The first we know of God, there is a holy awe that comes over us. When we want God to work, to cause His presence to be felt in our midst, we must feel He has the power to work among His people; and it is a terrible thing to resist.

---

[5] See Acts 5:17-20.

[6] See Acts 5:22-23.

[7] Joshua 23:10, paraphrased.

[8] Psalm 111:10 and Proverbs 9:10.

We must get on the full armor and rush into the battle. Press the battle to the gates. Vain is the help of man. There is no shelter except in the wounded side of Jesus. It is the only place on earth to which we can flee. We learn there the way of righteousness, and we know what awaits the sinner if he does not accept this shelter.

In the Old Testament, we read of God's workings among His people. When someone was sent with a message, it often seemed very foolish, humanly speaking. What was the outcome? God will always show Himself and put His seal upon His work. When the message was delivered, He came forth with the supernatural, with the sign of His invisible presence.

He manifested His presence in miraculous ways. That put His fear upon the heathen. They said there is no God like the Hebrews', because of His wonderful works. He was a God to be feared.

In the New Testament, signs and wonders were done before the people. Wherever Jesus went the people followed Him. God was with Him, putting fear upon the people through miracles, signs, and wonders God wrought through Him.

He said, "I do not these things of myself. The Father, he doeth the works."[9] The apostles said the same: "By the mighty power of the Holy Ghost, Jesus doeth the works." Not I, but Christ. It is the same today.

In the signs and wonders today it is "Not I, but Christ." He dwells in these bodies, and the work is done by the mighty power of the Holy Ghost. "Know ye not that your body is the temple of the Holy Ghost?"[10] Jesus Christ dwells in us. We are God's powerhouses.

It was by the hands of the apostles, not of angels, that God did His mighty works; and people believed when the signs followed. Jesus commanded the unclean spirits to come out and they had to come. The power of the Holy Spirit went through the apostles' hands and that is just the way God works today.

The apostles were not afraid of persecution, the sword, or anything else. They faced death in any form rather than disgrace the cause of

[9] John 14:10, paraphrased.

[10] 1 Corinthians 6:19.

Christ by being cowards. It is a mighty God we serve, and today, Jesus Christ who ascended into heaven is here by my side. He will lead His hosts on to victory. Let us press the battle to the gates.

This sect is always spoken against, misrepresented, and lied about, but Jesus Christ is leading on His hosts. God permitted Jesus to be nailed to the cross and laid in the grave, but He came forth like the sun. God permitted the apostles to be arrested and put in prison; then He had an opportunity to show His power. He sent His angel and delivered them. The angel of the Lord is with His own. Our citizenship is in heaven. We are children of the King.

Around us day and night are ministering spirits sent to minister to those who are heirs of salvation.[11] We can afford to be misrepresented or even put in prison, if only we are looking for the manifestation and the glory of translation to go sweeping through the gates.

The apostles were persecuted and the meeting broken up in Jerusalem, where the Lord was crucified. The meeting was held in Solomon's porch, one of the prominent places in the city. It seems the apostles were in this great porch, and they brought the sick into the street on beds and couches and every way and laid them all around: sick, blind, and those vexed with unclean spirits, a great multitude.

What would the preachers think if we brought the sick around the church in this way? When they were preaching one of those fine sermons, "firstly, secondly, thirdly," if someone dropped a sick person down in the midst, they would send for a policeman quickly. You know they would.

The paralytic did not break up the meeting when brought to Jesus and dropped down through the roof when He was preaching. He is our example. He was glad to have something like that because it gave Him a chance to show His power. He forgave him all his sins and then made him rise, take up his bed, and walk.[12]

The people began to shout, "Glory," the same way you do here. You cannot help you[rself]. If you have not done it, you will. A

[11]See Hebrews 1:14.

[12]See Luke 5:18-26.

consumptive woman was brought in here in her night robe. I did not care what she had on—she was healed. Hallelujah!

When the paralytic was healed, they gave glory to God. People say today, "You never heard such a cranky set." If they had only heard them then! We have something to make a fuss about. Dead people never make much noise, do they? There is not much noise in a graveyard.

Some people are frozen and have their feet in grave clothes. May God take off the grave clothes and set us free! David danced before the Lord with all his might. His wife did not like it. She thought he had disgraced her before the handmaidens and she began to grumble.

He said he was not dancing before the handmaidens but before the Lord. It is dangerous to lay your hand on the work of the Lord. She had no child to the day of her death. It was a great disappointment to the Jewish woman, as each one hoped to be the mother of the Lord.[13]

Do not lay your hand upon the work of the Lord. It meant sudden death to lay your hand upon the ark of the Lord. Beware of sin against the Holy Ghost. That is the unpardonable sin and cannot be forgiven. Sometimes the Holy Ghost comes like a mighty rushing wind from heaven and makes a great commotion among the people, sometimes silently. He comes to us here.

You want to take down your umbrellas and get your buckets right side up. God will fill the vessels and make you a powerhouse for Him; then God will show Himself mighty to pull down the strongholds of the devil and build up the kingdom of Christ.

You will have power to preach, and signs and wonders will be wrought as in the days of the apostles. The Lord was with them. He was invisible but He was with them, confirming the Word with signs and wonders; and He will never forsake us if we obey Him.

Signs and wonders following. Following what? The preaching of the Word. He is here and ye shall see Him with what we call visible signs. Peter said, "This you see is the Holy Ghost." If you are willing, you will see it here for God is coming in a wonderful way.

[13]See 2 Samuel 6:14-23.

They saw the fire on the apostles' heads and heard them speak in other tongues as the Spirit gave them utterance; they saw them stagger like drunken men. Wherever the Holy Ghost is poured out, you will see signs.[14]

That was a great meeting. The sick were brought on beds and cots, and God, at the hands of the apostles, wrought many signs and wonders. The fear of God fell on the people. Thousands and thousands were converted to God.

Their names were written in heaven; they were filled with the Holy Ghost, the glory of God. The power of God was so great they could not get close enough to have hands laid on all the sick. Peter seemed to be the leader in this divine-healing movement, and they tried to get them near enough that Peter's shadow might overshadow some of them.[15]

The power was of the Holy Ghost. He that believeth on Jesus Christ shall have such power that out of his inward parts shall flow rivers of living waters.[16] The Holy Spirit is like a river. Pentecost filled the apostles, and people were healed even watching for Peter's shadow.

The power of the Holy Ghost struck the sick ones and healed them, and the people marvelled. Jesus did many mighty works, and He told the apostles they should do greater things than these if they believed on Him.

Men and women, God wants you to get into that place. Don't you see God works through human instrumentality? God will use us if we are swallowed up in Him. In Chicago, people were healed sitting in their seats, and away up in the gallery some fell like dead people.

The power of God is going out while I am talking. You know I am speaking the truth. Believe it, accept it, and get more of Jesus. If we take in and take in and do not give out, we are like a sponge that needs to be squeezed. Let us get so full that it will run right out through us, not absorb and absorb and never give out.

---

[14]See Acts 2.

[15]See Acts 5:15.

[16]See John 7:38.

Many of you are baptized with the Holy Ghost; you ought to send the power this way while I send it that way, and when the two come together something would happen. I could not keep my feet if you would do this, glory! Glory to God!

Take a picture of the revival. Did they act like crazy folks? Some of the best people in Jerusalem took part in that revival. All classes were there. People were lying all around, getting healed, or running to bring someone else to be healed, and multitudes were saved.

It was the greatest revival; divine healing was the drawing card. When people are healed it does not mean simply healing, but it brings people to Christ. Take the man healed at the Beautiful Gate of the temple.

Peter took the miracle as his text and preached. The authorities laid hands on him and commanded him not to speak or teach in the name of Jesus, but Peter and John said, "We shall preach in that name anyway." They prayed and the Holy Ghost came in great power. The outgrowth of that healing in the temple was a great revival.[17]

Notice the mighty power that went from Peter's body. His very shadow healed people. Paul did special miracles; from his body were sent out handkerchiefs and aprons and the people were healed through them.[18] This is different than any other miracle in the New Testament, but God is doing the same thing today.

The Holy Ghost works through our hands, through our bodies! We are sending out thousands of handkerchiefs all over the country, over land and sea. I could tell you wonderful stories of the work they do; five were healed from one handkerchief.

As we hold up Jesus, God sends His power through us, as He did in apostolic days. Let us arise and shine and give God the glory.

When I first started out to preach, I did not know I was to pray for anyone to be healed, but God showed me I was to preach divine healing. The devil tried to keep me back, but thousands have been healed and saved through healing.

[17]See Acts 3.

[18]See Acts 19:11-12.

I lay on hands in the name of Jesus. 'Tis Jesus makes you whole. Sometimes the power is so great they are healed instantly, leaping and jumping and praising God. The Lord is here, we can have as great a revival as they had in Jerusalem, and the fear of God will be upon the people.

God wants you to march to the cross and give glory to Him. We want to get to work here. Let Him do the work in your soul first. We are going to have a revival here like the one in Jerusalem, with many signs and wonders.

Getting divine healing isn't like going to the doctor. Get baptized with the Holy Ghost before you leave; then when you get home you will not backslide. Glory to God!

"The Communings of Jesus"

> Not a sound invades the stillness,
> Not a form invades the scene,
> Save the voice of my Beloved,
> And the person of my King.
>
> Refrain
>
> > Precious, gentle, holy Jesus,
> > Blessed, Bridegroom of my heart,
> > In the secret inner chamber,
> > Thou wilt whisper what Thou art.
>
> And within these heavenly places,
> Calmly hushed in deep repose,
> There I drink with joy absorbing,
> All the love Thou wouldst disclose.
>
> Wrapt in deep adoring silence,
> Jesus, Lord, I dare not move,
> Lest I lose the smallest whisper,
> Meant to catch the ear of Love.
>
> Rest thou, O my soul, contented,
> Thou hast reached thy happy place,
> In the bosom of thy Savior,
> Gazing up in His dear face.[19]

Taken from *Signs and Wonders God Wrought in the Ministry of M. B. Woodworth-Etter.*

[19] Composer unknown.

Divine Healing and Signs and Wonders to Lead People to Christ

We all know, who have read the Acts of the Apostles, that their ministry was marvelously successful. Here are a few brief reports of some of their revivals.

Then they that gladly received his word were baptized: and the same day there were added unto them about three thousand souls.[1]

Howbeit many of them which heard the word believed; and the number of the men was about five thousand.[2]

And believers were the more added to the Lord, multitudes both of men and women.[3]

Then had the churches rest throughout all Judea and Galilee and Samaria, and were edified; and walking in the fear of the Lord, and the comfort of the Holy Ghost, were multiplied.[4]

While Peter yet spake these words, the Holy Ghost fell on all them which heard the word.[5]

And the hand of the Lord was with them: and a great number believed, and turned unto the Lord.[6]

And the next sabbath day came almost the whole city together to hear the word of God.[7]

But the word of God grew and multiplied.[8]

---

[1] Acts 2:41.

[2] Acts 4:4.

[3] Acts 5:14.

[4] Acts 9:31.

[5] Acts 10:44.

[6] Acts 11:21.

[7] Acts 13:44.

[8] Acts 12:24.

> And so were the churches established in the faith, and increased in number daily.[9]
>
> And some of them believed, and consorted with Paul and Silas; and of the devout Greeks a great multitude, and of the chief women not a few.[10]
>
> And the word of God increased; and the number of the disciples multiplied in Jerusalem greatly; and a great company of the priests were obedient to the faith.[11]
>
> Therefore many of them believed; also of honourable women which were Greeks, and of men, not a few.[12]
>
> And the Lord added to the church daily such as should be saved.[13]
>
> And this was known to all the Jews and Greeks also dwelling at Ephesus; and fear fell on them all, and the name of the Lord Jesus was magnified. And many that believed came, and confessed, and shewed their deeds. Many of them also which used curious arts brought their books together, and burned them before all men: and they counted the price of them, and found it fifty thousand pieces of silver. So mightily grew the word of God and prevailed.[14]

There are three reasons, or causes, that gave the disciples this phenomenal success:

First: They preached the Gospel of the kingdom, which is, as I have already stated, a full Gospel for spirit, soul, and body. They preached exactly as the Lord told Jeremiah to preach. "Thus saith the Lord; Stand in the court of the Lord's house, and speak unto all the cities of Judah, which come to worship in the Lord's house, all the words that I command thee to speak unto them; diminish not a word" (Jeremiah 26:2).

---

[9] Acts 16:5.

[10] Acts 17:4.

[11] Acts 6:7.

[12] Acts 17:12.

[13] Acts 2:47.

[14] Acts 19:17-20

And as He told Jonah to preach: "And the word of the Lord came unto Jonah the second time, saying, Arise, go unto Nineveh, that great city, and preach unto it the preaching [that] I bid thee" (Jonah 3:1-2).

The apostles did not diminish a word of the Gospel of the kingdom. They preached precisely the Gospel that Christ bade them preach. And such preaching, God will always honor and bless.

In the second place, they preached this Gospel under the power of the Holy Ghost. This they received on the Day of Pentecost. This is such an essential and all-important factor in preaching that Jesus would not permit them to enter upon their great life work until they had received the divine anointing.

Had they not tarried in Jerusalem until this anointing came, there would never have been any Acts of the Apostles written, for there would not have been any acts upon their part needing to be recorded, and the revivals mentioned above would never have been reported.

In the third place, God bore witness to their preaching with signs and wonders and with diverse miracles and gifts of the Holy Ghost. This was as important a factor in their success as either of the others. I am satisfied that without these miracles, the Gospel would have made but little progress in pushing its way through the heathen world.

Notice the apostles' prayer, which shows the estimation they placed upon miracles, especially the miracle of healing, as an auxiliary in their work: "And now, Lord, behold their threatenings: and grant unto thy servants, that with all boldness they may speak thy word, by stretching forth thine hand to heal; and that signs and wonders may be done by the name of thy holy child Jesus" (Acts 4:29-30).

Notice now a significant fact. Read the following:

> And by the hands of the apostles were many signs and wonders wrought among the people. . . . Insomuch that they brought forth the sick into the streets, and laid them on beds and couches, that at the least the shadow of Peter passing by might overshadow some of them. There came also a multitude out of the cities round about unto Jerusalem, bringing sick folks, and them which were vexed with unclean spirits: and they were healed every one.
>
> Acts 5:12-16

The significant fact is, that in this passage is a parenthesis which reads as follows: "(and they were all with one accord in Solomon's porch. And of the rest durst no man join himself to them.... And believers were the more added to the Lord, multitudes both of men and women.)"[15]

Why did Luke insert that parenthesis? Did those miracles have anything to do with that multitude of believers, both men and women, being added to the Lord? They constituted a powerful factor in that revival.

That was the result in nearly every instance where miracles were performed, great revivals followed. Read these words: "And the word of God increased; and the number of disciples multiplied in Jerusalem greatly; and a great company of the priests were obedient to the faith. And Stephen, full of faith and power, did great wonders and miracles among the people" (Acts 6:7-8).

Is there any relation between the miracles that Stephen wrought and the multiplication of disciples in Jerusalem? There is a most intimate and vital relation.

Take another case:

> Then Philip went down to the city of Samaria, and preached Christ unto them. And the people with one accord gave heed unto those things which Philip spake, hearing and seeing the miracles which he did. For unclean spirits, crying with loud voice, came out of many that were possessed with them: and many taken with palsies and that were lame, were healed. And there was great joy in that city.
>
> Acts 8:5-8

Did the miracles of casting out unclean spirits and healing the lame have anything to do with the people giving heed with one accord to the things that Philip spake, and filling that city with joy? Very much.

Take another case:

[15] Acts 5:12-14.

> And it came to pass, as Peter passed throughout all quarters, he came down also to the saints which dwelt at Lydda. And there he found a certain man named Aeneas, which had kept his bed eight years, and was sick of the palsy. And Peter said unto him, Aeneas, Jesus Christ maketh thee whole: arise, and make thy bed. And he arose immediately. And all that dwelt at Lydda and Saron saw him, and turned to the Lord.
>
> Acts 9:32-35

Raising Dorcas to life was another case with the same effect. "And it was known throughout all Joppa; and many believed in the Lord."[16]

If ministers could cast out devils today in the name of Jesus and lay hands on the sick and have them restored to health, they would not preach to empty benches, nor mourn over the dearth of revivals. On the contrary, every minister who could do that would have crowded houses and a perpetual revival. And that is what God wants His ministers to do, and it is not His fault if they are not able to do it.

There is nothing the devil hates with more infernal malignity than divine healing. That is something that is visible, tangible, real, and valuable. When a lame man is made to walk, or a poor epileptic made well, there is something the unsaved world can see and appreciate. And it convinces them of the goodness and lovingkindness of God.

A book is lying before me entitled, *Back to the Bible*. I see another advertised, *Back to Pentecost*. Does it occur to these authors that to get back to the Bible and to Pentecost is to get back to miracle-working power?

Such a return would not only secure the baptism of the Spirit, but it would secure the gifts of the Spirit in the working of miracles. Is there anyone taking the back track in that direction?

Taken from *Acts of the Holy Ghost*.

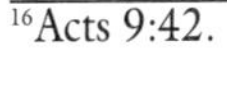

[16]Acts 9:42.

Miracle-Working Faith

esus has all power in heaven and earth, but we have to touch Him by faith.[1] Don't think you will get anything if you doubt.[2] The Lord Jesus never did anything without faith on the part of someone. You can never have faith without meeting His conditions. When you meet the conditions of surrender and obedience, He will drop the faith right down in your heart; it is the gift of God.[3] Jesus will not do anything today without faith. You must have not only faith in God, but you must have the very faith of Jesus Christ, the faith that Jesus Himself had. When God said a thing, He knew that God was going to do it; and that is the faith that He will give to you. All the miracles that He ever did were through the faith of someone. When Jesus turned the water into wine, it was through the faith of His mother and the servants. She said to them, "Whatsoever he saith unto you, do it." There was a need and she expected Him to do something to meet that need. He said to the servants, "Go and fill the water pots to the brim." The servants had faith to prepare the water pots, knowing that Jesus was going to do something.[4]

Peter walked all right while he had faith, but when he doubted he began to sink. Jesus rebuked him, not because he was doing something so great as to be presumptuous, but because he did not have faith to walk right on.[5] The centurion had great faith. He did not feel that he needed to have Jesus come to his house. He said, "I know that you have the power to heal with a word. Speak the word, and my servant will be healed." Jesus was surprised at such faith, and He healed the servant.[6]

---

[1] See Matthew 28:18.

[2] See James 1:6-7.

[3] See Ephesians 2:8.

[4] See John 2:1-11.

[5] See Matthew 14:28-31.

[6] See Matthew 8:5-10.

We read of a father whose child was dying. He went a long journey to find the wonderful Nazarene. Jesus said to him, "Except ye see signs and wonders ye will not believe." The father said, "Sir, come down ere my child die." As the man talked with Jesus, as he got near to Him, he believed. Jesus put him to the test and said, "Go thy way, thy son liveth." The man started off, and he did not have the witness till the next day when he got home. He did not urge Jesus to go home with him because he felt sure that the Lord had kept His word; and on his way home the servants met him and said, "Thy son liveth." The son was healed, but not perfectly strong yet. If he had been, he would have run out to meet him. The father asked at what hour the fever left him. They said, "At the seventh hour." The father wanted to know the hour that he might give God the glory. It was at the same hour when Jesus spoke the word to the father that the fever left his son and he began to amend. This healing was brought about by the faith and obedience of the father. He believed God, though he did not get the witness till he got home.[7]

When Lazarus was raised from the dead, it was through the faith of Martha. That is a most beautiful picture of what God can do through faith. Jesus loved those two sisters and Lazarus. It all rested with Martha whether or not that brother should be raised from the dead. He said, in substance, "If you will only believe my word, you are going to see something marvelous." But Martha was not through yet. There was a stone to be rolled away. It may be that you have a stone to be rolled away before your child can be healed, or before you can get your baptism.

According to the custom no one would dare to touch that stone but by order of the family. So Martha had to cooperate with Jesus when He gave the order. But at first she objected and said, "Master, by this time he is offensive." Just as though the master did not know His own business! He looked at her and said, "Said I not unto thee, that if thou wouldest believe, thou shouldest see the glory of God? How is it that you are so forgetful, Martha?" Then she got her eyes on Jesus and looked away from the corpse of Lazarus. I seem to see her step forth like a queen giving the order to roll the stone away.

[7] See John 4:46-53.

Jesus lifted up His eyes and thanked His Father that He had heard Him and that He knew that He heard Him always. He wanted the unbelieving people to know that His Father heard Him that they might see and believe. Beloved, do you want to be healed, or do you want to be baptized with the Holy Ghost that God may be glorified, that men and women may see the mighty miracles that He does and believe God? He said to His Father, "Thou hearest me always," and He will always hear your prayer if you believe God. Then Jesus went forth and cried with a loud voice, "Lazarus, come forth." And the dead came back to life, and many saw this mighty miracle and many believed. What a happy time they had as they went back to that home and took supper together.[8]

But you say, "Why does not God hear me?" Just because you do not obey Him, and you would not give Him a bit of glory if He did heal you.

When that sick man was carried up to the roof, do you not think that took some faith on his part, as well as on the part of those who carried him? How the finger of scorn was pointed at them all along the road. But the sick man did not expect to be carried back. They broke up the roof and let the man down in the midst before Jesus. "And when he saw their faith He said unto him, Man, thy sins are forgiven thee." He forgives all and heals all. Ring the bells of heaven, for thy sins are forgiven. Then he said, "Arise, and take up thy couch, and go unto thine house." The man knew he could not arise, but as Jesus spoke the word, he made the effort in faith, and "immediately he rose up before them."[9]

The very minute you begin to exercise faith, God begins to work. Do not come up here to have prayer offered for your healing unless you expect to be healed at once. Forget your disease and look at Jesus. Do you believe that God is going to take it away? Well, then, clap your hands and shout victory. It is faith and obedience that bring the healing. It is not long prayers but it is the look of faith. When you see the people begin to clap their hands and look for Jesus to come in, you see a change come into their faces. If you give

[8] See John 11:1-45.

[9] See Mark 2:3-12.

your sickness to God, you have not got it. When He tells you to arise and walk, you will have to do it and show your faith by your acts like a well person.

We say to them, move your feet, move your hands by faith. We want your whole body set free. If you do not think God is going to do something, don't come up here. That palsied man did not expect to be carried back. He walked back and carried his bed. As the disease begins to go, the virtue of Jesus begins to come in. So this man had faith to rise up and carry his couch. He had to take God at His Word and so have you. You see him standing there, healed, moving his hands and moving his feet, and making a great noise praising the Lord just like an old "crank"! Some of you would not do that after prayer was offered for you, but you would make a beeline to get right back in bed! But he did not forget what the Lord said, to carry his bed, as well as to rise up and walk. He felt like jumping over the bed. He did not say, "Don't ask me to run until tomorrow. Don't ask me to carry my bed for they will laugh at me, and I will never hear the last of it." I suppose he was shouting for joy like a crazy person. He broke up the meeting, but it was Jesus' meeting, and He did not say, "Stop making that noise," but He said, "Let him alone."

Faith comes by hearing the Word.[10] When Paul was preaching at Lystra, there was a cripple who had never walked. Paul perceived that he had faith to be healed. God is waiting for someone to have faith so He can get a chance to work a miracle. Paul said with a loud voice, "Stand upright on thy feet. And he leaped and walked."[11]

If you will venture the leap in faith, the Lord will catch you. Most people do not have faith in God. God smiled His approval on the Son of God by confirming His Word with signs and wonders. God baptized Jesus with the Holy Ghost and fire, also the disciples on the Day of Pentecost; so when God baptizes you with the Holy Ghost and fire, signs and wonders will follow. There is no limit to His power if we believe Him. The winds and the waves obeyed Him, and the fig tree was withered by His Word.[12] He said that they

[10]See Romans 10:17.

[11]See Acts 14:8-10.

[12]See Matthew 8:27, Luke 8:25, and Matthew 21:19.

who believed on Him could pluck up the sycamine[13] tree by the roots and cast the mountain into the sea and even do greater things than He did on earth because He went to His Father.[14]

The time has come for greater things, beloved. On the Day of Pentecost, the greater things began. On the Day of Pentecost He did something that had never been done before; many miracles had been wrought, but the disciples had never spoken in tongues. They were gathered together praising God the best they could when the Holy Ghost came upon them in a fiery baptism and spoke through them in new tongues; this was what broke up the unbelief in many of the Jewish people. They were amazed and said, "What does this mean? How hear we every man in our own tongue wherein we were born?" And here is a beautiful point, "We do hear them speak in our tongue the wonderful works of God."[15]

That was what brought three thousand people to their knees that day. God had said, "In the last days I will pour out my Spirit; I will pour out a cloudburst of power and glory upon My people. They shall speak with new tongues, they shall prophesy, they shall cast out devils."[16] Don't be tired of hearing people speak in new tongues; don't call anything common or unclean that God does.[17] It is the Holy Ghost let down from heaven. The Word says, "With stammering lips and another tongue will *he* speak to this people."[18]

I have seen hundreds healed in one day. God is showing the people the double cure of Calvary, for soul and body. Every time you hear God speaking through someone in tongues, it is the voice of God saying, "Get ready." The Great Tribulation is going to break sooner than you think. The Word says that in the last days knowledge shall be increased.[19] Think of the wonderful inventions in these last days.

---

[13] "sycamine"—a tree mentioned in the Bible (Luke 17:6), believed to be a mulberry *(Morus nigra)* with dark fruit *(Webster's N. W.*, 1997).

[14] See Matthew 21:20-21 and John 14:12.

[15] See Acts 2:1-12.

[16] See Joel 2:28 and Acts 2:16-18.

[17] See Acts 10:28.

[18] Isaiah 28:11, emphasis Maria Etter's.

[19] See Daniel 12:4.

The saints also are getting knowledge of what is coming. Great troubles are coming, tidal waves, earthquakes, etc. We warned San Diego when we were there. They wanted us to stay another month, but God did not lead us to do so, and the storm broke the very day we left there. So the Lord does warn His children. I have known the Lord to turn aside storms and cyclones in answer to prayer, and I have known Him to do mighty miracles.

When we were holding meetings and it was so hot and dusty, several times we have asked God to sent the rain to lay the dust and to cool the air so the people could come, and God has sent rain just around the locality. One time He led me to have meetings out in a wilderness, where we were five miles from the nearest railroad station. I did not know what God did this for, but I did know one thing, and that was that God wanted to show forth His power and glory. A great mass of people came, and the Lord led me to take that text, "What went ye out into the wilderness to see? A reed shaken with the wind?"[20] There were a number of Jewish brethren there, and I said, "That rain was in answer to prayer. Did you have any rain at Mt. Pleasant?" They turned pale as they realized the power of God.

The very earth was shaken with the power of God at Muncie, Indiana, where we were holding meetings. A great mass of people were there, and they had to stand, as we could not provide seats for them. They would fall against each other under the power of God. At two or three places God sent the sound of His armies in the treetops. The Lord said, "You must have more power among these people." I said to them, "We must have more of the power of God here. I am never going to preach another time to this people till God comes in power that you have never seen. Those of you who will take this stand and stay with me till the Lord comes in power, get down on your knees by me here." They began to be frightened. But I said, "If you do not come and wait on God with me I will go away." They did not want me to go away, so they came and got on their knees.

When you get down before God with such a determination as that, you do not have to wait very long. I would keep quoting Scripture and the power of God settled down upon us, and there was a holy

[20]See Matthew 11:7 and Luke 7:24.

awe. Some infidels laughed but they were frightened enough before we got through. Then we heard a sound in the tops of the trees, a sort of roaring. Some thought it was a great storm coming, but the Lord told me to look up and see the moon and stars shining. There was no sign of a storm. I gave a shout and said, "It is the armies of the Lord. Hallelujah!" I don't remember all that happened, but God came in great power. Some of the people were frightened, but I said, "Stand your ground. The Lord will strike you down under His power in your homes if you run away from this meeting." The people began to get converted all over the country. You remember how David heard "the sound of a going in the tops of the mulberry trees" when the Lord went forth to fight for him against his enemies.[21] Are we waiting to hear from heaven today?

God is going to do great things in these last days. We are living in very solemn times, and God is doing His strange work of judgment. Jesus is coming soon, and we will need to trust God to hide us away from the coming storm. The Son of Man is near, even at the doors. Awful tribulation is coming. The signs and wonders that He is now giving confirm the message that the last days are upon us. The damning sin of unbelief is all around us. But God is even raising the dead, here and there. A woman was dead, and the Lord gave me the prayer of faith; and in that big congregation I commanded her to come back to life in the name of Jesus.

Get on the whole armor of God.[22] Have faith in God, simple faith that will ask no questions. Keep low under the blood of Jesus. He says, "My people shall never be ashamed."[23] Terrible times are coming even in this land. Everything will be shaken except the people of God who are hidden away in the secret place of the Most High. If you do not take the warning messages that have been given here, I will witness against you in that day. "Let no man take your crown."[24]

---

[21] See 2 Samuel 5:24.

[22] See Ephesians 6:13-18.

[23] See Joel 2:26-27.

[24] Revelation 3:11, paraphrased.

"Hold fast till I come," Jesus says.[25] We will go up to meet Him in the clouds.[26] Now may God seal this message for His glory.

San Francisco, January 29, 1916

Transcribed by Mrs. Carrie Judd Montgomery from an address given by Mrs. Etter given in San Francisco, January 29, 1916, at Mid-winter Convention. *Triumphs of Faith.* February, 1916.

[25] Revelation 2:25.

[26] See 1 Thessalonians 4:17.

Work of the Holy Ghost

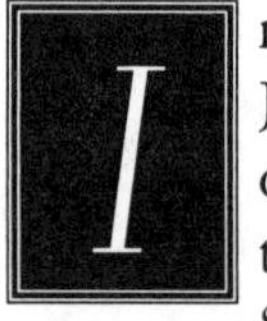

In John 15:26, Jesus is speaking of the coming of the Holy Ghost: "But when the Comforter is come, whom I will send unto you from the Father . . . he shall testify of me."

He is the Holy Ghost. The Lord speaks of the Holy Ghost as a person as much as He would of one of the apostles. On the Day of Pentecost, they were all of one accord, in one place, and something happened.[1] It will every day if you have the Spirit. "Suddenly there came a sound from heaven as of a mighty rushing wind."[2] This was the Holy Ghost when He came to stay. "There appeared unto them cloven tongues like as of fire, and it sat upon each of them. And they were all filled with the Holy Ghost, and began to speak with other tongues, as the Spirit gave them utterance."[3]

"When this was noised abroad, the multitude came together." What was noised abroad? That these people were all speaking in other languages. The news went through Jerusalem, and "the multitude came together, and were confounded, because that every man heard them speak in his own language."[4] And those who came were men out of every nation under heaven.

They heard these hundred and twenty speak in their own language wherein they were born. This is what gathered the people and confounded them. "They were all amazed and marvelled, saying one to another, Behold, are not all these which speak Galileans? And how hear we every man in our own tongue, wherein we were born? . . . we do hear them speak in our tongues the wonderful works of God."[5]

[1] See Acts 2:1.

[2] Acts 2:2.

[3] Acts 2:3-4.

[4] Acts 2:6.

[5] Acts 2:7-8,11.

The Holy Ghost is a wonderful person, not a myth or shadow. Pentecost is the greatest thing that ever happened in God's work when the Holy Ghost came in to stay. He came and took possession of one hundred and twenty men and women. He sat upon their heads in cloven tongues of fire and went in and took possession of their bodies, then of their vocal organs; and they spoke, every one, as He gave them utterance.

They spoke in languages they had never learned. They did not know what they were saying. The Holy Ghost took possession of their tongues and spoke through them. He spoke through the clay as you would speak through a telephone. [He] told about Jesus. "He shall testify of me."[6]

Jesus told the apostles that they should be witnesses.[7] The Holy Ghost, when He came, knew all about it; and He told through them of the wonderful works of God. When this was noised abroad, multitudes gathered. It was the speaking in tongues that drew the people. When they heard them, they were confounded and said, "What meaneth this?"[8]

I want you to notice this point—it was speaking in tongues that confounded them. The Holy Ghost spoke through these unlearned men who had never been to college to learn other languages. It was one of the most wonderful things God ever did; it is now, when God speaks through you.

The Lord said through the prophet, many hundred years ago, "Whom shall he teach knowledge? . . . them that are weaned from the milk."[9] The wisdom of the world was to be confounded through these unlearned people, and it proved to be so.

Jesus had been on earth, healed the sick, cast out devils, cleansed the temple, but the Jews rejected and crucified Him. Now, on the Day of Pentecost when they heard the Holy Ghost speak through these one hundred and twenty unlearned men and women, they

[6] John 15:26.

[7] See Acts 1:8.

[8] Acts 2:12.

[9] Isaiah 28:9.

were confounded. They heard them tell of Jesus, whom they had crucified, and were convinced that this was the work of divine power. Some said, "These people are drunk, filled with new wine," but Peter said, "They cannot be drunk so early in the day."[10]

He went back to the Old Testament scriptures and told what the prophet had said about the coming of the Holy Ghost. "This is that which was spoken by the prophet Joel."[11] The Holy Ghost had been with the apostles in a wonderful way, but they had not spoken with other tongues until Pentecost. Isaiah prophesied, "With stammering lips and another tongue will he speak to this people . . . yet they would not hear."[12] God Almighty was speaking through other tongues. Pentecost was proving the prophecy was fulfilled.

They would not believe Jesus, so they had to be convinced by the Word of God that what they heard was the Holy Ghost, as spoken by the prophets. Peter preached to them, taking the Old Testament as proof. They were convicted of sin and converted, three thousand of them.[13] They cried out for mercy, "We have crucified the Lord. What shall we do?" They got saved and baptized in the Holy Ghost. Peter said to them, "This you see is from the Father; repent of what ye did; turn to God and you shall receive the gift of the Holy Ghost."[14]

"The promise is unto you, and to your children." You can all have the same power we have and do the same things, you and your children. You can get this baptism and teach it to your children; they can have it. And "all that are afar off, even as many as the Lord our God shall call."[15]

God sends the Holy Ghost to come into the human body; He takes charge of the vocal organs and the person has nothing to do about it. But for all that, God does such a wonderful thing some of you will not believe it. Tongues are for a sign to unbelievers; they were

---

[10]Acts 2:13 and 15, paraphrased.

[11]Acts 2:16.

[12]Isaiah 28:11-12.

[13]See Acts 2:41.

[14]See Acts 2:36-38.

[15]Acts 2:39.

the worst kind of unbelievers; they had crucified the Lord, but they were made to believe in Jesus Christ by this sign.[16] They were convinced by this sign that Jesus was the Messiah, when everything else had failed.

These were unlearned men, all Galileans, yet they spoke all these tongues representing the different nations, in a wonderful way. It takes years and years to master other languages and very few speak them fluently like natives. These were unlearned people, yet they spoke fluently like natives, because God Almighty spoke through them.

Everyone who is baptized in the Holy Ghost today, as he ought to be, speaks in another language; and the first words almost always are, "Jesus is coming soon!" The pouring out of the Holy Spirit in this way is a sign that we are in the last days. When He comes in His fullness, He shall take possession and talk through you of the death, resurrection, and ascension of Jesus. When Jesus went away, he said, "Do not preach; but tarry at Jerusalem until ye receive power, after the Holy Ghost comes upon you."[17]

After their training of three years, they had much to tell, but He told them not to talk about it. He told them to stay together and watch until the power should come and then they should testify of Him. Now, when the Holy Ghost came and took possession of them, remember they kept still until the Holy Ghost testified through them; then they could be witnesses.

They had to keep still until the Holy Ghost testified through every one of them. He told the wonderful works of God—Jesus died and rose again, went to God's right hand, and sent the Holy Ghost to testify of Him. It is so wonderful to me, the Holy Ghost speaking first and the rest waiting until He had finished.

He took the Scriptures, for the people always believed in the prophets. He took the witness stand and brought to them the proof that the promise of the Father had literally come to pass in the fullness of time. God had spoken in other tongues through men. Peter

[16]See 1 Corinthians 14:22.

[17]Acts 1:4 and 8, paraphrased.

took up the Word, and confirmed what the Holy Ghost had done.[18] He confirmed it by the Old Testament.

Jesus said, "When the Holy Ghost comes in, He shall testify of Me, then you shall be witnesses. In the mouth of two or three witnesses shall every word be established."[19] When the Holy Ghost comes in to abide, He comes into the body like rivers of living water.[20] The power comes from the heart, not the head. *We* talk through the intellect; the Holy Ghost talks through the spirit. The Holy Ghost testifies when it is God's work.

Peter said, "This is that," this special thing. These, acting like drunken men, these talking in other languages—all this is "that spoken by the prophet." God said when His Spirit was poured out He would speak with stammering lips and another tongue; but some will not believe it.

The cloven tongues are seen. In Dallas and Chicago, fire was seen upon the heads of some. It is the same Holy Ghost speaking in other tongues; why not see the cloven tongues of fire?

When the Holy Ghost comes in, He will take possession of the house, take the uppermost seat, and speak Himself. Paul shows it is a wonderful thing for God to speak through you in unknown tongues by the Holy Ghost. He quotes the prophets of thousands of years ago.

Paul said, "I thank my God, I speak with tongues more than ye all: Yet in the church I had rather speak five words with my understanding, that by my voice I might teach others also, than ten thousand words in an unknown tongue."[21] "I would that ye all spake with tongues."[22] "Forbid not to speak with tongues."[23]

This is one of the last signs of the soon coming of Jesus. Most everyone that is baptized with the Holy Ghost, the first words they

[18]See Acts 2:14-36.

[19]John 15:26 and Acts 1:8, paraphrased; 2 Corinthians 13:1.

[20]See John 7:38-39.

[21]1 Corinthians 14:18-19.

[22]1 Corinthians 14:5.

[23]1 Corinthians 14:39.

speak in an unknown tongue when interpreted is, "Jesus is coming soon, get ready." Everyone that speaks in an unknown tongue should pray that he might interpret.[24]

Paul said, "Desire spiritual gifts . . . he that speaks in an unknown tongue speaketh not unto men, but unto God: for no man understandeth him; howbeit in the spirit he speaketh mysteries. He that speaketh in an unknown tongue edifieth himself; except he interpret, that the church may receive edifying."[25]

Tongues are for a sign to unbelievers that Jesus is coming soon and that the Holy Ghost is poured out. Those who have the *gift* of tongues can speak at will or anytime that the Spirit is moving. Some even lose their experience and still speak anytime, anything they want to, casting reflections on the cause; this is in the flesh and not of God.

John the Baptist was filled with the Holy Ghost from his birth, yet he was under the law.[26] The mother of Jesus was filled with the Holy Ghost but had to receive the baptism with the rest.[27] The apostles had received the Holy Spirit and had the love of God shed abroad in their hearts, yet [they] were baptized on the Day of Pentecost.[28]

Follow on and get the real baptism, and you will be filled with all the fullness. Jesus did not have the fullness of power until He finished His work, laid down His life, and God raised Him from the dead.

When He arose He was a mighty conqueror; then He had all authority and power. He breathed upon the apostles and said, "Receive ye the Holy Ghost."[29] Their understanding was opened, and they knew more than they ever did before. They were wonderfully blessed.

You must be full of joy before you get the baptism. They were full of joy and all of one mind and one spirit. Glory to God! They went to the Upper Room, they were ready, they believed, and they waited

[24]See 1 Corinthians 14:13.

[25]1 Corinthians 14:1-5, paraphrased.

[26]See Luke 1:15.

[27]See Luke 1:35.

[28]See John 20:22 and Romans 5:5.

[29]John 20:22.

at Jerusalem; they continued with one accord, not praying and begging all the time, but waiting.

Stop begging and get joy in your heart, and then you will get something. God had been moving in power and they had cast out devils; but now they waited until the power came upon them, and they spoke in new tongues.

Just as far as you believe, you will receive. Everyone, after the baptism, is supposed to speak with tongues. They had the testimony of the prophets, and Christ said they should speak with tongues. They were prayed up to date, they believed, expected, praised, and the Holy Ghost came down upon them.

They were full of joy; every doubt was gone. They did not care about the results—only that He came; and everyone was filled with the Holy Ghost. You must have something else, the other gifts: casting out devils, healing the sick. Poison or the deadly serpent shall not harm you.[30]

The apostles had nearly all the gifts; they looked for tongues. Many have only spoken with tongues once; they are not looking for other gifts. Just as far as you believe, you will get every blessing. We ask God to sanctify us and bless us, and just as far as our faith reaches out, we get what we ask for.[31]

In these days, we have too much light of God to wink at ignorance. We see miracles done, showing that the Holy Ghost is poured out; and God wants us to step out for all the gifts. There is the poison, some running sores, putrid and full of poison. People come here like that; when we ask God to rebuke that and believe He will, it will be cleansed.

If you accidentally drink poison, believe, give Him the glory, and the poison won't hurt you. A serpent fastened on Paul's hand, he shook it off and suffered no harm, and they thought he was a god and wanted to worship him.[32] All these things are the work of the Holy Ghost.

[30] See Mark 16:18 and Luke 10:19.

[31] See Matthew 7:7-8.

[32] See Acts 28:3-6.

Many people teach today that no one has the Holy Spirit until baptized with the Holy Ghost. The Holy Ghost comes in different degrees: the filling of the Spirit and the baptism in the Spirit. The baptism comes down on your head like a cloud.

When the prophets were anointed, the oil was poured over their heads; then the Holy Ghost came into them.[33] The Holy Ghost must come upon our heads, then all through us, taking possession of us. Many people do not think of anything but speaking in tongues; they lay everything else aside.

Thirty-five years ago, I was baptized with the Holy Ghost and fire; and I stood alone. When the Pentecostal movement broke out and some said they would not have anything but tongues, I was kept back and could not do much with the movement at first. There was so much false teaching, the Holy Ghost was driven away from many people. They wanted the Holy Ghost to work this way and not that way. Let the Holy Ghost work in any way that agrees with the Word of God.

The apostles had faith; they knew they were going to have power as they had never had it before. God has given us light, and He expects us to have faith that we shall receive the Holy Ghost in such a wonderful way that He will speak through us.

I believe the Holy Ghost will speak in tongues through everyone who receives the baptism, and you will receive the other gifts also if you believe for them. In these last days, God is raising up a people who will blow the trumpet.

How can we sing in the heavenly choir unless we are filled with the Holy Ghost? John heard the song of the redeemed like the rushing of mighty waters.[34] It is the Holy Ghost; it rolls up and sounds like the rushing of many waters. We have heard the heavenly music and many times there are sounds like instruments playing. The Holy Ghost sings through the people. God is working in mysterious ways these days, and I bless Him for it.

The early rain and the latter rain, much more abundant, were promised in the same month, with the same power and gifts as in

[33]See Exodus 29:7.

[34]Possibly a mixed allusion to Revelation 1:15 and 5:9-13.

the early Church.[35] "Greater things shall ye do, because I go to the Father."[36] He has left His work in our hands. It means something wonderful to be baptized in the Holy Ghost. The Jews were unbelieving until they heard the Holy Ghost speaking in other tongues through those unlearned people. They knew it was God; they realized they had crucified the Lord, that He had risen and gone to glory, and they cried out, "What shall we do?"

Jesus prayed on the cross, "Father, forgive them; for they know not what they do."[37] When the Holy Ghost came, they knew what they had done. The "tongues" were a sign to unbelievers; it is today one of the greatest things God ever did.

The Holy Ghost will sing through us. He is training us to sing at the marriage supper of the Lamb. We shall not all die, but we shall all be changed; we shall have a glorious body like Jesus and shall rise to meet Him in the air, full of joy.[38]

People who are healed are full of joy and sometimes jump and dance when the healing power comes into them. The Holy Ghost takes all the deadness and stiffness out of them; sometimes God slays them and lays them down so He can talk to them.

Men and women, rejoice! Seek the baptism and receive the gifts. You shall have them if you believe for them, and you shall be witnesses. May God seal this to some heart, in the name of Jesus.

Taken from *Signs and Wonders God Wrought in the Ministry of M. B. Woodworth-Etter.*

[35] See Joel 2:23.

[36] John 14:12, paraphrased.

[37] Luke 23:34.

[38] See 1 Corinthians 15:51-52 and 1 Thessalonians 4:17.

THE SPIRIT REVEALS THE DEEP THINGS OF GOD

The Knowledge of God the Result of Divine Revelation

This is not understood by anyone except he has the Holy Ghost.

Eye hath not seen, nor ear heard, neither have entered into the heart of man, the things which God hath prepared for them that love him. But God hath revealed them unto us by his Spirit: for the Spirit searcheth all things, yea, the deep things of God.

1 Corinthians 2:9-10

Many today apply this [verse] to eternity, to the other world; they think we can never know these things until we get into another world. I am glad the scripture explains itself. "Eye hath not seen," in the natural state. "God hath"—in the present time—"revealed them unto us by His Spirit." The new birth brings us into the realm of the supernatural. How [did He] revealed them? By His Spirit in this world. "The Spirit searcheth all things; yea, the deep things of God."

I desire to call your attention, especially, to the fourteenth verse: "The natural man receiveth not the things of the Spirit of God: for they are foolishness unto him: neither can he know them, because they are spiritually discerned."[1] The natural man (anyone who has not received the new birth) cannot understand this wonderful scripture.

There are two classes of man: the spiritual man and the natural man. The natural man is in the "gall of bitterness."[2] The spiritual man is born of God and walks in the Spirit; he gets out into the deep. The natural man can never discern spiritual things; he can never hear and understand the work of the Lord; these things pass all human understanding. The wisdom of this world—intellect and science—can never understand the spiritual things of God.

[1] 1 Corinthians 2:14.

[2] See Acts 8:23.

There are two kinds of wisdom. The wisdom of this world is foolishness with God.[3] The wisdom from above, the natural man cannot comprehend. It never enters his imagination to think of the things God hath prepared for those who love Him.

He hath prepared already and He hath revealed them to us by His Spirit. His Spirit lets us down into the deep things, even the deep things of God. This is what we preach, what we practice, and what we stand on. The work of the Spirit is foolishness to the natural man, but he that hath the Spirit can discern spiritual things.

Various Kinds of Spirits

There are many kinds of power and many spirits going out in the world today. We are told to try the spirits for they are many.[4] Everything is revealed by God through the blessed Holy Ghost. There is only one Spirit we want anything to do with, not our own spirit, nor any other spirit, but the Spirit of the living God. "As many as are led by the Spirit of God, they are the sons of God"; and "He will lead us into all truth,"[5] all the way. He will lead us where we can get the truth. The child of God will be led into the baptism of the Holy Ghost and fire, which is the Pentecostal baptism.

Then we can go from one deep thing to another. The Holy Ghost is sent to us by Jesus Christ, and all spiritual gifts come through the Holy Ghost. Jesus said, "He shall not speak of Himself, but of Me; He will speak to you and show you the things to come."[6] We believe it. Glory to God!

This is the Holy Ghost who came at Pentecost and turned Jerusalem upside down; and Jesus said that when the Holy Ghost came, He should abide with us forever, even unto the end.[7] The work of the Spirit is foolishness to the natural man; he cannot comprehend it.

Unless you hear the voice of God, the voice of the natural man will make you attribute what you see to excitement or to some other

[3] 1 Corinthians 3:19.

[4] See 1 John 4:1.

[5] Romans 8:14 and see John 16:13.

[6] John 16:13, paraphrased.

[7] See John 14:16.

power. When the Holy Ghost is poured out, there are always two classes—one is convinced and convicted and accepts it; the other says, "If I accept, I will have to lead a different life and be a gazing stock for the world and suffer persecution." They are not willing to pay the price, so they begin to draw back. First they wonder at the strange acts; then when they won't accept, they begin to despise. Everyone who continues to despise the works of the Holy Ghost will perish.

Satanic Power

There are many powers in the world that are not of God, but are counterfeit; but where there is a counterfeit there is always a genuine. No one ever tries to counterfeit anything that is not genuine; that is sure evidence that it is genuine.

The devil shows his power in a good many ways to deceive people. He tries to substitute some other power for the power of God. It was so in the time of Moses and the time of the prophets. God's power was especially in the world at certain times, and then magicians would come up with their power and show something that seemed similar. One was of God; the other was of the devil. Moses went to Egypt to lead the people out. Before Pharaoh he threw down his rod and it became a live serpent. The magicians said they had the same power, so they threw their rods down, and they became serpents.[8] One was of God, and the other was of the devil. Moses did not get scared and run away; he knew God and wouldn't have run if all the serpents in Egypt had come before him.

He stood his ground, and I admire him for it; I do not like a coward. What was the result? Moses' serpent swallowed the others up, head and tail! There was nothing left of them. Those who are trying to overthrow the power of God and substitute something else will have a day of judgment. The time is coming when the Almighty God will manifest His power then they, too, will be swallowed up.

The Lamb of God left the realms of glory and came down here to be footsore, dusty, weary, spat upon. He said, "I come to do thy

[8] See Exodus 7:9-12.

will, O God."[9] If He had not borne all these things, if he had not gone all the way to the cross, the Holy Ghost never could have come. If He had been left in the tomb, the Holy Ghost never could have come. As soon as He arose from the dead and ascended into heaven, the Holy Ghost could come.

Christ's Sovereignty

God gave His Son the highest place before all the hosts of heaven; then He sent the Holy Ghost to dwell in these bodies, His temple. The Holy Ghost is a great power; He is compared to wind, water, and fire.

At Pentecost He came like a cyclone—a mighty, rushing wind.[10] He is to come like rivers of living water.[11] He comes as fire. Tongues of fire sat upon each of them at Pentecost.[12] Wind, water, and fire—the most destructive elements we have, yet the most useful.

God uses them to denote the mighty power of the Holy Ghost. He was to be given after Jesus was glorified. We see many demonstrations of His mighty power; and we can but "speak of the things we have seen and heard" of His glory, His majesty.[13] When we know these things, we are witnesses to His power, His majesty, and His glory. Glory to God!

He is a mighty power, and He lives in these bodies. He lets down an "eternal weight of glory" upon us here, and when we are filled with this glory we have to give vent to it sometimes or we would explode.[14] What are we? Only worms of the dust; we cannot stand the glory of God; one breath from Him lays us prostrate.

In the Bible we read how men fell to the ground when they had a glimpse of God's glory. Saint Paul tells us there are those who have a form of godliness, but deny the power thereof; from such we are to

[9] Hebrews 10:9.

[10] See Acts 2:2.

[11] See John 7:38.

[12] See Acts 2:3.

[13] See Acts 4:20, 22:15, John 3:32, and 1 John 1:3.

[14] 2 Corinthians 4:17.

turn away.[15] "In the last days perilous times shall come," and those who have reprobate minds shall withstand God's children to their faces, even as the magicians withstood Moses.[16]

In the last days there will be some people living very near to God; but the devil will have his workers too, who will attribute signs and wonders to any power except the power of Christ. The Lamb of God, the lion of the tribe of Judah, has never lost His power and never will lose His power, and I would hate to say by my actions that I thought the devil had more power than God.

God's Power Unlike Any Other

There is a wonderful difference between the power of God and any of those other powers. The Holy Ghost comes only in Christ; He only comes into the bodies of those who love God. When He takes possession of us, He takes us away into the sweetest experience this side of heaven—alone with God. He talks to us and reveals to us "things to come."[17]

It is wonderful! God puts us under the power and God takes us out. No man can bestow this power upon another; it comes only through Jesus Christ. There are two kinds of power, and people who do not know the difference will stand up today and say wisdom is foolishness.

Many people today have an intellectual faith, a historical faith; they believe. Well, the devils believe and tremble;[18] belief is one thing, faith is another. "The letter killeth: the spirit giveth life."[19] If the truth is hid, it is hid to those who are lost.

We may have intellectual imaginations, go through a course of study learning the doctrines of men; yet there is none but the Holy Ghost who can give us a real abiding, tangible, definite knowledge of the things of God. They seem foolish to the natural man. Sometimes the

---

[15]2 Timothy 3:5.

[16]2 Timothy 3:1 and 8.

[17]See John 16:13.

[18]See James 2:19.

[19]2 Corinthians 3:6, paraphrased.

Holy Ghost gives a spirit of laughter and sometimes of weeping, and everyone in the place will be affected by the Spirit.

I have stood before thousands of people and could not speak, just weeping. When I was able to see, people were weeping everywhere. That is one way the Holy Ghost works. I have stood an hour with my hands raised, held by the mighty power of God. When I came to myself and saw the people, their faces were shining.

"God moves in a mysterious way/His wonders to perform."[20] He is the God I worship. Jesus says, "Here am I and the children Thou hast given Me."[21] We believe in signs and wonders, not from beneath, but from above. We are a people to be wondered at; we are for a sign among the people.[22]

Citizenship

The heaven of heavens cannot contain God, yet He tabernacles with men; He comes and dwells in us. His gifts are demonstrated through us, that people may know God dwells in Zion; we have a bodyguard of angels. The angels of the Lord encamp around those who love God.[23] "Our citizenship is in heaven,"[24] and we are on the way.

The Holy Ghost works in many ways. People saw the fire on the disciples' heads at Pentecost; they staggered like drunken men; then the Holy Ghost took possession of their tongues. God Almighty spoke through one hundred and twenty of His children, and they were telling of His wonderful works. They did not know what they were saying, but every man heard them speak in his own tongue wherein he was born.[25]

I am glad God does the same thing today. People who are not saved hate the power of God; the cold, dead formalists cannot understand

[20] A hymn, "God Moves in a Mysterious Way" (1774), William Cowper (1731-1800), Lines 1-2.

[21] See John 17:9,11.

[22] Zechariah 3:8, Deuteronomy 28:46, Isaiah 20:3.

[23] See Psalm 34:7.

[24] See Ephesians 2:6,19 and Philippians 3:20

[25] See Acts 2:8.

the power of God; it is foolishness to them. They think people are excited, hypnotized, have lost their mind.

May God have mercy upon us if we do not know God's power from hypnotic power or devil power! If any man speak against the Holy Ghost, it shall never be forgiven him. To attribute the work of the Holy Ghost to the devil or to any unclean spirit cannot be forgiven; that is the unpardonable sin.[26]

Some people are calling the Holy Ghost the devil, and they had better beware. There are different kinds of spirits and different kinds of power; and the natural man cannot understand the work of the Holy Spirit—shining faces, singing, shouting as one, to make one sound (See 2 Chronicles 5:13); sometimes staggering and falling, "drunken, but not with wine"[27]; sometimes speaking with other tongues.

Spiritual Manifestations in Angelic Singing

Praise God, some of the redeemed are getting so filled with the Holy Ghost that He is singing through them songs that none but the redeemed can sing, "There are diversities of operations, but the same Spirit."[28] Paul tells us, "The Spirit will work in you in one way and in someone else in another way; you know it is the same Spirit, and you do not get jealous because the other is blessed; no matter how the Spirit works, every member of the body is profited."[29]

People look on these things; they see us lift up holy hands to God, and they don't like it. They are too dead. They could not get their hands up. Paul says, "I will therefore that men pray every where, lifting up holy hands."[30] The Psalmist says, "O clap your hands, all ye people; shout unto God with the voice of triumph."[31]

People go to the theatre and clap their hands; but when we are raised from the spiritually dead and we get our grave clothes off and

[26]See Matthew 12:31-32, Mark 3:28-29, and Luke 12:10.

[27]See Ephesians 5:18.

[28]1 Corinthians 12:4,6, paraphrased. Maria Etter refers here to singing in the Spirit, in which spontaneous melodies and harmonies are sung in tongues and also in the native language of the worshipper.

[29]See 1 Corinthians 12.

[30]1 Timothy 2:8.

[31]Psalm 47:1.

begin to clap our hands, they think it an awful thing. David danced with all his might before the ark, and sometimes the Spirit of God gets into our feet and makes them like "hinds' feet."[32] David says, "By my God have I leaped over a wall."[33] How much more in these last days when we are getting ready for a flight in the air! We must get a good supply of this power; the same power that took Jesus up will take us up one day.

We want more of it, don't we? More of this mighty power. No matter what people say—foolishness, hypnotism, and every other thing—that doesn't make it so. The Spirit will take us out into the deep things, even "the deep things of God."[34]

Old Testament Types Revealed by the Spirit in the New

Many things recorded in the Old Testament are types of the work of the Spirit in the New. Many of the movements of God through His children seemed foolishness, and the messages He gave His prophets to carry, humanly speaking, seemed very foolish.

He gave Noah a plan of the ark—only one window, only one door. He built it according to God's plan, not heeding the jeers of the people, who thought he was losing his mind. He was a gazing stock for everybody, but he went on with the building and proved the wisdom of God in the end.

He built the ark and God provided the water, more water than they wanted—too much water for them. What happened? God took those who believed Him into the ark and shut the door. The water rose and the ark went above the treetops—as we are going someday. God is building the ark now, and the works of the Holy Ghost are foolishness to the people who are fighting them.

The ark sailed away and the world went down, all except Noah and his family.[35] Not many are going into the ark God is building; people are crying, "foolishness!" One time there was a great battle, the enemy had gathered like grasshoppers. God knew there were a

[32] See 2 Samuel 22:34, Psalm 18:33, and Habakkuk 3:19.

[33] 2 Samuel 22:30 and Psalm 18:29.

[34] 1 Corinthians 2:10.

[35] See Genesis 6-9.

lot of cowards among His people, and He tested them until only three hundred were left to meet the enemy.

The Leader—The Signal—The Result

God can work by the few as well as the many. He told Gideon what to do. He divided the men into three companies and "put a trumpet in every man's hand with empty pitchers and lamps within the pitchers," he said. "When I give the signal, blow the trumpet and say, 'The sword of the Lord and of Gideon.'"

As they obeyed their leader, something happened (God always has a leader). At the signal, they blew the trumpets and broke the pitchers, revealing the lamps, and they shouted, "The sword of the Lord and of Gideon."

At the shout and the light, the enemy was frightened to death and started to run, but God sent confusion among them. That little band of three hundred "cranks" put the whole host of the enemy to flight. What they did seemed foolish, did it not? But what was the outcome? The whole army of the enemy was conquered.[36]

God used a vision—He does sometimes. He let Gideon go down to the enemy's camp, and he heard a man tell his fellows a vision or dream of how a "cake of barley bread tumbled into the host of Midian and came into a tent and smote it that it fell and overturned it, that the tent lie alone." The other interpreted it, "This is nothing else save the sword of Gideon; into his hand hath God delivered Midian and all the hosts." So Gideon believed and took courage.[37]

Children of God who think you are something—you are nothing. When you realize you are nothing, God fights for you. How foolish seemed the method of fighting the Midianites! Israel might have said, "If we break the pitchers, the lamps will show the enemy where we are and they will shoot us." When God speaks, go forward, obey Him; He takes care of His own.

Truly, God moves in a mysterious way. Remember the fall of Jericho? It had great walls around it, and all the people were shut in. God said to Joshua that he and his men of war should march

[36]See Judges 7:2-8:4.

[37]Judges 7:14, paraphrased.

around the city once a day for six days, seven priests bearing before the ark seven trumpets of rams' horns. On the seventh day theywere to march around the city seven times, the priests blowing with the trumpets; and when they made a long blast the people were to shout, and the walls should fall down.[38]

It took faith to do all that marching without any sign of victory and to shout—anyone can shout *after* the walls fall. Humanly speaking, how foolish this all was! Don't you see? No preparation for war, only marching and blowing rams' horns; but that was God's way, and they were simple enough to obey God! What was the result? The walls went down.

So we could go all through the Word of God; so many things that seem so silly, things people would laugh at, but it was God's way, and His servants were willing to obey Him. The result showed the wonderful wisdom and brought victory through a visible display of His power.

Apparent Ignorance in the Natural Is Height Upon Height in Wisdom in the Spiritual

When these visible signs came, they put a fear of God upon the people; it is so with the works of the Holy Ghost. The ways of God are foolishness to the natural man, and the works of the Spirit are foolishness to the natural man; but what is the outcome?

Paul said, "If any man among you seemeth to be wise in this world, let him become a fool, that he may be wise."[39] Later he said, "I will come to visions and revelations of the Lord."[40] He said he was carried away to the third heaven—whether in the body or out of the body, he could not tell—he could not tell whether his whole body went or not; he was so light he could not tell whether he had left his body here or not.[41]

He said, "God knoweth," and he heard unutterable things. At another time Paul was praying in the temple and fell under the power of God; he fell into a trance. To the world he appeared to be unconscious, but he was never so wide-awake to God in his life.[42]

[38] See Joshua 6.

[39] 1 Corinthians 3:18.

[40] 2 Corinthians 12:1.

[41] 2 Corinthians 12:2, paraphrased.

[42] See Acts 22:17.

It is then that the Spirit of God lets us down into the deep things, even the deep things of God. Peter fell into a trance upon the housetop, and God spoke to him three times.[43] Paul and Silas started out to visit converts. Paul had a vision; he saw a man of Macedonia holding out his hands and saying, "Come over and help us." He knew it was the call of God, so they changed their course and went to this place, altogether different from their plans.[44]

When they began to preach and were arrested, they might have thought they had been mistaken; but Paul knew God, and he never doubted it was God's voice that had called him. They might have said, "If we had not come here, we would have had many people to preach to; now we have come to this strange place, have been put in prison, with our feet fast in the stocks." The devil put them in there, but God permitted it, and God delivered them.

There are many wonderful things all about us in these last days, things the natural man cannot understand, demonstrations of God's power. There are other powers too, and many do not know the difference. God's power is the greatest and is the only power that will bring peace to your soul.

God wants you to be pure and holy, filled with the Holy Ghost; but the devil is right here, too, and if you do not know the difference you will be listening to him. He comes sometimes as an angel of light.[45] One word in the Garden of Eden upset the world; the little word "not."[46]

When God talks to you, the message agrees with the written Word. The Holy Ghost never says anything that doesn't correspond with the Word. A message that comes from heaven must correspond with the Word; if otherwise, do not accept it.

The things of the Spirit that seem foolishness to the world antagonize the devil, and he sometimes does things that look very similar, but to him who understands there is a wonderful difference.

---

[43]See Acts 10:9-16.

[44]See Acts 16:9-10.

[45]See 2 Corinthians 11:14.

[46]See Genesis 2:17.

I have been carried away in the Spirit many, many times. Once, I was seven hours under the power of God. I have been examined at such a time by medical doctors and found to be in a normal condition. Many I know of have been honest enough to say the power was not hypnotic, even while they could not understand it.

Celebrated Hypnotist Baffled

One of the greatest hypnotists in the world came to our meeting in Saint Louis; he had been there two or three days before I knew anything about it. He was surprised to see a man lying there whom hundreds of hypnotists had tried to get under their power. He himself had tried it.

He went to him and tried to bring him out, but could not. After a while the hypnotist came to me to have an interview with me. He said he was going to call his friends together and tell them he had found something he could not understand.

He said, "If there is a God, I believe this is His power." He could not put anyone under that power, nor bring anyone out. When the doctors examined me when I was lying under the power, they said my pulse was regular, my blood flowing naturally, and my heart was in a natural condition.

I am told that when a person is hypnotized, the blood does not flow naturally; the person is unconscious and simply does what he is told. Someone has to put him in that state and bring him out again.

God does lay His people down under His power, and then He talks to them. I have known people to be a whole week under the power of God. May He seal these truths to our hearts!

I know nothing about hypnotic power. I never saw a person hypnotized; but I do know something of the power of God, of the power of the Holy Ghost. It is God Himself who sends this power; we can press the button, but God sends the power. Talk about excitement! This power is the best thing in the world to settle the nerves. These people go down praising God; while they are there and when they are up, they are still giving God praise.

"Let every thing that hath breath praise the Lord."[47] People ask why we tell them to praise the Lord. If you do not feel it at first, praise as a "sacrifice" and after a while the praise will come of itself, from a soul filled with joy. Hallelujah!

If you will search your Bible, you will find the things I have told you are true. My words do not amount to anything unless they are backed by God's Word. The Lord gave me this message tonight and I have written it to you.

When the power of the Spirit has been so maligned, it is time for you to take a stand for the truth. When a ship is in danger the sailors come to the front, if they are not cowards. Let us come to the front, not run away.

I stand here in defense of the Gospel. If we are faithful, all things must work together for God's glory. Praise His name.

Taken from *Spirit-Filled Sermons.*

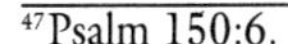

[47]Psalm 150:6.

TRY THE SPIRITS

Sermon Preached to Ministers and Workers at Montwait, Massachusetts

"Beloved . . . try the spirits."[1] There are many spirits we do not want to have anything to do with. There is our own spirit, the flesh, and the devil. There are many spirits contending, and many times we let our own spirit rule and make ourselves think it is God's. And we do the same with the flesh and the devil.

Sometimes we know it is not God, but we want to have our own way. If we have the Holy Ghost we can prove the spirits, because everything the Holy Ghost does is confirmed by the Word. We do not want to trust to tongues and interpretations; you must measure things by the Word. We must measure tongues and demonstrations by the Word; and if they do not agree with the Word, we must not accept them; everything must be measured by the Word.

We do know God and the voice of God, but the devil can come as an angel of light.[2] When you are in the Holy Ghost, that is the time the devil tries to get in and lead you astray. The Holy Ghost is revealing some secret things; at the same time the devil comes in; and if you are not careful, you will listen to what he has to say and follow him.

Once I was having a wonderful vision and right in the midst of it, the devil said to me, "You are going to die." I was very poorly and was worked nearly to death, and I listened to the devil for a minute; then I stopped to hear what God wanted to teach me.

I said, "What is this God is showing me? Does this agree with what God is showing?" I saw there was a big difference. God touched my forehead, the seat of intellect and reason; my mouth, signifying

[1] 1 John 4:1.

[2] See 2 Corinthians 11:14.

courage and power to give forth the message; and I could not die if I was to do this. If I was to give the people His message, I was not going to die.

There was someone in the meeting here God was blessing. He wanted to use her, but the devil came in and made her think she could do any outrageous thing and it would be of God. See how the devil can lead us off? She was talking in tongues and praying, and she said, "Lord, if You want me to kill anyone, I will do it; if You want me to set the camp on fire, I will do it."

That is the way in spiritualism; the Holy Ghost never does anything like that. He does not come to kill and knock people's heads off; He deals with them in love and tenderness. People have even offered up children in sacrifice. If you listen to God, the devil will be put to one side.

These things hurt the Pentecostal movement. God is in it, but the devil is in it, too. Many people are honest, but they do not understand. God shows great things that are going to happen, and the devil comes in and makes them set a date.

Daniel did not understand the vision he had. For some time, an angel appeared to him to make him understand the vision. Be careful the devil does not come in and give you another meaning all together different from what God wants you to have.

So many prophesy this or that and it never comes true; the prophecy was not according to the Word of God. Someone gives a person a message and he believes God sent it when it is not according to the Word.

When God calls you out for His work, He will take care of you, give you something to eat and clothe you. There are so many who run before they are sent; better not go at all. Sometimes the devil uses tongues to upset things generally. The devil can speak in tongues and your flesh can.

When God speaks in tongues, it means something and you want to look for interpretation. God says ask for interpretation.[3] Sometimes God gives it through someone else, but give the person who speaks

[3] See 1 Corinthians 14:13.

in tongues a chance to interpret. Be careful you do not give an interpretation in your own spirit; this hurts the work everywhere. Let us try the spirits and not get in the flesh.

Some people, if they do not like someone, will give a message in tongues, or a rebuke, and nearly knock the person's head off. This is the work of the devil. Then someone will get up—some people are so silly—and say, "Don't lay hands on that; it is the Holy Ghost."[4] And no one dares to touch it, and the devil has the whole thing.

It goes out that the leader sanctions all that and people do not want to have anything to do with it. The leader may have discernment but someone will pull his coattail and say, "Don't lay hands on that." Instead of being so afraid, let us search the Scriptures. God never told anyone to rebuke in an ugly tone.[5]

There was a great work being done in the West. One woman, especially, said the United States was going to be destroyed, and they should go to Japan. They went. People who could not spare the money helped them; they went to escape the wreck.

The whole thing was of the devil. The United States was not destroyed. They could not speak the Japanese language, they were stranded, and a number backslid. They tried to raise money for a great building, but never accomplished it. They had been doing a good work here, but other spirits got in.

God gave me a special commission to take the precious from the vile, and I do not want you to get into the snare of the devil. So many young people, after their baptism, give up work and go to preaching. In a few days they tell all they know, then tell something they don't know; bread and butter does not come in, and many of them backslide.

If God doesn't send you out, don't give up your work. Then you will have something to give. This mistake is made by many missionaries who go abroad; some sell all they have, break up their homes, separate from their wives, and God has not called them.

[4] "Don't lay hands on that"—Maria Etter means that people mistakenly say, "Don't hinder that person or criticize their message since it is from the Holy Spirit" when it is from the flesh and should be dealt with.

[5] See Ephesians 4:15.

The Holy Ghost makes us levelheaded. Those who stayed in the camp got as much as they who went.[6] Be God's stewards and give the Lord His part. The cattle upon a thousand hills are His, but He works through our instrumentality.[7] He gives you everything you have, physical, financial, and spiritual; and He expects you to use all your powers for Him. If you give out, He will supply.

He expects you to take Him into partnership, give Him what belongs to Him, and He will bless you. The Gospel has to be supported. Water is free, but it costs money to lay the pipes and keep the water running. Angels can fly, but men have to pay fare, and someone has to help.

If you keep the pipes in order, the Gospel will be given out; and you need to help with your prayers—hold up the hands of those who work. If you trust God and walk with Him, that is the work God wants of you.

Don't take up with every vision that comes along. In the Pentecostal movement in some places, they have discarded the Word of God. They don't want a leader and God always had a leader; when there is none, the devil takes the chair. God hath set some pastors and teachers.[8]

How does anyone know when God calls them to the ministry? Someone has said that when God calls anyone to do His work, you can hardly get him into the pulpit; but when the devil calls him, you can't keep him out of it.

Some people want to talk so much, bringing in a bone of contention. It is hurting the work everywhere. Leave outside issues. God will teach people what to eat, what to wear, and where to go. Many of God's children are nagging about these things. The Lord said, if you do not think it right to eat meat, don't do it; but don't judge another.[9]

---

[6] See 1 Samuel 30:24.

[7] See Psalm 50:10.

[8] See Ephesians 4:11.

[9] See Romans 14:17-23, 1 Corinthians 6:12-13 and 8:8-13, Colossians 2:16, and 1 Timothy 4:1-5.

When we open our mouths, let us say something. If you have the baptism, you need not tell it; people will know it. Let God speak to you. Do not wait for someone to speak in tongues and tell you God wants you to go to India; let God speak to you. People who go because someone else says so get homesick and discouraged and try to get back again. Let the Lord be our guide; if we do His will, we shall know His will.

Hold up Jesus and try to get the people so full of the Holy Ghost that they will live in unity. We do not want to lay hands on anyone suddenly.[10] If we do anything in a spirit of contention, the first thing we know everything is in a jumble and we have done more harm in one meeting than can be imagined.

Hold up Jesus and the resurrection. Let us walk in the light, as He is in the light.[11] Christ is the great headlight and I am on the stretch for more light than I ever saw in my life. You have fellowship when you walk in the light. We are the lower lights and He will show us what to do next.

He will say to you, "Now you can do this." You may say, "I did not know before that You would trust me." And again His answer, "You can do it now."

Until God shows you a thing, it is not a sin, but after He shows it to you, if you do it, it is a sin.[12] Consecrate everything to God, day by day. He will not call you to do a thing unless He is going to give you strength and grace.

When you go into a meeting, listen to the teaching. If it does not suit you and you want something else, the best thing you can do is to go out quietly and drum up a crowd yourself. Some say, "You have no need that any man should teach you."[13] The natural man cannot teach you, but the spiritual man can teach you. We know what we are talking about; the spiritual man can teach you. We know nothing as we should, and there is so much for us to know.

---

[10] 1 Timothy 5:22.

[11] See 1 John 1:7.

[12] See James 4:17.

[13] See 1 John 2:27.

Be careful not to lay hands suddenly on anyone. Regarding the recent disturbance here,[13] we profess to be saints; and we want to show forth the Spirit of Christ. We must be firm, but kind. Do not speak roughly. The crowd wants to see. I would have nearly broken my neck when I was young to see what you are seeing.

When they became noisy, it would have been useless to attempt to use force. It would only have ended in a fight and the plan of the enemy would have been accomplished. God led me in the only way by which the disturbance could be quelled and order restored; God fought for us. Do not speak roughly to the boys; each one is some mother's boy. God can smite with conviction; the battle is His, not ours.[14]

"Try the spirits." In one of our meetings there was a colored woman who had a wonderful experience spiritually; that is the kind the devil gets after. One day she commenced to go about on her knees, twisting about like a serpent. God does not tell anyone to do that. She spoke in tongues, then she said, "I don't want to do it; I don't want to do it."

Everyone knew it was not of God and I said to her, "That is not God; the enemy has got hold of you." At first, she didn't want to give up, but the next day God showed her and she asked to be delivered. The devil had got in and made her do things that were not right to kill her influence.

A woman came to me and said, "I am afraid this spirit on me is not of God. I was baptized in the Holy Ghost, and I went into a mission where they did everything by tongues. They got me so mixed up; I did not know where I was. Then, this spirit got hold of me; it shakes my head and makes my head ache."

That is spiritualism. Some people, when they pray for anyone and lay on hands, throw the slime off.[15] That is spiritualism. Don't ever do anything like that. When you lay hands on a person, God takes care of the evil spirit. If you are filled with the Holy Ghost, the devil

[13]Maria Etter refers here to the hoodlums who disrupted her meetings because of the notoriety she gained as a result of the arrests of herself and two of her associates for practicing medicine without a license. See "Aver They Are Cured," August 27, 1913, and the subsequent news articles.

[14]See 1 Samuel 17:47.

[15]That is, they affect others with "slime" or evil. Slime comes off them and gets on those they touch.

is outside you—keep him out. Be careful who lays hands on you, for the devil is counterfeiting God's work.

For two years, that woman could not give a testimony. God rebuked the shaking spirit, the power of God came in her hands and in her voice, and she gave a testimony for God.

That is what ails the Pentecostal movement; so much of this has crept in. Some people take every foolish thing for the Holy Ghost. There are two extremes: one keeps the Holy Ghost from working, except in a certain channel; and the other thinks everything is of the Holy Ghost, "don't lay hands on it." One is as bad as the other. Let everything be done by the Word of God.

We are living in the last days and there has got to be a higher standard for the Pentecostal movement. Christ is coming and we cannot move along in the old rut. God is sifting us today and we have got to rise above errors; we have to rise up and go forward. By the grace of God we will. Praise His name!

"Where the Blood Can Heal"

> Do you seek relief for your sin-sick soul?
> You to Christ, then, must make appeal.
> There's no other one who can make you whole,
> You must come where the blood can heal!
>
> Refrain
>
> > You must come where the blood can heal,
> > You must come where the blood can heal;
> > There's no other one who can make you whole,
> > You must come where the blood can heal!
>
> Vain are all your hopes of another cure,
> Be persuaded, you now, to feel,
> Help alone, thro' Christ, that you can secure,
> You must come where the blood can heal!
>
> Other proffered aids can but you deceive,
> At your will, unto life, they steal!
> You must look to Christ if you'd hope receive,
> You must come where the blood can heal!

Hear you not? 'Tis there a decoying voice,
Striving ever to quench thy zeal;
Would you from Him turn, refuge safe to find,
You must come where the blood can heal!

If you would arise from your bed of pain,
To the counsel of Christ then kneel,
'Tis prescribed by Him, and your only hope,
You must come where the blood can heal!

Taken from *Signs and Wonders God Wrought in the Ministry of M. B. Woodworth-Etter.*

The Wonderful Power of the Word of God, When Preached in the Demonstration of the Spirit

We are God's Mouthpieces

Human Eloquence Is Often Preferred to God's Word

Whosoever therefore shall be ashamed of me and of my words in this adulterous and sinful generation; of him also shall the Son of man be ashamed, when he cometh in the glory of his Father with the holy angels.

Mark 8:38

In the beginning was the Word, and the Word was with God, and the Word was God. The same was in the beginning with God. All things were made by him; and without him was not any thing made that was made. . . . And the Word was made flesh, and dwelt among us.

John 1:1-3,14

That which was from the beginning, which we have heard, which we have seen with our eyes, which we have looked upon, and our hands have handled, of the Word of life; (For the life was manifested, and we have seen it, and bear witness, and shew unto you that eternal life, which was with the Father, and was manifested unto us;) That which we have seen and heard declare we unto you, that ye also may have fellowship with us: and truly our fellowship is with the Father, and with his Son Jesus Christ.

1 John 1:1-3

The words of God have been sent down from heaven to us by Jesus Christ and the holy apostles, spoken with the Holy Ghost. They are from God and go forth a living power.

"Believest thou not that I am in the Father, and the Father in me? the words that I speak unto you I speak not of myself: but the Father that dwelleth in me, he doeth the works. Believe me that I am in the Father, and the Father in me: or else believe me for the very works' sake" (John 14:10-11). "They testify that the Father is in Me, and with Me."

God spake the worlds into existence. God said, "Let there be light: and there was light."[1] As He spake the Word—the earth, land, light, darkness, seas, lakes, mountains, valleys, with all the fruits and flowers—sprang into life, into existence and beauty. He spake the Word and every living creature stood before Him; from the mighty monsters of the sea, the lions of the forest, and wild beasts of every kind, down to the little singing bird; they stood looking in wonder and awe at the Mighty God that had, by the Word of His mouth and the power of His voice, called them into this beautiful world, saying by their very presence, "We know Thou are the great Jehovah! The God that inhabitest eternity."

When the high priest sent the officers to bring Jesus, the question was asked them, "Why have you not brought him?" They said, "Never man spake like this man" (John 7:45-46, paraphrased). "With his voice the dead are raised, the lepers cleansed, the blind see, they have their sight restored. The raging storm on the Sea of Galilee was hushed at His Word, and the roaring sea became as a sea of glass."

We Are God's Mouthpieces

The words of God spoken by the Holy Ghost have the same effect today. There is as much power in the name of Jesus now. Through the Holy Ghost, His words come like coals of fire burning in the brains and hearts of men. They are shot out like arrows dipped in the blood of Jesus; like lightning, piercing the king's enemies in the

---

[1] Genesis 1:3.

[2] See Luke 7:22, Matthew 11:5, and Mark 4:39-41.

head and lodging in the heart. They fall like dead men. They are like David's little pebbles, we throw them at a venture, and God directs them so that they never return void, but they bring life or death; heaven or hell.[3] They stand forever, for by the Word we will be justified or condemned.

When the disciples were arrested and put into prison as recorded in the fifth chapter of Acts, verses 19 and 20, "The angel of the Lord by night opened the prison doors, and brought them forth, and said, Go, stand and speak in the temple to the people all the words of this life." You see, God sent the angel to set them free and to tell them to go back amidst all the threats and the danger and to preach all the words of this life. His words are life; do not hold back any of the message.

Jesus says, "Whosoever shall be ashamed of me and of my words, of him shall the Son of man be ashamed, when he shall come in his own glory, and in his Father's."[4] Oh! God help all that pretend to preach the Word to see what is at stake. Will you please men or God? Will you deceive the people and come up at the judgment with your hands dripping with the blood of souls?

> Behold, the Lord's hand is not shortened, that it cannot save; neither his ear heavy, that it cannot hear. . . .
>
> For your hands are defiled with blood, and your fingers with iniquity; your lips have spoken lies, your tongue hath muttered perverseness. . . .
>
> The way of peace they know not; and there is no judgment in their goings: they have made them crooked paths: whosoever goeth therein shall not know peace.
>
> Isaiah 59:1,3, and 8

Do We Love the Praise of Men More Than the Praise of God?

You have given them smooth sayings, trusting to good works, and a moral life. "In vain do ye worship me, teaching the doctrines,

[3] See Isaiah 55:11.

[4] Luke 9:26.

commandments, and traditions of men,"[5] that will perish with the using.

Jesus tells us what He will do when He comes in all His glory. Yes, He is coming soon. This is the time of the end; we see the signs everywhere. In this wicked and adulterous generation, in these last days, the churches have gone after the wisdom and power of men instead of the wisdom and power of God. "Having a form of godliness, but denying the power thereof: from such turn away."[6] Read the third chapter of the second epistle of Timothy.

God is calling as never before, in thunder[ous] tones, to those who pretend to preach His Word, to "blow the trumpet in Zion," and to "sound an alarm in the holy mountain." Let all the people tremble. What is the signal to make the people tremble? The Day of the Lord is at hand. It is even at your doors.

> Blow ye the trumpet in Zion, and sound an alarm in my holy mountain: let all the inhabitants of the land tremble: for the day of the Lord cometh, for it is nigh at hand.
>
> Joel 2:1

> The great day of the Lord is near, it is near, and hasteth greatly, even the voice of the day of the Lord: the mighty man shall cry there bitterly. That day is a day of wrath, a day of trouble and distress, a day of wasteness and desolation, a day of darkness and gloominess, a day of clouds and thick darkness, A day of the trumpet and alarm against the fenced cities, and against the high towers. And I will bring distress upon men, that they shall walk like blind men, because they have sinned against the Lord: and their blood shall be poured out as dust, and their flesh as the dung. Neither their silver nor their gold shall be able to deliver them in the day of the Lord's wrath; but the whole land shall be devoured by the fire of his jealousy: for he shall make even a speedy riddance of all them that dwell in the land.
>
> Zephaniah 1:14-18

[5] See Matthew 15:9 and Mark 7:7.

[6] 2 Timothy 3:5.

Hear the angel shout, "The hour of his judgment has come; repent and worship God, that made heaven, and earth, and the sea, and all that are therein."[7]

Human Eloquence Is Preferred to God's Word

"The time has come when men will not endure sound doctrine, but turn the people to cunningly devised fables, turning away from the truth. Men of corrupt minds, reprobate concerning the truth, having a form of godliness but denying the power thereof: from such turn away, for of him who does not will I be ashamed when I come in all My glory."[8]

The last invitation is going forth, "Come to the marriage of the Lamb, and to the supper of the Lamb."[9] The Gospel of His coming kingdom is being preached as a witness to all nations. This work will soon be done. What are you doing? The Lord said, "Preach all the words of this life."[10] Oh! What a calling. Oh! What a privilege. The angels that stand before the throne cannot do this work.

Jesus said, "Tarry ye . . . until ye be endued with power from on high. Ye shall receive power, after that the Holy Ghost is come upon you. Then you shall cast out devils, you shall speak with new tongues, and if you take up serpents, or drink deadly poisons, they will not hurt you. You shall lay hands on the sick, and they shall recover. Your young men shall see visions."[11]

Tell them Jesus is coming soon. Show them the signs. The wise shall know the times. The wise shall shine as the firmament.[12] They shall reign, be kings, with kingly authority and bless the people as priests, for one thousand years.[13]

---

[7] Revelation 14:7, paraphrased.

[8] 2 Timothy 4:3-4, 2 Timothy 3:5, and Luke 9:26, paraphrased.

[9] See Revelation 19:9 and 17.

[10] Acts 5:20, paraphrased.

[11] Luke 24:49, Acts 1:8, Mark 16:17-18, and Acts 2:17, paraphrased.

[12] Daniel 12:3, paraphrased.

[13] See Daniel 12:3 and Revelation 20:4,6.

Maria Woodworth-Etter stands second from the right with friends and associates.

Time Will Soon Merge Into Eternity

Do you not think that it will pay to be a true messenger, or herald, of His soon coming when we shall be like Him and shall have glorious bodies like His? "He that is ashamed of my words, of him will I be ashamed when I come in all my Father's glory."[14] Oh! Can you not understand? He is coming as a Prince of glory, to meet His bride in the air, to escort His bride back to the great city, to the wedding, the marriage of the Lamb—when Jesus will present His bride to the Father. He will welcome His Son's wife. He is coming in all the glory of all His holy angels.

Oh! What a picture. Oh! What brightness. See, oh see! The shining hosts! Gabriel that stands before God! Oh, they are getting ready! They are tuning up the heavenly choir. They are coming! They are coming to meet us in the air! "For the Lord himself shall descend from heaven with a shout, with the voice of the archangel, and with the trump of God: and the dead in Christ shall rise first" (1 Thessalonians 4:16). They will come in the clouds of glory. We will all be caught up, changed in a moment, have glorious bodies like our Lord and Savior, Jesus Christ, and be forever with the Lord.[15] Oh, this is wonderful, but it is true.

Oh! Dear brethren in the ministry, can we miss this eternal weight of glory? When Jesus comes, will He be ashamed of us? Will you miss all for a high position or a high salary or a social position or to please the people?

Oh! What can you do in that day?

Oh! God help us to preach all the words of this life and earnestly contend for the faith once delivered to the saints.

As God sent Jesus into the world to deliver His message, so Jesus sends us into the world as His ministers, to preach His Gospel faithfully. Woe to us if we do not preach the whole truth or are ashamed or offended at any of His mighty works.

Taken from *Spirit-Filled Sermons.*

---

[14] Luke 9:26, paraphrased.

[15] See 1 Thessalonians 4:17.

Will Ye Also Go Away? Or, the Great Decision

After Seeing the Miracles Men Are Without Excuse—Qualify Now for High Positions in God's Eternal Kingdom

s the living Father hath sent me, and I live by the Father: so he that eateth me, even he shall live by me. This is that bread which came down from heaven: not as your fathers did eat manna, and are dead: he that eateth of this bread shall live for ever.

John 6:57-58

If he keeps on eating and believing he shall never die spiritually. Many of His disciples said, "This is an hard saying; who can hear it?"[1] Jesus knew their murmuring, and He gave them a little insight into the great Resurrection: "What and if ye shall see the Son of man ascend up where he was before. . . . And he said, Therefore said I unto you, that no man can come unto me, except it were given unto him of my Father."[2] That is a wonderful truth. No man ever made his way to Jesus without God. No man ever made his way to Jesus unless the Father sent His Spirit out and drew him. "From that time many of his disciples went back, and walked no more with him. Then said Jesus unto the twelve, Will ye also go away?"[3]

I think He never was more sad. He saw the multitude turn away, for they would not walk in the light. "Then Simon Peter answered him,

[1] John 6:60.

[2] John 6:62,65.

[3] John 6:66-67.

Lord, to whom shall we go? thou hast the words of eternal life. And we believe and are sure that thou art that Christ, the Son of the living God."[4]

Many do not believe that today; they do not know that that is the key to the whole Word of God. "And we believe and are sure that thou art that Christ, the Son of the living God." As the living Father has sent me, and I live by the Father, so we must live the same way, by the power of the Almighty God and the resurrection life of Christ within us. Glory to God.

Multitudes Follow the Christ

In the Word, we see that the Lord had many thousands of followers by this time. His fame had gone out all over the land. He had five thousand converts with Him when He supplied them with bread in the wilderness.[5] At another time, seven thousand saw the mighty power of the Almighty God manifested through Jesus Christ, when they ate and were filled; and many baskets were filled with what was taken up of what remained of the few loaves and fishes.[6]

Thousands came to Him for salvation and healing, and when they were healed they got salvation also. He gave them the double cure. He asked which is easier, to take away sins, or heal the body?[7] One is as easy as the other.

Behold, thou are made whole: sin no more, lest a worse thing come unto thee.[8] They got the double cure, they were saved and healed.

They were by this time pretty well acquainted with the Christ and had experienced His love and His mercy and delivering, healing, and protecting power. They had heard of His fame, and every day His power was greater and more wonderfully demonstrated. We

[4] John 6:68-69.

[5] Matthew 14:15-21, Mark 6:35-44, Luke 9:12-17, and John 6:1-14.

[6] "seven thousand"—The feeding of four thousand is found in Mark 8:1-9. The feeding of the five thousand is in Mark 6:35-44. In both cases, this number referred to the number of men, which meant the total number of people including women and children was much higher.

[7] See Matthew 9:5, Mark 2:9, and Luke 5:23.

[8] John 5:14.

find one day when out on the waters of the Sea of Galilee, He fell asleep and a great tempest arose. The ship was going down, for the waves were sweeping over it; and all were about to be drowned. His disciples were afraid and came and called Him. He arose and said, "Peace be still."

The terrible wind ceased, and the rolling waves suddenly became as a sea of glass, through the mighty power of Christ. The power of God fell upon the people also; and they came forward and said, "What manner of man is He, anyway? Is there no limit to His power? This man, this Messiah, says He is the Son of God. We are following Him from day to day, and every day we see more and more of His mighty power; there is no limit to it; see even the winds and the waves obey Him. All the people in the ship fell at His feet and acknowledged Him as the Son of God."[9] So His fame went everywhere, not so much by what He said, but because of the manifestations of His power.

After Seeing the Miracles, Without Excuse

He said, "If you don't believe what I say, believe Me for the works' sake. These are they which testify of Me that I came from God and am the Son of the living God." Though He spake as never man spake, they still had a cloak to cover their sins.[10] In the presence of the mighty signs and wonders, they stood naked before God. They had seen the miracles, had heard Him speak, had seen His majesty and power in many ways; now He began to turn and chide them. He commenced to tell them about getting filled with God and about being baptized with the Holy Ghost and kept by the power of God. He said, "By the living Father I live"—by the power and presence of the living God He was sustained and kept continually, for the Father never left Him for a moment.[11]

He said, "The works that I do I do not do, but my Father doeth the works. The words that I say, I do not say, but my Father gives me the words. Whatsoever the Father tells me to do I do."[12] He

[9] See Matthew 8:24-27, Mark 4:37-41, and Luke 8:22-25.

[10] See John 14:10-11.

[11] See John 6:57.

[12] See John 14:10 and 6:19.

gave the Father credit for everything. As Jesus was sustained by the mighty power of the living God, so we, too, must come to the point where we can be sustained and kept the same way by the power of God through Jesus Christ. We are not to live by natural bread alone. To do the works of God and at last enter heaven, we must have the spiritual man sustained and fed by the bread of heaven—we must be supported by the Holy Ghost. We need to drink from the fountain that never runs dry. We should desire and ask for the living water; whosoever drinks whereof never thirsts.[13] We should with joy draw water out of the wells of salvation.[14]

They Had More Light Than They Were Willing to Walk In

But they did not understand because they did not want to. So many don't want to walk in the light, and they turn away and are lost forever. "Who then can be saved?"[15] His hearers began to murmur and grumble as many do today. God knows when they grumble. Like the children of Israel, they often perish in the wilderness and are destroyed of the destroyers. (See 1 Corinthians 10:10.) Many thousands of those people who were saved and had all those blessings turned away and never followed the Son of God any more. Jesus looked at the few left and His heart must have been broken for those who were so blind. And He is today looking sorrowfully at His followers, for so many are backslidden and going off into delusions—it is the sifting time as never before. There must needs be also heresies among you, that they that are approved may be manifest among you (1 Corinthians 11:19, paraphrased).

God is looking at us and especially those who are baptized—"Will ye also go away?"[16] Will you also forsake Me? Will you also turn back, or will you go forward all the way?

Peter said, "To whom shall we go? We cannot find a better way. This has been a glorious way and we are willing to go all the way. And besides, thou alone hast the words of eternal life."[17] We don't

[13]See John 4:13-14.

[14]See Isaiah 12:3.

[15]See Matthew 19:25, Mark 10:26, and Luke 18:26.

[16]John 6:67.

[17]See John 6:68.

guess, but we know of a truth that thou art the Christ, the Son of the living God.

Jesus said, "What, and if ye shall see the Son of man ascend up where He was before?" He wanted to show them the mighty power of the Holy Ghost, of the resurrection life, and that the saints would go up by the same power.[18] "I am the living bread that cometh down from heaven. He that eateth me shall live by me and if he continues to eat he will never die spiritually."[19]

He said to the few who remained, "Will ye also go away?"

And they answered, "We know of a truth that thou art the Christ, the Son of the living God, that you have been telling us about." Glory to God!

Dear friends, God's people were always the least in number of all the peoples on earth. He said to the children of Israel, "I did not choose you because you were the wisest people or the wealthiest people, but you were the fewest of all the people of the earth." (See Deuteronomy 7:7.) I have called you, chosen you, and put My love upon you.

We find the previous followers of the Lord always diminished instead of increased. We find from the beginning of Bible history at the time of the Flood when the ark finally floated away, only a few, that is eight souls, had faith enough to enter into the ark; and all the rest went down in destruction to an awful doom. They saw the mighty signs and wonders, but they would not believe God. They laughed at the signs and thought Noah was a fool and that the ark was the craziest building they ever saw. They turned away after having had the light.[20]

Even at the great conflagration on the plains, when the judgment of God and the fire of God came down and destroyed those proud cities of Sodom and Gomorrah, God sent two angels from heaven to warn them; yet only three souls escaped to the mountains.[21] Others

[18]See John 6:62-69.

[19]John 6:57-58, paraphrased.

[20]See Genesis 6-8.

[21]See Genesis 19:1-16.

had the chance and they too had the opportunity of salvation, but they turned back and took the wrong way. God showed and offered mercy first until finally His mercy ceased. They had lost their opportunity, and judgment followed. Judgment always followed and always will follow the backslider who refuses to obey God. It is judgment unto death. Where Christ is, they never can go. Yes, we find all through the Word of God there were only a few. Before the destruction of Jerusalem, they had the call; they all had a chance, but not many escaped.[22]

Only a Few Qualify to Be Chosen

Now I turn again to our text. After these multitudes went back and there were only twelve left, the question was asked by our Lord Jesus. "Will ye also go away?" As to the rest, they never followed Him anymore; we never hear anything more of them. These people had been saved, but they did not follow the Son anymore. "It had been better for them not to have known the way of righteousness, than, after they have known it, to turn from the holy commandment delivered unto them" (2 Peter 2:21).

After Christ rose from the dead, He appeared to His disciples. He asked for fish and ate it in their presence; called Thomas to come and put his finger into His side and proved to them that He had the same body that was laid in the grave. At many different times He appeared to them in order to remove every doubt and prove He was indeed the risen Christ, the Son of the living God, who would soon ascend back to God where He was before. Several different times He met with them; at one time He was seen of over five hundred disciples—after He arose from the dead.[23] Many believe it was at this time that He ascended on high; that He went out on the mountain and talked to them for the last time and gave the Last Commission. They watched Him ascend up into heaven, until the angels appeared and said, "Why stand ye gazing up into heaven? this same Jesus, which is taken up from you into heaven, shall so come in like manner as ye have seen him go into heaven."[24]

[22]See Matthew 23:37-39.

[23]See Matthew 28:9,16-17; Mark 16:9,12,14; Luke 24:15,34,36; and John 20:14,19,26, and 21:1-14.

[24]Acts 1:11.

They remembered that He had charged them: Don't preach sermons or teach the people or do anything, but tarry at Jerusalem until ye be endued with power from on high.[25] Glory to God! I want you to see that Christ wanted to select men and women to set up His spiritual kingdom. He wanted to qualify them to establish the Holy-Ghost religion in the world. But after all they had seen and heard and after these five hundred had seen Jesus and were thoroughly convinced that He was the Son of God, even then there were only one hundred and twenty out of the five hundred (to say nothing about any of the rest) who really believed and were willing to "face the music"—to bear death or anything else—until God qualified and sent them out. See how His work had diminished after He was taken.

Only a Few Gave Heed

God help you to see whose fault it was that they did not all come up there and tarry to be initiated into the Holy Ghost baptism and the secrets of heaven. Only one hundred and twenty believed that God would fulfill the promise made hundreds of years before to the prophets and confirmed by Jesus. When the Day of Pentecost came, there were only a little company there with God to be qualified to establish the Holy-Ghost Church. They were saved and full of joy. They believed they would receive the Holy Ghost; therefore, they went back to Jerusalem and tarried, continually blessing and praising God until they were filled with joy.[26] Now you people who are seeking the baptism: get saved first, get filled with joy, get off the judgment seat; be of one accord, of one mind, and continue praising the Lord.

Christ's Church was set up in a blaze of Pentecostal power. Common, unlearned men and women went there trusting God, and the power of heaven came down. Suddenly, while they were praising and blessing God (they knew God was coming; and they were not criticizing as to how He would come, for they were willing to leave all that in His hands), suddenly they heard a sound from

[25] See Luke 24:49.

[26] See Acts 1 and 2.

heaven like a rushing mighty wind and the whole building was shaken and the tidal wave of God's Spirit from heaven filled the place. The power of God struck them and the Holy Ghost came and sat on each of them like tongues of fire.[27]

God was initiating them into the deep things of eternity and making them pillars in the Church of the living God. This was where and when the Church was organized and established, the Church of the Firstborn, glory to God! And these were all that the Lord had to depend on to establish the Church and spread the glad news of what had happened.

"You shall receive power after the Holy Ghost has come upon you, and then you shall know how to testify of Me; tell them in a way that people will believe, and I will be with you always; and when you preach the Word, you will see the signs of the living Christ right in your midst."[28] Glory to God! They began to preach the wonderful things, filled with the Holy Ghost; and the Lord Jesus Christ was with them. He was invisible. He was a coworker together with them, and He is working with His saints today. The Lord Jesus Christ confirms the Word with signs and wonders following.[29]

There Were Different Opinions About God's Work

But when the news went out and the crowds came to see what was taking place on the Day of Pentecost, they said these people are all drunk. They began to lie about the Holy Ghost and they have been lying about Him ever since. Peter referred to the old prophets and said, "You believe the prophets; hear what they say: 'This is that.' (Just what they said was coming, this is that which God said should take place in the last days). This which you see with the natural eye and which you hear—and we know they felt it—this is the power of God.[30] It is the Holy Ghost sent down from heaven." But the great company of people that had followed Him before and had seen the mighty miracles, refused to walk in the light.

[27]See Acts 2:3.

[28]Acts 1:8, paraphrased.

[29]See Mark 16:20.

[30]See Acts 2:16.

When we are born of the Spirit, we have some of the light of heaven in our souls. Jesus is giving us more light and giving us degrees of glory; and as long as we walk in that light, we shall have fellowship with one another, and the blood of Jesus Christ, His Son, cleanses us from all sin.[31] You are either going forward or backward. As long as we walk in that light, we have fellowship and love for each other and have a present salvation. But when we refuse to walk in the light, we go back and we lose that sweet fellowship with God and with the saints.

God is testing us just like He did the Jews and will continue to do so down to the end of the age. "Fear not, little flock; for it is your Father's good pleasure to give you the kingdom."[32] He said He would not come unless there was a falling away first.[33] God knows there is a falling away today. The Church of Jesus Christ was inaugurated in a blaze of glory and celestial fireworks, but she must be taken up in a greater blaze of glory. The Holy Ghost will continue to take us down into the deep things of God; and we shall be filled with all the fullness of God, with our garments white and our lamps brightly burning.

The Church will soon leave this world in a cloud of glory. God is calling out a people for a prepared place and preparing a people in the Church of the living God to finish up His work. She must be a glorious Church, pure and white, and clothed with the power of Almighty God: a prepared people; a peculiar nation; a called out nation, from all the nations of the earth; a separate nation; a holy priesthood; children of the living God—God's sons and daughters.[34]

So now the Lord is calling us to eat the strong meat, calling the saints of God to get deeper in Him.[35] They must be filled with the Holy Ghost and eat of the living bread. By continually eating we will never die spiritually. The time has come that we must have strong meat, and we must receive it or be left behind in the Great

---

[31]See 1 John 1:7.

[32]Luke 12:32.

[33]See 2 Thessalonians 2:3.

[34]See John 14:2-3, Titus 2:14, 1 Peter 2:9, and Ephesians 5:27.

[35]See Hebrews 5:12-14.

Tribulation that is coming. One calamity after another is sweeping over the earth. Unless we get deep in God, the waves and tribulations will sweep us away. Blessed is that servant, when Jesus comes to catch His bride away, whom He shall find giving the saints of God their meat in due season. The Gospel of the kingdom must be preached unto all nations, then shall the end come.[36] This Gospel must be backed up by mighty signs and wonders, people filled with the Holy Ghost and baptized in the fire.

People don't want to walk in the light, they don't like the way. People say, "We will be despised and called all kinds of names." If they can call us any worse than they did the Son of God, I'd like to know it. But if we suffer with Him, we shall reign with Him.[37] He has promised us everything in this life, with persecutions. We all want the good things, but not the persecutions. They that will live godly shall suffer persecutions.[38] Bless God, He is around us like a wall of fire. He that is in us and around us is more than he that is against us.[39]

Will you belong to the royal line, accept the invitation, and eat of the strong meat? Will you be baptized in the Holy Ghost? God help us to say, yes. Will you go up on the mountaintop and help make up the little flock who will fill the earth with a blaze of glory? For the wise, they that are deep, when Jesus comes, shall shine as the sun.[40] Those that are wise will put the sun in the shade. Don't you see how you can glorify God? He is coming in the glory of His Father, in the glory of all the angels, coming for His bride; and the saints that are alive in that day will be taken up alive. We shall not all sleep, but we shall all be changed.[41] Bless God. He makes our feet like hinds' feet, makes us jump and dance with joy with His resurrection power.[42]

---

[36]Matthew 24:14, paraphrased.

[37]See 2 Timothy 2:12.

[38]See Mark 10:30 and 2 Timothy 3:12.

[39]See Zechariah 2:5, Romans 8:31, and 1 John 4:4.

[40]See Daniel 12:3.

[41]See 1 Thessalonians 4:17 and 1 Corinthians 15:51.

[42]See Psalm 18:33.

Better the World Should Call Us Fools, Than God

But you say, "Oh! I would not be a fool!" But you are one already. I would rather be a fool for God than for the devil. To everyone that is not saved, he says, "Thou fool!" I would rather be one of God's wise little ones if all the people in the world called me a fool. But the wisdom of this world is foolishness in the sight of God.[43] The wisdom of this world shall perish.

Men are trusting in their money and education and all those things which have to do with this world instead of trusting in the arm of the Almighty God. All these things shall perish. I look at the Great White Throne, see the river of life, and see the wonderful things God is preparing. The things we see here shall perish, but the things we see in the spiritual will last forever. (See 2 Corinthians 4:18.) God will gather us up and take us where the people never get old, where there is no death nor harm, no children crying for bread, no prairie fires, and no wars. Bless God!

We are going, don't you want to join the procession? Don't you want to sell out, leave the City of Destruction and run from the storm?[44] Don't tarry in the plain, but escape for your life. Prepare to meet God. Prepare for the coming of the Lord, because He is coming soon. Let us not be foolish like the great company of those disciples who once had the light. Some had been healed, many had been saved and come to know that God is good.

"My Minister Does Not Believe That"

But people are saying today like they did then, "Have any of the priests believed?"

"No, not many."

"Well, I guess I won't then." Priests will go to hell and ministers, too, if they don't get right with God. Priests and ministers all have to go the same way through the little gate, wash in the fountain, and be made white, to get eternal life. If you expect to go up you

[43]See 1 Corinthians 3:19.

[44]An allusion to the city from which Christian runs in John Bunyan's *The Pilgrim's Progress.*

must tarry at your Jerusalem and be filled.[45] The Holy Ghost will quicken the mortal body and like David you will say, "For by thee I have run through a troop; by my God have I leaped over a wall."[46] Power to make you join in the holy dance!

Get out of the mud and run up the mountains, bless God![47] Let us get out of the mud and get cleaned up and dressed up for heaven. Join in the race for the prize. God is filling the people today. There are great degrees of glory, and everyone can take another degree and another and another (and they won't have to pay a lot of money either) until you come into the perfect image of Jesus Christ. But you say, "I don't want to give u[p] this and I don't want to give u[p] that." If you had any of the love of God in your heart, you would not want to do those things that are valueless and that mean death, because you would be a new creature.[48] Old things would pass away and everything would become new, but the trouble is you don't want to walk in the light.

Will They Laugh You Out of Heaven?

Many people see the light but they are too stubborn to walk in it. They say, "You don't want to go that way and be laughed at." Dear friends, what should you care? How many draw back through fear!—fear of being laughed at, fear you will lose your position or be thrown out of the synagogue. Bless God, they cannot turn you out of heaven. God is pouring out His Spirit and many have had the real Pentecostal power, but they are not willing to acknowledge it. They are not willing to go forward; therefore, they begin to draw back, sinning against light. While refusing to walk in the light, they get

[45] See Matthew 7:13 and Luke 13:24. "little gate"—A reference to the wicket gate in *The Pilgrim's Progress,* a gate that symbolizes the moment of assurance of salvation. "fountain"—A reference to the fountain in the Delectable Mountains in *The Pilgrim's Progress* where Christian washes after he escapes from the Doubting Castle and the Giant Despair.

[46] 2 Samuel 22:30 and Psalm 18:29.

[47] "mountains"—The Delectable Mountains of *The Pilgrim's Progress* where Christian learns from the shepherds how to live the Christian life.

[48] See 2 Corinthians 5:17.

leanness of soul. First thing you know if you fail to walk in the light, you cease to have fellowship with Jesus and one another; then the blood ceases to cleanse, and you begin to invent excuses to ease your own guilty conscience.[49]

You were not willing to acknowledge you did not know it all. Behold, I show you a new thing—you did not know it yesterday. Behold, I show you the new things from this day. Things you never knew before.[50] So many of us do not want to acknowledge that we don't know it all. We don't know anything as we ought to, and there is so much more for us to learn. Let us cut the shoreline, and get out where the Spirit lets us down into the deep things of God. So many people are not willing to walk in the light; that is chiefly why thousands of people who have come up against the Pentecostal movement have declared it was of the devil. When we refuse to walk in the light it is death to our souls, especially if we lay hands on the ark. It is spiritual death to that man's soul if he does not make it right.

They Look Unto Him and Are Radiant

A great many just born are being filled with God and baptized in the Holy Ghost, and God is revealing wonderful things to them. They are going on and on, thanking God for what they have and taking degrees in glory. Some are coming up through the press where everything is against them, all the devil's old rubbish. They are going upstream or toiling upward, and they will land on the mountaintop ready when Jesus comes to catch His bride away. But this is the sifting time.[51]

We find that after Jesus takes this little flock away, He will bring them back again on white horses. We are told that Jesus is coming back on a great white horse with a great army from heaven behind Him, all on white horses, the bride of Christ shouting "Glory to Him that bought us with His own blood." He takes them away from earth and takes them home to heaven and makes them kings

[49] See 1 John 1:6-7 and Psalm 106:15.

[50] See Isaiah 43:19.

[51] See Amos 9:9.

and priests to God, and they will reign with Him one thousand years.[52] And this little flock will be taken up very soon.

The time came at Pentecost when the few (out of many thousands) were willing to be called fanatics and God, true to His Word, owned and accepted them with a cloudburst of glory and filled their bodies with the Holy Ghost, when God spoke through them in other languages. They were ignorant, unlearned people; but God took possession and got hold of their tongues and spoke through them as He said, "For with stammering lips and another tongue will he speak to this people."[53] Yet for all that some don't want to hear. They could well afford to be laughed at and brought to death to have such a visitation from heaven and have God smile on them.

Gladly We Acclaim Him Worthy

He must become to us the fairest among ten thousand and the one altogether lovely.[54] We must be willing to leave everything and everyone on earth to follow Jesus. And the great holy Bridegroom is getting ready to come and take away His bride. "Fear not, little flock; for it is your Father's good pleasure to give you the kingdom."[55]

Are we going to backslide instead of walking in the light? Are we going to eat the strong meat, or are we going to say, "The way is too hard," and go off and grumble and growl and be lost forever? We are a royal line, king's daughters, a company of nobles, children of the living God who will go up, a great company. Everyone will be a king and priest. Bless God. We are going to ride on the white horses and come back to the Battle of Armageddon, but we must have the white robes on down here and follow the Lord wherever He goes.

If you are persecuted for Christ's sake, great is your reward in heaven. But if you are persecuted because you walk crooked, you ought to be persecuted enough to get down and get right. If you are wrong it will take persecution to get you right; but if you are a

[52]See Revelation 19:11,14; 5:12; 1 Thessalonians 4:17; Revelation 1:6; 5:10, and 20:4,6.

[53]Isaiah 28:11.

[54]See Song of Solomon 5:10,16.

[55]Luke 12:32.

child of God and those persecutions come, then you can look up and rejoice because great is your reward in heaven.[56]

Jesus is coming soon. He is giving you an invitation to the wedding, will you accept it? Will you be one of the little flock? The angels are holding back the four winds, and they are crying, "Shall we let loose?" No, not until we have sealed the servants of God with the seal of the living God in their foreheads.[57] Perhaps you are a servant of God; you want to be sealed, be baptized in the Spirit, filled with new life. And some of these days we will burst these earthly bonds and go up to meet the Lord in the air.[58] You that love Jesus will be tested.

God is asking us that question, "Will you also go away?" Is the way too hard? Is the price too great? Make up your mind you will stand on the rock. And if the whole world should leave, you will stand firm because Christ is and will be sufficient. We are going to be tested as never before. It is going to be harder every day, even among the people of God if only because so many false teachers are coming in. It is a day of delusion—all kinds of delusions are coming. Keep under the blood, keep white, keep holy, keep pure, and God will give us wisdom. Glory to God!

Taken from *Spirit-Filled Sermons.*

---

[56]See Matthew 5:10-12 and Mark 10:30.

[57]See Revelation 7:1-3.

[58]See 1 Thessalonians 4:17.

God's Work, His Acts, His Strange Acts

Tarry ye and wonder; cry ye out and cry; they are drunken but not with wine; they stagger, but not with strong drink.[1]

Behold, I will proceed to do a marvellous work among this people, even a marvellous work and a wonder: for the wisdom of their wise men shall perish, and the understanding of their prudent men shall be hid.[2]

Whom shall he teach knowledge? and whom shall he make to understand doctrine? them that are weaned from the milk, and drawn from the breasts. . . . For with stammering lips and another tongue will he speak to this people. . . . For the Lord shall rise up as in mount Perazim, he shall be wroth as in the valley of Gibeon, that he may do his work, his strange work; and bring to pass his act, his strange act. Now therefore be ye not mockers, lest your bands be made strong: for I have heard from the Lord God of hosts a consumption, even determined upon the whole earth.[3]

Right through these chapters God is speaking of the outpouring of the Holy Ghost and the latter rain and those who mock and make light of this wonderful work of God. The Jewish people despised this work of God and thereby sealed their own doom as a nation, and it was not long before judgment came upon them. In these last days it applies to us with more force. God is doing a marvelous and wonderful work amongst the people and those who make light and despise it will be given over to believe a lie. Despising these works is committing the unpardonable sin.[4]

[1] Isaiah 29:9, paraphrased.

[2] Isaiah 29:14.

[3] Isaiah 28:9,11, and 21-22.

[4] See Matthew 12:31-32.

At the time that Jerusalem was destroyed, the people that had received this wonderful baptism had the mark of God upon them. God gave them a sign that He was coming and by the Holy Ghost [would] lead His people out into a place in the country, where they were kept in perfect safety, so that there was not one of them [who] went down in the awful massacre.

So in these last days, those who sigh and cry are sealed with the Holy Ghost and are getting ready to take a flight in the golden chariots in the air, and not one of them will be left to go through the Great Tribulation. Of the rest that will go over to the Antichrist and his army, two-thirds of them will go down in the pestilences, storms, earthquakes, etc.[5]

The "strange work" mentioned in the text is the work of the Holy Ghost: His strange work, like when Joshua commanded the sun and moon to stand still. Woe to ye mockers lest ye go over the deadline: for I have heard from the Lord God of hosts a consumption determined on the whole earth. God will make a speedy riddance of these things. Through calamities God is warning the people. The display of the Holy Ghost power indicates that there is some crisis at hand.

Of all the wise men in the Sanhedrin, there was not one who acknowledged that Jesus was coming or acknowledged Him when He did come. None of those wise men understood it. Whom shall I send? Who will stand in the gap? To whom shall I give knowledge?[6] Those just converted, just weaned; those who cannot boast of their learning.

The Jews were confounded and astonished. Their education and talents did not amount to anything in the presence of the Holy Ghost. They said, "What does it mean anyway? Are they not ignorant men?" God spake with men of other lips and other tongues, yet for all that they would not believe.[7] It shows that the heavenly power will take full control of the whole body of those that God is

[5] See Matthew 24.

[6] An allusion to Isaiah 6:8, Ezekiel 22:30, and Jeremiah 6:10.

[7] See Acts 2.

going to work with, and make them in some things like drunken men, and that they would speak with other tongues and lips. So today it is the same way. The deep things of God are a sealed book to those that are lost; but the Holy Ghost searches the deep things of God and reveals them to us; God wants a people who understand His Word as He intended it should be understood.[8]

This is God's time for people to get ready to go up when Jesus comes, for them to get the baptism of the Holy Ghost. "Who[m] shall I send?"[9] God takes the weak things. David was the least in his father's house.[10] Gideon was the weakest in his father's house.[11] Paul says God has chosen the weak things that their faith may not stand in the oratory, eloquence, and wisdom of men that they have learned, but in the power of God.[12]

The last thing that will be done before Jesus comes is to scatter the power of the holy people. "Ye shall have power after that the Holy Ghost has come upon you."[13] The acts of the apostles was God working through the clay. It was His strange work, giving the Jews the last call, and they turned away and rejected it. So today, though people do not mock at an earthquake, they do at the power of God. Don't mock lest your bands be made strong, lest you commit the unpardonable sin.[14]

There is one point that I never could understand until God showed me. That is why the hundred and twenty on the Day of Pentecost began to speak in tongues. The speaking in tongues comes by faith, and I did not see that they were taught so as to have faith for this manifestation. The facts are that they were well taught on this point, for not only had Jesus told them (Mark 16:17) that they were to speak in tongues, but He also taught them to believe according to the Old Testament scriptures. The New Testament scriptures

[8] See 1 Corinthians 2:9-14.

[9] Isaiah 6:8.

[10] See 1 Samuel 16:11-12.

[11] See Judges 6:15.

[12] See 1 Corinthians 1:27-29.

[13] Acts 1:8, paraphrased.

[14] See Isaiah 28:22.

were not then written. "In the last day, that great day of the feast, Jesus stood and cried, saying, If any man thirst, let him come unto me, and drink" (John 7:37). That is, be born of the Spirit. And then what? "He that believeth on me, *as the scripture hath said,* out of his belly shall flow rivers of living water. (But this spake he of the Spirit, which they that believe on him should receive: for the Holy Ghost was not yet given: because that Jesus was not yet glorified.)" (John 7:38-39, emphasis by Etter).

Notice, "as the scripture hath said" refers to the scriptures I have already read, where Isaiah says, "With stammering lips and another tongue will He speak to this people" (Isaiah 28:11). Many have believed and received wonderful blessings and been greatly used; but being untaught on this point they could not believe "as the scriptures hath said," and so never spoke in other tongues.

"Faith comes by hearing."[15] They had heard and were well taught by Jesus and, being familiar with the Scripture, tarried, and believed until "they were all filled with the Holy Ghost, and began to speak with other tongues."[16] And now in the next verse (Isaiah 28:12), what does God say about this fullness of the Spirit that causes one to stammer and speak in tongues? Hear it: "This is the rest wherewith ye may cause the weary to rest; and this is the refreshing: yet they would not hear." After the sinner is saved, he finds a wonderful rest, and then if he reads the Scripture and believes, it will lead him into the baptism in the Holy Ghost, which is the rest that remaineth for the children of God.[17] Isaiah says so in the scripture just quoted.

"I proceed to do a marvelous work," saith the Lord. There are two classes of people; the one will glorify God and the other, fight. The law puts wonderful force on the speaking in other tongues. "In the law it is written, With men of other tongues and other lips will I speak unto this people; and yet for all that will they not hear me, saith the Lord" (1 Corinthians 14:21). Paul refers to the scripture

[15] Romans 10:17, paraphrased.

[16] Acts 2:4.

[17] See Hebrews 4:9.

in Isaiah. He says, "yet for all that," showing God puts much force on it.

The one hundred and twenty had faith because they had read the Scriptures and were familiar with what they read. Jesus said, "You are going to get the baptism, I am going to pour out the Holy Ghost."

Jesus said, "He shall bear witness and testify of me."[18] The Holy Ghost gives utterance, He is testifying of Jesus. "Devout men out of every nation were gathered there, and they said, 'They all speak in the language of our own native home.'"[19] They all heard them speak of the *wonderful* works of God. Before Peter preached, *God preached* to them in other tongues.

The Holy Ghost, when He comes in this way, testifies of Christ. About the first thing He says is, "Jesus is coming soon." The tongues are the sign of His coming soon. Peter said, "This that you hear and see."

> This is that which was spoken by the prophet Joel; And it shall come to pass in the last days, saith God, I will pour out of my Spirit upon all flesh: and your sons and your daughters shall prophesy, and your young men shall see visions, and your old men shall dream dreams: And on my servants and on my handmaidens I will pour out in those days of my Spirit; and they shall prophesy.[20]
>
> In the law it is written, With men of other tongues and other lips will I speak unto this people; and yet for all that they will not hear me, saith the Lord.
>
> 1 Corinthians 14:21

Those that God uses to turn the world upside down are all like a lump of clay in the potter's hand. Shall the vessel say, "You have not made me a vessel to suit me"?[21]

When any great and important machinery is invented in these days, they always have some power to move it; and your body is the

---

[18] See John 15:26.

[19] See Acts 2:5-8.

[20] Acts 2:16-18.

[21] See Isaiah 45:9.

temple of the Holy Ghost.[22] God sends the third person of the Trinity to take possession of this powerhouse. When God works through us, let us be passive and thank Him that He uses us at all.

The wisdom of this world is foolishness in the eyes of God, but *we speak the wisdom of God*. The wise of this world did not know Jesus and therefore He said to them, "Behold, your house is left unto you desolate."[23]

The wisdom of this world is perishing. I would rather have a thimbleful of God's wisdom than all the wisdom of this world today.

We are a people to be wondered at. "Here am I and the children thou hast given me."[24] We are for signs and wonders in Israel, from the Lord God that dwelleth in Zion or among His people.[25] "Behold the heaven of heavens cannot contain Him."[26] You cannot build a building large enough to contain the Lord, and yet He does come down and dwells in these temples.

To say there is no joy in the religion of the Lord is a lie. We are often talking of going to heaven; but I am trying to bring heaven down to you that you may have a heaven to go to heaven in, for we are workers together with Christ.

"And the Lord was with them."[27] I thought you said He went to heaven? He did in person, but He was present in Spirit. The Lord was with them and when they worked and preached, God put His sign on it, as He does here. Every time you see a miracle, it is God putting His seal on the Word preached.

God Gave the Gifts and Signs to His Church

> For the perfecting of the saints, for the work of the ministry, for the edifying of the body of Christ.
>
> Ephesians 4:12

[22]See 1 Corinthians 6:19.

[23]Matthew 23:38.

[24]John 17:9, paraphrased.

[25]Isaiah 8:18, paraphrased.

[26]See 2 Chronicles 6:18.

[27]Acts 11:21, paraphrased.

I am glad I am one of those who need these things and must have them. You people in this tent night after night see this marvelous work and wonder like those that God spake of through Isaiah the prophet. You see men and women staggering and falling like dead people; you see men and women carried in dying, get up and shout and run and walk; those born deaf and dumb healed; you hear men and women and children speak in other tongues and sing heavenly music, and yet for all that some of you will not believe.

I proceed to do a marvelous work. Yet some of you won't believe, but are stiff-necked. But praise God, some of the weakest ones get the baptism. This is the refreshing. (See Acts 3:19.)

God is pouring out His Spirit all over the world today. When the Holy Ghost came He would witness by speaking in other tongues. God does many works, but this is a marvelous one.

The Lord showed us that that is how the apostles got the light that the Holy Ghost would speak in other tongues. I never before understood how the apostles spake in tongues, as they come by faith, but now I see it plainly. "He that believeth on me, as the scripture hath said, our of his belly shall flow rivers of living water" (John 7:38).

There are so many gifts for us all—salvation, divine healing, wisdom, love, and power. "In the law it is written, With men of other tongues and other lips will I speak unto this people; and yet for all that they will not hear me, saith the Lord" (1 Corinthians 14:21).

God is sending His angels, His baptized people, with a great sound of the trumpet to gather His elect together, His people who have made a covenant with God by sacrifice, who have given up or sacrificed everything that stands in the way of their being caught away in the rapture and doing all they can to help others to get ready, blowing the trumpet—preaching in the power of the Holy Ghost with the outpouring of the Spirit on the people and the acts and signs and wonders and miracles manifested in the congregation before sinners, the world, and the saints.

The last thing to be done before the rapture is this power must be seen scattered among the saints everywhere. We must not only talk and say we ought to have these demonstrations, but we must produce the goods. The signs must be many and more wonderful than ever in the world, that the household of faith may be perfected, led into the baptism, and sealed with the knowledge to class us among the wise who shall shine as the firmament, that by these visible signs that they see and hear and feel, the lost world will get its last warning.

In the midst of these signs of the glory and presence of God, many will call on Him and be saved before the great and notable Day of the Lord comes, and those who turn away and reject will have no excuse. Amidst all the acts and wonders of the workings of the Spirit, the speaking in other tongues seems to be God's last or greatest warning to sinners, and it is a sign to unbelievers.[28] Hear His voice from heaven, "For with stammering lips and other tongues will I speak to this people, and yet *for all that* they will not believe me." It is a sign to all that Jesus is coming soon.

The Lord is doing His marvelous work here in Dallas. At every meeting the tent looks like a battlefield. Men, women, and children struck down and lying all around like dead men and speaking in tongues; angels seen by many; Jesus seen up over the people in bright glory; stars and great lights in and over the tent. This is going out and will go all over the world, growing in power till Jesus comes.

> Behold, I will do a new thing; now it shall spring forth; shall ye not know it?
>
> Isaiah 43:19

> Behold, the former things are come to pass, and new things do I declare: before they spring forth I tell you of them.
>
> Isaiah 42:9

Taken from *Acts of the Holy Ghost.*

[28] See 1 Corinthians 14:22.

Dancing in the Spirit Is Victory

Has a Place in the Church—Is the Expression of Holy Joy

avid danced with all his might before the Lord.[1] There is much in the Word about dancing. Where dancing in the Bible is mentioned, it always signifies victory for the Lord's hosts. It was always done to glorify God. The Lord placed the Spirit of power and love of the dance in the Church; and wherever the Scripture speaks of dancing, it implies that they danced by inspiration and were moved by the Spirit; and the Lord was always pleased and smiled His approval. But the devil stole the dance away and made capital of it.

In these last days when God is pouring out His Spirit in great cloudbursts and tidal waves from the floodgates of heaven and the great river of life is flooding our spirit and body and baptizing us with fire and resurrection life and divine energy, the Lord is doing His acts, His strange acts, which include dancing in the Spirit and speaking in other tongues and many other operations and gifts. The Holy Ghost is confirming the last message of the coming King, with great signs and wonders and miracles.

Dancing Has a Place in the Church

If you read carefully what the Scripture says about dancing, you will be surprised and will see that singing, music, and dancing have a humble and holy place in the Lord's Church:

> Let them praise his name in the dance: let them sing praises unto him with the timbrel and harp.
>
> Psalm 149:3

[1] See 2 Samuel 6:14.

> Praise him with the timbrel and dance: praise him with stringed instruments and organs.
>
> Psalm 150:4

> Then shall the virgin rejoice in the dance, both young men and old together.
>
> Jeremiah 31:13

"David danced before the Lord with all his might" (2 Samuel 6:14). His wife did not like it. She scolded him and made light of him; said he was dancing before the maidens like a lewd fellow; made out as if he was base and low. He answered, "I was not dancing before men, but before the Lord,"[2] showing that he had lost sight of the world and what they thought or said and was moved and controlled entirely by the Holy Ghost for the glory of God. All the great company were blessed but Michal, and she was stricken with barrenness till the day of her death.[3] So you see, she sinned making light of the power of God in the holy dance and attributed it to the flesh or the devil, just as some do today. They always lose out, and many are in darkness till death.

The Spirit of God Prompts the Dancing

The news of David's great victory (how before he became king, he had killed the giant Goliath and destroyed the great army of the Philistines) spread quickly over the land; and as David returned from the slaughter, the women came out of all the cities of Israel, singing and dancing, to meet the king with joy and playing on instruments of music.[4]

Now notice, in all their cities the women went out in the streets and danced with their music. Men are not mentioned there, just maidens and women danced unto the Lord in honor of God and David. They were prompted by the Spirit of God to praise him in the dance. It took courage to honor David in this way, but the Lord

[2] 2 Samuel 6:21, paraphrased.

[3] See 2 Samuel 6:23.

[4] See 1 Samuel 18:6.

smiled His approval by having it written by holy men of old and sent down to us in His precious Word.

> And he stood up, and leaped and praised God.
>
> Acts 3:8, paraphrased

> [Paul] said with a loud voice, Stand upright on thy feet. And he leaped and walked.
>
> Acts 14:10

> And Miriam the prophetess . . . took a timbrel in her hand; and all the women went out after her with timbrels and with dances. And Miriam answered them, Sing ye to the Lord, for he hath triumphed gloriously; the horse and his rider hath he thrown into the sea.
>
> Exodus 15:20-21

God has never done a greater miracle nor demonstrated His presence in so great a cloud of glory as at this time. While under the inspiration and light of His presence, their whole bodies and spirits [were] going out in love, the whole multitude of women, Miriam the prophetess and leader, leading them forth to praise the Lord with dancing, shouting, and music, singing a new song just given by the Spirit that had never been sung before. Do you call that foolishness? No, they were praising the Lord in the dance and song as they were moved by the mighty power of God.

Music Is Heard From Invisible Instruments

Moses also led the hosts in the same way, with music and dancing and a new song given for the occasion by the Spirit. So the Holy Ghost is falling on the saints of God today, and they are used in the same way. Those who never danced one step are experts in the holy dance, and those who do not know one note from another are expert musicians in playing many different instruments. Often the sound of invisible instruments from the platform is heard all over the house. And I say in the fear and presence of God, the singing and demonstration put fear of God on the people and cause a holy hush to come over the congregation. The strange acts are coming more and more, showing that Jesus is coming soon; and the Lord is getting His bride ready to be translated and dance and play at the great marriage of the Lamb, which will soon take place for the bride is making herself ready.

The Dance Gives Expression to Holy Joy

Jesus told us about a certain man whose prodigal son returned home. His elder son was in the field, and as he came near the house he heard music and dancing (Luke 15:25). He asked, "What does all this mean?"

They said, "Thy brother has come home, and thy father has killed the fatted calf, because he has received him safe and sound." And he was angry and would not go in, but the feast and rejoicing went on just the same.

The father said, "It was meet that we should be merry and rejoice for thy brother who was dead is alive again and was lost and is found."[5]

All will agree with me, this was intended by our Lord to prefigure and describe an old-fashioned, Holy-Ghost revival where at least one soul has been saved. The lost son is a sinner whom the Spirit brought out of darkness into light; the saints are filled with the Spirit, rejoicing because of his regeneration.

I was very slow to accept the dancing in the Spirit for fear it was in the flesh, but I soon saw it was the "cloud of glory" over the people that brought forth the dancing and playing of invisible instruments. The sounds of sweet, heavenly music could often be heard. Several times I asked that those of the congregation who had heard this music from the platform (where they knew there were no instruments to be seen) to be honest and raise their hands. Many hands went up from saints and sinners.

The stillness of death went over the people when they heard the sounds of music accompanied with the heavenly choir. Often a message in tongues was given in one or more languages and the interpretation. As I saw the effect on the people by the Holy Ghost

[5] See Luke 15:26-32.

in convincing them that they were in the presence of God, I concluded that this is surely the Lord's strange work and His strange acts. I saw as many as nine of the most noted ministers dancing at one time on the platform; they danced singly, with their eyes closed. Often some fell, slain by the mighty power of God. These things convinced me.

I also saw men and women who have been crippled join in the dance with wonderful grace. One lady who had been walking on crutches five years and who got healed in her seat afterwards danced over the platform, singing heavenly music. The virgins, the young men, and the old men all join in the dance together. Praise the Lord. "Let us be glad and rejoice, and give honour to him: for the marriage of the Lamb is come, and his wife hath made herself ready" (Revelation 19:7). The Lord is quickening our mortal bodies, an earnest of the translation.

Taken from *Spirit-Filled Sermons.*

[6] See Romans 8:11.

VISIONS

VISIONS AND TRANCES

Visions Are Promised by God

Where there is no vision, the people perish.

Proverbs 29:18

This fact has been proven all through the Bible. When the people of God were true and faithful, the Lord made known His presence *by* visible signs and revealed Himself and many things to them in visions. Then they always prospered in every way, and the fear of God fell upon the heathen nations; and they fled before them and cried out, "There is no God like the God of Israel;"[1] and God's cause was glorified in the earth.

But when they were backsliders and disobedient, God hid His face. There were no visions and the people perished in every way. They went on from one sin to another, substituting form and solemn feast and outward offering, polluted sacrifices; and trusting to human wisdom and works, instead of the power and Spirit of God.

People Without Visions in Darkness

Then He took away His Spirit and visions and signs of His presence. They were left in darkness over three hundred years till Christ came, and then they did not know Him. They crucified the Lord of glory and turned loose a murderer on helpless women and children.[2] Nearly the whole Jewish nation perished. All this happened because they would not be led of the Spirit of God.

When the new and living way was ushered in, the Lord gave many visions to show that Christ had come; that the Son of God was on earth; that no one need perish, but whosoever would be born of the Spirit, Christ would come and dwell in them and abide with them forever and manifest and reveal Himself to them through the Holy Ghost. The Holy Ghost would glorify Him by revealing the things of God to us and by showing us things to come.[3]

[1] See 2 Kings 5:15, Psalm 126:2, and Ezekiel 39.

[2] See Mark 15:7-15 and 1 Corinthians 2:8.

[3] See John 16:13.

On the Day of Pentecost, when the Holy Ghost was seen, heard, and felt, thousands were brought into the spiritual kingdom of God. Peter stood up in a blaze of Holy-Ghost power and glory and said when God poured out His Spirit on His sons and daughters, they would see visions and dream dreams and prophesy. He told them that these signs would be sure to follow the outpourings of the Spirit.[4]

The Lord said to Miriam, "If there be a prophet among you, I the Lord will make myself known unto him in a vision, and will speak unto him in a dream."[5]

Moses said, "Would to God all the Lord's people were prophets and all would prophesy."[6]

Peter says we will all prophesy when we have the Spirit of God, and visions is one of the signs that we have the Spirit.[7]

The Lord says if we are prophets He will make Himself known in visions. The heathen, or Gentiles, were perishing; they knew nothing of the religion of Jesus. God used two visions to bring about a great revival, where the whole congregation was converted and filled with the glory of God. This was the first Holy-Ghost revival among the heathens. It was a sample of all that was to follow. When the people saw the visible signs of the presence of God in their midst and He revealed Himself to them, everyone felt they were in the presence of God; and sinners came rushing to the loving arms of Christ and were saved from the awful doom that awaits the unsaved.

"Where there is no vision, the people perish."[8] Those who are opposing the demonstration of the Spirit today say we do not need these things; we are progressing with the age; we want an intellectual religion; we must explain and present the Word from a human standpoint, in a scientific way.[9]

---

[4] See Acts 2:17-18.

[5] Numbers 12:6.

[6] Numbers 11:29, paraphrased.

[7] See Acts 2:17-18.

[8] Proverbs 29:18.

[9] Maria Etter refers here to the textual studies of the biblical texts that were receiving a great deal of attention in the universities during the nineteenth century. Many scholars questioned the existence of miracles in the Bible in these studies.

In these last days the masses of so-called religious teachers belong to the class, Paul said, who have a form of godliness but deny the power. From such, turn away.[10] They will not endure sound doctrine; will turn the people away from the truth.[11]

These false teachers are in a worse condition than the Jews were. They are sinning against much greater light. They are willingly blind and are teaching their followers to hide behind a refuge of lies, trusting to doctrines and traditions of men which are vain worship.[12]

The judgments of God in the most awful way are coming upon the false church.

God Chooses to Give Visions

We might say they did not need these visions in the revival at Corinth. Why did not the Lord call all the apostles and the thousands of holy men and women who were filled with the Holy Ghost together and let them do the work? No, He was going to show them, and us, that it is not by human power, wisdom, or a great multitude, but by His power and Spirit that the people must be saved. They knew nothing about the great work till it was over and the waves of salvation swept all over the country till they reached the apostles.

It was four days from the time of Cornelius' vision till Peter came with six Jewish brethren. The news of the wonderful vision and that such a servant of God was coming to lead them to Christ, spread. They believed that God had been in their midst and was coming in great power to save. They were convinced and convicted; left all their work and came together; were just waiting for the kingdom of heaven to come in their hearts with power and glory.[13]

Some say Peter did all this mighty work. God did it all, through the Holy Ghost. Peter only preached one sermon. He preached that

[10] See 2 Timothy 3:5.

[11] See 2 Timothy 4:3-4.

[12] Mark 7:7.

[13] See Acts 10:30-33..

repentance and faith in a living, risen Christ would bring a present salvation and a living Christ in their hearts to abide with them forever.

The Wisdom of God Is Foolish to the Unsaved

The ways and wisdom of God are foolishness to the unsaved, but God hath revealed them to His chosen ones; yea, the deep things of God![14] Oh, praise the Lord for the wisdom and knowledge, the fellowship and presence of the Lord who lives and walks with us continually.

Stephen was not an apostle, but he was full of faith and the Holy Ghost; and we all are commanded to be filled with the same power.[15] He did great miracles among the people. When he so nobly defended the risen Christ, fearless of losing his life, his false accusers looked on his face and said it looked like the face of an angel.[16]

The pure Gospel accompanied by the power of the Holy Ghost cut them to the heart. They would not accept it and they rushed upon him with their teeth. (See Acts 7:54-56.) "But he, being full of the Holy Ghost, looked up stedfastly into heaven, and saw the glory of God, and Jesus standing on the right hand of God, and said, Behold, I see the heavens opened, and the Son of man standing on the right hand of God [vv. 55-56]."

Saul, who was one of the best scholars of his day and had a polished form of religion, would not believe in or accept visions or visible demonstrations of the power of God; so when he saw the glory of God and heard Stephen tell the wonderful vision he had seen, when the howling mob gathered around, Saul helped them on and consented to his death.[17]

God Definitely Deals with Saul

Now the great persecution commenced. Saul, like a bloodhound who had got the smell of blood, followed the trail, filling the prisons, and putting the saints to death. (See Acts 26:10-12.)

[14] See 1 Corinthians 1:18 and 2:10.

[15] See Ephesians 5:18.

[16] See Acts 6:15.

[17] See Acts 8:1.

While on his way to Damascus to take the saints from prison to put them to death, about noon, when the sun was shining in all its strength, this man who did not believe in the visible power of God said he saw a light from heaven above the brightness of the sun "shining round about me and them which journeyed with me."[18] He and all of his party were struck to the earth as dead men. There was no loud praying or singing or religious excitement to put these strong men in that condition. God had sent a shock from the battery of heaven.

Saul, who had hated demonstrations of the Spirit, saw at once he was lost and on the way to hell. The Lord showed him while lying under the power of the Holy Ghost that he must preach the Gospel; and wherever he went, he must tell about all he had seen and heard and things that the Lord would show to him in the future. Jesus appeared to him, then and talked to him face-to-face and many times after in visions.[19]

The Lord used three visions to bring about the conversion of Saul, one of the brightest scholars of the Jewish church. He was under deep conviction, neither ate nor drank for three days and nights. He counted the cost. When he accepted Christ he was filled with the Holy Ghost. The first thing he did was to preach a living Christ and to throw open the prisons and stop the awful persecution and show the despised followers of Jesus that he was their friend and brother.[20] The churches all had rest, and the waves of salvation swept over all the land. See the glorious results to the Church and the world. All brought about by three visions. Where there is no vision the people perish.

Paul never doubted the power of God nor any demonstration. He knew more about the personality of the Holy Ghost and His many offices, gifts, visions, revelations, diverse operations, leadings, teachings, and power and taught more about these things than any or all the rest of the apostles; and he proved clearly that all this power would be for the people of God forever.

---

[18] Acts 26:13.

[19] See Acts 26:16, 16:9, and 18:9.

[20] See Acts 9:19-20.

The Book of Visions

The book of Revelations is (*sic*) the most wonderful of all in the Bible. Christ appeared to John in person and gave him one vision after another. He showed him the heavenly city, the great city, the city of gold, and the jasper walls. The city lieth four squares—fifteen hundred miles high, as long and wide as it was high; told about the climate, the inhabitants, their occupations. He had visions of the Great Judgment Day, of the lake of fire and brimstone and all the lost swept into it. The Lord told him to write all that he saw and heard and show it to the churches, and they were to show it to the world.

The prophet said the time would come, if anyone had a vision, when they would be ashamed to tell it.[21] That time is here. The masses of church leaders look upon everything supernatural as a disgrace and cry out, "hypnotism!" "excitement!" "drunkenness!" or some other power. Just like the Jews, progressing with the age, they are satisfied with dead form.

The churches are filled with unconverted people. *Where there are no visions the people perish. If there is not power enough for visions, there is not enough to save a soul.*

Visions Are Promised by God

The gift of visions was especially promised in the last days.

> And it shall come to pass in the last days, saith God, I will pour out my Spirit upon all flesh: and your sons and your daughters shall prophesy, and your young men shall see visions, and your old men shall dream dreams: And on my servants and on my handmaidens I will pour out in those days of my Spirit; and they shall prophesy.
>
> Acts 2:17-18

Thank the Lord, those days are here; and God is revealing Himself to those who come to Him in the right way in special gifts, in healing all manner of diseases, in all the fullness of the Holy-Ghost power. Hundreds are having wonderful visions; and wherever these signs follow the Word, all classes flock to Christ.

[21] See Zechariah 13:4.

Dr. Talmage[22] went into the Brooklyn tabernacle one Sunday morning and said to his congregation: "I have been to heaven; I have just got back and will tell you what I saw." The first one he met in heaven was his mother, who had been dead thirty-two years. He knew her and talked to her. He saw many he knew while here on earth and many were made known unto him that he had never known; saw white horses hitched to golden chariots standing at the doors of mansions, and others driving through streets, etc.

Many noted men and women and all classes of the children of God are bringing messages from heaven to earth. These things, with many other signs of the times, show us the Lord is coming soon for His saints and to punish a lost world. The Lord help those who profess to love Him to have enough of His Spirit to know the power of God!

Where there are no visions the people perish.

Paul says, while he was praying in the temple he fell into a trance. Paul said he would come to revelations and visions of the Lord. He was carried away to the third heaven. Whether in the body or out of the body, he could not tell, but God knew. He heard and saw wonderful things.[23]

That was a wonderful experience. He could not tell whether he was carried away soul and body or whether his spirit left the body for a while. But he was conscious of being carried away and knew it was the power of God. Paul said when the church came together, if anyone had a revelation, to tell it. (See 1 Corinthians 14:26).

Taken from *Life and Experience of Mrs. M. B. Woodworth-Etter.*

[22]Thomas Dewitt Talmage (1832-1902), a nineteenth-century preacher whose New York tabernacle hosted D. L. Moody and other evangelists.

[23]See Acts 22:17 and 2 Corinthians 12:1-4.

A Vision of the Coming of the Lord

n March 24th, 1904, when I fell under the operation of the power of God, while praying for the healing of the last one at the altar, I saw the Savior on the cross and sinners coming to Him. I saw steps leading across to the pearly gates of heaven. All those who plunged into the fountain were at once placed on the steps. Each one carried a light, which grew brighter as they went higher. There was not a spot of defilement on their robes. I was made to understand that they were the light of the world, that their lamps were lighted in heaven. They had Christ in their souls. Each one had a bodyguard of angels of God, escorting them on the upward journey. At the top of the steps were the pearly gates, where the heavenly hosts waited to welcome the pilgrims of earth.

I also saw that the world is in great darkness and that saints are very few. "Many are called but few chosen," or will accept.[1] Many were under conviction, but trusted to water baptism, to confirmation, or to church membership, but unless they are carrying the light from God, they are worse than an open sinner.

The whole world lies in great darkness, except just a few. I saw the preparation in heaven and earth for the soon coming of Christ. Heaven seemed to be in a commotion. The Lord was marshalling His hosts; getting the horses and chariots ready. The armies of heaven were moving; the gates were open. An angel came out of the gates blowing a great trumpet, the Savior was taking the lead with all the glory of heaven, shouting to the saints in a loud voice, *that awakened the dead.*

The Lord showed me He was judging His saints, separating the wheat from the tares, that the household of faith was getting their portion of meat in this, God's due season. The angel was sealing the last ones of the members of the bride with the seal of the living God. They were a little flock and the last one would soon be sealed,

[1] Matthew 20:16, paraphrased.

then the Lord would come in a cloud of glory to take His bride to the marriage feast, or supper.

God help all who read this vision to take warning and repent, for the judgment of God is at hand.

Another Remarkable Vision

While holding a revival in Fostina, Ohio, in March 1894, while in my bed I had a vision of God. I thought I was in a day meeting and was standing by the pulpit. Some man in the congregation spoke in a loud voice, saying, "Sister Woodworth, look at the hand above the door." I looked in that direction, and right above the door coming from the vestibule, I saw a large hand, wrist, and part of the arm. The wrist was bare for several inches. There was a soft, flowing sleeve that hung down about eight inches. It was white and very soft looking. The fingers were all bent a little, except the little and index fingers; they pointed out each way. The hand and arm were lovely. The sleeves and all were white and shining. The hand and arm moved about and pointed all over the congregation again and again, then pointed the index finger to me and waved the hand and fingers as if beckoning me, or calling me to come. The hand continued to move over the people, then pointed. Every eye saw the wonderful hand sight. I cried out in a loud voice, "Oh! That is the hand of God!"

There was a very large window on the same side of the house. The transom was open and a hand just like the other came through the transom and did just like the other, both warning and pointing the people to me. Both lovely hands pointed over the house, then to me. I cried out again and again, "Oh! That is the hand of God!" They both went away at once.

It seemed the congregation could not move. Then I said, "Oh! I believe it is the hand of God, and it means something wonderful to the people and especially to me." Just then I saw through the transom of the same window and clear up to heaven, a path twenty feet or more wide. It reached from heaven down and was full of stars and light. As I looked I saw one of the hands and nearly all of the arm with the flowing, soft sleeve come out of heaven and come down the shining path. Then it came across the window, through the transom without stopping, and over the congregation, with the index finger and arm pointing to me. The finger touched me on the forehead. The little finger or thumb, or both, touched my face. The hand and arm waved over me. I felt the everlasting arms and the soft sleeves around me. Everyone saw it then. It was straight across the congregation and out of the window and up to heaven without stopping. I cried out with a loud voice, "It is the hand of God. It was the everlasting arms." I said, "God is going to reveal Himself to me in a wondrous way, writing His laws on my mind with the finger of God. Perhaps He is soon going to take me home." For the devil came also to make me believe I was going to die, but I said, no.

The Lord showed me the vision is concerning the soon coming of Christ. The warning, the hands pointing over the people, then pointing them to me and to heaven, was God drawing the people to me to get light on the speedy coming of our Lord, and to get ready to meet Him; that it would be only a few years; that I would pass through several changes in my life and work; that would be for my good and the glory of God. This vision was not of Christ, but of God that inhabits eternity, the Father of our Lord and Savior, Jesus Christ. The great fatherhood and love of God was revealed to me as never before, as a personal God. God is as much person as Jesus Christ. Jesus said, "I am the express image of my Father's person."[2] God is a spirit form. He alone had immortality; but through Christ's obedience unto death on the cross, He brought life and immorality to light.[3]

It was the arm of God and the finger of God that touched my forehead. He showed me He would seal me with, and reveal unto me, the wisdom of God and the knowledge of His glorious plan of the ages; the winding up of this harvest; of the calling and preparation of the bride; of the soon coming of Christ, the Bridegroom; that the Gentile door will soon be closed; of the great time of trouble that will follow the Rapture of ascension of the bride.

All that are left will go down in, or through, this great day or time of trouble that the angel Gabriel told Daniel of—such as never was,

[2] See John 14:9. The phrase "express image" appears in Hebrews 1:3.

[3] See 2 Timothy 1:10.

or ever shall be again.[4] The whole world will be taken in a snare at the winding up of that awful time, with the great battle of God Almighty with the armies of earth, when He comes back with His saints to set up the glorious millennial kingdom, which will last one thousand years, when Christ and His bride shall judge the nations.[5]

In that vision the Lord gave me a special call for this work and to give the household of faith their meat in due season; to give the last call to the Gentile sinners, the last call to the marriage supper of the Lamb, for His wife is about ready to enter into the marriage relation, and the door will be closed never to be opened again; and to get those who have been called to be established, to be faithful and true, that they may be anointed with the Holy Ghost and with power, and sealed with the proper knowledge of His coming and of their great work during the millennial reign of one thousand years, when the saints shall judge the world and angels, when all the families of the earth shall be blessed.

The Lord showed me He would enlighten and reveal these things to me by His Word; through the Spirit He would write them in my forehead, or mind and heart. He touched my mouth with His thumb and finger, showing me He would put words in my mouth and give me wisdom to explain these things as fast as He gave them to me, that this was, and is, His due time when we must know these things. He put His loving arms around me, showing His loving care and protection, that He gave me a new lease of life for this word, which was to be devoted to this preparation work of warning the people and getting the bride ready.

I have been very near death several times, but the memory of the wonderful vision has inspired me to new life. I have been wonderfully enlightened during all these years. I understand all these things better every day, as God is leading me to separate the wheat from the tares with His Word and by His Spirit. Christ, the great reaper in white, clothed in power, is with me in this great harvest work. He gives me the light every day. The time is very short! The Lord is showing me many things on this line. I never loved the blessed,

[4] See Daniel 12:1 and Matthew 24:21.

[5] See 1 Corinthians 6:2.

loving Father so much as now. I never had an idea that His plans were so great and glorious. Oh! Praise His name forever.

The Lord revealed to me in this vision many vicissitudes and changes that I would pass through in the following four years of my life. These revelations have and are being fulfilled.

Notes in 1916

It has been fifteen years since the Lord gave me this vision. Read it carefully and see if you do not see the hand of God and know that God gave the vision. See how the Lord gave me courage to prophesy how He was going to use me to write another book and send it out quickly. In four months' time we had out ten thousand of the sixth volume of a new book called *The Acts of the Holy Ghost.*

This book has gone almost over the entire world and different parts of it have been translated into several languages, and the Lord has blessed the book far beyond all expectations, in enlightening and convicting and stirring up people of all classes to seek more of God. We get letters from all parts of the world asking for help for both soul and body. We get thousands of handkerchiefs, asking us to pray over them; and like God worked special miracles through the hands of Paul, insomuch that they sent handkerchiefs and aprons and they went out from Paul's body.[6] Devils were cast out and they were healed; so He is working today the same way, and we receive letters from across the seas and also from the Atlantic to the Pacific shouting, "Glory to God! I am healed and filled with God!"

Many times they are healed while we are praying for them, and many times while they are reading the letter, the power of God falls on them and they apply the handkerchief; they are healed immediately and very often they are converted, and some have received the baptism of the Holy Ghost; and at the same time many of the worst diseases and the worst cripples are made to leap and praise God for perfect healing.

In the last two years and a half, I have traveled over twenty-two thousand miles. This is the month of May, and I have received calls from twenty-seven states and one from Washington, D.C., and two

[6] See Acts 19:11-12.

calls from Canada to hold conventions or camp meetings for one month or more, and many from small places in these states.

Please read carefully the different accounts of the meetings and see the wonderful work God hath wrought, and you will have to confess that God gave the vision and that the vision and the prophecy have come true. Then be very careful how you receive these great and marvelous works of God, for He hath taken one of the weakest of all to confound the mighty so that no flesh shall glory.[7]

God is continually revealing to His children the mysteries of the kingdom, which are hidden from the "wise and prudent." (See Matthew 11:25.) "God's children have supernatural revelations and see visions: otherwise the Bible could not be the Word of God, for it is *(inter alia)*[8] the result and record of visions."[9]

Someone said that they thought that those who said they had had a vision just imagined it. If that is so, after the Crucifixion Mary did not see Christ, but only imagined it; and when she saw the two angels, she just imagined that also; and when Jesus appeared to her, why she just imagined that.[10] If that is so, the apostles who testified that they saw Him only imagined they saw Him,[11] and after that, when Jesus was seen by the five hundred brethren, seen by all of them at the same time; why those five hundred men just imagined it, imagined all together, at precisely the same time (1 Corinthians 15:6). And everyone that saw Jesus after His resurrection from the dead just imagined it. On what ground then do you believe that Jesus rose from the dead if you reject supernatural testimony? Spiritual things are spiritually discerned.[12]

After receiving the new birth into the spiritual kingdom, God's children know those things which are mysteries and forever secret and hidden from the eyes of the simply natural, unregenerate men,

[7] See 1 Corinthians 1:27.

[8] *inter alia:* among other things. *(Webster's N. W.,* 1997).

[9] Source of quotation unknown.

[10] See Matthew 28:5-10, Mark 16:9-10, Luke 24:4-6, and John 20:11-18.

[11] See Matthew 28:17; Mark 16:12-14; Luke 24:15-31, 36; and John 20:19-29; 21:1-25.

[12] See 1 Corinthians 2:14.

however wise, learned, and intelligent they may be, and to whatever high degree of acumen and understanding they may have attained.

When Elisha's servant at Dothan saw that the city was compassed round by a host, both with horses and chariots, he came to his master and said, "Alas, my master, how shall we do?" Elisha prayed, "Open his eyes that he may see." And behold the mountain was full of horses and chariots of fire about Elisha.[13] If Elisha's servant could see, why not we?

Paul had a vision in the temple; Peter on the housetop had a vision; John the revelator had visions, and numerous others.[14]

One of the elementary and fundamental doctrines of the Christian religion is the immutability of the omnipotent God; or in ordinary parlance, it is the fixed belief that God *has not changed, and will not change, in His dealings with mankind, as long as this dispensation lasts;* that He is all-powerful, and that He has not lost any of His power during the centuries that have elapsed since the days of the early Church; that He is still faithful and true to fulfil all that He has promised to do on the conditions specified in His Word; that He has not lost any of the love that He once had for mankind; and that under the same circumstances and conditions will do as much for us as He ever did for anyone else.

"We repeat that the doctrine and belief in 'The Immutability of an Omnipotent God' is one of the fundamental doctrines of the Christian religion, which has been adhered to all down the ages, by the Christian Church of all denominations; *and that no one can deny that God reveals Himself in visions to His servants, and remain an orthodox Christian.*"[15]

Written at Dallas, Texas

It could be truly said, as Peter said on the Day of Pentecost, that this you see and hear and feel is the promise of the Father, the wonder-working Holy Ghost.[16]

---

[13] See 2 Kings 6:15-17.

[14] Paul's vision is recorded in Acts 22:17-21, Peter's in Acts 10:9-20, and John's in the entire book of Revelation.

[15] Source of quotation unknown.

[16] See Acts 2:33.

With great "signs and wonders" the Lord has stretched forth His hand in working mighty miracles; healing all manner of diseases; casting out demons; laying the people out as dead; many of the meetings look like a battlefield; sinners struck down in their sins; and saints lying like Peter and Paul as dead; the saints have been given great visions and revelations and prophecies from heaven.

The Holy Ghost has been seen as cloven tongues, as rays of light, and as a great cloud of glory over the pulpit and the altar, and the Lord has been seen by many walking through the tent and about the altar.

Thousands of people are stirred and are writing to us for help, both spiritual and physical. The Macedonian cry is, "Come, come and help us or send help."[17]

God has called the saints, the brethren in the ministry, and the evangelists and workers from all parts. They have all fallen in line and rejoiced in the unity and love and power of God in our midst and went away feeling convinced of the need of more power of the living God in us and through us and in our midst.

At the end of five months, as we are about to close our work here, the interest which has been increasing from the first is now deeper and the presence of God is more manifest than ever.

As we are expecting to leave soon, the people are improving the opportunity and rushing here from all parts. There are twelve just arrived from Canada, one from England, and others are on their way.

The Lord showed a brother in a vision that the bands of angels that sang at the birth of Jesus were singing through the saints.

The Lord is manifesting His presence more and more to His children and encouraging us in every way that we may be ready and be weaned away from the world and be ready for His soon coming.

I have every reason to praise the Lord that He has wonderfully sustained me during these five months; I have been laboring very hard, not only in the meetings, but outside of meetings.

[17]See Acts 16:9.

I would say to the reader that the contents of my books are as a drop in the ocean compared to the many meetings and wonderful things that have never been mentioned and no account given of them.

I am sending books forth in the name of the Lord. The Lord showed me that I must make haste and get the books out, for He is going to send them all over the world. They will not only be used to help to gather the saints together and prepare for the marriage and the great work of the future, but it will be a great help to those who are left to go through the tribulation.

I ask the prayers of all the saints that shall read these lines that I may be kept continually in His will and covered with His mighty love and power; that God though me can finish the work that He has called me to do that He may have all the glory.

Mrs. Woodworth-Etter
December 12th, 1912

Taken from *A Diary of Signs and Wonders,* Harrison House Edition.

Divine Healing

I Am the Lord That Healeth Thee

Healing Is Part of Salvation—Satan Binds, Christ Sets Free

nd God said:

> If thou wilt diligently hearken to the voice of the Lord thy God, and wilt do that which is right in his sight, and wilt give ear to his commandments, and keep all his statutes, I will put none of these diseases upon thee, which I have brought upon the Egyptians: for I am the Lord that healeth thee.
>
> Exodus 15:26

We find in the twenty-eighth chapter of Deuteronomy that health is only promised to the children of God with all the blessings there mentioned, on condition that we serve God with a pure heart and claim these promises for us, individually, as our inheritance purchased on the Cross and left in the will and Testament which our Lord sealed with His blood, saying Himself took our infirmities and our sicknesses (See Matthew 8:17).

If we backslide or do not trust the Lord, we may expect all or any of these curses. "Because of the wickedness of thy doings, whereby thou hast forsaken me" (verse 20).[1] The pestilence shall cleave unto thee until thou be consumed from off the land. The Lord shall smite thee with consumption, and with a fever, and with an inflammation, and with an extreme burning, and with madness, with blindness, with the scab and itch wherein thou canst not be healed. Long pining, sickness, and death are promised to our seed, and every sickness and plague and unknown disease that come on the heathen, the enemy of Christ and His Church, is also promised to a backslidden people.[2]

[1] Deuteronomy 28:20.

[2] See Deuteronomy 28:21-22,27-29.

You see this scripture fulfilled. There is all manner of sickness and many unknown diseases among the professed followers of Christ today. The sins of the parents are visited upon the third and fourth generation.[3]

"The Lord will take away from thee all sickness" (Deuteronomy 7:15). No difference whether we get our sickness from our own past sinful life or inherited it from sins of past generations or of our parents, we have the promise, "I will take away all sickness from you." If we give ourselves soul and body to the Lord for all time, to be used for His glory and exercise present faith, we will feel that we are made whole, soul and body.

Exercise Present Faith

We can keep well by claiming the promise, "I will not put any of these diseases upon you, for I am the Lord that healeth you."[4]

Threescore years and ten is the allotted time of man.[5] There are very few deaths recorded in the Bible from sickness, except from their immediate sins or someone else's sin.

Satan is the cause of all sin, and sin is the cause of all sickness. Nearly all sickness is the result of our own sins. Sometimes it is caused by others. Abraham and his wife sinned and Abimelech's family was smitten. They repented. Abraham prayed unto God, and He healed Abimelech and his wife and his maidservants (See Genesis 20:17).

Miriam, one of the three leaders of the children of Israel, sinned. The Lord came down and made her confess her sins. She lost her experience, fell from grace, and was smitten with leprosy. She was in a lost condition and would have died an awful death, but she repented and Aaron called on Moses to offer the prayer of faith. Moses cried unto the Lord, saying, "Heal her now, O God, I beseech thee" (Numbers 12:13).[6]

[3] See Exodus 20:5, Numbers 14:18, and Deuteronomy 5:9.

[4] See Exodus 15:26.

[5] See Psalm 90:10.

[6] Maria Etter's original scripture notation was Numbers 12:8,13.

We find the chosen people of God murmured and sinned. They were smitten with a terrible plague. The dead and dying were lying all over the camp. In a short time, nearly fourteen thousand of those who a few hours before were right with God were lying cold in death.

Moses and Aaron Interceded

Moses and Aaron interceded and offered an atonement and the plague was stayed (See Numbers 16:48-49).

And the Lord sent fiery serpents among the people, and they bit the people; and many people of Israel died. Therefore the people came to Moses and said, "We have sinned, for we have spoken against the Lord, and against thee; pray unto the Lord, that He take away the serpents from us."

And Moses prayed for the people. And the Lord said to Moses, "Make thee a serpent of brass and put it upon a pole: and it shall come to pass, that everyone that is bitten, when he looketh upon it, shall live."

And Moses made a serpent of brass and put it upon a pole, and it came to pass, that if a serpent had bitten any man, when he beheld the serpent of brass, he lived. (See Numbers 21:6-9)

We see right in the church in the wilderness on account of their sins, they were suffering from the awful plague caused by the poisonous bite of the serpent; the high and low, the rich and poor lay dead or dying in every tent all over the campground.

These people would have lived many years if they had obeyed the Lord and trusted the promise He made in the words of our text. When they began to realize the awful work of death around them and knew they would soon all be dead, they repented of their sins and asked Moses to pray that the serpents might be taken away.

They did not ask to be healed; but as they repented, the Lord took away the serpents and provided a remedy that, through faith, they might be healed. The serpent was put high on a pole. The good news was shouted through the camp. The Lord says, "Everyone that looks at the brazen serpent shall live." That was a wonderful divine-healing meeting. There was nothing in the serpent; but God said, "Look and live." It was their faith in God's Word that brought about the healing. No matter how near dead they were, [even if it were] with the last gasping breath, if they got their eyes on the serpent, the disease left; and they were on their feet ready to help someone else.

Healing Is Part of Salvation

As Moses lifted up the serpent in the wilderness, even so must the Son of God be lifted up: That whosoever believeth in Him shall not perish. (See John 3:14-15.) Jesus was lifted up on the Cross for our sins and our sicknesses. You cannot preach the Gospel of our Lord and Savior Jesus Christ without preaching divine healing for the body as well as the soul.

King "Saul died for his transgression which he committed against the Lord, even against the word of the Lord, which he kept not, and also for asking counsel of one that had a familiar spirit, to enquire of it" (1 Chronicles 10:13).

King Jehoram's sins were visited upon his family till they all pined away and went into an early grave. He was smitten with an incurable disease. After two years of awful suffering, his bowels fell out by reason of his sore disease. (See 2 Chronicles 21:14-15,18-19.)

King Uzziah was a mighty man of God. [He] had great power with God and man, but his heart was lifted up to his destruction. He sinned against the Lord and was smitten with leprosy and was a leper until the day of his death. [He] was cut off from the house of the Lord and lived alone, dying a lingering, awful death. He was shut away from the living and went down to an early grave. If he had repented and prayed the prayer of faith, he would have lived. (See 2 Chronicles 26:16-21.)

Asa and the Doctors

King Asa was diseased in his feet until his disease was exceedingly great; yet, in his disease, he sought not to the Lord, but to the physicians. Asa died. He was sick from one to two years, went from one physician to another, but did not go to the Lord; and the result was he died. (See 2 Chronicles 16:12-13.)

Israel sinned. They were smitten with a pestilence. Seventy thousand men fell. The plague had reached Jerusalem. David lifted up his eyes and saw the Angel of the Lord stand between the earth and the heavens, having a drawn sword in his hand stretched out over Jerusalem. Then David and the elders of Israel, who were clothed in sackcloth, fell upon their faces; and David confessed his sin and prayed unto the Lord; and the plague was stayed. (See 1 Chronicles 21:14-27.)

We read very few cases in the Bible where anyone died of sickness or was sick, except they had brought it on themselves by their own sins. Whenever they repented and offered the prayer of faith, claiming the promise God had made, saying, "I will take away all sickness from you, for I am the Lord that healeth thee," they were restored to God's favor, made well in body and soul and lived many years to serve the Lord.

Whenever we commit a known sin, if we die without repenting we are lost forever. All the good deeds or work we ever did will not atone for one known sin, but for the sin we committed we shall die and be lost, when we take ourselves out of God's hands.

He that committeth sin is a child of the devil. We are then in a condition to receive any of the cursings that the Lord said should come upon those who would not be true to Him.

Satan Binds—Christ Sets Free

Satan has powers to afflict or bring on any infirmities or sickness. Jesus said: "Ought not this woman [to] be loosed whom Satan hath bound, lo, these eighteen years?" (See Luke 13:16.) Jesus cast the spirit out. The woman was made whole. She glorified the Lord more in one hour than in all those years the devil had her bound. The law of the Spirit of life makes us free from satanic power.

The wicked do not live out half their days. If you notice carefully what we have written, you will see this is true. It was not God's will that they should be cut off, but it was on account of their sins and disobedience. The devil has power over death (See Hebrews 2:14). If we are the sons of God, we are born of the Spirit; we are led by the Spirit.[7]

[7] See Romans 8:14.

"If ye abide in me, and my words abide in you, ye shall ask what ye will, and it shall be done unto you" (John 15:7). If we meet the conditions, He will bring our petition to pass if He has to bring all heaven down. Thousands are sick and dying today in the Church on account of their sins, not living out half their days.

King Jeroboam laid his hand on the prophet of the Lord to arrest him, and his hand was withered. He could not take it back. The prayer of faith was offered, and his hand was restored like the other. He was like thousands of ministers today: He had left God's way and substituted and counterfeited and had a form similar in many ways to God's—enough to deceive the people. When God sent His servant to tell him the awful judgment that was coming upon him and his people, instead of repenting he laid his hand on God's work and his hand was withered. (See 1 Kings 13:4-6.)

Anyone who lays his hands on the scriptural ark, or work of God, is smitten with spiritual barrenness. He loses his experience and power. Paul says of such: "Having a form of godliness, but denying the power thereof: from such turn away.[8] They will not endure sound doctrine, but are despisers of those that are good or godly; men of corrupt minds; reprobate concerning the faith.[9] The power of God always accompanies the faith of our Lord Jesus Christ and His doctrine.

Hezekiah Prevails in Prayer

Hezekiah was sick with a lingering, painful sickness—unto death. The messenger came to him saying, "Thus saith the Lord, Set thy house in order: for thou shalt die, and not live" (Isaiah 38:1, paraphrased). He saw his body was going down to the grave of corruption, that he was dying before his time, that he could be more faithful and do more for the Lord than he had done. He wept and prayed to God to heal him. The Lord sent the messenger back, saying: "I have heard thy prayer, I have seen thy tears: behold, I will add unto thy days fifteen years" (Isaiah 38:5).

[8] 2 Timothy 3:5.

[9] 2 Timothy 4:3, 3:3, and 3:8, paraphrased.

He had faith. He said, "so wilt thou recover me, and make me to live" (Isaiah 38:16). He broke forth in prayer, saying, "Thou hast in love to my soul delivered it from the pit of corruption [the grave]: for thou hast cast all my sins behind thy back. . . . The Lord was ready to save me: therefore we will sing my songs to the stringed instruments all the days of our life in the house of the Lord" (See Isaiah 38:17-20).

King David Sick Because of His Sins

King David committed awful sins. The Lord spared his life and gave him time to repent; but his child that he loved took sick and died because of his sins.[10] Many children die because of their parents' sins.

David did not confess his sins to get right with God, and there came a long sickness upon him. He said:

> There is no soundness in my flesh because of thine anger; neither is there any rest in my bones because of my sin.
>
> My wounds stink and are corrupt because of my foolishness.
>
> My loins are filled with a loathsome disease.[11]

His enemies made sport of him and said, "When shall he die, and his name perish? An evil disease . . . cleaveth fast unto him: and now that he lieth he shall rise up no more" (38 and 41 Psalm).[12]

The people knew what power he had with God in the past; and on seeing him now, groaning and weeping all night on account of his terrible suffering, they said, "Where is his God?" He confessed his sins; and when he said, "Heal me, oh, Lord, for thy praise,"[13] the Lord was ready to save and heal. He said, "O, Lord my God, I cried unto thee, and thou hast healed me. Thou hast turned for me my mourning; into dancing . . . and girded me with gladness."[14]

---

[10]See 2 Samuel 12:14,18.

[11]Psalm 38:3,5,7.

[12]Psalm 41:5,8; paraphrased.

[13]See Psalm 51:14-15.

[14]Psalm 30:2,11

> Bless the Lord, O my soul, and forget not all his benefits: Who forgiveth all thine iniquities; who healeth all thy diseases.
>
> Psalm 103:2-3

Praise the Lord! He is just as willing to save and heal us today as He was David.

Partaking of the Lord's Supper Unworthily the Cause of Sickness

> For he that eateth and drinketh unworthily, eateth and drinketh damnation to himself, not discerning the Lord's body. For this cause many are weak and sickly among you, and many sleep.
>
> 1 Corinthians 11:29-30

It is only God's permissive will for you to be sick when partaking unworthily.

Paul is speaking to the backsliding church members at Corinth and those who had never had anything else but a religious profession. They were keeping up the outward profession and form, even taking the wine and bread—the emblems of the broken body and shed blood of the Lord—making an outward show and pretense of love and obedience. For this cause they had not only brought damnation to their own souls, but many were sickly and getting weaker; and many were dead already and many more were dying.

May the Holy Ghost open the eyes of those who read these words. The Lord help you to be willing to receive the truth. Look at these suffering and dead church members in the light of Paul's preaching—pining away, going down to an early grave and down to hell on account of their sins. The Lord has nothing to do with it, only that He permits it on account of their sins.

Paul did not say the Lord did it to chasten or bring them near Him, but tells them they brought it on themselves by making a false profession of religion.

One of the worst sins we can be guilty of is having an outward form without the life and power of the Spirit of Christ. We set the religion of Jesus in a false light, as if He had not power to keep us in health, and give the lie to the living Christ who dwells with every child of God. There are hundreds of such church members and professors, dead and dying, over our land today.

Some are languishing on beds for years for this same cause and instead of the minister showing them their condition and getting their souls right and then pointing them to Christ, who healeth all our diseases and takes our infirmities and bears our sicknesses and suffering; instead of offering the prayer of faith that will save the sick, that the Lord may raise them up, the majority of teachers will make them think they are all right and that it is God who is making them suffer.

Many religious teachers will come up at the judgment reeking with the blood of souls. They will not be able to say with Paul: "My hands and my heart are pure of the blood of all men's souls."[15]

Taken from *Spirit-Filled Sermons.*

[15] Acts 20:26, paraphrased.

DIVINE HEALING

Health for Body, Soul, and Spirit

"Himself took our infirmities, and bare our sicknesses, in His own body on the tree."[1] If we really believe this wonderful truth, we will claim our deliverance and step out, acting as we believe.

In seeking healing for our bodies, we are so apt to look at feelings or symptoms and believe we are healed just in proportion to the amount we see and feel when in reality, we are healed when we believe. "Whatsoever ye desire when ye pray, believe that ye have received and ye shall have."[2] The work was all finished on Calvary. On Calvary's tree the remedy is found that will heal all sicknesses and diseases of the soul and body. Jesus offers it unto us free. It is "look and live."[3] Therefore, all we have to do is to appropriate it to our own individual needs. Sometimes it is instantly realized in the body, but more often it is a gradual deliverance, requiring us to step out in faith before we see any signs of having it.

We take salvation the same way—claiming it by faith before we feel any change in our hearts. So we must see with the eye of faith, our bodily healing, before it can be made manifest in us.

Now faith is not natural sight; if it was it would no longer be faith, but reality. Faith is believing God and His Word and that He will do all that He has promised. "It counts the things which be not (like perfect, well bodies) as though they were";[4] and the things which be (like feelings and symptoms) as though they were not, because God said so and what He says is true.

This sermon was printed as a tract.

[1] Matthew 8:17 and 1 Peter 2:24, paraphrased.

[2] Mark 11:24, paraphrased.

[3] See Numbers 21:8-9.

[4] See Romans 4:17.

Faith looks away from the natural, from the things of the senses, and sees the fulfillment of the promise through Christ's complete work on Calvary. It sees every need supplied through the atonement. It then believes and acts and will soon bring forth the fruit—a healthy body.

We must believe after the prayer of faith has been given, for "Whatsoever ye desire when ye pray, believe that ye have received, and ye shall have."[5] We must cling to the promises of Jesus instead of looking at our feelings, or go[ing] by them, for our senses are false witness[es] unto us when we step out in faith.

If we are looking and going by our feelings, we are believing them instead of believing God. We are to believe as we pray. We often ask God to heal us and then we begin to note how we feel, and worry and fret about the things that are seen. We concluded because we didn't feel any better, that God had not healed or heard our prayers. What's the matter? Simply, we were believing feelings instead of God and His Word. The believing is not in accordance with the praying.

The Lord Jesus healed, though medical man abounded—there were "many physicians." (See Mark 5:26.) The Lord Jesus healed without inquiry, whether people were taking medicine or not. The Lord Jesus healed, without exception, all who came or were brought to Him. (See Matthew 8:16.)

The Lord Jesus sometimes healed without the result being apparent at once. (See Luke 17:14.) The Lord Jesus sometimes healed gradually. (See John 4:49-52.) The Lord generally healed on the spot, instantaneously. (See Matthew 15:30-31.) The Lord Jesus sometimes indicated healing would be in the near future. (See John 9:7.) The Lord Jesus sometimes removed a man from his surroundings before healing him. (See Mark 8:22-23.)

The Lord Jesus healed all manner of diseases (see Matthew 4:23-24), including lunacy, epilepsy, leprosy, palsy, fever, paralysis, blindness, lameness, deafness, withered limbs, a sword cut, etc. The Lord healed illness associated with devils. (See Luke 9:42.) The Lord

[5] Mark 11:24, paraphrased.

Jesus healed people at a distance without going to them. There is an instance of His healing someone sixteen miles away. (See John 4:46-53.) The Lord Jesus healed by a touch, by others touching Him, by His taking people by the hand, by command, by a word. (See Matthew 8:3; Luke 8:44; Mark 1:31; Luke 6:10; and Mark 7:34.)

The Lord Jesus transmitted this power to others: to the twelve disciples (see Luke 9:1); to the seventy who were not apostles (see Luke 10:1-9); to believers generally, if they claimed the power (see John 14:12-14); to Peter's shadow (see Acts 5:14-15).

When a tree is cut down, it is then a dead tree. As long as the sap is in the branches, the leaves and branches will flourish; but as soon as the sap is exhausted, they will wither and dry up. So with our healing—as soon as diseases and sickness are smitten, it is dead; symptoms may remain for a time, but if we believe the work done and cause removed, the symptoms will vanish.

In Christ is all we need. With Him all things are possible; without Him we can do nothing.[6]

One of the secrets of obtaining these things of the Lord is to see Jesus—looking away from ourselves and see[ing] Him. This connects us to Him; then seeing Him, praise Him and pull down all we need for body and soul.

Cast all doubts, fears, and unbelief on Him, who is the burden bearer; and as you do this, He is responsible for even our believing. Then stand in faith, counting the work as done until health and strength are made manifest in the flesh.[7]

The prayer of faith through the anointed cloth is based on Acts 19:11-12. It says, "God wrought special miracles by the hands of Paul: So that from his body were brought unto the sick handkerchiefs or aprons, and the diseases departed from them, and the evil spirits went out of them." Paul was wonderfully used of God in his ministry. This gave the people great faith in his prayer in their behalf, so that they brought aprons and handkerchiefs for him to bless and pray over. When these were put on the sick and afflicted,

[6] See Ephesians 1:3, Matthew 19:26, Mark 10:27, and John 15:5.

[7] See Psalm 55:22 and Ephesians 6:13.

they were healed, as they believed, just like the woman was healed when by faith she touched Jesus' garments.[8]

In my ministry of about forty-five years, thousands of handkerchiefs have been prayed over and anointed and sent out again. We have received all kinds of wonderful testimonies of healings as a result of this part of the ministry. The cloth is only the medium through which faith is exercised. The woman that came to Jesus said, "If I can only touch the hem of His garment, I shall be made whole."[9] By faith, she touched Him and received her healing. You can do so, too. You may put the cloth on any part of the body, if not convenient to put it on the diseased part, and leave it on as you feel led, but do not doubt Jesus afterwards. If the woman who touched Jesus had doubted, she would not have been healed. The same way with us today.

This tract is written to help you, dear one. Be of good cheer and have a childlike faith in all that Jesus has promised, and the Lord will do great and marvelous things for you.[10]

Taken from a tract by the same title.

---

[8] See Matthew 9:20-22.

[9] Matthew 9:21, paraphrased.

[10] The tract continues, "Always send stamp for reply. Many people forget to do this. –Mrs. Woodworth Etter, 2114 Miller St., Indianapolis, Ind." The address is no longer valid.

PRAYER OF FAITH SHALL SAVE THE SICK

The prayer of faith shall save the sick.

Is any sick among you? let him call for the elders of the church; and let them pray over him, anointing him with oil in the name of the Lord: And the prayer of faith shall save the sick, and the Lord shall raise him up; and if he (has) committed sins, they shall be forgiven him. Confess your faults one to another, and pray one for another, that ye may be healed. The effectual fervent prayer of a righteous man availeth much. (Elijah) was a man subject to like passions as we are, and he prayed earnestly that it might not rain: and it rained not on the earth for the space of three years and six months.[1]

James 5:14-17

The apostle James sends this letter out over the world to all churches, ministers, and to every member of the body of Christ. All these teachings and blessings are for every child of God that will accept them. He wants the Church to know that the power to heal the sick and teach divine healing was not confined to the apostles, but elders of each and every church had the gift of healing or the power to heal and that by meeting the conditions given, every one of the followers of Christ would positively be healed.

He delivered this doctrine of divine healing of the body to be taught and practiced in every church, that each member would know their privilege and duty to God. If he or she were sick, instead of sending for a doctor, perhaps an infidel doctor, they should send at once for the elders and let God glorify Himself by manifesting the healing power in raising him up.

This is the longer version of "Divine Healing Included in the Atonement." The subtitles from the shorter version have been inserted here.

[1] Words in parentheses are Maria Etter's emendation.

Let God Glorify Himself

Some teachers refuse to walk in the God-given light and say this text means "spiritual healing." I am glad the Word of God is so plain that anyone who wants the light can have it: "The prayer of faith shall save the sick, and the Lord shall raise him up; and if he have committed sins, they shall be forgiven him."[2] You see the line between the raising up of the sick one and the forgiving of sin? If they backslid, or sinned in any way that brought on the sickness, the sick ones should have faith in the promises of God in sending for the elders as God had commanded.

The elders come and anoint with oil, a symbol of the Holy Ghost or healing virtue that must come from Jesus, on and through the sick one—soul and body. They pray together the prayer of faith, and having met the conditions, the Lord honors the faith and comes with His mighty power and raises up the sick one to health and restores to him peace and joy in his soul.

The Lord Honors the Faith

> "Pray one for another, that you may be healed."[3]

You see, the power of the Lord is ever present with His children to heal. The command is given to every child of God. If the elder cannot come, then get a few of God's children together in the true Spirit of Christ, and pray for one another, that you may be healed.

Some have gifts of casting out devils and healing by laying on hands. Oh! Let us not forget these blood-bought benefits. He forgiveth all our iniquities, He healeth all our diseases.[4] He promises to heal soul and body; the verb is in the present tense. "The effectual fervent prayer of a righteous man availeth much."[5]

---

[2] James 5:15

[3] James 5:16, paraphrased.

[4] See Psalm 103:3.

[5] James 5:16.

Unwavering Faith

The Lord shows us that we must have the righteousness of Christ, meet every other condition, and ask the Lord for what we want in faith, without wavering. If we waver, or doubt, we need not expect anything, for God will not hear us.[6]

The prayer of faith God will answer, if He had to bring all heaven down to prompt us to greater faith to ask the Lord for greater things.

He refers us back to the dark days of dearth[7]and condemnation in which Elijah lived and says, "He was a man, subject to like passion, as we are." He was not an angel, but a man, with the same human nature and passions as we have. He prayed earnestly, that it might not rain, and the heavens were shut up for three years and six months; he prayed again, and the rain came. He prayed for God to send fire from heaven, that the people might know there was a true God and that he was God's servant and the Lord was leading him.[8]

The Lord Wants Us to Ask

The Lord wants us to ask for great signs and wonders. The fire that came from heaven and brought the people down before God was a symbol of the Holy Ghost. The Lord wants to send into our midst signs and wonders in answer to our prayers.

Elijah represents Christ—[Elisha,][9] the Church. When Elijah was taken up to heaven, a double portion of his spirit came upon Elisha, and Elisha did many more signs and wonders than Elijah did.[10]

"Verily, verily, I say unto you, He that believeth on me, the works that I do shall he do also; and greater works than these shall he do; because I go to my Father. And whatsoever ye shall ask in my name, that will I do, that the Father may be glorified in the Son. If

---

[6] See James 1:6-7.

[7] "dearth"—scarcity. This may be a typographical error, and Etter may have said "death."

[8] See 1 Kings 17:1 and 2 Kings 1.

[9] The version of the sermon in *Spirit-Filled Sermons* adds Elisha's name here.

[10] See 2 Kings 2:9-15.

ye shall ask anything in my name, I will do it" (John 14:12-14, paraphrased). "If ye abide in me, and my words abide in you, ye shall ask what ye will, and it shall be done unto you" (John 15:7). You see, Christ's will and our will come together with the same desire to glorify the Father, the Spirit of Christ prompting us to ask for great things, that the Lord will have a chance to let down His right hand of power and let the people see the visible signs of the Lord of Hosts, that dwelleth in Zion.

Every one of us ought to be anointed with the same power and gifts that God hath set in the Church, that the world may believe that the Father has sent Christ into the world and that the Father hath loved us, as He loved Him—Christ.[11] "In my name shall they cast out devils; they shall lay hands on the sick and they shall recover."[12]

These are the special gifts. I praise the Lord! He hath given these gifts to me, and in His name, through His name, thousands of unclean spirits are cast out. The deaf, dumb, lame, blind, paralytic, and cancer devils have been driven out. Thousands of diseases have fled by laying on my hands, in His name, and they were made whole.

Healing in the Atonement

Divine healing is taught in the Atonement, as much as the salvation of the soul. Isaiah, 53rd chapter, says: "He was wounded for our transgressions, he was bruised for our iniquities: the chastisement of our peace was upon him; and with his stripes we are healed."[13]

Matthew 8:17 says: "That it might be fulfilled which was spoken by Isaiah [Esaias] the prophet, saying, Himself took our infirmities, and bare our sicknesses."

> For by one Spirit are we all baptized into one body. . . .Ye are the body of Christ.
>
> 1 Corinthians 12:13,27[14]

[11] An allusion to John 17:21.

[12] Mark 16:17-18, paraphrased.

[13] Isaiah 53:5.

[14] Etter's text in at least two versions has 1 Corinthians 12:13 and 12:27 quoted separately without notation, followed by the scripture notation, "1 Cor. 12:12," which she may have meant as an introductory commentary on the next section.

God has set some in the Church or body: Firstly, apostles; secondarily, prophets; thirdly, teachers.[15]

> For to one is given by the Spirit the word of wisdom; to another the word of knowledge by the same Spirit; To another faith by the same Spirit; to another the gifts of healing by the same Spirit; To another the working of miracles; to another prophecy; to another discerning of spirits; to another divers kinds of tongues; to another the interpretation of tongues.
>
> 1 Corinthians 12:8-10

Together we have the promise of apostles, prophets, teachers, and evangelists, in the coming Church of Christ.[16] What a glorious Church is the real body and bride of our Lord!

The signs were to follow their works: "For the perfecting of the saints, for the work of the ministry, for the edifying of the body of Christ" (Ephesians 4:12).

You see that God placed all the gifts and working of the Spirit in the Church and they were to remain with the people of God, "till all come in the unity of the faith[17] by the same Spirit . . . to every man is given the manifestation of the Spirit to profit withal; but all these worketh the selfsame Spirit—one Lord and one Spirit.[18]

The Holy Ghost is the agent of Christ sent by God to work through the Church, the body of Christ, and each member is to possess one or more of these gifts as we walk in the light and believe and accept these blessings, or gifts.

Paul says, "Concerning spiritual gifts, brethren, I would not have you ignorant, concerning the knowledge of the Son of God, till we all come in the unity of the faith unto a perfect man, unto the measure of the stature of the fullness of Christ."[19]

---

[15] See 1 Corinthians 12:28.

[16] See Ephesians 4:11.

[17] Ephesians 4:13, paraphrased.

[18] See 1 Corinthians 12:7 and 11.

[19] 1 Corinthians 12:1 and Ephesians 4:13, paraphrased.

Dear reader, when will we all come up to this measure? Not until the last one of the little flock is ready to be translated. We must be filled with the fullness of God, with wisdom and power. These signs and gifts must follow until the Church goes out to meet the Lord—the Bridegroom. She will go out to meet Him with the same power that the apostles had after they were filled with the Holy Ghost on the Day of Pentecost. Oh! Praise the Lord, all these signs are with us and are manifested in our meetings.

Taken from *Acts of the Holy Ghost.*

James' Commission to the Church to Pray for the Sick

In the last chapter of James, verse fourteen is for the Church. Remember, it is not for sinners.

> Is any sick among you? let him call for the elders of the church; and let them pray over him, anointing him with oil in the name of the Lord: And the prayer of faith shall save the sick, and the Lord shall raise him up; and if he have committed sins, they shall be forgiven him.[1]

"Confess your faults one to another." You have to be pretty straight when you come to God. "Pray one for another, that ye might be healed. The effectual fervent prayer of a righteous man availeth much."[2]

"Elijah was a man like other men, not an angel, and he prayed that it might not rain, and it rained not for three years and six months. He prayed again and God heard him and sent the rain."[3] This chapter is for us; it applies to us. All through the chapter it refers to the days we are living in.

When these things come to pass know that the end draweth near.[4] This chapter brings us down to the last days.

Verse 7. In the east they had the early rain to start the grain. They could not tell anything about the harvest until they received the latter rain. If it came abundantly, there would be a good harvest. The apostle says to us, "Wait for the latter rain; be ye also patient unto the coming of the Lord." When the latter rain is falling, we

---

[1] James 5:14-15.

[2] James 5:16, both quotations.

[3] James 5:17-18, paraphrased.

[4] See James 5:8.

know the coming of the Lord is near. We are getting the early rain and will get the latter rain before long. He is getting the bride ready.

The apostle is speaking to the Church. If anyone is sick among you, don't run for the doctor or send him to the hospital, but let the sick ones send for the elders. The elders were supposed to be men endued with the Holy Ghost, who would come and pray over him, anointing him with oil, and he should be raised up. And if he had sinned in any way, he must confess it, and through prayer, be forgiven.

Some people say this is spiritual healing. They are blind because they want to be. Anointing with oil is a symbol of the anointing with the Holy Ghost. A barrel of oil would not heal, but if you are anointing with faith and obedience, you get the blessing.

It is the healing virtue of Jesus—the power of God. After the disease is cast out, the healing power of Jesus comes in. The prayer of faith shall save the sick; the power of God cleanses the soul; and the sick one is raised up, both soul and body.

Any of God's children, filled with the Holy Ghost, can pray with the sick, anointing with oil in the name of the Lord; and you can rely upon it, the person will be raised up. You can do that without any special gift. Pray for one another. People may die before help can reach them. Call in the neighbors and unite in prayer. If there has been any backbiting, confess it.

The prayer of faith is effectual and availeth much. If you cannot get anyone with a special gift, pray for each other. I know many people who have not had a doctor in the family; parents pray for the children, and children pray for the parents; little ones who can hardly talk will pray and the sick are raised up.

Pray one for another. Wherever you are, Jesus is. He is the healer and also the baptizer. He gives the resurrection life. Many today are wonderfully healed while alone with God. God is moving in a marvelous way. We must exercise faith and obedience.

Elijah had great power with God, and he was a man just like you. Elisha had twice as much power as Elijah.[5] Moody[6] says we ought

---

[5] See 2 Kings 2:9.

[6] Dwight Lyman Moody (1837-1899) was a well-known American evangelist.

to have much more and do greater things than he did. This was away back (*sic*) in the moonlight of the Church. We, in the sunlight today, ought to do four times as many miracles as they did.

Great miracles ought to be performed; and they are being performed in these days when the bride is getting herself ready to meet the Bridegroom and go up into the air with Him. God will do greater works in the last days.

All the people that are baptized in the Spirit believe that Jesus is coming soon. One-half know it. How? By the Word and signs. God wants to move His people; when the Gospel of the coming King shall be preached to all the world, then the Lord will come.

This Gospel of the coming King is to girdle the earth and give every professing child of God a chance to come into the power of the Holy Ghost. If we do not blow the trumpet and give forth the right sound, the Tribulation will be upon us and their blood will be required at our hands.

We are told to watch and pray as we see the Day approaching.[7] What is the signal of danger? The great Day of the Lord is at hand. How could we blow the trumpet, if we did not know the signal? I am glad we do know it.

This chapter shows the power of God in the Church. Every child of God should have power enough to bring down a blessing. There must be faith and obedience. Expect something from the Lord just now and He answers quickly.

You see how quickly prayer is answered and different diseases healed; you see it here every day. God says the prayer of faith will save the sick.[8] Everyone does not have to anoint with oil; some have gifts; there are different gifts.

Jesus said, "These signs shall follow them that believe; In my name shall they cast out devils . . . they shall lay hands on the sick, and they shall recover."[9]

---

[7] See Mark 13:33 and Hebrews 10:25.

[8] See James 5:15.

[9] Mark 16:17-18.

One point I want to make clear: It says anoint with oil, but it does not say pray for every sinner; it is for the saints. If they have backslidden, let them confess and they will be forgiven.

Sinners cannot expect to be healed unless they give their hearts to God. Jesus said, "Thy sins are forgiven,"[10] then He healed. God expects you to come the same way. I cannot pray for your body unless you give yourself to God. If you want God to heal you, you must stop sinning.

If you promise me you will, God will take your promise through our faith. God did not promise to heal sinners and let them go forth to serve the devil. He said, "Sin no more, lest a worse thing come upon you."[11] You will sin unless you get saved.

They should know in every church what to do: send for the elders. Until recently very few persons would lay hands on the sick without anointing with oil; I have been criticized for this, all the way.

I received my anointing thirty-five years ago when God raised me up from the sickbed. God showed me I must preach healing, and I told the people how God raised me up. After awhile, I was holding a meeting in Indiana and worked nearly to death, sometimes nearly all night.

The Spirit of the Lord came upon me; God was trying to show me He wanted me to preach healing for the sick, but I was afraid it was the enemy; it seemed like presumption. Many souls would be saved through divine healing and the devil knew it.

Healing is the great drawing card in the New Testament. Finally, I settled the question. I knew it was the Lord, and I said, "Whenever you want me to pray for someone, bring them to me, or take me to them, and I will do it."

The first place I went, we had a wonderful meeting. There was a man who had been a great skeptic; I met a man who asked me to go and visit the man's daughter, who was dying. Five doctors had given her up. She had been converted a few weeks before in our meeting. I did not see how I could go, but I felt the hand of the Lord was in it, and I said, "If I cannot go, I will pray for her and I believe God will heal her."

---

[10] See Matthew 9:2, Mark 2:5, and Luke 5:20.

[11] John 5:14, paraphrased.

The next morning I was very weak, but felt I must go to her when the Lord said to me, "You pray for her and I will heal her." A few days later, in another town, word was brought me that He had fulfilled His promise. You talk about hypnotic power or my power; I never saw this woman.

About laying on of hands: I was holding a meeting in Indiana [and] there were few people to pray the power down. Dr. Daggett, a physician, came to the meetings whenever he could and would lead in prayer.

Sometimes he had to go out, he suffered so with pain in his knees. The Lord began to say to me, "That man ought to be healed." He impressed this upon me so much, I had to go to him and say, "I wish you did not have to go out; I need you here." He said, "I am very sorry, but I suffer so I have to go." I asked him if he did not believe God could heal him and told him that I believed God wanted to heal him.

God was working with him in the same way. I called the congregation together and said, "Are there any Christians here who believe God can heal? If you really believe, come and help me. I am going to pray for healing."

Several came. I did not know what to do any more than a baby. I began to pray; the power of the Lord raised my right arm up until it was over the knee and then stopped, for I did not like to touch it. The power of God was in my hand and He wanted me to lay my hand on the man's knee. When I understood what God wanted, I laid my hand on the knee and asked God to take the disease out. [The man] sprang to his feet, healed. He had been that way twelve years; everyone knew him and everyone was amazed.

Once when there were thousands of people present, I called out, "Is Dr. Daggett in the congregation?" He was making his way through the crowd, running to a place on the platform. He told how wonderfully he was healed, and I heard of him twelve years afterward.

That was the first one I ever laid hands on. "They shall lay hands on the sick, and they shall recover."[12] That was the way God led me

[12]Mark 16:18.

out. I have been criticized all along the line by those who anoint with oil. After Pentecost, you never read of the apostles anointing with oil. They did as Jesus directed, they laid their hands on the sick and they recovered.

God does not lead everyone alike. Anyone He leads to anoint, it is all right, but God did not lead me that way. He led me to pray the prayer of faith and lay hands on and cast out demons in the name of Jesus.

Anyone who has faith to comply with the commission James gives can pray the prayer of faith for the sick and they will be healed.

Taken from *Signs and Wonders God Wrought in the Ministry of Maria B. Woodworth-Etter*

Questions and Answers on Divine Healing

Preface

There has been such a great demand for "Questions and Answers on Divine Healing" that the first edition of fifteen thousand is entirely exhausted. This booklet has proved itself such a great blessing to the people who are seeking light on divine healing, that I feel constrained to publish this present, enlarged and revised edition, *Questions and Answers on Divine Healing,* which will be sent prepaid to you for 25 cents.

Those who want more light on this subject and on things pertaining to the kingdom of God should in no wise fail to get all of my literature.

Marvels and Miracles, published by myself (January, 1922), has nearly six hundred pages. This book gives a condensed account of my life and ministry, up to the present time—a period of nearly fifty years. It will be sent prepaid to you for $1.65.

Spirit-Filled Sermons contains over a score of sermons, delivered and carefully selected and arranged by myself, to give God's people the necessary light for these last days, and particularly on the soon coming of Jesus Christ. This book will be sent prepaid to you for 65 cents.

These two books, together with *Questions and Answers on Divine Healing (Revised and Enlarged)* will be sent prepaid to one address, the three for $2.50. We should do all we can to circulate them.

May God greatly bless all who read this literature and give everyone a part in bringing it to hungry souls, is my prayer. Missionaries call for it and have already translated much of my writings into the language of their people. What we do must be done quickly. Amen.

Questions and Answers on Divine Healing

Q. What is divine healing?

A. Divine healing is the act of God's grace, by the direct power of the Holy Spirit, by which the physical body is delivered from sickness and disease and restored to soundness and health.

Q. Have we any promise in the Bible that divine healing was ever intended to be an attainable blessing to the people of God?

A. Yes. There are many such promises. We find it given to the people of Israel in a special covenant promise.

> If thou wilt diligently hearken to the voice of the Lord thy God, and wilt do that which is right in his sight, and wilt give ear to his commandments, and keep all his statutes, I will put none of these diseases upon thee, which I have brought upon the Egyptians: for I am the Lord that healeth thee.
>
> Exodus 15:26

> And ye shall serve the Lord your God, and he shall bless thy bread, and thy water; and I will take sickness away from the midst of thee.
>
> Exodus 23:25

> And he said unto them, Go ye into all the world, and preach the gospel to every creature. . . . And these signs shall follow them that believe; In my name shall they cast out devils; they shall speak with new tongues . . . they shall lay hands on the sick, and they shall recover.
>
> Mark 16:15-18

Q. Does the Bible prove that any of the people of God ever enjoyed this blessing?

A. Yes. We read that even before this covenant blessing was promised, the physical condition of the people was perfect, which indicates plainly that God had a special interest in their health. (See Psalm 105:37.) There were at least two and one-half million people in the Exodus from Egypt, "and there was not one feeble person among their tribes." Moses enjoyed this blessing in a special manner. "And Moses was an hundred and twenty years old when he died: his eye was not dim, nor his natural force abated" (Deuteronomy 34:7). So also did Caleb, in an unusual experience of preservation and health, live to an old age. (See Joshua 14:10-11.) David personally knew of the benefits and blessings of healing. (See Psalm 6:2; 30:2; and 103:1-4.) Whenever Israel lived up to the covenant conditions, they all had the benefits of healing and health. (See Psalm 107:20 and 2 Chronicles 30:20.) Hezekiah had a personal experience of the same. (See 2 Kings 20:1-5.)

Q. Was this blessing ever promised to anyone else than the Jews?

A. Yes. It is given in prophecy as a redemption blessing, which, together with all other gospel blessings through Christ, is offered to both Jew and Gentile. (See Galatians 3:27-29.)

Q. What does prophecy say about divine healing?

A. There is more said about it in prophecy than we have time at present to read, but I will just quote a few verses, and the rest can be read at your leisure. "Then the eyes of the blind shall be opened, and the ears of the deaf shall be unstopped. Then shall the lame man leap as an hart, and the tongue of the dumb sing" (Isaiah 35:5-6). This very prophecy is referred to by Jesus Himself in Matthew 11:5, where it was daily being fulfilled, "The blind receive their sight, and the lame walk, the lepers are cleansed, and the deaf hear, the dead are raised up, and the poor have the gospel preached to them."

Another very plain prophecy is found in Isaiah 53:4: "Surely he hath borne our griefs, and carried our sorrows." The fulfillment of this wonderful voice of inspiration is found in Matthew 8:17: "Himself took our infirmities, and bare our sicknesses." It is admitted by all reliable translators and the most eminent Hebrew scholars, such as Barnes, Magee, Young, and Lesser, that Isaiah 53:4 in its literal rendering corresponds exactly with Matthew 8:17. We see, therefore, that the latter is a direct reference to the former. Then the beautiful prophecy of salvation and healing is found in the following verse, viz. Isaiah 53:5: "But he was wounded for our transgressions, he was bruised for our iniquities: the chastisement of our peace was upon him; and with his stripes we are healed."

These prophecies all point to the redemptive work of Jesus, which finds its center in the Cross. The apostle Peter refers to this verse just quoted in the following language: "Who his own self bare our sins in his own body on the tree, that we, being dead to sins, should live unto righteousness: *by whose stripes ye were healed*" (1 Peter 2:24).

The following references will enable you to see that more is said in prophecy about healing: Isaiah 42:7; 61:1—fulfilled in Luke 4:18-21. Prophecy in Malachi 4:2—fulfilled in Matthew 4:16 and Luke 1:78-79. These are all fulfilled in redemption.

These promises of God are all fulfilled in this day of grace and Holy-Ghost dispensation. They are all part of God's glorious redemptive work. It is His holy will to glorify Himself by restoring His children to perfect bodily health, and thus manifesting to all mankind His love, faithfulness, tender mercy, and truth.

The deliverance of the body from the destructive power of Satan and its restoration to health is an integral part of salvation. Were this lacking, God's glorious perfect salvation would be incomplete and imperfect. The Lord Jesus would have failed to completely deliver us from Satan's dominion and destructive power; and this marvelous, wonderful, and glorious *salvation* of the human race, the product of the wisdom, love, and power of the Almighty, would have been a partial failure after all!

Q. Do you believe that the Bible teaches divine healing as a redemption blessing?

A. Yes. Do you not see how plain this is made in the prophecies just quoted and in their fulfillment? Jesus worked in every respect in His life, ministry, death, and resurrection, just according to the redemption plan. His words and deeds are the divine expression of this redemption plan, and we can clearly see that healing for the body is placed upon an equality with healing for the soul. Both are obtained upon the same grounds: obedience and faith.

Q. Can a person possess salvation without healing?

A. Yes, he may. While both are obtained by faith, yet they may not be obtained by the same act of faith. Jesus will be to us just what our faith takes Him for.

Q. Did Jesus heal everybody?

A. Yes, all who came to Him in faith. Read Matthew 4:23-24 and 12:15.

Q. But they did not seem to have faith, did they?

A. Yes. If you read the references just mentioned, you will notice the people "came to him" for healing and "followed him." At Nazareth, His own town, where He had been brought up, He could do no great work among them, because of their unbelief.[1] At Capernaum, where some of the most remarkable healings were wrought, the people were a believing people.[2] Out of nineteen of the most prominent individual cases of healing in the ministry of Christ and the apostles, there are twelve of these where their faith is spoken of.[3] The rest are mentioned sufficiently plain to show that faith brought the healing in every case.

Q. Did not Jesus heal arbitrarily, for the sole purpose of establishing His divinity?

A. No. He healed according to the law of redemption and because of His great compassion to suffering humanity. (See Matthew 14:14.)

Q. Did not healing cease when Jesus finished His earthly ministry?

A. No. It was more wonderfully manifested in the ministry of the apostles, after the Day of Pentecost. (See Acts 3:1-16; 5:12-16; 8:6-8; 9:17-18,33-42; 14:8-10,19-20; 19:11-12; 20:8-12; 28:3-6,8.) This proves clearly that divine healing is a redemption blessing for the entire Holy-Spirit dispensation.

Q. But we are taught that it was only for the beginning of the gospel dispensation. How about that?

A. The Bible does not teach any such doctrine.

[1] See Matthew 13:54-58.

[2] See Matthew 8, Mark 2-3,5, and Luke 4:31-43.

[3] See Matthew 8:10; 9:2,29; and 15:28; Mark 2:5; 5:34; and 10:52; Luke 5:20; 7:50; 8:48; 17:19; and 18:42.

Q. But it does teach that "when that which is perfect is come, then that which is in part shall be done away" (1 Corinthians 13:10.) How about this?

A. This Scripture has no reference to divine healing or any of the redemption blessings that they shall be done away in this dispensation. If there ever has been a time in this dispensation when it could have been said with reference to the full possession and manifestation of the gospel blessings, that "that which is perfect is come," it was when the Holy Spirit came at Pentecost; but we see after this, mighty works of salvation and healing; and they were in no sense "done away" with, but were greatly increased. So you see the "done away" argument has no scriptural basis whatever. As long as the dispensation of grace shall last, so long shall the benefits of grace be extended to "whomsoever will."

Q. Well then, when was divine healing done away?

A. In the design of God it was never done away, nor was it ever taken away, abolished, or withdrawn. There is not a single word in the Bible to that effect. The statement originated from the adversary of mankind in an endeavor to retain his power and deprive mankind of some of the great advantages of the Atonement; and to prevent his victims, bound, oppressed, and tortured by him, from obtaining their freedom.

The Lord Jesus came to set the captives free and to deliver those who are bound, (See Isaiah 61:1), and His work is being continued today by His representatives on earth. He is with them always, even unto the end of the dispensation, or "consummation of the age" (Matthew 28:20 RV[4]), working with them, accompanying the proclamation of the Gospel of deliverance and salvation from Satan's power, with the manifestation of His presence and healing power. "They shall lay hands on the sick, and they shall recover" (Mark 16:18).

[4] "RV"— RV stands for *Revised Version,* which denotes a Bible translation that came out between 1881-1884. A group of English and American scholars translated this version using manuscripts that hadn't been available to the King James Version translators. (Frank Charles Thompson, editor and compiler, *The New Chain Reference Bible* [Indianapolis: B. B. Kirkbride Bible Co., Inc., 1964] p. 181.)

This great salvation is declared by His messengers and confirmed by "God also bearing them witness, both with signs and wonders, and with divers miracles, and gifts of the Holy Ghost" (Hebrews 2:4).

Q. Do you mean to say that it was perpetuated in the primitive Church?

A. Certainly it was. History shows that for several centuries there was no other means of healing practiced in the Church.

Q. But what happened after that?

A. Just what crowded out all other gospel truths—the superstitions and unbelief of the apostasy. But, thank God, the darkness is past and the Son of "righteousness with healing in his wings"[5] is shining salvation and health to all who will forsake all their old doctrines, creeds, and superstitions and get back upon the old apostolic foundation, the Word of God.

Q. But how may I know that it is still God's will to heal?

A. Just as you may know that it is His will to save—by His Word. His Word is His will. Whatever is for God's glory, that is what He wants to do. It is for His glory to heal His servants. It shows how much He loves them and manifests His power. One case of healing in the name of Jesus, accompanied by the joy of the knowledge of sins forgiven and the peace that passeth all understanding,[6] is sufficient to demonstrate the divinity and resurrection of Jesus Christ and therefore convict and convince sinners.

Q. But it may be His will not to heal me.

A. You must go outside of God's Word to find standing ground for such a conclusion; for there is nothing inside of the Bible about healing but what corresponds with our blessed text: "Himself took our infirmities and bare our sicknesses." Most people who argue that it might not be God's will to heal them are at the same time taking medicine and employing every possible human agency to get well. Why be so inconsistent? Why fight against

[5] Malachi 4:2, paraphrased.

[6] See Philippians 4:6-7.

God's will? If it is His will for you not to get well, then die. Stop fighting against God.

Q. But does not sickness come from God as a blessing?

A. No. It never comes from God, only in a permissive sense, the same as a temptation comes to us; and sickness is never a blessing to us, only as any other temptation or trial may be considered a blessing. The blessing is in the deliverance and healing. Every person who has ever experienced the healing touch of God knows what a blessing to the soul comes with it. Sickness is an abnormal condition of the body and cannot be a blessing from God.

Q. If it does not come from God, then where does it come from?

A. It comes from the devil and was always dealt with by Jesus in His earthly ministry as a work of the devil. The Word of God plainly teaches us that the devil is the author of disease. (Read Job 2:7; Luke 13:16; and Acts 10:38.)

Q. But are there not some other scriptures that teach us that sickness comes from God?

A. Only in a permissive sense.

Q. Does the Bible teach us that God intends to be the healer of His people without the use of medicine?

A. Yes. It nowhere recommends or commands the use of medicine with prayer and faith. [See note below.]

Q. But how about Hezekiah's figs, the blind man's clay, and Timothy's wine?

A. It is true Isaiah told Hezekiah to take a lump of figs, but this has nothing to do with the New Testament means of healing. Also it is very evident that the figs did not heal him; but God said, "I will heal thee."[7]

Editor's note: During Maria Etter's time, medicine was a young science and medicines were not regulated. This meant that some medicines were often poisonous mixtures sold to unwitting buyers. Her natural distrust of medicine at this period of time is understandable. Healing evangelists like Kathryn Kuhlman, Oral Roberts, or Kenneth Hagin all advocate staying on medication until the healing manifests. This means a diabetic should stay on insulin until the blood sugar levels show an improvement that allows a reduction or elimination of the medication.

[7] See Isaiah 38.

Jesus did not use the clay on the eyes of the blind man for any curative power, for He commanded the man at once to go and wash it off. No one has heard of blindness from birth being healed by the use of clay as a medicine since then, or ever before. It is evident that the spittle and clay were used by Jesus as a requirement of submission and obedience from the blind man. The thought must have been repulsive and humiliating to him as the clay was applied to his eyes, but, like Naaman, he submitted and obeyed and received the blessing unspeakable, of healing.[8]

The juice of the grape was recommended to Timothy as an article of diet, and would not be objectionable today, in its proper use, under similar circumstances.[9]

Q. Are not medicines recognized in the Word of God?

A. Yes. Let us read how it recognizes them. "Thou hast no healing medicines" (Jeremiah 30:13). "In vain shalt thou use many medicines" (Jeremiah 46:11). "A merry heart doeth good like a medicine" (margin, "to a medicine," showing that the merry heart is better than the medicine, Proverbs 17:22). "And the fruit thereof shall be for meat, and the leaf thereof for medicine" (Ezekiel 47:12). This latter reference does not mean any material remedy but is prophetical of the Tree of Life and divine healing. (See Revelation 22:2.) Thus we see the Word of God places no intrinsic value upon medicine.

Q. Is not the ministry of physicians for the body designed of God, the same as the ministry of the Gospel for the soul?

A. No. The greater portion of the physicians of the land are ungodly people, many of them professed infidels, and were never designed of God to administer drugs and poisons to anyone; much less to the people of God, whose bodies are the sacred temples of the Holy Spirit. "The Lord [is] for the body" (1 Corinthians 6:13). The ministers of the Gospel are the ministers for soul and body. "And they departed, and went through the towns, preaching the gospel, and healing every where"

[8] See John 9:1-11 and 2 Kings 5.

[9] See 1 Timothy 5:23.

(Luke 9:6). "And they went forth, and preached every where, the Lord working with them, and confirming the word with signs following" (Mark 16:20).

Q. But is not the ministry of physicians recognized in the Bible?

A. Yes. Let us read how it recognizes them. "But ye are forgers of lies, ye are all physicians of no value" (Job 13:4). "And Asa in the thirty and ninth year of his reign was diseased in his feet, until his disease was exceeding great: yet in his disease he sought not to the Lord, but to the physicians. And Asa slept with his fathers" (2 Chronicles 16:12-13).

He died.

[Here is another scripture that refers to physicians:]"And had suffered many things of many physicians, and had spent all that she had, and was nothing bettered, but rather grew worse" (Mark 5:26). These scriptures show that the Bible gives no very favorable recognition of physicians.

Q. Was not the anointing with oil the mode of doctoring in Bible times?

A. No. While some kinds of oil may have some medical value for some kinds of disease, it was not at all designed for any such use in connection with the prayer of faith in healing the sick. If anointing was the mode of doctoring, the Church would have had no need of instruction in this respect; for it would have been a common practice everywhere by the doctors. Had this been the mind of the apostle, then he would have assigned the work of anointing to the doctors; and his instructions would have to have been given something after the following ridiculous manner, which ought to make every divine-healing-fighter hide his face with shame. "Is any sick among you? Let him send for the doctor and let him anoint him, and the anointing shall save the sick. The effectual fervent use of such anointing availeth much."

It would be wisdom for professed ministers of the Gospel to take an attitude toward God's Word which would harmonize with it. It would be more honest to declare outright that they do not believe the Bible than to try to cover up their unbelief by perverting it. God has assigned this sacred ministry of anointing and praying the prayer of faith for healing the sick to the elders of His Church.

Q. But do you not think we ought to employ a physician and then ask God to bless the medicine?

A. No. That is not God's way of healing; and furthermore, it is a question to many intelligent and scientific people as to whether good or evil results from the use of poisonous drugs and medicines which are so generally used today.

Q. What! Do you mean to say there is no healing virtue in medicines and drugs?

A. According to many of the medical authorities there is not. Whatever benefit there may be in them, there is evidently much more harm done by their use than there is good. Dr. J. B. of Boston, an eminent physician and believer in divine healing, in writing about the blind faith of people in the use of patent medicines, says: "But to be faithful, I must also warn you against the use of drugs by physicians. Narcotics, sedatives, stimulants, tonics, quinine, antipyrine, and hundreds of others are injuring brains and nerves, stomachs, and livers, bringing on heart failure, and doing far more harm than good." [See note below.]

Where is Koch's Tuberculosis Lymph[10] that was to cure that disease? Dr. Talmage[11] preached a sermon about the salvation of humanity from tuberculosis by Dr. Koch. The Emperor of

[10]"Koch's Tuberculosis Lymph"—Robert Koch (1843-1910) discovered something called tuberculin in the late nineteenth century, which he thought would be a cure for tuberculosis and also a vaccine against it. After his announcement in1896, he was famous for having found the cure for tuberculosis. Soon after it became apparent that tuberculin didn't work for either a cure or a vaccine. Koch didn't die of tuberculosis, but went on to make many other discoveries. This comment, probably written in 1899, occurs at a time when public disappointment was high.

[11]Thomas Dewitt Talmage (1832-1902), a well-known New York preacher and evangelist.

Germany ennobled him, and they gave him a large sum of money for his wonderful discovery. But Professor Virchow, the greatest pathologist in Germany, dissected more than a score of bodies of persons who had died after taking Koch's lymph and found that the effect of the lymph was to drive the parasites out of the tubercles which they had formed, increase their number, drive them into the healthy tissues, and quickly destroy life. Dr. Virchow demonstrated that Koch's lymph was a creator of tuberculosis (consumption) and not a destroyer. You would not find a doctor in Chicago today that would give a drop of it, and yet they nearly all praised it at first as a wonderful discovery. The last I read of Professor Koch was that he was dying of tuberculosis.

Dr. W. H. said that if all the drugs were cast into the sea, it would be better for humanity but worse for the fishes. Dr. Bell said: "I believe that if the advice of Dr. H. were followed and physicians would confine themselves to giving good advice, and mechanical and surgical aid when needed, the mortality would improve four or five percent; or in other words, there would be a savings of about three thousand lives (annually) in New England alone, and probably much more than that." In speaking of the belief of some who would take medicine and then ask God to bless it, he says, "If what Dr. H. says is true, it would require a miracle to save the fishes, and how much more to save the people; how much more divine power, so to speak, to overcome both the disease *and* the ill effect of the drug?" Many testimonials of noted and honored men who have spent their lives in the study and practice of medicine can be given, which show the danger and uncertainty of drugs. Watson,[12] a renowned author of London, says: "After all, it is God that healeth our diseases and redeemeth our life from destruction."[13]

[12]"Watson"—A 17th-century puritan, Thomas Watson, rector of Saint Stephen's Walbrook, London, who was known for his sermons and books, such as *A Divine Cordial*, *The Ten Commandments*, and *The Lord's Prayer.*

[13]See Psalm 103:3-4.

Q. Would you advise every child of God to trust God alone for healing and health?

A. Certainly, for this is God's way. It is what He desires us to do. "It is better to trust in the Lord than to put confidence in man" (Psalm 118:8). It honors Him to get in line with His divine plan, and it is a great spiritual benefit to everyone.

Q. But would not such a position, if every child of God take it, affect the practice of many Christian physicians?

A. Well, yes, it might affect it somewhat, but we are not responsible for that. And then there will always be plenty of sinners and unbelieving Christian professors who will always furnish employment to every reliable and worthy physician; and we shall always feel grateful if there does prove to be a worthy physician who may be a blessing to those who know not the way of the Lord.

Q. What attitude do physicians generally take toward divine healing?

A. We will let Dr. B. answer. He says: "I would say, . . . there can be no antagonism between the medical profession and divine healing. (Of course, he must have reference to good, conscientious people of the profession.) First, because of the vast number of incurable cases for which medical or surgical treatment can do little or nothing. New England has 4,600,000 inhabitants, of whom 1,500 die every year of cancer, 15,000 of consumption, and about 80,000 from all causes. Can you believe that the medical profession would not welcome the incoming of a measure of divine power which should save all this suffering and prolong all these lives, or, at least, of the useful and saved ones, till threescore years and ten? Or if only a few should have the faith to grasp this blessing, what physician can there be found who would not rejoice? It is not the MDs but the DDs[14] who oppose this teaching.

Q. Why do the DDs oppose it?

A. Because of their shameful cowardice. Many of them, if not all, cannot but see the precious doctrine in the Bible; but there are very few, if any, of these men who are preaching for salary, who

[14] "MDs" and "DDs"—Medical doctors and doctors of divinity, i. e. educated pastors and theologians.

have the moral or Christian courage to preach the full Gospel. Their salary and reputation are at stake, and they are very careful to preach nothing that will offend their worldly supporters. This is a great wrong and every man who thus keeps back the truth from the people will have to answer for it at the great Day of reckoning. Because they are afraid to preach the truth they try to make themselves disbelieve it; and to justify themselves they must oppose it.

Q. Was not Luke spoken of as the beloved physician?

A. Yes (in Colossians 4:14) but this does not signify that he was practicing after he went into the gospel work. There is no record, nor the slightest intimation, that he did. It was evident that he was present with Paul at Troas where the young man Eutychus was restored to life[15]. However, there is nothing said about Luke interfering with any medical suggestions. He was called the physician in this reference, very likely because of his former profession.

Q. If healing is for us all, how can we ever die?

A. The same as the patriarchs, prophets, apostles, the saints of the first three centuries, and many of them in the nineteenth century. Without disease, "like as a shock of corn cometh in in his season."[16] There were many also whose lives were cut short by martyrdom. There is not the slightest shadow of intimation in the Bible that we must die with disease.

Q. Why is it then that so many of our fathers and mothers have died with disease?

A. Because divine healing has been so little taught. Many never heard anything about it, only that it could not be obtained in this life.

Q. Why are there some who believe in healing and seemingly fail to obtain it?

A. There are many reasons why. Many people do not give God a fair chance to heal them, because they will not meet all the

[15]See Acts 20:4-12.

[16]Job 5:26.

conditions of His Word. There are thousands of secret sins, each one of them enough to hinder their faith from laying hold upon God. The apostle says, "Beloved, if our heart condemn us not, then we have confidence toward God. And whatsoever we ask, we receive of him, because we keep his commandments, and do those things that are pleasing in his sight" (1 John 3:21-22). It means much to live in God's sight where our hearts condemn us not.

Some also who come to God for healing come only to "try healing" as they would try some new doctor. They would be glad to buy it with money; but when they find that it costs every sin and requires a holy walk with God, they become offended and get nothing from God. Jesus said in connection with healing (Matthew 11:6): "Blessed is he, whosoever shall not be offended in me." Others, whose faith is not sufficient at the time to grasp the promises and get the blessing, become discouraged and give up; whereas they should keep upon believing ground until the blessing comes.

Q. But are there not a few who seem to have met every condition and still fail to get the blessing?

A. Yes, apparently so. Yet it is evident that some of the conditions have not been met. It may be no fault on the part of the individual, only that it may be the lack of determined faith; but whatever it may be, there is a lack on the part of the individual somewhere; for God's part is complete; and when ours is, the work must be done. As the Church advances in spiritual light and power, there will be a better understanding of some of these cases.

Q. What are the conditions on which God promises to heal us?

A. We must forsake all our sins and then claim the virtue of the atoning blood, by faith, till we come to know that the free and unmerited divine favor and promises are ours.

We must have away down (*sic*) in our hearts a settled resolve to serve God better than we ever have before.

We should be willing to minister to the saints as opportunity offers and cooperate with them in God's work. God's work is the turning of sinners from sin unto holiness. We should have compassion for all men and a desire to help them. We should be seeking to know God's will better and be zealous in carrying it out in our lives.

We should search the Scriptures and study and meditate on them till we know it is God's will to heal us and believe, when prayers are offered on our behalf, that God hears and answers them.

Q. Should a person who cannot seem to get the blessing then go to taking medicine?

A. No. He should get nearer to God and wait upon Him in importunity until his faith brings the blessing.[17]

Q. How about innocent children and persons whose afflictions render them incapable of exercising faith?

A. In such cases intercessory faith will bring the blessing for them.

Q. What is intercessory faith?

A. It is the exercise of faith by one person for another. Parents can exercise faith for the healing of their children, or any child of God can help another.

Q. Can intercessory faith bring healing to another person who is responsible to obey and believe for himself?

A. Yes, there may be cases where this is done for the time; but in every case each responsible person must, sooner or later, come to the place where his individual responsibility must be acted upon and perfect obedience rendered to God.

Q. What steps must be taken to obtain healing?

A. Obedience and faith. People seeking healing should come forsaking all their sins forever; claiming the atonement of the blood of Christ on their behalf, believing the Word of God and His promises, and with determination to serve God better than before and to walk in all the light from His Word.

Q. What means must be used?

A. There are different scriptural means.

1. Anointing with oil and the prayer of faith. James 5:14.

[17]Other healing evangelists disagree with this stand and have suggested that many times until believers have enough faith to be healed, they should remain under the care of a physician.

2. Laying on of hands of them that believe. Mark 16:18.
3. The prayer of faith individually. John 15:7 and 2 Kings 20:1,5.
4. The prayer of faith through one or more intercessors. John. 4:49, Matthew 8:5-13; 9:2-8.

Q. Is Christian Science the same as divine healing?

A. No. It is vastly different. In its origin it differs as widely as night from day. Christian Science is less than forty years old; while the first mention of divine healing dates back to Abraham when he prayed for Abimelech.[18] Christian Science was conceived and given birth to by Mrs. Mary B. G. Eddy of Boston, Massachusetts. Divine healing is given to man by the God of heaven.

As a science, Christian Science is a conglomeration of illogical, ridiculous, and impractical theories, which no Christian Scientist (so-called) has ever yet, nor ever will be able to demonstrate. It claims that there is no sickness, pain, sin, evil, devil, nor death—all these things are but delusions and can be overcome by intelligence and understanding. It is known also as a mind cure, mental medicine, and metaphysical healing. If it made no other claim than scientific, there would be little danger of it doing any harm, but its doctrines as a religion make it a dangerous and Christ-dishonoring foe. It perverts the sacred Word of God and assails the plan of redemption, ignoring the blood of Christ and denying the deity of the Lord Jesus Christ.

A few points only can be noticed here. It denies the depravity of man and teaches that every man is the reflection of God and possesses inherent divinity regardless of regeneration. It rejects the second and third chapters of Genesis, the history of the fall of man. It teaches that man has never fallen and needs no redemption, only in the sense that he must be brought to an understanding of Christian Science. It totally ignores the doctrine of vicarious atonement and therefore is of the devil. Its doctrines are based upon such skillfully perverted and misapplied texts of Scripture that many souls are led astray by its delusions.

[18]See Genesis 20:17-18.

Q. How about spiritualism?[19]

A. Spiritualism is closely allied to Christian Science. It is another of the antichrist doctrines that denies the [redemption] plan, being direct counterfeits of divine healing.

Q. Is it possible that people may be healed through satanic power?

Q. Yes. The devil has power to work miracles (see Revelation 16:13-14) and when souls can be the easier deceived by them, he will give the deception. He is the author of disease and has the power to remove it, if by so doing he can more easily hold his subjects in darkness. Every professed healer or teacher of healing and everyone who claims healing, who denies the blood of Christ as the sacrifice for sin, is antichrist and of the devil; no matter what miraculous manifestations of healing, or otherwise, they may claim to produce. (See Galatians 1:8-9.)

Q. Can any be healed by animal magnetism?[20]

A. There may be some material results upon disease through this power, but this is not divine healing. It is but a natural cause producing a natural effect and can be practiced by any person who may possess it, regardless of any scriptural or true spiritual condition. In many cases these professed healers have proved to be hypocrites and frauds, claiming to possess divine power to heal, deceiving souls for advantage and gain and reproaching the cause of Christ.

Q. How may we know the difference between these counterfeits and the teachers of divine healing?

A. Every true minister of the Gospel preaches divine healing to a greater or less extent, depending upon the light received, and

---

[19] "spiritualism"—The belief that the dead still live and communicate to the living through mediums. It was a popular fad in the nineteenth century, arising from a crisis of faith in Europe and America.

[20] "animal magnetism"—A concept developed and popularized by Anton Mesmer, who believed that the forces of life in living things could be transferred. He advocated healing by laying the fingers or hands in certain positions to transfer the force to the ailing person or to free the flow of their own life for use. (Robert H. Wozniak "Trance and Trauma; Functional Nervous Disorders and the Subconscious Mind" Webpage. Accessed: 22 May 2000, Web address: http://serendip.brynmawr.edu/mind/trance.html).

always demands the Bible requirements of every sinner—"repentance toward God, and faith toward our Lord Jesus Christ"[21]—and never claims to heal anyone, but simply prays the prayer of faith and attributes all healing power to God through Jesus Christ.

Q. Does not God give the "gifts of healing" to some?

A. Yes. This is one of the gifts of the Holy Spirit (see 1 Corinthians 12:9,30), which is given to such persons in the Church of God as can glorify Him therewith. The gifts of healing are the various spiritual means designed of God to be used in cases of emergency by every true minister and child of God; but as an individual endowment, it is given to certain ones who are called and qualified by the Holy Spirit to the ministry of healing in casting out devils and laying on hands.

Q. What is the grace of healing?

A. It is our redemption right to healing, the same as justification and sanctification, purchased for us through the Atonement and offered to all who will meet the Bible conditions.

People seeking healing should believe it is God's time to heal them and have faith enough to believe He hears the prayers offered on their behalf. When they are prayed for, they should believe the disease is gone and try to act their faith. The cause is gone and the effects of the disease sometimes do not go till later.

If you say, "If it is God's will He will save me," you could pray till the judgment trumpet sounds and you would not get salvation. So it is with healing. You should be convinced all disease is from Satan and that it is God's will to heal you; if you are unsaved, when you forsake all your sins; if you are saved, when you are prepared to keep all your vows to the Most High and to walk in all the light He gives you.

You never get faith to be healed till you surrender. Give up your own will and way and mode of life and yield yourself to Christ, carrying out the directions of His Word and Spirit and desiring Him to work through you to establish His kingdom amongst men.

[21] Acts 20:21.

Do not say, "I will be healed if it is His will." "If" implies doubt. Let not him that doubteth think that he shall receive anything from the Lord. When we waver and doubt, it is like the waves of the sea casting up filth in the face of the Almighty.[22]

"If ye abide in me, and my words abide in you, ye shall ask what ye will, and it shall be done unto you" (John 15:7). We should abide in Him, in His service, having His mind, filled with His Spirit.

Whatever is for God's glory, that is what He wants to do. It is for His glory to heal His saints; it shows how much He loves them and manifests His power. One case of healing in the name of Jesus, accompanied by the joy of the knowledge of sins forgiven, is sufficient to demonstrate the divinity and resurrection of Jesus, and therefore convince sinners.

"If ye shall ask any thing in my name, I will do it" (John 14:14). This is not merely making mention of His name, it means anything that is for the good of His kingdom.

If a clerk obtains anything in the name of the firm he represents, it is understood it is for the glory and upbuilding of the firm and to be used to carry on their business. He would not be allowed to obtain things in the name of the firm and then use them for his individual private use. The firm we work for is the Father, Son, and Holy Ghost. Some ask in the name of Christ, but He is not going to get any good out of it, because they do it from a selfish motive. God cannot be deceived, and He does the healing. Is He going to get anything out of your healing? Is His kingdom and mankind going to be benefited?

Q. Is it right then for us always to pray for each other's healing and health?

A. Yes. "Beloved, I wish (pray) above all things that thou mayest prosper and be in health, even as thy soul prospereth" (3 John 2 [addition Etter's]). "Confess your faults one to another, and pray one for another, that ye may be healed" (James 5:16).

Intercession

Q. Do the intercessions of Jesus mean much to us?

[22] See James 1:6-8.

A. The most pathetic aspect of the redemptive methods is the intercession of the Lord Jesus—our Great High Priest gone into the heavenly place; hidden behind the veil; reappearing at the high court of the majesty on high as the advocate of man, suing for mercy and reconciliation; the eternal God listening to His plea for sinners who, coming in their own name, would be refused audience, would be consumed by the divine indignation. Had any common Jew appeared in the presence of Ahasuerus to ask the revocation of the royal edict, he would have been slain in the courts of the palace; but to Esther the queen, clad in her royal attire (the insignia of state), the king could hold out the golden scepter.[23]

The Most High God of holiness and truth, at the head of His universe, framed in purity and fashioned for righteousness, could not treat[24] face to face in His open court in presence of His holy and law-abiding angels, with rebels and conspirators; with creatures who had denied His name and joined hand and cause with an invading traitor. The first effect of sin was to suspend communication between God and man. The Almighty could not listen to His enemies in arms or to any being spotted by disloyalty.

Q. But is not the heavenly Father eternally and infinitely pitiful?[25]

A. Yes, and eternally just, as well. And if a holy Sovereign would have a loyal universe, He must rule the moral races in exact equipoise of divine attributes. His scepter must be held in the clasped hands of justice and mercy. To make mercy "a darling attribute" would unsettle the integrity of the divine administration. To have condoned the offense of the first pair, and through them, of the whole race by a great act of amnesty, would have set a premium on rebellion—a bestowment of special favor because of treason. A finite ruler can rarely do this with safety with finite subjects; and infinite Sovereign with finite rebels, never. Justice must not waver in the hands of One who demands the allegiance of all worlds.

There must be no compromise with evil in a perfect jurisprudence. This, we may believe, is the reason why the offended

[23] See Esther 5:1-2.

[24] "treat"—negotiate.

[25] "pitiful"—full of pity for others.

Lord did not call the faithless twain[26] to repentance and pardon directly, without the intervention of a third person. For some will not cease to make light of the doctrine of Christ's expiation in vicarious suffering for the race and ridicule the necessity of a mediator between a loving God and penitent offenders. But the necessity of an intercessor at the court of heaven is as clearly taught in both Testaments as of a sin-bearer—a Savior. Even pardoned and renewed men, while in a state of probation, have no privilege of access to the Father save through the mediation of another, even Jesus the Lamb of God: "Wherefore also he is able to save to the uttermost them who draw near unto God through him seeing he ever liveth to make intercession for them" (Hebrews 7:25 RV[27]).

Q. Just what do the Scriptures mean by "Intercession," "Intercessor," "Advocate"?

A. Intercession—To meet with, to come between, to intercede, as in our text, Hebrews 7:25 and Romans 8:27, 8:38[-39], and 11:2. Intercessor—One who intercedes, or comes between parties who are unable to meet in their own name, for some reason. Advocate—One called in, a helper, as in 1 John 2:1. "If any man sin, we have an advocate (at the throne[28]) . . . Jesus Christ the righteous." He pleads our cause, presents our case.

Q. On what ground does Jesus undertake and maintain our case?

A. Not merely in suppliance for mercy or pleading for clemency; but His plea is righteousness, not in His client, but in Himself. "We have an advocate . . . Jesus Christ the righteous." He presents not our merits but His own. Wherein our cause is weak, He covers it with His own virtue. The claims of justice against us He meets and cancels by the merit of His suffering in our stead. To the record of our sins, He pleads that He "bore them in his own body on the tree."[29] If justice flaunts its death warrant against us,

[26] "twain"—two, i. e. Adam and Eve.

[27] RV stands for *Revised Version,* which denotes a Bible translation that came out between 1881-1884. (Frank Charles Thompson, editor and compiler, *The New Chain Reference Bible* (Indianapolis: B.B. Kirkbride Bible Co., Inc., 1964) p. 181.)

[28] Addition Etter's.

[29] 1 Peter 2:24, paraphrased.

running forever, He nullifies it by the testimony that "He tasted death for every man."[30] If some angel, jealous for the dignity of the throne, insists that the holy Lord cannot treat with sinners, He enjoins that it is not sinners who are speaking, but Himself in the sinner's stead; and He "knew no sin." He is "righteous."[31]

We may be reminded that it is said in the Book that the Spirit intercedes for us.[32] True. And a glorious truth it is, for the exposed and hunted people of God, surrounded by evil and pursued by devils, need special divine attention in both worlds, not only advocacy at the throne but also defense and guidance in their struggle to maintain, against principalities and powers and spiritual wickedness in high places, vital and vigorous relations with Him who represents them before the Father. Someone has beautifully said, "Christ pleads for us above, and the Spirit pleads in us here below." —Selected[33]

Facts Worth Remembering

God in Person Does the Healing—Jesus said, "I am the way and the truth and the life," and He has ever been revealed to His people in all the ages by the covenant name, Jehovah-Rophi,[34] or "I am Jehovah that healeth thee." (See John 14:6 and Exodus 15:26.)

The Lord Jesus, the Christ, Is Still the Healer—He cannot change, for "Jesus, the Christ, is the same yesterday and today, yea and forever;"' and He is still with us, for He said: "Lo, I am with you all the days, even unto the consummation of the age."[35] (See Hebrews 13:8 and Matthew 28:20.) Because He is unchangeable and because He is present, in spirit, just as when in the flesh, He is the healer of His people.

Disease Can Never Be God's Will—It is the devil's work, consequent upon sin, and it is impossible for the work of the devil ever to be

---

[30] Hebrews 2:9, paraphrased.

[31] 2 Corinthians 5:21 and 1 John 2:1.

[32] See Romans 8:26.

[33] Source unknown.

[34] "Rophi"—Rapha.

[35] Possibly taken from the RV version.

the will of God. The Christ came to "destroy the works of the devil," and when He was here on earth He healed "all manner of disease and all manner of sickness," and all these sufferers are expressly declared to have been "oppressed of the devil." (See 1 John 3:8, Matthew 4:23, and Acts 10:38.)

The Gifts of Healing Are Permanent—It is expressly declared that the "gifts and calling of God are without repentance," and the gifts of healings are amongst the nine gifts of the Spirit to the Church. (See Romans 11:29 and 1 Corinthians 12:8-11.)

Partaking Worthily of the Lord's Supper Should Ensure Health—We can also see that divine healing was included in the Atonement because it is shown in 1 Corinthians 11:29-30, that those who eat the Lord's Supper worthily will not die premature death or be sick.

Some of God's Promises

Will we trust God or flee to man?

> Cursed be the man that trusteth in man, and maketh flesh his arm.
>
> Jeremiah 17:5

> And Jesus went about all Galilee, teaching in their synagogues, and preaching the gospel of the kingdom, and healing all manner of sickness and all manner of disease among the people.
>
> Matthew 4:23

> And when he had called unto him his twelve disciples, he gave them power against unclean spirits, to cast them out, and to heal all manner of sickness and all manner of disease.
>
> Matthew 10:1

Our pastors tell us to follow Christ. I ask, "Are they doing it?" "And heal the sick that are therein, and say unto them, The kingdom of God is come nigh unto you" (Luke 10:9). This command is to all that preach Christ today. "And he sent them to preach the kingdom of God, and to heal the sick" (Luke 9:2). Are they doing it now?

> And they brought unto him all sick people that were taken with divers diseases and torments, and those which were possessed with devils . . . and he healed them.
>
> Matthew 4:24

> He is the same yesterday and to day and for ever.[36]

> Now when the sun was setting, all they that had any sick with divers diseases brought them unto him; and he laid his hands on every one of them, and healed them.
>
> Luke 4:40

> And the whole multitude sought to touch him: for there went virtue out of him, and healed them all.
>
> Luke 6:19

Christ is no respecter of persons; the same faith brings the same power today.

> And a great multitude followed him, because they saw his miracles which he did on them that were diseased.
>
> John 6:2

> And besought him that they might only touch the hem of his garment: and as many as touched were made perfectly whole.
>
> Matthew 14:36

> Bless the Lord, O my soul, and forget not all his benefits: Who forgiveth all thine iniquities; who healeth all thy diseases.
>
> Psalm 103:2-3

[36] Hebrews 13:8, paraphrased.

If the Lord heals all, there is none left for the doctors. God can and will do these things without man's ways, for He says, "My ways are not man's ways.[37] For I will restore health unto thee, and I will heal thee of thy wounds, saith the Lord" (Jeremiah 30:17).

> The diseased have ye not strengthened, neither have ye healed that which was sick, neither have ye bound up that which was broken, neither have ye brought again that which was driven away, neither have ye sought that which was lost; but with force and with cruelty have ye ruled them.
>
> Ezekiel 34:4

This is to the minister; God help them to heed it. They were commanded to heal the sick as well as preach the Gospel, and that command is on all until the Gospel is preached to all the world and every creature.[38]

> The Spirit of the Lord is upon me, because he hath anointed me to preach the gospel to the poor; he hath sent me to heal the brokenhearted, to preach deliverance to the captives, and recovering of sight to the blind, to set at liberty them that are bruised.
>
> Luke 4:18

> And the power of the Lord was present to heal them.
>
> Luke 5:17

> But unto you that fear my name shall the Sun of righteousness arise with healing in his wings; and ye shall go forth, and grow up as calves of the stall.
>
> Malachi 4:2

> In vain shalt thou use many medicines.
>
> Jeremiah 46:11

[37] See Isaiah 55:8.

[38] See Mark 16:15-18.

> And Joseph commanded his servants the physicians to embalm his father.
>
> Genesis 50:2

The only place in the Bible where the doctors are called is to the dead.

> Then he called his twelve disciples together, and gave them power and authority over all devils, and to cure diseases.
>
> Luke 9:1

> Insomuch that they brought forth the sick into the streets, and laid them on beds and couches, that at the least the shadow of Peter passing by might overshadow some of them.
>
> Acts 5:15

> Fools, because of their transgression, and because of their iniquities, are afflicted. . . . Then they cry unto the Lord in their trouble, and he saveth them out of their distresses. He sent his word, and healed them, and delivered them from their destructions.
>
> Psalm 107:17,19-20

> Verily, verily, I say unto you, He that believeth on me, the works that I do shall he do also; and greater works than these shall he do; because I go unto my Father.
>
> John 14:12

> But seek ye first the kingdom of God, and his righteousness; and all these things shall be added unto you.
>
> Matthew 6:33

Recapitulation

Man was created in perfect health and it was God's will for him so to remain. God loved him and as long as he was grateful and obedient kept him from suffering and disease. (See Genesis 1:31.)

Sickness, infirmity, and disease are all the work of the devil, either directly or through the agency of his subordinate devils. (See Luke 13:16 and Acts. 10:38.)

When Eve and Adam yielded to the temptation of Satan and disobeyed God, sin entered into the world, and they became subjects of Satan. (See Romans 5:19.) He deceived them. Instead of being "as gods, knowing good and evil,"[39] they laid themselves open to the punishment which God inflicted upon them by permitting the devil to have power over them and afflict their bodies with pains and aches, with disease and sickness and premature death. (See Hebrews 2:14, 1 Corinthians 11:29-30, and Psalm 55:23.)

The blessed Lamb of God, the Lord Jesus Christ, undertook the fight for the redemption of our race. He overcame and is today crowned victor, but only after He hung lifted up on the cross between earth and sky, proof and manifestation of divine love and mercy triumphant over hell, for e'er. He breathed His last and declared, "It is finished."[40]

The devil has been deceiving and imposing on mankind to a great extent ever since that it is not finished as far as the healing of the body is concerned, but that you must bear your diseases and sicknesses and bodily pains and suffering (though perhaps your sins may be remitted) unless doctors and medicines can heal or help you.

Those who are free from condemnation, who have passed from death unto life can say, "The law of the Spirit of life in Christ Jesus hath made me free from the law of sin and death" (Romans 8:2). The law of sin and death produced disease and sickness and bodily afflictions and infirmities, which all belong to the kingdom of Satan and are the consequences and effects of his supremacy over his subjects. Let us renounce him, his works, together with all subjectiveness[41] and submission to his power, and claim our blood-bought privileges and immunity.

[39] Genesis 3:5.

[40] John 19:30.

[41] "subjectiveness"—Here Etter means the act of being subject to Satan's power. She does not mean being subjective and determining truth from our individual experience.

Jesus declared He has come to set the captives free and to open the prison to them that are bound. (See Luke 4:18 and Isaiah 61:1.) We have been translated from the dominion of Satan into the kingdom of Christ (see Colossians 1:13), who has conquered, defeated, judged, and bound Satan and all the hosts of hell (who are the authors of all disease) on behalf of all who will believe and claim it. (See John 16:11 and 12:31.)

As far as God's children are concerned, Satan is a deceiver, usurping power over their bodies, taking advantage of their ignorance and unbelief in God's love and power and His Word and promises. Claim the freedom of your bodies from his power to inflict disease; resist his encroachments; repudiate his work; and fight his power, calling on God for faith, strength, and healing. Act as though you trusted God for health and as though you had confidence in His ability and willingness to heal you; that is, if you are walking in all the light He gives you.

God claims and desires to demonstrate to an unbelieving world, "I am the Lord that healeth thee" (Exodus 15:26). If you have recourse to doctors, medicines, and remedies, is it not giving this statement the lie? For the unsaved will surely believe it is the doctor and his medicines that healeth thee. Take God as your Savior for the body. (See 1 Corinthians 6:13, Ephesians 5:23, and Romans 12:1.) The Lord Jesus is the great healer who delivers us from the oppressor, Satan.

It is said that there was an old Negro, for many years a slave in one of the southern states of America, living on a plantation remote from railways and means of communication. Many months after President Lincoln had signed the proclamation, freeing all slaves in America, a traveler chanced that way and asked the old slave why he chose to work in bondage and forego his rights to freedom and liberty under the proclamation. He found the old man had never heard and did not know that he was free. But was he free? He was a slave!

Dear reader, sick and ailing in body, if you can read your title clear to mansions in the skies, you are in the same class as the Negro, a free man legally in God's sight if you claim it, yet at present in unnecessary bondage. The Lord Jesus has the rule, the dominion, and the power. He has purchased your freedom. He has proclaimed the acceptable day of the Lord, the day of redemption, when you can be healed in your body and go free from disease. If hitherto you have been in ignorance, hear the Lord say: "I am the Lord that healeth thee." Claim it and go free. Amen. God grant it. "He that believeth . . . hath the witness" (1 John 5:10).

The Heavenly Call

Many who read this book have [either] never heard of me or [have heard] very little of my life's work as a minister and an evangelist. For your good and the glory of God, I will tell a little of the work at this time.

Over forty-five years ago, the Lord called me in a wonderful way and led me into the baptism of the Holy Ghost, which came with mighty power and like great waves as of liquid fire, accompanied by a band of angels. I was caught up and tossed in the midst of this as in a whirlwind.

As I went forth in the ministry, the power of God has always stayed with me, accompanied with all the gifts, the Lord demonstrating His Word with signs and wonders all these years till the present time. The Lord has always been working with me, blessing my labors with great success in the salvation of the lost and in healing thousands of the sick of all manner of diseases, including the lame, halt, and blind; baptizing with the Holy Ghost; and sending thousands of ministers, evangelists, and workers out into the field. The Word went forth, for multitudes published it. I have published many books and a number of tracts. They are now being used in many parts of the world and especially in Europe.

There is quite a demand for a work like *Questions and Answers on Divine Healing*. This is why I am led to publish it: that hungry souls may have the light on healing for soul and body. The time is urgent to obey the call, to gather in the sick and blind and the shut-in ones that the house may be furnished with guests all ready for the soon coming of the Lord. Behold, He cometh quickly! He comes! The end is here! The end is here! It hasteth greatly!

In my past ministry I have published and sent out many accounts of the wonderful works of God. I feel like the disciples of old, that there is no limit to His wonderful display of power in signs and miracles.

Signs and Miracles

As the disciples of old traveled with the Master, they were continually surprised and amazed at His miraculous power. Every day He brought forth something new and greater than the day before. When He calmed the tempest and saved the crew of the ship, how the fear of God fell on them all, and they said, "Behold, what manner of man is He?"[42]

We are living in the last days of the Gentile dispensation when He has promised to do His greatest work through His children. He is now pouring out His Spirit and calling out a people for His bride. The last message is, "Jesus is coming soon," and it must be confirmed by miracles. Visible signs that it is the Word of the Most High God accompany this message as it is being heralded forth in the power of the Spirit.

The Tabernacle

I praise God that He is continually putting His seal on the work in the new tabernacle, which was dedicated on May the 19th, 1918. His presence has been, and is being, gloriously manifested in various ways in the lighthouse of God.

Three-and-a-half years have gone by since the dedication of the tabernacle while I am getting out this (Revised and Enlarged) edition of *Questions and Answers on Divine Healing*. During this time the work of soul saving has been going on with unabated interest and very satisfying results. Meetings are held nearly every night of the week in the tabernacle, and then three or four times a year we have special revival campaigns which God greatly blesses. Hundreds of people have come into these meetings to get help in body and spirit. They received what they came for and went home rejoicing. The Word goes forth and a multitude of people publish it. At the water baptisms, at the time when we have the sacred sacrament, and at many other special and ordinary meetings, the power comes

[42] Matthew 8:27, Mark 4:41, and Luke 8:25, paraphrased.

in waves of glory so that many are prostrated under the mighty power of God. We praise God for what He is doing.

In the last days—days of His preparation—He is pouring out His Spirit, giving the early and latter rain in the same month, to prepare the bride for His coming.[43] He is now confirming His Word with a great display of His presence, giving visible signs and working miracles. The glory of God is being seen at times in various parts of the tabernacle. It has rested over the pulpit like a purple cloud. A band of angels has also been seen a number of times. The song of the redeemed—the song of the dove—in the Spirit is wonderful. Angels and also heavenly instruments have been heard, making melody in harmony with the song. The presence of heaven generally rests on the congregation. Sometimes, when the glory comes and breaks like a cloud, saints in various parts of the house begin to dance before the Lord in the Spirit. Among them are old men and women, young men and virgins, old men of eighty and children of two years. People are amazed at the manifestation of God's power.

Waves of peace, love, and joy sweep over the congregation. They are in the banqueting hall of the great King of eternity, whose banner over them is love.[44] They are refreshed and their strength [is] renewed and their hearts rejoice in partaking of the fruit of the Spirit. They look unto Him, and their faces are radiant and shine with the glory of God.[45]

I have felt several times as if we were going to be translated and that Jesus had come. Lately, many strong men and women have been struck down by the power of God and saints have lain from sixteen to twenty hours as dead. During this time they hardly moved; they received wonderful visions of things that are coming and have prophesied—some of which things have already come true. Strong messages in tongues, with interpretations, have been given by those in this condition while under the power of God.

People are coming from nearly all the states and from Canada, for healing and for the baptism of the Holy Ghost. Many of these have proved that the Lord is present to heal.

[43]See Joel 2:23.

[44]See Song of Solomon 2:4.

[45]See Psalm 34:5.

Healed of Chronic Nervousness

A young woman came to the meeting from Richmond, Indiana, with chronic nerve trouble, from which she had been in torment day and night for nine years. The doctor told her that her case was turning into Saint Vitus' Dance. Out of twenty-four hours she could only sleep about two; a restless, shaking spirit had taken hold of her. When prayer was offered for her, this nervous spirit went out and she slept for nine hours, something she had not done in nine years. She sleeps like a little child now and has even fallen asleep while on duty in daytime. She gains rapidly in strength and weight and has been carried away in the spirit a number of times, laying all night and part of the day under the power of God, eighteen hours at one time. More than three years have gone by since this woman was prayed for, and today she is still healed.

Healed of Floating Kidney

> For over a year my wife was sick with a floating kidney. My family physician, also a specialist, after a thorough examination said nothing but an operation would save her life. She got so bad that something had to be done at once.
>
> For some years my wife and I had taken Jesus as our physician for both soul and body, so I went earnestly in prayer for her and found that in a short time she was carried away in a vision under the power of God. Sister Etter had been out West for some time, and God showed my wife while in this condition that she [Sister Etter] was now at home. I went out the next day to see if this was true and found that she had just arrived home a few days before. I took my wife and my mother out to have them prayed for. Both of them fell under the power as Sister Etter laid her hands on them and they were completely healed.
>
> My mother had a bleeding cancer for two years or more and the same doctors advised an operation for her, too, but I thank God that she also got perfectly healed.

> Neither my wife nor my mother have had a sign or a symptom of their trouble since.
>
> JOHN BRAMLETT
>
> 2122 MILLER STREET
>
> INDIANAPOLIS, INDIANA [Address no longer current]

I would like to see many of the saints move here to Indianapolis to stay, that they might be here to help as part of the Lord's host in the battle against the powers of darkness. This is a Holy-Ghost school; and if God calls you, heed His call and come and get the preparation to meet Jesus when He comes. Amen.

THE PRAYER OF FAITH THROUGH THE ANOINTED HANDKERCHIEF

> And God wrought special miracles by the hands of Paul: So that from his body were brought unto the sick handkerchiefs or aprons, and the diseases departed from them, and the evil spirits went out of them.
>
> Acts 19:11-12

We notice by these two verses that Paul must have been filled with the Holy Spirit and his body had become a powerhouse for the Lord. The sick and afflicted had handkerchiefs and aprons brought unto him over which he prayed the prayer of faith and no doubt anointed them. When the sick and afflicted received these anointed articles again, the Scriptures say that the diseases departed from them and the evil spirits went out. This is wonderful. Paul so lived, walked, and talked that he got filled with the Spirit of God and evil spirits became subject to him. (See Acts 19:15.) Jesus says, "Verily, verily, I say unto you, He that believeth on me, the works that I do shall he do also; and greater works than these shall he do; because I go unto my Father" (John 14:12).

We are living in the last days at the close of the Gentile times, when God is cutting His work short in righteousness. He is rapidly restoring the gifts, which were in the early Church, to His people again. He is pouring out His Spirit once more as He did in the days of Pentecost. (See Acts 2:1-4.) People get filled with God and speak with new tongues. Devils are being cast out and the sick are being healed.

In my ministry thousands of anointed pieces of cloth have been and are being sent out after they have been prayed over and anointed. A large number of these go across the waters.

Like in Paul's day, evil spirits are being cast out and people are healed of all manner of diseases. We get wonderful reports of healing[s] and deliverances as a result of this work. Many people who have been given up by the best of doctors have been and are being wonderfully healed.

If you are suffering, dear one, and you desire deliverance through the prayer of faith, you may write me and very briefly describe your case. I will be glad to assist you in whatever way I can. If you have not got my literature, you should get it, because it helps you to get faith.

When you send for a handkerchief, put it on your body or on the diseased part in Jesus' name. It is prayed over and set apart for your special case if sent to you. We send these handkerchiefs out dipped by faith in the blood of Jesus. As long as the cloth lasts, the power of God will operate, if faith is exercised. It can be used on one or more sick persons. Jesus said, *"I will come and heal you"* (Matthew 8:7, paraphrased). In verse 17 Jesus says He bore our sicknesses. In Isaiah 53:5, He says by His stripes we are healed.

Listen, dear suffering one. The body of Jesus was broken and bruised as our substitute. He suffered pain and was tormented so that He could take pain and torment from you and me and heal us. This is why He says *He bore our sicknesses.* He has all power now and is in heaven. He told you and me to call upon Him when we are sick. When we do this He hears us and sends forth His Word and heals us. (See Psalm 107:20.) Have the faith as of a grain of mustard seed.[46] Say "Yes, Jesus, I believe. I can, I will, I do believe that Jesus heals me now." Before you say these words very long, the Word that Jesus has sent to heal you will reach you and the healing power will go all through your body. You will soon be shouting, "Glory! Hallelujah!" as you realize that Jesus hath made you whole. After this, do not look to any of the devil's counterfeit symptoms, but look to Jesus only. Amen.

[46]See Matthew 17:20 and Luke 17:6.

We are located in West Indianapolis, Indiana, where we have a tabernacle and are permanently established. Meetings are being held constantly, and I personally hope to spend nearly all my time here. Our Christmas, New Year's, Easter, and mid-summer revival campaigns we hope to make an annual affair. So prepare beforehand to attend them.

Saints, workers, and ministers are cordially invited to stop off at this place and spend some time with us worshiping God in the Spirit and in getting body, soul, and spirit revived. This is a Holy-Ghost work or school. Saints are moving here to get their preparation so as to be ready to be caught up by Jesus when He comes. (See 1 Thessalonians 4:16-17.) "Behold, I come quickly; and my reward is with me."[47] May God help each one of us to be ready when He comes. Amen.

Entire text of *Questions and Answers on Divine Healing,* booklet form.[48]

[47] Revelation 22:12.

[48] Note: In his book on Etter, Wayne Warner makes a convincing argument that the question-and-answer section of *Questions and Answers on Divine Healing* (1919) was borrowed from chapter 9 of a book published in serial form in 1898 and in book form in 1899 by J. W. Byers. Notwithstanding issues of plagiarism (which Warner believes may have been committed by her editors without Etter's knowledge), the booklet has been included here because Etter herself believed it faithfully represented her teachings on healing. (See Wayne Warner, *The Woman Evangelist: The Life and Times of Charismatic Evangelist Maria B. Woodworth-Etter* (Studies in Evangelicalism, No. 8),(Lanham, Maryland: Scarecrow Press, 1986) pp.194-199.).

Women in Ministry

WOMEN'S RIGHTS IN THE GOSPEL

nd when the Day of Pentecost was fully come, they were all with one accord in one place.

Acts 2:1

> And it shall come to pass in the last days, saith God, I will pour out of my Spirit upon all flesh: and *your sons and your daughters* shall prophesy, and your young men shall see visions, and your old men shall dream dreams.
>
> Acts 2:17 & Joel 2:28-29[1] [emphasis Etter's]

> And suddenly there came a sound from heaven as of a rushing mighty wind, and it filled all the house where they were sitting. And there appeared unto them cloven tongues like as of fire, and it sat upon each of them. And they were *all* filled with the Holy Ghost, and began to speak with other tongues, as the Spirit gave them utterance.
>
> Acts 2:2-4 [emphasis Etter's]

There was a wonderful excitement; the people came rushing in great multitudes from the city to see what was the matter. They saw these men and women, with their faces shining with the glory of God, all preaching at once, all anxious to tell what God had done for them and a dying world. Conviction went like daggers to their hearts. And, just as it is today when the power of God is manifest, instead of yielding, they cried out, "too much excitement," and began to fight against God. They said, "These people are mad, are drunken with new wine," and mocked them.[2]

Peter gets up to defend the cause of Christ. He refers to Joel 2:28-29:

> And it shall come to pass in the last days, saith God, I will pour out of my Spirit upon all flesh: and your sons

[1] The passage quotes Acts 2:17, which is a paraphrase of Joel 2:28-29.

[2] Acts 2:12-13.

Maria Woodworth-Etter wore white clothes while preaching and ministering.

> and your daughters shall prophesy, and your young men shall see visions, and your old men shall dream dreams: And on my servants and on my handmaidens I will pour out in those days of my Spirit; and they shall prophesy.

(Acts 2:17-18, 1 Corinthians 14:22-26, and 1 Corinthians 1-5),

Paul speaks as if it were very common for women to preach and prophesy. "Every woman that prayeth or prophesieth with her head uncovered dishonoureth her head" (1 Corinthians 11:5). "The same man had four daughters, virgins, which did prophesy" (Acts 21:9, see Ephesians 4:11).

Paul worked with the women in the Gospel more than any of the apostles. Priscilla and Phebe traveled with Paul preaching and building up the churches. (Acts 18:2,18,25; Romans 16.)

He and Phebe had been holding revivals together; now she is called to the city of Rome. Paul cannot go with her, but he is very careful of her reputation and that she is treated with respect. He writes a letter of recommendation: "I commend unto you Phoebe our sister, which is a servant of the church (which signifies a minister of the church) . . . at Cenchrea: That ye receive her in the Lord, as becometh saints, and that ye assist her in whatsoever business she hath need of you: for she hath been a succourer of many, and of myself also" (Romans 16:1, parenthetical statement Etter's addition).

This shows that she had authority to do business in the churches and that she had been successful in winning souls to Christ. He is not ashamed to say she had encouraged him; he speaks in the highest praise of a number of sisters who had been faithful workers in the work of the Lord, who had risked their lives in the effort to save souls; and not he alone, but all the churches of the Gentiles sent their thanks.

Paul said, "Let your women keep silence in the churches." So saith the law. We are not under law but under grace. "And learn of their husbands at home."[3] What will those do who have no husbands? Do you suppose they will remain in ignorance and be lost? And if some women had to depend on their husbands for knowledge, they would die in ignorance.

[3] See 1 Corinthians 14:34-35.

Paul referred to contentions in the churches. Paul [also] says you had better not marry. How many agree with Paul? How many obey? He is referring to contentions in the churches, that it is a shame to bring up questions and have jangling in the house of God. He writes to the brethren, "I hear that there be divisions among you; and I partly believe it" (1 Corinthians 11:18). "Help those women which laboured with me in the gospel, with Clement also, and with other my fellowlabourers, whose names are in the book of life" (Philippians 4:3). There were also several women who were prophetesses. (Luke 2:36, 2 Kings 22:13-15.) Huldah, the prophetess, the wife of Shallum, dwelt in Jerusalem, in the college, and they communed with her, and she said unto them, "Thus saith the Lord God of Israel."[4] Exodus 15:20; [also] Micah 6:4 says, "I sent before thee, Moses, Aaron, and Miriam."

And in Judges 4:4, it says, "Deborah, a prophetess, the wife of Lapidoth, she judged Israel at that time." See the responsible position that God gave her, to sit and judge the hosts of the children of Israel. The children of Israel had sinned and God would not fight their battles, and for twenty years the nations arose against them and defied them to come out to battle. Barak dared not meet the enemy unless Deborah led the van. This brave woman, ever ready to defend the cause of God, said, "I will surely go." God's people must not be taken by the enemies. Oh, no; call our the armies of the Lord. Sisera's mighty host is gathering. Every soldier to his post. See the brave woman riding with Barak, the commander, at the head of the army, cheering on the hosts to victory, shouting victory as she led on the armies, sweeping through the enemies' ranks, carrying death and destruction till the king leaped from his chariot and fled for his life, but was captured and killed by a woman. Every man was put to the sword; not one was left to tell of the defeat.[5]

The mother of Sisera looked out of the window for the return of the king, her son, from the battle and cried, "Oh, why does he not come, why is his chariot so long in coming? Why, oh, why does he tarry so long?" While she is weeping for her son's return, he is lying

[4] See 2 Kings 22:14-15 or 2 Chronicles 34:22-23.

[5] Judges 4:4-16

cold in death in the tent where he has been captured and killed by a woman.[6]

Queen Esther intercedes at the king's court, and the sad decree of the king is reversed so that her life and the life of the Jewish nation are saved.

Paul says there is no difference, but that male and female are one in Christ Jesus. (See Galatians 3:28.) Let us take Jesus for our pattern and example and see no man, save Jesus only.

Women were called and commissioned by the angel sent from heaven, and by the Lord Jesus Christ, to preach the Gospel. (See Matthew 28:5-10.)

The cowardly disciples had forsaken the Savior and fled. Peter denied the Savior and swore he never knew Him, but many women followed him and stood by the cross and went to the sepulcher and saw the body laid away. The great stone was rolled against the door. (See Matthew 27:55-61.) These women went home sad and brokenhearted, but they returned to pay a last tribute to their dear friend. They spent the night in preparing spices to embalm the body of their Lord. They came to the sepulcher as it was coming day. The grave was empty. The Lord was not there. As they stood weeping, two angels stood by them and said:

> "Fear not ye: for I know that ye seek Jesus, which was crucified. He is not here: for he is risen, as he said, Come, see the place where the Lord lay. And go quickly, and tell his disciples that he is risen from the dead; and, behold, he goeth before you into Galilee; there shall ye see him: lo, I have told you."[7]

They started at once with joy and rejoicing. They could not walk fast enough; they ran to hunt up the brothers, to tell the Good News. As they were going, Jesus met them, and they fell at His feet and worshipped Him. He said: "Be not afraid: go tell my brethren that they go into Galilee, and there shall they see me."[8]

[6] See Judges 4:17-22; 5:28-30.

[7] Matthew 28:5-7.

[8] Matthew 28:10

It was not only the twelve that were to tell the Good News. There were several hundred brethren; yes, thousands of followers at this time. They never thought of bloodthirsty soldiers who had put their master to death and were seeking for His friends who would dare to defend Him.

Observe the wonderful mission that Jesus had entrusted to these weak women to preach the first resurrection sermon; to risk their lives in gathering together the followers of Christ, where the wonderful meeting was to be held. But just like many today, they would not believe. Peter said, "I will not believe your report."[9] Thomas said, "I will not believe except I see the prints in His hands and feet."[10]

In the midst of all these discouragements, they went on with the work and had grand success. Jesus met with and preached to them; they were all made to rejoice. They were called by angels, and the Lord from glory, and sent to preach the Gospel. The names of four women were given and there were many others.[11]

God is calling the Marys and the Marthas today all over our land to work in various places in the vineyard of the Lord; God grant that they may respond and say, "Lord, here am I; send me."[12] This call was made after Christ had risen. (Turn also to John 4:10-29,39-42.)

"I will pour out in the last days of my Spirit"—that refers in a special manner to these last days in which we are now living. God is promising great blessings and power to qualify His handmaidens for the last great harvest, just before the notable Day of the Lord comes. We must first be baptized into Christ by the one Spirit, that is, to be born of the Spirit; then we ought to be anointed with power and wisdom. The Spirit ought to be poured out like oil on our heads, to give us knowledge of the deep things of God. The Lord says we shall prophesy.

Paul says, "Desire spiritual gifts, but rather that ye may prophesy" (1 Corinthians 14:1). It makes no difference how many gifts we have, if we have not the gift of talking and teaching, it will not avail

---

[10]See John 20:25.

[11]See Luke 24:10 amd Mark 16:1; Mary Magdalene, Mary The Mother of James, Joanna, and Salome are named specifically and Luke states there were others also.

[12]Isaiah 6:8.

us much. The Lord has promised this greatest gift to His handmaidens and daughters. In the third verse, Paul explains what it is to prophesy. "He that prophesieth speaketh unto men to edification and exhortation, and comfort." He that prophesieth edifieth the Church. No one can talk for God, only by the enlightening power of the Holy Ghost. Moses said, "Would God that all the Lord's people were prophets, and that the Lord would put his spirit upon them!" (Numbers 11:29).

While Jesus sat at Jacob's well to rest, there was a poor woman, one who was living in sin, who came to the well to get water; although she had fallen very low and was despised by her friends so that she had no one to lift her up and tell her of a better way, Jesus came to seek the lost, to lift up the fallen.

God help us to follow His example; if they feel that their feet are slipping into the pit of hell, Jesus is a mighty Savior. He can lift them up and make them children of a King.

Jesus preached salvation; the woman was converted; she left her pitcher and took the well of salvation with her, and running to the city, went up one street and down another, with her face shining with the glory of God. Perhaps the people would have scorned her an hour before; now they saw and felt the change.

"Look what he has done for me. He will do the same for you."

The people left their stores, their places of business, left their parlors and kitchens and came out in great multitudes to see the Savior of the world. There was a great revival there at the well. Jesus went into the city and stayed two days. The wave of salvation went on and on. This was the result of one sermon by a weak woman. Many were converted and made to rejoice in a Savior's love by the preaching of the woman who said, "He told me all the things that ever I did."[13]

They came to her and said, "We know now for ourselves," and, like the Queen of Sheba, said "The half was not told."[14]

My dear sister in Christ, as you hear these words, may the Spirit of God come upon you and make you willing to do the work the Lord

[13]See John 4:1-30.

[14]See John 4:39-42, 1 Kings 10:1-13, and 2 Chronicles 9:6-12.

has assigned to you. It is high time for women to let their lights shine; to bring out their talents that have been hidden away rusting and use them for the glory of God, and do with their might what their hands find to do, trusting God for strength, who has said, "I will never leave you."[15]

Oh, the fields are white, for the harvest is great and ripe, and it is ready for the gospel sickle; oh, where are the laborers to gather the golden grain into the Master's garner?[16]

The world is dying, the grave is filling, hell is boasting; it will all be over soon.

God left the glorious work of saving souls in the hands of the Church. What is the Church composed of? Men, women, and children. We are putting up a building of God. Everyone has a part in this building. If we cannot be a pillar or cornerstone, let us be a spike or a nail or a brick; let us not despise the day of small things.[17] Whatever we do for Jesus, with the right motive, is precious in His sight. God's Church is a workshop—no idlers allowed there. There should be bills posted, "To work, to work. Everyone at his post." You and I should say when Satan tempts us, like Nehemiah, "I am doing a great work, so that I cannot come down. I am commissioned by the King of heaven to work for Him."[18] The work is great and the time is short. He offers a great reward. Like the blind man, we will tell what God has done for us. "Once I was blind, now I can see."[19]

> The Spirit and the bride say, Come. And let him that
> heareth say, Come . . . And whosoever will, let him
> take the water of life freely.[20]

If we have been, like David, taken away from that horrible pit, over which we were hanging by the thread of life; if our feet have been taken out of the mire and clay; if the chains of Satan which were around us, like brass and iron, have been broken; if our feet have

[15] See Hebrews 13:5.

[16] See John 4:35-38, Matthew 9:37-38, and Luke 10:2.

[17] See Zechariah 4:10.

[18] See Nehemiah 6:1-4.

[19] See John 9:25.

[20] Revelation 22:17.

been set on solid rock, and a new song put into our mouths; if we have been adopted into the family of God, of which part are in heaven and part on earth; if our names are written in the Book of Life—then we have the gift of eternal life. We are heirs to the bank of heaven, to an eternal inheritance, to a mansion in the golden city, to a robe and a crown. We are sons and daughters of the Most High God. Should we not honor our high calling and do all we can to save those who sit in the valley and shadow of death?

Let us not plead weakness; God will use the weak things of this world for His glory. When He wanted to introduce His glorious Gospel to a dying world, He did not go to the Jewish Sanhedrin and select the wise and mighty. He went along the sea of Galilee and chose twelve ignorant men and said to them, "Follow me, and I will make you fishers of men."[21] They started in the strength of God, setting up the kingdom of our Lord Jesus. They were led on by the mighty conqueror and today He sways His scepter from the rivers to the ends of the earth.

Oh, hear the Master calling for soldiers! He says He will lead us on to victory. Oh, who will respond to the call? Who will place his name on the heavenly roll? Who will enlist in the war and help to conquer the mighty foe? Who will help to beat back the powers of darkness? He does not ask you to die, but to live forever. He will give a glorious bounty—eternal life.

Let us work for rewards. We shall be rewarded according to our work. "They that turn many to righteousness shall shine as the stars, forever and ever."[22] We do not want to have starless crowns. Oh, let us win stars for the Master's glory.[23]

---

[21] Matthew 4:19.

[22] Daniel 12:3.

[23] In another version of this sermon a six-stanza poem, "The Starless Crown" is included in which the narrator dreams of going to heaven and being asked about a crown:

> And then in solemn tone He said, "Where is the diadem
> that ought to sparkle on thy brow, adorned with many a gem?
> I know thou hast believed on Me, and life through Me is thine.
> But where are all those radiant stars that in thy crown should shine,
> Yonder thou see'st a glorious throng, and stars on every brow;
> For every soul they led to Me they wear a jewel now;
> And such thy bright reward had been, if such had been thy deed,
> If thou hadst sought some wondering feet in paths of peace to lead.

(Poet unknown, stanza 4, *Acts of the Holy Ghost,* Maria Woodworth-Etter [Indianapolis: Maria Woodworth-Etter, 1912], p.486).

"Blessed are they that mourn: for they shall be comforted."[24] If we weep and mourn now on account of poor sinners, we shall laugh through all eternity. Oh, let us work now, and by and by our weeping will be over. We shall come rejoicing, bringing in the sheaves.[25] We can say, "Here am I, Father, and the children Thou hast given me."[26]

A child was dying. "Father," said she, "I have come to the river and am waiting for the ferrymen to take me over."

"Does it seem dark and cold, my child?"

"Oh, no, there is no darkness here. The river is covered with solid silver. The boats, they are solid light. I am not afraid of the ferrymen. Oh, I see over the river! There is a great and beautiful city, all filled with light. The angels are making music. Oh, I see the most beautiful form! He beckons me to come. Oh! I know who it is—it is blessed Jesus. He has taken me in His bosom." And thus she passes over the river of death, made like a silver stream by the presence of her Redeemer.

Taken from *A Diary of Signs and Wonders: A Classic* (Tulsa, OK: Harrison House, [Original printing by Maria Woodworth-Etter, 1916]), pp. 210-216.

[24]See Psalm 126:6.

[25]See John 27:9,11.

[26]Matthew 5:4

THE LAST DAYS

The Transfiguration on the Mount

Or the Healing of the Lunatic, a Type of the Imminent Rapture of the Saints, the Binding of Satan, and the Destruction of the Antichrist and His Army

erily I say unto you, There be some standing here, which shall not taste of death, till they see the Son of man coming in his kingdom. And after six days Jesus taketh Peter, James, and John his brother, and bringeth them up into a high mountain apart, And was transfigured before them: and his face did shine as the sun, and his raiment was white as the light. And, behold, there appeared unto them Moses and Elias talking with him.

Matthew 16:28-17:3

Jesus says the wise shall know when we are in the time of the end, or the days of the Son of Man. They shall know when Jesus is coming for His bride. The words of the text come in thundering tones to this class that are living today. They shall not taste of death till they (or rather we) see Jesus coming in all His glory. We know by all the signs and by the fulfillment of all the prophecies that His coming is near, even at our doors. Daniel said none of the wicked shall know, none but the wise; those that have been baptized with the Holy Ghost and power; those that God is sealing with the deep things of God, with the things of the Spirit of God.[1] God is revealing His secrets to this class now of the condition of the world and of the children of the Lord and of the time and manner of His coming and of the future when we shall sit with Him on His throne, executing judgments on

[1] See Daniel 12:9-10.

the world and on the Antichrist and his army.[2] And of how we shall-reign kings and priests, with power and authority, for one thousand years, with Christ on the earth.[3]

Here in the Holy-Ghost school is where we graduate, we will get our diploma and be promoted to high position, when Jesus comes.

Jesus spoke these words: They should not taste of death till they saw a miniature picture of His glorious coming.[4] Not one who heard understood Him, but six days after He revealed the secret to only three. This six days applies to us, as only a short time, a very few years at most. Out of all His followers and all His disciples, He only trusted three with these deep and glorious truths and counted them worthy to see His glory. They were not even to tell anyone of this wonderful display of His glorious coming kingdom.[5] This proves that of all the baptized people of the Lord, only a very few will be of the wise, of the bride, and sit with Him on His throne.

He took those three away from all the rest, apart up into a high mountain. The high mountain means the hill of the Lord, or the manifestation of the sons of God, or the rapture in the skies.[6]

Jesus was transfigured, changed, and glorified before them. He shone as bright as the sun. His garments were whiter than light, shining bright with all the glory of heaven. It was a small picture of His coming glory and the glory and brightness of His saints, that will comprise, or make up His kingdom for our bodies will be changed and made like His glorious body.[7] "They that be wise shall shine as the brightness of the firmament."[8]

The great God, the loving Father, shouted down from the bright cloud that was over them, acknowledging His Son, showing how He will come in all His Father's glory. That our loving Father will come

[2] See 1 Corinthians 6:2.

[3] See Revelation 5:10 and 20:6.

[4] See Matthew 16:28, Mark 9:1, and Luke 9:27.

[5] See Matthew 17:9.

[6] See Psalm 24:3, Romans 8:19, and 1 Thessalonians 4:17.

[7] See 1 Corinthians 15:51-54.

[8] Daniel 12:3.

to welcome the bride, the Lamb's wife, back to the city to the marriage in the skies, with all the music and glory of the eternal world.

The world was not disturbed, neither did any of them see or know where Jesus and His disciples had gone. They did not know or see any of the brightness or glory that was transpiring on the mountain. It will be just the same when Jesus comes, no one will see or know anything about the glorious rapture until the saints have all gone to glory. Then they will miss them and remember what we have told them, and then they will realize what they have missed.

The hinderer, the Holy Ghost, will go up with the bride, then the devil will be let loose.[9] The Antichrist will show his power. The Great Tribulation will burst in awful fury on a lost world. The time that Jesus and His disciples were on the mountain represents the time of the devil being loose and the time of the dreadful persecution of the saints by the Antichrist and his army, such a time of trouble as never has been nor ever shall be.[10]

In the type of the devil in the lunatic, whom Jesus found when He came down from the mountain, note that there was a great commotion; the disciples seemed to be frightened and to have lost their faith.[11] Those in power will show their authority, they will persecute the Christians, casting them into the fire, throwing them into the water, trying in every way to put them to death for not receiving the mark of the Beast.

When Jesus comes back with His bride, all the world will see Him and those that have escaped from the persecutions will rush to Him for mercy and pardon. That Jesus cast out the devil from the lunatic and told him not to enter him again, shows His power over the devil, the old serpent. He will bind and cast him into the bottomless pit, and He will destroy the Antichrist and all his armies.[12]

In the fifteenth chapter of the book of Acts, James says, "Simeon hath declared how God at the first did visit the Gentiles, to take out

[9] See 2 Thessalonians 2:6-7.

[10] See Matthew 24:21.

[11] See Matthew 17:14-18.

[12] See Revelation 20:2-3 and 19:20-21.

of them a people for his name." Verse 16: "After this I will return, and will build again the tabernacle of David, which is fallen down; and I will build again the ruins thereof, and I will set it up: That the residue of men might seek after the Lord, and all the Gentiles, upon whom my name is called, saith the Lord, who doeth all these things."[13]

You see that out of all nations, there will be a people left who will seek after the Lord because it says, "the Gentiles who call on his name." Then all the nations or tribes of the Jews will seek the Lord. One third of all the earth will go through or survive the tribulations or fires of judgments and will seek the Lord.

In the nineteenth chapter of the book of Revelation John says,

> And I saw heaven opened, and behold a white horse; and he that sat upon him was called Faithful and True . . . . on his head were many crowns. . . . And he was clothed with a vesture dipped in blood. . . . And the armies which were in heaven followed him upon white horses, clothed in fine linen, white and clean . . . And I saw an angel standing in the sun; and he cried with a loud voice, saying to all the fowls that fly in the midst of heaven, Come and gather yourselves together unto the supper of the great God (verses 11-17).

Jesus comes to take a people for His name. The bride takes the name of her husband.

At the close of the time of trouble, He comes back with His bride, clothed in white, on white horses of power, purity, honor, and glory, to fight the last battle, destroying the Antichrist's army. He takes possession of the whole earth and sets up His Millennium (*sic*) kingdom for one thousand years, after two-thirds of the whole earth is destroyed. One-third will pass through the Great Tribulation "That the residue of men might seek after the Lord, and all the Gentiles, upon whom my Name is called."[14] So you see that not only the Jews, but all nations of the earth, the Gentiles, that call on His name will hear the voice of the Prophet.

[13]Acts 15:14,16-17.

[14]See Acts 15:17.

All these will witness the battle of the great day and see the supper of the great God, when the blood will flow up to the horses' bridles.[15] Ride on, conquering Jesus, until You conquer every foe and bring the whole world back to God, when the glory of God shall cover the earth, as the waters cover the mighty deep.[16]

The voice of praise shall go up from the rising to the setting of the sun, when Jesus with His glorified saints shall reign kings and priests for one thousand years.[17] Oh readers, let us get ready that we may escape all these things that are coming on the earth and be caught away to meet the Bridegroom in the air.

Two-thirds of the people will die of famine, pestilence, war, or earthquakes or be destroyed by the Antichrist or killed in this last battle of the great day of God Almighty, when the blood will be up to the horses' bridles. Oh, in the name of God, reader, will you escape that awful day and be ready to meet the Lord when He takes His great power to reign on the earth for one thousand years?

And it shall come to pass that everyone who will not hear the voice of the prophet shall be destroyed from among the people, or cut off.[18] Today is the day of salvation; harden not your hearts, lest you be destroyed.[19] Hear Him calling today.

Taken from *Acts of the Holy Ghost.*

---

[15]See Revelation 14:20.

[16]See Habakkuk 2:14, paraphrased.

[17]See Psalm 113:3.

[18]See Acts 3:23.

[19]See 2 Corinthians 6:2 and Hebrews 3:8.

Some Shall Not Taste Death: The Rapture and Binding of Satan

Verily I say unto you, There be some standing here, which shall not taste of death, till they see the Son of man coming in his kingdom. And after six days Jesus taketh Peter, James, and John his brother, and bringeth them up into an high mountain apart, And was transfigured before them: and his face did shine as the sun, and his raiment was white as the light.

Matthew 16:28-17:2

For He was the Son of Man and He was the Son of God. He "shall come in the glory of his Father with his angels; and then he shall reward every man according to his works,"[1] according to the deeds done while in the body.

> Verily I say unto you, There be some standing here, which shall not taste of death, till they see the Son of man coming in his kingdom. And after six days (literal days) Jesus taketh Peter, James, and John his brother, and bringeth them up into an high mountain apart, And was transfigured before them: and his face did shine as the sun, and his raiment was white as the light. And, behold, there appeared unto them Moses and Elias talking with him. Then answered Peter, and said unto Jesus, Lord, it is good for us to be here (but he did not know what he was talking about): if thou wilt, let us make here three tabernacles; one for thee, and one for Moses, and one for Elias.[2]

But God settled the question.

[1] Matthew 16:27.

[2] Matthew 16:28-17:4; parenthetical comments are Maria Etter's.

> While he yet spake, behold, a bright cloud overshadowed them: and behold a voice out of the cloud (another person called attention), which said, This is my beloved Son, in whom I am well pleased; hear ye him.
>
> Matthew 17:5

Glory to God! Hallelujah! Glory to Jesus!

There is a great deal in this lesson. It shows both the kingdom of Christ, which is very near at hand now, and the translation of the saints, and it shows the Tribulation that is coming on the earth. And it shows the close of the Tribulation when Christ comes back with His saints, binds the devil, destroys the Antichrist and His army, and sets up the glorious Millennium.

Six days—the Lord was speaking to the apostles and He meant six, natural, literal days. For just six days after, they saw what He said they should see. But it applies to us—a day for a year and a day with the Lord is a thousand years,[3] and it was four days before Christ came—four thousand years—and the two last days bring us down to today and makes six thousand years. So we are on the stage of action today, right at the close of the last day. On the sixth day close to the seventh day, we will be ushered into the great Millennium—the thousand years of rest—the Sabbath day. Jesus speaks to us with as much force tonight, and He applies it to us as He did to them.

A Display of Heavenly Glory

"Only a little while, six days I say to you, some of you who are standing here shall never taste of death until you see My coming kingdom, for I shall come in all the glory of My Father's kingdom with all the holy angels, and I shall come in My own kingly glory. I will give you a display of this glory in a few days—you shall never taste of death until you see this thing." They did not understand. Six days after that it came to pass. He took Peter, James, and John, those who seemed to be always nearest the Master—more anxious to stand by Him than the rest—and they were initiated into a good many things the rest did not know.

[3] See 2 Peter 3:8.

He took these three and slipped away from the rest and took them up into the mountain. Six natural days from the time He said, "Some of you shall not taste of death until you see this glory. I am going to reveal it to you." Hallelujah to Jesus! Let us think about it. The prophecies are fulfilled and it will be just a very short time now according to God's Word. I say to you tonight, this applies to us. "I am coming in My kingdom in all the glory of the eternal world to catch My bride away." Some of you will never taste of death until you see this and take part in it. Glory to God! Hallelujah!

God Turns to His People Again

Those prophecies point to this time—this is the end of the Gentile age—the Gentile age is to wind up at the close of the sixth day. The Jews are saying, "Come, let us return to the Lord, for we have been wounded and bruised and He will heal us up; and the second day He will revive us; and early in the morning of the third day, He will raise us up."[4] This is the second day. The Jews are being wonderfully revived all over the land—they never had such notoriety. They are reviving; their bands are being broken. But early in the morning, it will only be a few days—bless God!—He will raise us up. And He will raise them up from the grave and wonderful things are going to take place.

Before the Great Tribulation, the saints will be taken up—Jesus Christ shall stand up for His people, and there will be such a time of trouble on the earth as the world never knew and never will know again—when the dead in Christ shall rise and the saints shall be taken up.[5] So we are coming into the time when these prophecies are coming on the earth—the beginning of sorrows—and if this is only the beginning, what will the end be?[6] This is the preparation time when He will scatter the power of the holy people all over the world as a witness. God shall rise up in His power and majesty, and God shall work His strange work by the Holy Ghost through His saints.[7] Natural men do not understand.

---

[4] See Hosea 6:1-2.

[5] See Daniel 12:1, Matthew 24:21, and 1 Thessalonians 4:16.

[6] See Matthew 24:8.

[7] See Isaiah 28:21.

Jesus is coming in His kingdom. Get out of the City of Destruction;[8] run up on the mountain—bless God. Be ready for the manifestations of the sons of God.[9] This is the preparation time. The last message—"this Gospel of My kingdom shall be preached in the last days of my preparation for a witness to all the world"—to every nation, not to every person. Then shall the end be.[10] Christ will come and take a prepared people out for Himself—a people for His bride, and then the awful darkness will cover the earth; the Tribulation time will set in—the time of trouble will continue until the Battle of Armageddon when the Antichrist shall be destroyed and two-thirds of all the earth will go down in war, famine, and pestilences and be devoured by wild beasts.

But one-third will withstand the Antichrist and escape all the troubles and calamities that come in this earth—[they will] go through the fire, persecution, famine; and when Jesus comes back to bind the devil and cast him into the pit, one-third of the earth will run out to meet Him and acknowledge Him as their Lord of Lords. And He will call them His people and forgive their sins and they will call Him their God and they will be restored at Jerusalem. God has said it. For He says after He takes His bride away at the end of this Tribulation, He shall return with His bride riding on the white horse of power; and He will come back to build up the waste places of Jerusalem—that the residue of men might seek after the Lord, and all the Gentiles that have called on His name will be in that company of the one-third that won't go down in the tribulations. He is coming back with the saints at the end of the Tribulation to destroy the Antichrist and the blood will be up to the horses' bridles.[11]

There will soon be three suppers—the supper in the skies at the marriage of the Lamb.

The prophet John saw a great angel standing in the sun calling with a loud voice to the fowls of the air: "Come gather yourselves together

---

[8] "City of Destruction"—An allusion to *The Pilgrim's Progress.* Christian runs from the City of Destruction to become a Christian.

[9] See Romans 8:19.

[10] See Matthew 24:14.

[11] See Revelation 14:20.

for the great supper of the great God, that you may eat the flesh of the kings and of the mighty men of the earth and those that sat upon horses and eat the flesh of the horses and drink their blood at the supper of the great God."[12]

The Antichrist and his army will be destroyed when God will call the wild beasts and the fowls of the air to eat their carcasses at the time when Jesus will come back and bind the devil and cast him into the pit [for] one thousand years. But the one-third that have gone through everything and by the hand of God escaped will come out to meet the Lord with gladness. And He will accept them and forgive them, and He will call them His people, and they shall be established. And the glorious Millennium will be ushered in. But before this the saints of God will be caught away. He is coming to take His people out and everyone that is not ready to go up will be left behind and go down when the Antichrist comes forth.

The time of the awful Tribulation is near. May the Lord help us to understand this, dear friends. The enemies of the Lord today are getting worse and worse—the cup of iniquity is full—the harvest of the earth is ripe and ready to be cut down and cast into the wine press of the wrath of God Almighty.[13] So God is pouring out His Spirit. Glory hallelujah! Causing signs and wonders through the holy vessels which shall be as clay to scatter the power of God through the land. And the great angels are saying, "Cannot we loose?"[14] When will all these wonders cease? These great [modern] inventions [of our day] are coming up in the preparation time. Not because they are, but because it is God's time of preparation. There is no end to inventions.

God's Day of Preparation

"I will rise up and work my strange works in the day of preparation. Therefore be ye not mockers."[15] Behold, I have the message from the Lord—"the decree has gone forth and I will make a speedy

[12]Revelation 19:17-18, paraphrased.

[13]See Revelation 14:19-20.

[14]Revelation 7:1-3.

[15]See Isaiah 28:21-22.

riddance of all the mockers on the face of the earth." They don't laugh at a cyclone, they don't laugh at a great fire, but they will laugh and mock at God's strange work. Be ye not mockers, for I got the message from the Lord. It came from heaven and the decree has already gone forth. God will make a speedy riddance of all the mockers on the face of the earth.

This is God's work. He is giving the people a warning, pouring out His Spirit upon the earth for the last time to warn the people just before the notable Day of the Lord comes. Every nation will be warned through the mighty display of God's power. Repent and turn to the Lord and you shall be saved—[we have] the visible signs that God is here, the visible manifestations that this is God's message—the last message and that God through His people is scattering the Holy Ghost. We haven't a dead God or a dead Christ, but He ever liveth and He is right here tonight. God is scattering power over the land and warning the people against the things that are coming. And everyone that has the mark of fire and blood will be taken out alive. Every last one. And then the Antichrist will come forth—the Man of Sin, the awful Antichrist—he will come forth in his awful power after the hinderers are taken out.[16] Who are the hinderers? The body of Christ.

"Ye are the light of the world."[17] And He shines in the heart just as He shines through the faces of the saints. Glory to God!

So God is warning you through His saints and getting people ready, sending out the warning in every direction to escape from the City of Destruction, and don't tarry in the plains. Get on your wedding garments, accept the invitation, and get ready to take the flight through the air. When the saints are taken out, there will be no restraining power—the devil will be let loose. People will sigh for one of these days, sigh and cry, "There is no prophet anymore, no priests. We don't hear from heaven"—no light, all darkness—when the Holy Ghost goes up with the body of Christ in the bride.

There will be awful darkness and the door will be shut, and no one will have an opportunity to join the bride. The bride is being made

[16]See 2 Thessalonians 2:6-7.

[17]Matthew 5:14.

up now. May God help us to see this. So the message is for you. Some of you here tonight will never taste death until you see the Son of Man. Never, until you see the Son of Man coming in the clouds of heaven. Hallelujah! Keep looking up. Are you ready to go? If you are not, come tonight.

After six days, the disciples did not understand this, but He took those who were nearest, watching and praying and looking for those things to come true, took three of them and slipped away from everybody—nobody knew where He was—and He took them up into a high mountain (and that is a good place to be—way up above the world with the devil under your feet).[18] How beautiful on the mountain are the feet of those who are running up and hurling back the glad tidings that Jesus is coming.[19] That is a good place to go to pray if you pray right. Bless the Lord, it is not the long prayer or the loud prayer, but hallelujah!—the prayer of faith. They were praying and something happened. He said, "I am coming in all my Father's glory and in all the glory of the holy angels, and some of you here are going to see this."[20]

Peter, just before he went away, said, "There will be lying wolves, but don't forget what you have heard. I have been telling you that He is coming again and I have not been telling you cunningly devised fables, but I am telling you the truth. I saw the King transfigured and I heard the voice of the great God of heaven. He came down to welcome the bride—He came down to be at the wedding—the cloud of glory settled over us and out of that cloud a great voice, the voice of God Almighty, and He introduced the bride to His Son. This is my Son, He is my Son, He is King of Glory. I am pleased at the selection of His bride."[21] Hallelujah!

In the Twinkling of an Eye

They saw the manifestations. They saw Him just exactly as it is going to be when the saints go up. They had the picture—the vision.

[18] See Matthew 17:1-13 and Mark 9:2-13.

[19] See Isaiah 52:7.

[20] Matthew 16:27-28, paraphrased.

[21] See 2 Peter 1:14-18.

"Fear not, little flock."[22] In that vision He brought before their eyes the saints that are going up some of these days. There are some living here that will never taste of death until they see Jesus come. He brought the picture before them in a vision. Every tribe, tongue, and nation on earth will be in that company, witnesses out of every nation.[23] These three disciples were permitted to see them all changed, just like they will be when He comes. We shall be all changed, we will not all sleep, but we shall be changed in a moment, in the twinkling of an eye.[24] We will have a glorious body like the Son of God and we shall be like Him, for we shall see Him as He is.[25]

Now then, John saw this picture twice. God has not left us in the dark. John was a man like we are, but God reveals the deep things of God to His saints.[26] John had been banished to the Isle of Patmos. One time when he was talking to the Lord, behold the Spirit of God was all over and around him; and he saw an open door and in a minute he was translated to heaven. He saw the saints go up and he went up with them. He saw thrones and those that sat upon them, and he saw Christ on the throne of His Father.[27] "To him that overcometh will I grant to sit with me in my throne, even as I also overcame, and am set down with my Father in his throne."[28]

He overcame the devil at the very last and we must not only commence, but go to the end. When He overcame the last, He went up and God gave Him a seat at His right hand—the highest place in the courts of glory—and He is there today.[29] Stephen saw the glory of God and saw Jesus sitting at the right hand of God in majesty on high.[30]

---

[22] Luke 12:32.

[23] See Revelation 14:6.

[24] See 1 Corinthians 15:51-52.

[25] See 1 John 3:2.

[26] See 1 Corinthians 2:9-10.

[27] See Revelation 1.

[28] Revelation 3:21.

[29] See Ephesians 1:20 and Hebrews 1:3.

[30] See Acts 7:55-56.

"To him that overcometh will I grant to sit with me in my throne, even as I also overcame, and am set down with my Father in his throne."[31] He has not taken His throne yet. John saw the saints go up the second time—then He saw Jesus take His throne and went up to the marriage supper. Blessed and holy are they that are called to the marriage supper of the Lamb.[32] Blessed are they that shall eat bread at that supper and drink wine in my Father's kingdom. We are going to be substantial people, aren't we? Glory to God! Sit down to the marriage supper of the Lamb. That is the place He is preparing for you. O glory to God! Don't you want to be there?

We are a nation despised and hated—a nation not desired. The devil hates us and all his imps hate us, but He says, "Come, hide you away, come together—bind yourselves together and get ready for the manifestations of the sons of God. Fear not, it is your Father's good will to give you the kingdom."[33] He shall make us kings and priests in the sight of our God.[34] Kings and priests, glory to God! So Jesus comes out and takes the throne and the bridal company will be the highest in heaven. There are great degrees of glory, but the overcomers—the bridal party—will sit with Jesus Christ the Lamb of God on His Great White Throne through all the ages. They will follow the Lamb whithersoever He goes. They are the class that Daniel saw. They that turn many to righteousness shall shine as the sun.[35] There are degrees to glory. I would rather be one of the wise ones.

The glory of God knocked Paul blind and he said it put the noonday sun in the shade.[36] And when the saints of God burst forth and their bodies are changed, they will eclipse the sun. Don't you think it will be great? Don't you think you had better take a degree of glory tonight?

---

[31] Revelation 3:21.

[32] See Revelation 19:9.

[33] See Luke 12:32.

[34] See Revelation 1:6 and 5:10.

[35] See Daniel 12:3.

[36] See Acts 26:13.

He said to Peter, James, and John, "Don't tell any man about the vision until after I have gone to glory."[37] So they saw something the rest did not know, because they were nearer to God. They wanted God to let them down in[to] the deep things of God. That teaches us a lesson, dear friends. There are degrees of glory. They that be wise shall shine as the firmament and they that be wise shall know when Jesus comes. Do you suppose God would not reveal these things to His waiting bride? I tell you yes. We know a few things now. We know it is very soon.

You are not left in the dark—you are all the children of light and of the day.[38] You have been illuminated from heaven. You will not be overtaken by surprise. Are we ready, are we watching? Be ready to stand when the Son of Man comes. Watch and pray always.[39] Watch the signs and watch the prophecies that you may be counted worthy to escape the awful tribulations and stand before the Son of Man when He comes. Watch and pray. You know the signs. You will not be overtaken as a thief because I am warning you.[40] You are the children of day and you shall know. Glory to God!

So the Lord shows us now all these awful calamities coming on the earth. He says: "Be ye not fearful when you see these awful things coming. Look up and rejoice. Lift your heads and see the break of day. The sun is rising. Lift up your heads. Rejoice, for your redemption draweth nigh."[41] Glory!

The secret of the Lord is with those who love Him.[42] Those He can trust. So God is revealing these things to us from day to day.[43] We will not be surprised. When you see certain signs, know that it is even at your door. We know that now. We don't know the day or hour, but God gives us to understand; we shall know a little while before we are taken up.[44] And when you get where you cannot do anything else, just stand, wait for the Son of Man to come and catch His waiting bride away.

[37]Mark 9:9, paraphrased.

[38]See 1 Thessalonians 5:5.

[39]See Mark 13:33.

[40]See 1 Thessalonians 5:4.

[41]Luke 21:28, paraphrased.

[42]See John 14:21.

[43]See 1 Corinthians 2:10.

[44]See Matthew 25:13.

Beautiful Fine Needlework

Get this lesson; there are great degrees of glory. Don't you want to be the beautiful bride and stand before the King of Glory? Her clothes are so beautiful with fine needlework and Oh, how she loves her Bridegroom. She doesn't worship anybody but Him. She is not trifling with many lovers, but He has become the fairest among ten thousand—[she is] willing to leave all and go with her strange lover.[45]

Sometimes a lady here marries a stranger and there is lots of kicking. "If you go I will disinherit you." But she leaves her parents, home, money.

"O I love my lover best. He is mine and I am his.[46] I will have to go and leave you." So she leaves everything and she gets into the ship and sails with her strange lover to a strange land, where she has never been, and among strange people that she has never known. And he is so proud of her. And she is so proud of him. He is strange to the world, but he is mine and I am his. I will be glad to go.

There are degrees of glory. He said, "The wise shall know."[47] Don't think it strange that none of the wicked shall know about the coming of the Lord. Daniel saw the saints robed in white on land and sea, God scattering the Holy Ghost through them. Daniel, the wise, shall know. He reveals His secrets to the wise. Are you one of the wise? Is God letting you down into the deep things? Bless God He will! We are in the Holy-Ghost school, going from one room to another, from one school to another, graduating, getting our diploma. God wants us to get down into the deep things. He reveals His secrets to us just like to those three. "Don't you tell anyone until after I am raised from the dead." It was hid from the rest. That shows us, dear friends, there are degrees in glory. Some shall shine as stars and some will eclipse the sun. A great many people will not know when Jesus comes. The wise shall know when Jesus comes.

At that time there will be two sleeping in one bed, one will be taken and the other left; two grinding at the mill, one will be taken and

[45]See Song of Solomon 5:10.

[46]Song of Solomon 2:16.

[47]Daniel 12:10, paraphrased.

the other left.[48] Many people think they will know and they will be left. God is showing us these things and giving us this lesson. After Jesus went up, they were all in the dark. They lost their faith. All power will be taken away when Christ has gone and the saints are gone. The devil will be let loose and the Antichrist will begin to show his power. We find a type of this period in the story of the man that had the demons in him. The disciples could not cast them out. The father brought him to Jesus and said, "The demons try to drown him, burn him, and knock his brains out." Jesus cast the demons out and commanded that they enter no more into him.[49] So the Antichrist will burn some and drown some and knock the heads off of others as in the dark days. And then Jesus comes back, binds the devil, and destroys the army of the Antichrist—two-thirds of all the earth—and only one-third who went through all the fires trusting God the best they could are going to escape.

Taken from *Holy-Ghost Sermons.*

[48] See Matthew 24:40-41.

[49] See Matthew 17:15-18.

The Outpouring of the Holy Spirit in the Last Days—According to Joel's Prophecy

The Lord is in our midst. Be still and know the voice of God. "The Lord is in his holy temple: let all the earth keep silence before him."[1] Let us try to realize His wonderful presence. We must all meet Him sooner or later, as individuals; it is a good thing to get acquainted with Him now.

Acts 2:17. This Scripture applies to us today:

> It shall come to pass
> in the last days, saith God, I will pour out of my Spirit upon all flesh: and your sons and your daughters shall prophesy, and your young men shall see visions, and your old men shall dream dreams: And on my servants and on my handmaidens I will pour out in those days of my Spirit; and they shall prophesy: And I will shew wonders in heaven above, and signs in the earth beneath; blood, and fire, and vapour of smoke: The sun shall be turned into darkness, and the moon into blood, before that great and notable day of the Lord come.[2]

This is a wonderful scripture and many do not understand it. There is a certain time spoken of here when certain great and wonderful things shall take place, and people shall know that prophecy is being fulfilled. "It shall come to pass in the last days, I will pour out My Spirit," and there shall be signs in the heavens and the earth—signs of His coming. The Holy Ghost will be poured out before the "notable day of the Lord" comes.

[1] Habakkuk 2:20.

[2] Acts 2:17-20.

This prophecy was first spoken eight hundred years before Jesus came to earth.[3] Peter, standing up on the Day of Pentecost, rehearses the prophecy and confirms it. Under the inspiration of the Holy Ghost, on fire with the Holy Ghost from head to foot, speaking with tongues of fire, he said these things would come to pass in the last days.

We believe and know by the Word of God and by the signs that we are now living in the last days, the very times Peter spoke about when we were to know by the mighty things taking place. We are the people and this is the time just before the "notable day of the Lord" bursts upon the world. We believe we are the people, yea we *know* it. We have a right to our belief, for it is based upon the Word of God, and no man or woman has any right to denounce our teaching or to injure us in any way until it can be proved by the Word of God that the things we teach are not true.

You should give us a hearing, then take the same Word of God and prove by it that the things we teach are not true—if you can. You must first prove that the Holy Ghost working in all His mighty, miraculous power is done away with before you have any right to denounce us as frauds and hypocrites on account of these things which we say come from God.

Whenever anyone, minister or lawyer, can take the platform and prove by the Word of God that the Holy Ghost and His mighty, miraculous power have been taken away from the Church, we are willing to go to prison—not before. It cannot be done. God never recalls His gifts; God never changes.[4] My Bible says, "Jesus Christ the same yesterday, and to day, and for ever."[5] There are many ways besides the working of the Holy Ghost by which we know we are in the last days.

Joel, in speaking of the last days, tells us many things we cannot mention today, which show us that we are in this time. Nahum tells us when this time comes it will be the "day of His preparation,"

[3] See Joel 2:28.

[4] See Romans 11:29 and Malachi 3:6.

[5] Hebrews 13:8.

preparing men that they may be taken out of the world first before the Tribulation comes.[6]

Before the Flood, Noah was commanded to build an ark. He was just five years building the ark—though many believe it was much longer than that—and the time he was building it was the preparation time in those days. Noah, at God's command, was preparing a place for himself and [his] family where they should be in safety, above the storm that was coming, above the waves and billows. At the same time the old world was getting a warning, Noah was building the ark.[7]

Jesus compares that day of preparation to this time in these last days.[8] It is a short period and has been going on for some time. It is prophesied that there will be great signs in the earth: blood, fire, and smoke; earthquakes, great destruction. All these things have been coming upon the earth in the last few years. God has a time for everything. Daniel says that in the time of the end, knowledge shall be increased, and many shall run to and fro.[9] And Nahum says, "The chariots shall rage in the streets . . . they shall seem like torches, they shall run like the lightnings."[10] (See sermon on "The Second Coming of Christ.")

Jesus sent the Holy Ghost with mighty signs and wonders. He took possession of men, and they staggered like drunken men. They were drunk, but not with wine. They spoke with "stammering lips and another tongue."[11] The things happened when Pentecost first came, to set up the Church in power; that was the early rain.

In the last days, the time of preparation, God will cause to come again the early rain as at Pentecost, and He will also give the latter rain abundantly in the same month.[12] What do you think of that?

---

[6] Nahum 2:3.

[7] See Genesis 6.

[8] See Luke 17:26-27.

[9] See Daniel 12:4.

[10] Nahum 2:4.

[11] Isaiah 28:11.

[12] See Joel 2:23.

The early disciples went by the death route. It will take a double portion of the Spirit to fill our bodies, to make us sound in spirit, soul, and body. When Jesus comes like a flash of lightning, He shall change these bodies of ours in a moment, and they shall be made like His glorious body.[13]

"I show you a mystery . . . we shall all be changed," and shall rise to meet the Lord in the air.[14] When are these things to be? At the end of the day of preparation, just before the Tribulation bursts upon the world. We are to watch for the signs and not forsake the assembling of ourselves together; and so much the more as we see the day approaching![15] Glory to God! The Jews understood something of this. They say one to another, "We have been wounded, we have gone through many troubles; let us turn to the Lord. "After two days will he revive us: in the third day he will raise us up."[16] The Holy Ghost was first poured out at Pentecost.

We are now down at the end of the second thousand years since Christ set up His kingdom. What about the Jews? The Jews today have great liberty in Palestine; so much so that they are going back by [the] thousands and building up the waste places. Modern improvements are there today and they are hoping for something, they do not know what. After the Tribulation the Jews will return to the Lord.

"I will pour out my Spirit in the last days;" not sprinkle a few drops, but *pour out* on all *flesh*—a cloudburst! Just at the end. It will continue until the saints are taken away, then the Tribulation will burst upon the earth. The signs will be, your (some, not everybody) sons and your daughters shall prophesy. It is very plain that everyone may understand. There is to be a wonderful ministry in the last days. Paul says male and female are one in Christ.[17] Both shall prophesy in the last days. That is the effect of the outpouring of the Holy Ghost. Other signs: Devils shall be cast out, hands shall be laid on the sick and they shall recover; many shall speak with new

[13]See 1 Corinthians 15:51-54 and Philippians 3:21.

[14]1 Corinthians 15:51, paraphrased. See also 1 Thessalonians 4:17.

[15]See Hebrews 10:25.

[16]Hosea 6:2.

[17]See Galatians 3:28.

tongues; if anyone drinks poison accidentally, it shall not hurt him; serpents shall not be able to hurt in the last days.[18]

See the power given man today? He has even chained the lightning. It is the day for preparation. Men run to and fro and fly over the land. Hurry up! The ark will soon be finished and then God will say, "Come up."[19] The ark went up above the waters; the world went down. God is preparing His spiritual ark today; the body of Christ will soon be complete, and when it is complete it will go above the treetops to meet our Lord and King in the air. We are in the day of preparation of the King of Glory and His bride is making herself ready. Rejoice and be glad, for the marriage of the Lamb is at hand. The bride must be arrayed in white linen, the robe of righteousness, clothed in the power of the mighty God through His poured-out Spirit.

She is getting her garments ready to meet the Bridegroom. I praise the Lord I am living in this day. The bride will be caught up just before the Tribulation bursts upon this sin-cursed earth. The bride must be very beautiful. She is represented as a queen dressed in a robe of finest needlework. What is that fine wedding dress, the garments the bride will wear when she meets the Lord in the air? She will shine with the gifts and jewels of the Holy Ghost.

We have this treasure in earthen vessels; but they that be wise shall shine as the brightness of the sun.[20] The wise shall know when these things are coming, when the ark is about ready to go up. The Lord will not keep any secrets from them, as there is perfect confidence between bride and Bridegroom, so Jesus will reveal secrets to His bride. He will show us the deep things of God, and we shall know when the end is drawing near.[21] You must make your own wedding garments; you cannot hire them made.

The time is coming; people do not usually begin to make wedding garments until the wedding day is near. A bride is very happy, is willing to forsake her father's house, her friends—everything—and

[18]See Mark 16:17-18.

[19]See Revelations 11:12.

[20]See 2 Corinthians 4:7 and Daniel 12:3.

[21]See 2 Corinthians 2:9-10.

go with her bridegroom, even to a foreign country. She loves those she leaves, but he is dearer to her than anything else. We must be willing to leave anything and everything to go with Jesus. The bride will be taken out from among men, and the men and women will be left. You may say, "I do not believe it." *I believe it!*

Do you suppose I would leave home, friends, my only child that I have to spend my life for others if I did not know these things were so? God has revealed these things by His Word and by signs, and I know they are true. God is almighty, is putting His seal upon this truth every day; He is putting the seal of the Holy Ghost upon people every day. The Holy Ghost is a witness to you, by mighty signs and wonders, that we are preaching the Word of God. I call God to witness that the Holy Ghost is putting His seal upon the work here. There are signs here every day. What are you going to do about it? If you believe the Bible, you must accept it. We have the eternal Word to stand on, and stronger is He that is with us than all that can be against us.[22]

After Pentecost, they went out and preached the Holy Ghost sent by the ascended Jesus, and He confirmed the Word with signs following.[23] I say before God, He is confirming the Word here every day, and these miracles are put down in heaven's record. Jesus Christ is the healer and the baptizer. John the Baptist said, "He that cometh after me is mightier than I . . . he shall baptize you with the Holy Ghost, and with fire," and I praise God that some of the fire has struck this place.[24] You can make flowery speeches and the devil laughs; but this work stirs the devil. It is "by my spirit," saith the Lord.[25]

Paul said his teaching was not with enticing words of man's wisdom, but in demonstration of the Spirit and of power.[26] That shakes the world; and it is just the same today. You say, "I do not like this power." Well, the devil does not like it either. I have been out in the work thirty-five years and people fell under the power by thousands before

[22]See 1 John 4:4 and Romans 8:31

[23]See Acts 2:43.

[24]Matthew 3:11.

[25]Zechariah 4:6.

[26]See 1 Corinthians 2:4.

I preached healing. There were mighty outpourings of the Spirit that made the devil howl. It shows how little we know of the real Gospel when we take the letter of the law; it is like skimmed milk.

No man can understand the deep things of God except by the Spirit.[27] Paul had much knowledge, but he said the wisdom of this world was foolishness in the sight of God.[28] True wisdom comes from heaven. The Word must be preached in simplicity. Jesus had the eloquence of high heaven at His command, yet He used language that the most uneducated could understand.

Preach in a simple way and demonstrate. The seal is put upon the Word by the Holy Spirit. Many say that when we lay hands upon the people, they get mesmerized. I am sorry they do not know more of the power of God. There was a great revival at Samaria; Simon the sorcerer was baptized, but none of them had been baptized with the Holy Ghost. Peter and John went to Samaria and laid their hands on them, and they received the Holy Ghost. He was imparted to them in some way through the laying on of the apostle's hands. Simon recognized the power was different from sorcery and he wanted it. He offered them money to give him this power that whomsoever he laid hands on, they might receive the Holy Ghost.[29]

The apostles were horrified. They said, "Thy money perish with thee, because thou hast thought that the gift of God may be purchased with money."[30] The Holy Ghost and His power are gifts of God; you cannot buy them. Many people today do not understand any more than Simon did. The apostles told him to repent or he would be lost. "Thou art in the gall of bitterness."[31] May God open the eyes of the people!

By the laying on of the apostles' hands, something happened; the Holy Ghost fell on those people and they had great blessing. There were great demonstrations in those days when the Holy Spirit fell

[27] See 1 Corinthians 2:10-11.

[28] See 1 Corinthians 3:19.

[29] See Acts 8:5-24.

[30] Acts 8:20.

[31] Acts 8:23.

on the people. The thought is that ***when hands were laid on, something happened.*** They spoke in other languages, their mouths were filled with laughter, and sometimes they fell like dead men.[32]

You must prove that God has taken this power away before you judge us harshly. Peter said the things they saw on the Day of Pentecost were the things the prophets said should come. You ask why the people go down? What is our little strength under the power of God? Whenever people get a glimpse of God's glory, they lose their strength and fall.

Paul said that in his vision he did not know whether he was in the body or out of the body, God knew.[33] John the Revelator, when he saw the glory of God in a vision, fell as one dead.[34] In Daniel's vision he fell upon his face; then a hand touched him and set him upon his knees and hands (you have never seen anything like that). Then he was taken up, strengthened, and saw a great vision. The men that were with Daniel fled, so they did not see the vision. But Daniel fled not, and he saw it; but he fell prostrate.[35] Just a little manifestation of God's power and we lose our strength and go down.

Some of you do not understand the working of the Spirit; you are not near enough to God to know it is the work of the Spirit. Peter was on the housetop praying and he lost his strength and went down. A voice from heaven called him three times.[36] Sometimes God teaches us more in ten minutes when we are lost to this world than we would otherwise learn in months. Paul, as he journeyed to Damascus persecuting the Christians, was stricken to the earth when the light shone from heaven; and those who were with him also fell to the earth. Paul says the light was above the brightness of the sun; yet it was at midday when the sun was at its strength. All those men fell from their horses and rolled in the dust when the glory of God passed by. Paul was struck blind and was blind for three days.[37]

---

[32]See Psalm 126:2.

[33]See 2 Corinthians 12:2.

[34]See Revelation 1:17.

[35]See Daniel 10:4-10.

[36]See Acts 10:9-13.

[37]See Acts 9:1-9 and 26:13-14.

When Jesus went to the grave He went down a corpse, but when He arose from the dead, the soldiers were stricken down at the manifestation of God's power and glory.[38] You must prove God no longer manifests His power and glory before you condemn us. Remember the first martyr, Stephen; he was a man full of faith, wisdom, and power—full of the Holy Ghost. The wise men tried to confound him but could not do it; then they were jealous and wanted to get rid of him. They hired men of the baser sort—that is the kind for that work—who lied about this mighty servant of God.[39]

They arrested him, and there he was before the great assembly. He did not try to defend himself, but he took the opportunity offered to preach to them about Jesus. He was filled with the Holy Ghost. His face was as the face of an angel and those who swore his life away saw it.[40] He did not look like a liar and a hypocrite. He was a servant of Almighty God.

You can see that light today sometimes in the faces of God's children. Stephen looked up into heaven and saw the glory of God. He saw Jesus who had risen from the dead, standing at the right hand of God, and he told the people. Oh Lord, open the eyes of these people, and let them see the angels of the Lord encamped around about us and Jesus standing in the midst! When Stephen told what he saw, they gnashed their teeth; they did not intend to repent. They dragged him out and stoned him to death, but the Lord received him and permitted it.[41]

God promises His people shall be protected and it is no sign He forsakes them because trouble comes. Stephen's enemies did not like it because God received him, nor did they like to see his face shine with the glory of God. His body was lying a bruised mass, but *he* rose to meet the Lord. He had a glorious vision.[42] Do you believe he

[38]See Matthew 28:4.

[39]See Acts 6:5,8.

[40]See Acts 17:5.

[41]See Acts 6:15.

[42]See Acts 7:54-60.

saw the throne and Jesus standing there? People talk about these things as though they were fables.

God says before Jesus comes these same "signs and wonders" shall come to pass: the sick shall be healed, devils cast out, people shall speak with tongues—just before He comes.[43] I am so glad for these days. When Jesus came before, He rebuked the Jewish leaders. He told them they could discern the face of the sky, but not the signs of the times. "How is it ye did not look for me?"[44] How much more shall He upbraid people when He returns? "Why didn't you see the signs? Why didn't you listen to My messenger? Why didn't you look at the Word and see whether they were telling the truth or were imposters." Excuses won't do when we stand before Jesus. The light has come. Let us arise and shine and give God the glory![45]

Nothing but the mighty Holy Ghost will ever take you up in the clouds. He will quicken these mortal bodies, and they will be changed.[46] We shall not have wings, but our hands and feet will be made light. Our feet will be like "hinds' feet,"[47] run, skip, and almost fly. We shall know the power of the resurrection life. We will be so filled with the Holy Ghost that our bodies will be made light. Sometimes my body is made so light, I can hardly stay.

My feet are on the earth, but my hands seem on the throne. Christ arose from the dead, and He is the resurrection and the life. People want to get the blood of Jesus over them, over their diseased bodies, in His name.

Do you believe right now? If you believe then praise the Lord in faith [that] it shall be done. If you do not feel the joy, offer praise as a sacrifice and ask God to give you the joy. When the unclean spirit is driven out, the disease goes and the resurrection life comes in. Then you lose your little strength and go down like Daniel, John, and the rest of them and lie down in green pastures.[48]

[43] See Mark 16:17-18, Joel 2:23, and Zechariah 10:1. Etter believed that the signs referred to by Mark will be displayed in greater abundance, in a "latter rain" which will come before the end times.

[44] See Matthew 16:3 and Luke 12:56.

[45] See Isaiah 60:1.

[46] See Romans 8:11 and 1 Corinthians 15:51-52.

[47] See Psalm 18:33 and Habakkuk 3:19.

[48] See Psalm 23:2.

Some dance, shout, and praise the Lord as the life of Jesus thrills through them. I declare to you on the authority of God and from my own experience, I know it is the power of God through Jesus Christ. It does not take Jesus long to do the work, but it takes some of us a long time to get there. Five minutes will do the work. Then the peace of God will flow through you like a river, and you will have joy in the Holy Ghost. As you go home, don't think about your sins. Don't commit any more, and don't worry about the past, it is under the blood.

God gave me a message, and He has given me the strength to stand here and deliver it. He asks you in a loving way to meet the Lord in the air, to attend the marriage supper. Will you meet me there? He is coming so soon; I often think I shall live until He comes. I praise Him today, that I know these things. Sometimes people get into the flesh and make too much demonstration, but that is better than never to talk, pray, or sing. Let us not condemn, but let us all try to get nearer to God. That is what I am striving for today.

> *Oh, God, I have held up your Son today; I have honored His name with all the strength You have given me. Take the scales off the eyes of those who do not see and make them to see the truths that have been brought out! May they think of them again and again, and may they go unto You to find out whether these things are so.*
>
> *You know how I have pleaded with people not to lay hands on the ark or on the Lord's anointed. Open the eyes of those who have only known dead forms and make them to know I am Thy servant. Lord, I want the joy bells to ring in heaven because they are on the way, but You cannot take them against their will. I pray I may meet them at the marriage supper of the Lamb.*

Taken from *Signs and Wonders God Wrought in the Ministry of Maria B. Woodworth-Etter.*

The Last Call of Mercy

Make Your Calling and Selection Sure—The Reward of the Overcomer

e give thee thanks, O Lord God Almighty, which art, and wast, and art to come; because thou hast taken to thee thy great power, and hast reigned. And the nations were angry, and thy wrath is come, and the time of the dead, that they should be judged, and that thou shouldest give reward unto thy servants the prophets, and to the saints, and them that fear thy name, small and great; and shouldest destroy them which destroy the earth.

Revelation 11:17-18

And I saw another angel fly in the midst of heaven, having the everlasting gospel to preach unto them that dwell on the earth, and to every nation, and kindred, and tongue, and people, Saying with a loud voice, Fear God, and give glory to him; for the hour of his judgment is come: and worship him that made heaven, and earth, and the sea, and the fountains of waters.

Revelation 14:6-7

Fear God and give glory to Him; worship God — the God of heaven who made the heavens and the earth, the land and sea and waters of the earth. Glory to God.

I saw an angel, a great angel flying over the earth, having the everlasting Gospel to preach to every nation, kindred, and tongue on earth—the message to repent and fear God. He was preaching the everlasting Gospel with a voice of thunder. Warn the people, sound the alarm, fear God, worship Him, and give glory to Him who made heaven and earth and the sea and the fountain of waters and the starry firmament. Worship God for the hour of His judgment is come.

The Last Message

In God's Word, angels are often used to represent His servants. These angels represent the saints of God in these last days going with rapidity over the land, baptized in the Holy Ghost, running up the mountain, and hurling back the glad tidings that Jesus is coming. It is the Gospel of salvation from sin and the baptism of the Holy Ghost with all the signs and wonders about the time of the coming of Christ. This glorious Gospel is concerning the kingdom of Christ, the last message being given out before Jesus comes.

When the disciples asked how the people should know when the time of the end came, He answered, "This Gospel of My kingdom must be preached to the last generation. It must be preached as a witness to every nation, tribe, kindred, and tongue."[1] Not to every person but to every nation. Every nation must be represented in the peoples, tribes, kindreds, and tongues that will make up the bridal company.

This Gospel must be preached in all parts of the world through God's people by the Holy Ghost, and when He has accomplished to scatter (*sic*) the power (the demonstrations and signs by the Holy Ghost), then will the end come. It is the last message to go forth in power, the power of the Holy Ghost; and God will back it up with signs and wonders and put His seal on it. God shall bear witness by the Holy Ghost by signs, by wonders, by mighty works, and by diverse operations of the Spirit to prove that the end is near. This He is doing today.

Not All Now Alive Will Die

There are people living today that will be caught away to heaven without dying. There are people now living that will have the mark of the Beast. There are also those who will not be able to buy or sell because they will not take the mark of the Beast.[2] There are those now living who will go on living in this world until the last great Battle of Armageddon. God help us to see this.

[1] Matthew 24:14, paraphrased.

[2] See Revelation 13:17.

Let us look up and worship Him, give glory to Him for the dead to be raised and for the saints to get their reward and for judgment to be poured out upon the wicked. The restitution of all things is near at hand when the wicked shall be cut off from the face of the earth. Jesus is coming and the saints of God are carrying the Word of God over the water, through the air, and over the mountains by printing press, telephone, and wireless. God is pouring out His Spirit upon the earth and people from every church and from every religion on earth are baptized in the Holy Ghost and have the mark of blood and fire and are sealed with the seal of the living God, and God is girding the earth today with these baptized saints.

This glorious Gospel that Jesus is coming soon, backed up by signs and gifts of the Spirit, is girding the earth today. Distance does not make any difference; the necessary money comes in some way—they are not afraid of the warships, nor sharks, nor other dangers of the deep, but start and they land over in England, Europe, Africa, giving the last message, "Jesus is coming soon; prepare to meet God."

We Are to Sound the Alarm

So a great angel means the mighty power of God calling with a loud voice—"Prepare to meet God. Blow the trumpet—blow the trumpet in Zion, sound the alarm, let all the people tremble. Give the signal of danger—the time is near, it is at the door, it hasteth greatly."[3] Days of destruction, days of darkness, days of tribulation are even now upon earth. Don't you see the waves of darkness coming this way? Look out today in our own country, look at the destruction, look at the raging fires, look at the high waters sweeping away property, look at the commotion among the people, the quarrel between labor and capital—don't you see it is ready to spread all over the land? Don't you see the signs of the coming of the Lord? His coming shall be very tempestuous, preceded by great storms, earthquakes, calamities, thunderings, lightnings, and awful things.

It shall be tempestuous also for the saints of God. They got this salvation with great joy, but also with awful persecution, awful trials,

[3] See Joel 2:1.

and awful tribulations. People hate the Holy Ghost, they always did—they don't want any joy. We are a nation despised, hated, and not desired. O hasten and hide you away, get deep in God that you may be hid away from the great tempest that will burst upon the face of the earth.[4] May God wake up the people here tonight. Every sign that Jesus said should come has come. God's people have always been hated, despised, criticized, and misrepresented. The work of the Spirit of God is foolishness to natural men, but it is the power of God and the wisdom of God to everyone that accepts.[5] God's children have a hard time. The world tries to discourage them in every way, tries to drive them out—but they hated Him before they hated you.[6]

Prepare to Meet God

But Jesus is coming on the white horse of power, leading us on to victory.[7] We are running up the mountain hurling back the warning, "Prepare, prepare, prepare to meet God. Jesus is coming! Get ready, jump into the fountain, get washed from your sins, and get on the white garment. Behold, the time is come for Him to take His great power and reign, time for the dead to be raised, and time for the saints to get their reward. Repent, worship God, and give glory to God, for the hour of His judgment is here. People of America, wake up. The trumpet is sounding. The alarm is being given. Wake up before God shuts the door of mercy and you are shut out forever."

O God awaken the people! Glory to God. O you are going to sleep, just like they did in Jerusalem. But those who were sealed with the blood and the fire mark were taken out just before the gates were shut—the rest were shut in. They had asked about the sign; and He had told them, "When you see a certain sign get ready—and when you see another sign, get out: don't stop to take anything—turn not back to take your cloak!"[8]

---

[4] See Psalm 31:20 and Isaiah 26:20.

[5] See 1 Corinthians 2:14.

[6] See John 15:18.

[7] See Revelation 6:2 and 19:11.

[8] See Matthew 24:15-18, Mark 13:14-16, and Luke 21:20-21.

How Shall We Escape if We Neglect the Warning?

Now He is warning us. Watch the signs and search the Scriptures. You see, every sign is being fulfilled today right before our eyes. Watch and pray and be up and doing. "Forsake not the assembling of yourselves together, but much more so as you see the day approaching."[9] And the angels that are holding back the four winds cry out, "May we let loose?" But the great angel flying through the midst of heaven says, "Hold back a little longer—hold back the sun that it may not scorch the people. Hold back the tidal waves. Hold back the greatest forest fires. Hold back until we have sealed the servants of the Lord with the seal of the living God in the forehead."[10] O God, waken the people. Can't you see He is calling out a people and preparing a people and sealing a people? Hallelujah! The bride of Christ must be pure and holy. The whole being must be purified, and we must have some of the resurrection power in our bodies.

Worship God, fear God. Get your eyes off men's wisdom. Get free from all the delusions of the devil and get your eyes upon the Almighty God. There are many gods today. People are worshipping all kinds of gods—gods of money, gods of education, gods of science, and a hundred others. But none of them amount to anything; all who trust in them will be lost and go down to destruction. God is warning you to get your eyes on the living God—the true God—the great Spirit-being. God Almighty is a great, spiritual, holy being—Jesus Christ was, too. He was with God before the world was made, another beautiful, spiritual, holy being—the image of the Father.[11] And He came down and took upon Him the form of man, and it must have been exactly like the spiritual form. So many don't want to believe in Jesus and don't believe that Jesus was the Son of God. If He was not what He said He was, He is the meanest man that ever lived.

---

[9] Hebrews 10:25, paraphrased.

[10] See Revelation 7:1-3.

[11] See John 1:1.

God Chooses Us and Reveals Christ to Us

They don't believe He was the Son of God and that through the sacrifice on the Cross and the blood flowing on Calvary, the fountain was opened to the house of David for the remission of sins. But if you don't go to heaven by the way of the Cross, you will never get there at all.[12] No one who worships God can reach God if they leave out Jesus. No man ever can reach God if he leaves out Jesus Christ, and he cannot come except the Father draw him.[13] God sends His Holy Spirit, gentle as a dove, to lead you to Jesus Christ. If you follow, He will lead you repentant right to the bleeding feet of the Son of God, and when you accept Him, God saves you and the Spirit of God comes in. When you find Him, it is knowledge.

The Holy Spirit reveals Christ as your Savior, and Christ introduces you to the Father and you cry out, "Abba Father," right there. They both work together. You can't get saved without God—you can't get saved without Christ. No man ever came to Christ except the Father drew him and no man ever got to God except he came through Christ. When you come to Christ in the right way, the Holy Spirit makes it known. Christ reveals God as a great, holy being, too holy to look upon. No man can ever look upon the face of God Almighty.[14] Moses wanted to see God and God said to Moses, "You climb into the cleft of that rock and hide, and I will pass by and you shall see a little of My glory."[15]

Moses hid in the rock and God put His hand over the cleft of the rock and passed by, and Moses was permitted to see a little of the glory of God but he did not see God.[16] God wants you and I (*sic*) to hide in this Rock and God will reveal His glory. He wants to fill us with His glory; how else can one chase a thousand and two put ten thousand to flight?[17] O bless God, we want to see more of His glory tonight. The great personal Savior, the wonderful, beautiful spirit

[12] See John 14:6.

[13] See John 6:44.

[14] See 1 Timothy 6:15-16.

[15] See Exodus 33:22.

[16] See Exodus 33:18-23.

[17] See Leviticus 26:8.

being! You need Jesus revealed to you as a risen Savior and God revealed to you as a great loving Father with great loving arms reaching out to take the whole world in. That is the God to worship in these days.

The Last Call of Mercy

He is giving you the last call now. Take your eyes off all the other things and worship the God of heaven. The fear of God is the beginning of wisdom.[18] "Fear God and give Him glory—worship Him and give Him glory for the hour of His judgment is come." Our God is a consuming fire.[19] You will never find Him as a Savior in the time of His wrath if you don't come to Him in the time of His mercy. He can only be found in the straight and narrow way.[20] Jesus says, "I am the way, the truth, and the life."[21] The way is a narrow one, but it is wide enough for you and Jesus to walk in.

If you have any other god, you had better get away from him tonight and get acquainted with the God of heaven and earth—the God who will pour out His wrath on those who trample the blood of Jesus under their feet as something unholy. Don't be like the Jews before the destruction of Jerusalem. They said God did not care, [that] God has forsaken the earth.[22] But He is wonderfully alive and "It is a fearful thing to fall into the hands of the living God."[23] The door of mercy will be closed unless you repent, and you will fall into the hands of the living God. God help us to see this.

The Delusion That Jesus Is His Own Father

Many people are being led away and trying to hold Jesus up and at the same time are tearing Him down by denying the existence of the

[18]See Psalm 111:10 and Proverbs 9:10.

[19]See Hebrews 12:29 and Deuteronomy 4:24.

[20]See Matthew 7:14.

[21]John 14:6.

[22]See Ezekiel 8:12 and 9:9.

[23]Hebrews 10:31. This is also a possible allusion to Jonathan Edwards' (1703-1758) "Sinners in the Hands of an Angry God" (1741).

Father.[24] This is the biggest delusion the devil ever invented. You endeavor to tear God off His throne—the God of heaven and all His love and mercy. Take away God, and Jesus Christ will suffer. Tear God out of the Bible and you take the whole foundation out of the Bible and there is nothing left at all. But it is all a sign that Jesus is coming soon and that this is the great sifting time. May God help us and open our eyes.

God has so many things to show us. Don't you see the fulfillment of prophecy? Don't you see the time is at hand when the Messiah should come? Jesus said to the Pharisees, "You can discern the clouds and the sky but you cannot discern the time is here for the Messiah to be revealed."[25] And there are a thousand more signs today for us of the nearness of the coming of Jesus: His being right at the door and we being more blind than the Jews. Many are married to this world and the things of this world, which will all be swept away. The awful judgments will come—the Antichrist will arise—the clouds of judgment will burst and God's wrath will be poured out without measure.

See the awful things that are going on now? These are only the beginning of sorrows. He will soon make a speedy riddance of all mockers on the face of the earth. The Lord will take out a people who are prepared. The world will go right on. The Antichrist will reign. It will be the hour of tribulations and of judgments. The Antichrist will rule, some say forty years, and some say three years and a half—no one knows how long, but it will be long enough.

Make Your Calling and Selection Sure

Be always in an attitude or prayer or praise that you may be accounted worthy to escape all these awful calamities. The angels are holding back the worst of these things until the saints of God are sealed in the forehead with the seal of the living God.

Soon the Man of Sin is coming. Read the book of Revelations (*sic*); read the prophecies; it will almost make your hair stand up. When this

[24]Maria Etter here refers to the Jesus-Only or Oneness doctrine which began in a revival at which she spoke in Los Angeles in 1913.

[25]Matthew 16:3 and Luke 12:56, paraphrased.

Man of Sin reigns, the time will come when you cannot buy or sell unless you have the mark of the Beast.[26]

Thousands will be put to death and there will be worse things than death—torture and cruelties worse than ever before known, even in the Dark Ages. This Antichrist will come and rule, and every person that won't worship the Beast he will have put to death. This Man of Sin is on the earth at some place. There is a move to organize a great federation. Don't touch it; it is bound to go to pieces. They will make threats against you. Don't be forced to join in with them but fear God. Keep out of the federation. Fear God and worship Him. Give glory to Him, for the hour of His judgment is come—the time is come for Him to take His great power and reign—the time for the dead to be raised. Fear God—the God who made heaven and earth and the sea and the fountains of living waters. Give glory to Him. For the hour of His judgment is come. It is, whether you believe it or not. O God.

The Time of the Gentiles Is Dying Out

"Blow ye the trumpet in Zion, and sound an alarm in my holy mountain."[27] Let all the people of the land tremble at the sound of the trumpet, which is the signal of danger, for the great Day of the Lord cometh. It is nigh at hand, it hasteth greatly. It is at the door! Prepare, prepare to meet your God. Blow the trumpet. Warn the people that Jesus is coming. Hallelujah! The time of the Gentiles is dying out. Black darkness shall cover the earth and gross darkness, the people. Soon men and women will gnaw their tongues because of their pain and this awful darkness.[28]

The time is at hand when the sun shall scorch men and women, when wild beasts will be let loose and serpents. These animals and reptiles will be starving in times of famine, and they will therefore be worse than ever before. He says all these things are going to burst on the earth. He says in that day of Great Tribulation, if you escape the famine, the wild beasts will get you. If you shall escape

[26]See Revelation 13:17.

[27]Joel 2:1.

[28]See Revelation 16:10.

the wild beasts and the wars and the famine and wander into your own house to lean up against the wall and rest, a poisonous serpent will bite you.[29] There will be famine, pestilence, and all these things at the same time. Even now these things are coming; even the insects are full of poison.

A Great Catastrophe Impending—Shall We Escape It?

Get ready for the coming of the Lord. Get the mark of fire and blood on you, for the destroying weapon will not come near the man or woman that has the mark of God upon them. Not one of the children of God who had the mark of blood and fire—the Holy Ghost—went down in the awful slaughter at the destruction of Jerusalem.[30] God took them out of the way. God led them out to a place of safety. God took care of His own. But when they saw the signs coming closer and closer, they left their property, left everybody that would not go with them, and they had to go alone. They could not take their property, nor can you. You had better use it now.

Blow the trumpet! Sound the alarm in Zion! God Almighty is giving to us the same signs, even plainer than He did to them. We believe God and are preparing for flight. Get ready, for some of these days Jesus is coming. When the day comes, everyone that has the blood and fire mark will be caught up alive, taken up just before hell is let loose. Before the Antichrist takes power, we will be taken away. Jesus will catch His waiting bride away. Glory to God. He is preparing a people to take flight through the air. See the signs coming closer and closer.

And that is why we don't rest hardly three or four minutes a day (*sic*). People are coming thousands of miles and living in little old tents on half rations, just to help us to warn the people and to take their stand for God. What will money amount to pretty soon? When Jesus comes you cannot take it along. Bless God, we are going to the city of God, where the streets of the city are gold and the great gates are like pearls; and the streets are fifteen hundred miles high,

[29] See Amos 5:19.

[30] See Ephcsians 1:13. "The mark of blood and fire"—The mark of the Passover lamb and the tongue of fire from the baptism of the Holy Spirit. (See also Exodus 12:7,13.)

fifteen hundred miles long, and square.[31] That is where we are going—going to be hid away. There will be no storms there to blow it over, no fires can burn it down. It is more beautiful than anything on earth—twelve gates of pearl. Oh, won't you look up and by faith see the city John saw? It is beautiful: bright and glorious.

"Lift up your heads ye everlasting gates and let the King of glory in. Who is this King of glory? The Lord God of hosts."[32] It is Jesus Christ the King of glory coming home with His Bride. Lift up your doors and let the King of glory in with his beautiful Bride. That will take place pretty soon.

The Reward of the Overcomer

He will change these vile bodies and they will be made like His glorious body.[33] He says to us, "To him that overcometh will I grant to sit with me in my throne, even as I also overcame, and am set down with my Father in his throne."[34]

You can be an overcomer if you want to. Jesus has not taken His throne and won't take it until the bride goes up. John saw the bride go up and then he saw the throne. He saw Christ take His great throne and the bride will sit with Christ on the throne.

Don't you want to go? Don't you want to get ready for the Bridegroom when He comes in all His glory and all His majesty with all the holy angels? He is coming quickly. His loved saints will burst forth as quickly as you can wink your eye. We won't lose our identity or personality but just burst forth to shine like the firmament and we will eclipse the sun down here. Our sun that lightens the earth will be thrown in the shade by every one of God's wise ones as they burst forth and go up to meet the Lord in the air.[35]

The Night Cometh When No Man Can Work

Christ is the head and the bride is the body and the Holy Ghost (the light of the Gentile age) is setting the body of Christ and filling

[31] See Revelation 21.

[32] Psalm 24:7-10, paraphrased.

[33] See Philippians 3:21.

[34] Revelation 3:21

[35] See Daniel 12:3.

it up with resurrection life from the eternal shores. It is the power of God Almighty, through Jesus Christ, in these bodies of ours. God is holding back the four winds and giving the saints of God a little more time and opportunity to get busy.[36] They are warning the people to blow the trumpet and sound the alarm.[37] They are telling the Good News to the people of this last generation of every tribe and kindred and tongue, and that they must be sealed with the blood and the fire. Wake up and warn the people that they must be sealed with the seal of the living God in the forehead. May God give them the mind of Christ that all these things will be real to them.[38]

God is real to us—Christ is as real to us as you are. We know we have God in us and eternal life just as well as we know we have the natural body. When I start to preach and He gives me a new shock of power from His heavenly battery, I feel like I was about sixteen years old. Glory! That is the resurrection power that will take us up to meet the Lord in the air. They often tell me I had better be in bed. How can I go to bed? I have to tell the people about Jesus. Bless God. They say it would do me good to take a little rest. How can I rest when the people are soon going down to death in this Great Tribulation? By the grace of God I am going to warn you. Blow the trumpet, sound the alarm. Wake up the people from the sleep of death that they may repent and give glory to God. Worship God. Fear the God of heaven, for the hour of His judgment is at hand. God bless the people.

God's Word Will Not Return Void

Beloved, it ought to make you tremble to see the wonderful prophecies fulfilled right before your eyes. God says in the last days with stammering lips and other tongues[39] will I—Jehovah—speak to these people of America. The Spirit of God is telling these wonderful works of God through the lips of clay like you talk over a telephone. I, Jehovah, will speak from heaven. When it is interpreted, what is it? They all are telling the wonderful works of God.

[36]See Revelation 7:1-3.

[37]See Joel 2:1.

[38]See 1 Corinthians 2:16.

[39]See Isaiah 28:11.

On the Day of Pentecost the Rabbis said, "What does it mean?" They were confounded by the eloquence, power, and wisdom and cried, "Are these not all ignorant Galilean people, yet we do every one of us hear them speak in the language wherein we were born."[40]

It confounded them. What does it mean? With all the mighty wisdom of the Rabbis, they could not fathom it. With all their wonderful knowledge, it was like a closed book to them. They could not answer. God said the book should be closed.[41] Somebody has to tell them and He just called up these little Marys and Martha, Peter, and John and let them explain it.

He has given a wonderful message here tonight. God gave the messages in tongues and interpretations that terrible wars and pestilences are coming upon the earth in a very short time. Many of you dear boys here tonight are to be called out to the battlefront and will die in the trenches and on the battlefield and when dying, will remember of what I warned you today and get saved.

Do You Lightly Esteem God's Invitation?

You see, the Spirit and the Word agree, and if you are all of one mind it is like clockwork.[42] Every message tonight was on the line of the coming of the Lord, the pouring out of His wrath, and the saints going up. People, people, O get ready! Prepare to meet Him. He is coming soon.

Well, and what if you do not believe He will come? You will soon be cold in the grave anyway. But Jesus is coming, and you are not too old to live until He comes. I know it is so by the signs and by the Word. He says the wise shall know. And if you never had a warning before, you have one tonight. Everyone that gets this light and gets this power makes it plain. He will run. He will run to meet the Lord, and while he is running he is telling the people to get ready for Jesus is coming. Don't stay in the plain, but run to the mountain for Jesus is coming.[43]

---

[40]Acts 2:7-8, paraphrased.

[41]See Daniel 12:4.

[42]See 1 John 5:7-8.

[43]An allusion to Lot in Sodom and Gomorrah and also to the landscape in *The Pilgrim's Progress.*

Beloved, you ought to thank God that the mercy door has not been closed. Thank God that you still have another invitation. Will you accept it? Will you prepare your wedding robes? You must make them yourselves. You cannot make them at the last minute. You must make it yourself, and I am glad you have to do it. Revelation 19:7. And to the saints here and everywhere He says, "Rejoice and be glad for the marriage of the Lamb is come and the bride hath made herself ready — and blessed and holy are they that are called to the marriage supper of the Lamb."[44]

It will be pretty substantial, don't you think? Blessed are they that eat bread in my Father's kingdom. Rejoice and be exceeding glad my children because the day of your reward is at hand.[45] Lift up your heads, O ye righteous, for the King of Glory is nigh.[46] "Fear not, little flock; for it is your Father's good pleasure to give you the kingdom."[47] O my children! Do not fail Him but lift up your heads and be not ashamed, nor yet afraid of their faces.[48] Behold, have I not said that I am with you even unto the end of the world.[49] Lift up your heads, be glad and rejoice for your redemption draweth nigh.[50]

Taken from *Spirit-Filled Sermons.*

[44] Revelation 19:7 and 9, paraphrased.

[45] See Matthew 5:12.

[46] See Psalm 24:7-10.

[47] Luke 12:32.

[48] See Jeremiah 1:8.

[49] See Matthew 28:20.

[50] See Luke 21:28.

THE CLOSING OF THE GENTILE AGE

God's Judgments Are in the Earth—The Last Warnings Are Being Given

he Lord shall rise up as in mount Perazim, he shall be wroth as in the valley of Gibeon, that he may do his work, his strange work; and bring to pass his act, his strange act. Now therefore be ye not mockers, lest your bands be made strong: for I have heard from the Lord God of hosts a consumption, even determined upon the whole earth.

Isaiah 28:21-22

In all the history of the Bible and in all God's dealings with the world, He sent and offered them mercy and deliverance first. He did everything to persuade them to trust and obey Him and to escape the coming judgments. But they still kept on sinning till the pent-up wrath of God was poured out, and they were all destroyed. With a strong hand and a supernatural power, He was with His people in the Spirit of judgment and of strength, to them that turned the battle to the gate.

When mercy ceased to be a virtue, judgments came like a desolation and destruction like a whirlwind, and they then hear Him say, "You will seek me right early, but your cries come too late, I will answer. I will laugh at your calamities, and mock when your fear cometh."[1]

In all the threatened dangers and in the midst of awful judgments, the Lord caused His supernatural presence to be seen in signs through His children; while showing wrath, He worked His strange work through and by the Holy Spirit.

[1] Proverbs 1:26 and 28, paraphrased.

Heedless the World Rushes on to Its Doom

With all these past warnings and examples of mercy and awful calamities that came with or followed the rejection of the loving voice of God so tenderly calling them to come to Him from their evil ways, to fly to His outstretched arms—with all these past warnings and examples, the poor, blinded, debauched world does not, and will not, take warning; but after six thousand years she keeps on sinning; still seeks to take the management from God, saying, "God does not know, He does not care, we will run the world ourselves."[2]

People are running wild after wealth and form, exalting and worshipping the wisdom of man, his power and ability or mighty inventive powers. Even in their professed worship, they have left the fountainhead of living waters and have hewn out cisterns, broken cisterns that will hold no water.[3] They have turned their backs to God and are facing the sun of human wisdom and power that has risen and blinded them so that they are satisfied with the gods of this world.

Vain Is the Help of Man

Hear one of the last warning notes from the eternal throne, from the loving Father: "In vain ye worship Me, going after the doctrines and traditions of men, which will perish with the using."[4] You order your lives after worldly principles. Acting like Christians as far as churchgoing and talking is concerned, but living and acting like the world nevertheless.

The time of trifling is about over. God is calling the Elijah class, which is clothed with the power of God, and King Ahab to come face to face and test their gods. We must come to a halt and put our gods to a test; and the one that answers by fire and has the supernatural manifestation of God's approval and power, we will serve; that is God's test.[5]

[2] See Job 22:13-14 and Psalm 74:9-11.

[3] See Jeremiah 2:13.

[4] Matthew 15:9 and Mark 7:7, paraphrased.

[5] See 1 Kings 18:17-40.

"It shall come to pass, in the last days, saith the Lord, I will plead with all flesh, with the sword and fire, and the slain of the Lord shall be many."[6] The sword is the Word of God. The fire is the Holy Ghost. The slain of the Lord are those that fall under conviction, or lay prostrate like dead men and women, under the power of God.

Lightning of His Power

He will send out His arrows—His Word dipped in the blood of Jesus, shot out with the lightning of His power—and they shall wound the King's enemies in the head. They shall fall at His feet. Oh, praise His name. When God has His way the tent ground looks like a battlefield; men, women, and children lying in all parts like dead men. In the manifested presence of the Almighty, their natural strength fails them.

According to God's Word, the time of trouble such as men have never seen or known or ever will see again, has already commenced and will finish with the battle of the great God.

We are in the last days of His preparation, and Jesus is coming soon for His bride, and she is getting ready (1 Thessalonians 4:16-17). He is sending His angels, His servants, with a message like the sound of a trumpet, calling the elect together so that we may all be baptized with one faith, one Spirit, and one mind; that we may be amongst the wise that shall shine as the brightness of the firmament.[7]

In the chapter from which the text is taken, which refers to the time of the last or Laodicean church, which is the vine of the earth, the vine of man's planting, He shows that in that time of the awful destruction in which she will be utterly destroyed, the saints who are going through will be clothed with power.[8]

The workings of the Holy Ghost are foolishness to men. They cry out and say, "They are drunken"; but it is not with wine or strong drink.[9] They say, "They are hypnotized and mesmerized." Many are mockers, they see the strange and supernatural with the natural eye and hear with their ears the wonderful works of God. They confess

[6] Isaiah 66:16, paraphrased.

[7] See Daniel 12:3.

[8] See Isaiah 28.

[9] See Acts 2:13,15.

there was and is, great power. They cannot deny the great miracles. It makes them fear and tremble, but many turn away, drive off conviction, and become mockers.

They commit the unpardonable sin and their bands are made strong; they are lost forever. The Lord says He will consume them in His wrath. They will not mock then when the cyclone is raging, when the earth is rocking and reeling under the earthquake. But now they make much sport of God's work and say of the strange and supernatural, "It is true there is a work done, but it is the work of the devil."

In the vision, Daniel heard one saint ask another, "When shall all these wonders cease?" The answer was, "when he shall have accomplished to scatter the power of the holy people, then all these wonders shall cease."[10] The Gospel of His coming kingdom must first be preached, as a witness to all nations. God will have many witnesses out of every nation, tongue, and people on the earth.

Signs, Wonders, and Works

These signs, wonders, and demonstrations and the power of the Holy Ghost through the baptized saints must be scattered. God's strange acts must be done. This is our work today, calling the elect together that they may see, feel, and receive the baptism with the Holy Ghost and fire and burn with a holy zeal and be endued with power and be sealed with the knowledge of these things that they may be among the wise that shall know when Jesus is coming.[11] They shall shine as the sun in our Father's kingdom.

The Lord of Hosts is with us today for a crown of glory and a diadem of beauty unto the residue of His people and with great power to those that press the battle to the gates.[12]

He is giving His wisdom to the weak. To those who naturally have not the wisdom of this world, He is teaching knowledge and making us to understand. He is revealing and manifesting Himself to those that are weaned from the milk, little children, and those

[10]See Daniel 12:5-7.

[11]See Daniel 12:10.

[12]Isaiah 28:5-6, paraphrased.

who are not learned.[13] Yea, He reveals the deep things of God,[14] speaking in new tongues as the Spirit gives utterance,[15] showing the wonderful work of God.

He is speaking in other languages fluently, plainly, and distinctly and with power that which no one can learn at school, except after a long time. "With stammering lips and other tongues will I speak unto this people, *yet for all that* you will not believe."[16] Oh readers, be not mockers lest your bands be made strong, lest ye be consumed.[17] Hear Him say so. Hear, brother!

Paul says, referring to this solemn warning hundreds of years after it was spoken by the prophet, that it is one of the last signs that God is giving to the lost world that God is moving in their midst and that Jesus is coming.[18] Yes, it is a special sign that Jesus is coming soon (1 Thessalonians 4:16). "Yet with all this you will not believe." Be careful how you hear, how you act.[19] It is the last call. God is working His strange work and His strange act. The Holy Ghost is seen in many ways. He is seen in bright lights, in balls of fire, in hundreds of stars, and in bands of angels over, and in, the tent in our meetings.

The Lord of Hosts says He will work as He did when the sun and moon stood still at the command of Joshua.[20] We will not be surprised at anything our God does. His people are people of power.

> All thy works shall praise thee, O Lord; and thy saints shall bless thee. They shall speak of the glory of thy kingdom, and talk of thy power.
>
> Psalm 145:10-11

Taken from *Spirit-Filled Sermons.*

[13]See Isaiah 28:9.

[14]See 1 Corinthians 2:10.

[15]See Acts 2:4.

[16]1 Corinthians 14:21, paraphrased.

[17]See Isaiah 28:22

[18]See 1 Corinthians 14:22.

[19]See Isaiah 28:21.

[20]See Joshua 10:13.

THE SEAL OF GOD ON HIS PEOPLE

Gather yourselves together, yea, gather together, O nation not desired; Before the decree bring forth, before the day pass as the chaff, before the fierce anger of the Lord come upon you, before the day of the Lord's anger come upon you. Seek ye the Lord, all ye meek of the earth, which have wrought his judgment; seek righteousness, seek meekness: it may be ye shall be hid in the day of the Lord's anger.

Zephaniah 2:1-3

This call is not to sinners, but to God's servants, to His children to eat the strong meat.[1] "Ye meek of the earth who have wrought His judgments."

You see, you are saved and are working some for the Lord, but He calls you to seek the Lord in a different way and for a different meekness. He cries to you three times to seek the Lord, to seek meekness, and to seek righteousness.

He is giving you the call to the marriage supper, calling you to get oil in your vessels; to get baptized with the Holy Ghost; to be sealed with the seal of the living God in the forehead. The Holy Ghost will also witness through you in other tongues, for you may have any of the gifts. You shall have power after Holy Ghost has come in as a witness.[2]

The prophet here is warning you to escape the awful judgments that are now coming on the earth. It may be that you may be hid in the day of the Lord's anger. This is the only hope for you. To escape the awful destruction that is about to sweep over the world, there is no other hiding place, no safety in the world. Oh, that you may be hid in the day of His wrath!

[1] See Hebrews 5:14.

[2] See Acts 1:8.

Yes, you may be, but it depends on how far and how deep you get hid away in God's love and power and will, as to whether you will be hid in that day. You may be hid. He shows that His judgments will burst on the earth like a whirlwind and that the wicked will be like chaff.

Dear reader, there is no doubt according to God's Word and the signs all around us and the revelations and warnings the Lord is now giving us through His Spirit, that this is the time the prophet refers to and we are the people. We have no time to lose for, "behold he cometh, and is even now at the door."[3]

The text implies haste, "Awake, arise, rouse yourselves. Flee to Christ. Get oil in your vessels." *Shout* the cry, "Behold, the bridegroom cometh."[4] Trim your lamps.[5] Get sealed with wisdom, that we may be among the wise to sit with Christ on His Throne to judge the nations.[6] "Gather yourselves together, yea, gather together, o nation not desired." No one wants this people that have come out of darkness into this marvelous light,[7] this peculiar people, who appear foolish on account of the supernatural power and visible works of the Spirit. We are hated and despised and forsaken—our name cast out as evil, misrepresented, and counted as the offscourings of the earth, but we are very much beloved in heaven.

When the prophet Daniel was asking God to explain these things that we now see, Jesus appeared to him, and sent the angel to him, to make plain the vision. The angel said, "O Daniel, a man greatly beloved." Understand the vision and the words. Then again, "O man greatly beloved, fear not: peace be unto thee."[8]

The Sound of the Bugle Call

We are the people that the Lord was showing him. Now the same loving words of cheer come to us through His Spirit, to "the little

[3] See Revelation 3:20.

[4] Matthew 25:6.

[5] See Matthew 25:7.

[6] Revelation 3:21.

[7] See 1 Peter 2:9.

[8] Daniel 10:11 and 19.

flock"[9]—the bride that is making herself ready. "To him that overcometh will I grant to sit with me in my throne. Fear not, for I am with you, you are much beloved."[10]

The Lord is sounding the bugle call in a most wonderful way through some—by the Holy Ghost. It makes the people tremble. He is calling His saints together, to see eye to eye when He shall bring us to heavenly Zion. Blow ye the trumpet in Zion. Sound an alarm in the Holy mount, among the saints. Let all the people tremble.[11] Go gather My saints together, who have made a covenant with Me by sacrifice.[12] God help us to make the right kind of sacrifice. Oh, praise the Lord, that is my calling today, to get the saints together in one spirit, one faith, and one mind, filled with love and oneness in Christ—lost and swallowed up in Him and in His love and power.

In the preceding chapter, He shows us the awful trials and the time of the great tribulations. From the fourteenth verse to the last of the chapter,

> The great day of the Lord is near, it is near, and hasteth greatly. . . . a day of trouble and distress, a day of wasteness and desolation, a day of darkness and gloominess, and a day of clouds and thick darkness. . . . And I will bring distress upon men, that they shall walk like blind men, because they have sinned against the Lord: and their blood shall be poured out as dust, and their flesh as the dung. Neither their silver nor their gold shall be able to deliver them in the day of the Lord's wrath; but the whole land shall be devoured.
>
> Zephaniah 1:14-18

After giving us this fearful warning, "Gather yourselves together, O gather together, that you may be hid in the day of His wrath."[13]

[9] See Luke 12:32.

[10] Revelation 3:21, Isaiah 43:5 and Daniel 10:19, paraphrased.

[11] See Joel 2:1.

[12] Psalm 50:5, paraphrased.

[13] See Zephaniah 2:1-3.

We are a nation among the nations: "Ye are a chosen generation, a royal priesthood, an holy nation, a peculiar people; that ye should shew forth the praises of him who hath called you out of darkness into his marvellous light" (1 Peter 2:9).

We are called out in this generation. We are a holy nation, a nation of kings and priests, called out from among men. We are royal because we are children of a King; a holy priesthood, heirs to a throne.

> Unto him that loved us, and washed us from our sins in his own blood, And hath made us kings and priests unto God and his Father; to him be glory and dominion for ever and ever. Amen.
>
> Revelation 1:5-6

> Thou wast slain, and hast redeemed us to God by thy blood out of every kindred, and tongue, and people, and nation; And hast made us unto our God kings and priests: and we shall reign on the earth.
>
> Revelation 5:9-10

This shouting was going on in heaven after Jesus had taken His bride up to heaven.

They had been counted worthy to be hidden away in the city of gold, the prepared place that Jesus had promised. The great marriage had taken place. The long-waiting bride was made the Lamb's wife. They were all enjoying the great marriage supper of the Lamb. They were receiving their crowns and positions in glory, taking their thrones and exalted stations that their diplomas called for, that they had gained down here in the Holy-Ghost school. Hear the shouting; they make the heavens ring, amidst all the brightness and glory of heaven. Oh, the meeting of the loved ones to never part! They are safe, safe home at last.

Jesus is the attraction. He is the One, all eyes are on Him, all are trying to get nearest Him and give Him all honor and glory, for through His blood and power they have entered into His glory. He hath made us kings and priests to God and we shall reign on the earth a thousand years.[14]

[14] See Revelation 5:10 and 20:6.

Yes, they were safe in heaven while the dreadful work of destruction was going on in the earth. They knew they were coming back to earth to rule with kingly authority, to bless the people with priestly power. The saints shall judge the world. They were rejoicing because they were coming back to earth.

Taken from *Spirit-Filled Sermons.*

THE BLOOD AND FIRE MARK

The Despised Ones Delivered—Momentous Events Are Impending

zekiel 9: God gave the prophet the vision in this chapter nearly twenty-seven hundred years ago. We are living amidst the same conditions and the same things are taking place today as took place at the time of the destruction of Jerusalem.

> He cried also in mine ears with a loud voice, saying, Cause them that have charge over the city to draw near, even every man with his destroying weapon in his hand. And, behold, six men came from the way of the higher gate [men of authority], which lieth toward the north, and every man a slaughter weapon in his hand; and one man among them was clothed with linen, with a writer's inkhorn by his side.
>
> Ezekiel 9:1-2

He with the writer's inkhorn represents the baptized saints before the destruction of Jerusalem, with the Holy Ghost in them, going around baptizing the people with blood and fire.

> He called to the man clothed with linen, which had the writer's inkhorn (which represents the Church today, the Holy Ghost working through us). "Go through the midst of the city, through the midst of Jerusalem, and set a mark upon the foreheads of the men that sigh and cry for the abominations."
>
> And to the others (the destroying army) he said in my hearing, "Go after him through the city, and smite—let not your eye spare, neither have pity; slay utterly old and young, both maids, and little children, and women, but come not near any man upon whom is the mark; and begin at my sanctuary." Then they began at the ancient men which were before the house. And he said

> unto them, "Defile the house, and fill the courts with the slain: go ye forth." And they went forth, and slew in the city.
>
> And it came to pass, while they were slaying them, that I fell upon my face, and cried, and said, "O, Lord God, wilt thou destroy all the residue of Israel in thy pouring out of thy fury upon Jerusalem?"
>
> Then said he unto me, "The iniquity of the house of Israel and Judah is exceeding great, and the land is full of blood, and the city is full of perverseness: for they say, The Lord hath forsaken the earth."[1]

That is what they say today—the Lord doesn't see anymore.

> As for me also (He made me know that He lives), mine eye shall not spare, neither will I have pity, but I will recompense their way upon their head. And, behold, the man clothed with linen, which had the writer's inkhorn by his side, came back and reported the matter, saying, "I have done as thou hast commanded."[2]

The Lord said unto him, "Go through the midst of the city, through the midst of Jerusalem, and set a mark upon the foreheads of the men that sigh and cry for all the abominations that be done in the midst thereof." And when it was done he came back and reported, "It is done, I have finished, the last one is sealed, the door of mercy is closed."

A Wonderful Vision

The prophet had this vision nearly six hundred years before Jesus came, before the destruction of Jerusalem; and now it makes about twenty-seven hundred years since he saw that vision—that vision of Jerusalem; of the Church; of the conditions of the world, especially the Church. But we are living in a parallel time today in the world and the Church; and the same wonderful things are taking place today just before the Great Tribulation, just before the wrath of God is poured out without mercy on the people. The same things are

[1] Ezekiel 9:3-9, paraphrased. Parenthetical comments are Mrs. Etter's.

[2] Ezekiel 9:10-11, paraphrased.

going on today. The Lord showed the prophet the awful condition of the Church, and these things came upon the Jewish nation, but this time they are coming upon the whole world.

God gave the law from Mount Sinai amidst mighty signs and wonders.[3] And when the temple was dedicated, the presence of God was seen.[4] God appeared, gave them priests and prophets and revelations from heaven. Spiritual signs, visions, and angels appeared. God talked from heaven and did these things while His people obeyed, but by and by, they got proud and haughty and lifted up. And they began to glory in multiplying numbers, taking in people from other nations who were unsaved and whose hearts were not right with God; and [He] gave them high places in the Church; giving them authority and power, giving them charge of God's holy vessels; and they ruled the holy people with a rod of iron.

God warned them and warned them and finally began to show them that they had left the fountainhead of living waters.

Broken Cisterns Won't Hold Water

But they hewed them out broken cisterns that could not hold water.[5] They began to follow the wisdom of men. The glory of God appeared to the prophet, picked him up by the hair of the head, and carried him through space between heaven and earth and set him down at Jerusalem and told him to look and see the awful things—the holy places filled with pictures of serpents like devil worship today, and things that were unclean.[6] God showed him the abominations; took him into the holiest place, where he found twenty-seven men sitting with their back to God and worshipping the sun[7] and then told him, "Now you go and take the pattern of the Church in all its glory, when the glory of God filled the house. You warn these people and take the pattern of the glorious Church and go and compare it with the pattern today, and show them where they failed and see if they will repent."[8]

[3] See Exodus 19:18 and 24:16.

[4] See 1 Kings 8:10-11.

[5] See Jeremiah 2:13.

[6] See Ezekiel 8:3,10.

[7] See Ezekiel 8:16.

[8] See Ezekiel 43:10-11.

He said, "They will never do it."

But God does not say for us to run things to suit ourselves. They were warned. Son of man, I am sending you not among the heathen but among the people of Israel.[9] But they would not hear. They failed to know that the prophet of God was in their midst. So he stood and warned them, but it did not do any good, and pretty soon the last prophet came and they rejected him. And the love and mercy and glory of God left them.

A God-Forsaken People

For nearly four hundred years, perhaps more, the children of Israel were left without holy priests, without prophets, without visions or revelations—except a few little ones, brokenhearted little ones who were true to God. They began to say, "Oh, God, how long? There is none that can tell us anymore. We have no prophet, priests, visions."[10] When people were right with God they saw signs of the invisible God. But when they backslid, they lost the connection with heaven. The pipe got filled up; the flow of living water stopped. They trusted in broken cisterns, man's wealth and knowledge, which are an abomination without God. That is the condition the Jews were in when Christ came; and after they had been looking for Him for nearly four hundred years, they did not know Him. He said to them, "Why is it you do not discern the signs of the time? Your prophecy is fulfilled and you are living in the days when the Son of Man should come."[11]

They had been saying, "God has forgotten; God doesn't see; God has left the earth, and the signs and wonders are all gone,"[12] and they began to follow men's wisdom. But they did not want the power of God. They left the fountain of living water. They did not want to hear a shout in the camp; did not want to see God's power.

Before Jesus came His coming was prophesied, and when He came the Jewish nation had another chance—He offered them the kingdom. But they spurned Him and turned Him away, and finally

[9] Ezekiel 3:5-9, paraphrased.

[10] See Psalm 74:9.

[11] See Matthew 16:3.

[12] See Ezekiel 9:3.

one day He wept over them bitterly and spread out His hands—just as He is doing today. "Oh, Jerusalem! How often would I have gathered you from the destruction that is coming; now I leave you."[13]

Blood Shall Flow Like Rivers

"This time your house is left unto you desolate; your city shall be destroyed; the enemy is coming; armies are coming in to lay your place desolate, and blood shall flow like rivers."[14] But God warned His people.

He had a people that had accepted Christ and they had followed the Lamb. They tarried at Jerusalem until baptized with the Holy Ghost, and God revealed Himself to them and revealed the Word to them. He said one day, when speaking of the temple, "The day is coming when that beautiful temple will be destroyed; not one stone will be left on another and the city will be destroyed."

The disciples said, "Lord, tell us when the evil thing will happen, we want to know what will be the sign of Thy second coming and of the end of the world."[15]

So Jesus told them and gave us signs how we will know today. Jesus is soon coming. The signs show He will come back soon. We are concerned about the signs. They asked questions, they did not talk for foolishness, and the Lord told them how they should know. He gave them signs and said when you see certain signs, prepare to flee to the mountains. Make ready to escape and finally there will be a certain sign. When you see this last sign, if you have not made all preparations for flight, if you are on the housetop, go not into the house; if you are in the field, do not turn back to take your cloak, but flee to the mountains. Get out of the city because the gates will be closed and you will be shut in.[16]

They believed what God said; they took His Word by faith. They believed the Word, they felt responsibility, they loved their people; but they knew unless they accepted Jesus Christ, they would not

[13]See Matthew 23:37-38 and Luke 13:34-35.

[14]See Ezekiel 6:4-7.

[15]Matthew 24:2-3, Mark 13:2-4, and Luke 21:5-7, paraphrased.

[16]See Matthew 24, Mark 13, and Luke 21.

escape. They were sighing and crying because of their own people according to the flesh and their neighbors, sighing and crying on account of the awful things going on, but they were shut in with God. They had the mark of God upon them.

When you see the things that are making the world turn pale and tremble, lift up your heads and rejoice, when this comes. Rejoice because every calamity shows it will soon be over. So, although they sighed and cried, still they rejoiced because they knew they were saved.

The Mark in the Forehead

The man with the inkhorn represents the Holy Ghost. In a short time, all these things are coming. Get busy; warn the people; whether they will hear or forbear, warn the people. We see the saints of God filled with the Holy Ghost. We see them go through the offices and stores and business places; and here are the people going back and forth about their business, that if they remain unsealed, will help form the great armies of the Antichrist. The man with the inkhorn was to do the work of sealing or marking those who will escape destruction, getting ready for the great work of destruction; but no one knew what was going on. And the saints of God are going everywhere, warning the people the best they can. "Judgment is coming; destruction is coming; the city will be taken." They are laughed at as fools and fanatics and everything else. They will not listen.

Before Jerusalem was destroyed the saints knew destruction was coming and the city would be taken; their business would be no good; the enemy would take everything. The only thing they could do was warn the people that destruction was coming. Their money and their homes and silver and land would not do them any good. Neither will it do you any good. God help you to see, [so] that you may use your time and means to spread the Gospel.

Blow the trumpet in Zion. Jerusalem will be taken; tribulation is coming; the Day of the Lord is near, it hasteth greatly, it is even at the door. Warn the people that they must have the seal of God on their foreheads. So we are going around getting the people saved, giving them the Word in the Holy Ghost that they may be baptized with the Holy Ghost and sealed with the finger and mark of the living God in the forehead.[17] They had to have the mark of God in the forehead to understand these things. Go through the city, note those who cry and sigh and put the blood mark upon them and the fire mark on them. Seal them with the finger of God—that is what God is doing today. Glory to God!

The Despised Ones Delivered

That is what they did. The Word went out. They were laughed at and scorned and persecuted and everything else, but they saw the signs coming faster; and the more they warned them, the more they laughed at them and the more they persecuted them. They made huts away in the mountains and every day felt worse about their friends and neighbors. They would go to the city in haste and try to show the people these things were true. They did not believe. But that did not change the fact. At the time of the great feast, the rabbis and many people from all over the world were there in the city. The people of the Jewish nation were gathered there in the city. It was full for the great feast. The Lord had told them, "When you see a certain signal get out quick (*sic*)." Don't go back to get anything out of your houses, but make haste to get out of the city. Don't go back to take anything, but get out of the city quick. The rest (those who would not take the warning) stayed in the city. They would not believe anything; they were having a good time.

All at once the certain signal came, the gates were closed, they were shut in, and they never got out. Those who had the seal of the living God upon them were caught up, taken out just like we will be when the time comes. Josephus,[18] the historian, tells us that not one of the followers of Jesus Christ went down in the slaughter. They believed God and prepared for flight and escaped. There was not one of them permitted to be locked up in that city because they believed God and made preparations for flight. Hallelujah!

---

[17]See Ephesians 1:13.

[18]Josephus (37-*circa* 100), a Jewish historian who witnessed and recorded the fall of Jerusalem.

We are a nation that is hated, a nation not desired, a nation despised.[19] As Paul said, "This sect is spoken against everywhere but I am glad I am one of them."[20] When Jesus comes you will be willing to be called a fanatic, a Holy Roller, or anything. God help you to see it. In Jerusalem they were all having a good time and were taken unaware. The enemy came and the gates were shut, and the greatest calamity that the world ever heard of fell upon the Jews.

The army went into the city and unto the inner court where the holy men sat, twenty-seven of them, with their backs to God worshipping the sun. They commenced at these fat priests and heads of the Church; and they were slaughtered first, like oxen. We are told they had no provisions, did not expect any danger, and were shut in there and literally starved to death. Delicate women ate their own children. Delicate women, who would not put a foot to the ground, ate their own children during the siege.[21] Never had such a thing happened before. You know all about those things. Some were carried away in captivity; only a few despised little ones left as slaves. But God's people, those who had the mark—those who had sighed and cried—everyone was taken out. Oh, Hallelujah!

The prophet Ezekiel saw these things twenty-seven hundred years ago. But they refer to us today. When Jesus comes there will be such a tribulation on the earth as was never known before. That was only a little storm. The great preparation is now going on over our country and all the world.

The darkness will be so great it can be felt. There will be such a time, as the world never heard of, when Jesus comes to catch His bride away. He will take all that sigh and that cry for the abominable things that are going on in the world. Those who have the mark are the children of light. They will not be overtaken as a thief in the night. The wise shall know.[22] Glory to God. Oh, I praise God!

Now then, you see, they escaped. They believed and obeyed. History tells us that many rich men, many great men, went down in the slaughter. But those that they had called fools, that were wanderers

---

[19]See Matthew 24:9.

[20]See Acts 28:22-23.

[21]See Deuteronomy 28:56-57.

[22]See Daniel 12:10.

and pilgrims, who had to leave their homes and leave their wealth, they escaped with their life and a few little things they could take away to provide for their comfort.

When Jesus comes you won't take anything. All will be left for the devil to war over because the world is going on much as it does now. When Jesus comes it is not the end of the world, but the saints will be taken out when He comes.

It Behooves Us to Watch

Every day we should be watching and ready: "And ye yourselves like unto men that wait for their lord, when he will return from the wedding; that when he cometh and knocketh, they may open unto him immediately" (Luke 12:36).

You had better get ready quickly. If you do not hurry, escape will be cut off suddenly.

Dear friends, we are living in a time parallel to that. Jesus is coming again. God is visiting the earth again, pouring out His Spirit. The Church has gone back. When I was a girl the Methodist church was the most powerful and the most spiritual. The people fell under the power of God, shouted, danced, got healed from diseases, and did lots of other things. They had an amen corner in every church; and when the preacher would come in, he would not stop for anything, but go to the pulpit, open the Bible, and begin. There were no secondlys nor thirdlys nor anything of that kind; they did not have time, and the amens came from all over the house. They obeyed God, and they were happy people; they had great power. But now they are just like the Jews we have been considering.

Today they are saying, "We don't know God. He left us. We don't see Him." So today there is not an amen nor a shout from anybody. They do not like any fuss or see any need for it. And if one sister gets blessed and the power of God comes on her and she shouts, three or four good sisters get around and she never shouts again.

War, Famine, and Pestilence

Dear friends, if they (your own fathers and mothers and grandfathers) were right then, you would not like to have anyone say they were crazy. If they were right before God, someone is wrong today.

But today, whenever they see any people get together, shout, and praise God, they set them down as cranks. The stiff-necked Jews wished they had been amongst the despised ones when they found they were the ones who had been spared. They found out when it was too late. After we that they call cranks are taken away, they will say those people were not so cranky after all.

God is pouring out His Spirit again on all nations of the earth all over the world, and today God has a baptized people; saints of every nation, church, and tribe, baptized in the Holy Ghost and fire. They are warning the people. Get under the blood and get the mark of the living God in the forehead. God is visiting you again, and we are just on the eve of the awful Tribulation. Men and women will eat their own children. There will be war, famine, and pestilence and all things at the same time. If you escape the war, the wild beasts will get you. If you escape the lion and bear and stagger around in your own house for a quiet place to die, a serpent will bite you.[23]

Great God, don't you see these things are coming? Watch the signs and read the Word—read the Word of God and watch the signs. These moving pictures[24] were seen by the prophet twenty-seven hundred years ago. A day with the Lord is only a little while and a thousand years only a day.[25] He saw us, the people on the stage of action today. (Multitudes of the people who are living today will be in this great army of slaughter.) But the saints will be taken out, those who will become saints here on the earth today. Some of those living here tonight will never see death until they see the Son of God coming in glory.

So we see every day the signs being fulfilled everywhere that Jesus is coming. And that is why the saints today are making such an effort to go through the world, running the risk of everything to enlighten the people; to find hearts that will receive the message and get saved and let God mark and seal them with the seal of the living God in their foreheads. Make the vision plain.[26] God help me.

[23]See Amos 5:19.

[24]"moving pictures"—Mrs. Etter is comparing prophetic visions to silent films which were becoming a familiar media in the early twentieth century.

[25]See 2 Peter 3:8.

[26]See Habakkuk 2:2.

Will the people see that we are actors in this vision? Make it plain so that the one who hears may understand and run to get ready. That is what we are doing today.

Now, beloved, we must have this mark of God. We must be not only saved, but also sealed with the seal of the living God. It may be, if you get deep enough, that you will be hid away from all these awful things that are coming on the earth. Be shut in with God today.

The Loosing of Judgment

The angels represented as holding back the four winds of the earth are letting loose now as sure as God lives.[27] Another great angel cries, "Hold on a little longer." We wonder about these things. Angels see the awful condition of the earth; the cup of iniquity is full. "O Lord, can't we let loose, may we let loose? Can the sun be turned on to scorch men; may the cyclones tear down the cedars; may the tidal waves sweep the towns away; may the earthquakes come?"

But the great angel who carries the Gospel of Jesus Christ says, "Hold on a little while, hold on a little longer; don't let loose. Hold back the power of the sun; hold back the greatest tidal waves, the greatest cyclones, the greatest earthquakes, and the greatest calamities until we have sealed the servants of God with the seal of God in their foreheads.

You who are servants of God must be sealed with the seal of God—have the blood and fire mark—sealed with the seal of the living God. "Hold back the great calamities—it would be a great inconvenience to My servants. They are the lights of the world. For the sake of the souls that want to be saved, I will give My people a little more chance to work." Hold back! What for? Hold back until we have sealed the saints of God with the seal of the living God in the forehead. My people help these people to see why the sun did not get two or three degrees hotter and kill millions. Don't you see the signs of what is coming? One hundred fell in Chicago in the heat.[28] A few more degrees and millions would have gone down.

---

[27] See Revelation 7:1.

[28] Summer heat waves in Chicago often cause heat-related deaths. Etter speaks of one here that occurred in 1916.

Shall We Escape the Great Tribulation?

Watch and pray. Be in an attitude of prayer or praise all the time that you may be counted worthy to escape these awful calamities and stand before the Son of God. Don't you see we have no time for telling what this or that one said? I am here to tell you what Jesus Christ said.

Two will be working in the fields: one will be taken and the other left.[29] One will be watching and praying, the other idly talking and jesting; and you will answer him because you have to listen. But suddenly the one doing the foolish talking will look around in surprise because he does not get any answer and ask, "Where are you Tom? What is the matter?" He will get no answer because he is alone. His companion is gone. Where did he go? Find him if you can. He escaped—Jesus caught him away. Two will be sleeping in the same bed. One will be caught away, and the other snore away. One escaped before the gate was shut. Glory to God—caught away.

It is going to be just that way when Jesus comes. He will take them up alive—they will be changed quicker than a wink—they will not have another body, but this body will be so light.[30] We are not waiting for wings, but we are looking for the dynamo from heaven to lighten these bodies. We will rise like He did—hands and feet like wings—we will go sailing through the air over the stars up to meet Him with a shout—"Glory to God!"

A Fountain of Tears

For those who are left here, it will be so different. Those who reject Christ will be left to perish. Oh, God, how we ought to be sighing and crying for the people that will be left—we don't sigh and cry enough. But at the same time, we are so full of joy it seems like we have to give vent or explode. Be glad because you are living in the time of the latter rain. Rejoice! Be glad. Yet at the same time, we are sighing and crying because of the corrupt state of the world and the calamities that are coming. Several times I cry out—the Holy Ghost within me cries out—and I recall what the prophet said when he

[29]See Matthew 24:40.

[30]See 1 Corinthians 15:52.

was speaking of this day. Oh, my bowels—my bowels![31] His body seemed to be bursting and his head was a fountain of tears for the destruction that is coming on the earth. Jesus is weeping as He did over Jerusalem; and how the Holy Ghost weeps through me! It seems as though I would cry until I would die, but I go on. God is putting a mark on those that sigh and cry for all the abominable things that are done in the earth and because of the needless tribulations men insist on bringing on themselves.

Dear friends, don't you see the angels want to let loose the four winds? "Oh, can we let loose—they are so wicked and the people perish."

"No, not yet, not until we have sealed the servants of God with the seal of the living God in the foreheads."[32]

Go through the streets and put a mark upon everyone that sighs and cries—put the mark of God on them. Tell them to be baptized with the Holy Ghost. Jesus Christ will baptize you with the Holy Ghost and fire. He will give us wisdom—the mind of Christ—seal us with knowledge; and we will not be left in the darkness of ignorance, but we shall be children of light.

You who are saved and living pure and holy lives, if you don't get down and seek more of God and be sealed, you are going to be left. Get where you feel the everlasting arms of Jesus around you [or] you will be carried away in the press by and with the crowd; and you will not be ready to go up when Jesus comes. Oh, loosing angels, hold back until the servants of God get the light and until they are sealed with the seal of the living God in their foreheads. But there is not much time. Are we about our Master's business? No wonder I don't rest. I am trusting God to carry me through. I know these things are true. God help us, we are getting pretty near shut in now. There are so many false doctrines of the devil coming and so many people getting deluded. You must be kept under the blood or you will be carried away.

---

[31] See Jeremiah 4:19.

[32] Revelation 7:3, paraphrased.

Momentous Events Are Impending

I praise God for the knowledge that Jesus is coming soon. Praise His name forever. Some of these awful things are already on the earth to some extent. You know the Lord said when certain things happen, it is the beginning of sorrows.[33] The nations are mad. They are crazy, filled with jealous hatred, killing one another. One nation is against another; several have gone down—look at them. No one knows the real truth. May God help you to see it. This is the beginning of sorrows. The four angels are going to let loose as sure as you live.

Let me ask you travelers to the Bar of God.[34] If all this is the beginning of sorrows, what will the end be? You may escape the worst things and be hid away. The prophet looking down at the last days saw the saints going up. He says, "Come up, My people, and enter into the place prepared for you and shut the doors after you and hide you for a little while, for the Lord cometh down to punish the inhabitants of the earth and their blood shall flow like the dust and their flesh lay like dung and they will not be buried."[35] In the European war[36] tens of thousands have been buried in piles and others lay rotting—you know these things—nobody knows where they are.

Isn't Scripture being fulfilled now? If this is only the beginning of sorrows, what is the end to be? God is holding back the worst thing. Europe has had the call. They have been warned and warned. God gave a wonderful vision to a man that was raised for a Catholic priest. Two angels visited him in the night and revealed to him things that are about to come to pass and told him he must go and warn a great congregation, about two thousand of them, and tell them how Europe had been warned; but they turned their

[33] See Matthew 24:4-8.

[34] "Bar of God"—The law court of God.

[35] Isaiah 26:20-21 and Zephaniah 1:17, paraphrased.

[36] "European war"—World War I; Etter is preaching this sermon at a time when Europe is at war, but America has not yet declared war on Germany. This is the summer of the Battle of Verdun and the Battle of Sommes in which over two million lives were lost.

backs and rejected him, and now he is warning them at the mouth of the cannon.

This country is the same way. God is giving them the last call—the last chance to be sealed with the seal of the living God, but they turn Him away. The last one will soon be sealed. God will call at the mouth of the cannon. This country will be bathed in blood after awhile. The best thing we can do is to hide away. God help us to be up and doing, to be clothed in white linen, which is the power of the Holy Ghost working through us, and instructing them to ask God for knowledge and wisdom and get the resurrection power in their body; and when Jesus comes they may be snatched out of this world.

Not Dead, but Gone Before

We who are alive will not prevent those that are asleep, but the dead in Christ will rise first and shake all the dust and worms like dew and will go up with a shout. Praise the Lord! They will meet us.[37] Don't be afraid about the dead who died in Christ, for when Jesus comes God will bring the dead with Him—so God is coming in honor of His Son's wedding to meet the bride. We do not need to worry about the dead ones. They will be made alive. Oh, the time is near! It won't be very long until we who are alive will meet them in the air. Some will be laid away the very day He comes. I will meet my husband that died a few years ago.[38] He said, "I am not looking to the grave at all." But his body is there, and different saints in visions have seen him come up in his glorified body; and he will be one of the first to meet me when I rise in the air. Many dear saints have died shouting and gone to glory. They will be raised and I will meet them. Oh, dear friends, all that have died in Christ will be raised first. We will rise in our glorified, immortal bodies to meet the Lord in the air.

Now, beloved, don't let this message run off. Let it go down and burn in your heart because it is a message from the Lord. Hallelujah! It is something you have never heard before, but you hear it

[37]See 1 Thessalonians 4:16-17.

[38]Samuel Etter died in 1914.

now. You see the parallel, between the time we are living in and the time of the prophet Ezekiel. You see the danger. You are being warned. Take your Bible, ask God about these people up here that you think are so lightheaded. I am glad I am lightheaded enough to believe God. I am glad I am light enough to go up in the air when He comes. Hallelujah! Glory! I have of the resurrection power! Praise the Lord! I am looking forward to going up in the sky—up in the air—not to the grave. Glory to God! Hallelujah!

Taken from *Spirit-Filled Sermons.* This is a revised and expanded version of a sermon originally given in Petoskey, Michigan, in July, 1916, and first published in *Signs and Wonders God Wrought in the Ministry of Maria B. Woodworth-Etter.*

CHRIST AND HIS BRIDE

The Rapture of the Saints— A Royal Nation in Royal Robes

nd to the angel of the church in Philadelphia write; These things saith he that is holy, he that is true, he that hath the key of David, he that openeth, and no man shutteth; and shutteth, and no man openeth; I know thy works: behold, I have set before thee an open door, and no man can shut it: for thou hast a little strength, and hast kept my word, and hast not denied my name. Behold, I will make them of the synagogue of Satan, which say they are Jews, and are not, but do lie; behold, I will make them to come and worship before thy feet, and to know that I have loved thee. Because thou hast kept the word of my patience, I also will keep thee from the hour of temptation, which shall come upon all the world, to try them that dwell upon the earth. Behold, I come quickly: hold that fast which thou hast, that no man take thy crown. Him that overcometh will I make a pillar in the temple of my God, and he shall go no more out: and I will write upon him the name of my God, and the name of the city of my God, which is new Jerusalem, which cometh down out of heaven from my God: and I will write upon him my new name.

Revelation 3:7-12

THE PHILADELPHIA CHURCH

Here, Jesus Himself is giving John a description of the Philadelphia church, whose name signifies love: "A glorious church, not having spot, or wrinkle, or any such thing; but that it should be holy and without blemish" (Ephesians 5:27).

She must be a glorious church, not having spot or wrinkle or any such thing[1]—holy and without blemish. Oh! Brother, it means much to be a member of this church.

[1] See Ephesians 5:27.

The book of Revelations (*sic*) is the most wonderful of the New Testament. Jesus had said to Peter in answer to his question, "And what shall this man do?", "If I will that he tarry till I come, what is that to thee? follow thou me."[2] The report went out that John would never die.

When John was quite old, the enemies of Christ tried to kill him. They threw him into a kettle of boiling oil, but the Lord did not let it hurt him.[3] Then they were frightened and banished him to the lonely isle called Patmos, and he was left there to die.[4] He had been such a true witness for Jesus and His Word that it was the darkest hour of his life; but he was alone with God, filled with the Spirit.

The book of Revelations (*sic*) is a wonderful book. About sixty-four years after John and the other disciples saw Jesus go up to heaven, He came back to earth to John and gave him great moving pictures of the future of the Church, starting from Pentecost. What a light in those dark days!

Jesus came back to John in all His kingly power and glory. He had been gone a long time. The change was so great that John felt so little in His presence that when he saw Him, he fell at His feet as one dead.[5]

John said, "He laid his right hand upon me, saying unto me, Fear not; I am the first and the last: I am he that liveth, and was dead; and, behold, I am alive for evermore."[6]

"John do you know Me? We fished together, walked together, and slept together. Many times you have rested your weary head on my bosom." Can we imagine the joy when John heard the old familiar voice of the Galilean, that had quieted their fears so often, when the sweet voice said, "It is I. Do not be afraid. I have come back to

---

[2] John 21:21-22.

[3] Tertullian (circa A. D. 160-220) writes that John went to Rome, where he was "plunged, unhurt into boiling oil" *(Nelson's Illustrated Bible Dictionary,* [Thomas Nelson Publishers, 1986] *PC Bible,* 2.1J [Seattle: Biblesoft, 1998]).

[4] See Revelation 1:9.

[5] See Revelation 1:17.

[6] Revelation 1:17-18.

bring you important messages, I want you to write all you hear, and send it to the churches."[7]

The first three chapters of Revelations (*sic*) give the career of Christ's body, or Church, from the time she was established at Pentecost down to the last overcomer, to the close when the Church is taken up to glory and seated on the throne with Jesus, executing judgment on the lost world and showing all that would take place down to the end of the one thousand years.

The first thing John heard was a great voice, like a trumpet. He looked to where the voice came from, and he saw seven golden candlesticks, representing the seven churches, or assemblies of Christians, down to the last. He saw Jesus in the midst of the candlesticks, in all His power and glory.[8]

His eyes were as a blaze of fire. His feet like a blazing furnace of brass. His voice like the sound of many waters; in His right hand were seven stars; out of His mouth went a two-edged sword. His countenance was like the sun shining in all its strength. Oh glory to God! What a Prince! What a King! What a living, wonder-working power is our Christ, in His Church, in us, also beneath us, and around us, like a wall of fire![9]

He shows us that our greatest trials and battles will be with the devil in the enemies of Christ, in His true Church. But hear Him say, "Behold I will make them come, and fall at our feet, and acknowledge that God loves us, and that we are His true witnesses."[10]

Christ is now on trial for His honor and glory, as never before. When so-called "great preachers" are denying the necessity for the atoning blood and almost everything else of much value, but the dead letter, hear Him say, "I hold the key, I will open for you."[11] No man or power can close the door against us if we will keep His Word and not deny His name or be ashamed of His works.

---

[7] Revelation 1:19-20, paraphrased.

[8] See Revelation 1:10,12-13.

[9] See Revelation 1:14-16.

[10] Revelation 3:9, paraphrased.

[11] See Revelation 3:7.

He warns us we will have trouble, will be persecuted and misrepresented by false prophets, who call themselves Jews or Christians and great leaders, but who are of the synagogue of Satan, who lie, and do not the truth.[12]

Come out of the Laodicean church and become a Philadelphian.

The Rapture of the Saints

The fourth chapter of Revelations (*sic*) shows the rapture of the saints and that their seat is on His throne. Jesus gives the description of the Church all through this dispensation. It applies and His message is to us who are now living on earth today.

The Laodicean church is the last and great church of today, including all organizations, incorporated religious institutions, and bodies in the world, having a nice form of godliness, but denying the power thereof; "from such turn away."[13] They have a religion but do not let it affect their mode of life.

There has been a falling away from the doctrine of Christ and the Holy Ghost and apostolic power and wisdom to a cold form and to a teaching of the doctrines and traditions of men.

> And unto the angel of the church of the Laodiceans write; These things saith the Amen, the faithful and true witness, the beginning of the creation of God; I know thy works, that thou art neither cold nor hot: I would thou wert cold or hot. So then because thou art lukewarm, and neither cold nor hot, I will spue thee out of my mouth. Because thou sayest, I am rich, and increased with goods, and have need of nothing; and knowest not that thou art wretched, and miserable, and poor, and blind, and naked: I counsel thee to buy of me gold tried in the fire, that thou mayest be rich; and white raiment, that thou mayest be clothed, and that the shame of thy nakedness do not appear; and anoint thine eyes with eyesalve, that thou mayest see. As many as I love, I rebuke and chasten: be zealous therefore, and repent. Behold, I stand at the door, and knock: if any man hear my voice, and open the door, I will come in to him, and

[12]See Revelation 3:9-10.

[13]2 Timothy 3:5.

> will sup with him, and he with me. To him that overcometh will I grant to sit with me in my throne, even as I also overcame, and am set down with my Father in his throne. He that hath an ear, let him hear what the Spirit saith unto the churches.
>
> Revelation 3:14-22

This is what concerns us. God is calling His people out of her. Thousands have heard the call, "Come out of her, my people, that ye be not partakers of her sins, and that ye receive not of her plagues." The last call is going forth. The Lord is shouting in a voice of thunder, through His bride, "Come out quickly." You may have time to be an overcomer in the temple of my God, and of such He says, "He shall go out no more."[14]

High Rank of the Family of God

The bride must qualify for her high position in God's glorious eternal kingdom; she must successfully pass through many tests and must graduate with the highest honors of the Holy Ghost. Those who sit on His throne will be the highest rank of all the whole family of God. They will be heirs of God, equal with Christ; they will have kingly power with Christ to rule the nations for one thousand years. They are called the wise and are those that Daniel saw: "And they that be wise shall shine as the brightness of the firmament; and they that turn many to righteousness as the stars for ever and ever" (Daniel 12:3).

The wise shall shine as the brightness of the firmament (there are degrees of glory, one of the sun, one of the moon), or as the stars forever. We thought years ago that the winning of souls was the greatest work. "They that turn many to righteousness shall shine as the stars for ever and ever," but "the wise shall shine as the brightness of the firmament." They shall shine as the sun in my Father's kingdom.

None of the wicked shall know anything about when Jesus comes, but the wise shall know. Hear Him shout, "To him that overcometh will I grant to sit with me in my throne, even as I also overcame,

[14] See Revelation 3:12, paraphrased.

and am set down with my Father in his throne."[15] Oh! Praise the Lord, the wise shall sit with Christ on His throne.

They shall know just when Jesus will come for His bride. They will be pillars in His temple, in his body, or Church. They will be initiated into the deep things of God and know His secrets. They will go in, to go out no more. Oh! Let us be sure that we are faithful and true; then He will select us as worthy to be saved from that hour of trial, or tribulation, that is coming on all the world as a snare.

He will come Himself to take His bride and to take us, if we are part of His bride, to the marriage supper of the Lamb in the skies.[16]

He says, "I am coming quickly,"[17] or soon. Hold fast to all you have received till He comes. See that no man takes your crown. "Him that overcometh will I make a pillar in My Church."[18]

Watch and pray that you may be counted worthy to escape all these things that are coming on earth and to stand before the Lord.

A Royal Nation in Royal Robes

We are strangers in a strange land,[19] we are princes in disguise, our royal robes shine, but the world cannot see them. They cannot see the table our Father hath prepared for us, spread out in shining brightness and snowy whiteness. It is covered with royal dainties, rich wine to make us glad, meat to make us strong, heavenly bread to keep us alive forevermore, and oil to make us shine, bright lights in this dark world.

Our enemies cannot taste of the feast. Oh! Praise the Lord; He is calling out a people for a special purpose in these last days. He calls them the wise ones, a chosen generation, a called-out nation, from among the nations; a royal, kingly nation, or nation of kings; an holy priesthood; a peculiar people; His very own whose lives confess that they are not of this world but that they seek a city to come whose

---

[15] Revelation 3:21.

[16] See Revelation 19:7.

[17] Revelation 3:11, paraphrased.

[18] Revelation 3:12, paraphrased.

[19] See Exodus 2:22 and Hebrews 11:13.

builder and maker is God; for our citizenship and kingdom is not of this world. We confess we are pilgrims and strangers.[20]

As living stones we are built up a spiritual house.[21] Oh! Glory to God. We are God's temple, in which He lives and moves, and He uses the clay to show His glorious presence and that the world can see that the treasure is in our earthen vessels and that it is all of God.[22]

We are a holy priesthood to offer up spiritual sacrifices to God through Jesus Christ. We are a living Church, a spiritual body of Jesus, who is the living head. Christ is the head, and we are the living members of His body.[23]

Christ is the firstborn. It has pleased God through Jesus, the captain of our salvation to bring many sons and daughters into the kingdom;[24] for He does not call us servants but sons; and because we are the sons of God, He hath sent forth the Spirit of His Son, into our hearts crying "Abba Father."[25]

The Church of God, and of our Lord Jesus Christ, was set up on the Day of Pentecost in a blaze of glory. It was built on the foundation laid by the apostles and prophets—Jesus Christ being the cornerstone.[26] The apostles were the pillars of the one hundred and twenty that were present and received the Pentecostal baptism and of the three thousand that were saved, who received the gift of the Holy Ghost and became lively stones[27] and were placed in the building that day.

Oh! Blessed are those that are called to the marriage of the Lamb. "Kings' daughters were among his honourable women: upon thy right hand did stand the queen in gold of Ophir. . . . The king's daughter is all glorious within: her clothing is of wrought gold"

[20]See 1 Peter 2:9,11 and Hebrews 11:10,13.

[21]See 1 Peter 2:5.

[22]See 2 Corinthians 4:7.

[23]See Colossians 2:19.

[24]See Hebrews 2:10.

[25]See Galatians 4:6-7.

[26]Ephesians 2:20, paraphrased.

[27]See 1 Peter 2:5.

(Psalm 45:9,13). "And His wife hath made herself ready" (Revelation 19:7).

The Rejoicing of the Angelic Hosts

Oh! Hear the shouts around the throne, from one end to the other, as the voice of a great multitude, as the voice of many waters, as the voice of mighty thunderings, shouting, "Alleluia: for the Lord God omnipotent reigneth!"[28] Oh! Beloved, what is all this about? Do we comprehend that the Lord Jesus and His bride are causing all this rejoicing?

All heaven is waiting to hear the shout, "Go forth to meet her." There is something wonderful soon going to take place.

The mighty God that inhabiteth eternity, with all the heavenly hosts, has been waiting thousands of years for this great event, for the mystical body to come together. Christ, our living head, the bride, the living body, for the marriage of the Son of God, the great Jehovah. Very, very soon they will say, "For the marriage of the Lamb has come."[29]

Oh dearly beloved, let us abstain from worldly lusts, which war against the soul.[30] Let us refrain from indulging the cravings of our earthly nature. Let our words be few and well chosen.[31] Let us live and act as we believe they do in heaven. By faith, we can almost hear the bugle call of the angels, getting the armies of heaven ready for marching. We can almost hear the angel choir tuning their harps of gold; all heaven is getting agitated and expectant.

"To him that overcometh will I grant to sit with me in my throne, even as I also overcame, and am set down with my Father in his throne."[32]

Jesus has not yet taken His throne and will not do so until He takes up His bride.

---

[28] Revelation 19:6.

[29] Revelation 19:7, paraphrased.

[30] 1 Peter 2:11, paraphrased.

[31] See Colossians 4:6.

[32] Revelation 3:21.

This promise is only to the wise of the bridal party; those who will sit with Christ on His throne will have the highest rank of all the hosts of heaven. This is only promised to the overcomers in the last days, to those who will be taken up from among men. This is the close of the bride's career on earth.

The first verse of the fourth chapter of Revelations (*sic*) prefigures the Church translated to heaven. John was carried to heaven. He represents the Rapture: "Immediately I was in the spirit: (or changed, as we will be in the twinkling of an eye) and, behold, a throne was set in heaven, and one sat on the throne. And he that sat was to look upon like a jasper and a sardine stone."[34]

The brightest jewels are mentioned to help us to comprehend a little of the brightness and splendor and of the glory of Christ and His bride.

John saw Jesus taking His throne and seating the bride with Him in the midst of the throne: "Out of the throne proceeded lightnings and thunderings and voices: and there were seven lamps of fire burning before the throne, which are the seven Spirits of God. And before the throne there was a sea of glass like unto crystal: and in the midst of the throne, and round about the throne, were living ones full of eyes before and behind."[34]

The Glory of the Bride

The description of these living ones is symbolic of power, the wings and the eyes signifying they were full of light, power, and knowledge. They were so swallowed up in sunlight of glory, as it were, that their crowns cannot be seen.

An unfortunate translation calls them the "four beasts," but more accurate translations state they are "living ones." These are not beasts, but the overcomers, shining as the brightness of the sun; seated with Christ on His throne just like He promised.

We see the twenty-four crowned heads seated around the throne, as if in council, but not on the throne. We hear these overcomers shouting the loudest praises to the Lamb and to the Lord God

[33] Revelation 4:2-3; parenthetical comment by Mrs. Etter.

[34] Revelation 4:5-6, paraphrased.

Almighty, who was and is and who has come to take His great power, and to reign.[35]

Now the overcomers give glory to Him that sitteth on the throne, who liveth forever and ever. (See Revelation 19:4.) The overcomers do not otherwise take part, but the four and twenty elders fall before the throne and worship Him that sits on the throne, casting their crowns at His feet, saying, "Thou art worthy, O Lord, to receive glory and honour and power."[36] You see the beasts, or overcomers, on the throne did not fall down, but the others fell down in honor and confirmation of what the living creatures had said.

We read,

> And when he had taken the book, the four beasts and four and twenty elders fell down before the Lamb, having every one of them harps, and golden vials full of odours, which are the prayers of saints. And they sung a new song, saying, Thou art worthy to take the book, and to open the seals thereof: for thou wast slain, and hast redeemed us to God by thy blood out of every kindred, and tongue, and people, and nation; And hast made us unto our God kings and priests: and we shall reign on the earth.
>
> Revelation 5:8-10

You see the living creatures, or rather, overcomers, and elders fall down before the Lamb, having every one of them harps of gold and golden vials full of odors, which are the prayers of the saints. Oh! Hear the shouts of the overcomers with the elders, "Thou art worthy, for thou wast slain and has redeemed us to our God by thy blood out of every kindred and tongue and people and nation and has made us unto our God kings and priests, and we shall reign on the earth."

In the thirteenth verse we hear all the hosts of heaven raise a shout, giving glory to Him that sitteth on the throne; and the four living creatures say, "Amen."[37] And the four and twenty elders fell down and worshipped Him that liveth forever and ever.

[35]See Revelation 4:4, 10-11 and 11:16-17.

[36]Revelation 4:11.

[37]See Revelation 5:14.

When the overcomers said, "Amen," the elders fell down and worshipped, but the living creatures did not fall down, showing that though they were redeemed by His blood from all nations, yet they were clothed with the highest honor and power next to Christ, in power and glory.

In the sixth chapter of Revelations, (*sic*) you see the living creatures, the overcomers, on the throne with Christ executing judgments on the earth, during the Great Tribulation. As one after another shouts, "Come and see," one judgment after another comes on the earth. "Do ye not know that the saints shall judge the world?" (1 Corinthians 6:2). And that saints shall judge fallen angels.[38]

They shall come back with Christ to fight the last great battle, when the Antichrist and all his army shall be destroyed; after which they shall reign, kings and priests for one thousand years, when all the residue of men shall seek after the Lord and all the Gentiles shall call on His name. Oh, hasten the day when the knowledge of God shall cover the earth as the waters cover the great and mighty deep.

Taken from *Spirit-Filled Sermons.*

[38]See 1 Corinthians 6:3.

The Marriage Supper of the Lamb

A Vision of the New Jerusalem— The Time is at Hand

lessed are they which are called unto the marriage supper of the Lamb.

Revelation 19:9

Oh beloved, have you been called? Let us be glad and rejoice and give honor to Him, for the call to the marriage of the Lamb has come. The bride must be arrayed in linen, pure and white.[1]

Yes, in the time our text refers to, His wife has made herself ready. See the King coming out of His ivory palace that He has all ready to receive His bride. His garments are flooded with sweet odors. They smell of myrrh and aloes and cassia.[2]

She is rejoicing in His love. Hearken! Oh, daughters! Beloved, are we among the blessed that are called to the banquet—to this heavenly marriage supper in the skies? Oh, consider, and incline your ears to hear the whispers of His love.[3]

Christ Must Have Preeminence

We must forget our own people and our father's house.[4] Our beloved Bridegroom is very jealous.[5] We must love Him with our whole heart and our whole being. We must long for Him so that He will greatly desire our beauty, for He is our Lord, and we must worship Him.

---

[1] See Revelation 19:8.

[2] See Psalm 45:8.

[3] See Revelation 19:9.

[4] See Genesis 2:24; Maria Etter alludes to Ephesians 5:31-32, but does not use its exact meaning, which has Christ leaving the Father to cleave to the Church.

[5] See James 4:4-5 and Exodus 34:14.

We must be ready to leave all at any moment that the herald shall shout, "Behold, the Bridegroom. Behold, He cometh, go ye forth to meet Him."[6] Oh, are you ready to leave all to sail away with our beloved to that heavenly kingdom, to those mansions in the city of gold that He has been preparing and adorning for so many years with all the wealth and jewels of heaven? Oh, that city of gold!

Do our hearts leap for joy? Do we cry, "Come, oh come quickly, my Redeemer, my beloved and my King? Oh! Most mighty, with Thy glory and Thy majesty, Thou art fairer than all the sons of men!"[7] "Thy throne, O God, is for ever and ever: the sceptre of thy kingdom is a right sceptre" (Psalm 45:6).

Oh! Look at the lovely bride. They are all honorable women, kings' daughters. Behold, on His right hand stands the queen robed in the shining glory of Ophir.[8] The King's daughter is all glorious within. Her clothing is of wrought gold. She shall be brought to the King in raiment of needlework. The virgins, her companions that follow her, shall be brought unto her.[9] Oh! Glory to God! Look at the virgins, the guests at the wedding; they shall go in with gladness. Rejoicing with great joy, they will be brought into the King's palace.[10]

Streets Like Transparent Glass

Oh! The very gates of solid pearl. The walls jasper, and the city is pure gold, like clear glass. The streets are pure gold, like transparent glass.[11]

The very foundations are built and garnished with all manner of precious stones.[12]

Oh! Behold! Let us rise on the wings of faith and in the Spirit take a view of our eternal home. The city lieth four square—fifteen hundred miles high.[13] Oh, those pearly gates and jasper walls! How they shine in the glorious brightness and light of God and the Lamb.

---

[6] Matthew 25:6, paraphrased.

[7] See Psalm 45:2.

[8] See Psalm 45:9.

[9] See Psalm 45:14.

[10] See Matthew 25:1-13.

[11] See Revelation 21:11,18,21.

[12] Revelation 21:19, paraphrased.

[13] See Revelation 21:16.

A Vision of the New Jerusalem

A brother recently had a vision of the New Jerusalem. He says: "I began to dimly outline the grandest and most ravishing scene my eyes had ever yet beheld. The scenery before me was far distant, yet the objects were bright and shining as the sun. I saw, as it were, a great and high mountain city with a shining gemmed wall about it and bright and living forms passing over the city and upon it, and at many places disappearing into the city.

"I was astonished to see the streets ran through the city in every direction, up and down, and into it to the north, to the south, to the east, and to the west; and also along the sides of the city. Every division in the city has a street upon its sides above, below, and on either side thereof; and the streets appeared clear like the purest water. Within the city, which was brighter and more glorious toward the top and upon which was a light bright as the sun, I saw an innumerable number of forms with shining mantles upon them, but I could distinguish nothing definitely because of the great distance. Sweet, low, and faint sounds did also occasionally greet my ears, yet I could distinguish no voice or language."

Oh, beloved, if the outside is so glorious, what will it be to live in the city, to roam through the courts of glory?

Our Lord says we shall go in with joy and rejoicing.[14] Oh, our Lord will have many surprises for us as He takes us through our mansions fair. We shall sit with Him in His throne and be surrounded with all the brightness and glory of heaven.

We shall see the river of life running out from beneath the throne of God, like a sea of clear glass. There will be the nation of kings with their gold-crowned heads.[15]

We Shall Eat of the Tree of Life

We shall eat of the Tree of Life that bears twelve manner, or kinds, of fruit every month.[16] Oh, these beautiful trees on each side of the

[14]See Psalm 45:15.

[15]See Revelation 22:1 and 21:24.

[16]See Revelation 22:2.

river. We shall eat of the fruit. Jesus said, "I say unto you, I will not drink henceforth of this fruit of the vine, until that day when I drink it new with you in my Father's kingdom" (Matthew 26:29).

Yes, we shall eat and drink with our Bridegroom in His kingdom. Jesus said, "I appoint unto you a kingdom, as my Father hath appointed unto me; That ye may eat and drink at my table in my kingdom" (Luke 22:29-30).

Oh, praise the Lord, this is strong proof that the kingdom is literal and substantial. It shall be free from the curse of sin. "Blessed are they that are called to the marriage supper of the Lamb."[17]

See the feast, "In this mountain shall the Lord of hosts make unto all people a feast of fat things, a feast of wines on the lees, of fat things full of marrow, of wines on the lees well refined" (Isaiah 25:6). "He will swallow up death in victory; and the Lord God Himself will wipe all tears from off all faces. The reproach will be forever taken off His people."[18]

Oh! Hasten the day when the kingdoms of this world shall become the kingdoms of our Lord and His Christ; and He shall reign, and we shall reign with Him for the ages of ages.[19] Oh, blessed King! Come and take up Thy great power and reign.

We are now bearing the image of Adam, the first man, but our fleshly bodies will be changed and made like unto His glorious body.[20] Our mortal body will be changed to an immortal body. Jesus ate with His disciples after He arose from the dead with the same body immortalized; and so will we, for we will be like Him.[21]

Brethren, "We shall not all sleep, but we shall all be changed, In a moment, in the twinkling of an eye" (1 Corinthians 15:51-52). "Then we which are alive and remain shall be caught up together with them [the glorified and risen dead] in the clouds, to meet the

[17]Revelation 19:9, paraphrase.

[18]Isaiah 25:8, paraphrased.

[19]See Revelation 11:15.

[20]See 1 Corinthians 15:45-52.

[21]See Luke 24:41-43 and John 21:5-14.

Lord in the air: and so shall we ever be with the Lord" (1 Thessalonians 4:17).

The time is about up when Jesus will come to take out a people for His bride. His delight is in her, and He will give her His name. Yes, we shall be called the bride, the Lamb's wife. We will be His pride and glory. He will be glorified in us through the ages of the ages.

As Jesus and His bride travel through the many beautiful worlds and He presents her in all her beauty, she, too, in her majesty and glory points to her royal Bridegroom and tells of His wonderful redeeming love.

The Time Is at Hand

Yes, the time is at hand. Jesus has given us many signs so that we should know when to look for His return and assuredly know that His coming is near, even at the doors. He said that the wise should know.[22] "And they that be wise shall shine as the brightness of the firmament" (Daniel 12:3).

Oh, beloved, are we watching? Are we waiting? Will we be chosen to escape all the awful things that are coming on the earth? To many, it will be a day of darkness; and there will be no light in it for them. He will come as suddenly as a flash of lightning and we will be taken as quickly, or our desolation will overtake us just as suddenly.[23]

He will come with all the brightness of heaven. The saints will see all His glory and will hear all the bells of heaven ringing. Amidst the singing of the great angelic choir, they will be caught away, swallowed up, and immersed in all this brightness and glory. But the poor, lost world will sleep on, not knowing what has happened. Two will be sleeping in one bed, the one taken and the other left, to sleep on. Two will be at the mill grinding, one taken, the other left. Two will be in the field, the one taken, the other left.[24]

[22]See Daniel 12:10.

[23]See Matthew 24:27.

[24]See Matthew 24:40-41 and Luke 17:34-36.

So suddenly shall this appear that they that are left will not know it until too late. Then they will realize what has happened, when they see that all these they reckoned foolish cranks have disappeared.

No, the world is too blinded in sin and darkness; she cannot behold the glory of the rapture as the saints go shouting through the air.

Hark! By faith we might almost hear them marshalling the hosts of heaven, the angels tuning their harps of gold. We can almost see the banquet, the table spread for the marriage supper in the air. Many, in visions, have seen the supper reaching across the skies. Oh, dear reader, will you accept the invitation to the marriage supper in the skies? Oh! Glory to God, I will meet you there!

Taken from *Spirit-Filled Sermons.*

The Second Coming of Christ

A Startling Manifesto—Philadelphia Conference on the Return of the Lord

For this we say unto you by the word of the Lord, that we which are alive and remain unto the coming of the Lord shall not precede them which are asleep. For the Lord himself shall descend from heaven with a shout, with the voice of the archangel, and with the trump of God: and the dead in Christ shall rise first: Then we which are alive and remain shall be caught up together with them in the clouds, to meet the Lord in the air; and so shall we ever be with the Lord.

1 Thessalonians 4:15-17, paraphrased.

The Lord Jesus shall be revealed from heaven with his mighty angels, In flaming fire taking vengeance on them that know not God, and that obey not the gospel of our Lord Jesus Christ: Who shall be punished with everlasting destruction from the presence of the Lord, and from the glory of his power.

2 Thessalonians 1:7-9

This is the first resurrection. Blessed and holy is he that hath part in the first resurrection: on such the second death hath no power, but they shall be priests of God and of Christ, and shall reign with him a thousand years.

Revelation 20:5-6

The subject of the resurrection is grand and glorious to contemplate. It should be taught and explained in all our churches. It is the hope of the Church; it was the theme of the prophets' and apostles' preaching.

The atonement and resurrection are the keynotes of the New Testament.

We believe we are living in the last days, that the coming of the Lord draweth nigh.

A prophetic conference met in New York, November 1878—there were one hundred and forty bishops and ministers from the different states and across the waters. They met to compare the prophecies referring to the coming of Christ. They concluded that Daniel's "seventy weeks" are about expired.[1]

A Startling Manifesto

On the front page of the *Chicago Herald* on 6th December 1917, there appeared a report reprinted from the London *Christian World* that prominent clergymen of the Protestant churches of England have issued a manifesto, consisting of seven sections, expressing the view that the Millennium is at hand.

"The Significance of the Hour"

It is entitled, "The Significance of the Hour," and is as follows:

1. *That the present crisis points toward the close of the times of the Gentiles.*
2. *That the revelation of our Lord may be expected at any moment when He will be manifested as evidently as to His disciples on the evening of His resurrection.*
3. *That the completed Church will be translated to be "forever with the Lord."*
4. *That Israel will be restored to its own land in unbelief and be afterward converted by the appearance of Christ on its behalf.*
5. *That all human schemes of reconstruction must be subsidiary to the Second Coming of our Lord because all nations will be subject to His rule.*
6. *That under the reign of Christ there will be a further great effusion of the Holy Spirit on all flesh.*

[1] See Daniel 9:24.

7. *That the truths embodied in this statement are of the utmost practical value in determining Christian character and action with reference to the pressing problems of the hour.*

Amongst the signers of the manifesto are clergymen of international reputation, including:

Dr. Dixon, for many years pastor of the Moody church in Chicago and now minister of one of the largest Baptist churches in England, he being successor of the late Charles H. Spurgeon.

Dr. F. B. Meyer, minister of Christ Church of London and secretary of the Free Church Council of England.

Dr. Morgan of Northfield and Winona fame, who was once sought as pastor of the Fifth Avenue Church of New York, and recently pastor of Westminster Congregational Church of London.

Dr. Young, who has occupied some of the principal Methodist pulpits of England; Alfred Bird, Congregationalist; William F. Gooch, Presbyterian; I. Stewart Holden, H. Webb Peploo, and Frank S. Webster, Episcopalians.

Philadelphia Conference 1918

A conference on the soon coming of the Lord and the fulfillment of prophecy was held for three days at Philadelphia, Pennsylvania, in 1918. The large hall was filled to overflowing, and it was attended by many of the most eminent clergymen from the various denominations and noted Bible teachers. They passed a resolution endorsing the above manifesto from their English brethren. Dr. Scofield, the publisher of the well-known *Scofield Bible,* was unable to be present at the last moment, but sent the following telegram:

> *Ashuelot, New Hampshire, May 25th, 1918. To the Philadelphia Conference on the Return of our Lord. Greetings: I pray that God may guide all your proceedings, especially in the putting forth of a fearless warning that we are in the awful end of the Times of the Gentiles, with no hope for humanity except in the personal return of the Lord in glory. C. I. Scofield.*

Daniel's Prophecy

Daniel spoke of many things that the angel revealed to him that should take place before the coming of Christ that have already come to pass. He spoke of the war between the North and the South; that the South should rebel and rise up against the North; that the North should come with a mighty army and conquer the South. She should come with great ships of war. He spoke of the cars, the express trains, the chariots rushing through the land like a whirlwind. You remember that for months and years our trains went like whirlwinds, crowded with men of war. (See Daniel 11:40.) This was to be near the end.

He spoke of the loss of life and property by fire and floods. Whole towns have been swept away; thousands and thousands of families have been left homeless and without a penny by these destroying elements. Over two hundred thousand were swept into eternity by accidents and pestilence in one year. Over one hundred thousand were swallowed up in one terrible earthquake. Daniel asked the angel, "What shall be the end of these things? When he shall have accomplished to scatter the power of the holy people, all these things shall be finished."[2] This is the last prophecy.

> So likewise ye, when ye shall see all these things, know that it is near, even at the doors.
>
> Matthew 24:33

There Shall Arise False Christs

> As (Jesus) sat upon the mount of Olives, the disciples came unto him privately, saying, Tell us, when shall these things be? and what shall be the sign of thy coming, and of the end of the world? And Jesus answered and said unto them, Take heed that no man deceive you. For many shall come in my name, saying, I am Christ; and shall deceive many.
>
> Matthew 24:3-5 (Parenthetical addition by Maria Etter.)

[2] Daniel 12:7, paraphrased.

It is said there are thirty-two persons in the world today claiming to be the Christ and each of these have a large following. Perhaps the most notable of them all is a Persian, Abdul Baha, whose home is in the Valley of Akka. He is the founder of the Bahaian (*sic*) movement, a false system of religion that has spread over the United States during the past few years and which has caused many of our best educated and cultured men and women to worship at his shrine.

Some of our wealthiest people in New York and Boston have made special trips to Persia for the sole purpose of obtaining an interview with this false Christ; and they have brought back to the United States, teachers and followers of this cult and have furnished the means for promulgating the creed until the Bahaian (*sic*) movement has swept across our country and today is to be found in all of the larger cities.

Wars and Rumors of Wars

> And ye shall hear of wars and rumours of wars: see that ye be not troubled: for all these things must come to pass.
>
> Matthew 24:6

From the time of our own Civil War, which drenched our land in blood, almost every country has been plunged into the horrors of war. The great conflict between China and Japan in 1895 was followed by the Spanish-American War in 1898. Scarcely had the war clouds between us and Spain rolled away when the world was reading the details of another bloody strife, this time between Great Britain and the Boers;[3] and for three years South Africa was deluged in awful carnage.

Just two years later occurred the Russo-Japanese War, which was the bloodiest of all recent conflicts. Then came the Great European War in 1914,[4] which is too recent to need much description, with its indescribable and untold suffering, agony, and despair; and when the people in some places were massacred by the thousands, like cattle; it seemed as if all the horrors of hell were let loose and scores went insane from the lust of the horrible butchery.

[3] "Boers"—South Africans of Dutch descent.

[4] "Great European War"—World War I.

Today, communism, nihilism, socialism, anarchism, and Bolshevism are threatening the foundations of the strongest thrones, and not a crowned head today is safe from the assassin's bullet:[5] "For nation shall rise against nation, and kingdom against kingdom: and there shall be famines, and pestilences, and earthquakes, in divers places. All these are the beginning of sorrows" (Matthew 24:7-8).

EARTHQUAKES

> There shall be earthquakes in divers places.
>
> Matthew 24:7, paraphrased

Now, as we come to the subject of earthquakes, we find that during the past few years practically every country has been visited one or more times by a great convulsion of nature, and they have been increasing at an alarming rate. I mention only those that have been disastrous to life and property.

In 1898, six villages were destroyed and seven others damaged by an earthquake in Russia in which one thousand people lost their lives. In the same year, in Asia Minor, over sixteen hundred deaths occurred from the same cause, while many others were injured.

Most of us can recall the earthquake in South Carolina in which three-fourths of the city of Charleston was destroyed and about one hundred people perished. This same seismic disturbance traveled across the Atlantic and visited France and Italy, two thousand people perishing in the latter country.

Let me give you the awful destruction of life and property through earthquakes and volcanic eruptions, for just one year, 1892.

In Turkestan, there were ten thousand deaths and fifteen thousand houses destroyed; and at another time during the same year, there were nearly seven hundred deaths and one thousand injured. On the Island of Saint Vincent, two thousand people perished through a volcanic eruption. We all remember quite vividly the eruption of Mount Peelee, which resulted in the destruction of Martinique, where two thousand people were swept into eternity and large numbers injured. And all this in one year! What an awful record!

[5] In this context Maria Etter probably refers to the murders of the Romanov family by the Bolsheviks in Russia.

In the first three years of the present century, there were forty-eight earthquakes. Allowing the same number for each successive three years, should the world stand, we would have the amazing record of sixteen hundred earthquakes for this century.[6]

[AUTOMOBILES]

> The chariots shall be with flaming torches in the day of his preparation. . . . The chariots shall rage in the streets, they shall justle one against another in the broad ways: they shall seem like torches, they shall run like the lightnings.
>
> Nahum 2:3-4

Automobiles: We have had them now for years, and we have become so familiar with these big, awkward chariots with their immense lights, constantly passing to and fro in our streets, jostling one against another and running like lightning, that we have forgotten that they are only another fulfillment of God's prophecy for the last days.

THE PREVALENCE OF TRAVEL AND KNOWLEDGE

> Shut up the words, and seal the book, even to the time of the end: many shall run to and fro, and knowledge shall be increased.
>
> Daniel 12:4

Today, when an event of any note occurs, it is flashed around the world in thirty minutes so we can readily see the wonderful strides knowledge has made within the past few years, thus fulfilling Daniel's prophetic vision.

The first steam locomotive ever seen in the old Garden of Eden is today puffing noisily back and forth, hauling material to construct a mighty dam, which will create a new channel for the river Euphrates and thereby irrigate Mesopotamia, the land originally given to Abraham and which is today being resettled through the Zionistic Society.

[6] According to the U. S. Geological Survey, from 1900-1999, eighteen major earthquakes and one great earthquake (7.0 magnitude or greater) per year have been the steady average. The first three years' average of sixteen was below normal. (USGS National Earthquake Information Center, "Are Earthquakes Really on the Increase?" Webpage. Updated: 18 January 2000. Accessed 18 April 2000. *http://www.neic.cr.usgs.gov/neis/general/handouts/increase_in_earthquakes.html*

And Knowledge Shall Be Increased

When we stop to consider that we have gone from ox carts to flying machines in one generation and that we have gone from no means of communication except letter and stage coach to the immense public press, the telephone and telegraph and wireless with their ceaseless stream of news and information, which cover the earth with their ever-increasing circulation like falling leaves from some mighty tree of knowledge, we can readily see the fulfillment of Daniel's prophecy.

Airships

The airships of today that are to be seen flying about the country in different nations are another sign of the last days. The prophet Isaiah looked down through the centuries and saw the airships of these last days and was made to inquire, "Who are these that fly as a cloud, and as the doves to their windows?" (Isaiah 60:8). We have now a U. S. Mail, Air Service.

The angel told Daniel to seal up these prophecies until the time of the end, in the day of His preparation. The signs of the coming of Christ, spoken of by Daniel, Nahum, and others, have been sealed through all ages, until the last fifty years.

Today the cars run over and under the river. "The gates of the rivers shall be opened."[7] "The chariots shall rage in the streets, they shall justle one against another in the broad ways" (Nahum 2:4). The Lord says: "When ye shall see all these things, know that it is near. . . . Verily I say unto you, This generation shall not pass, till all these things be fulfilled" (Matthew 24:33-34).

These chariots or coaches should run in the day of His preparation. (See Nahum 2:3-4.) These things are to take place in the end of the harvest, the time we are now living in, when the last call is being given, the summons just before the Gentile age closes. These cars were not to run over all the land, but they were to reach Jerusalem, and the Jews were to see these signs of His preparation in Palestine to enable them to know the end of the dispensation and the coming of Christ was near. The cars are now running from Joppa to Jerusalem.

[7] Nahum 2:6.

The electric cars are also said to be running there, and sewerage and all modern improvements are now seen. Every car or train that passes there is speaking to them and to us in tones of thunder as a warning voice from God saying, "The harvest will soon be passed and the summer ended. The preparation days are closing. Christ is coming; go ye out to meet Him."[8]

SUBMARINES

The prophet Habakkuk prophesied concerning the submarine in the following words.

> And makest men as the fishes of the sea, as the creeping things, that have no ruler over them? They take up all of them with the angle, they catch them in their net, and gather them in their drag: therefore they rejoice and are glad. Therefore they sacrifice unto their net, and burn incense unto their drag; because by them their portion is fat, and their meat plenteous. Shall they therefore empty their net, and not spare continually to slay the nations?
>
> Habakkuk 1:14-17

Men have become as fish in moving about on the bed of the ocean. The submarine is a creeping thing. There was no power able to cope with them for a while. But soon they began to take them with an angle, with grappling irons; they made large nets of steel wire and caught them and were jubilant at their success.

FIG-TREE BUDS

Jesus cursed the fig tree and the Jewish nation in Palestine.[9] The rain and dews were taken away from the land; it became a barren waste and has been for two thousand years. The Lord told them when they, the Jews or anyone, would see the fig tree again bearing and the latter rains and dews in Palestine, they would know the coming of the Son of Man was near, even at your door.[10]

[8] See Matthew 25:6.

[9] See Matthew 21:19-20 and Mark 11:13-14,20-21.

[10] See Matthew 24:32-33 and Mark 13:28-29.

Dear readers, these signs are seen today by all who visit the Holy Land. For several years God has been sending the rains and dews; the fig trees are bearing and [also trees of] many other kinds of fruit. The flowers are blooming. The Jews are going back by the thousands. This is one of the strongest signs. Oh! Praise the Lord that we are living in the close of this last generation and are permitted to give the household of faith their portion in this His due person. At this same time He promised to pour out His Spirit and give us the rains of spiritual power; that Christ, the chief reaper, would be with us in a cloud of glory and [with] the Holy-Ghost power to reap the harvest and gather in the wheat.[11] Thank God we will have the pleasure of being one of the reapers.

He says to us, "Watch and pray always that you may escape all these things that are coming on the earth and stand before the Son of Man."[12]

We Live in the Shadows of the Great Tribulation

In the twelfth chapter of Daniel, Gabriel told Daniel that Michael, the prince, or Christ, would come for His bride, to deliver His people, to take her to Himself and from the earth, and that there would be such a time of trouble as never was. No, nor never should be again.[13] The world will not be burned up. Two will be grinding at the mill, one shall be taken up, the other left; the whole world will be taken in a snare. Christ will take out His people for His name, or bride. They will all go up to meet the Lord in the air and to the marriage feast of the Lamb.[14]

The angels that are now holding back the powers of darkness will soon be commanded to let loose the four winds of God's wrath.[15] This awful time of trouble will last some years. We think about three and one half years. Then Christ will come back with His bride to begin the Millennium reign of one thousand years, when the Jews will accept Christ.

---

[11]See Matthew 13:24-30,36-43.

[12]Luke 21:36, paraphrased.

[13]See Daniel 12:1.

[14]See Matthew 24:40, 1 Thessalonians 4:17, and Revelation 19:9.

[15]See Revelation 7:1.

"The residue of men might seek after the Lord" (Acts 15:17). The judgments will last one thousand years. One day with the Lord is as a thousand years.[16] The six days are about passed, or six thousand years. The last, or seventh, is now about coming in. The saints will sit with Christ to judge the nations and angels all through this Judgment Day. "Do ye not know that the saints shall judge the world?"[17] The Lord is preparing His little flock now for this work. Reader, will you be among that number?

Your Redemption Draweth Near

Jesus, in speaking of the signs of the last days, says: "Behold the fig tree, and all the trees; When they now shoot forth, ye see and know of your own selves that summer is now nigh at hand. So likewise ye, when ye see these things come to pass, know ye that the kingdom of God is nigh at hand" (Luke 21:29-31). "And this gospel of the kingdom shall be preached in all the world for a witness unto all nations; and then shall the end come" (Matthew 24:14).

Our missionaries tell us the Gospel has been sent into all the inhabitable parts of the earth; so today the power of the holy people is scattered over the earth. In every nation and kindred and tribe and tongue, there are those who are witnesses that Jesus has power on earth to forgive sins. So today the knowledge of the Lord covers the whole earth—a theoretical knowledge at least.

The lion of the tribe of Judah hath prevailed. The mighty conqueror is marching on from the rivers to the ends of the earth. Today, He is reigning in the hearts of His people all over our land.

Dear brother in the Lord, cheer up; the end and your redemption draweth near, much nearer than when we first believed.[18] Some, even ministers, pray for the time to hasten when the whole world will be converted. That is contrary to the teachings of the Word of God. Jesus says the people shall wax worse and worse and do more wickedly.[19] As in the days of Noah, they ate, they drank, they married and went on in their wickedness, till the very day that the floods

[16]See 2 Peter 3:8.

[17]1 Corinthians 6:2.

[18]See Luke 21:28 and Romans 13:11.

[19]See Matthew 24:12. Etter may also be thinking of 2 Timothy 3:13.

came and swept them all away: as, in the days of Lot, they bought and sold, builded (*sic*) and mocked at God's messengers, and although God sent angels to warn them, only eight were saved from the storm of fire and brimstone; so it shall be at the coming of the Son of Man.[20]

The Apostasy Approaches

Jesus says that time will not come except there will be a falling away in the churches. False teachers will rise up, "having a form of godliness, but denying the power thereof: from such turn away."[21] There are hundreds of such teachers today. They are blind leaders of the blind.[22] They are going down to hell together. This is a visible sign of the coming of Christ.

Since that late great war[23] our churches have been decreasing in spiritual power and growing rich in fine houses, swelling the membership, but making little effort to get the people converted; taking in members without conversion—dead weights. The abomination of desolation that Daniel spoke of has been set up in the churches.[24] Did you ever consider it takes six living men to carry one dead one? They come in without the wedding garments on, with the black robes of sin around them, while God's children are feasting on the heavenly manna.[25] They sit back and criticize. They dare not taste of the feast. They fight against God and all the workings of the Holy Ghost. The devil has them blinded. He appears as an angel of light, trying to deceive the very elect.[26] We are told to watch; to be on our guard; that we shall be tried as with fire and be pure as gold.[27]

Jesus will send His angels to gather the wheat from the tares; God help us, dear friends, to be among the wheat.[28]

[20] See Matthew 24:37-39. See also Genesis 7:9; 9:19 and 19:15,26. In the case of Noah, eight were saved from the Flood. In the case of Lot, four fled the storm of fire and brimstone and three survived.

[21] 2 Timothy 3:5.

[22] Matthew 15:14.

[23] "late great war"—World War I.

[24] See Matthew 24:15 and Mark 13:14. See also Daniel 11:31 and 12:11.

[25] See Matthew 24:24 and Revelation 2:17.

[26] See Galatians 1:8.

[27] See 1 Peter 1:7.

[28] See Matthew 13:24-40.

In a spiritual sense, the Sun of righteousness[29] has gone down, or out of, most of all the churches. The moonlight is very pale; black, spiritual darkness is setting down all over the land. It is so thick that it can be felt. The old serpent is dragging down many bright lights or stars. Many bright lights are going out in awful darkness.[30] We see those that seemed to be the best established, that we thought would suffer most anything for Christ's honor and glory, now compromising with those that have no power, but only a form.[31] From such, the Lord said, turn away. Many others go off into fanaticism, accepting delusions, that they might be damned. There never was such a time.

Fanatical teachers are swarming like bees in the large cities and going about to every place deceiving and being deceived and if it were possible, they would deceive the very elect.[32]

The Christian Life a Test of Endurance

The perilous times are here. They will not endure the faith of the glorious Gospel of our Christ. "He that shall endure unto the end, the same shall be saved" (Matthew 24:13). "Blessed is the man that endureth temptation" (James 1:12). "Behold, we count them happy which endure" (James 5:11).

Neither will they tolerate it much longer, they try to crush it out in every way. The Lord said to work while it is day, for the night would come when no man could work.[33] "Having done all, to stand" (Ephesians 6:13).

We are going through that time now. The spiritual famine is upon us, but the Lord said He would sustain us in that time and care for those that trust Him. We see the Laodicean church is being spewed out of His mouth. His Spirit is withdrawn from them; the next call will be to judgment. The most (*sic*) of the salt of the professors of religion has lost its saving qualities.

[29]See Malachi 4:2.

[30]See Revelation 6:12-13 and Ezekiel 32:8.

[31]See 2 Timothy 3:5.

[32]See Matthew 24:24.

[33]See John 9:4.

It is only a little flock that is holding the angels in check and the world from awful wreck and ruin. The servants of God will all soon be sealed, and then the Lord will take the bride, who is the light of the world, out.[34] She is as fair as the morn, as bright as the sun, and as terrible as an army with banners.

Christ is a perfect Savior; He came to restore all that was lost in Adam's fall. When Adam fell, he lost his holy nature; sickness and death came to the body. If Christ could not restore soul and body, He would not be a perfect Savior. The believer's soul is made perfect in this life, pure and white; the body will be subject to disease, until the coming of Christ.

The Translation or Rapture

Paul says, "He shall change our vile body, that it may be fashioned like unto his glorious body."[35] The last enemy that Christ will conquer is death; the time is coming when they that are in their graves shall hear His voice and shall come forth; "They that have done good, unto the resurrection of life; and they that have done evil, unto the resurrection of damnation,"[36] in the image of the devil, their father.

Elijah went to heaven in a golden chariot, soul and body.[37] Enoch went up in a whirlwind.[38] Christ took the same body to heaven that was nailed to the cross and was laid in the grave.[39]

Paul speaks of being perfect in one sense and not in another. He is already perfect in heart; but "If by any means I might attain unto the resurrection of the dead,"[40] when he would be perfect, soul and body united and completely delivered forever from the power and dominion of Satan. When they are clothed upon with immortality, then the saints will shout victory over death, hell, and the grave.[41]

[34] See Revelation 7:1-3 and Matthew 5:14.

[35] Philippians 3:21, paraphrased.

[36] John 5:29.

[37] See 2 Kings 2:11.

[38] See Genesis 5:24. Etter is interpreting "Enoch walked with God: and he was not; for God took him" to mean he went the same way as Elijah.

[39] See John 20:17, 20, 27 and Acts 1:9.

[40] Philippians 3:11.

[41] See 1 Corinthians 15:53-55.

The Nearness of the Rapture

"Behold, I come quickly."[42] He expects to hear a hearty response from everyone who is true to Him, "Even so, come, Lord Jesus."[43] God's true children are ready, watching morning, noon, and night for the coming of the Bridegroom, in the hour of death or in the clouds. They have their lamps trimmed and burning;[44] they are making every effort to gather in their friends and neighbors before the storm of God's wrath shall burst in awful fury on a lost and ruined world.

Jesus is preparing the mansions for the bride;[45] He is preparing the marriage supper. He is gathering the hosts of angels together; His chariots are almost ready. The angel is standing on the sea and saying that time is no longer, that is, that there shall be no longer delay. For the bride hath made herself ready.[46] "Blessed are they which are called unto the marriage supper of the Lamb."[47]

When the herald shall shout, "*Behold, the bridegroom cometh; go ye out to meet him.*"[48] Oh! What a sight will burst on our raptured vision as we see the King of heaven coming! The Bridegroom, in His royal robes, with all the glory of the heavenly world and His golden chariot; with all the shining angels to escort the bride, the Lamb's wife, to the golden city, the New Jerusalem, with the spirits of the saints coming back for their bodies. "Oh grave! Give us our bodies!" The mighty conqueror unlocks the grave and with a shout that penetrates the caverns of the sainted dead, the graves fly open, the sleeping saints come forth from dusty beds, set free from all the effects of sin.[49] Old age, gray hair, withered limbs, deformities, death, disease are all the effects of sin. Jesus came to save us from the curse of sin, to restore all that was lost by the Fall.

---

[42] Revelation 3:11 and 22:7.

[43] Revelation 3:20.

[44] See Matthew 25:4,7.

[45] See John 14:2.

[46] See Revelation 19:7.

[47] Revelation 19:9.

[48] Matthew 25:6.

[49] See 1 Thessalonians 4:16 and 1 Corinthians 15:52.

The Grand Reunion in the Skies

Jesus died in the prime of life, in the strength and vigor of manhood. We shall be like Him;[50] these vile bodies shall be changed and made like unto the glorious Son of God, not that we shall be unclothed, but clothed upon with immortality.

Oh, what a happy meeting that will be! Whole families and friends will rise up from the old churchyards and clasp each other in a long embrace which will last forever; mothers and children shall meet, husbands and wives, brothers and sisters, friends and neighbors, pastors and flocks.

Those who are alive will be changed in a moment, set free from the effect of sin, and be clothed with the glory of heaven.[51] Then a mighty shout of victory will go up from the millions of saints: "O death, where is thy sting? O grave, where is thy victory?"[52] But thanks be to God for victory over death, hell, and the grave.

The Bliss of the Redeemed

Oh, the rapture as we shall march through the streets of pure gold! We shall raise our voices, which shall sound like rushing waters, like mighty thunders, and unite in singing glory of the Lamb, who has bought us and washed us in His own precious blood. With harps and palms in our hands and crowns on our heads—Jesus will place the shining crowns with His own hands upon our heads—then we shall march through the streets of the city, accompanied with all the music of the hosts of heaven saying, "Alleluia: for the Lord God omnipotent reigneth."[53] Let us be glad and rejoice and give honor to Him for the marriage of the Lamb is come and His wife hath made herself ready.[54]

Jesus will lead us to the Great White Throne, and say, "Here, Father, am I and the children thou hast given me."[55] We will prostrate ourselves before the throne and cast our crowns at His feet

[50] 1 John 3:2.

[51] See 1 Corinthians 15:52.

[52] 1 Corinthians 15:55.

[53] Revelation 19:6.

[54] See Revelation 19:7.

[55] See John 17:24.

saying, "Holy, holy, holy, is the Lord God of hosts. Worthy is the Lamb that was slain to receive power, and riches, and wisdom, and strength, and honour, and glory, and blessing."[56]

We shall all sit down to the marriage supper of the Lamb. Oh! What a company—apostles, martyrs, fathers, mothers, children, friends and neighbors, brothers and sisters in the Lord, ministers and converts. Oh, what a reunion, what a gathering that will be as we look along the table at the bright and shining faces! Then to behold the dear Savior smiling on His children! Dear friends, will you be there?

> *Are you ready for the bridegroom when He comes?*
> *Behold, He cometh! Behold, He cometh!*
> *Be robed and ready, for the bridegroom cometh!*

CHORUS

> *Behold the bridegroom, for He comes!*
> *Behold, He cometh! Behold, He cometh!*
> *Be robed and ready, for the bridegroom comes!*[57]

I proceed to do a marvelous work.[58] Yet some of you won't believe, but are stiff-necked, but praise God, some of the weakest ones get the baptism. God is pouring out His Spirit all over the world today. When the Holy Ghost came, He would witness by speaking in other tongues. God does many works, but this is a marvelous one.

The Lord showed us that it was from Isaiah that the apostles got the light that the Holy Ghost would speak in other tongues.[59] I never before understood how the apostles spake in tongues, as they came by faith, but now I see it plainly, "He that believeth on me, as the scripture hath said, out of his belly shall flow rivers of living water" (John 7:38).

Other Tongues Seems to Be the Last Resort of God

There are so many gifts for us all—salvation, divine healing, wisdom, love, and power.

[56]See Revelation 4:8,10 and 5:12.

[57]Source of hymn unknown.

[58]See Isaiah 29:14.

[59]See Isaiah 28:11.

"In the law it is written, With men of other tongues and other lips will I speak unto this people; and yet for all that will they not hear me, saith the Lord."[60]

God is sending His angels or messengers, His baptized people, with voices like the sound of the trumpet, to gather His elect together. To gather His people who have made a covenant with God by sacrifice, who have given up or sacrificed everything that stands in the way of their being caught away in the rapture and are doing all they can to help others to get ready, blowing the trumpet, preaching in the power of the Holy Ghost with the outpouring of the Spirit on the people and the acts and signs and wonders and miracles manifested.

The last thing to be done before the rapture is this power must be seen scattered among the saints everywhere.[61] We must not only talk and say we ought to have these demonstrations, but we must produce the goods. The signs must be many and more wonderful than ever in the world, so that the household of faith may be perfected[62]—that they may be led into the baptism[63] and sealed with the knowledge that Jesus is coming again, that they may be classified among the wise who shall shine as the firmament.[64] Also, that by these visible signs that they see and hear and feel, the lost world may get its last warning.

In the midst of these signs of the glory and presence of God, many will call on Him and be saved before the great and notable Day of the Lord comes, and those who turn away and reject will have no excuse. Amidst all the acts and wonders of the workings of the Spirit, the speaking in other tongues seems to be God's last or greatest warning to sinners, and it is a sign to unbelievers.[65] Hear His voice from heaven, "For with stammering lips and other tongues will I speak to this people, and yet for all that they will not believe Me."[66] It is a sign to all that Jesus is coming soon.

Taken from *Spirit-Filled Sermons.*

---

[60] 1 Corinthians 14:21.

[61] See Daniel 12:7.

[62] See Galatians 6:10 and Ephesians 4:12-13.

[63] "baptism"—the baptism of the Holy Spirit.

[64] See Daniel 12:3.

[65] See 1 Corinthians 14:22.

[66] Isaiah 28:11-12, paraphrased.

Prepare for War—Marshalling of the Nations

or, behold, in those days, and in that time, when I shall bring again the captivity of Judah and Jerusalem, I will also gather all nations, and will bring them down into the valley of Jehoshaphat. . . . Proclaim ye this among the Gentiles; Prepare war, wake up the mighty men, let all the men of war draw near; let them come up: Beat your plowshares into swords, and your pruninghooks into spears: let the weak say, I am strong.

Joel 3:1-2, 9-10

But in the last days it shall come to pass, that the mountain of the house of the Lord shall be established in the top of the mountains, and it shall be exalted above the hills; and people shall flow (into) it.

And many nations shall come, and say, Come, and let us go up to the mountain of the Lord, and to the house of the God of Jacob; and he will teach us of his ways, and we will walk in his paths: for the law shall go forth of Zion and the word of the Lord from Jerusalem.

And he shall judge among many people, and rebuke strong nations afar off; and they shall beat their swords into plowshares, and their spears into pruninghooks: nation shall not lift up a sword against nation, neither shall they learn war any more.

But they shall sit every man under his vine and his fig tree; and none shall make them afraid: for the mouth of the Lord of hosts hath spoken it.

Micah 4:1-4 [parenthetical emendation by Maria Etter.]

These two quotations from Joel and Micah sound a little contradictory. I have heard people say so. But the statements refer to two different parties and times.

The first, "Beat your plowshares into swords, and your pruninghooks into spears," means, "Get ready for battle," and it refers to this present time, a time of war. The second, "Beat their swords into plowshares, and their spears into pruninghooks," means, "Get ready for a time of great farming."

The one [calls us] to prepare for the greatest battle the world has ever heard of; the other refers to the time when war shall be no more.

The first text in this sermon, "Prepare for war; wake up the mighty men of war. Let the nations gather together for battle," refers to this time of the end that we are now living in when the Gentile time is full or closing.

You see the awful slaughter, massacre, deadly hatred, causing them to kill and destroy each other. God has risen up like a mighty man of war. He shall roar and shout out from Jerusalem till all nations are gathered in deadly combat, till the blood flows like a river.[1]

In the text in Joel the call is primarily to the Holy Land, where the great battle of God Almighty will be fought: the battle of the great day of God while the angel is standing in the sun, calling all the fowls of the air to come to the supper of the great God to eat the flesh of all the mighty men, the great men of the world, and the rich men. They are invited to eat and drink the blood and get fat on the flesh, on the carcasses of kings and princes of the world who will soon fall in the notable Day of the Lord.[2]

The Lord shall awake and shout out as a man of war. He shall roar out of Zion and shall utter His voice from Jerusalem. The heavens shall shake and the earth, when the nations are gathering for this great battle with the Lamb and His army from heaven.[3]

John said, "I saw heaven opened, and behold a white horse, and him that sat upon him. His eyes were as a flame of fire. On his head were many crowns, and he was clothed in a vesture dipped in blood.

And the armies which were in heaven followed him on white horses, clothed in white linen, white and clean."[4]

[1] See Joel 3:16 and Revelation 14:20.

[2] See Revelation 19:17-18.

[3] See Joel 3:16.

[3] Revelation 19:11-14, paraphrased.

Oh, praise the Lord! The saints have been translated to heaven. The marriage of the Lamb and His bride has taken place with shouting and hallelujahs that have shaken all heaven and earth. The great marriage supper, with all its grandeur and glory and greatness, is over. And they have been with the Lord, executing judgments of the earth during the awful Tribulation.

Now the cup of wickedness is full. They have defied the God of heaven long enough. He has stood up in His wrath. All nations of the earth are gathering to the Valley of Jehoshaphat.[5] The Lord of Lords and King of Kings, with all His armies of heaven, comes riding in triumph, down through the skies. Enoch saw the Lord coming with ten thousand of His saints.[6] The Antichrist has gathered his army and is about to destroy God's children. They will gather all their armies together against Jerusalem to fight, but then the Lord comes from heaven and fights this great battle. The saints do not have to fight; the Lord Himself does the fighting.[7]

Then the millennial kingdom is set up, and Satan will be chained during that thousand years.[8] During that time, the curse and its effects, including all weeds, thistles, and that which would produce disease, etc., have been taken away. "Nothing shall hurt or destroy in all my holy mountain."[9] The time is coming when they shall cease to make war,[10] and the devil is taken out of the hearts of the people.

Today they are just like wild beasts, thirsting for each other's blood. They are burying the living and the dead together. Pestilence also has already begun its deadly havoc. Did you ever hear of a great war breaking out so quickly? For years past the most talented men have been inventing to see who could get the most deadly weapons.

God has been holding back the tidal waves and the other destructive forces. His angel has shouted back, "Wait till the servants of God are sealed with the seal of God."[11]

---

[5] See Joel 3:2.

[6] See Jude 14.

[7] See Revelation 19:15.

[8] See Revelation 20:3.

[9] Isaiah 11:9, paraphrased.

[10] See Psalm 46:9.

[11] Revelation 7:2-3, paraphrased.

The division of the book of Joel into chapters is bad. The first verses of the third chapter are a continuation of the last verses of the second chapter and should not be divided from them.

"In the last days I will pour out my Spirit."[12] [God will] baptize with the Holy Ghost, and scatter the power of the holy people.[13]

God said, "I will rise up in my wrath in that day."[14] When the judgments of God are in the earth, some will repent. "In the last days I will pour out My Spirit."[15] God says, wake up the heathen. God is sealing His saints, but that sealing time is pretty nearly over.[16] That they speak in new tongues is a sign that the Lord is coming.

"The power of the holy people shall be scattered."[17] These are they that are clay in the potter's hand.[18] They are just clay, having no control of themselves at all. God Almighty speaks through them, "With stammering lips and other tongues will I speak unto this people, but *for all that* they will not hear."[19]

Proclaim and tell it to the people. Blow the trumpet. Sound the alarm in the holy mountain. What is the danger? *The great Day of the Lord is coming, it is near at hand.*[20]

God's people are blowing the trumpet. They are sounding the alarm in Zion. What is the signal of danger? *The great Day of the Lord is near.* It is time for the saints to get this knowledge if they do not already know it. How can we give the signal if we do not know? How could we warn the people of danger?

If they escape when the sword is coming, good. But warn them anyhow. If we do not warn them, their blood will be on our hands.[21]

---

[12]See Joel 2:28.

[13]Daniel 12:7.

[14]See Joel 3:16 and the surrounding verses concerning God's judgment.

[15]Joel 2:28.

[16]Revelation 7:3.

[17]See Daniel 12:7.

[18]Isaiah 64:8 and Jeremiah 18:4-6.

[19]Isaiah 28:11 and 1 Corinthians 14:21, paraphrased.

[20]Joel 2:1.

[21]See Ezekiel 3:18-19.

Wake up the heathen. Call up your mighty men. Call the soldiers into line. Get them ready. Get the weapons of war ready for the world's great conflict. There never has been anything like it, nor ever will be again.

There will be a scarcity of steel. They cannot make enough of it. The nations are all the time building new warships and manufacturing so many deadly weapons. It takes a good deal of steel to make these warships, such monster vessels!—each nation trying to build the largest ships and invent the most deadly weapons.

Still, they are crying, "Peace, peace."[22] Right in the midst of this false peace and security, death and war and destruction have come like a whirlwind.

There is a lack of steel. Where are they going to get it? Pretty soon they will not be able to meet the demand for it. Then men will be hunting around the farmyards, old barns, stables, and sheds, everywhere, for old plowshares and pruninghooks, for everything that they can beat into swords and spears to kill their neighbors with.[23]

The time is coming in this glorious America when parties and factions will rise up. Labor against Capital, and other parties and factions. There will be no safety to him that goes out or goes in. And at that time they will not be able to buy or sell, unless they have the mark of the Beast.[24] It will be death, and to have the mark of the Beast will mean the second death.

There will be no safety or hiding place to him that goes out or in. "As if a man did flee from a lion, and a bear met him; or went into the house, and leaned his hand on the wall, and a serpent bit him" (Amos 5:19).

It is implied that the land will be infested with poisonous serpents, reptiles, and insects, and they will be turned loose among the people with their deadly power to bite, sting, and destroy.[25] So that if you run away from the sword and pestilence and try to hide in the house, you will lay your hand on the wall and be bitten by a deadly serpent. There will be no safety to him that goes in or out.

[22]See 1 Thessalonians 5:3 and Jeremiah 6:14.

[23]See Joel 3:10.

[24]See Revelation 13:17.

[25]See Revelation 9:1-6.

There will be awful, deadly hatred among the people, and they will be banded together hand in hand, and they will make weapons of steel with which to kill and destroy one another. I read not long ago that the powers were crying out because of the scarcity of steel. Your neighbor will be hunting round for a piece of old steel to kill his neighbor with. In Europe now they are calling out young men and boys to fight and to be destroyed.

It is time to wake up from the sleep of death and call on God to give you life.

According to the Word of God and the signs of the times, we are now living in the commencement of these awful times, when many who read these lines will see a great deal more than I have written. You and your children will go down in death or go through this dreadful time of trouble such as never has been nor ever will be again.

Many of the best Bible students say that the eleventh chapter of Daniel refers to the Sultan, or ruling powers of Turkey. "He shall plant the tabernacles of his palace between the seas in the glorious holy mountain; yet he shall come to his end, and none shall help him" (Daniel 11:45). And they think that the book of Obadiah also refers to him.

The passage in Daniel does not refer to the Antichrist, for he will not be revealed or take his power till after the hinderer is taken away,[26] till Christ takes out a people for His name from among the Gentiles, till He comes and takes His bride.

He shall come to his end, the time of the end, and at that time Michael the great prince shall stand up for his people and all will be delivered whose names are written in the Book of Life.[27] And the wise, who know these things shall shine as the brightness of the firmament.[28]

The way the war is raging against Turkey, it looks as if she might lose her capital, Constantinople, and be compelled to leave her head-quarters almost any day. How natural it would be for her to transfer

[26]See 2 Thessalonians 2:6-7.

[27]See Daniel 12:1.

[28]See Daniel 12:3.

her government to the Holy Land, of which she still has control, in haste: she could occupy almost any building for that purpose.

It is reported that the Turks are building a large palace, or building, and they are keeping it quiet and will not tell anyone what it is for. "He shall plant the tabernacles of his palace between the seas in the glorious holy mountain; yet he shall come to his end, and none shall help him."[29] But he will not stay there very long; little by little, he will go down till he is entirely destroyed.

The Holy Land was to be trodden down of the Gentiles until the time of the end. Then, and at that time, Christ will come. The Jews will flock to Jerusalem and again possess the Holy Land. Most of those who have gone through the Tribulation will have had enough, and they will be ready to listen to the voice of that prophet.

If the angels are loosed, it will not be long before we take our flight. When these things begin to come fast, we shall soon be taken out of the world. The worst trouble will come after the saints are taken out.[30] The Antichrist will deny the blessed Christ and cause people to take his mark or to be put to death.[31] Those who do not go with Christ will have to go through this or go down in it.

Jesus comes to take a people out for His name, for His bride. He comes and takes her away to the heavens. The great marriage supper takes place after which they will be sitting with Christ on His throne and helping to execute judgment during this awful Tribulation.

Look at the awful death and carnage and destruction if you do not go up with the bridal company.

Those who go up when Christ comes are the Lamb's wife. He returns to build up the waste places of Jerusalem. The soil will all be fertile then, and the people will not need to do much work. It will be like a holy camp meeting all the time during the millennial age.

The first time Jesus comes, none see Him but the bride. The world hates her and cares nothing for her, and Jesus is going to take her away.

---

[29]Daniel 11:45.

[30]See 1 Thessalonians 4:16.

[31]See Revelation 13:16-17.

Christ will come as quickly as the lightning flashes from the east to the west; just that quick He will snatch His bridal company away, while the world sleeps in a drunken stupor.[32]

But the next time He comes, all will know it. "Every knee shall bow and every tongue shall confess"; every eye shall see Him, and every slanderous tongue will have to confess before the world that these were God's chosen vessels.[33]

This honor belongs to the saints. They will have to confess that we were right and that they were wrong. God is very proud of His bride. Children of God now deny themselves many of the things of the world, but we are heirs of the kingdom, though many of us are poor in this world and having hard times. There is going to be a change in this old world. God is calling you to behold. Don't go a step further. Don't step over the mangled body of Christ anymore or it may be the last time.

The first time the bride will be caught away; the second time she will come riding on white horses.[34] Jesus will stand on Mount Olivet, and they that pierced Him shall see Him.[35] You know now down in your hearts that Jesus is the Christ, that we people are every one in earnest, that we hear something more than natural men hear: the wisdom we get from God who gives liberally.[36] That has been my prayer more than anything else, "Give me wisdom." Almost a blind man can see if he looks at the signs of the times.

Daniel says the wise shall know when the Lord comes.[37] You may say you don't believe. You don't want to believe and that day will overtake you as a thief in the night.[38] None of the wicked shall understand the signs of Jesus' coming. Ye who are children of the light shall know, and that day will not overtake you unexpectedly. God gave Daniel a picture of the lost world, none of whom should know when He comes.

---

[32] See Matthew 24:27.

[33] Romans 14:11, paraphrased.

[34] See Revelation 19:14.

[35] See Zechariah 14:4.

[36] See James 1:5.

[37] See Daniel 12:10.

[38] See 1 Thessalonians 5:4.

Who are the wise? Those who know the time of the Lord's coming. "They that turn many to righteousness shall shine as the stars. But they that be wise shall shine as the brightness of the firmament.[39] They that be wise shall know.

Don't be looking to the grave. Look, for behold He cometh. Oh, glory to God in the Highest. Come, oh Redeemer, come quickly.

ADDENDA

"World's Great War Tragedy Is Filled With Blood Scenes

"Every man in a French force penetrating Ft. Douaumont was killed in a German charge. Men are fighting in dark, underground tunnels, using hand searchlights and knives and bombs.

"Hundreds of French and Germans have been buried alive in the wrecking of underground works by shell fire.

"Scores have gone insane from the lust of the horrible butchery.

"Surgeons, amputating arms and legs without anesthetics, report wounded French and Germans continuing the struggle with knives though unable to stand.

"A French captain reported seven thousand dead heaped along a seven-hundred-yard front."

— Extract from Daily Paper, USA, 1916.

MAY 1916

"PREPAREDNESS" THE CRY OF THE HOUR IN NEW YORK

"The civilians in the mammoth preparedness demonstration in New York last Saturday are shown passing the New York Public Library. An idea of its magnitude may be gained when it is remembered that the marching columns composed of twenty men abreast extended for twenty miles."

MARSHALLING OF THE NATIONS

"By common consent, the European war was written down from its very beginning as the greatest titanic struggle ever waged by man; such a marshalling of the nations was never before seen on earth.

[39] Daniel 12:3, paraphrased.

"After eighteen months' conflict, President Wilson said in an address at Cleveland, Ohio, January 29th, 1916: 'While a year ago it seemed impossible that a struggle upon such a large scale should last a whole year, it has now lasted a year and a half, and the end is not yet in sight.'"

— *Washington Post,* January 30, 1916

The Toll of War

"The blackest eighteen months known to the modern world! The net result has been 2,990,000 men in the very prime of life killed, more than 2,200,000 made prisoners, and more than 9,830,000 wounded."

— International News Service

"So over the whole world is heard the sound of the trumpet and of the alarm of war, and 'two-thirds of the world is at war.' I know that daily we are treading amidst the most intricate dangers, that the world is on fire and sparks are likely to drop anywhere," President Wilson said.

— *Washington Post,* January 30th, 1916

Time foretold in prophecy. (See Joel 3:9,14; Revelation 11:18; and Jeremiah 25:31,33.) Two things are plainly seen in these scriptures. First, that when the Day of the Lord is near, the nations of the world will be making gigantic preparations for war. "Prepare war, wake up the mighty men, let all the men of war draw near; let them come up: Beat your plowshares into swords, and your pruning-hooks into spears: let the weak say, I am strong."[40]

If this had been written by a present-day observer of events, it could not have described the international situation more accurately.

Armageddon

The last conflict of the nations of the European conflict, terrible and far reaching as it is, is not the Armageddon of the nations of which the Scriptures tell us, but it surely is a forerunner of the last great clash of the world empires.

Taken from *A Diary of Signs and Wonders.*

[40]Joel 3:9-10.

Death & Judgment

DEATH IS CERTAIN! WHAT WILL FOLLOW?

This World Is Not Your Home—All We Do Fade As a Leaf

Thus saith the Lord, Set thine house in order: for thou shalt die, and not live.

Isaiah 38:1

My prayer is that the Lord will arrest every sinner who reads these words and that you will take the warning in the text to mean you, and flee from the wrath to come by taking the nearest way to the Cross, and throw yourself at the bleeding feet of the dying Lamb of God. Let Him cleanse and wash out all sin and filth from your heart and mind; let the Lord Jesus come in and take possession of your body, or the house, fill you with His love and presence, be the keeper of the house, and speak that you may obey like a dear child. His sheep hear His voice. When He leads, they follow.[1]

THIS WORLD IS NOT YOUR HOME

Jesus has spoken to you many times by His Spirit and told you, "The world is not your home," and that it is not all of life to live nor all of death to die, but after death comes the judgment.[2]

He has shown you that you are a sinner, lost and undone, that the wrath of God hangs over you. If you die in your sins it will be an awful thing to fall into the hands of the living God.[3]

If you go on in your sins, you will be arrested by the sheriff of heaven and bound hand and foot and cast into outer darkness, where the inhabitants weep and wail and gnash their teeth.[4] The Lord has told you the time will come when you will cry for mercy. The mercy door will be closed and God will not hear you. He will

[1] See John 10:3-4.

[2] See Hebrews 11:13 and 9:27.

[3] Hebrews 10:31, paraphrased.

[4] See Matthew 8:12, 22:13, and 25:30.

laugh and mock at your fears and calamity. He will say, "Depart from me, ye accursed, into everlasting fire,"[5] a place prepared for the devil and his angels.

Heaven was prepared for you; but if you are not pure in heart, the pearly gates will be closed against you. This world will be wrapped in flames and will burn as pitch and tar, and the wicked will be swept off into destruction.

In view of the awful doom the text implies, make the preparation at once. You must die, and there is no repentance in the grave. As you go down in death, you will rise in the judgment. Death is coming, that awful eternity is before you! Before the sun rises or sets again, you may be cold in death and your soul lost.

The Pale Horse

You will soon hear the clatter of the feet of the pale horse and his rider, the monster, Death, bearing down upon you.[6] You will have a race with the pale horse, and he will run you down into the cold, icy river of death.

The Lord says, "Prepare for death, for thou shalt die." "As I live, saith the Lord God, I have no pleasure in the death of the wicked; but that the wicked turn from his way and live" (Ezekiel 33:11).You will die soon and meet your God, whether you are ready or not. He will not always chide, neither will He hold His anger forever.[7]

Hear Him call. Seek the Lord while He may be found. Call upon Him while He is near.[8] God has warned you through the rolling thunder, the flashing lightning, and the whirling cyclone. The voice of God has spoken to you saying, "Take warning, fly to Christ and seek shelter from the storms of the great Judgment Day."

The day of His wrath is coming, and who will be able to stand?[9] Every funeral procession you see tells you that you, too, must soon

[5] Matthew 25:41, paraphrased.

[6] See Revelation 6:8.

[7] Psalm 103:9, paraphrased.

[8] Isaiah 55:6, paraphrased.

[9] Revelation 6:17, paraphrased.

die. Are you ready? When you stood by the bedside of one struggling in death or looked on the face in the coffin, the Lord said to you, "Prepare for death and follow Me."

Every fall you look upon the withered flowers and falling leaves. They tell you of death. Death is written on the breezes. Everything points to death and shows you that you will soon be laid away in the silent city of the dead and soon be forgotten by the living.

All We Do Fade as a Leaf

You hear the solemn moaning of the winds through the leafy trees. They say to you: "This world is not your home; you did not come here to stay forever." Seek a home in heaven, a house not built with hands, whose builder and maker is God, where you will soon meet all the loved ones, to be forever with the Lord.[10]

When you walk over the withered flowers and faded leaves and as they rustle beneath your feet, the voice of God speaks to you, saying, "You are passing away; you will soon be lying 'neath the sod and be forgotten." The thoughtless throng will walk over your moldering form and think no more of you than you do of the dead leaves you are crushing beneath your feet.

Dear reader, if you have not given your heart to Jesus, drop on your knees, confess your sins to Him, and accept Him as your personal Savior. Never rise till the light of heaven shines down in your soul and you know you are saved. If you do not, you will soon find yourself swept out on the shores of eternity, lost—lost forever!

The Great Judgment Morning

I dreamed that the Great Judgment morning
Had dawned, and the trumpet had blown;
I dreamed that the nations had gathered
To judgment before the White Throne,
From the Throne came a bright-shining angel
And stood on the land and the sea,
And swore with his hand raised to Heaven.
That time was no longer to be.

[10]See Hebrews 11:10, 2 Corinthians 5:1, and 1 Thessalonians 4:7.

Chorus
And, oh, what a weeping and wailing
When the lost ones were told of their fate;
They cried for the rocks and the mountains,
They prayed, but their prayers were too late.[11]

Taken from *Spirit-Filled Sermons.*

[11]Composer unknown.

The Unpardonable Sin

God's Deadline—The Folly of Procrastination

Wherefore I say unto you, All manner of sin and blasphemy shall be forgiven unto men: but the blasphemy against the Holy Ghost shall not be forgiven unto men. And whosoever speaketh a word against the Son of man, it shall be forgiven him: but whosoever speaketh against the Holy Ghost, it shall not be forgiven him, neither in this world, neither in the world to come.

Matthew 12:31-32

But he that shall blaspheme against the Holy Ghost hath never forgiveness, but is in danger of eternal damnation.

Mark 3:29

The question has been asked a thousand times, "What is the unpardonable sin?" But how often is it answered? Jesus explains: "Because they said, He hath an unclean spirit" (Mark 3:30). "This fellow doth not cast out devils, but by Beelzebub the prince of the devils" (Matthew 12:24). To commit that awful sin is to attribute the power of the Holy Ghost to the power of the devil. It is to rob God of His glory and give it to the devil.

There is one sin unto death: the sin against the Holy Ghost.[1] To avoid committing that sin, you must know what and who the Holy Ghost is and what is His office.

The Holy Ghost is the third person in the Trinity—the Father, the Son, and the Holy Ghost. They all agree, have different offices, but the same Spirit.[2] [For example,] three men are engaged in partnership

[1] See Mark 3:29 and Luke 12:10.

[2] See 1 John 5:7-8.

in a business firm; they all agree and have the same spirit, but have different offices to perform.

The Comforter

The Holy Ghost is a person as much as Christ is. "But the Comforter, which is the Holy Ghost, whom the Father will send in my name, he shall teach you all things" (John 14:26). You see, He is our teacher: "I will pray the Father, and he shall give you another Comforter, that he may abide with you for ever" (John 14:16). You will see He is a person. Jesus said He was going away, but He would not leave them alone.[3] He would send the Holy Ghost, and He was to stay with the Church forever.

Blasphemy against God and all kinds of sin against Him and against mankind will be blotted out; but whosoever speaks against the Holy Ghost hath no forgiveness, neither in this world nor the world to come.[4] Christ said this because they said He had an evil spirit and did His mighty works through that agency. So, you see, it is an unpardonable sin to attribute any of the mighty works of the Holy Ghost to the devil. There has never been a time since the early Church when there was so much danger of people committing the unpardonable sin as there is today, since the Pentecostal fire has girdled the earth and tens of thousands have received the Holy Ghost, backed up by signs and wonders and diverse operations of the Spirit.

Let Every Man Be Slow to Speak

When men and women come in contact with this work of the Holy Ghost, hearing His words and seeing His works, there is danger less (*sic*) they attribute the power there present to some other agency other than the Spirit of God. There is danger less (*sic*) they condemn the power and condemn God's servants. How often have we heard ministers say, when they heard men and women and children speaking in other tongues, "Oh, it is the work of the devil." Now you hear what God says about it; they are speaking against the Holy Ghost.

He will not only come in healing power, but will manifest Himself in many mighty ways. On the Day of Pentecost, Peter said, "God

[3] See John 16:7.

[4] Matthew 12:32, paraphrased.

hath poured forth this which ye see and hear."[5] And from what theyheard and saw, three thousand owned it was the power of God and turned to Christ.[6] Others stifled conviction and turned away saying, "This is the work of the devil." When the Holy Ghost is poured out, it is either life unto life or death unto death to those who blaspheme against the Holy Ghost. So we want to be careful what we say against the diverse operations, supernatural signs, and workings of the Holy Ghost. Some people look on and say, "It looks like hypnotism," or "I believe it is mesmerism." To others it appears mere foolishness, even as Scripture says of the natural man: "The things of the Spirit of God are foolishness unto him and he cannot know them because they are spiritually discerned."[7]

God's Deadline

Now you may see the danger of committing the unpardonable sin. In every community there are those who have stepped over the "deadline," the line that separates them forever from the mercy of God and exposes them forever to His wrath.

It is awful to see men and women going about with the black pall of death resting on them, giving every indication that they are forsaken of God. They are as sure of hell as that they are alive; they have no desire to be Christians and go on without a ray of hope. "My spirit shall not always strive with man,"[8] said the Lord. When the Holy Ghost leaves you the last time, your doom is sealed. We meet a great many such persons in our meetings who we must believe have committed this sin, for "Whosoever speaketh against the Holy Ghost hath never forgiveness, but is in danger of eternal damnation" (See Mark 3:29).

The Folly of Procrastination

You need not go so far as to make fun or speak lightly of the workings of the Spirit and power of God, but just continue to procrastinate a little too long. "He will reprove the world of sin, and of righteousness (of a change of heart, of the need of a Savior), and of judgment."[9]

[5] Acts 2:33, paraphrased.

[6] See Acts 2:41.

[7] 1 Corinthians 2:14, paraphrased.

[8] Genesis 6:3.

[9] John 16:8, parenthetical comment by Maria Etter.

That is what the Holy Ghost will do for the sinner. This is conviction. He warns you of your awful doom in rejecting Christ. The man who has been converted and lost his first love and is in a lukewarm condition, should he die without doing his first works over, is lost.

You often hear the remark: "I have a little spark left."

"I would that you were cold or hot."[10] Don't you know you are presuming on God's love and mercy? You are guilty every moment you live. Jesus warns you to repent and get out of this condition, for you are sailing under false colors. "I will come and spew you out of my mouth."[11] I will remove the candlestick and take away that little spark.[12] It is done, and you have crossed the deadline after having tasted the power of God in the soul and after knowing that you were saved.[13] You knew you were saved, but should you now deny it, saying, "There is no reality in the religion of Jesus," your doom is sealed.

A False Peace Without Salvation

There is a class that is past feeling, being alienated from the life of Christ; and there is another class whose hearts are calloused as if seared with a hot iron.[14] They have no feeling. The Spirit of God has left them. They cannot repent nor have godly sorrow. Then the devil comes as an angel of light and makes them "believe a lie that they may be damned."[15] They think they are all right. They will laugh in your face and go down to the jaws of death and wake up in hell before they will realize their peril. God will send them strong delusions for not receiving the truth. Many classes are deluded.

There are no real unbelievers until God gives them over to believe a lie. The Lord came again and again. The truth was presented to them, but they fought instead of yielding and tried to believe what they knew to be a lie, thinking to ease their guilty consciences. When God shuts up a man, there can be no opening. There is a sin

[10] Revelation 3:15, paraphrased.

[11] Revelation 3:16, paraphrased.

[12] Revelation 2:5, paraphrased.

[13] See Hebrews 6:4-6.

[14] See Ephesians 4:18 and 1 Timothy 4:2.

[15] See 2 Thessalonians 2:11-12.

unto death we need not pray for.[16] The Lord says, "When you spread out your hands in prayer I will not hear you; let this people alone that I may consume them."[17] Today if you hear His voice, harden not your hearts.[18] Tomorrow may be too late.

Taken from *Spirit-Filled Sermons.*

[16]See 1 John 5:16.

[17]See Exodus 32:9-10. See also Jeremiah 7:16, 11:14.

[18]See Hebrews 3:7-8,15, and 4:7.

The Pale Horse and His Rider

Are You Ready for the Other World?—Comparative Worthlessness of the World's Rewards

If thou hast run with the footmen, and they have wearied thee, then how canst thou contend with horses? and if in the land of peace, wherein thou trustedst, they wearied thee, then how wilt thou do in the swelling of Jordan?

Jeremiah 12:5

There are just two classes of people, and there are two racetracks. And we must all run the race, either with the footmen or the horseman, which is the pale horse and his rider, the black angel of death with his clanking chains, taking his prisoner down to death and hell, or with the redeemed for the prize of eternal joy.

We must all run one of these races. One we enter with joy, running, marching, singing, and shouting as we run up the shining way, where the pearly gates swing open, and we are met and welcomed by the hosts of heaven, who have been watching and waiting for us.

The other race with the horseman, you will be forced to run when the sheriff of heaven is sent to arrest you. He will read the death warrant and show [that] you must suffer the penalty of God's broken laws.

Our Death Warrant Needs Canceling

You have been tried at heaven's court and found guilty; the sentence is passed. The hour of execution has come, "Bring the prisoner, bind him hand and foot, and take him away and cast him into outer darkness, where there is weeping and wailing and gnashing of teeth."[1]

[1] Matthew 22:13, paraphrased.

It will be a fearful thing to fall into the hands of the living God,[2] to go out in darkness, and to be a wandering star in the darkness of eternity.

All that are traveling the broad road are getting ready for the race with the horseman.

Paul was acquainted with eastern races, where thousands were gathered to see them enter the races and run for the prize, which was only a perishable crown made of leaves. Many ran, but only one got the prize. All who ran for the crown made a great sacrifice and self-denial. They laid aside every weight;[3] all their garments; everything that would be in their way, and wore a perfectly tight-fitting garment so that nothing would weigh them down or be in their way. Everything that might hinder them from running the race to the end was gladly laid aside.

They paid no attention to how they looked or what the cloud of witnesses[4] might say. It was the prize that they were running for. Thousands of friends were cheering and shouting victory for them as they ran, clapping hands and cheering them on to victory, while their enemies were doing all they could as they looked on to discourage them and make them stumble on the track. If one fell he was thrown aside or out of the track, lest he should be a stumbling-block in the way of others.

Lay Aside Every Weight and the Sin You Indulge In

Paul said the crown lay at the end of the race. While he was running the race, he never looked back, but kept his eyes on the prize of the high calling of Christ Jesus.[5] The crown of rejoicing that he saw was all ready to be placed on his head. He said, "Behold the cloud of witnesses looking on."[6]

---

[2] Hebrews 10:31, paraphrased.

[3] See Hebrews 12:1.

[4] See Hebrews 12:1.

[5] See Philippians 3:14.

[6] See 1 Corinthians 9:25, Philippians 3:14, and Hebrews 12:1-2.

All heaven is leaning out over the battlements and are looking out at the pearly gates, down on the white-robed, blood-washed soldiers who have entered the race from earth to glory. They have laid aside every weight or sin. They have gone through the dressing room and have put on their white garments and girdle and the gospel shoes.[7]

While the saints of God are cheering and encouraging each other, all the world is looking on with all the hosts of hell. The black cloud of witnesses are mocking, sneering, lying, and throwing all manner of stumbling blocks in our way. All hell is shouting when they cause one to fall.

Remember that all who start or enter the race do not reach the end.[8] You may be almost to the end, the crown in sight, then fall and be thrown from the track, out of the way of others.

Jesus says, "Hold fast till I come.[9] See that no man takes your crown."[10] That warning is given to us who are waiting for the coming of the Lord, who hope to see the manifestation of the sons of God. So many are fainting and falling, so many bright lights going out when the blazing glory of the bright morning is bursting on our spiritual vision.[11]

The Comparative Worthlessness of the World's Rewards

Oh, see what sacrifice, expense, and trouble men and women will make for a little popularity or notoriety to receive worldly honors, which are all like a fading leaf that will perish with them and soon be forgotten.[12]

How little sacrifice most of those who profess Christ are willing to make. They will not give their money or time to the true work of the

[7] See Ephesians 6:14-15.

[8] See 1 Corinthians 9:24.

[9] See Revelation 2:25.

[10] See Revelation 3:11.

[11] See Ezekiel 32:8.

[12] See 1 Corinthians 9:25.

Lord. It is given to the popular side when they blow the trumpet before them, and when everyone says, "How charitable, how good, how kind."[13] They get their reward in the eyes of the world, but how will they stand in the Judgment?[14] These are all on the outside of the racetrack to heaven. Not everyone that says, "Lord, Lord," will inherit the kingdom, but they that follow the Lamb where He leads.[15]

When the children of Israel crossed the Jordan, the waters overflowed the banks and the crossing was very dangerous. The text refers to the swelling of the Jordan of death for the sinner to cross, showing how awful it will be to die without Christ; but God parted the waters and made a dry path through the howling river. The children of Israel passed through on the dry ground; their enemies looked and expected to see them swallowed up.[16] But when they were in the middle, the most dangerous place, their feet were on dry ground.

Earth Is Receding—
Heaven Is Opening—God Is Calling

So is the death of the Christian; the friends are standing around the bed. They have done all they could, all that living hands could do; now they watch to see the last breath, to hear the last word. The earth is receding; he is losing sight of loved ones, but look at the light in the eye and in the face. "I have fought a good fight.[17] The time of departure has come; I see the light from the other shore. I hear the music of heaven and the songs of the angels."

"Look, they come, they are in my room, around my bed, to carry me home." While loved ones are weeping, she is crossing on dry land. There is no river to cross, only a little brook. The angels have come with a golden chariot to take the battle-scarred soldier from the battles of life, to the solders' reunion around the throne of God.

Paul says we go to be present with the Lord.[18] Oh! What a change to be admitted into the shining splendor of the golden mansions

---

[13]See Matthew 6:2,5.

[14]See Mathew 6:1 and Luke 16:15.

[15]See Matthew 7:21-22, Luke 6:46, and 13:25.

[16]See Exodus 14:15-16.

[17]See 2 Timothy 4:7.

[18]See 2 Corinthians 5:8.

and palaces of the city of God, to see the Great White Throne, the crystal sea, the Tree of Life, the angel choir, the pearly gates, the loving Father, the loving Savior, the host of heaven, and the loved ones who are waiting to welcome us.

Oh! We will fall before the throne and cry, "Holy, holy, holy is the Lord God Almighty and worthy is the Lamb forever and ever, who loved us and bought us and washed us in His blood and brought us to enjoy the mansions prepared for us."[19]

Oh! Backslider, you that have fallen and are sidetracked; you got weary in the race. How can you contend with the horse and his rider? And you that was (*sic*) afraid or ashamed to run with the footmen and despised those in the race, what will you do in the swelling of Jordan?

Are You Ready to Meet Christ?

In such an hour, as ye think not,[20] death will overtake you. It will not always be at your neighbor's door that the pale horse will stop. He will soon call for you.[21]

The strong man or woman will be laid helpless on a bed, racked with pain or scorched with fever. The doctor will say he cannot live. The house will be darkened.

They will step softly, weeping; loved ones will stand around your bed. Hark! What is that you hear? Your eyes open, you tremble at the sound. It is the clatter of the hoofs of the pale horse, as he comes nearer and nearer with his rider, the monster—Death, the sheriff of heaven. You hear the rattling of chains; he comes nearer and dashes through the door.

He shouts, "Wife stand back," or "Husband stand back, this is my prisoner."

As he draws near, you hear the clanking of the chains as he binds you hand and foot. The hour of execution has come. You cannot bribe the jury or the judge; all your money will not save you an hour's time or your life. Your friends cannot save you; they would

[19] See Revelation 4:8; 5:9,12.

[20] See Matthew 24:44.

[21] See Revelation 6:8.

not take your place if they could. He lifts you, bound and helpless, onto the pale horse and bears you away, down in the swelling of Jordan. See the rolling billows; hear the roaring of the waves as he bears you down in the cold, icy river of death.

Oh! How cold, how dark, there is no light on the other side; all is darkness and despair. Oh! Sinner, how will you do in the swelling of Jordan? It is not all of death to die—after death comes the judgment[22]—for we must all appear before the judgment seat of Christ.[21]

Oh, may the convicting Spirit of Christ get hold of you as you read these warnings. Hurry away to Christ before you fall into the hands of the living God.[24]

Taken from *Spirit-Filled Sermons.*

[22]Hebrews 9:27, paraphrased.

[23]See Romans 14:10 and 2 Corinthians 5:10.

[24]See Hebrews 10:31.

MISCELLANEOUS

THE CITY OF GOD

lorious things are spoken of thee, O city of God.

Psalm 87:3

The whole of this text refers literally to the ancient city of David, yet is undoubtedly an epitome of the glory and privileges of the Christian Church, of which Jerusalem was a type. Jerusalem was exalted and fortified by its situation, but much more so by the favor and protection of Jehovah.

> His foundation is in the holy mountains. The Lord loveth the gates of Zion more than all the dwellings of Jacob.[1]

What Jerusalem was, that the Christian Church now is—built by God, "Upon the foundation of the apostles and prophets, Jesus Christ himself being the chief corner stone; In whom all the building fitly framed together groweth unto an holy temple in the Lord: In whom ye also are builded together for an habitation of God" (Ephesians 2:20-22).

God loved His Church beyond the kingdoms and empires of the earth, which rise and fall only to subserve His purposes concerning her.

ITS LITERAL MEANING

Jerusalem was truly the "city of God," the city which He particularly chose, and the one to which He paid especial regard. It was the capital of the kingdom of Judah and the scene of the most extraordinary event in which men and angels have, and must forever have, the deepest interest. This was the place selected by the Almighty for His dwelling and here His glory was rendered visible. Of this place David speaks, saying: "Walk about Zion, and go round about her: tell the towers thereof. Mark ye well her bulwarks, consider her palaces; that ye may tell it to the generation following" (Psalm 48:12-13).

[1] Psalm 87:1-2.

He says further, that the city is "Beautiful for situation, the joy of the whole earth, is mount Zion."[2] It was indeed, at one time, "the perfection of beauty and the glory of the land."[3] Here David sat and tuned his harp and sang the praises of Jehovah. Hither the tribes came up to worship. Here enraptured prophets saw bright visions of the world above and received messages from on high for guilty man. Hither our Lord and Savior came in the form of a servant and groaned and bled and wept and poured out His soul unto death to redeem us from sin and save us from the pains of hell. This ancient city was the emporium of Jewish commerce and the seat of oriental learning.

Above all others, these glorious things were spoken of *this* city. There was the seat of the civil government. There were the splendid courts of the kings of Judah. "There," says the psalmist, "are set thrones of judgment."[4] There the princes and nobles resided and from thence issued the mandates by which the people were governed.

There the divine ordinances were celebrated. There were the ark, the altar, the sacrifices, and stupendous temple of Solomon. There was the testimony of Jehovah. There were the visible symbols of the divine glory of the King of heaven dwelling in the midst of His people. "I have chosen and sanctified this house, that my name may be there for ever: and mine eyes and mine heart shall be there perpetually."[5] David said, "God is known in her palaces for a refuge."[6]

There was held the general assemblage of all the Israelitish (*sic*) tribes. Three times a year, all the males from all the Jewish dominion, came up to Jerusalem to worship. How interesting it must have been to see such multitudes all assembled to praise God in the beauty of holiness,[7] playing on sacred instruments, singing beautiful songs, and making solemn processions.

[2] Psalm 48:2.

[3] See Psalm 50:2 and Lamentations 2:15.

[4] Psalm 122:5.

[5] See 2 Chronicles 7:16.

[6] Psalm 48:3.

[7] See Psalm 29:2 and 96:9.

It was honored with the presence of our Lord Jesus Christ, who was and still is "The Prince of Peace."[8]

Its Typical Application to the Church of Christ

"Jerusalem which is above is free, which is the mother of us all" (Galatians 4:26); that is, all believers. Hence Christians are represented (Ephesians 2:19) as fellow citizens of this spiritual Jerusalem. Now of this spiritual city, glorious things are spoken.

She has been gloriously founded by the living God. She is built upon Jesus Christ, the sure foundation and precious cornerstone. "For other foundation can no man lay than that is laid, which is Jesus Christ."[9]

"Thou art Peter, and upon this rock (Christ) I will build my church."[10] The general Church then is built by God and securely founded on Jesus Christ.

He purchased the Church with His own blood:

> Who is this that cometh from Edom, with dyed garments from Bozrah? this that is glorious in his apparel, travelling in the greatness of his strength? I that speak in righteousness, mighty to save. Wherefore art thou red in thine apparel, and thy garments like him that treadeth in the winevat? I have trodden the winepress alone; and of the people there was none with me.[11]

He quickens every member by His own Spirit, "And you hath he quickened, who were dead in trespasses and sins."[12]

God protects and supports her by His own power. He has all power in heaven and on earth. He says, "The gates of hell shall not prevail against" His Church.[13] He who is an inhabitant of the spiritual Jerusalem is safe. The Church will live when her enemies are all dead and their names have perished from the annals of human events.

---

[8] Isaiah 9:6.

[9] 1 Corinthians 3:11.

[10] Matthew 16:18, parenthetical addition by Maria Etter.

[11] Isaiah 63:1-3.

[12] Ephesians 2:1.

[13] Matthew 16:18.

She possesses glorious privileges. All ancient enfranchised cities had various immunities and privileges, but none ever had such as are enjoyed in the spiritual Jerusalem.

We enjoy in the Church spiritual illumination. Christ says,

> I will pray the Father, and he shall give you another Comforter, that he may abide with you for ever; even the Spirit of truth; whom the world cannot receive.[14]
>
> But the Comforter, which is the Holy Ghost, whom the Father will send in my name, he shall teach you all things, and bring all things to your remembrance, whatsoever I have said unto you.[15]

We have peace with God. "There is no peace, saith the Lord, unto the wicked."[16] But the apostle says, "Being justified by faith, we have peace with God."[17]

"The love of God is shed abroad in our hearts by the Holy Ghost which is given unto us."[18]

Solomon says, "Let the children of Zion (the Church) be joyful in their King."[19] The apostle says, "We joy and rejoice greatly."[20]

Peter says, "Whom having not seen, ye love; in whom, though now ye see him not, yet believing, ye rejoice with joy unspeakable and full of glory."[21]

We are protected from danger:

> Surely he shall deliver thee from the snare of the fowler, and from the noisome pestilence. He shall cover thee with his feathers, and under his wings shalt thou trust:

[14] John 14:16-17.

[15] John 14:26.

[16] Isaiah 48:22.

[17] Romans 5:1.

[18] Romans 5:5.

[19] Psalm 149:2.

[20] 1 Thessalonians 3:9, paraphrased.

[21] 1 Peter 1:8.

> his truth shall be thy shield and buckler. Thou shalt not be afraid for the terror by night; nor for the arrow that flieth by day; Nor for the pestilence that walketh in darkness; nor for the destruction that wasteth at noonday. A thousand shall fall at thy side, and ten thousand at thy right hand; but it shall not come nigh thee.[22]

We enjoy the constant presence and favor of Christ. He says, "I will never leave thee, nor forsake thee."[23] Again, "Lo, I am with you alway, even unto the end of the world."[24] "And where I am, there shall also my servant be."[25]

The spiritual Jerusalem contains glorious inhabitants. They are all free. Paul says, "We are not children of the bondwoman, but of the free."[26]

> Being made free from sin, and become servants to God, ye have your fruit unto holiness, and the end everlasting life.[27]

They are a heavenly race, suitable to the dignity of the founder of the city. They are born of God. "Whosoever is born of God doth not commit sin."[28] And, "Whatsoever is born of God overcometh the world."[29]

They are sons of God. "Behold, what manner of love the Father hath bestowed upon us, that we should be called the sons of God."[30] John further says, "Beloved, now are we the sons of God."[31]

Paul says they are "heirs of God, and joint-heirs with Christ."[32]

---

[22] Psalm 91:3-7.

[23] Hebrews 13:5.

[24] Matthew 28:20.

[25] John 12:26.

[26] Galatians 4:31.

[27] Romans 6:22.

[28] 1 John 3:9.

[29] 1 John 5:4.

[30] 1 John 3:1.

[31] 1 John 3:2.

[32] Romans 8:17.

They are a holy people. "Every man that hath this hope in him purifieth himself, even as he is pure."[33] "The blood of Jesus Christ his Son cleanseth us from all sin."[34] "Whosoever abideth in him sinneth not."[35] "Whosoever is born of God doth not commit sin."[36] It is written, "Ye are an holy nation."[37] Their robes have all been washed in the blood of the Lamb.[38]

They are priests and kings. The apostle Peter says, referring to the inhabitants of the spiritual Jerusalem, "But ye are a chosen generation, a royal priesthood, an holy nation, a peculiar people."[39] The revelator says of Christ, "[He] hath made us kings and priests unto God."[40] They shall see the Great White Throne and have crowns on their heads and palms in their hands and reign forever and ever.[41]

Considered in Reference to Heaven Itself

Heaven is emphatically the city of God; the city of the great king;[42] a city which hath foundations, which is come; the city which the ancient patriarchs sought,[43] and the city which John saw in a vision[44] and afterwards described; the future home of the saints, as represented by various figures, calculated to convey the sublimest ideas of durability and perfection—such as, a house, mansion, city, and inheritance.[45]

It is a located place, a city within bounds. Jesus said, "I go to prepare a place for you. And if I go and prepare a place for you, I will come again, and receive you unto myself; that where I am, there ye may be also."[46]

---

[33] 1 John 3:3.

[34] 1 John 1:7.

[35] 1 John 3:6.

[36] 1 John 3:9.

[37] 1 Peter 2:9, paraphrased.

[38] See Revelation 7:14.

[39] 1 Peter 2:9.

[40] Revelation 1:6.

[41] See Revelation 7:9-17.

[42] See Psalm 48:2.

[43] See Hebrew 11:10.

[44] See Revelation 21:2.

[45] See Ephesians 2:19, John 14:2, Hebrews 11:10, and Ephesians 1:11.

[46] John 14:2-3.

That place is heaven, and glorious things are spoken of it in the oracles of God. It is surpassingly grand in magnificence. There the throne of supreme glory is erected and there manifestations of God are witnessed.

The sun is a splendid object here; the radiance of the stars and the beauty of the firmament impress our senses strongly; but these and all other resplendent objects which glitter in mortal eyes have no glory by reason of that which excelleth them.

The Revelator says, or rather God through him,

> Come up hither, and I will shew thee things which must be hereafter. And immediately I was in the spirit: and, behold, a throne was set in heaven, and one sat on the throne. . . . and there was a rainbow round about the throne, in sight like unto an emerald. And round about the throne were four and twenty seats: and upon the seats I saw four and twenty elders sitting, clothed in white raiment; and they had on their heads crowns of gold. And out of the throne proceeded lightnings and thunderings and voices: and there were seven lamps of fire burning before the throne. . . . And before the throne there was a sea of glass like unto crystal.
>
> Revelation 4:1-6

The Revelator further says,

> He . . . shewed me that great city, the holy Jerusalem, descending out of heaven from God, Having the glory of God: and her light was like unto a stone most precious, even like a jasper stone, clear as a crystal; And had a wall great and high, and had twelve gates, and at the gates twelve angels. . . . And the wall of the city had twelve foundations. . . . And the city lieth foursquare, and the length is as large as the breadth. . . . In the midst of the street of it, and on either side of the river, was there the tree of life, which bare twelve manner of fruits, and yielded her fruit every month. . . . And there shall be no night there; and they need no candle, neither light of the sun; for the Lord God giveth them light: and they shall reign for ever and ever.
>
> Revelation 21:10-22:5

Such is the description of heaven, the saints' future home. Is it not surpassingly grand and magnificent? It is complete in its enjoyments. This will appear when we consider it perfectly excludes all evil.

> *Those holy gates forever bar*
> *Pollution, sin, and shame,*
> *And none shall gain admittance there,*
> *But followers of the Lamb.*[47]

The inhabitants have washed their robes and made them white in the blood of the Lamb. The question has been asked, "Who shall ascend into the hill of the Lord?" The answer is, "He that hath clean hands, and a pure heart."[48] "The pure in heart shall see God."[49]

We will enjoy the utmost perfection of soul and body. These bodies, no longer subject to aches, pains, and diseases, will be free and light-winged as thought itself; and our enraptured spirits will drink in the glory of the celestial world; and our enraptured souls will be filled with the glory of the King of Kings and dwell with the ransomed hosts of heaven. We will sing through all eternity, "I've been redeemed, been washed in the blood of the Lamb."[50] Glory to God.

Glorious visions! We shall see God, Christ, angels, and our brethren and friends that have gone before. "They shall be like him, for they shall see him as he is."[51] "The pure in heart shall see God."[52] "Now we see through a glass, darkly; but then face to face."[53] "They shall see the King of beauty."[54]

The most glorious and amicable society will be enjoyed in heaven, and the most pleasing engagements will be enjoyed by the blood-washed throng, for the marriage supper of the Lamb has come.

[47] Source of verse unknown.

[48] Psalm 24:3-4.

[49] Matthew 5:8, paraphrased.

[50] Allusion to "Redeemed," Lyrics: Fanny J. Crosby (1820-1915), Music: William Kirkpatrick (1838-1921).

[51] 1 John 3:2, paraphrased.

[52] Matthew 5:8, paraphrased.

[53] 1 Corinthians 13:12.

[54] Isaiah 33:17, paraphrased.

Glory to God, the city is almost in sight. Dear friends, travelers to the judgment bar[55] of God, will you not go with us? God is calling you today. Oh, come and be a soldier for Jesus, that you may enjoy a better country and walk the gold-paved streets with Christ the Redeemer and the saints of light.

The city above is eternal in its duration. Built in Jehovah, it rests on His goodness, power, and truth; an immovable basis, "The saints shall reign forever and ever."[56] "Believers shall not perish, but have everlasting life."[57]

> There is a city mine eyes doth see,
> In visions of enraptured thought;
> So bright! That all which spreads between,
> Is with its radiant glory fraught.
>
> A land upon whose blissful shore,
> There rests no shadow, falls no stain,
> There those who meet shall part no more,
> And those long parted shall meet again.[58]

"Glorious things are spoken of thee, O city of God."[59]

> "When we've been there ten thousand years,
> Bright shining as the sun,
> We've no less days to sing God's praise
> Than when we first begun."[60]

Taken from *Acts of the Holy Ghost.*

[55] "bar"—court of law.

[56] Revelation 22:5, paraphrased.

[57] John 3:16 and John 6:40, paraphrased.

[58] Source and title of hymn unknown.

[59] Psalm 87:3.

[60] "Amazing Grace" (1779), seventh verse, John Newton (1725-1807).

Etter and ministry associates in Indiana, 1924, the year she died.

Neglect Not the Gift That Is in Thee

Instructions to Ministers and Christian Workers

"Note—One of the most deeply solemn meetings was that in which seventy elders, evangelists, and helpers had hands laid on them that they might receive a fresh anointing of the Spirit and have more power in their ministry. A holy hush fell on all, and the slaying power of the Lord was strongly manifested. One after another they were prostrated under the power until the large platform looked like a battlefield.

"Then came a cry from those who worked in hospitals and visited the sick, that they might have more power to bring blessings to the suffering; and Sister Etter and several of the brethren prayed for nearly fifty. Again, as other ministers and workers came in at the close of the month's meetings, there was another service of this nature on Sunday, July 27th, in which fifty more were prayed for. All present were deeply affected by seeing the mighty power of God resting upon His workers. The faces of many were wet with tears as they looked upon the scene.

"On July 17th, before giving a talk to the ministers and Christian workers, Sister Etter made a few introductory remarks in which she said she was not sending them out with license to preach but that she did believe in many there were gifts lying dormant and that she felt part of her mission was to stir up the gifts in her brethren. She said: 'I have no authority to send you out. My prayer is that God will give you authority. We can be of the same mind and same spirit though separated a thousand miles. God has wonderfully blessed me by imparting gifts and many have received the baptism when I laid hands on them. You are going out with a courage you never had before. We don't want to be a hissing and a byword. We don't want to run ahead of the Lord nor lag behind. Let us get deep in the Spirit, so the power will come on us this morning.'

"Brother Argue spoke of the fresh anointing that had come to many at the Los Angeles camp meeting through a similar service and also emphasized the fact that these ministers who were about to be prayed for with the laying on of hands were not being sent out by Sister Etter or to claim any authority from her or the Stone Church, but that they might go away from this service with more power, a new courage, and a stronger faith. He spoke of the great need of wisdom, that some had not exercised wisdom and had gone out claiming authority from certain missions because hands were laid on them in that place. Everyone was committed to God and made to feel his responsibility to God. Many other valuable instructions were given fitting the hour, but lack of space forbids us recording them further. We give below the address given by Mrs. Etter. All felt the hush of the presence of the Lord, and it was a time of real solemnity to many hearts."

> And this gospel . . . shall be preached unto all the world for a witness . . . and then shall the end come.[1]

> The Holy Ghost said, Separate me Barnabas and Saul for the work whereunto I have called them.[2]

They had been called and were working, but now they were to be set apart in a special way. The Holy Ghost has to call you, qualify you. Jesus Christ has to send you forth: "And when they had fasted and prayed, and laid their hands on them, they sent them away. So they, being sent forth by the Holy Ghost, departed."[3]

Has God sent you? The Holy Ghost has to qualify you. Our laying on of hands would do no good unless the Holy Ghost comes in to work mightily. The Holy Ghost said, "Separate." These men had been called and chosen—chosen for the special work to which they had already been called.

---

[1] Matthew 24:14, paraphrased.

[2] Acts 13:2.

[3] Acts 13:3-4.

Now in the tenth chapter of Luke we read that the Lord appointed the seventy and sent them forth two and two before His face. He said, "Behold, I send you forth as lambs"—let us remain lambs and not become wolves to bite and snatch and tear and antagonize everybody. "Behold I send you forth as lambs among wolves"—but remember the wolves won't devour you. "Carry neither purse nor scrip." Don't be over anxious about anything.[4]

Verse 19: "Behold, I give unto you power to tread on serpents and scorpions, and over all the power of the enemy: and nothing shall by any means hurt you."[5]

Then He tells them not to rejoice that the spirits are subject unto them, but rather rejoice that they are children of God.[6] Don't be puffed up by the miracles; don't get your eyes on them, but keep your eyes on Jesus. You are not saved by miracles. You are saved and kept by the power of God. The miracles are the works of the Holy Ghost. You will get a reward for the works of the Holy Ghost that are wrought through you; they are going to make your crown, but they will never save you. If a hundred thousand were healed through my prayer today, I could not pin my salvation to that. We are not saved by works, but through faith in Jesus,[7] through living, constant faith and prayer. We are kept by the power of God. The works are thrown in, and there will be a great reward for them; our crown will be the brighter.

Now in Moses' day the work was great as it is now, and the time came when the force of workers had to be enlarged. The Lord told Moses to select seventy men of good report, elders of the people, and bring them together to the tent of meeting that He might take of the Spirit that was upon Moses and put it on them. He said that they should be used in the same way as Moses; and so it was, the Spirit that rested on Moses came upon the seventy, and they all began to prophesy. Then they were sent out to work.[8]

[4] See Luke 10:1-4 and Philippians 4:6.

[5] Luke 10:19.

[6] See Luke 10:20.

[7] See Ephesians 2:8-9.

[8] See Numbers 11:16-25.

When the Spirit of God comes on you, you are not going to sit around idle and do nothing. And the Spirit fell upon two men who had stayed in the camp. They had not been brought into the tent by Moses, yet the Spirit fell upon them.[9] That made some feel jealous, and you will find the same spirit today—jealousy of those who are being blessed. Are you jealous for the cause or jealous for yourself? It wasn't for God's glory that Joshua asked Moses to forbid the prophesying of these men. Thank God for Moses' answer, "Would God that all the Lord's people were prophets."[10]

You must have the Spirit resting upon you if you are to do anything for God, either at home or abroad. You are not fit for work unless you have it, and those who serve at home must have it the same as those who go to China or Africa. God is not calling everyone to the foreign field, but God is calling everyone in some way. Many make the mistake of going out whom God has not called, and many spend all their time running around to camp meetings. Let us make every place a tent of meeting with the Lord and the Spirit may fall on us as on Eldad and Medad, who were not called to the tent of meeting.

And if you are not called to the foreign field, get to work in the place in which God does call you to labor. If you cannot get victory for God, you are not called. The hardest place God sends you is just the place where He is going to give the greatest victory. But if you have not the Spirit and power of the Holy Ghost to energize you, you will be stranded. God expects us to be qualified by the Spirit resting upon us even more in these last days than in the time of Moses. The seventy that Christ sent out had power, and how much more should we have power now that Christ is glorified? So we are expected to do all these great things set forth in the last chapter of Mark.

Now in the twenty-fourth chapter of Matthew it says, "This gospel of the kingdom shall be preached to all nations as a witness and then shall the end come."[11] Friends, you and I cannot go out and preach as we used to do. Many sermons that God wonderfully blessed in the past I cannot preach now. I used to preach hellfire, so you could

---

[9] See Numbers 11:26-28.

[10] Numbers 11:29.

[11] Matthew 24:14, paraphrased.

nearly see the fire, and it took effect then; but the call today is for a different ministry. It is not so much in the might of preaching, but in the demonstration of the Spirit. Sinners are more hard-hearted than they used to be. You can preach hell until they see the blaze, and yet they will stand and look you calmly in the face; but let them see the mighty power of God manifested, and they are convicted.

The disciples came to Jesus privately and asked Him what should be the sign of His coming and of the end of the world, and He answered these questions.[12] The same questions are being asked today. "How will people know when You are coming back again?" And then, "What will be the sign of the end when the Tribulation is over?" Now we are given signs that we may know Jesus is coming soon. He goes on to tell many things that will happen by which we may know. He says this Gospel must be preached all over the world as a witness, and then shall the end come. This is our business, to sound the midnight cry, to herald the King. It is our mission to blow the trumpet in Zion among the saints,[13] for the day of the Lord is at hand. It is near, even at the door.

Jesus says in the same chapter, "Now from the fig tree learn her parable; when the branch putteth forth its leaves, ye know that the summer is nigh; even so ye also when ye see all these things, know that He is nigh, even at the doors."[14]

He had just been saying that the Lord would send forth His angels with the great sound of the trumpet to gather together the elect from the four winds.[15] These are not actual angels but God's servants. The Greek word translated "angel" means "messenger." You see the heralds going forth giving this last message of the kingdom, having power in the Holy Ghost, signs and wonders following; then know that the coming of the Lord is near at hand.

The Lord has given me a special mission to bring about a spirit of unity and love, and God is raising up people in every land who are reaching out after more of God and saying, "Come and help us. We

[12] See Matthew 24:3.

[13] See Joel 2:1.

[14] Matthew 24:32-33, paraphrased.

[15] See Matthew 24:31.

want the spirit of love. We want the signs and wonders." The Lord showed me last night as I lay awake most of the night, to gather together the ministers as far as I could that we might see eye to eye, preach the same Gospel, and have the same signs following. The Word is going forth and the multitude is going to take it up and publish it everywhere—this Gospel of the kingdom, our last commission. So you see the saints going out to give this last message, telling the people that Jesus is coming soon.

Our Lord told us [that] as it was in the days of Noah, so shall it be in our day.[16] While the great mass of people are busy with the affairs of this life, a little band like Noah and his family are preparing to be hidden away in Christ from the disaster that will come upon the world. And we are told that in the time of the end, the book of Daniel will be read and understood. Daniel had called upon God to show him the future, and he was given a vision of great things taking place; but the Lord said, "It is not for this people, Daniel. It is for the people you ask about in the time of the end. Seal up the book; they won't know anything about it now."[17]

The book of Daniel is for our time, and God is now opening His Word. The light of heaven is shining upon it; God is unveiling it to us. He is giving us light on these things as never before. He says positively, "They that be wise shall understand."[18] We are going to know before Jesus comes. Nearly everyone that is carried away in a vision gets the message, "Jesus is coming soon. Tell the people to be ready."

God expects us as ambassadors, as teachers, as messengers of His kingdom to blow the trumpet that sounds the alarm to those who are not ready for His coming. He expects us to prove by His Word and by the signs and wonders following our ministry, make it plain that Jesus is coming soon. His ambassadors must stop all contention; all hair-splitting theories must be dropped; this hobby and that hobby with continual harping on finished work or sanctification[19]

[16]See Matthew 24:37.

[17]See Daniel 12:9.

[18]Daniel 12:10, paraphrased.

[19]"finished work or sanctification"—During Maria Etter's ministry, the discussion among Christians concerning the stages of spiritual growth and how power over sin could be achieved was often divisive. Sanctification was considered by John Wesley to be a second stage or "the second blessing" in which the Christian obtained power to live a righteous life.

that antagonizes the saints must be put away. We are to go out and lift up Jesus.

Not many sinners come in by our preaching red-hot judgment these days. Paul says preaching has to be with demonstration of the Spirit and of power.[20] The Holy Ghost bears witness with signs and miracles; unless these attend our ministry, we cannot succeed. There are scores and hundreds getting saved. They come from all parts of the country to get healed. The ministry of healing brings people more than anything else; and if you can lay hands on the sick and they recover, you won't have to preach to empty seats. You produce the goods of heaven and people want the goods. Let the Word go forth in demonstration and power, so people can see what God has for them. There will be no failure in your ministry when they see the power of the Lord present to heal.

The main thing to keep before the people is the near coming of Jesus. We are not to set the day—God forbid—but the saints will know as the day draws nigh. We can tell by the signs that it is near. God expects you to preach as one having authority. This is a generation that will go up without dying. Christ looked down the ages to our day and saw the whole world in unbelief, men fainting and their hearts failing them with fear of the things that were coming upon the earth, and Daniel prophesied and said the wicked should grow worse and worse and none of the wicked should understand; but the wise shall understand.[21]

Then the Lord gave Daniel[22] another picture. He saw on the land and on the sea, here and there, messengers blowing the trumpet, hailing each other as they pass along. For years back whenever I met a child of God, my greeting has been, "Watchman, what of the night?" and from those who have much of the Spirit of God the answer comes, "The morning cometh."[23] But the night is here, too. We have to preach that. We know the darkness of hell is spreading

[20] See 1 Corinthians 2:4.

[21] See Luke 21:26 and Daniel 12:10.

[22] Maria Etter is thinking of Isaiah here.

[23] See Isaiah 21:11-12.

over this earth and it will soon be a fearful scene, a regular deluge of blood. We have to sound the alarm and give the message that the King is coming. Some will be accounted worthy to escape all these things and stand before the Son of Man.

There is loving unity here. So far as I can see, there is not a dissentient voice. There is not much wildfire. God will not permit it, and no one dares to chime in saying, "I am a dove," when he is a raven. No one dares to join us but to magnify God. Those just starting in the life of the Spirit will run off in the flesh more or less; but if they are honest, they will recover themselves and fall into their places. There is room for everything in a meeting but the devil. We don't want to give him a place. I haven't heard any hobby aired here. Christ finished the work on Calvary, the wonderful plan of salvation; but I do not consider the great work of the baptism was finished until after He went to glory because the Holy Ghost could not be poured forth until after His ascension. That brings us into the heavenly places and leads us on in the way. There are powers and gifts and greater gifts; we are to go on from glory to glory.[23] God didn't send us out to ride hobbies,[24] to hold up this term or that term, but to hold up Jesus. He didn't send us out to tear down churches.

When Christ sent out His workers He said, "If you go to a city, don't be gadding about. Abide in one place and be much in prayer; and don't be worried about the money not coming in, for the laborer is worthy of his hire."[25] Give yourself wholly to your ministry. If you are in the will of God, He will provide for you. And eat such things as are set before you; don't have some fad about diet. Don't say, "I don't eat this," and "I don't eat that." If you don't eat it, let it alone; but don't air your opinion about it. The Lord says, "He that receiveth you in My name receiveth Me," and we want to represent Him worthily.[26]

As for forbidding to marry or having spiritual affinities—shun such things as you would a deadly viper. But you don't need to talk about these things. Just hold up Jesus. God doesn't want you to be personal about these sins. Let Jesus have the preeminence. The more

[23] 2 Corinthians 3:18.

[24] "ride hobbies"—to pursue favorite interests obsessively.

[25] See Luke 10:4-9.

[26] See Mark 9:37, Luke 9:48, and John 13:20.

He is held up, the deeper people get in love with Him, the quicker they will drop everything else. So let us hold up Jesus and herald the coming of the King. Show them the great danger of the Tribulation. Preach Jesus and hold on to God until the signs follow. There is something wrong unless they do follow. Don't wait until you have any special gifts. Believe you can do it, and it will be done. Not only send forth the prayer, but look to God for courage; command the devil to go and you will see victory perched on your banner. People are affected every day by seeing the wonderful miracles. There are different degrees in heavenly places; there are the moon and the sun and the stars. The time has come when we have to be something more than the moon. We have to be as the sun. "They that be wise shall shine as the brightness of the firmament."[27]

Don't denounce churches. Don't denounce the Catholics. Catholics won't come in for fear you will denounce them. I never mention Catholics. I never denounce any particular church. We can show the signs of the formalist in a general way, and they see they have been fed on chaff; and they know they are frozen to death and will want to get alive. Let us hold up Jesus; and if we do that, these antagonistic spirits will get ashamed. They will find themselves lacking. If you blow the trumpet, show the people a supernatural God, and give them the light on what is coming in the millennial age—that they will be kings and priests—they will realize that the King is in our midst in power and might and glory.

Anyone that will call upon God in the right way shall be saved. He is pouring out His Spirit upon the sons and daughters. There is a special ministry for the women in these days. The sign that brought the people together when the five thousand were converted was healing, and there would have probably been ten thousand if they hadn't broken up the meeting. Five thousand as a result of this one man healed, and from that healing the disciples preached the mighty works of God.[28]

So the great revivals all through the New Testament were the result of somebody getting healed. Eneas was eight years afflicted, like the

---

[27]Daniel 12:3.

[28]See Acts 3 and 4:4.

man the other day, only this man was probably in a worse condition than Eneas; he could not bend himself, could not open his mouth, could not even move his eyes or his head. Soon he was able to stand on his feet; he had been carried in and while we were singing, he ran down the aisle and down the stairs without taking hold of the banisters, and down the street. And all that saw him glorified God as the people did when Eneas was healed.[29] There are scores to get saved and healed, so you will always have the miraculous, if the signs follow. God is going to draw in such as can be saved to see the mighty works.

Paul said to Timothy, "Stir up the gift of God, which is in thee."[30] If there is any gift God is showing you [that] you ought to have, you can receive it by the laying on of hands. It is not so much what you say about the baptism in the Holy Spirit, but what they see you have. We can talk until we are hoarse and they won't be convinced, but the power of God convinces them. Don't wait for manifestations before you go forth and do something. When you are weakest, then you are strong.[31] Let us go out and work miracles. Then the people will glorify God.

In the Stone Church, July 17, 1913

Taken from *The Latter-Rain Evangel*, August 1913.

[29] See Acts 9:32-35.

[30] 2 Timothy 1:6.

[31] See 2 Corinthians 12:10.

Gospel Witness

Faith, Prayer, and Love

What a valuable combination! Faith without prayer is worthless; and faith and prayer without love would be profitless. (See 1 Corinthians 13:1-3.) Prayer without faith is a nullity.

Love presupposes both prayer and faith: for both of these latter are means to love as an end. Prayer and faith establish love. The prayer of faith brings in the Holy Spirit (Galatians 3:2), and enthrones Christ in the heart (Ephesians 3:17); and when Christ becomes the real King of one's heart, love becomes the dominant power therein. (See 1 Corinthians 13:4-8). When perfect love or the Christ-like nature, controls one's whole being, then prayer—the prayer of faith—will be spontaneous; for in this event, the Holy Spirit will breathe into the love-dominated being every prayer the Father wishes to answer and with the prayer will give the faith also to receive an answer.

True prayer, then, in its higher aspects is but the out-breathing of love, whether unuttered or expressed, accompanied by the faith that accepts the answer; or deeper still, the true prayer of faith is the out-working of the life of Christ in the soul; the petition proceeding from the Father through the Son and by the Holy Spirit. Such prayer is the voice of God echoing in the spirit of one who is being developed unto the stature of Christ, through the mighty inworkings of the Holy Trinity.

What wonderful possibilities open to us along this line! Were we so pliable in the hands of God, as that the Spirit could awaken in us every prayer that the Father is willing to answer—imparting along with the prayer the faith to receive what we ask for—what could God not accomplish in us and through us! Surely, in this event, we would ultimately reach God's highest thought for us and be at our best as instruments in His hands. (See John 14:12 and John 7:38.)

O Father, inbreathe the spirit of prayer into each one of Thy dear children who is seeking to belong to the small company of full overcomers; giving to each the faith that will appropriate the full answer to every petition issuing from Thee through Thy Son and by the Spirit! Then speedily the bride will be made ready, and all things will soon mature for the coming of the Bridegroom! O blessed Christ, speed the time!

Taken from *Life & Experience of Maria B. Woodworth-Etter.*

Books For Further Study

A Diary of Signs & Wonders, M.B. Woodworth, Maria Beulah Woodworth-Etter (Tulsa: Harrison House, Inc., 1981).

Holy Ghost Sermons: Timeless Spirit-Filled Messages for the Last Days, Maria Woodworth-Etter (Tulsa: Harrison House, Inc., 1997).

Holy Ghost Sermons: A Living Classic Book, Maria Beulah Woodworth-Etter (Tulsa: Harrison House; 1997).

The Holy Spirit, Maria Beulah Woodworth-Etter (New Kensington, PA: Whitaker House, 1998).

The Lessons of Maria Woodworth-Etter On Miracles, Maria Beulah Woodworth-Etter, Larry Keefauver, Ed. (Lake Mary, FL: Creation House Press, 1997).

Maria Woodworth-Etter: A Complete Collection of Her Life Teachings, Roberts Liardon (Tulsa: Albury Publishing Company, 2000).

The Original Maria Woodworth-Etter Devotional (Charisma Classic), Maria Beulah Woodworth-Etter, Larry Keefauver, Ed. (Lake Mary, FL: Creation House,1997).

Signs and Wonders, Maria Beulah Woodworth-Etter (New Kensington, PA: Whitaker House, 1997).

The Spirit-Filled Woman's Devotional: Alyse Lounsberry, Alyse A. Lounsberry (Editor), J. W. Martin, Ed. (Lake Mary, FL: Creation House, 1997).

The Woman Evangelist: The Life and Times of Charismatic Evangelist Maria B. Woodworth-Etter (Studies in Evangelicalism, No 8), Wayne E. Warner (Lanham, MD: Scarecrow Press, 1986).

Readers may also wish to visit the Flower Pentecostal Heritage Center, which has a valuable collection of materials regarding Maria Woodworth-Etter (Address: 1445 Boonville Avenue, Springfield, Missouri 65802, E-mail: Archives@ag.org).

Alphabetical Title Index

Topical Index

Acts of the Holy Ghost

Biographical

Bride of Christ

Churches Established

Conversions

Death & Judgment

Divine Healing

Faith

Heaven

Interviews

Ministry

News Articles Containing Sermon Excerpts

Opinions and Editorials

Persecution/Opposition

Rapture

Revival Reports

Salvation

Second Coming

The Last Days

Visions and Trances

Water Baptism

Women in Ministry

About the Author

Blessed with a gift of unusually strong preaching, Roberts Liardon has answered a world-wide calling of God, which came to him when he was an eight-year-old boy. Having preached in ninety-three nations, Roberts Liardon is founder and senior pastor of Embassy Christian Center and Spirit Life Bible College, which is fully accredited, and was twice elected the Most Outstanding Young Man in America.

A best-selling author, Roberts' books have been translated into over 33 languages, and his audio and video tapes have helped strengthen and change the body of Christ all over the world!

Through his compilation of *The Maria Woodworth-Etter Collection*, Roberts preserves the treasure of our Christian heritage.

Church History Is Valuable To Us

If you have any materials pertaining to Church history, we would like to know about them. Roberts Liardon Ministries is committed to preserving Christian archives in our Reformers and Revivalists Historical Museum. Memorabilia from our past is very valuable and vital to future Church growth.

We are looking for magazines, letters, books, manuscripts, photographs, audio and videotapes, movies, diaries, scrapbooks, and any other personal items that would portray our Church history. Thank you for desiring to bless the world with your historical treasures.

Please contact us at our ministry addresses.

Roberts Liardon Ministries International Offices:

EUROPE

Roberts Liardon Ministries
P. O. Box 295
Welwyn, Garden City
Herts, AL7 2ZG England
Phone and Fax: 44 1707 327 222

SOUTH AFRICA

Roberts Liardon Ministries
P. O. Box 3155
Kimberley 8300, South Africa
Phone and Fax: 27 538 321 207

Philippines

Roberts Liardon Ministries
PO Box 154
Ilo Ilo, 5000
Philippines
Phone: 63 33 329 4537

USA

Roberts Liardon Ministries
P. O. Box 30710
Laguna Hills, California 92654
Phone: (949) 833-3555
Fax: (949) 833-9555
or
www.robertsliardon.org

Books by Roberts Liardon

Maria Woodworth-Etter:
The Complete Collection of Her Life Teachings

The Quest for Spiritual Hunger
(A Compilation of *Holding to the Word of the Lord*, *The Quest for Spiritual Hunger*, *The Price of Spiritual Power*, and *Spiritual Timing*)

Breaking Controlling Powers
(A Compilation of *How to Survive an Attack*, *Breaking Controlling Powers*, and *Learning to Say No Without Feeling Guilty*)

Run to the Battle
(A Compilation of *The Invading Force*, *A Call to Action*, and *Run to the Battle*)

John G. Lake:
The Complete Collection of His Life Teachings

Smith Wigglesworth Speaks to Students of the Bible

Sharpen Your Discernment

Smith Wigglesworth:
The Complete Collection of His Life Teachings

God's Generals

Cry of the Spirit:
Unpublished Sermons by Smith Wigglesworth

Forget Not His Benefits

Haunted Houses, Ghosts, & Demons

I Saw Heaven

Kathryn Kuhlman:
A Spiritual Biography of God's Miracle-Working Power

Religious Politics

Also Available:

God's Generals Video Collection
(12 Video Tapes)

Additional copies of this book and other book titles
from **ALBURY PUBLISHING** are
available at your local bookstore.

ALBURY PUBLISHING
Tulsa, Oklahoma

For a complete list of our titles,
visit us at our website:
www.alburypublishing.com

For international and Canadian orders,
please contact:

Access Sales International
2448 East 81st Street
Suite 4900
Tulsa, Oklahoma 74137
Phone 918-523-5590   Fax 918-496-2822